PRINCIPLES AND IMPLEMENTATION OF DATA WAREHOUSING

PRINCIPLES AND IMPLEMENTATION OF DATA WAREHOUSING

By

RAJEEV A. PARIDA
Software Engineer
SSI Education
New Delhi

FIREWALL MEDIA
(An Imprint of Laxmi Publications Pvt. Ltd.)
BANGALORE • CHENNAI • COCHIN • GUWAHATI • HYDERABAD
JALANDHAR • KOLKATA • LUCKNOW • MUMBAI • RANCHI
NEW DELHI • BOSTON, USA

Published by :

FIREWALL MEDIA

(An Imprint of Laxmi Publications Pvt. Ltd.)
113, Golden House, Daryaganj,
New Delhi-110002

Phone : 011-43 53 25 00
Fax : 011-43 53 25 28

www.laxmipublications.com
info@laxmipublications.com

Price : ₹ **375.00** *Only.*

First Edition : 2006
Reprint : 2007, 2008, 2013

OFFICES

Bangalore	080-26 75 69 30	**Chennai**	044-24 34 47 26
Cochin	0484-237 70 04, 405 13 03	**Guwahati**	0361-251 36 69, 251 38 81
Hyderabad	040-24 65 23 33	**Jalandhar**	0181-222 12 72
Kolkata	033-22 27 43 84	**Lucknow**	0522-220 99 16
Mumbai	022-24 91 54 15, 24 92 78 69	**Ranchi**	0651-220 44 64

FPR-2843-375-PRIN IMP DATA WAREHOUSE-PAR
Typeset at : ABRO Enterprises, Delhi.

C—5330/012/06
Printed at : Sanjeev Offset Printers, Delhi.

PREFACE

In an increasingly complex business operating environment, organizations around the world face the twin challenge of creating and deploying information technology application infrastructure for information capture and sharing, and for making effective use of the information in decision making.

Even when data is efficiently captured and stored, it may remain relatively useless for reporting and decision making purposes. Transaction and other data often need to be combined in order to provide useful information for those requiring it, be it senior decision makers or individual employees doing their assigned jobs. Data warehouses provide a mechanism for storing and combining data from a large number of sources for the purpose of querying, reporting and decision-making. Data warehouses are different from online transaction processing databases. They are "subject-oriented, integrated, time-variant, non-volatile collection of data" used to support decision making.

Data warehousing was initially viewed as a way to solve the problems associated with independently maintained legacy data. Legacy data systems were originally developed to support functional activities such as accounting, sales and human resources. They often contained duplicate, dissimilar, or inaccurate information about the same entity. For example, three databases may have different renderings of the address of the same company. However, creating a single data warehouse to address the problems associated with non-integrated legacy data has itself proved to be difficult and problematic. Some of the difficulties relate to the nature of the data in a data warehouse, the cost and complexity of building and maintaining it, and the challenges associated with using the data contained in the warehouse.

Since single, large-scale data warehouses are proving to be too difficult to build and maintain, there is a move to develop distributed data warehouses. Distributed data warehouses, especially those built around Internet technology, hold the promise for increased functionality and usability, as well as reduced deployment costs.

Once a data warehouse is built, a number of issues related to obtaining useful information out of the warehouse arise. These include data quality, techniques for mining the data, and the correctness and relevance of the data.

This book is intended for Information Technology (IT) professionals who have been hearing about or have been tasked to evaluate, learn or implement data warehousing technologies.

Far from being just a passing fad, data warehousing technology has grown much in scale and reputation in the past few years, as evidenced by the increasing number of products, vendors, organizations and yes, even books, devoted to the subject. Enterprises that have successfully implemented data warehouses find it strategic and often wonder how they ever managed to survive without it in the past.

As early as 2003, a IDC survey of Fortune 500 IT managers found that 90 percent of all organizations had planned to implement data warehouses by 2005. Virtually all Top-100 US banks will actively use a data warehouse-based profitability application by 2004. Nearly 30 percent of companies that actively pursue this technology have created a permanent or semipermanent unit to plan, create, maintain, promote, and support the data warehouse.

If you are an IT professional who has been tasked with planning, managing, designing, implementing, supporting, or maintaining your organization's data warehouse, then this book is intended for you.

Rajeev A. Parida

ACKNOWLEDGEMENT

This book, like so many others, this is the product of team of people working behind the scene. I would like to take a minute to acknowledge and thank those who pitched into push this project over the finish line.

First of all I am grateful to Mr. Abhiram Behera, Data Warehousing Architect, HCL Perot System, NJ, USA for his guidance, suggestion and supervision throughout this project.

I would like to express my gratitude to Mrs. Anupama Parida and Mr. Ayush Parida for editing and proof reading the manuscript.

I am thankful to Mr. Ranjan Parida, Director Data Matrix Solutions Pvt. Ltd., Mr. Dilip Pattanik, Lecturer GNIM who have helped me frame picture in their respective position in this book. Without their generosity this book would have sorely lacked visual impact.

I would like to extend my sincere thanks to Mr. Santnoo Pattanik, HOD Computer Science Department, GNIM, New Delhi for his cooperation and help.

Furthermore, my special thanks to Mrs. Nirupama Behera, Priyadarshini Behera and Shreya Behera for formulating the original concept and made many suggestion for the topic covered in this book via e-mail from Florida, USA.

Finally, I would express my gratitude to Mr. Niranjan Parida, Mrs. Savita Parida and Mr. Parveen Sharma for their endless inspiration and love.

Rajeev A. Parida

CONTENTS

1 DATA WAREHOUSING CONCEPTS AND DESIGNS

WHAT IS A DATA WAREHOUSE?

For any business to be successful, fast access to information is critical. Information is extracted from existing data. Important decisions are based on information available at any point in time. In order to get the right information at the right time, data about the business has to be stored on a computer system (such as Database Management System). Database Management System is the combination of two components like *Database* and *Database Management System.*

A database is a collection of interrelated data stored from which information can be extracted to many users for different purposes. The collection of data must be logically coherent with inherent meaning. The database can handle business inventory accounting, payroll and filing and use the information in its files to prepare summaries, estimates and other reports. There can be a database which stores books, magazines, novels, movie and photograph. A database is designed and built for a specific purpose, keeping in the mind the needs of applications that are going to use it and the end user of those applications. It is managed by software package known as Database Management System.

A Database System consist of two parts namely : *Database Management System* and *Database Application*. A Database Management System is a general purpose software system that enables uses to define and manipulate databases. It provides and environment, where in data can be stored an retrieved from databases easily and most efficiently. The Database Management System is the software used to create and maintain the database. Whereas Database Application is the program that lets us view, retrieve and update information stored in the Database Management System.

An evolutionary path has been witnessed in the database industry in the development of following functionalities: *data collection and data creation, data management* (including data storage and data retrieval and database transaction processing), and *data analysis and understanding* (involving data warehousing and data mining). For instance, the early development of data collection and database creation mechanisms served as a prerequisite for later development of effective mechanisms for data storage and query and transaction processing. With database system offering query and transaction processing as common practice, data analysis and understanding has naturally become the next target.

Since the 1960s, database and information technology has been evolving systematically from primitive file processing systems to sophisticated and powerful database systems. The research and development in database systems since the 1970s has progressed from early hierarchical and network database systems to the development of relational database systems (where data are stored in relational table structures), data modeling tools, and indexing and data organization technique. In addition, user gained convenient and flexible data access through query languages, user interfaces, optimize query processing and transaction management. Efficient methods for on-line transaction processing (OLTP), where a query is viewed as a read only transaction, have contributed substantially to the evolution and wide acceptance of relational technology as a major tool for efficient storage, retrieval, and management of large amounts of data.

Database technology since the mid-1980s has been characterized by the popular adoption of relational technology and an upsurge of research and development activities on new and powerful database systems. These employ advanced data model such as extended-relational, object-oriented, object-relational, and deductive models. Application oriented database system, including spatial, temporal, multimedia, active and scientific databases, knowledge bases, and office information bases, have flourished. Issues related to the distribution, diversification and sharing of data have been studied extensively. Heterogeneous database system and internet based global information systems such as World Wide Web (WWW) have also merged and play a vital role in the information industry.

The steady and amazing progress of computer hardware technology in the past three decades has led to large supplies of powerful and affordable computers, data collection equipment and storage media. This technology provides a great boost to the database and information industry and makes a huge number of databases and information repositories available for transaction management, information retrieval and data analysis.

Data now be stored in many different types of databases. One database architecture that has recently emerged is the data warehouse, a repository of multiple heterogeneous data sources, organised under unified schema at a single site in order to facilitate management decision making.

A data warehouse is a relational database that is designed for query and analysis rather than for transaction processing. It usually contains historical data derived from transaction data, but it can include data from other sources. It separates analysis workload from transaction workload and enables an organization to consolidate data from several sources.

In addition to a relational database, a data warehouse environment includes an extraction, transportation, transformation, and loading (ETL) solution, an online analytical processing (OLAP) engine, client analysis tools, and other applications that manage the process of gathering data and delivering it to business users.

A common way of introducing data warehousing is to refer to the characteristics of a data warehouse as set forth by William Inmon:

- Subject oriented
- Integrated
- Nonvolatile
- Time variant.

Subject Oriented

Data warehouses are designed to help you analyze data. For example, to learn more about your company's sales data, you can build a warehouse that concentrates on sales. Using this warehouse, you can answer questions like "Who was our best customer for this item last year?" This ability to define a data warehouse by subject matter, sales in this case, makes the data warehouse subject oriented.

Integrated

Integration is closely related to subject orientation. Data warehouses must put data from disparate sources into a consistent format. They must resolve such problems as naming conflicts and inconsistencies among units of measure. When they achieve this, they are said to be integrated.

Nonvolatile

Nonvolatile means that, once entered into the warehouse, data should not change. This is logical because the purpose of a warehouse is to enable you to analyze what has occurred.

Time Variant

In order to discover trends in business, analysts need large amounts of data. This is very much in contrast to **online transaction processing (OLTP)** systems, where performance requirements demand that historical data be moved to an archive. A data warehouse's focus on change over time is what is meant by the term time variant.

Contrasting OLTP and Data Warehousing Environments

Figure 1.1 illustrates key differences between an OLTP system and a data warehouse.

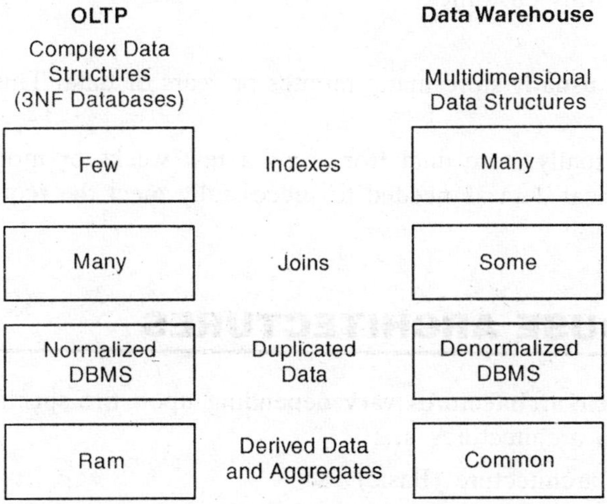

Figure 1.1 Contrasting OLTP and Data Warehousing Environments.

One major difference between the types of system is that data warehouses are not usually in **third normal form (3NF),** a type of data normalization common in OLTP environments.

Data warehouses and OLTP systems have very different requirements. Here are some examples of differences between typical data warehouses and OLTP systems:

- **Workload**

  Data warehouses are designed to accommodate *ad hoc* queries. You might not know the workload of your data warehouse in advance, so a data warehouse should be optimized to perform well for a wide variety of possible query operations.

  OLTP systems support only predefined operations. Your applications might be specifically tuned or designed to support only these operations.

- **Data modifications**

  A data warehouse is updated on a regular basis by the ETL process (run nightly or weekly) using bulk data modification techniques. The end users of a data warehouse do not directly update the data warehouse.

  In OLTP systems, end users routinely issue individual data modification statements to the database. The OLTP database is always up to date, and reflects the current state of each business transaction.

- **Schema design**

  Data warehouses often use denormalized or partially denormalized schemas (such as a star schema) to optimize query performance.

  OLTP systems often use fully normalized schemas to optimize update/insert/delete performance, and to guarantee data consistency.

- **Typical operations**

  A typical data warehouse query scans thousands or millions of rows. For example, "Find the total sales for all customers last month."

  A typical OLTP operation accesses only a handful of records. For example, "Retrieve the current order for this customer."

- **Historical data**

  Data warehouses usually store many months or years of data. This is to support historical analysis.

  OLTP systems usually store data from only a few weeks or months. The OLTP system stores only historical data as needed to successfully meet the requirements of the current transaction.

DATA WAREHOUSE ARCHITECTURES

Data warehouses and their architectures vary depending upon the specifics of an organization's situation. Three common architectures are:

- Data warehouse architecture (Basic)
- Data warehouse architecture (with a Staging Area)
- Data warehouse architecture (with a Staging Area and Data Marts)

Data Warehouse Architecture (Basic)

Figure 1.2 shows a simple architecture for a data warehouse. End users directly access data derived from several source systems through the data warehouse.

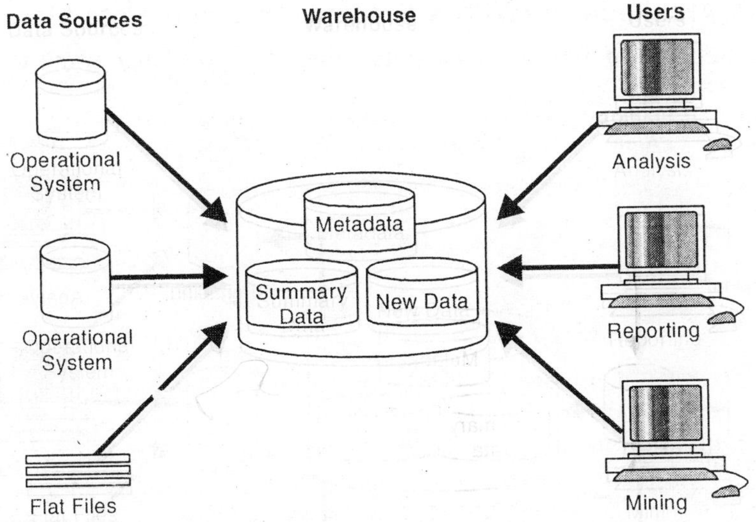

Figure 1.2 Architecture of a Data Warehouse.

In figure 1.2, the metadata and raw data of a traditional OLTP system is present, as is an additional type of data, summary data. Summaries are very valuable in data warehouses because they pre-compute long operations in advance. For example, a typical data warehouse query is to retrieve something like August sales. A summary in Oracle is called a **materialized view.**

Data Warehouse Architecture (with a Staging Area)

In figure 1.2, you need to clean and process your operational data before putting it into the warehouse. You can do this programmatically, although most data warehouses use a **staging area** instead. A staging area simplifies building summaries and general warehouse management. Figure 1.3 illustrates this typical architecture.

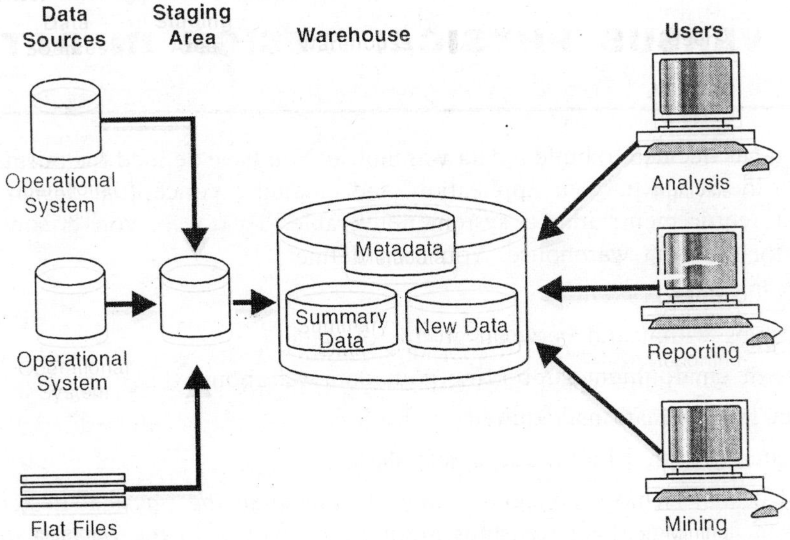

Figure 1.3 Architecture of a Data Warehouse with a Staging Area.

Data Warehouse Architecture (With a Staging Area and Data Marts)

Although the architecture in figure 1.3 is quite common, you may want to customize your

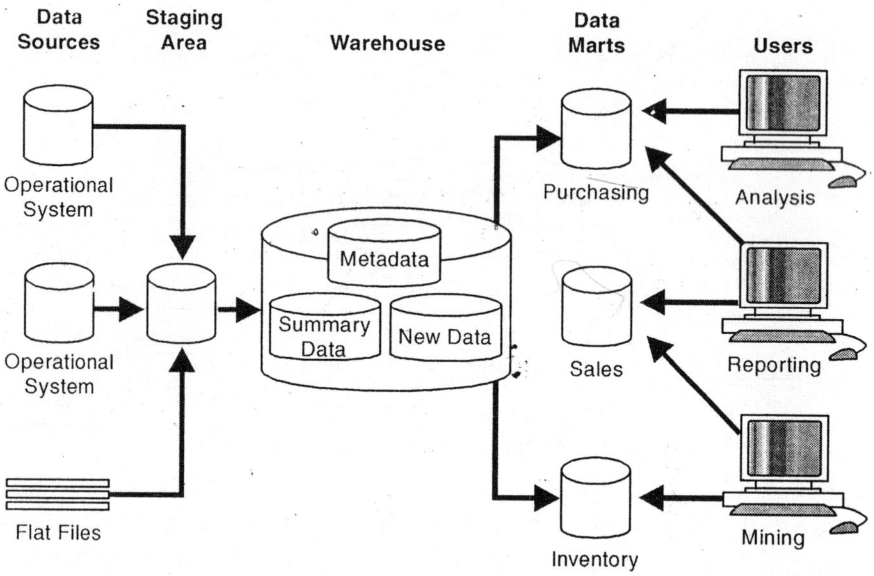

Figure 1.4 Architecture of a Data Warehouse with a Staging Area and Data Marts.

warehouse's architecture for different groups within your organization. You can do this by adding **data marts,** which are systems designed for a particular line of business. Figure 1.4 illustrates an example where purchasing, sales, and inventories are separated. In this example, a financial analyst might want to analyze historical data for purchases and sales.

LOGICAL VERSUS PHYSICAL DESIGN IN DATA WAREHOUSES

Your organization has decided to build a data warehouse. You have defined the business requirements and agreed upon the scope of your application, and created a conceptual design. Now you need to translate your requirements into a system deliverable. To do so, you create the logical and physical design for the data warehouse. You then define:

- The specific data content
- Relationships within and between groups of data
- The system environment supporting your data warehouse
- The data transformations required
- The frequency with which data is refreshed.

The logical design is more conceptual and abstract than the physical design. In the logical design, you look at the logical relationships among the objects. In the physical design, you look at the most effective way of storing and retrieving the objects as well as handling them from a transportation and backup/recovery perspective.

Orient your design toward the needs of the end users. End users typically want to perform analysis and look at aggregated data, rather than at individual transactions. However, end users might not know what they need until they see it. In addition, a well-planned design allows for growth and changes as the needs of users change and evolve.

By beginning with the logical design, you focus on the information requirements and save the implementation details for later.

CREATING A LOGICAL DESIGN

A logical design is conceptual and abstract. You do not deal with the physical implementation details yet. You deal only with defining the types of information that you need.

One technique you can use to model your organization's logical information requirements is entity-relationship modeling. Entity-relationship modeling involves identifying the things of importance (entities), the properties of these things (attributes), and how they are related to one another (relationships).

The process of logical design involves arranging data into a series of logical relationships called entities and attributes. An **entity** represents a chunk of information. In relational databases, an entity often maps to a table. An **attribute** is a component of an entity that helps define the uniqueness of the entity. In relational databases, an attribute maps to a column.

To be sure that your data is consistent, you need to use unique identifiers. A **unique identifier** is something you add to tables so that you can differentiate between the same item when it appears in different places. In a physical design, this is usually a primary key.

While entity-relationship diagramming has traditionally been associated with highly normalized models such as OLTP applications, the technique is still useful for data warehouse design in the form of dimensional modeling. In dimensional modeling, instead of seeking to discover atomic units of information (such as entities and attributes) and all of the relationships between them, you identify which information belongs to a central fact table and which information belongs to its associated dimension tables. You identify business subjects or fields of data, define relationships between business subjects, and name the attributes for each subject.

Your logical design should result in (1) a set of entities and attributes corresponding to fact tables and dimension tables and (2) a model of operational data from your source into subject-oriented information in your target data warehouse schema.

You can create the logical design using a pen and paper, or you can use a design tool such as Oracle Warehouse Builder (specifically designed to support modeling the ETL process) or Oracle Designer (a general purpose modeling tool).

DATA WAREHOUSING SCHEMAS

A schema is a collection of database objects, including tables, views, indexes, and synonyms. You can arrange schema objects in the schema models designed for data warehousing in a variety of ways. Most data warehouses use a dimensional model.

The model of your source data and the requirements of your users help you design the data warehouse schema. You can sometimes get the source model from your company's enterprise data model and reverse-engineer the logical data model for the data warehouse from this. The physical implementation of the logical data warehouse model may require some changes to adapt it to your system parameters—size of machine, number of users, storage capacity, type of network, and software.

Star Schemas

The **star schema** is the simplest data warehouse schema. It is called a star schema because the diagram resembles a star, with points radiating from a centre. The centre of the star consists of one or more fact tables and the points of the star are the dimension tables, as shown in figure 1.5

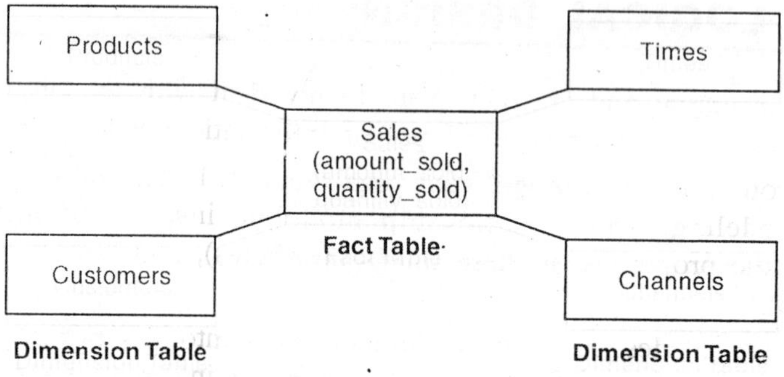

Figure 1.5 Star Schema.

The most natural way to model a data warehouse is as a star schema, only one join establishes the relationship between the fact table and any one of the dimension tables.

A star schema optimizes performance by keeping queries simple and providing fast response time. All the information about each level is stored in one row.

Other Schemas

Some schemas in data warehousing environments use third normal form rather than star schemas. Another schema that is sometimes useful is the snowflake schema, which is a star schema with normalized dimensions in a tree structure.

DATA WAREHOUSING OBJECTS

Fact tables and dimension tables are the two types of objects commonly used in dimensional data warehouse schemas.

Fact tables are the large tables in your warehouse schema that store business measurements. Fact tables typically contain facts and foreign keys to the dimension tables. Fact tables represent data, usually numeric and additive, that can be analyzed and examined. Examples include `sales`, `cost`, and `profit`.

Dimension tables, also known as lookup or reference tables, contain the relatively static data in the warehouse. Dimension tables store the information you normally use to contain queries. Dimension tables are usually textual and descriptive and you can use them as the row headers of the result set. Examples are `customers` or `products`.

Fact Tables

A fact table typically has two types of columns: those that contain numeric facts (often called measurements), and those that are foreign keys to dimension tables. A fact table contains either detail-level facts or facts that have been aggregated. Fact tables that contain aggregated facts are often called summary tables. A fact table usually contains facts with the same level of aggregation. Though most facts are additive, they can also be semi-additive or non-additive. Additive facts can be aggregated by simple arithmetical addition. A common example of this is sales. Non-additive facts cannot be added at all. An example of this is averages. Semi-additive facts can be aggregated along some of the dimensions and not along others. An example of this is inventory levels, where you cannot tell what a level means simply by looking at it.

Creating a New Fact Table

You must define a fact table for each star schema. From a modeling standpoint, the primary key of the fact table is usually a composite key that is made up of all of its foreign keys.

Dimension Tables

A dimension is a structure, often composed of one or more hierarchies, that categorizes data. Dimensional attributes help to describe the dimensional value. They are normally descriptive, textual values. Several distinct dimensions, combined with facts, enable you to answer business questions. Commonly used dimensions are customers, products, and time.

Dimension data is typically collected at the lowest level of detail and then aggregated into higher level totals that are more useful for analysis. These natural rollups or aggregations within a dimension table are called hierarchies.

Hierarchies

Hierarchies are logical structures that use ordered levels as a means of organizing data. A hierarchy can be used to define data aggregation. For example, in a `time` dimension, a hierarchy might aggregate data from the `month` level to the `quarter` level to the year level. A hierarchy can also be used to define a navigational drill path and to establish a family structure.

Within a hierarchy, each level is logically connected to the levels above and below it. Data values at lower levels aggregate into the data values at higher levels. A dimension can be composed of more than one hierarchy. For example, in the product dimension, there might be two hierarchies—one for product categories and one for product suppliers.

Dimension hierarchies also group levels from general to granular. Query tools use hierarchies to enable you to drill down into your data to view different levels of granularity. This is one of the key benefits of a data warehouse.

When designing hierarchies, you must consider the relationships in business structures. For example, a divisional multilevel sales organization.

Hierarchies impose a family structure on dimension values. For a particular level value, a value at the next higher level is its parent, and values at the next lower level are its children. These familial relationships enable analysts to access data quickly.

Levels

A level represents a position in a hierarchy. For example, a `time` dimension might have a hierarchy that represents data at the `month`, `quarter`, and `year` levels. Levels range from general to specific, with the root level as the highest or most general level. The levels in a dimension are organized into one or more hierarchies.

Level Relationships

Level relationships specify top-to-bottom ordering of levels from most general (the root) to most specific information. They define the parent-child relationship between the levels in a hierarchy.

Hierarchies are also essential components in enabling more complex rewrites. For example, the database can aggregate an existing sales revenue on a quarterly base to a yearly aggregation when the dimensional dependencies between quarter and year are known.

Typical Dimension Hierarchy

Figure 1.6 illustrates a dimension hierarchy based on `customers`.

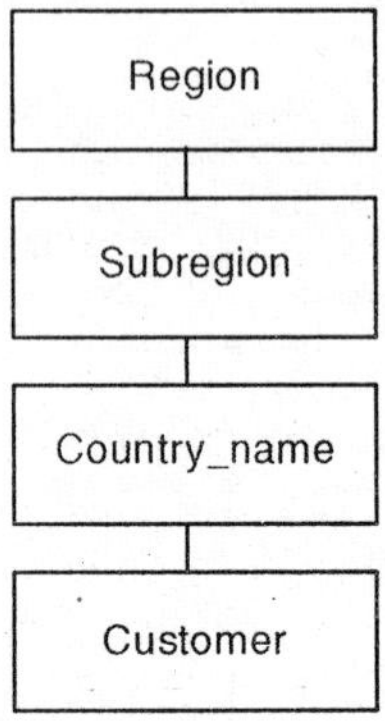

Figure 1.6 Typical Levels in a Dimension Hierarchy.

Unique Identifiers

Unique identifiers are specified for one distinct record in a dimension table. Artificial unique identifiers are often used to avoid the potential problem of unique identifiers changing. Unique identifiers are represented with the # character. For example, `#customer_id`.

Relationships

Relationships guarantee business integrity. An example is that if a business sells something, there is obviously a customer and a product. Designing a relationship between the sales information in the fact table and the dimension tables products and customers enforces the business rules in databases.

Example of Data Warehousing Objects and Their Relationships

Figure 1.7 illustrates a common example of a `sales` fact table and dimension tables `customers`, `products`, `promotions`, times, and `channels`.

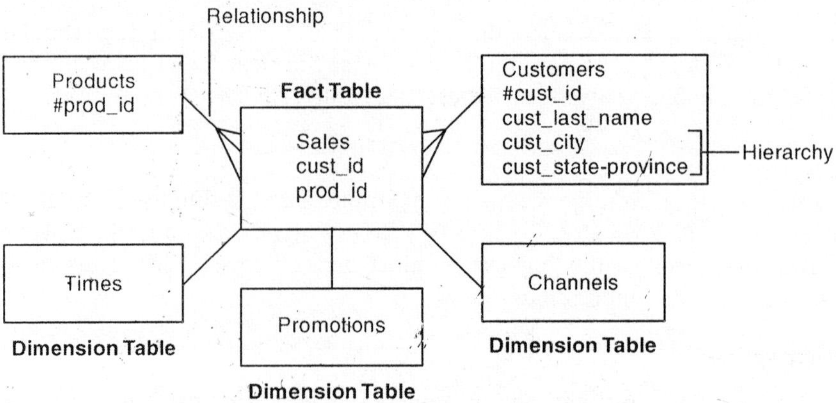

Figure 1.7 Typical Data Warehousing Objects.

MOVING FROM LOGICAL TO PHYSICAL DESIGN

Logical design is what you draw with a pen and paper or design with Oracle Warehouse Builder or Designer before building your warehouse. Physical design is the creation of the database with SQL statements.

During the physical design process, you convert the data gathered during the logical design phase into a description of the physical database structure. Physical design decisions are mainly driven by query performance and database maintenance aspects. For example, choosing a partitioning strategy that meets common query requirements enables Oracle to take advantage of partition pruning, a way of narrowing a search before performing it.

PHYSICAL DESIGN

During the logical design phase, you defined a model for your data warehouse consisting of entities, attributes, and relationships. The entities are linked together using relationships. Attributes are used to describe the entities. The **unique identifier** (UID) distinguishes between one instance of an entity and another.

Figure 1.8 offers you a graphical way of looking at the different ways of thinking about logical and physical designs.

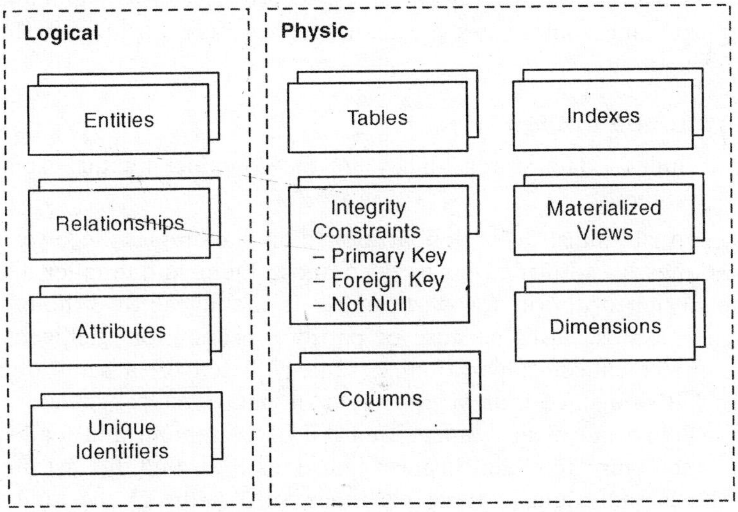

Figure 1.8 Logical Design Compared with Physical Design.

During the physical design process, you translate the expected schemas into actual database structures. At this time, you have to map:

- Entities to tables
- Relationships to foreign key constraints
- Attributes to columns
- Primary unique identifiers to primary key constraints
- Unique identifiers to unique key constraints.

Physical Design Structures

Once you have converted your logical design to a physical one, you will need to create some or all of the following structures:

- Tablespaces
- Tables and partitioned tables
- Views
- Integrity constraints
- Dimensions.

Some of these structures require disk space. Others exist only in the data dictionary. Additionally, the following structures may be created for performance improvement:

- Indexes and partitioned indexes
- Materialized views.

Tablespaces

A tablespace consists of one or more datafiles, which are physical structures within the operating system you are using. A datafile is associated with only one tablespace. From a design perspective, tablespaces are containers for physical design structures.

Tablespaces need to be separated by differences. For example, tables should be separated from their indexes and small tables should be separated from large tables. Tablespaces should also represent logical business units if possible. Because a tablespace is the coarsest granularity for backup and recovery or the transportable tablespaces mechanism, the logical business design affects availability and maintenance operations.

Tables and Partitioned Tables

Tables are the basic unit of data storage. They are the container for the expected amount of raw data in your data warehouse.

Using partitioned tables instead of nonpartitioned ones addresses the key problem of supporting very large data volumes by allowing you to decompose them into smaller and more manageable pieces. The main design criterion for partitioning is manageability, though you will also see performance benefits in most cases because of partition pruning or intelligent parallel processing. For example, you might choose a partitioning strategy based on a sales transaction date and a monthly granularity. If you have four years' worth of data, you can delete a month's data as it becomes older than four years with a single, quick DDL statement and load new data while only affecting 1/48th of the complete table. Business questions regarding the last quarter will only affect three months, which is equivalent to three partitions, or 3/48ths of the total volume.

Partitioning large tables improves performance because each partitioned piece is more manageable. Typically, your partition is based on transaction dates in a data warehouse. For example, each month, one month's worth of data can be assigned its own partition.

Data Segment Compression

You can save disk space by compressing heap-organized tables. A typical type of heap-organized table that you should consider for data segment compression is partitioned tables.

To reduce disk use and memory use (specifically, the buffer cache), you can store tables and partitioned tables in a compressed format inside the database. This often leads to a better scaleup for read-only operations. Data segment compression can also speed up query execution. There is, however, a cost in CPU overhead.

Data segment compression should be used with highly redundant data, such as tables with many foreign keys. You should avoid compressing tables with much update or other DML activity. Although compressed tables or partitions are updatable, there is some overhead in updating these tables, and high update activity may work against compression by causing some space to be wasted.

Views

A view is a tailored presentation of the data contained in one or more tables or other views. A view takes the output of a query and treats it as a table. Views do not require any space in the database.

Integrity Constraints

Integrity constraints are used to enforce business rules associated with your database and to prevent having invalid information in the tables. Integrity constraints in data warehousing differ from constraints in OLTP environments. In OLTP environments, they primarily prevent the insertion of invalid data into a record, which is not a big problem in data warehousing environments because accuracy has already been guaranteed. In data warehousing environments, constraints are only used for query rewrite. `NOT NULL` constraints are particularly common in data warehouses. Under some specific circumstances, constraints need space in the database. These constraints are in the form of the underlying unique index.

Indexes and Partitioned Indexes

Indexes are optional structures associated with tables or clusters. In addition to the classical B-tree indexes, bitmap indexes are very common in data warehousing environments. Bitmap indexes are optimized index structures for set-oriented operations. Additionally, they are necessary for some optimized data access methods such as star transformations.

Indexes are just like tables in that you can partition them, although the partitioning strategy is not dependent upon the table structure. Partitioning indexes makes it easier to manage the warehouse during refresh and improves query performance.

Materialized Views

Materialized views are query results that have been stored in advance so long-running calculations are not necessary when you actually execute your SQL statements. From a physical design point of view, materialized views resemble tables or partitioned tables and behave like indexes.

Dimensions

A dimension is a schema object that defines hierarchical relationships between columns or column sets. A hierarchical relationship is a functional dependency from one level of a hierarchy to the next one. A dimension is a container of logical relationships and does not require any space in the database. A typical dimension is city, state (or province), region, and country.

OVERVIEW OF HARDWARE AND I/O CONSIDERATIONS IN DATA WAREHOUSES

Data warehouses are normally very much concerned with I/O performance. This is in contrast to OLTP systems, where the potential bottleneck depends on user workload and application access patterns. When a system is constrained by I/O capabilities, it is I/O bound, or has an I/O bottleneck. When a system is constrained by having limited CPU resources, it is CPU bound, or has a CPU bottleneck.

Database architects frequently use RAID (Redundant Arrays of Inexpensive Disks) systems to overcome I/O bottlenecks and to provide higher availability. RAID can be implemented in several levels, ranging from 0 to 7. Many hardware vendors have enhanced these basic levels to lessen the impact of some of the original restrictions at a given RAID level. The most common RAID levels are discussed later in this chapter.

Why Stripe the Data?

To avoid I/O bottlenecks during parallel processing or concurrent query access, all tablespaces accessed by parallel operations should be striped. Striping divides the data of a large table into small portions and stores them on separate datafiles on separate disks. As shown in figure 1.9, tablespaces should always stripe *over at least as many devices as CPUs.* In this example, there are four CPUs, two controllers, and five devices containing tablespaces.

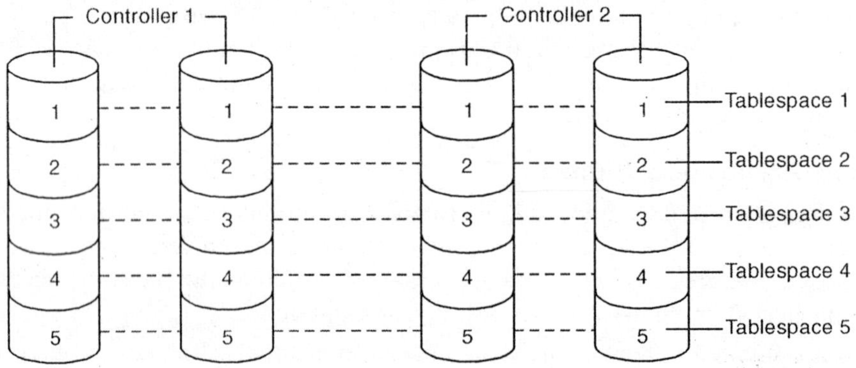

Figure 1.9 Striping Objects Over at least as Many Devices as CPUs.

You should stripe tablespaces for tables, indexes, rollback segments, and temporary tablespaces. You must also spread the devices over controllers, I/O channels, and internal buses. To make striping effective, you must make sure that enough controllers and other I/O components are available to support the bandwidth of parallel data movement into and out of the striped tablespaces.

You can use RAID systems or you can perform striping manually through careful data file allocation to tablespaces.

The striping of data across physical drives has several consequences besides balancing I/O. One additional advantage is that logical files can be created that are larger than the maximum size usually supported by an operating system. There are disadvantages however. Striping means that it is no longer possible to locate a single datafile on a specific physical drive. This can cause the loss of some application tuning capabilities. Also, it can cause database recovery to be more time-consuming. If a single physical disk in a RAID array needs recovery, all the disks that are part of that logical RAID device must be involved in the recovery.

Automatic Striping

Automatic striping is usually flexible and easy to manage. It supports many scenarios such as multiple users running sequentially or as single users running in parallel. Two main advantages make automatic striping preferable to manual striping, unless the system is very small or availability is the main concern:

- For parallel scan operations (such as full table scan or fast full scan), operating system striping increases the number of disk seeks. Nevertheless, this is largely offset by the large I/O size (DB_BLOCK_SIZE * MULTIBLOCK_READ_COUNT), which should enable this operation to reach the maximum I/O throughput for your platform. This maximum is in general limited by the number of controllers or I/O buses of the platform, not by the number of disks (unless you have a small configuration or are using large disks).
- For index probes (for example, within a nested loop join or parallel index range scan), operating system striping enables you to avoid hot spots by evenly distributing I/O across the disks.

Oracle Corporation recommends using a large stripe size of at least 64 KB. Stripe size must be at least as large as the I/O size. If stripe size is larger than I/O size by a factor of two or four, then trade-offs may arise. The large stripe size can be advantageous because it lets the system perform more sequential operations on each disk; it decreases the number of seeks on disk. Another advantage of large stripe sizes is that more users can work on the system without affecting each other. The disadvantage is that large stripes reduce the I/O parallelism, so fewer disks are simultaneously active. If you encounter problems, increase the I/O size of scan operations (for example, from 64 KB to 128 KB), instead of changing the stripe size. The maximum I/O size is platform-specific (in a range, for example, of 64 KB to 1 MB).

With automatic striping, from a performance standpoint, the best layout is to stripe data, indexes, and temporary tablespaces across all the disks of your platform. This layout is also appropriate when you have little information about system usage. To increase availability, it may be more practical to stripe over fewer disks to prevent a single disk value from affecting the entire data warehouse. However, for better performance, it is crucial to stripe all objects over multiple disks. In this way, maximum I/O performance (both in terms of throughput and in number of I/Os per second) can be reached when one object is accessed by a parallel operation. If multiple objects are accessed at the same time (as in a multiuser configuration), striping automatically limits the contention.

Manual Striping

You can use manual striping on all platforms. To do this, add multiple files to each tablespace, with each file on a separate disk. If you use manual striping correctly, your system's performance improves significantly. However, you should be aware of several drawbacks that can adversely affect performance if you do not stripe correctly.

When using manual striping, the degree of parallelism (DOP) is more a function of the number of disks than of the number of CPUs. First, it is necessary to have one server process for each datafile to drive all the disks and limit the risk of experiencing I/O bottlenecks. Second, manual striping is very sensitive to datafile size skew, which can affect the scalability of parallel scan operations. Third, manual striping requires more planning and set-up effort than automatic striping.

Local and Global Striping

Local striping, which applies only to partitioned tables and indexes, is a form of non-overlapping, disk-to-partition striping. Each partition has its own set of disks and files, as illustrated in figure 1.10. Disk access does not overlap, nor do files.

An advantage of local striping is that if one disk fails, it does not affect other partitions. Moreover, you still have some striping even if you have data in only one partition.

A disadvantage of local striping is that you need many disks to implement it—each partition requires multiple disks of its own. Another major disadvantage is that when partitions are reduced to a few or even a single partition, the system retains limited I/O bandwidth. As a result, local striping is not optimal for parallel operations. For this reason, consider local striping only if your main concern is availability, rather than parallel execution.

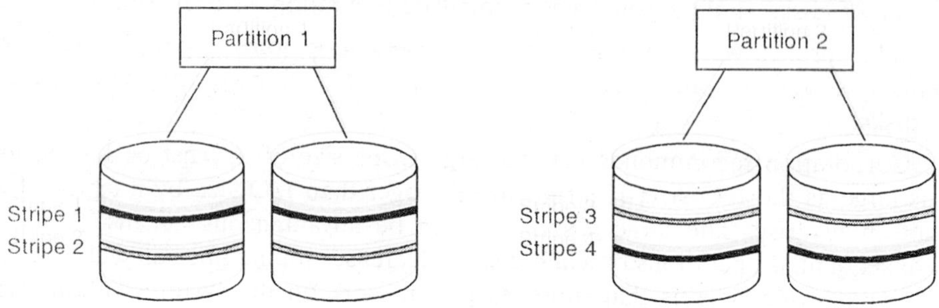

Figure 1.10 Local Striping.

Global striping, illustrated in figure 1.11, entails overlapping disks and partitions.

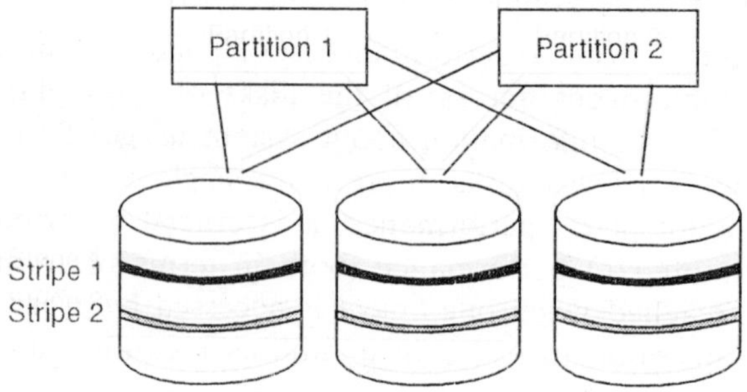

Figure 1.11 Global Striping.

Global striping is advantageous if you have partition pruning and need to access data in only one partition. Spreading the data in that partition across many disks improves performance for parallel execution operations. A disadvantage of global striping is that if one disk fails, all partitions are affected if the disks are not mirrored.

Analyzing Striping

Two considerations arise when analyzing striping issues for your applications. First, consider the cardinality of the relationships among the objects in a storage system. Second, consider what you can optimize in your striping effort: full table scans, general tablespace availability, partition scans, or some combinations of these goals. Cardinality and optimization are discussed in the following section.

Cardinality of Storage Object Relationships

To analyze striping, consider the relationships illustrated in figure 1.12.

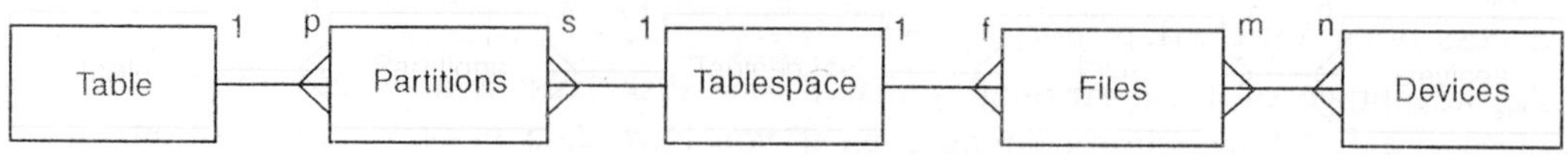

Figure 1.12 Cardinality of Relationships.

Figure 1.12 shows the cardinality of the relationships among objects in a typical Oracle storage system. For every table there may be:

- p partitions, shown in figure 1.12 as a one-to-many relationship
- s partitions for every tablespace, shown in figure 1.12 as a many-to-one relationship
- f files for every tablespace, shown in figure 1.12 as a one-to-many relationship
- m files to n devices, shown in figure 1.12 as a many-to-many relationship.

Striping Goals

You can stripe an object across devices to achieve one of the three goals:

- Goal 1: To optimize full table scans, place a table on many devices
- Goal 2: To optimize availability, restrict the tablespace to a few devices
- Goal 3: To optimize partition scans, achieve intra-partition parallelism by placing each partition on many devices.

To attain both Goals 1 and 2 (having the table reside on many devices, with the highest possible availability), maximize the number of partitions p and minimize the number of partitions for each tablespace s.

To maximize Goal 1 but with minimal intra-partition parallelism, place each partition in its own tablespace. Do not use striped files, and use one file for each tablespace.

To minimize Goal 2 and thereby minimize availability, set f and n equal to 1. When you minimize availability, you maximize intra-partition parallelism. Goal 3 conflicts with Goal 2 because you cannot simultaneously maximize the formula for Goal 3 and minimize the formula for Goal 2. You must compromise to achieve some of the benefits of both goals.

Striping Goal 1: Optimize Full Table Scans

Having a table reside on many devices ensures scalable full table scans.

To calculate the optimal number of devices for each table, use this formula:

$$\text{Number of devices per table} = \frac{p \times f \times u}{s \times m}$$

You can do this by having t partitions, with every partition in its own tablespace, if every tablespace has one file, and these files are not striped.

$t \times 1/p \times 1 \times 1$, up to t devices

If the table is not partitioned, but is in one tablespace in one file, stripe it over n devices.

$1 \times 1 \times u$ devices

There are a maximum of t partitions, every partition in its own tablespace, f files in each tablespace, each tablespace on a striped device:

$t \times f \times u$ devices

Striping Goal 2: Optimize Availability

Restricting each tablespace to a small number of devices and having as many partitions as possible helps you achieve high availability.

$$\text{Number of devices per tablespace} = \frac{f \times u}{m}$$

Availability is maximized when $f = n = m = 1$ and p is much greater than 1.

Striping Goal 3: Optimize Partition Scans

Achieving intra-partition parallelism is advantageous because partition scans are scalable. To do this, place each partition on many devices.

$$\text{Number of devices per partition} = \frac{f \times u}{s \times m}$$

Partitions can reside in a tablespace that can have many files. You can have either a striped file or many files for each tablespace.

RAID CONFIGURATIONS

RAID systems, also called disk arrays, can be hardware- or software-based systems. The difference between the two is how CPU processing of I/O requests is handled. In software-based RAID systems, the operating system or an application level handles the I/O requests while in hardware-based RAID systems, disk controllers handle I/O requests. RAID usage is transparent to Oracle. All the features specific to a given RAID configuration are handled by the operating system and Oracle does not need to worry about them.

Primary logical database structures have different access patterns during read and write operations. Therefore, different RAID implementations will be better suited for these structures. The purpose of this chapter is to discuss some of the basic decisions you must make when designing the physical layout of your data warehouse implementation. It is not meant as a replacement for operating system and storage documentation or a consultant's analysis of your I/O requirements.

There are advantages and disadvantages to using RAID, and those depend on the RAID level under consideration and the specific system in question. The most common configurations in data warehouses are:

- RAID 0 (Striping)
- RAID 1 (Mirroring)
- RAID 0+1 (Striping and Mirroring)
- RAID 5

RAID 0 (Striping)

RAID 0 is a non-redundant disk array, so there will be data loss with any disk failure. If something on the disk becomes corrupted, you cannot restore or recalculate that data. RAID 0 provides the best write throughput performance because it never updates redundant information. Read throughput is also quite good, but you can improve it by combining RAID 0 with RAID 1.

Oracle does not recommend using RAID 0 systems without RAID 1 because the loss of one disk in the array will affect the complete system and make it unavailable. RAID 0 systems are used mainly in environments where performance and capacity are the primary concerns rather than availability.

RAID 1 (Mirroring)

RAID 1 provides full data redundancy by complete mirroring of all files. If a disk failure occurs, the mirrored copy is used to transparently service the request. RAID 1 mirroring requires twice as much disk space as there is data. In general, RAID 1 is most useful for systems where complete redundancy of data is required and disk space is not an issue. For large datafiles or systems with less disk space, RAID 1 may not be feasible, because it requires twice as much disk space as there is data. Writes under RAID 1 are no faster and no slower than usual. Reading data can be faster than on a single disk because the system can choose to read the data from the disk that can respond faster.

RAID 0+1 (Striping and Mirroring)

RAID 0+1 offers the best performance of all RAID systems, but costs the most because you double the number of drives. Basically, it combines the performance of RAID 0 and the fault tolerance of RAID 1. You should consider RAID 0+1 for datafiles with high write rates, for example, table datafiles, and online and archived redo log files.

Striping, Mirroring, and Media Recovery

Striping affects media recovery. Loss of a disk usually means loss of access to all objects stored on that disk. If all datafiles in a database are striped over all disks, then loss of any disk stops the entire database. Furthermore, you may need to restore all these database files from backups, even if each file has only a small fraction of its total data stored on the failed disk.

Often, the same system that provides striping also provides mirroring. With the declining price of disks, mirroring can provide an effective supplement to, but not a substitute for, backups and log archives. Mirroring can help your system recover from disk failures more quickly than using a backup, but mirroring is not as robust. Mirroring does not protect against software faults and other problems against which an independent backup would protect your system.

You can effectively use mirroring if you are able to reload read-only data from the original source tapes. If you have a disk failure, restoring data from backups can involve lengthy downtime, whereas restoring from a mirrored disk enables your system to get back online quickly or even stay online while the crashed disk is replaced and resynchronized.

RAID 5

RAID 5 systems provide redundancy for the original data while storing parity information as well. The parity information is striped over all disks in the system to avoid a single disk as a bottleneck during write operations. The I/O throughput of RAID 5 systems depends upon the implementation and the striping size. For a typical RAID 5 system, the throughput is normally lower than RAID 0 + 1 configurations. In particular, the performance for high concurrent write operations such as parallel load can be poor.

Many vendors use memory (as battery-backed cache) in front of the disks to increase throughput and to become comparable to RAID 0+1. Contact your disk array vendor for specific details.

The Importance of Specific Analysis

A data warehouse's requirements are at many levels, and resolving a problem at one level can cause problems with another. For example, resolving a problem with query performance during the ETL process can affect load performance. You cannot simply maximize query performance at the expense of an unrealistic load time. If you do, your implementation will fail. In addition, a particular process is dependent upon the warehouse's architecture. If you decide to change something in your system, it can cause performance to become unacceptable in another part of the warehousing process. An example of this is switching from using database files to flat files during the loading process. Flat files can have different read performance.

This chapter is not meant as a replacement for operating system and storage documentation. Your system's requirements will require detailed analysis prior to implementation. Only a detailed data warehouse architecture and I/O analysis will help you when deciding hardware and I/O strategies.

2 PARALLELISM AND PARTITIONING IN DATA WAREHOUSES

Data warehouses often contain large tables and require techniques both for managing these large tables and for providing good query performance across these large tables. This chapter discusses two key methodologies for addressing these needs: parallelism and partitioning.

OVERVIEW OF PARALLEL EXECUTION

Parallel execution dramatically reduces response time for data-intensive operations on large databases typically associated with decision support systems (DSS) and data warehouses. You can also implement **parallel execution** on certain types of online transaction processing (OLTP) and hybrid systems. Parallel execution is sometimes called **parallelism.** Simply expressed, parallelism is the idea of breaking down a task so that, instead of one process doing all of the work in a query, many processes do part of the work at the same time. An example of this is when four processes handle four different quarters in a year instead of one process handling all four quarters by itself. The improvement in performance can be quite high. In this case, each quarter will be a **partition,** a smaller and more manageable unit of an index or table.

When to Implement Parallel Execution

The most common use of parallel execution is in DSS and data warehousing environments. Complex queries, such as those involving joins of several tables or searches of very large tables, are often best executed in parallel.

Parallel execution is useful for many types of operations that access significant amounts of data. Parallel execution improves processing for:

- Large table scans and joins
- Creation of large indexes
- Partitioned index scans

- Bulk inserts, updates, and deletes
- Aggregations and copying.

You can also use parallel execution to access object types within an Oracle database. For example, use parallel execution to access LOBs (large objects).

Parallel execution benefits systems that have *all* of the following characteristics:

- Symmetric multi-processors (SMP), clusters, or massively parallel systems
- Sufficient I/O bandwidth
- Underutilized or intermittently used CPUs (for example, systems where CPU usage is typically less than 30%)
- Sufficient memory to support additional memory-intensive processes such as sorts, hashing, and I/O buffers.

If your system lacks any of these characteristics, parallel execution might not significantly improve performance. In fact, parallel execution can reduce system performance on overutilized systems or systems with small I/O bandwidth.

GRANULES OF PARALLELISM

Different parallel operations use different types of parallelism. The optimal physical database layout depends on the parallel operations that are most prevalent in your application or even of the necessity of using partitions.

The basic unit of work in parallelism is called a granule. Oracle divides the operation being parallelized (for example, a table scan, table update, or index creation) into granules. Parallel execution processes execute the operation one granule at a time. The number of granules and their size correlates with the degree of parallelism (DOP). It also affects how well the work is balanced across query server processes. There is no way you can enforce a specific granule strategy as Oracle makes this decision internally.

Block Range Granules

Block range granules are the basic unit of most parallel operations, even on partitioned tables. Therefore, from an Oracle perspective, the degree of parallelism is not related to the number of partitions.

Block range granules are ranges of physical blocks from a table. The number and the size of the granules are computed during runtime by Oracle to optimize and balance the work distribution for all affected parallel execution servers. The number and size of granules are dependent upon the size of the object and the DOP. Block range granules do not depend on static preallocation of tables or indexes. During the computation of the granules, Oracle takes the DOP into account and tries to assign granules from different datafiles to each of the parallel execution servers to avoid contention whenever possible. Additionally, Oracle considers the disk affinity of the granules on MPP systems to take advantage of the physical proximity between parallel execution servers and disks.

When block range granules are used predominantly for parallel access to a table or index, administrative considerations (such as recovery or using partitions for deleting portions of data) might influence partition layout more than performance considerations.

Partition Granules

When Oracle uses partition granules, a query server process works on an entire partition or subpartition of a table or index. Because partition granules are statically determined by the structure of the table or index when a table or index is created, partition granules do not give you the flexibility in parallelizing an operation that block granules do. The maximum allowable DOP is the number of partitions. This might limit the utilization of the system and the load balancing across parallel execution servers.

When Oracle uses partition granules for parallel access to a table or index, you should use a relatively large number of partitions (ideally, three times the DOP), so that Oracle can effectively balance work across the query server processes.

Partition granules are the basic unit of parallel index range scans and of parallel operations that modify multiple partitions of a partitioned table or index. These operations include parallel creation of partitioned indexes, and parallel creation of partitioned tables.

PARTITIONING DESIGN CONSIDERATIONS

In conjunction with parallel execution, partitioning can improve performance in data warehouses. The following are the main design considerations for partitioning:

- Types of partitioning
- Partition pruning
- Partition-wise joins.

Types of Partitioning

This section describes the partitioning features that significantly enhance data access and improve overall application performance. This is especially true for applications that access tables and indexes with millions of rows and many gigabytes of data.

Partitioned tables and indexes facilitate administrative operations by enabling these operations to work on subsets of data. For example, you can add a new partition, organize an existing partition, or drop a partition and cause less than a second of interruption to a read-only application.

Using the partitioning methods described in this section can help you tune SQL statements to avoid unnecessary index and table scans (using partition pruning). You can also improve the performance of massive join operations when large amounts of data (for example, several million rows) are joined together by using partition-wise joins. Finally, partitioning data greatly improves manageability of very large databases and dramatically reduces the time required for administrative tasks such as backup and restore.

Granularity can be easily added or removed to the partitioning scheme by splitting partitions. Thus, if a table's data is skewed to fill some partitions more than others, the ones that contain more data can be split to achieve a more even distribution. Partitioning also allows one to swap partitions with a table. By being able to easily add, remove, or swap a large amount of data quickly, swapping can be used to keep a large amount of data that is being loaded inaccessible until loading is completed, or can be used as a way to stage data between different phases of use. Some examples are current day's transactions or online archives.

Partitioning Methods

Oracle offers four partitioning methods:

- Range partitioning
- Hash partitioning
- List partitioning
- Composite partitioning.

Each partitioning method has different advantages and design considerations. Thus, each method is more appropriate for a particular situation.

Range Partitioning

Range partitioning maps data to partitions based on ranges of partition key values that you establish for each partition. It is the most common type of partitioning and is often used with dates. For example, you might want to partition sales data into monthly partitions.

Range partitioning maps rows to partitions based on ranges of column values. Range partitioning is defined by the partitioning specification for a table or index in `PARTITION BY RANGE (column_list)` and by the partitioning specifications for each individual partition in `VALUES LESS THAN (value_list)`, where `column_list` is an ordered list of columns that determines the partition to which a row or an index entry belongs. These columns are called the partitioning columns. The values in the partitioning columns of a particular row constitute that row's partitioning key.

`value_list` is an ordered list of values for the columns in the column list. Each value must be either a literal or a `TO_DATE` or `RPAD` function with constant arguments. Only the `VALUES LESS THAN` clause is allowed. This clause specifies a non-inclusive upper bound for the partitions. All partitions, except the first, have an implicit low value specified by the `VALUES LESS THAN` literal on the previous partition. Any binary values of the partition key equal to or higher than this literal are added to the next higher partition. Highest partition being where `MAXVALUE` literal is defined. Keyword, `MAXVALUE`, represents a virtual infinite value that sorts higher than any other value for the data type, including the null value.

The following statement creates a table `sales_range` that is range partitioned on the `sales_date` field:

```
CREATE TABLE sales_range
(salesman_id   NUMBER(5),
salesman_name  VARCHAR2(30),
sales_amount   NUMBER(10),
sales_date     DATE)
COMPRESS
PARTITION BY RANGE(sales_date)
(
PARTITION sales_jan2000 VALUES LESS THAN(TO_DATE('02/01/2000','DD/MM/YYYY')),
PARTITION sales_feb2000 VALUES LESS THAN(TO_DATE('03/01/2000','DD/MM/YYYY')),
PARTITION sales_mar2000 VALUES LESS THAN(TO_DATE('04/01/2000','DD/MM/YYYY')),
PARTITION sales_apr2000 VALUES LESS THAN(TO_DATE('05/01/2000','DD/MM/YYYY'))
```

Hash Partitioning

Hash partitioning maps data to partitions based on a hashing algorithm that Oracle applies to a partitioning key that you identify. The hashing algorithm evenly distributes rows among partitions, giving partitions approximately the same size. Hash partitioning is the ideal method for distributing data evenly across devices. Hash partitioning is a good and easy-to-use alternative to range partitioning when data is not historical and there is no obvious column or column list where logical range partition pruning can be advantageous.

Oracle uses a linear hashing algorithm and to prevent data from clustering within specific partitions, you should define the number of partitions by a power of two (for example, 2, 4, 8).

The following statement creates a table `sales_hash`, which is hash partitioned on the `salesman_id` field:

```
CREATE TABLE sales_hash
(salesman_id   NUMBER(5),
salesman_name  VARCHAR2(30),
sales_amount   NUMBER(10),
week_no        NUMBER(2))
PARTITION BY HASH(salesman_id)
PARTITIONS 4;
```

List Partitioning

List partitioning enables you to explicitly control how rows map to partitions. You do this by specifying a list of discrete values for the partitioning column in the description for each partition. This is different from range partitioning, where a range of values is associated with a partition and with hash partitioning, where you have no control of the row-to-partition mapping. The advantage of list partitioning is that you can group and organize unordered and unrelated sets of data in a natural way. The following example creates a list partitioned table grouping states according to their sales regions:

```
CREATE TABLE sales_list
(salesman_id   NUMBER(5),
salesman_name  VARCHAR2(30),
sales_state    VARCHAR2(20),
sales_amount   NUMBER(10),
sales_date     DATE)
PARTITION BY LIST(sales_state)
(
PARTITION sales_west VALUES('California', 'Hawaii') COMPRESS,
PARTITION sales_east VALUES('New York', 'Virginia', 'Florida'),
PARTITION sales_central VALUES('Texas', 'Illinois')
);
```

Partition `sales_west` is furthermore created as a single compressed partition within `sales_list`. For details about partitioning and compression, see **"Partitioning and Data Segment Compression"**.

An additional capability with list partitioning is that you can use a default partition, so that all rows that do not map to any other partition do not generate an error. For example, modifying the previous example, you can create a default partition as follows:

```
CREATE TABLE sales_list
(salesman_id   NUMBER(5),
salesman_name  VARCHAR2(30),
sales_state    VARCHAR2(20),
sales_amount   NUMBER(10),
sales_date     DATE)
PARTITION BY LIST(sales_state)
(
PARTITION sales_west VALUES('California', 'Háwaii'),
PARTITION sales_east VALUES ('New York', 'Virginia', 'Florida'),
PARTITION salés_central VALUES('Texas', 'Illinois')
PARTITION sales_other VALUES(DEFAULT)
);
```

Composite Partitioning

Composite partitioning combines range and hash or list partitioning. Oracle first distributes data into partitions according to boundaries established by the partition ranges. Then, for range-hash partitioning, Oracle uses a hashing algorithm to further divide the data into subpartitions within each range partition. For range-list partitioning, Oracle divides the data into subpartitions within each range partition based on the explicit list you chose.

Index Partitioning

You can choose whether or not to inherit the partitioning strategy of the underlying tables. You can create both local and global indexes on a table partitioned by range, hash, or composite methods. Local indexes inherit the partitioning attributes of their related tables. For example, if you create a local index on a composite table, Oracle automatically partitions the local index using the composite method.

Oracle supports only range partitioning for global partitioned indexes. You cannot partition global indexes using the hash or composite partitioning methods.

Performance Issues for Range, List, Hash, and Composite Partitioning

This section describes performance issues for:

- When to use range partitioning
- When to use hash partitioning
- When to use list partitioning
- When to use composite range-hash partitioning
- When to use composite range-list partitioning.

When to Use Range Partitioning

Range partitioning is a convenient method for partitioning historical data. The boundaries of range partitions define the ordering of the partitions in the tables or indexes.

Range partitioning organizes data by time intervals on a column of type DATE. Thus, most SQL statements accessing range partitions focus on timeframes. An example of this is an SQL statement similar to "select data from a particular period in time." In such a scenario, if each partition represents data for one month, the query "find data of month 98-DEC" needs to access only the December partition of year 98. This reduces the amount of data scanned to a fraction of the total data available, an optimization method called partition pruning.

Range partitioning is also ideal when you periodically load new data and purge old data. It is easy to add or drop partitions.

It is common to keep a rolling window of data, for example keeping the past 36 months' worth of data online. Range partitioning simplifies this process. To add data from a new month, you load it into a separate table, clean it, index it, and then add it to the range-partitioned table using the EXCHANGE PARTITION statement, all while the original table remains online. Once you add the new partition, you can drop the trailing month with the DROP PARTITION statement. The alternative to using the DROP PARTITION statement can be to archive the partition and make it read only, but this works only when your partitions are in separate tablespaces.

In conclusion, consider using range partitioning when:

- Very large tables are frequently scanned by a range predicate on a good partitioning column, such as ORDER_DATE or PURCHASE_DATE. Partitioning the table on that column enables partition pruning.
- You want to maintain a rolling window of data.
- You cannot complete administrative operations, such as backup and restore, on large tables in an allotted time frame, but you can divide them into smaller logical pieces based on the partition range column.

The following example creates the table sales for a period of two years, 1999 and 2000, and partitions it by range according to the column s_salesdate to separate the data into eight quarters, each corresponding to a partition.

```
CREATE TABLE sales
  (s_productid  NUMBER,
   s_saledate   DATE,
   s_custid     NUMBER,
   s_totalprice NUMBER)
  PARTITION BY RANGE(s_saledate)
 (PARTITION sal99q1 VALUES LESS THAN (TO_DATE('01-APR-1999', 'DD-MON-YYYY')),
  PARTITION sal99q2 VALUES LESS THAN (TO_DATE('01-JUL-1999', 'DD-MON-YYYY')),
  PARTITION sal99q3 VALUES LESS THAN (TO_DATE('01-OCT-1999', 'DD-MON-YYYY')),
  PARTITION sal99q4 VALUES LESS THAN (TO_DATE('01-JAN-2000', 'DD-MON-YYYY')),
  PARTITION sal00q1 VALUES LESS THAN (TO_DATE('01-APR-2000', 'DD-MON-YYYY')),
  PARTITION sal00q2 VALUES LESS THAN (TO_DATE('01-JUL-2000', 'DD-MON-YYYY')),
  PARTITION sal00q3 VALUES LESS THAN (TO_DATE('01-OCT-2000', 'DD-MON-YYYY')),
  PARTITION sal00q4 VALUES LESS THAN (TO_DATE('01-JAN-2001', 'DD-MON-YYYY')));
```

When to Use Hash Partitioning

The way Oracle distributes data in hash partitions does not correspond to a business or a logical view of the data, as it does in range partitioning. Consequently, hash partitioning is not an effective way to manage historical data. However, hash partitions share some performance characteristics with range partitions. For example, partition pruning is limited to equality predicates. You can also use partition-wise joins, parallel index access, and parallel DML.

As a general rule, use hash partitioning for these purposes:

- To improve the availability and manageability of large tables or to enable parallel DML in tables that do not store historical data.

- To avoid data skew among partitions. Hash partitioning is an effective means of distributing data because Oracle hashes the data into a number of partitions, each of which can reside on a separate device. Thus, data is evenly spread over a sufficient number of devices to maximize I/O throughput. Similarly, you can use hash partitioning to distribute evenly data among the nodes of an MPP platform that uses Oracle Real Application Clusters.
- If it is important to use partition pruning and partition-wise joins according to a partitioning key that is mostly constrained by a distinct value or value list.

NOTE

*In hash partitioning, partition pruning uses only equality or **IN**-list predicates.*

If you add or merge a hashed partition, Oracle automatically rearranges the rows to reflect the change in the number of partitions and subpartitions. The hash function that Oracle uses is especially designed to limit the cost of this reorganization. Instead of reshuffling all the rows in the table, Oracle uses an "add partition" logic that splits one and only one of the existing hashed partitions. Conversely, Oracle coalesces a partition by merging two existing hashed partitions.

Although the hash function's use of "add partition" logic dramatically improves the manageability of hash partitioned tables, it means that the hash function can cause a skew if the number of partitions of a hash partitioned table, or the number of subpartitions in each partition of a composite table, is not a power of two. In the worst case, the largest partition can be twice the size of the smallest. So for optimal performance, create a number of partitions and subpartitions for each partition that is a power of two. For example, 2, 4, 8, 16, 32, 64, 128, and so on.

The following example creates four hashed partitions for the table `sales_hash` using the column `s_productid` as the partition key:

```
CREATE TABLE sales_hash
   (s_productid   NUMBER,
   s_saledate     DATE,
   s_custid       NUMBER,
   s_totalprice   NUMBER)
   PARTITION BY HASH(s_productid)
   PARTITIONS 4;
```

Specify partition names if you want to choose the names of the partitions. Otherwise, Oracle automatically generates internal names for the partitions. Also, you can use the `STORE IN` clause to assign hash partitions to tablespaces in a round-robin manner.

When to Use List Partitioning

You should use list partitioning when you want to specifically map rows to partitions based on discrete values.

Unlike range and hash partitioning, multi-column partition keys are not supported for list partitioning. If a table is partitioned by list, the partitioning key can only consist of a single column of the table.

When to Use Composite Range-Hash Partitioning

Composite range-hash partitioning offers the benefits of both range and hash partitioning. With composite range-hash partitioning, Oracle first partitions by range. Then, within each range, Oracle creates subpartitions and distributes data within them using the same hashing algorithm it uses for hash partitioned tables.

Data placed in composite partitions is logically ordered only by the boundaries that define the range level partitions. The partitioning of data within each partition has no logical organization beyond the identity of the partition to which the subpartitions belong.

Consequently, tables and local indexes partitioned using the composite range-hash method:

- Support historical data at the partition level
- Support the use of subpartitions as units of parallelism for parallel operations such as PDML or space management and backup and recovery
- Are eligible for partition pruning and partition-wise joins on the range and hash dimensions.

Using Composite Range-Hash Partitioning

Use the composite range-hash partitioning method for tables and local indexes if:

- Partitions must have a logical meaning to efficiently support historical data
- The contents of a partition can be spread across multiple tablespaces, devices, or nodes (of an MPP system)
- You require both partition pruning and partition-wise joins even when the pruning and join predicates use different columns of the partitioned table
- You require a degree of parallelism that is greater than the number of partitions for backup, recovery, and parallel operations.

Most large tables in a data warehouse should use range partitioning. Composite partitioning should be used for very large tables or for data warehouses with a well-defined need for these conditions. When using the composite method, Oracle stores each subpartition on a different segment. Thus, the subpartitions may have properties that differ from the properties of the table or from the partition to which the subpartitions belong.

The following example partitions the table `sales_range_hash` by range on the column `s_saledate` to create four partitions that order data by time. Then, within each range partition, the data is further subdivided into 16 subpartitions by hash on the column `s_productid`:

```
CREATE TABLE sales_range_hash(
  s_productid  NUMBER,
  s_saledate   DATE,
  s_custid     NUMBER,
  s_totalprice NUMBER)
   PARTITION BY RANGE (s_saledate)
   SUBPARTITION BY HASH (s_productid) SUBPARTITIONS 8
  (PARTITION sal99q1 VALUES LESS THAN (TO_DATE('01-APR-1999', 'DD-MON-YYYY')),
   PARTITION sal99q2 VALUES LESS THAN (TO_DATE('01-JUL-1999', 'DD-MON-YYYY')),
   PARTITION sal99q3 VALUES LESS THAN (TO_DATE('01-OCT-1999', 'DD-MON-YYYY')),
   PARTITION sal99q4 VALUES LESS THAN (TO_DATE('01-JAN-2000', 'DD-MON-YYYY')));
```

Each hashed subpartition contains sales data for a single quarter ordered by product code. The total number of subpartitions is 4×8 or 32.

In addition to this syntax, you can create subpartitions by using a subpartition template. This offers better ease in naming and control of location for tablespaces and subpartitions. The following statement illustrates this:

```
CREATE TABLE sales_range_hash(
  s_productid  NUMBER,
  s_saledate   DATE,
  s_custid     NUMBER,
  s_totalprice NUMBER)
   PARTITION BY RANGE (s_saledate)
   SUBPARTITION BY HASH (s_productid)
   SUBPARTITION TEMPLATE(
  SUBPARTITION sp1 TABLESPACE tbs1,
  SUBPARTITION sp2 TABLESPACE tbs2,
  SUBPARTITION sp3 TABLESPACE tbs3,
  SUBPARTITION sp4 TABLESPACE tbs4,
  SUBPARTITION sp5 TABLESPACE tbs5,
  SUBPARTITION sp6 TABLESPACE tbs6,
  SUBPARTITION sp7 TABLESPACE tbs7,
  SUBPARTITION sp8 TABLESPACE tbs8)
  (PARTITION sal99q1 VALUES LESS THAN (TO_DATE('01-APR-1999', 'DD-MON-YYYY')),
  PARTITION sal99q2 VALUES LESS THAN (TO_DATE('01-JUL-1999', 'DD-MON-YYYY')),
  PARTITION sal99q3 VALUES LESS THAN (TO_DATE('01-OCT-1999', 'DD-MON-YYYY')),
  PARTITION sal99q4 VALUES LESS THAN (TO_DATE('01-JAN-2000', 'DD-MON-YYYY')));
```

In this example, every partition has the same number of subpartitions. A sample mapping for `sal99q1` is illustrated in table 2.1. Similar mappings exist for `sal99q2` through `sal99q4`.

Table 2.1 Subpartition Mapping

Subpartition	Tablespace
sal99q1_sp1	tbs1
sal99q1_sp2	tbs2
sal99q1_sp3	tbs3
sal99q1_sp4	tbs4
sal99q1_sp5	tbs5
sal99q1_sp6	tbs6
sal99q1_sp7	tbs7
sal99q1_sp8	tbs8

When to Use Composite Range-List Partitioning

Composite range-list partitioning offers the benefits of both range and list partitioning. With composite range-list partitioning, Oracle first partitions by range. Then, within each range, Oracle creates subpartitions and distributes data within them to organize sets of data in a natural way as assigned by the list.

Data placed in composite partitions is logically ordered only by the boundaries that define the range level partitions.

Using Composite Range-List Partitioning

Use the composite range-list partitioning method for tables and local indexes if:

- Subpartitions have a logical grouping defined by the user

- The contents of a partition can be spread across multiple tablespaces, devices, or nodes (of an MPP system)
- You require both partition pruning and partition-wise joins even when the pruning and join predicates use different columns of the partitioned table
- You require a degree of parallelism that is greater than the number of partitions for backup, recovery, and parallel operations.

Most large tables in a data warehouse should use range partitioning. Composite partitioning should be used for very large tables or for data warehouses with a well-defined need for these conditions. When using the composite method, Oracle stores each subpartition on a different segment. Thus, the subpartitions may have properties that differ from the properties of the table or from the partition to which the subpartitions belong.

This statement creates a table `quarterly_regional_sales` that is range partitioned on the `txn_date` field and list subpartitioned on `state`.

```
CREATE TABLE quarterly_regional_sales
(deptno NUMBER,
  item_no VARCHAR2(20),
  txn_date DATE,
  txn_amount NUMBER,
  state VARCHAR2(2))
PARTITION BY RANGE (txn_date)
SUBPARTITION BY LIST (state)
(
PARTITION q1_1999 VALUES LESS THAN(TO_DATE('1-APR-1999','DD-MON-YYYY'))
(SUBPARTITION q1_1999_northwest VALUES ('OR', 'WA'),
  SUBPARTITION q1_1999_southwest VALUES ('AZ', 'UT', 'NM'),
  SUBPARTITION q1_1999_northeast VALUES ('NY', 'VM', 'NJ'),
  SUBPARTITION q1_1999_southeast VALUES ('FL', 'GA'),
  SUBPARTITION q1_1999_northcentral VALUES ('SD', 'WI'),
  SUBPARTITION q1_1999_southcentral VALUES ('NM', 'TX')),
PARTITION q2_1999 VALUES LESS THAN(TO_DATE('1-JUL-1999','DD-MON-YYYY'))
(SUBPARTITION q2_1999_northwest VALUES ('OR', 'WA'),
  SUBPARTITION q2_1999_southwest VALUES ('AZ', 'UT', 'NM'),
  SUBPARTITION q2_1999_northeast VALUES ('NY', 'VM', 'NJ'),
  SUBPARTITION q2_1999_southeast VALUES ('FL', 'GA'),
  SUBPARTITION q2_1999_northcentral VALUES ('SD', 'WI'),
  SUBPARTITION q2_1999_southcentral VALUES ('NM', 'TX')),
PARTITION q3_1999 VALUES LESS THAN (TO_DATE('1-OCT-1999','DD-MON-YYYY'))
(SUBPARTITION q3_1999_northwest VALUES ('OR', 'WA'),
  SUBPARTITION q3_1999_southwest VALUES ('AZ', 'UT', 'NM'),
  SUBPARTITION q3_1999_northeast VALUES ('NY', 'VM', 'NJ'),
  SUBPARTITION q3_1999_southeast VALUES ('FL', 'GA'),
  SUBPARTITION q3_1999_northcentral VALUES ('SD', 'WI'),
  SUBPARTITION q3_1999_southcentral VALUES ('NM', 'TX')),
PARTITION q4_1999 VALUES LESS THAN (TO_DATE('1-JAN-2000','DD-MON-YYYY'))
(SUBPARTITION q4_1999_northwest VALUES('OR', 'WA'),
  SUBPARTITION q4_1999_southwest VALUES('AZ', 'UT', 'NM'),
  SUBPARTITION q4_1999_northeast VALUES('NY', 'VM', 'NJ'),
  SUBPARTITION q4_1999_southeast VALUES('FL', 'GA'),
  SUBPARTITION q4_1999_northcentral VALUES ('SD', 'WI'),
  SUBPARTITION q4_1999_southcentral VALUES ('NM', 'TX')));
```

You can create subpartitions in a composite partitioned table using a subpartition template. A subpartition template simplifies the specification of subpartitions by not requiring that a subpartition descriptor be specified for every partition in the table. Instead, you describe subpartitions only once in a template, then apply that subpartition template to every partition in the table. The following statement illustrates an example where you can choose the subpartition name and tablespace locations:

```
CREATE TABLE quarterly_regional_sales
(deptno NUMBER,
  item_no VARCHAR2(20),
  txn_date DATE,
  txn_amount NUMBER,
  state VARCHAR2(2))
PARTITION BY RANGE (txn_date)
SUBPARTITION BY LIST (state)
SUBPARTITION TEMPLATE(
SUBPARTITION northwest VALUES ('OR', 'WA') TABLESPACE ts1,
SUBPARTITION southwest VALUES ('AZ', 'UT', 'NM') TABLESPACE ts2,
SUBPARTITION northeast VALUES ('NY', 'VM', 'NJ') TABLESPACE ts3,
SUBPARTITION southeast VALUES ('FL', 'GA') TABLESPACE ts4,
SUBPARTITION northcentral VALUES ('SD', 'WI') TABLESPACE ts5,
SUBPARTITION southcentral VALUES ('NM', 'TX') TABLESPACE ts6)
(PARTITION q1_1999 VALUES LESS THAN(TO_DATE('1-APR-1999','DD-MON-YYYY')),
  PARTITION q2_1999 VALUES LESS THAN(TO_DATE('1-JUL-1999','DD-MON-YYYY')),
  PARTITION q3_1999 VALUES LESS THAN(TO_DATE('1-OCT-1999','DD-MON-YYYY')),
  PARTITION q4_1999 VALUES LESS THAN(TO_DATE('1-JAN-2000','DD-MON-YYYY')));
```

Partitioning and Data Segment Compression

You can compress several partitions or a complete partitioned heap-organized table. You do this by either defining a complete partitioned table as being compressed, or by defining it on a per-partition level. Partitions without a specific declaration inherit the attribute from the table definition or, if nothing is specified on table level, from the tablespace definition.

To decide whether or not a partition should be compressed or stay uncompressed adheres to the same rules as a nonpartitioned table. However, due to the capability of range and composite partitioning to separate data logically into distinct partitions, such a partitioned table is an ideal candidate for compressing parts of the data (partitions) that are mainly read-only. It is, for example, beneficial in all rolling window operations as a kind of intermediate stage before aging out old data. With data segment compression, you can keep more old data online, minimizing the burden of additional storage consumption.

You can also change any existing uncompressed table partition later on, add new compressed and uncompressed partitions, or change the compression attribute as part of any partition maintenance operation that requires data movement, such as `MERGE PARTITION`, `SPLIT PARTITION`, or `MOVE PARTITION`. The partitions can contain data or can be empty.

The access and maintenance of a partially or fully compressed partitioned table are the same as for a fully uncompressed partitioned table. Everything that applies to fully uncompressed partitioned tables is also valid for partially or fully compressed partitioned tables.

Data Segment Compression and Bitmap Indexes

If you want to use data segment compression on partitioned tables with bitmap indexes, you need to do the following before you introduce the compression attribute for the first time:

1. Mark bitmap indexes unusable.
2. Set the compression attribute.
3. Rebuild the indexes.

The first time you make a compressed partition part of an already existing, fully uncompressed partitioned table, you must either drop all existing bitmap indexes or mark them `UNUSABLE` prior to adding a compressed partition. This must be done irrespective of whether any partition contains any data. It is also independent of the operation that causes one or more compressed partitions to become part of the table. This does not apply to a partitioned table having B-tree indexes only.

This rebuilding of the bitmap index structures is necessary to accommodate the potentially higher number of rows stored for each data block with data segment compression enabled and must be done only for the first time. All subsequent operations, whether they affect compressed or uncompressed partitions, or change the compression attribute, behave identically for uncompressed, partially compressed, or fully compressed partitioned tables.

To avoid the recreation of any bitmap index structure, Oracle recommends creating every partitioned table with at least one compressed partition whenever you plan to partially or fully compress the partitioned table in the future. This compressed partition can stay empty or even can be dropped after the partition table creation.

Having a partitioned table with compressed partitions can lead to slightly larger bitmap index structures for the uncompressed partitions. The bitmap index structures for the compressed partitions, however, are in most cases smaller than the appropriate bitmap index structure before data segment compression. This highly depends on the achieved compression rates.

NOTE *Oracle will raise an error if compression is introduced to an object for the first time and there are usable bitmap index segments.*

Example of Data Segment Compression and Partitioning

The following statement moves and compresses an already existing partition `sales_q1_1998` of table `sales`:

```
ALTER TABLE sales
MOVE PARTITION sales_q1_1998 TABLESPACE ts_arch_q1_1998 COMPRESS;
```

If you use the `MOVE` statement, the local indexes for partition `sales_q1_1998` become unusable. You have to rebuild them afterward, as follows:

```
ALTER TABLE sales
MODIFY PARTITION sales_q1_1998 REBUILD UNUSABLE LOCAL INDEXES;
```

The following statement merges two existing partitions into a new, compressed partition, residing in a separate tablespace. The local bitmap indexes have to be rebuilt afterward, as follows:

```
ALTER TABLE sales MERGE PARTITIONS sales_q1_1998, sales_q2_1998
INTO PARTITION sales_1_1998 TABLESPACE ts_arch_1_1998
COMPRESS UPDATE GLOBAL INDEXES;
```

Partition Pruning

Partition pruning is an essential performance feature for data warehouses. In partition pruning, the cost-based optimizer analyzes FROM and WHERE clauses in SQL statements to eliminate unneeded partitions when building the partition access list. This enables Oracle to perform operations only on those partitions that are relevant to the SQL statement. Oracle prunes partitions when you use range, LIKE, equality, and IN-list predicates on the range or list partitioning columns, and when you use equality and IN-list predicates on the hash partitioning columns.

Partition pruning dramatically reduces the amount of data retrieved from disk and shortens the use of processing time, improving query performance and resource utilization. If you partition the index and table on different columns (with a global, partitioned index), partition pruning also eliminates index partitions even when the partitions of the underlying table cannot be eliminated.

On composite partitioned objects, Oracle can prune at both the range partition level and at the hash or list subpartition level using the relevant predicates. Refer to the table sales_range_hash earlier, partitioned by range on the column s_salesdate and subpartitioned by hash on column s_productid, and consider the following example:

```
SELECT * FROM sales_range_hash
WHERE s_saledate BETWEEN (TO_DATE('01-JUL-1999', 'DD-MON-YYYY')) AND
  (TO_DATE('01-OCT-1999', 'DD-MON-YYYY')) AND s_productid = 1200;
```

Oracle uses the predicate on the partitioning columns to perform partition pruning as follows:

- When using range partitioning, Oracle accesses only partitions sal99q2 and sal99q3.
- When using hash subpartitioning, Oracle accesses only the one subpartition in each partition that stores the rows with s_productid=1200. The mapping between the subpartition and the predicate is calculated based on Oracle's internal hash distribution function.

Pruning Using DATE Columns

In the earlier partitioning pruning example, the date value was fully specified as four digits for the year using the TO_DATE function, just as it was in the underlying table's range partitioning description. While this is the recommended format for specifying date values, the optimizer can prune partitions using the predicates on s_salesdate when you use other formats, as in the following example:

```
SELECT * FROM sales_range_hash
WHERE s_saledate BETWEEN TO_DATE('01-JUL-99', 'DD-MON-RR') AND
   TO_DATE('01-OCT-99', 'DD-MON-RR') AND s_productid = 1200;
```

Although this uses the DD-MON-RR format, which is not the same as the base partition, the optimizer can still prune properly.

If you execute an EXPLAIN PLAN statement on the query, the PARTITION_START and PARTITION_STOP columns of the output table do not specify which partitions Oracle is accessing. Instead, you see the keyword KEY for both columns. The keyword KEY for both columns means that partition pruning occurs at run-time. It can also affect the execution plan because the information about the pruned partitions is missing compared to the same statement using the same TO_DATE function than the partition table definition.

Avoiding I/O Bottlenecks

To avoid I/O bottlenecks, when Oracle is not scanning all partitions because some have been eliminated by pruning, spread each partition over several devices. On MPP systems, spread those devices over multiple nodes.

Partition-Wise Joins

Partition-wise joins reduce query response time by minimizing the amount of data exchanged among parallel execution servers when joins execute in parallel. This significantly reduces response time and improves the use of both CPU and memory resources. In Oracle Real Application Clusters environments, partition-wise joins also avoid or at least limit the data traffic over the interconnect, which is the key to achieve good scalability for massive join operations.

Partition-wise joins can be full or partial. Oracle decides which type of join to use.

Full Partition-Wise Joins

A full partition-wise join divides a large join into smaller joins between a pair of partitions from the two joined tables. To use this feature, you must equipartition both tables on their join keys. For example, consider a large join between a sales table and a customer table on the column customerid. The query "find the records of all customers who bought more than 100 articles in Quarter 3 of 1999" is a typical example of a SQL statement performing such a join. The following is an example of this:

```
SELECT c.cust_last_name, COUNT(*)
FROM sales s, customers c
WHERE s.cust_id = c.cust_id
     AND s.time_id BETWEEN TO_DATE('01-JUL-1999', 'DD-MON-YYYY') AND
     (TO_DATE('01-OCT-1999', 'DD-MON-YYYY'))
  GROUP BY c.cust_last_name HAVING
  COUNT(*) > 100;
```

This large join is typical in data warehousing environments. The entire customer table is joined with one quarter of the sales data. In large data warehouse applications, this might mean joining millions of rows. The join method to use in that case is obviously a hash join. You can reduce the processing time for this hash join even more if both tables are equipartitioned on the `customerid` column. This enables a full partition-wise join.

When you execute a full partition-wise join in parallel, the granule of parallelism, as described under **"Granules of Parallelism"**, is a partition. As a result, the degree of parallelism is limited to the number of partitions. For example, you require at least 16 partitions to set the degree of parallelism of the query to 16.

You can use various partitioning methods to equipartition both tables on the column `customerid` with 16 partitions. These methods are described in these subsections.

Hash-Hash

This is the simplest method: the `customers` and `sales` tables are both partitioned by hash into 16 partitions, on the `s_customerid` and `c_customerid` columns. This partitioning method enables full partition-wise join when the tables are joined on `s_customerid` and `c_customerid`, both representing the same customer identification number. Because you are using the same hash function to distribute the same information (customer ID) into the same number of hash partitions, you can join the equivalent partitions. They are storing the same values.

In serial, this join is performed between pairs of matching hash partitions, one at a time. When one partition pair has been joined, the join of another partition pair begins. The join completes when the 16 partition pairs have been processed.

NOTE *A pair of matching hash partitions is defined as one partition with the same partition number from each table. For example, with full partition-wise joins we join partition 0 of* `sales` *with partition 0 of* `customers`*, partition 1 of* `sales` *with partition 1 of* `customers`*, and so on.*

Parallel execution of a full partition-wise join is a straightforward parallelization of the serial execution. Instead of joining one partition pair at a time, 16 partition pairs are joined in parallel by the 16 query servers. Figure 2.1 illustrates the parallel execution of a full partition-wise join.

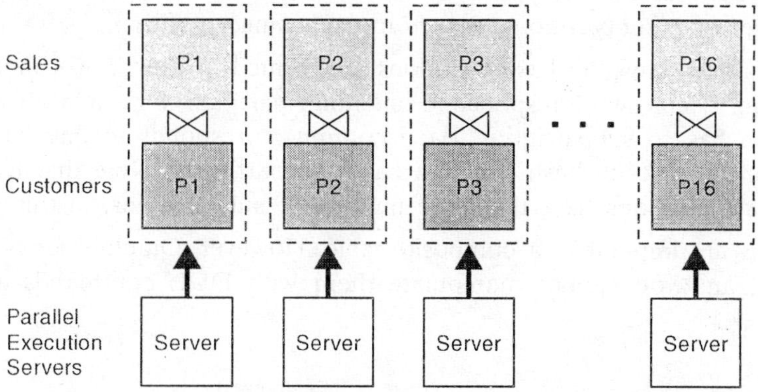

Figure 2.1 Parallel Execution of a Full Partition-wise Join.

In figure 2.1, assume that the degree of parallelism and the number of partitions are the same, in other words, 16 for both. Defining more partitions than the degree of parallelism may improve load balancing and limit possible skew in the execution. If you have more partitions than query servers, when one query server completes the join of one pair of partitions, it requests that the query coordinator give it another pair to join. This process repeats until all pairs have been processed. This method enables the load to be balanced dynamically when the number of partition pairs is greater than the degree of parallelism, for example, 64 partitions with a degree of parallelism of 16.

NOTE *To guarantee an equal work distribution, the number of partitions should always be a multiple of the degree of parallelism.*

In Oracle Real Application Clusters environments running on shared-nothing or MPP platforms, placing partitions on nodes is critical to achieving good scalability. To avoid remote I/O, both matching partitions should have affinity to the same node. Partition pairs should be spread over all nodes to avoid bottlenecks and to use all CPU resources available on the system.

Nodes can host multiple pairs when there are more pairs than nodes. For example, with an 8-node system and 16 partition pairs, each node receives two pairs.

(Composite-Hash)-Hash

This method is a variation of the hash-hash method. The `sales` table is a typical example of a table storing historical data. For all the reasons mentioned under the heading **"When to Use Range Partitioning"**, range is the logical initial partitioning method.

For example, assume you want to partition the sales table into eight partitions by range on the column s_salesdate. Also assume you have two years and that each partition represents a quarter. Instead of using range partitioning, you can use composite partitioning to enable a full partition-wise join while preserving the partitioning on s_salesdate. Partition the sales table by range on s_salesdate and then subpartition each partition by hash on s_customerid using 16 subpartitions for each partition, for a total of 128 subpartitions. The customers table can still use hash partitioning with 16 partitions.

When you use the method just described, a full partition-wise join works similar to the one created by the hash-hash method. The join is still divided into 16 smaller joins between hash partition pairs from both tables. The difference is that now each hash partition in the sales table is composed of a set of 8 subpartitions, one from each range partition.

Figure 2.2 illustrates how the hash partitions are formed in the sales table. Each cell represents a subpartition. Each row corresponds to one range partition, for a total of 8 range partitions. Each range partition has 16 subpartitions. Each column corresponds to one hash partition for a total of 16 hash partitions; each hash partition has 8 subpartitions. Note that hash partitions can be defined only if all partitions have the same number of subpartitions, in this case, 16.

Hash partitions are implicit in a composite table. However, Oracle does not record them in the data dictionary, and you cannot manipulate them with DDL commands as you can range partitions.

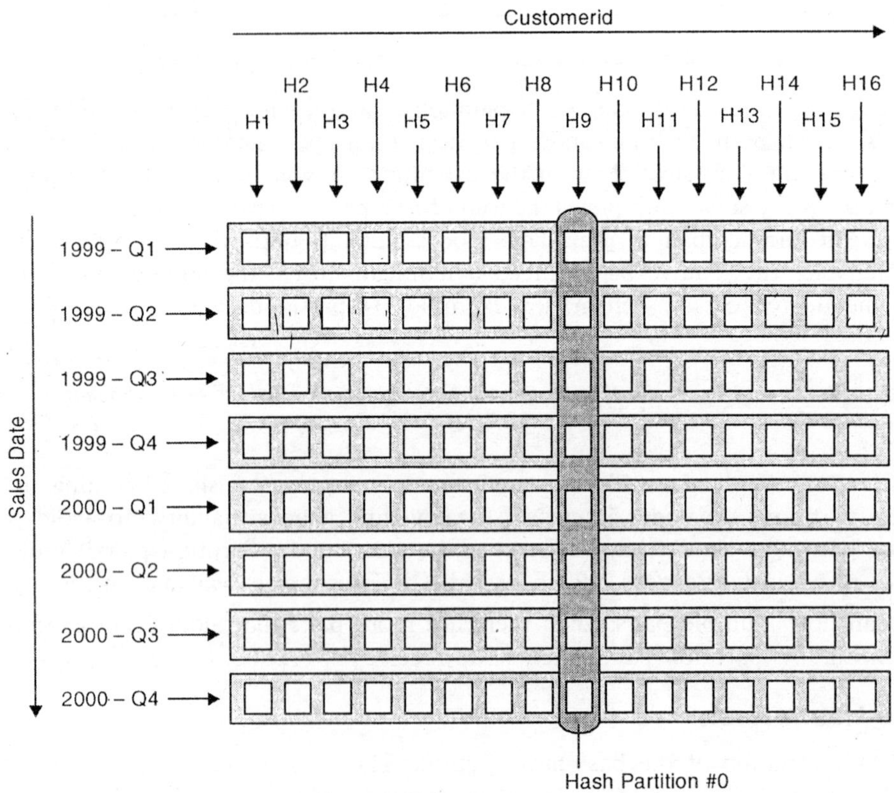

Figure 2.2 Range and Hash Partitions of a Composite Table

(Composite-Hash)-Hash partitioning is effective because it lets you combine pruning (on s_salesdate) with a full partition-wise join (on customerid). In the previous example query, pruning is achieved by scanning only the subpartitions corresponding to Q3 of 1999, in other words, row number 3 in figure 2.2. Oracle then joins these subpartitions with the customer table, using a full partition-wise join.

All characteristics of the hash-hash partition-wise join apply to the composite-hash partition-wise join. In particular, for this example, these two points are common to both methods:

- The degree of parallelism for this full partition-wise join cannot exceed 16. Even though the sales table has 128 subpartitions, it has only 16 hash partitions.
- The rules for data placement on MPP systems apply here. The only difference is that a hash partition is now a collection of subpartitions. You must ensure that all these subpartitions are placed on the same node as the matching hash partition from the other table. For example, in figure 2.2, store hash partition 9 of the sales table shown by the eight circled subpartitions, on the same node as hash partition 9 of the customers table.

(Composite-List)-List

The (Composite-List)-List method resembles that for (Composite-Hash)-Hash partition-wise joins.

Composite-Composite (Hash/List Dimension)

If needed, you can also partition the customer table by the composite method. For example, you partition it by range on a postal code column to enable pruning based on postal code. You than subpartition it by hash on customerid using the same number of partitions (16) to enable a partition-wise join on the hash dimension.

Range-Range and List-List

You can also join range partitioned tables with range partitioned tables and list partitioned tables with list partitioned tables in a partition-wise manner, but this is relatively uncommon. This is more complex to implement because you must know the distribution of the data before performing the join. Furthermore, if you do not correctly identify the partition bounds so that you have partitions of equal size, data skew during the execution may result.

The basic principle for using range-range and list-list is the same as for using hash-hash: you must equipartition both tables. This means that the number of partitions must be the same and the partition bounds must be identical. For example, assume that you know in advance that you have 10 million customers, and that the values for customerid vary from 1 to 10,000,000. In other words, you have 10 million possible different values. To create 16 partitions, you can range partition both tables, sales on c_customerid and customers on s_customerid. You should define partition bounds for both tables in order to generate partitions of the same size. In this example, partition bounds should be defined as 625001, 1250001, 1875001, ... 10000001, so that each partition contains 625000 rows.

Range-Composite, Composite-Composite (Range Dimension)

Finally, you can also subpartition one or both tables on another column. Therefore, the range-composite and composite-composite methods on the range dimension are also valid for enabling a full partition-wise join on the range dimension.

Partial Partition-wise Joins

Oracle can perform partial partition-wise joins only in parallel. Unlike full partition-wise joins, partial partition-wise joins require you to partition only one table on the join key, not both tables. The partitioned table is referred to as the reference table. The other table may or may not be partitioned. Partial partition-wise joins are more common than full partition-wise joins.

To execute a partial partition-wise join, Oracle dynamically repartitions the other table based on the partitioning of the reference table. Once the other table is repartitioned, the execution is similar to a full partition-wise join.

The performance advantage that partial partition-wise joins have over joins in non-partitioned tables is that the reference table is not moved during the join operation. Parallel joins between non-partitioned tables require both input tables to be redistributed on the join key. This redistribution operation involves exchanging rows between parallel execution servers. This is a CPU-intensive operation that can lead to excessive interconnect traffic in Oracle Real Application Clusters environments. Partitioning large tables on a join key, either a foreign or primary key, prevents this redistribution every time the table is joined on that key. Of course, if you choose a foreign key to partition the table, which is the most common scenario, select a foreign key that is involved in many queries.

To illustrate partial partition-wise joins, consider the previous `sales/customer` example. Assume that `s_customer` is not partitioned or is partitioned on a column other than `c_customerid`. Because `sales` is often joined with `customers` on `customerid`, and because this join dominates our application workload, partition `sales` on `s_customerid` to enable partial partition-wise join every time `customers` and `sales` are joined. As in full partition-wise join, you have several alternatives:

Hash/List

The simplest method to enable a partial partition-wise join is to partition `sales` by hash on `c_customerid`. The number of partitions determines the maximum degree of parallelism, because the partition is the smallest granule of parallelism for partial partition-wise join operations.

The parallel execution of a partial partition-wise join is illustrated in figure 2.3, which assumes that both the degree of parallelism and the number of partitions of `sales` are 16. The execution involves two sets of query servers: one set, labeled *set 1* in figure 2.3, scans the `customers` table in parallel. The granule of parallelism for the scan operation is a range of blocks.

Rows from `customers` that are selected by the first set, in this case all rows, are redistributed to the second set of query servers by hashing `customerid`. For example, all rows in `customers` that could have matching rows in partition `P1` of `sales` are sent to query server 1 in the second set. Rows received by the second set of query servers are joined with the rows from the corresponding partitions in `sales`. Query server number 1 in the second set joins all `customers` rows that it receives with partition `P1` of `sales`.

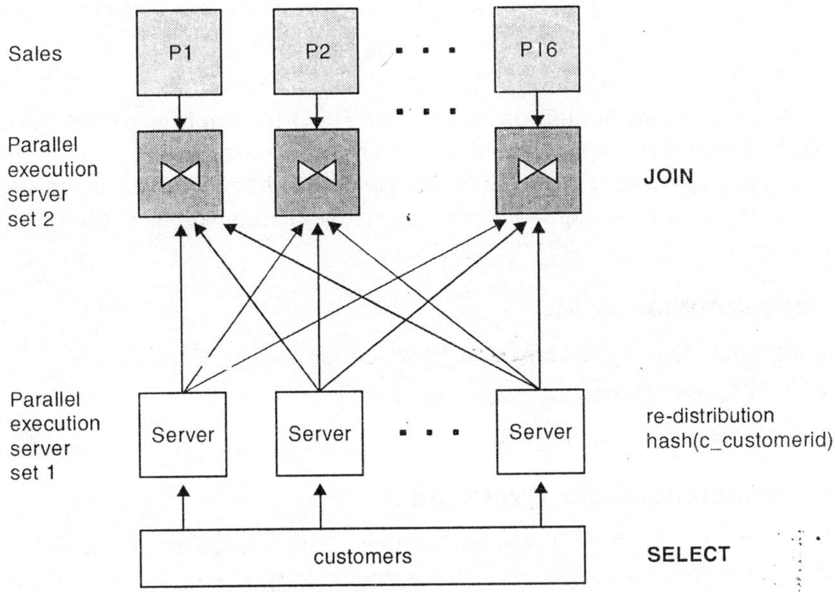

Figure 2.3 Partial Partition-wise Join.

NOTE *This section is based on range-hash, but it also applies for range-list partial partition-wise joins.*

Considerations for full partition-wise joins also apply to partial partition-wise joins:

- The degree of parallelism does not need to equal the number of partitions. In figure 2.3, the query executes with two sets of 16 query servers. In this case, Oracle assigns 1 partition to each query server of the second set. Again, the number of partitions should always be a multiple of the degree of parallelism.
- In Oracle Real Application Clusters environments on shared-nothing platforms (MPPs), each hash partition of `sales` should preferably have affinity to only one node in order to avoid remote I/Os. Also, spread partitions over all nodes to avoid bottlenecks and use all CPU resources available on the system. A node can host multiple partitions when there are more partitions than nodes.

Composite

As with full partition-wise joins, the prime partitioning method for the `sales` table is to use the range method on column `s_salesdate`. This is because `sales` is a typical example of a table that stores historical data. To enable a partial partition-wise join while preserving this range partitioning, subpartition `sales` by hash on column `s_customerid` using 16 subpartitions for each partition. Pruning and partial partition-wise joins can be used together if a query joins `customers` and `sales` and if the query has a selection predicate on `s_salesdate`.

When `sales` is composite, the granule of parallelism for a partial partition-wise join is a hash partition and not a subpartition. Refer to figure 2.2 for an illustration of a hash partition in a composite table. Again, the number of hash partitions should be a multiple of the degree of parallelism. Also, on an MPP system, ensure that each hash partition has affinity to a single node. In the previous example, the eight subpartitions composing a hash partition should have affinity to the same node.

NOTE *This section is based on range-hash, but it also applies for range-list partial partition-wise joins.*

Range

Finally, you can use range partitioning on `s_customerid` to enable a partial partition-wise join. This works similarly to the hash method, but a side effect of range partitioning is that the resulting data distribution could be skewed if the size of the partitions differs. Moreover, this method is more complex to implement because it requires prior knowledge of the values of the partitioning column that is also a join key.

Benefits of Partition-Wise Joins

Partition-wise joins offer benefits described in this section:

- Reduction of communications overhead
- Reduction of memory requirements.

Reduction of Communications Overhead

When executed in parallel, partition-wise joins reduce communications overhead. This is because, in the default case, parallel execution of a join operation by a set of parallel execution servers requires the redistribution of each table on the join column into disjoint subsets of rows. These disjoint subsets of rows are then joined pair-wise by a single parallel execution server.

Oracle can avoid redistributing the partitions because the two tables are already partitioned on the join column. This enables each parallel execution server to join a pair of matching partitions.

This improved performance from using parallel execution is even more noticeable in Oracle Real Application Clusters configurations with internode parallel execution. Partition-wise joins dramatically reduce interconnect traffic. Using this feature is for large DSS configurations that use Oracle Real Application Clusters.

Currently, most Oracle Real Application Clusters platforms, such as MPP and SMP clusters, provide limited interconnect bandwidths compared with their processing powers. Ideally, interconnect bandwidth should be comparable to disk bandwidth, but this is seldom the case. As a result, most join operations in Oracle Real Application Clusters experience high interconnect latencies without parallel execution of partition-wise joins.

Reduction of Memory Requirements

Partition-wise joins require less memory than the equivalent join operation of the complete data set of the tables being joined.

In the case of serial joins, the join is performed at the same time on a pair of matching partitions. If data is evenly distributed across partitions, the memory requirement is divided by the number of partitions. There is no skew.

In the parallel case, memory requirements depend on the number of partition pairs that are joined in parallel. For example, if the degree of parallelism is 20 and the number of partitions is 100, 5 times less memory is required because only 20 joins of two partitions are performed at the same time. The fact that partition-wise joins require less memory has a direct effect on performance. For example, the join probably does not need to write blocks to disk during the build phase of a hash join.

Performance Considerations for Parallel Partition-Wise Joins

The cost-based optimizer weighs the advantages and disadvantages when deciding whether or not to use partition-wise joins.

- In range partitioning where partition sizes differ, data skew increases response time; some parallel execution servers take longer than others to finish their joins. Oracle recommends the use of hash (sub)partitioning to enable partition-wise joins because hash partitioning, if the number of partitions is a power of two, limits the risk of skew.
- The number of partitions used for partition-wise joins should, if possible, be a multiple of the number of query servers. With a degree of parallelism of 16, for example, you can have 16, 32, or even 64 partitions. If there is an even number of partitions, some parallel execution servers are used less than others. For example, if there are 17 evenly distributed partition pairs, only one pair will work on the last join, while the other pairs will have to wait. This is because, in the beginning of the execution, each parallel execution server works on a different partition pair. At the end of this first phase, only one pair is left. Thus, a single parallel execution server joins this remaining pair while all other parallel execution servers are idle.
- Sometimes, parallel joins can cause remote I/Os. For example, on Oracle Real Application Clusters environments running on MPP configurations, if a pair of matching partitions is not collocated on the same node, a partition-wise join requires extra internode communication due to remote I/O. This is because Oracle must transfer at least one partition to the node where the join is performed. In this case, it is better to explicitly redistribute the data than to use a partition-wise join.

MISCELLANEOUS PARTITION OPERATIONS

The following partition operations are needed on a regular basis:

- Adding partitions
- Dropping partitions
- Exchanging partitions
- Moving partitions
- Splitting and merging partitions
- Truncating partitions
- Coalescing partitions.

Adding Partitions

Different types of partitions require slightly different syntax when being added. Basic topics are:

- Adding a partition to a range-partitioned table
- Adding a partition to a hash-partitioned table
- Adding a partition to a list-partitioned table.

Adding a Partition to a Range-Partitioned Table

Use the `ALTER TABLE ... ADD PARTITION` statement to add a new partition to the "high" end (the point after the last existing partition). To add a partition at the beginning or in the middle of a table, use the `SPLIT PARTITION` clause.

For example, consider the table, sales, which contains data for the current month in addition to the previous 12 months. On January 1, 1999, you add a partition for January, which is stored in tablespace tsx.

```
ALTER TABLE sales
      ADD PARTITION jan96 VALUES LESS THAN ('01-FEB-1999')
      TABLESPACE tsx;
```

You cannot add a partition to a range-partitioned table that has a MAXVALUE partition, but you can split the MAXVALUE partition. By doing so, you effectively create a new partition defined by the values that you specify, and a second partition that remains the MAXVALUE partition.

Local and global indexes associated with the range-partitioned table remain usable.

Adding a Partition to a Hash-Partitioned Table

When you add a partition to a hash-partitioned table, Oracle populates the new partition with rows rehashed from an existing partition (selected by Oracle) as determined by the hash function.

The following statements show two ways of adding a hash partition to table scubagear. Choosing the first statement adds a new hash partition whose partition name is system generated, and which is placed in the table's default tablespace. The second statement also adds a new hash partition, but that partition is explicitly named p_named and is created in tablespace gear5.

```
ALTER TABLE scubagear ADD PARTITION;
ALTER TABLE scubagear
      ADD PARTITION p_named TABLESPACE gear5;
```

Adding a Partition to a List-Partitioned Table

The following statement illustrates adding a new partition to a list-partitioned table. In this example, physical attributes and NOLOGGING are specified for the partition being added.

```
ALTER TABLE q1_sales_by_region
   ADD PARTITION q1_nonmainland VALUES ('HI', 'PR')
      STORAGE (INITIAL 20K NEXT 20K) TABLESPACE tbs_3
      NOLOGGING;
```

Any value in the set of literal values that describe the partition being added must not exist in any of the other partitions of the table.

You cannot add a partition to a list-partitioned table that has a default partition, but you can split the default partition. By doing so, you effectively create a new partition defined by the values that you specify, and a second partition that remains the default partition.

Local and global indexes associated with the list-partitioned table remain usable.

Dropping Partitions

You can drop partitions from range, composite, list, or composite range-list partitioned tables. For hash-partitioned tables, or hash subpartitions of range-hash partitioned tables, you must perform a coalesce operation instead.

Dropping a Table Partition

Use one of the following statements to drop a table partition or subpartition:

- ALTER TABLE ... DROP PARTITION to drop a table partition
- ALTER TABLE ... DROP SUBPARTITION to drop a subpartition of a range-list partitioned table

A typical example of dropping a partition containing data and referential integrity objects is as follows:

```
ALTER TABLE sales
  DISABLE CONSTRAINT dname_sales1;
ALTER TABLE sales DROP PARTITTION dec98;
ALTER TABLE sales
  ENABLE CONSTRAINT dname_sales1;
```

In this example, you disable the integrity constraints, issue the ALTER TABLE ... DROP PARTITION statement, then enable the integrity constraints. This method is most appropriate for large tables where the partition being dropped contains a significant percentage of the total data in the table.

Exchanging Partitions

You can convert a partition (or subpartition) into a nonpartitioned table, and a nonpartitioned table into a partition (or subpartition) of a partitioned table by exchanging their data segments. You can also convert a hash-partitioned table into a partition of a range-hash partitioned table, or convert the partition of the range-hash partitioned table into a hash-partitioned table. Similarly, you can convert a list-partitioned table into a partition of a range-list partitioned table, or convert the partition of the range-list partitioned table into a list-partitioned table.

A typical example of exchanging into a nonpartitioned table follows. In this example, table stocks can be range, hash, or list partitioned.

```
ALTER TABLE stocks
    EXCHANGE PARTITION p3 WITH stock_table_3;
```

Moving Partitions

Use the MOVE PARTITION clause to move a partition. For example, to move the most active partition to a tablespace that resides on its own disk (in order to balance I/O) and to not log the action, issue the following statement:

```
ALTER TABLE parts MOVE PARTITION depot2
     TABLESPACE ts094 NOLOGGING;
```

This statement always drops the partition's old segment and creates a new segment, even if you do not specify a new tablespace.

Splitting and Merging Partitions

The SPLIT PARTITION clause of the ALTER TABLE or ALTER INDEX statement is used to redistribute the contents of a partition into two new partitions. Consider doing this when a partition becomes too large and causes backup, recovery, or maintenance operations to take a long time to complete. You can also use the SPLIT PARTITION clause to redistribute the I/O load.

This clause cannot be used for hash partitions or subpartitions.

A typical example is to split a range-partitioned table as follows:

```
ALTER TABLE vet_cats SPLIT PARTITION
      fee_katy at (100) INTO ( PARTITION
      fee_katy1 ..., PARTITION fee_katy2 ...);
ALTER INDEX JAF1 REBUILD PARTITION fee_katy1;
ALTER INDEX JAF1 REBUILD PARTITION fee_katy2;
ALTER INDEX VET REBUILD PARTITION vet_parta;
ALTER INDEX VET REBUILD PARTITION vet_partb;
```

Use the `ALTER TABLE ... MERGE PARTITIONS` statement to merge the contents of two partitions into one partition. The two original partitions are dropped, as are any corresponding local indexes.

You cannot use this statement for a hash-partitioned table or for hash subpartitions of a range-hash partitioned table.

The following statement merges two subpartitions of a table partitioned using range-list method into a new subpartition located in tablespace `tbs_west`:

```
ALTER TABLE quarterly_regional_sales
   MERGE SUBPARTITIONS q1_1999_northwest, q1_1999_southwest
      INTO SUBPARTITION q1_1999_west
         TABLESPACE tbs_west;
```

Truncating Partitions

Use the `ALTER TABLE ... TRUNCATE PARTITION` statement to remove all rows from a table partition. Truncating a partition is similar to dropping a partition, except that the partition is emptied of its data, but not physically dropped.

You cannot truncate an index partition. However, if there are local indexes defined for the table, the `ALTER TABLE TRUNCATE PARTITION` statement truncates the matching partition in each local index.

The following example illustrates a partition that contains data and has referential integrity constraints:

```
ALTER TABLE sales
    DISABLE CONSTRAINT dname_sales1;
ALTER TABLE sales TRUNCATE PARTITTION dec94;
ALTER TABLE sales
    ENABLE CONSTRAINT dname_sales1;
```

In this example, you disable the integrity constraints, issue the `ALTER TABLE ... TRUNCATE PARTITION` statement, then re-enable the integrity constraints.

This method is most appropriate for large tables where the partition being truncated contains a significant percentage of the total data in the table.

Coalescing Partitions

Coalescing partitions is a way of reducing the number of partitions in a hash-partitioned table, or the number of subpartitions in a range-hash partitioned table. When a hash partition is coalesced, its contents are redistributed into one or more remaining partitions determined by the hash function. The specific partition that is coalesced is selected by Oracle, and is dropped after its contents have been redistributed.

The following statement illustrates a typical case of reducing by one the number of partitions in a table:

```
ALTER TABLE ouul
     COALESCE PARTITION;
```

❑❑❑

3 INDEXES CONSTRAINTS AND MATERIALIZED VIEWS

BITMAP INDEXES

Bitmap indexes are widely used in data warehousing environments. The environments typically have large amounts of data and ad hoc queries, but a low level of concurrent DML transactions. For such applications, bitmap indexing provides:

- Reduced response time for large classes of ad hoc queries
- Reduced storage requirements compared to other indexing techniques
- Dramatic performance gains even on hardware with a relatively small number of CPUs or a small amount of memory
- Efficient maintenance during parallel DML and loads.

Fully indexing a large table with a traditional B-tree index can be prohibitively expensive in terms of space because the indexes can be several times larger than the data in the table. Bitmap indexes are typically only a fraction of the size of the indexed data in the table.

NOTE *Bitmap indexes are available only if you have purchased the Oracle9i Enterprise Edition.*

An index provides pointers to the rows in a table that contains a given key value. A regular index stores a list of rowids for each key corresponding to the rows with that key value. In a bitmap index, a bitmap for each key value replaces a list of rowids.

Each bit in the bitmap corresponds to a possible rowid, and if the bit is set, it means that the row with the corresponding rowid contains the key value. A mapping function converts the bit position to an actual rowid, so that the bitmap index provides the same functionality as a regular index. If the number of different key values is small, bitmap indexes save space.

Bitmap indexes are most effective for queries that contain multiple conditions in the `WHERE` clause. Rows that satisfy some, but not all, conditions are filtered out before the table itself is accessed. This improves response time, often dramatically.

Benefits for Data Warehousing Applications

Bitmap indexes are primarily intended for data warehousing applications where users query the data rather than update it. They are not suitable for OLTP applications with large numbers of concurrent transactions modifying the data.

Parallel query and parallel DML work with bitmap indexes as they do with traditional indexes. Bitmap indexing also supports parallel create indexes and concatenated indexes.

Cardinality

The advantages of using bitmap indexes are greatest for columns in which the ratio of the number of distinct values to the number of rows in the table is under 1%. We refer to this ratio as the **degree of cardinality.** A gender column, which has only two distinct values (male and female), is ideal for a bitmap index. However, data warehouse administrators also build bitmap indexes on columns with higher cardinalities.

For example, on a table with one million rows, a column with 10,000 distinct values is a candidate for a bitmap index. A bitmap index on this column can outperform a B-tree index, particularly when this column is often queried in conjunction with other indexed columns. In fact, in a typical data warehouse environments, a bitmap index can be considered for any non-unique column.

B-tree indexes are most effective for high-cardinality data: that is, for data with many possible values, such as `customer_name` or `phone_number`. In a data warehouse, B-tree indexes should be used only for unique columns or other columns with very high cardinalities (that is, columns that are almost unique). The majority of indexes in a data warehouse should be bitmap indexes.

In ad hoc queries and similar situations, bitmap indexes can dramatically improve query performance. `AND` and `OR` conditions in the `WHERE` clause of a query can be resolved quickly by performing the corresponding Boolean operations directly on the bitmaps before converting the resulting bitmap to rowids. If the resulting number of rows is small, the query can be answered quickly without resorting to a full table scan.

Example 3.1 : Bitmap Index

The following example shows a portion of a company's `customers` table.

```
SELECT cust_id, cust_gender, cust_marital_status, cust_income_level
FROM customers;
         CUST_ID C  CUST_MARITAL_STATUS    CUST_INCOME_LEVEL
         -------------------------------------------------
             ...
              70 F                          D:  70,000  -  89,999
              80 F  married                 H: 150,000  - 169,999
              90 M  single                  H: 150,000  - 169,999
             100 F                          I: 170,000  - 189,999
             110 F  married                 C:  50,000  -  69,999
             120 M  single                  F: 110,000  - 129,999
             130 M                          J: 190,000  - 249,999
             140 M  married                 G: 130,000  - 149,999
     ...
```

Because `cust_gender`, `cust_marital_status`, and cust_`income_level` are all low-cardinality columns (there are only three possible values for marital status and region, two possible values for gender, and 12 for income level), bitmap indexes are ideal for these columns. Do not create a bitmap index on `cust_id` because this is a unique column. Instead, a unique B-tree index on this column provides the most efficient representation and retrieval.

Table 3.1 illustrates the bitmap index for the cust_gender column in this example. It consists of two separate bitmaps, one for gender.

Table 3.1 Sample Bitmap Index

	gender = 'M'	**gender = 'F'**
cust_id 70	0	1
cust_id 80	0	1
cust_id 90	1	0
cust_id 100	0	1
cust_id 110	0	1
cust_id 120	1	0
cust_id 130	1	0
cust_id 140	1	0

Each entry (or bit) in the bitmap corresponds to a single row of the `customers` table. The value of each bit depends upon the values of the corresponding row in the table. For instance, the bitmap `cust_gender='F'` contains a one as its first bit because the region is `east` in the first row of the `customers` table. The bitmap `cust_gender='F'` has a zero for its third bit because the gender of the third row is not `F`.

An analyst investigating demographic trends of the company's customers might ask, "How many of our married customers have an income level of G or H?" This corresponds to the following SQL query:

```
SELECT COUNT(*) FROM customers
WHERE cust_marital_status = 'married'
AND cust_income_level IN ('H: 150,000 - 169,999', 'G: 130,000 - 149,999');
```

Bitmap indexes can efficiently process this query by merely counting the number of ones in the bitmap illustrated in figure 3.1. The result set will be found by using bitmap or merge operations without the necessity of a conversion to rowids. To identify additional specific customer attributes that satisfy the criteria, use the resulting bitmap to access the table after a bitmap to rowid conversion.

status = 'married'		region = 'central'		region = 'west'						
0		0		0		0		0		0
1		1		0		1		1		1
1	AND	0	OR	1	=	1	AND	1	=	1
0		0		1		0		1		0
0		1		0		0		1		0
1		1		0		1		1		1

Figure 3.1 Executing a Query Using Bitmap Indexes.

Bitmap Indexes and Nulls

Unlike most other types of indexes, bitmap indexes include rows that have NULL values. Indexing of nulls can be useful for some types of SQL statements, such as queries with the aggregate function COUNT.

Example 3.2 : Bitmap Index

```
SELECT COUNT(*) FROM customers WHERE cust_marital_status IS NULL;
```

This query uses a bitmap index on cust_marital_status. Note that this query would not be able to use a B-tree index.

```
SELECT COUNT(*) FROM employees;
```

Any bitmap index can be used for this query because all table rows are indexed, including those that have NULL data. If nulls were not indexed, the optimizer would be able to use indexes only on columns with NOT NULL constraints.

Bitmap Indexes on Partitioned Tables

You can create bitmap indexes on partitioned tables but they must be local to the partitioned table—they cannot be global indexes. (Global bitmap indexes are supported only on nonpartitioned tables). Bitmap indexes on partitioned tables must be local indexes.

Bitmap Join Indexes

In addition to a bitmap index on a single table, you can create a bitmap join index, which is a bitmap index for the join of two or more tables. A bitmap join index is a space efficient way of reducing the volume of data that must be joined by performing restrictions in advance. For each value in a column of a table, a bitmap join index stores the rowids of corresponding rows in one or more other tables. In a data warehousing environment, the join condition is an equi-inner join between the primary key column or columns of the dimension tables and the foreign key column or columns in the fact table.

Bitmap join indexes are much more efficient in storage than materialized join views, an alternative for materializing joins in advance. This is because the materialized join views do not compress the rowids of the fact tables.

Example 3.3 : Bitmap Join Index

Using the example in "Bitmap Index", create a bitmap join index with the following sales table:

```
SELECT time_id, cust_id, amount FROM sales;
```

TIME_ID	CUST_ID	AMOUNT
01-JAN-98	29700	2291
01-JAN-98	3380	114
01-JAN-98	67830	553
01-JAN-98	179330	0
01-JAN-98	127520	195
01-JAN-98	33030	280
...		

```
CREATE BITMAP INDEX sales_cust_gender_bjix
ON sales(customers.cust_gender)
FROM sales, customers
WHERE sales.cust_id = customers.cust_id
LOCAL;
```

The following query shows how to use this bitmap join index and illustrates its bitmap pattern:

```
SELECT sales.time_id, customers.cust_gender, sales.amount
FROM sales, customers
WHERE sales.cust_id = customers.cust_id;
```

```
TIME_ID          C          AMOUNT
----------------------------------
01-JAN-98        M            2291
01-JAN-98        F             114
01-JAN-98        M             553
01-JAN-98        M               0
01-JAN-98        M             195
01-JAN-98        M             280
01-JAN-98        M              32
...
```

Table 3.2 illustrates the bitmap join index in this example:

Table 3.2 Sample Bitmap Join Index

	cust_gender = 'M'	**cust_gender = 'F'**
sales record 1	1	0
sales record 2	0	1
sales record 3	1	0
sales record 4	1	0
sales record 5	1	0
sales record 6	1	0
sales record 7	1	0

You can create other bitmap join indexes using more than one column or more than one table, as shown in these examples.

Example 3.4 :

You can create a bitmap join index on more than one column, as in the following example, which uses `customers(gender, marital_status)`:

```
CREATE BITMAP INDEX sales_cust_gender_ms_bjix
ON sales(customers.cust_gender, customers.cust_marital_status)
FROM sales, customers
WHERE sales.cust_id = customers.cust_id
LOCAL NOLOGGING;
```

Example 3.5 :

You can create a bitmap join index on more than one table, as in the following, which uses `customers(gender)` and `products(category)`:

```
CREATE BITMAP INDEX sales_c_gender_p_cat_bjix
ON sales(customers.cust_gender, products.prod_category)
FROM sales, customers, products
WHERE sales.cust_id = customers.cust_id
AND sales.prod_id = products.prod_id
LOCAL NOLOGGING;
```

Example 3.6 :

You can create a bitmap join index on more than one table, in which the indexed column is joined to the indexed table by using another table. For example, we can build an index on `countries.country_name`, even though the `countries` table is not joined directly to the `sales` table. Instead, the `countries` table is joined to the `customers` table, which is joined to the sales table. This type of schema is commonly called a **snowflake schema.**

```
CREATE BITMAP INDEX sales_c_gender_p_cat_bjix
ON sales(customers.cust_gender, products.prod_category)
FROM sales, customers, products
WHERE sales.cust_id = customers.cust_id
AND sales.prod_id = products.prod_id
LOCAL NOLOGGING;
```

Bitmap Join Index Restrictions

Join results must be stored, therefore, bitmap join indexes have the following restrictions:

- Parallel DML is currently only supported on the fact table. Parallel DML on one of the participating dimension tables will mark the index as unusable.
- Only one table can be updated concurrently by different transactions when using the bitmap join index.
- No table can appear twice in the join.
- You cannot create a bitmap join index on an index-organized table or a temporary table.
- The columns in the index must all be columns of the dimension tables.
- The dimension table join columns must be either primary key columns or have unique constraints.
- If a dimension table has composite primary key, each column in the primary key must be part of the join.

B-TREE INDEXES

A B-tree index is organized like an upside-down tree. The bottom level of the index holds the actual data values and pointers to the corresponding rows, much as the index in a book has a page number associated with each index entry.

In general, use B-tree indexes when you know that your typical query refers to the indexed column and retrieves a few rows. In these queries, it is faster to find the rows by looking at the index. However, using the book index analogy, if you plan to look at every single topic in a book, you might not want to look in the index for the topic and then look up the page. It might be faster to read through every chapter in the book. Similarly, if you are retrieving most of the rows in a table, it might not make sense to look up the index to find the table rows. Instead, you might want to read or scan the table.

B-tree indexes are most commonly used in a data warehouse to index unique or near-unique keys. In many cases, it may not be necessary to index these columns in a data warehouse, because unique constraints can be maintained without an index, and because typical data warehouse queries may not work better with such indexes. Bitmap indexes should be more common than B-tree indexes in most data warehouse environments.

LOCAL INDEXES VERSUS GLOBAL INDEXES

B-tree indexes on partitioned tables can be global or local. With Oracle8*i* and earlier releases, Oracle recommended that global indexes not be used in data warehouse environments because a partition DDL statement (for example, `ALTER TABLE ... DROP PARTITION`) would invalidate the entire index, and rebuilding the index is expensive. In Oracle9*i*, global indexes can be maintained without Oracle marking them as unusable after DDL. This enhancement makes global indexes more effective for data warehouse environments.

However, local indexes will be more common than global indexes. Global indexes should be used when there is a specific requirement which cannot be met by local indexes (for example, a unique index on a non-partitioning key, or a performance requirement).

Bitmap indexes on partitioned tables are always local.

WHY INTEGRITY CONSTRAINTS ARE USEFUL IN A DATA WAREHOUSE

Integrity constraints provide a mechanism for ensuring that data conforms to guidelines specified by the database administrator. The most common types of constraints include:

- `UNIQUE` constraints
  To ensure that a given column is unique
- `NOT NULL` constraints
  To ensure that no null values are allowed
- `FOREIGN KEY` constraints
  To ensure that two keys share a primary key to foreign key relationship

Constraints can be used for these purposes in a data warehouse:

- Data cleanliness
  Constraints verify that the data in the data warehouse conforms to a basic level of data consistency and correctness, preventing the introduction of dirty data
- Query optimization.

The Oracle database utilizes constraints when optimizing SQL queries. Although constraints can be useful in many aspects of query optimization, constraints are particularly important for query rewrite of materialized views.

Unlike data in many relational database environments, data in a data warehouse is typically added or modified under controlled circumstances during the extraction, transformation, and loading (ETL) process. Multiple users normally do not update the data warehouse directly, as they do in an OLTP system.

Many significant constraint features have been introduced for data warehousing. Readers familiar with Oracle's constraint functionality in Oracle7 and Oracle8 should take special note of the functionality described in this chapter. In fact, many Oracle7-based and Oracle8-based data warehouses lacked constraints because of concerns about constraint performance. Newer constraint functionality addresses these concerns.

OVERVIEW OF CONSTRAINT STATES

To understand how best to use constraints in a data warehouse, you should first understand the basic purposes of constraints. Some of these purposes are:

- Enforcement

  In order to use a constraint for enforcement, the constraint must be in the `ENABLE` state. An enabled constraint ensures that all data modifications upon a given table (or tables) satisfy the conditions of the constraints. Data modification operations which produce data that violates the constraint fail with a constraint violation error.

- Validation

  To use a constraint for validation, the constraint must be in the `VALIDATE` state. If the constraint is validated, then all data that currently resides in the table satisfies the constraint.

  Note that validation is independent of enforcement. Although the typical constraint in an operational system is both enabled and validated, any constraint could be validated but not enabled or vice-versa (enabled but not validated). These latter two cases are useful for data warehouses.

- Belief

  In some cases, you will know that the conditions for a given constraint are true, so you do not need to validate or enforce the constraint. However, you may wish for the constraint to be present anyway to improve query optimization and performance. When you use a constraint in this way, it is called a belief or `RELY` constraint, and the constraint must be in the `RELY` state. The `RELY` state provides you with a mechanism for telling Oracle9*i* that a given constraint is believed to be true.

Note that the `RELY` state only affects constraints that have not been validated.

Typical Data Warehouse Integrity Constraints

This section assumes that you are familiar with the typical use of constraints. That is, constraints that are both enabled and validated. For data warehousing, many users have discovered that such constraints may be prohibitively costly to build and maintain. The topics discussed are:

- UNIQUE constraints in a data warehouse
- FOREIGN KEY constraints in a data W
- Integrity constraints and partitioning warehouse
- RELY constraints
- Integrity constraints and parallelism
- View constraints.

UNIQUE Constraints in a Data Warehouse

A UNIQUE constraint is typically enforced using a UNIQUE index. However, in a data warehouse whose tables can be extremely large, creating a unique index can be costly both in processing time and in disk space.

Suppose that a data warehouse contains a table sales, which includes a column sales_id. sales_id uniquely identifies a single sales transaction, and the data warehouse administrator must ensure that this column is unique within the data warehouse.

One way to create the constraint is as follows:

```
ALTER TABLE sales ADD CONSTRAINT sales_unique
UNIQUE(sales_id);
```

By default, this constraint is both enabled and validated. Oracle implicitly creates a unique index on sales_id to support this constraint. However, this index can be problematic in a data warehouse for three reasons:

- The unique index can be very large, because the sales table can easily have millions or even billions of rows.
- The unique index is rarely used for query execution. Most data warehousing queries do not have predicates on unique keys, so creating this index will probably not improve performance.
- If sales is partitioned along a column other than sales_id, the unique index must be global. This can detrimentally affect all maintenance operations on the sales table.

A unique index is required for unique constraints to ensure that each individual row modified in the sales table satisfies the UNIQUE constraint.

For data warehousing tables, an alternative mechanism for unique constraints is illustrated in the following statement:

```
ALTER TABLE sales ADD CONSTRAINT sales_unique
UNIQUE (sales_id) DISABLE VALIDATE;
```

This statement creates a unique constraint, but, because the constraint is disabled, a unique index is not required. This approach can be advantageous for many data warehousing environments because the constraint now ensures uniqueness without the cost of a unique index.

However, there are trade-offs for the data warehouse administrator to consider with DISABLE VALIDATE constraints. Because this constraint is disabled, no DML statements that modify the unique column are permitted against the sales table. You can use one of two strategies for modifying this table in the presence of a constraint:

- Use DDL to add data to this table (such as exchanging partitions).
- Before modifying this table, drop the constraint. Then, make all necessary data modifications. Finally, re-create the disabled constraint. Re-creating the constraint is more efficient than re-creating an enabled constraint. However, this approach does not guarantee that data added to the sales table while the constraint has been dropped is unique.

FOREIGN KEY Constraints in a Data Warehouse

In a star schema data warehouse, FOREIGN KEY constraints validate the relationship between the fact table and the dimension tables. A sample constraint might be:

```
ALTER TABLE sales ADD CONSTRAINT sales_time_fk
  FOREIGN KEY (sales_time_id) REFERENCES time (time_id)
  ENABLE VALIDATE;
```

However, in some situations, you may choose to use a different state for the FOREIGN KEY constraints, in particular, the ENABLE NOVALIDATE state. A data warehouse administrator might use an ENABLE NOVALIDATE constraint when either:

- The tables contain data that currently disobeys the constraint, but the data warehouse administrator wishes to create a constraint for future enforcement.
- An enforced constraint is required immediately.

Suppose that the data warehouse loaded new data into the fact tables every day, but refreshed the dimension tables only on the weekend. During the week, the dimension tables and fact tables may in fact disobey the FOREIGN KEY constraints. Nevertheless, the data warehouse administrator might wish to maintain the enforcement of this constraint to prevent any changes that might affect the FOREIGN KEY constraint outside of the ETL process. Thus, you can create the FOREIGN KEY constraints every night, after performing the ETL process, as shown here:

```
ALTER TABLE sales ADD CONSTRAINT sales_time_fk
  FOREIGN KEY (sales_time_id) REFERENCES time (time_id)
  ENABLE NOVALIDATE;
```

ENABLE NOVALIDATE can quickly create an enforced constraint, even when the constraint is believed to be true. Suppose that the ETL process verifies that a FOREIGN KEY constraint is true. Rather than have the database re-verify this FOREIGN KEY constraint, which would require time and database resources, the data warehouse administrator could instead create a FOREIGN KEY constraint using ENABLE NOVALIDATE.

RELY Constraints

The ETL process commonly verifies that certain constraints are true. For example, it can validate all of the foreign keys in the data coming into the fact table. This means that you can trust it to provide clean data, instead of implementing constraints in the data warehouse. You create a RELY constraint as follows:

```
ALTER TABLE sales ADD CONSTRAINT sales_time_fk
  FOREIGN KEY (sales_time_id) REFERENCES time (time_id)
  RELY DISABLE NOVALIDATE;
```

RELY constraints, even though they are not used for data validation, can:

- Enable more sophisticated query rewrites for materialized views.

- Enable other data warehousing tools to retrieve information regarding constraints directly from the Oracle data dictionary.

Creating a `RELY` constraint is inexpensive and does not impose any overhead during DML or load. Because the constraint is not being validated, no data processing is necessary to create it.

Integrity Constraints and Parallelism

All constraints can be validated in parallel. When validating constraints on very large tables, parallelism is often necessary to meet performance goals. The degree of parallelism for a given constraint operation is determined by the default degree of parallelism of the underlying table.

Integrity Constraints and Partitioning

You can create and maintain constraints before you partition the data. Later chapters discuss the significance of partitioning for data warehousing. Partitioning can improve constraint management just as it does to management of many other operations.

View Constraints

You can create constraints on views. The only type of constraint supported on a view is a `RELY` constraint.

This type of constraint is useful when queries typically access views instead of base tables, and the DBA thus needs to define the data relationships between views rather than tables. View constraints are particularly useful in OLAP environments, where they may enable more sophisticated rewrites for materialized views.

OVERVIEW OF DATA WAREHOUSING WITH MATERIALIZED VIEWS

Typically, data flows from one or more online transaction processing (OLTP) databases into a data warehouse on a monthly, weekly, or daily basis. The data is normally processed in a **staging file** before being added to the data warehouse. Data warehouses commonly range in size from tens of gigabytes to a few terabytes. Usually, the vast majority of the data is stored in a few very large fact tables.

One technique employed in data warehouses to improve performance is the creation of summaries. Summaries are special kinds of aggregate views that improve query execution times by precalculating expensive joins and aggregation operations prior to execution and storing the results in a table in the database. For example, you can create a table to contain the sums of sales by region and by product.

The summaries or aggregates that are referred to in this book and in literature on data warehousing are created in Oracle using a schema object called a **materialized view.** Materialized views can perform a number of roles, such as improving query performance or providing replicated data.

Prior to Oracle8*i*, organizations using summaries spent a significant amount of time and effort creating summaries manually, identifying which summaries to create, indexing the summaries, updating them, and advising their users on which ones to use. The introduction of summary management in Oracle8*i* eased the workload of the database administrator and meant the user no longer needed to be aware of the summaries that had been defined. The database administrator creates one or more materialized views, which are the equivalent of a summary. The end user queries the tables and views at the detail data level. The query rewrite mechanism in the Oracle server automatically rewrites the SQL query to use the summary tables. This mechanism reduces response time for returning results from the query. Materialized views within the data warehouse are transparent to the end user or to the database application.

Although materialized views are usually accessed through the query rewrite mechanism, an end user or database application can construct queries that directly access the summaries. However, serious consideration should be given to whether users should be allowed to do this because any change to the summaries will affect the queries that reference them.

Materialized Views for Data Warehouses

In data warehouses, you can use materialized views to precompute and store aggregated data such as the sum of sales. Materialized views in these environments are often referred to as summaries, because they store summarized data. They can also be used to precompute joins with or without aggregations. A materialized view eliminates the overhead associated with expensive joins and aggregations for a large or important class of queries.

Materialized Views for Distributed Computing

In distributed environments, you can use materialized views to replicate data at distributed sites and to synchronize updates done at those sites with conflict resolution methods. The materialized views as replicas provide local access to data that otherwise would have to be accessed from remote sites. Materialized views are also useful in remote data marts.

Materialized Views for Mobile Computing

You can also use materialized views to download a subset of data from central servers to mobile clients, with periodic refreshes and updates between clients and the central servers.

This chapter focuses on the use of materialized views in data warehouses.

The Need for Materialized Views

You can use materialized views in data warehouses to increase the speed of queries on very large databases. Queries to large databases often involve joins between tables, aggregations such as `SUM`, or both. These operations are expensive in terms of time and processing power. The type of materialized view you create determines how the materialized view is refreshed and used by query rewrite.

You can use materialized views in a number of ways, and you can use almost identical syntax to perform a number of roles. For example, a materialized view can replicate data, a process formerly achieved by using the `CREATE SNAPSHOT` statement. Now `CREATE MATERIALIZED VIEW` is a synonym for `CREATE SNAPSHOT`.

Materialized views improve query performance by precalculating expensive join and aggregation operations on the database prior to execution and storing the results in the database. The query optimizer automatically recognizes when an existing materialized view can and should be used to satisfy a request. It then transparently rewrites the request to use the materialized view. Queries go directly to the materialized view and not to the underlying detail tables. In general, rewriting queries to use materialized views rather than detail tables improves response. Figure 3.2 illustrates how query rewrite works.

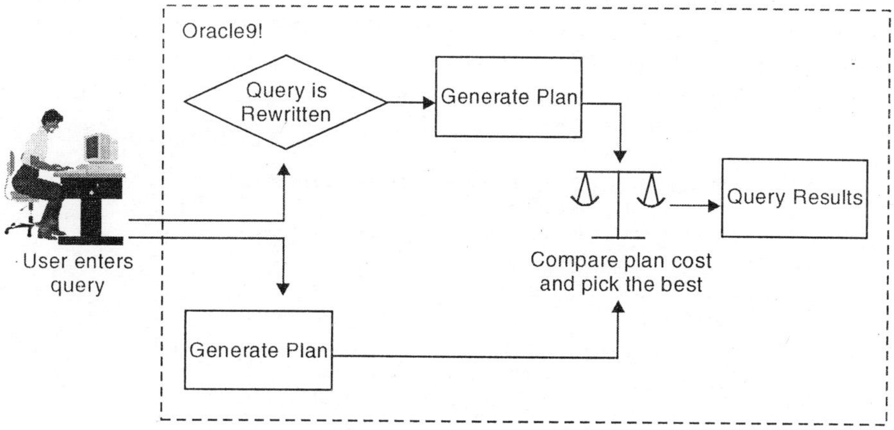

Figure 3.2 Transparent Query Rewrite.

When using query rewrite, create materialized views that satisfy the largest number of queries. For example, if you identify 20 queries that are commonly applied to the detail or fact tables, then you might be able to satisfy them with five or six well-written materialized views. A materialized view definition can include any number of aggregations (`SUM`, `COUNT(x)`, `COUNT(*)`, `COUNT(DISTINCT x)`, `AVG`, `VARIANCE`, `STDDEV`, `MIN`, and `MAX`). It can also include any number of joins. If you are unsure of which materialized views to create, Oracle provides a set of advisory procedures in the `DBMS_OLAP` package to help in designing and evaluating materialized views for query rewrite. These functions are also known as the Summary Advisor or the Advisor. Note that the OLAP Summary Advisor is different.

If a materialized view is to be used by query rewrite, it must be stored in the same database as the fact or detail tables on which it relies. A materialized view can be partitioned, and you can define a materialized view on a partitioned table. You can also define one or more indexes on the materialized view.

Unlike indexes, materialized views can be accessed directly using a `SELECT` statement.

NOTE *The techniques shown in this chapter illustrate how to use materialized views in data warehouses. Materialized views can also be used by Oracle Replication.*

Components of Summary Management

Summary management consists of:

- Mechanisms to define materialized views and dimensions.
- A refresh mechanism to ensure that all materialized views contain the latest data.
- A query rewrite capability to transparently rewrite a query to use a materialized view.
- A collection of materialized view analysis and advisory functions and procedures in the `DBMS_OLAP` package. Collectively, these functions are called the Summary Advisor, and are also available as part of Oracle Enterprise Manager.

Many large decision support system (DSS) databases have schemas that do not closely resemble a conventional data warehouse schema, but that still require joins and aggregates. The use of summary management features imposes no schema restrictions, and can enable some existing DSS database applications to improve performance without the need to redesign the database or the application.

Figure 3.3 illustrates the use of summary management in the warehousing cycle. After the data has been transformed, staged, and loaded into the detail data in the warehouse, you can invoke the summary management process. First, use the Advisor to plan how you will use summaries. Then, create summaries and design how queries will be rewritten.

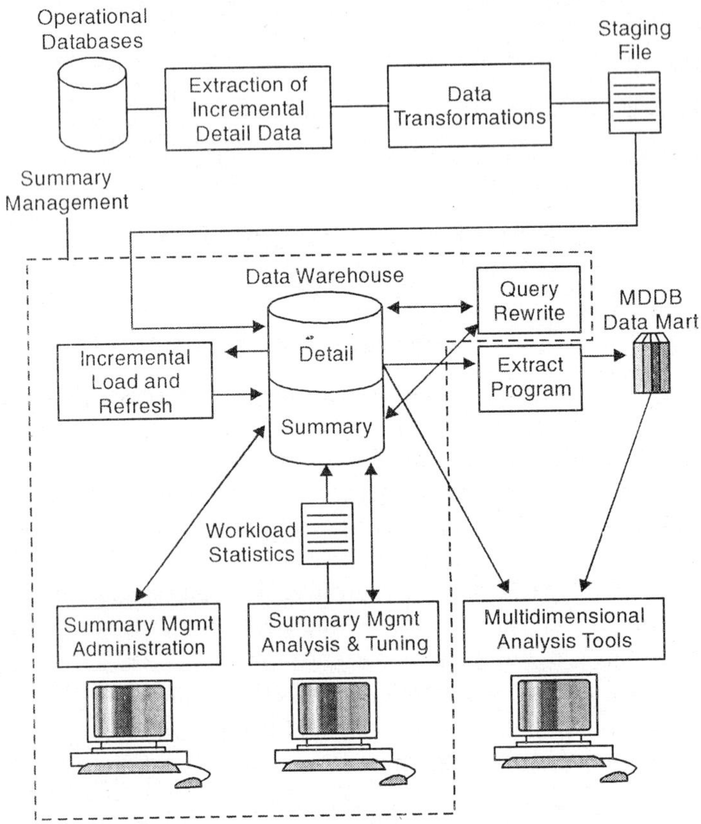

Figure 3.3 Overview of Summary Management.

Data Warehousing Terminology

Some basic data warehousing terms are defined as follows:

- **Dimension tables** describe the business entities of an enterprise, represented as hierarchical, categorical information such as time, departments, locations, and products. Dimension tables are sometimes called lookup or reference tables.

  Dimension tables usually change slowly over time and are not modified on a periodic schedule. They are used in long-running decision support queries to aggregate the data returned from the query into appropriate levels of the dimension hierarchy.

- **Hierarchies** describe the business relationships and common access patterns in the database. An analysis of the dimensions, combined with an understanding of the typical work load, can be used to create materialized views.

- **Fact tables** describe the business transactions of an enterprise. Fact tables are sometimes called detail tables.

The vast majority of data in a data warehouse is stored in a few very large fact tables that are updated periodically with data from one or more operational OLTP databases.

Fact tables include facts (also called measures) such as sales, units, and inventory.

- A simple measure is a numeric or character column of one table such as `fact.sales`.
- A computed measure is an expression involving measures of one table, for example, `fact.revenues - fact.expenses`.
- A multitable measure is a computed measure defined on multiple tables, for example, `fact_a.revenues - fact_b.expenses`.

Fact tables also contain one or more foreign keys that organize the business transactions by the relevant business entities such as time, product, and market. In most cases, these foreign keys are non-null, form a unique compound key of the fact table, and each foreign key joins with exactly one row of a **dimension table.**

- A materialized view is a precomputed table comprising aggregated and joined data from fact and possibly from dimension tables. Among builders of data warehouses, a materialized view is also known as a **summary.**

Materialized View Schema Design

Summary management can perform many useful functions, including query rewrite and materialized view refresh, even if your data warehouse design does not follow these guidelines. However, you will realize significantly greater query execution performance and materialized view refresh performance benefits and you will require fewer materialized views if your schema design complies with these guidelines.

A materialized view definition includes any number of aggregates, as well as any number of joins. In several ways, a materialized view behaves like an index:

- The purpose of a materialized view is to increase query execution performance.
- The existence of a materialized view is transparent to SQL applications, so that a DBA can create or drop materialized views at any time without affecting the validity of SQL applications.
- A materialized view consumes storage space.
- The contents of the materialized view must be updated when the underlying detail tables are modified.

Schemas and Dimension Tables

In the case of normalized or partially normalized dimension tables (a dimension that is stored in more than one table), identify how these tables are joined. Note whether the joins between the dimension tables can guarantee that each child-side row joins with one and only one parent-side row. In the case of denormalized dimensions, determine whether the child-side columns uniquely determine the parent-side (or attribute) columns. These relationships can be enabled with constraints, using the `NOVALIDATE` and `RELY` options if the relationships represented by the constraints are guaranteed by other means. Note that if the joins between fact and dimension tables do not support the parent-child relationship described previously, you still gain significant performance advantages from defining the dimension with the `CREATE DIMENSION` statement. Another alternative, subject to some restrictions, is to use outer joins in the materialized view definition (that is, in the `CREATE MATERIALIZED VIEW` statement).

You must not create dimensions in any schema that does not satisfy these relationships. Incorrect results can be returned from queries otherwise.

Materialized View Schema Design Guidelines

Before starting to define and use the various components of summary management, you should review your schema design to abide by the following guidelines wherever possible.

Guidelines 1 and 2 are more important than guideline 3. If your schema design does not follow guidelines 1 and 2, it does not then matter whether it follows guideline 3. Guidelines 1, 2, and 3 affect both query rewrite performance and materialized view refresh performance.

Schema Guideline	Description
Guideline 1 Dimensions	Dimensions should either be denormalized (each dimension contained in one table) or the joins between tables in a normalized or partially normalized dimension should guarantee that each child-side row joins with exactly one parent-side row. You can enforce this condition by adding FOREIGN KEY and NOT NULL constraints on the child-side join keys and PRIMARY KEY constraints on the parent-side join keys.
Guideline 2 Dimensions	If dimensions are denormalized or partially denormalized, hierarchical integrity must be maintained between the key columns of the dimension table. Each child key value must uniquely identify its parent key value, even if the dimension table is denormalized. Hierarchical integrity in a denormalized dimension can be verified by calling the VALIDATE_DIMENSION procedure of the DBMS_OLAP package.
Guideline 3 Dimensions	Fact and dimension tables should similarly guarantee that each fact table row joins with exactly one dimension table row. This condition must be declared, and optionally enforced, by adding FOREIGN KEY and NOT NULL constraints on the fact key column(s) and PRIMARY KEY constraints on the dimension key column(s), or by using outer joins. In a data warehouse, constraints are typically enabled with the NOVALIDATE and RELY clauses to avoid constraint enforcement performance overhead.
Guideline 4 Incremental Loads	Incremental loads of your detail data should be done using the SQL*Loader direct-path option, or any bulk loader utility that uses Oracle's direct-path interface. This includes INSERT ... AS SELECT with the APPEND or PARALLEL hints, where the hints cause the direct loader log to be used during the insert.
Guideline 5 Partitions	Range/composite partition your tables by a monotonically increasing time column if possible (preferably of type DATE).
Guideline 6 Dimensions	After each load and before refreshing your materialized view, use the VALIDATE_DIMENSION procedure of the DBMS_MVIEW package to incrementally verify dimensional integrity.
Guideline 7 Time Dimensions	If a time dimension appears in the materialized view as a time column, partition and index the materialized view in the same manner as you have the fact tables.

If you are concerned with the time required to enable constraints and whether any constraints might be violated, use the ENABLE NOVALIDATE with the RELY clause to turn on constraint checking without validating any of the existing constraints. The risk with this approach is that incorrect query results could occur if any constraints are broken. Therefore, as the designer, you must determine how clean the data is and whether the risk of wrong results is too great.

Loading Data

A popular and efficient way to load data into a warehouse or data mart is to use SQL*Loader with the DIRECT or PARALLEL option or to use another loader tool that uses the Oracle direct-path API.

Loading strategies can be classified as one-phase or two-phase. In one-phase loading, data is loaded directly into the target table, quality assurance tests are performed, and errors are resolved by performing DML operations prior to refreshing materialized views. If a large number of deletions are possible, then storage utilization can be adversely affected, but temporary space requirements and load time are minimized. The DML that may be required after one-phase loading causes multitable aggregate materialized views to become unusable in the safest rewrite integrity level.

In a two-phase loading process:

- Data is first loaded into a temporary table in the warehouse.
- Quality assurance procedures are applied to the data
- Referential integrity constraints on the target table are disabled, and the local index in the target partition is marked unusable
- The data is copied from the temporary area into the appropriate partition of the target table using INSERT AS SELECT with the PARALLEL or APPEND hint
- The temporary table is dropped
- The constraints are enabled, usually with the NOVALIDATE option

Immediately after loading the detail data and updating the indexes on the detail data, the database can be opened for operation, if desired. You can disable query rewrite at the system level by issuing an ALTER SYSTEM SET QUERY_REWRITE_ENABLED = false statement until all the materialized views are refreshed.

If QUERY_REWRITE_INTEGRITY is set to stale_tolerated, access to the materialized view can be allowed at the session level to any users who do not require the materialized views to reflect the data from the latest load by issuing an ALTER SESSION SET QUERY_REWRITE_INTEGRITY=true statement. This scenario does not apply when QUERY_REWRITE_INTEGRITY is either enforced or trusted because the system ensures in these modes that only materialized views with updated data participate in a query rewrite.

Overview of Materialized View Management Tasks

The motivation for using materialized views is to improve performance, but the overhead associated with materialized view management can become a significant system management problem. When reviewing or evaluating some of the necessary materialized view management activities, consider some of the following:

- Identifying what materialized views to create initially
- Indexing the materialized views
- Ensuring that all materialized views and materialized view indexes are refreshed properly each time the database is updated
- Checking which materialized views have been used
- Determining how effective each materialized view has been on workload performance
- Measuring the space being used by materialized views
- Determining which new materialized views should be created

- Determining which existing materialized views should be dropped
- Archiving old detail and materialized view data that is no longer useful.

After the initial effort of creating and populating the data warehouse or data mart, the major administration overhead is the update process, which involves:

- Periodic extraction of incremental changes from the operational systems
- Transforming the data
- Verifying that the incremental changes are correct, consistent, and complete
- Bulk-loading the data into the warehouse
- Refreshing indexes and materialized views so that they are consistent with the detail data.

The update process must generally be performed within a limited period of time known as the **update window.** The update window depends on the **update frequency** (such as daily or weekly) and the nature of the business. For a daily update frequency, an update window of two to six hours might be typical.

You need to know your update window for the following activities:

- Loading the detail data
- Updating or rebuilding the indexes on the detail data
- Performing quality assurance tests on the data
- Refreshing the materialized views
- Updating the indexes on the materialized views.

TYPES OF MATERIALIZED VIEWS

The `SELECT` clause in the materialized view creation statement defines the data that the materialized view is to contain. Only a few restrictions limit what can be specified. Any number of tables can be joined together. However, they cannot be remote tables if you wish to take advantage of query rewrite. Besides tables, other elements such as views, inline views (subqueries in the `FROM` clause of a `SELECT` statement), subqueries, and materialized views can all be joined or referenced in the `SELECT` clause.

The types of materialized views are:

- Materialized views with aggregates
- Materialized views containing only joins
- Nested materialized views.

Materialized Views with Aggregates

In data warehouses, materialized views normally contain aggregates as shown in example 3.7. For fast refresh to be possible, the `SELECT` list must contain all of the `GROUP BY` columns (if present), and there must be a `COUNT(*)` and a `COUNT(column)` on any aggregated columns. Also, materialized view logs must be present on all tables referenced in the query that defines the materialized view. The valid aggregate functions are: `SUM`, `COUNT(x)`, `COUNT(*)`, `AVG`, `VARIANCE`, `STDDEV`, `MIN`, and `MAX`, and the expression to be aggregated can be any SQL value expression.

Fast refresh for a materialized view containing joins and aggregates is possible after any type of DML to the base tables (direct load or conventional `INSERT`, `UPDATE`, or `DELETE`). It can be defined to be refreshed ON COMMIT or ON DEMAND. A REFRESH ON COMMIT, materialized view will be refreshed automatically when a transaction that does DML to one of the materialized view's detail tables commits. The time taken to complete the commit may be slightly longer than usual when this method is chosen. This is because the refresh operation is performed as part of the commit process. Therefore, this method may not be suitable if many users are concurrently changing the tables upon which the materialized view is based.

Here are some examples of materialized views with aggregates. Note that materialized view logs are only created because this materialized view will be fast refreshed.

Example 3.7 : Creating a Materialized View

```
CREATE MATERIALIZED VIEW LOG ON products
WITH SEQUENCE, ROWID
(prod_id, prod_name, prod_desc, prod_subcategory, prod_subcat_desc, prod_
category, prod_cat_desc, prod_weight_class, prod_unit_of_measure, prod_pack_
size, supplier_id, prod_status, prod_list_price, prod_min_price)
INCLUDING NEW VALUES;

CREATE MATERIALIZED VIEW LOG ON sales
WITH SEQUENCE, ROWID
(prod_id, cust_id, time_id, channel_id, promo_id, quantity_sold, amount_sold)
INCLUDING NEW VALUES;

CREATE MATERIALIZED VIEW product_sales_mv
PCTFREE 0  TABLESPACE demo
STORAGE (INITIAL 8k NEXT 8k PCTINCREASE 0)
BUILD IMMEDIATE
REFRESH FAST
ENABLE QUERY REWRITE
AS  SELECT p.prod_name, SUM(amount_sold) AS dollar_sales,
COUNT(*) AS cnt, COUNT(amount_sold) AS cnt_amt
FROM sales s, products p
WHERE s.prod_id = p.prod_id
      GROUP BY prod_name;
```

Above example creates a materialized view product_sales_mv that computes total number and value of sales for a product. It is derived by joining the tables sales and products on the column prod_id. The materialized view is populated with data immediately because the build method is immediate and it is available for use by query rewrite. In this example, the default refresh method is FAST, which is allowed because the appropriate materialized view logs have been created on tables product and sales.

Example 3.8 : Creating a Materialized View

```
CREATE MATERIALIZED VIEW product_sales_mv
   PCTFREE 0 TABLESPACE demo
   STORAGE (INITIAL 16k NEXT 16k PCTINCREASE 0)
   BUILD DEFERRED
   REFRESH COMPLETE ON DEMAND
   ENABLE QUERY REWRITE
```

```
AS
SELECT
  p.prod_name,
    SUM(amount_sold) AS dollar_sales
      FROM sales s, products p
      WHERE s.prod_id = p.prod_id
      GROUP BY p.prod_name;
```

Above example creates a materialized view `product_sales_mv` that computes the sum of sales by `prod_name`. It is derived by joining the tables `store` and `fact` on the column `store_key`. The materialized view does not initially contain any data, because the build method is `DEFERRED`. A complete refresh is required for the first refresh of a build deferred materialized view. When it is refreshed and once populated, this materialized view can be used by query rewrite.

Example 3.9 : Creating a Materialized View

```
CREATE MATERIALIZED VIEW LOG ON sales
WITH SEQUENCE, ROWID
(prod_id, cust_id, time_id, channel_id, promo_id, quantity_sold, amount_sold)
INCLUDING NEW VALUES;

CREATE MATERIALIZED VIEW sum_sales
  PARALLEL
  BUILD IMMEDIATE
  REFRESH FAST ON COMMIT
  AS
  SELECT s.prod_id, s.time_id,
          COUNT(*) AS count_grp,
  SUM(s.amount_sold) AS sum_dollar_sales,
          COUNT(s.amount_sold) AS count_dollar_sales,
  SUM(s.quantity_sold) AS sum_quantity_sales,
          COUNT(s.quantity_sold) AS count_quantity_sales
  FROM sales s
  GROUP BY s.prod_id, s.time_id;
```

Above example creates a materialized view that contains aggregates on a single table. Because the materialized view log has been created, the materialized view is fast refreshable. If DML is applied against the `sales` table, then the changes will be reflected in the materialized view when the commit is issued.

Requirements for Using Materialized Views with Aggregates

Table 3.3 illustrates the aggregate requirements for materialized views.

Table 3.3 Requirements for Materialized Views with Aggregates

If aggregate X is present, aggregate Y is required and aggregate Z is optional		
X	Y	Z
COUNT(expr)	-	-
SUM(expr)	COUNT(expr)	-
AVG(expr)	COUNT(expr)	SUM(expr)
STDDEV(expr)	COUNT(expr) SUM(expr)	SUM(expr * expr)
VARIANCE(expr)	COUNT(expr) SUM(expr)	SUM(expr * expr)

Note that COUNT(*) must always be present. Oracle recommends that you include the optional aggregates in column Z in the materialized view in order to obtain the most efficient and accurate fast refresh of the aggregates.

Materialized Views Containing Only Joins

Some materialized views contain only joins and no aggregates, such as in the following example, where a materialized view is created that joins the sales table to the times and customers tables. The advantage of creating this type of materialized view is that expensive joins will be precalculated.

Fast refresh for a materialized view containing only joins is possible after any type of DML to the base tables (direct-path or conventional INSERT, UPDATE, or DELETE).

A materialized view containing only joins can be defined to be refreshed ON COMMIT or ON DEMAND. If it is ON COMMIT, the refresh is performed at commit time of the transaction that does DML on the materialized view's detail table. Oracle does not allow self-joins in materialized join views.

If you specify REFRESH FAST, Oracle performs further verification of the query definition to ensure that fast refresh can be performed if *any* of the detail tables change. These additional checks are:

- A materialized view log must be present for each detail table.
- The rowids of all the detail tables must appear in the SELECT list of the materialized view query definition.
- If there are no outer joins, you may have arbitrary selections and joins in the WHERE clause. However, if there are outer joins, the WHERE clause cannot have any selections. Further, if there are outer joins, all the joins must be connected by ANDs and must use the equality (=) operator.
- If there are outer joins, unique constraints must exist on the join columns of the inner table. For example, if you are joining the fact table and a dimension table and the join is an outer join with the fact table being the outer table, there must exist unique constraints on the join columns of the dimension table.

If some of these restrictions are not met, you can create the materialized view as REFRESH FORCE to take advantage of fast refresh when it is possible. If one of the tables did not meet all of the criteria, but the other tables did, the materialized view would still be fast refreshable with respect to the other tables for which all the criteria are met.

A materialized view log should contain the rowid of the master table. It is not necessary to add other columns.

To speed up refresh, you should create indexes on the materialized view's columns that store the rowids of the fact table.

Example 3.10 : Materialized View Containing Only Joins

```
CREATE MATERIALIZED VIEW LOG ON sales
  WITH ROWID;

CREATE MATERIALIZED VIEW LOG ON times
  WITH ROWID;

CREATE MATERIALIZED VIEW LOG ON customers
  WITH ROWID;
```

```
CREATE MATERIALIZED VIEW detail_sales_mv
       PARALLEL BUILD IMMEDIATE
       REFRESH FAST
       AS
       SELECT s.rowid "sales_rid", t.rowid "times_rid", c.rowed "customers_rid",
       c.cust_id, c.cust_last_name, s.amount_sold,
       s.quantity_sold, s.time_id
       FROM sales s, times t, customers c
       WHERE  s.cust_id = c.cust_id(+) AND
              s.time_id = t.time_id(+);
```

In this example, to perform a fast refresh, `UNIQUE` constraints should exist on `c.cust_id` and `t.time_id`. You should also create indexes on the columns `sales_rid`, `times_rid`, and `customers_rid`, as illustrated in the following. This will improve the refresh performance.

```
CREATE INDEX mv_ix_salesrid
  ON detail_sales_mv("sales_rid");
```

Alternatively, if the previous example did not include the columns `times_rid` and `customers_id`, and if the refresh method was `REFRESH FORCE`, then this materialized view would be fast refreshable only if the sales table was updated but not if the tables `times` or `customers` were updated.

```
CREATE MATERIALIZED VIEW detail_sales_mv
       PARALLEL
       BUILD IMMEDIATE
       REFRESH FORCE
       AS
       SELECT
       s.rowid "sales_rid",
       c.cust_id, c.cust_last_name, s.amount_sold,
       s.quantity_sold, s.time_id
       FROM sales s, times t, customers c
       WHERE s.cust_id = c.cust_id(+) AND
             s.time_id = t.time_id(+);
```

Nested Materialized Views

A nested materialized view is a materialized view whose definition is based on another materialized view. A nested materialized view can reference other relations in the database in addition to referencing materialized views.

Why Use Nested Materialized Views?

In a data warehouse, you typically create many aggregate views on a single join (for example, rollups along different dimensions). Incrementally maintaining these distinct materialized aggregate views can take a long time, because the underlying join has to be performed many times.

Using nested materialized views, you can create multiple single-table materialized views based on a joins-only materialized view and the join is performed just once. In addition, optimizations can be performed for this class of single-table aggregate materialized view and thus refresh is very efficient.

Example 3.11 : Nested Materialized View

You can create a nested materialized view on materialized views that contain joins only or joins and aggregates.

All the underlying objects (materialized views or tables) on which the materialized view is defined must have a materialized view log. All the underlying objects are treated as if they were tables. All the existing options for materialized views can be used, with the exception of ON COMMIT REFRESH, which is not supported for a nested materialized view that contains, joins and aggregates.

Using the tables and their columns from the sh sample schema, the following materialized views illustrate how nested materialized views can be created.

```
/* create the materialized view logs */
CREATE MATERIALIZED VIEW LOG ON sales
  WITH ROWID;
CREATE MATERIALIZED VIEW LOG ON customers
  WITH ROWID;
CREATE MATERIALIZED VIEW LOG ON times
  WITH ROWID;

/*create materialized view join_sales_cust_time as fast refreshable at
   COMMIT time */
CREATE MATERIALIZED VIEW join_sales_cust_time
REFRESH FAST ON COMMIT AS
SELECT c.cust_id, c.cust_last_name, s.amount_sold, t.time_id,
       t.day_number_in_week, s.rowid srid, t.rowid trid, c.rowid crid
FROM sales s, customers c, times t
WHERE s.time_id = t.time_id AND
     s.cust_id = c.cust_id;
```

To create a nested materialized view on the table join_sales_cust_time, you would have to create a materialized view log on the table. Because this will be a single-table aggregate materialized view on join_sales_cust_time, you need to log all the necessary columns and use the INCLUDING NEW VALUES clause.

```
/* create materialized view log on join_sales_cust_time */
CREATE MATERIALIZED VIEW LOG ON join_sales_cust_time
WITH ROWID (cust_name, day_number_in_week, amount_sold)
INCLUDING NEW VALUES;

/* create the single-table aggregate materialized view sum_sales_cust_time on

   join_sales_cust_time as fast refreshable at COMMIT time */
CREATE MATERIALIZED VIEW sum_sales_cust_time
  REFRESH FAST ON COMMIT
  AS
  SELECT COUNT(*) cnt_all, SUM(amount_sold) sum_sales,
  COUNT(amount_sold)
        cnt_sales, cust_last_name, day_number_in_week
  FROM join_sales_cust_time
  GROUP BY cust_last_name, day_number_in_week;
```

This schema can be diagrammatically represented as in figure 3.4.

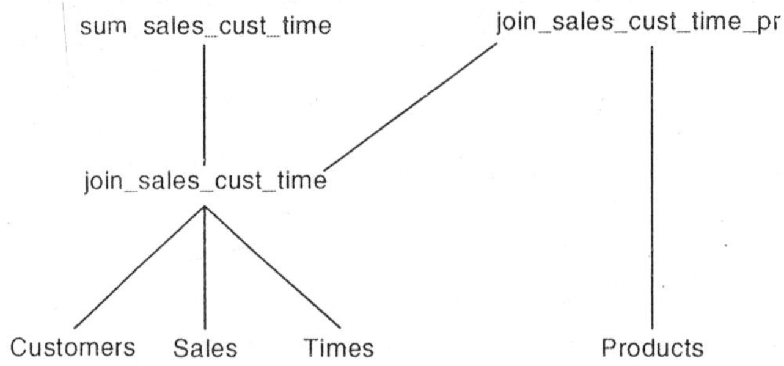

Figure 3.4 Nested Materialized View Schema.

Nesting Materialized Views with Joins and Aggregates

You can nest materialized views with joins and aggregates, but the ON DEMAND clause is necessary for FAST REFRESH.

Some types of nested materialized views cannot be fast refreshed. Use EXPLAIN_MVIEW to identify those types of materialized views. Because you have to invoke the refresh functions manually, ordering has to be taken into account. This is because the refresh for a materialized view that is built on other materialized views will use the current state of the other materialized views, whether they are fresh or not. You can find the dependent materialized views for a particular object using the PL/SQL function GET_MV_DEPENDENCIES in the DBMS_MVIEW package.

Nested Materialized View Usage Guidelines

You should keep the following in mind when deciding whether to use nested materialized views:

- If you want to use fast refresh, you should fast refresh all the materialized views along any chain. It makes little sense to define a fast refreshable materialized view on top of a materialized view that must be refreshed with a complete refresh.
- If you want the highest level materialized view to be fresh with respect to the detail tables, you need to ensure that all materialized views in a tree are refreshed in the correct dependency order before refreshing the highest-level. Oracle does not provide support for automatic refreshing of intermediate materialized views in a nested hierarchy. If the materialized views under the highest-level materialized view are stale, refreshing only the highest-level will succeed, but makes it fresh only with respect to its underlying materialized view, not the detail tables at the base of the tree.
- When refreshing materialized views, you need to ensure that all materialized views in a tree are refreshed. If you only refresh the highest-level materialized view, the materialized views under it will be stale and you must explicitly refresh them.

Restrictions When Using Nested Materialized Views

The following restrictions exist on the way you can nest materialized views:

- Fast refresh for ON COMMIT is not supported for a higher-level materialized view that contains joins and aggregates.

- DBMS_MVIEW.REFRESH APIs will not automatically refresh nested materialized views unless explicitly specified. Thus, if monthly_sales_mv is based on sales_mv, you have to refresh sales_mv first, followed by monthly_sales_mv. Oracle does not automatically refresh monthly_sales_mv when you refresh sales_mv or vice versa.
- If you have a table costs with a materialized view cost_mv based on it, you cannot then create a prebuilt materialized view on table costs. The result would make cost_mv a nested materialized view and this method of conversion is not supported.

CREATING MATERIALIZED VIEWS

A materialized view can be created with the CREATE MATERIALIZED VIEW statement or using Oracle Enterprise Manager. Example below creates the materialized view cust_sales_mv.

Example 3.12 : Creating a Materialized View

```
CREATE MATERIALIZED VIEW cust_sales_mv
PCTFREE 0 TABLESPACE demo
STORAGE (INITIAL 16k NEXT 16k PCTINCREASE 0)
PARALLEL
BUILD IMMEDIATE
REFRESH COMPLETE
ENABLE QUERY REWRITE
AS
SELECT  c.cust_last_name,
  SUM(amount_sold) AS sum_amount_sold
  FROM customers c, sales s
  WHERE s.cust_id = c.cust_id
  GROUP BY c.cust_last_name;
```

It is not uncommon in a data warehouse to have already created summary or aggregation tables, and you might not wish to repeat this work by building a new materialized view. In this case, the table that already exists in the database can be registered as a prebuilt materialized view.

Once you have selected the materialized views you want to create, follow these steps for each materialized view.

1. Design the materialized view. Existing user-defined materialized views do not require this step. If the materialized view contains many rows, then, if appropriate, the materialized view should be partitioned (if possible) and should match the partitioning of the largest or most frequently updated detail or fact table (if possible). Refresh performance benefits from partitioning, because it can take advantage of parallel DML capabilities.
2. Use the CREATE MATERIALIZED VIEW statement to create and, optionally, populate the materialized view. If a user-defined materialized view already exists, then use the ON PREBUILT TABLE clause in the CREATE MATERIALIZED VIEW statement. Otherwise, use the BUILD IMMEDIATE clause to populate the materialized view immediately, or the BUILD DEFERRED clause to populate the materialized view later. A BUILD DEFERRED materialized view is disabled for use by query rewrite until the first REFRESH, after which it will be automatically enabled, provided the ENABLE QUERY REWRITE clause has been specified.

Naming Materialized Views

The name of a materialized view must conform to standard Oracle naming conventions. However, if the materialized view is based on a user-defined prebuilt table, then the name of the materialized view must exactly match that table name.

If you already have a naming convention for tables and indexes, you might consider extending this naming scheme to the materialized views so that they are easily identifiable. For example, instead of naming the materialized view `sum_of_sales`, it could be called `sum_of_sales_mv` to denote that this is a materialized view and not a table or view.

Storage And Data Segment Compression

Unless the materialized view is based on a user-defined prebuilt table, it requires and occupies storage space inside the database. Therefore, the storage needs for the materialized view should be specified in terms of the tablespace where it is to reside and the size of the extents.

If you do not know how much space the materialized view will require, then the `DBMS_OLAP.ESTIMATE_SIZE` package, can estimate the number of bytes required to store this uncompressed materialized view. This information can then assist the design team in determining the tablespace in which the materialized view should reside.

You should use data segment compression with highly redundant data, such as tables with many foreign keys. This is particularly useful for materialized views created with the `ROLLUP` clause. Data segment compression reduces disk use and memory use (specifically, the buffer cache), often leading to a better scaleup for read-only operations. Data segment compression can also speed up query execution.

Build Methods

Two build methods are available for creating the materialized view, as shown in following table. If you select `BUILD IMMEDIATE`, the materialized view definition is added to the schema objects in the data dictionary, and then the fact or detail tables are scanned according to the `SELECT` expression and the results are stored in the materialized view. Depending on the size of the tables to be scanned, this build process can take a considerable amount of time.

An alternative approach is to use the `BUILD DEFERRED` clause, which creates the materialized view without data, thereby enabling it to be populated at a later date using the `DBMS_MVIEW.REFRESH` package .

Table 3.4 Build Methods

Build Method	Description
`BUILD IMMEDIATE`	Create the materialized view and then populate it with data
`BUILD DEFERRED`	Create the materialized view definition but do not populate it with data

Enabling Query Rewrite

Before creating a materialized view, you can verify what types of query rewrite are possible by calling the procedure `DBMS_MVIEW.EXPLAIN_MVIEW`. Once the materialized view has been created, you can use `DBMS_MVIEW.EXPLAIN_REWRITE` to find out if (or why not) it will rewrite a specific query.

Even though a materialized view is defined, it will not automatically be used by the query rewrite facility. You must set the QUERY_REWRITE_ENABLED initialization parameter to TRUE before using query rewrite. You also must specify the ENABLE QUERY REWRITE clause if the materialized view is to be considered available for rewriting queries.

If this clause is omitted or specified as DISABLE QUERY REWRITE when the materialized view is created, the materialized view can subsequently be enabled for query rewrite with the ALTER MATERIALIZED VIEW statement.

If you define a materialized view as BUILD DEFERRED, it is not eligible for query rewrite until it is populated with data.

Query Rewrite Restrictions

Query rewrite is not possible with all materialized views. If query rewrite is not occurring when expected, DBMS_MVIEW.EXPLAIN_REWRITE can help provide reasons why a specific query is not eligible for rewrite. Also, check to see if your materialized view satisfies all of the following conditions.

Materialized View Restrictions

You should keep in mind the following restrictions:

- The defining query of the materialized view cannot contain any non-repeatable expressions (ROWNUM, SYSDATE, non-repeatable PL/SQL functions, and so on).
- The query cannot contain any references to RAW or LONG RAW datatypes or object REFs.
- If the defining query of the materialized view contains set operators (UNION, MINUS, and so on), rewrite will use them for full text match rewrite only.
- If the materialized view was registered as PREBUILT, the precision of the columns must agree with the precision of the corresponding SELECT expressions unless overridden by the WITH REDUCED PRECISION clause.
- If the materialized view contains the same table more than once, it is possible to do a general rewrite, provided the query has the same aliases for the duplicate tables as the materialized view.

General Query Rewrite Restrictions

You should keep in mind the following restrictions:

- If a query has both local and remote tables, only local tables will be considered for potential rewrite.
- Neither the detail tables nor the materialized view can be owned by SYS.
- SELECT and GROUP BY lists, if present, must be the same in the query of the materialized view.
- Aggregate functions must occur only as the outermost part of the expression. That is, aggregates such as AVG(AVG(x)) or AVG(x)+ AVG(x) are not allowed.
- CONNECT BY clauses are not allowed.

Refresh Options

When you define a materialized view, you can specify two refresh options: how to refresh and what type of refresh. If unspecified, the defaults are assumed as ON DEMAND and FORCE.

The two refresh execution modes are: ON COMMIT and ON DEMAND. Depending on the materialized view you create, some of the options may not be available.The following table describes the refresh modes.

Table 3.5 Refresh Modes

Refresh Mode	Description
ON COMMIT	Refresh occurs automatically when a transaction that modified one of the materialized view's detail tables commits. This can be specified as long as the materialized view is fast refreshable (in other words, not complex). The ON COMMIT privilege is necessary to use this mode
ON DEMAND	Refresh occurs when a user manually executes one of the available refresh procedures contained in the DBMS_MVIEW package (REFRESH, REFRESH_ALL_MVIEWS, REFRESH_DEPENDENT)

When a materialized view is maintained using the ON COMMIT method, the time required to complete the commit may be slightly longer than usual. This is because the refresh operation is performed as part of the commit process. Therefore this method may not be suitable if many users are concurrently changing the tables upon which the materialized view is based.

If you anticipate performing insert, update or delete operations on tables referenced by a materialized view concurrently with the refresh of that materialized view, and that materialized view includes joins and aggregation, Oracle recommends you use ON COMMIT fast refresh rather than ON DEMAND fast refresh.

If you think the materialized view did not refresh, check the alert log or trace file.

If a materialized view fails during refresh at COMMIT time, you must explicitly invoke the refresh procedure using the DBMS_MVIEW package after addressing the errors specified in the trace files. Until this is done, the materialized view will no longer be refreshed automatically at commit time.

You can specify how you want your materialized views to be refreshed from the detail tables by selecting one of four options: COMPLETE, FAST, FORCE, and NEVER. The following table 3.6 describes the refresh options.

Table 3.6 Refresh Options

Refresh Option	Description
COMPLETE	Refreshes by recalculating the materialized view's defining query
FAST	Applies incremental changes to refresh the materialized view using the information logged in the materialized view logs, or from a SQL*Loader direct-path or a partition maintenance operation
FORCE	Applies FAST refresh if possible; otherwise, it applies COMPLETE refresh
NEVER	Indicates that the materialized view will not be refreshed with the Oracle refresh mechanisms

Whether the fast refresh option is available depends upon the type of materialized view. You can call the procedure DBMS_MVIEW.EXPLAIN_MVIEW to determine whether fast refresh is possible.

General Restrictions on Fast Refresh

The defining query of the materialized view is restricted as follows:

- The materialized view must not contain references to non-repeating expressions like SYSDATE and ROWNUM.
- The materialized view must not contain references to RAW or LONG RAW data types.

Restrictions on Fast Refresh on Materialized Views with Joins Only

Defining queries for materialized views with joins only and no aggregates have the following restrictions on fast refresh:

- All restrictions from "General Restrictions on Fast Refresh".
- They cannot have GROUP BY clauses or aggregates.
- If the WHERE clause of the query contains outer joins, then unique constraints must exist on the join columns of the inner join table.
- If there are no outer joins, you can have arbitrary selections and joins in the WHERE clause. However, if there are outer joins, the WHERE clause cannot have any selections. Furthermore, if there are outer joins, all the joins must be connected by ANDs and must use the equality (=) operator.
- Rowids of all the tables in the FROM list must appear in the SELECT list of the query.
- Materialized view logs must exist with rowids for all the base tables in the FROM list of the query.

Restrictions on Fast Refresh on Materialized Views with Aggregates

Defining queries for materialized views with joins and aggregates have the following restrictions on fast refresh:

- All restrictions from "General Restrictions on Fast Refresh".

Fast refresh is supported for both ON COMMIT and ON DEMAND materialized views, however the following restrictions apply:

- All tables in the materialized view must have materialized view logs, and the materialized view logs must:
  - Contain all columns from the table referenced in the materialized view.
  - Specify with ROWID and INCLUDING NEW VALUES.
  - Specify the SEQUENCE clause if the table is expected to have a mix of inserts/direct-loads, deletes, and updates.
- Only SUM, COUNT, AVG, STDDEV, VARIANCE, MIN and MAX are supported for fast refresh.
- COUNT(*) must be specified.
- For each aggregate AGG(expr), the corresponding COUNT(expr) must be present.
- If VARIANCE(expr) or STDDEV(expr) is specified, COUNT(expr) and SUM(expr) must be specified. Oracle recommends that SUM(expr *expr) be specified. See table 3.3 for further details.
- The SELECT list must contain all GROUP BY columns.
- If the materialized view has one of the following, then fast refresh is supported only on conventional DML inserts and direct loads.

- Materialized views with MIN or MAX aggregates
- Materialized views which have SUM(expr) but no COUNT(expr)
- Materialized views without COUNT(*).

Such a materialized view is called an insert-only materialized view.

- The COMPATIBILITY parameter must be set to 9.0 if the materialized aggregate view has inline views, outer joins, self joins or grouping sets and FAST REFRESH is specified during creation. Note that all other requirements for fast refresh specified previously must also be satisfied.
- Materialized views with named views or subqueries in the FROM clause can be fast refreshed provided the views can be completely merged.
- If there are no outer joins, you may have arbitrary selections and joins in the WHERE clause.
- Materialized aggregate views with outer joins are fast refreshable after conventional DML and direct loads, provided only the outer table has been modified. Also, unique constraints must exist on the join columns of the inner join table. If there are outer joins, all the joins must be connected by ANDs and must use the equality (=) operator.
- For materialized views with CUBE, ROLLUP, Grouping Sets, or concatenation of them, the following restrictions apply:
- The SELECT list should contain grouping distinguisher that can either be a GROUPING_ID function on all GROUP BY expressions or GROUPING functions one for each GROUP BY expression. For example, if the GROUP BY clause of the materialized view is "GROUP BY CUBE(a, b)", then the SELECT list should contain either "GROUPING_ID(a, b)" or "GROUPING(a) AND GROUPING(b)" for the materialized view to be fast refreshable.
- GROUP BY should not result in any duplicate groupings. For example, "GROUP BY a, ROLLUP(a, b)" is not fast refreshable because it results in duplicate groupings "(a), (a, b), AND (a)".

Restrictions on Fast Refresh on Materialized Views With the UNION ALL Operator

Materialized views with the UNION ALL set operator support the REFRESH FAST option if the following conditions are satisfied:

- The defining query must have the UNION ALL operator at the top level.

The UNION ALL operator cannot be embedded inside a subquery, with one exception: The UNION ALL can be in a subquery in the FROM clause provided the defining query is of the form SELECT * FROM (view or subquery with UNION ALL) as in the following example:

```
CREATE VIEW view_with_unionall_mv
AS
(SELECT c.rowid crid, c.cust_id, 2 umarker
 FROM customers c
 WHERE c.cust_last_name = 'Smith'
 UNION ALL
 SELECT c.rowid crid, c.cust_id, 3 umarker
 FROM customers c
 WHERE c.cust_last_name = 'Jones');

CREATE MATERIALIZED VIEW unionall_inside_view_mv
REFRESH FAST ON DEMAND
AS
SELECT * FROM view_with_unionall;
```

Note that the view view_with_unionall_mv satisfies all requirements for fast refresh.

- Each query block in the UNION ALL query must satisfy the requirements of a fast refreshable materialized view with aggregates or a fast refreshable materialized view with joins.

The appropriate materialized view logs must be created on the tables as required for the corresponding type of fast refreshable materialized view.

Note that Oracle also allows the special case of a single table materialized view with joins only provided the ROWID column has been included in the SELECT list and in the materialized view log. This is shown in the defining query of the view view_with_unionall_mv.

- The SELECT list of each query must include a maintenance column, called a UNION ALL marker. The UNION ALL column must have a distinct constant numeric or string value in each UNION ALL branch. Further, the marker column must appear in the same ordinal position in the SELECT list of each query block.
- Some features such as outer joins, insert-only aggregate materialized view queries and remote tables are not supported for materialized views with UNION ALL.
- Partition Change Tracking-based refresh is not supported for UNION ALL materialized views.
- The compatibility initialization parameter must be set to 9.2.0 to create a fast refreshable materialized view with UNION ALL.

ORDER BY Clause

An ORDER BY clause is allowed in the CREATE MATERIALIZED VIEW statement. It is used only during the initial creation of the materialized view. It is not used during a full refresh or a fast refresh.

To improve the performance of queries against large materialized views, store the rows in the materialized view in the order specified in the ORDER BY clause. This initial ordering provides physical clustering of the data. If indexes are built on the columns by which the materialized view is ordered, accessing the rows of the materialized view using the index often reduces the time for disk I/O due to the physical clustering.

The ORDER BY clause is not considered part of the materialized view definition. As a result, there is no difference in the manner in which Oracle detects the various types of materialized views (for example, materialized join views with no aggregates). For the same reason, query rewrite is not affected by the ORDER BY clause. This feature is similar to the CREATE TABLE ... ORDER BY capability that exists in Oracle.

Materialized View Logs

Materialized view logs are required if you want to use fast refresh. They are defined using a CREATE MATERIALIZED VIEW LOG statement on the base table that is to be changed. They are not created on the materialized view. For fast refresh of materialized views, the definition of the materialized view logs must specify the ROWID clause. In addition, for aggregate materialized views, it must also contain every column in the table referenced in the materialized view, the INCLUDING NEW VALUES clause and the SEQUENCE clause.

An example of a materialized view log is shown as follows where one is created on the table sales.

```
CREATE MATERIALIZED VIEW LOG ON sales
WITH ROWID
(prod_id, cust_id, time_id, channel_id, promo_id, quantity_sold, amount_sold)
INCLUDING NEW VALUES;
```

Oracle recommends that the keyword SEQUENCE be included in your materialized view log statement unless you are sure that you will never perform a mixed DML operation (a combination of INSERT, UPDATE, or DELETE operations on multiple tables).

The boundary of a mixed DML operation is determined by whether the materialized view is ON COMMIT or ON DEMAND.

- For ON COMMIT, the mixed DML statements occur within the same transaction because the refresh of the materialized view will occur upon commit of this transaction.
- For ON DEMAND, the mixed DML statements occur between refreshes. The following example of a materialized view log illustrates where one is created on the table sales that includes the SEQUENCE keyword:

```
CREATE MATERIALIZED VIEW LOG ON sales
WITH SEQUENCE, ROWID
(prod_id, cust_id, time_id, channel_id, promo_id,
 quantity_sold, amount_sold)
INCLUDING NEW VALUES;
```

Using Oracle Enterprise Manager

A materialized view can also be created by using Oracle Enterprise Manager by selecting the materialized view object type. There is no difference in the information required if this approach is used. However, you must complete three property sheets and you must ensure that the option **Enable Query Rewrite** on the **General** sheet is selected.

Using Materialized Views with NLS Parameters

When using certain materialized views, you must ensure that your NLS parameters are the same as when you created the materialized view. Materialized views with this restriction are as follows:

- Expressions that may return different values, depending on NLS parameter settings. For example, (date > "01/02/03") or (rate <= "2.150") are NLS parameter dependent expressions.
- Equijoins where one side of the join is character data. The result of this equijoin depends on collation and this can change on a session basis, giving an incorrect result in the case of query rewrite or an inconsistent materialized view after a refresh operation.
- Expressions that generate internal conversion to character data in the SELECT list of a materialized view, or inside an aggregate of a materialized aggregate view. This restriction does not apply to expressions that involve only numeric data, for example, a+b where a and b are numeric fields.

REGISTERING EXISTING MATERIALIZED VIEWS

Some data warehouses have implemented materialized views in ordinary user tables. Although this solution provides the performance benefits of materialized views, it does not:

- Provide query rewrite to all SQL applications
- Enable materialized views defined in one application to be transparently accessed in another application
- Generally support fast parallel or fast materialized view refresh.

Because of these limitations, and because existing materialized views can be extremely large and expensive to rebuild, you should register your existing materialized view tables with Oracle whenever possible. You can register a user-defined materialized view with the `CREATE MATERIALIZED VIEW ... ON PREBUILT TABLE` statement. Once registered, the materialized view can be used for query rewrites or maintained by one of the refresh methods, or both.

The contents of the table must reflect the materialization of the defining query at the time you register it as a materialized view, and each column in the defining query must correspond to a column in the table that has a matching datatype. However, you can specify `WITH REDUCED PRECISION` to allow the precision of columns in the defining query to be different from that of the table columns.

The table and the materialized view must have the same name, but the table retains its identity as a table and can contain columns that are not referenced in the defining query of the materialized view. These extra columns are known as unmanaged columns. If rows are inserted during a refresh operation, each unmanaged column of the row is set to its default value. Therefore, the unmanaged columns cannot have `NOT NULL` constraints unless they also have default values.

Materialized views based on prebuilt tables are eligible for selection by query rewrite provided the parameter `QUERY_REWRITE_INTEGRITY` is set to at least the level of `stale_tolerated` or `trusted`.

When you drop a materialized view that was created on a prebuilt table, the table still exists—only the materialized view is dropped.

When a prebuilt table is registered as a materialized view and query rewrite is desired, the parameter `QUERY_REWRITE_INTEGRITY` must be set to at least `stale_tolerated` because, when it is created, the materialized view is marked as unknown. Therefore, only stale integrity modes can be used.

The following example illustrates the two steps required to register a user-defined table. First, the table is created, then the materialized view is defined using exactly the same name as the table. This materialized view `sum_sales_tab` is eligible for use in query rewrite.

```
CREATE TABLE sum_sales_tab
  PCTFREE 0  TABLESPACE demo
   STORAGE (INITIAL 16k NEXT 16k PCTINCREASE 0)
    AS
    SELECT s.prod_id,
       SUM(amount_sold) AS dollar_sales,
       SUM(quantity_sold) AS unit_sales
         FROM sales s GROUP BY s.prod_id;

CREATE MATERIALIZED VIEW sum_sales_tab
ON PREBUILT TABLE WITHOUT REDUCED PRECISION
ENABLE QUERY REWRITE
AS
SELECT s.prod_id,
```

```
SUM(amount_sold) AS dollar_sales,
SUM(quantity_sold) AS unit_sales
FROM sales s GROUP BY s.prod_id;
```

You could have compressed this table to save space.In some cases, user-defined materialized views are refreshed on a schedule that is longer than the update cycle. For example, a monthly materialized view might be updated only at the end of each month, and the materialized view values always refer to complete time periods. Reports written directly against these materialized views implicitly select only data that is not in the current (incomplete) time period. If a user-defined materialized view already contains a time dimension:

- It should be registered and then fast refreshed each update cycle.
- You can create a view that selects the complete time period of interest.
- The reports should be modified to refer to the view instead of referring directly to the user-defined materialized view.

If the user-defined materialized view does not contain a time dimension, then:

- Create a new materialized view that does include the time dimension (if possible).
- The view should aggregate over the time column in the new materialized view.

PARTITIONING AND MATERIALIZED VIEWS

Because of the large volume of data held in a data warehouse, partitioning is an extremely useful option when designing a database.

Partitioning the fact tables improves scalability, simplifies system administration, and makes it possible to define local indexes that can be efficiently rebuilt. Partitioning the fact tables also improves the opportunity of fast refreshing the materialized view when the partition maintenance operation occurs.

Partitioning a materialized view also has benefits for refresh, because the refresh procedure can use parallel DML to maintain the materialized view.

Partition Change Tracking

It is possible and advantageous to track freshness to a finer grain than the entire materialized view. The ability to identify which rows in a materialized view are affected by a certain detail table partition, is known as Partition Change Tracking (PCT). When one or more of the detail tables are partitioned, it may be possible to identify the specific rows in the materialized view that correspond to a modified detail partition(s); those rows become stale when a partition is modified while all other rows remain fresh.

Partition Change Tracking can be used to identify which materialized view rows correspond to a particular detail table. Partition Change Tracking is also used to support fast refresh after partition maintenance operations on detail tables. For instance, if a detail table partition is truncated or dropped, the affected rows in the materialized view are identified and deleted. Identifying which materialized view rows are fresh or stale, rather than considering the entire materialized view as stale, allows query rewrite to use those rows that are fresh while in `QUERY_REWRITE_INTEGRITY=ENFORCED` or `TRUSTED` modes.

To support PCT, a materialized view must satisfy the following requirements:

- At least one of the detail tables referenced by the materialized view must be partitioned.

- Partitioned tables must use either range or composite partitioning.
- The partition key must consist of only a single column.
- The materialized view must contain either the partition key column or a partition marker of the detail table.
- If you use a `GROUP BY` clause, the partition key column or the partition marker must be present in the `GROUP BY` clause.
- Data modifications can only occur on the partitioned table.
- The `COMPATIBILITY` initialization parameter must be a minimum of 9.0.0.0.0.
- Partition Change Tracking is not supported for a materialized view that refers to views, remote tables, or outer joins.
- Partition Change Tracking-based refresh is not supported for `UNION ALL` materialized views.

Partition change tracking requires sufficient information in the materialized view to be able to correlate each materialized view row back to its corresponding detail row in the source partitioned detail table. This can be accomplished by including the detail table partition key columns in the select list and, if `GROUP BY` is used, in the `GROUP BY` list. Depending on the desired level of aggregation and the distinct cardinalities of the partition key columns, this has the unfortunate effect of significantly increasing the cardinality of the materialized view. For example, say a popular metric is the revenue generated by a product during a given year. If the `sales` table were partitioned by `time_id`, it would be a required field in the `SELECT` clause and the `GROUP BY` clause of the materialized view. If there were 1000 different products sold each day, it would substantially increase the number of rows in the materialized view.

Partition Marker

In many cases, the advantages of PCT will be offset by this restriction for highly aggregated materialized views. The `DBMS_MVIEW.PMARKER` function is designed to significantly reduce the cardinality of the materialized view. The function returns a partition identifier that uniquely identifies the partition for a specified row within a specified partition table. The `DBMS_MVIEW.PMARKER` function is used instead of the partition key column in the `SELECT` and `GROUP BY` clauses.

Unlike the general case of a PL/SQL function in a materialized view, use of the `DBMS_MVIEW.PMARKER` does not prevent rewrite with that materialized view even when the rewrite mode is `QUERY_REWRITE_INTEGRITY=enforced`.

Example 3.13 : Partition Change Tracking

The following example uses the `sh` sample schema and the three detail tables `sales`, `products`, and `times` to create two materialized views. For this example, `sales` is a partitioned table using the `time_id` column and `products` is partitioned by the `prod_category` column. `times` is not a partitioned table.

The first materialized view is for the yearly sales revenue for each product.

The second materialized view is for monthly customer sales. As customers tend to purchase in bulk, sales average just two orders for each customer per month. Therefore, the impact of including the `time_id` in the materialized view will not unacceptably increase the number of rows stored. However, most orders are large and contain many different products. With approximately 1000 different products sold each day, including the `time_id` in the materialized view would substantially increase the cardinality. This materialized view uses the `DBMS_MVIEW.PMARKER` function.

The detail tables must have materialized view logs for FAST REFRESH.

```
CREATE MATERIALIZED VIEW LOG ON SALES WITH ROWID
    (prod_id, time_id, quantity_sold, amount_sold)
    INCLUDING NEW VALUES;

CREATE MATERIALIZED VIEW LOG ON PRODUCTS WITH ROWID
    (prod_id, prod_name, prod_desc)
    INCLUDING NEW VALUES;
CREATE MATERIALIZED VIEW LOG ON TIMES WITH ROWID
    (time_id, calendar_month_name, calendar_year)
    INCLUDING NEW VALUES;

CREATE MATERIALIZED VIEW cust_mth_sales_mv
    BUILD DEFERRED REFRESH FAST ON DEMAND
    ENABLE QUERY REWRITE
AS
   SELECT s.time_id, p.prod_id, SUM(s.quantity_sold),
   SUM(s.amount_sold),
     p.prod_name, t.calendar_month_name, COUNT(*),
     COUNT(s.quantity_sold),     COUNT(s.amount_sold)
   FROM sales s, products p, times t
   WHERE  s.time_id = t.time_id AND s.prod_id = p.prod_id
   GROUP BY t.calendar_month_name, p.prod_id, p.prod_name, s.time_id;
```

cust_mth_sales_mv includes the partition key column from table sales (time_id) in both its SELECT and GROUP BY lists. This enables PCT on table sales for materialized view cust_mth_sales_mv. However, the GROUP BY and SELECT lists include PRODUCTS.PROD_ID rather than the partition key column (PROD_CATEGORY) of the products table. Therefore, PCT is not enabled on table products for this materialized view. In other words, any partition maintenance operation to the sales table will allow a PCT fast refresh of cust_mth_sales_mv. However, PCT fast refresh is not possible after any kind of modification to the products table. To correct this, the GROUP BY and SELECT lists must include column PRODUCTS.PROD_CATEGORY. Following a partition maintenance operation, such as a drop partition, a PCT fast refresh should be performed on any materialized view that is referencing the table upon which the partition operations are undertaken.

Example 3.14 : Creating a Materialized View

```
CREATE MATERIALIZED VIEW prod_yr_sales_mv
BUILD DEFERRED
REFRESH FAST ON DEMAND
ENABLE QUERY REWRITE
AS
     SELECT    DBMS_MVIEW.PMARKER(s.rowid),
               DBMS_MVIEW.PMARKER(p.rowid),
               s.prod_id, SUM(s.amount_sold), SUM(s.quantity_sold),
               p.prod_name, t.calendar_year, COUNT(*),
               COUNT(s.amount_sold), COUNT(s.quantity_sold)
       FROM    sales s, products p, times t
       WHERE   s.time_id = t.time_id AND
               s.prod_id = p.prod_id
       GROUP BY DBMS_MVIEW.PMARKER (s.rowid),
```

```
DBMS_MVIEW.PMARKER (p.rowid),
t.calendar_year, s.prod_id, p.prod_name;
```

prod_yr_sales_mv includes the DBMS_MVIEW.PMARKER function on the sales and products tables in both its SELECT and GROUP BY lists. This enables partition change tracking on both the sales table and the products table with significantly less cardinality impact than grouping by the respective partition key columns. In this example, the desired level of aggregation for the prod_yr_sales_mv is to group by times.calendar_year. Using the DBMS_MVIEW.PMARKER function, the materialized view cardinality is increased only by a factor of the number of partitions in the sales table times, the number of partitions in the products table. This would generally be significantly less than the cardinality impact of including the respective partition key columns.

A subsequent INSERT statement adds a new row to the sales_part3 partition of table sales. At this point, because cust_mth_sales_mv and prod_yr_sales_mv have partition change tracking available on table sales, Oracle can determine that those rows in these materialized views corresponding to sales_part3 are stale, while all other rows in these materialized views are unchanged in their freshness state. An INSERT INTO products statement is not tracked for materialized view cust_mth_sales_mv. Therefore, cust_mth_sales_mv becomes completely stale when the products table is modified in this way.

Partitioning a Materialized View

Partitioning a materialized view involves defining the materialized view with the standard Oracle partitioning clauses, as illustrated in the following example. This statement creates a materialized view called part_sales_mv, which uses three partitions, can be fast refreshed, and is eligible for query rewrite.

```
CREATE MATERIALIZED VIEW part_sales_mv
PARALLEL
  PARTITION BY RANGE (time_id)
  (PARTITION month1
      VALUES LESS THAN (TO_DATE('31-12-1998', 'DD-MM-YYYY'))
      PCTFREE 0 PCTUSED 99
      STORAGE (INITIAL 64k NEXT 16k PCTINCREASE 0)
      TABLESPACE sf1,
   PARTITION month2
      VALUES LESS THAN (TO_DATE('31-12-1999', 'DD-MM-YYYY'))
      PCTFREE 0 PCTUSED 99
      STORAGE (INITIAL 64k NEXT 16k PCTINCREASE 0)
      TABLESPACE sf2,
   PARTITION month3
      VALUES LESS THAN (TO_DATE('31-12-2000', 'DD-MM-YYYY'))
      PCTFREE 0 PCTUSED 99.
      STORAGE (INITIAL 64k NEXT 16k PCTINCREASE 0)
      TABLESPACE sf3)
BUILD DEFERRED
REFRESH FAST
ENABLE QUERY REWRITE
AS
SELECT s.cust_id, s.time_id,
  SUM(s.amount_sold) AS sum_dol_sales,  SUM(s.quantity_sold) AS sum_unit_sales
  FROM sales s GROUP BY s.time_id, s.cust_id;
```

Partitioning a Prebuilt Table

Alternatively, a materialized view can be registered to a partitioned prebuilt table as illustrated in the following example:

```
CREATE TABLE part_sales_tab(time_id, cust_id, sum_dollar_sales, sum_unit_sale)
  PARALLEL
  PARTITION BY RANGE (time_id)
  (
    PARTITION month1
      VALUES LESS THAN (TO_DATE('31-12-1998', 'DD-MM-YYYY'))
      PCTFREE 0 PCTUSED 99
      STORAGE (INITITAL 64k NEXT 16k PCTINCREASE 0)
      TABLESPACE sf1,
    PARTITION month2
      VALUES LESS THAN (TO_DATE('31-12-1999', 'DD-MM-YYYY'))
      PCTFREE 0 PCTUSED 99
      STORAGE (INITIAL 64k NEXT 16k PCTINCREASE 0)
      TABLESPACE sf2,
    PARTITION month3
      VALUES LESS THAN (TO_DATE('31-12-2000', 'DD-MM-YYYY'))
      PCTFREE 0 PCTUSED 99
      STORAGE (INITIAL 64k NEXT 16k PCTINCREASE 0)
      TABLESPACE sf3)
AS
SELECT s.time_key, s.cust_id,
  SUM(s.amount_sold) AS sum_dollar_sales,
  SUM(s.quantity_sold) AS sum_unit_sales
       FROM sales s GROUP BY s.time_id, s.cust_id;

CREATE MATERIALIZED VIEW part_sales_tab_mv
ON PREBUILT TABLE
ENABLE QUERY REWRITE
AS
SELECT s.time_id,  s.cust_id,
  SUM(s.amount_sold) AS sum_dollar_sales,
  SUM(s.quantity_sold) AS sum_unit_sales
       FROM sales s GROUP BY s.time_id, s.cust_id;
```

In this example, the table `part_sales_tab` has been partitioned over three months and then the materialized view was registered to use the prebuilt table. This materialized view is eligible for query rewrite because the `ENABLE QUERY REWRITE` clause has been included.

Rolling Materialized Views

When a data warehouse or data mart contains a time dimension, it is often desirable to archive the oldest information and then reuse the storage for new information. This is called the rolling window scenario. If the fact tables or materialized views include a time dimension and are horizontally partitioned by the time attribute, then management of rolling materialized views can be reduced to a few fast partition maintenance operations provided the unit of data that is rolled out equals, or is at least aligned with, the range partitions.

If you plan to have rolling materialized views in your warehouse, you should determine how frequently you plan to perform partition maintenance operations, and you should plan to partition fact tables and materialized views to reduce the amount of system administration overhead required when old data is aged out. An additional consideration is that you might want to use data compression on your infrequently updated partitions.

You are not restricted to using range partitions. For example, a composite partition using both a time value and a key value could result in a good partition solution for your data.

MATERIALIZED VIEWS IN OLAP ENVIRONMENTS

This section discusses certain OLAP concepts and how relational databases can handle OLAP queries. Next, it recommends an approach for using materialized views to meet OLAP performance needs. Finally, it discusses using materialized views with set operators, a common scenario for OLAP environments.

OLAP Cubes

While data warehouse environments typically view data in the form of a star schema, OLAP environments view data in the form of a hierarchical cube. A hierarchical cube includes both detail data and aggregated data: it is a data set where the data is aggregated along the rollup hierarchy of each of its dimensions and these aggregations are combined across dimensions. It includes the typical set of aggregations needed for business intelligence queries.

Example of a Hierarchical Cube

Consider a sales data set with two dimensions, each of which has a 4-level hierarchy:

- Time, which contains (all times), year, quarter, and month.
- Product, which contains (all products), division, brand, and item.

This means there are 16 aggregate groups in the hierarchical cube. This is because the four levels of time are multiplied by four levels of product to produce the cube. The following table shows the four levels of each dimension.

Table 3.7 ROLLUP By Time and Product

ROLLUP By Time	ROLLUP By Product
year, quarter, month	division, brand, item
year, quarter	division, brand
year	division
all times	all products

Note that as you increase the number of dimensions and levels, the number of groups to calculate increases dramatically. This example involves 16 groups, but if you were to add just two more dimensions with the same number of levels, you would have $4 \times 4 \times 4 \times 4 = 256$ different groups. Also, consider that a similar increase in groups occurs if you have multiple hierarchies in your dimensions. For example, the time dimension might have an additional hierarchy of fiscal month rolling up to fiscal quarter and then fiscal year. Handling the explosion of groups has historically been the major challenge in data storage for OLAP systems.

Typical OLAP queries **slice and dice** different parts of the cube comparing aggregations from one level to aggregation from another level. For instance, a query might find sales of the grocery division for the month of January, 2002 and compare them with total sales of the grocery division for all of 2001.

Specifying OLAP Cubes in SQL

Oracle9*i* can specify hierarchical cubes in a simple and efficient SQL query. These hierarchical cubes represent the logical cubes referred to in many OLAP products. To specify data in the form of hierarchical cubes, users can work with the extensions to `GROUP BY` clause introduced in Oracle9*i*.

You can use one of Oracle's new extensions to the `GROUP BY` clause, concatenated grouping sets, to generate the aggregates needed for a hierarchical cube of data. By using concatenated rollup (rolling up along the hierarchy of each dimension and then concatenate them across multiple dimensions), you can generate all the aggregations needed by a hierarchical cube. These extensions are discussed in detail in Chapter 18, "SQL for Aggregation in Data Warehouses".

Example of Concatenated ROLLUP

The following shows the `GROUP BY` clause needed to create a hierarchical cube for the 2-dimension example described earlier. The following simple syntax performs a concatenated rollup:

```
GROUP BY ROLLUP(year, quarter, month),
  ROLLUP(Division, brand, item);
```

This concatenated rollup takes the `ROLLUP` aggregations listed in the table of the prior section and perform a cross-product on them. The cross-product will create the 16 (4x4) aggregate groups needed for a hierarchical cube of the data.

Querying OLAP Cubes in SQL

Analytic applications treat data as cubes, but they want only certain slices and regions of the cube. Concatenated rollup (hierarchical cube) enables relational data to be treated as cubes. To handle complex analytic queries, the fundamental technique is to enclose a hierarchical cube query in an outer query that specifies the exact slice needed from the cube. Oracle9*i* optimizes the processing of hierarchical cubes nested inside slicing queries. By applying many powerful algorithms, these queries can be processed at unprecedented speed and scale. This enables OLAP tools and analytic applications to use a consistent style of queries to handle the most complex questions.

Example of a Hierarchical Cube Query

Consider the following analytic query. It consists of a hierarchical cube query nested in a slicing query.

```
SELECT month, division, sum_sales FROM
   (SELECT year, quarter, month, division, brand, item, SUM(sales) sum_sales,
       GROUPING_ID(grouping-columns) gid
    FROM sales, products, time
    WHERE join-condition
    GROUP BY
      ROLLUP(year, quarter, month),
      ROLLUP(division, brand, item)
  )
WHERE division = 25
  AND month = 200201
  AND gid = gid-for-Division-Month;
```

The inner hierarchical cube specified defines a simple cube, with two dimensions and four levels in each dimension. It would generate 16 groups (4 Time levels * 4 Product levels). The GROUPING_ID function in the query identifies the specific group each row belongs to, based on the aggregation level of the *grouping-columns* in its argument.

The outer query applies the constraints needed for our specific query, limiting Division to a value of 25 and Month to a value of 200201 (representing January 2002 in this case). In conceptual terms, it slices a small chunk of data from the cube. The outer query's constraint on the GID column, indicated in the query by *gid-for-division-month* would be the value of a key indicating that the data is grouped as a combination of division and month. The GID constraint selects only those rows that are aggregated at the level of a GROUP BY month, division clause.

Oracle removes unneeded aggregation groups from query processing based on the outer query conditions. The outer conditions of the previous query limit the result set to a single group aggregating division and month. Any other groups involving year, month, brand, and item are unnecessary here. The group pruning optimization recognizes this and transforms the query into:

```
SELECT month, division, sum_sales
FROM
  (SELECT  null, null,  month, division,
      null, null, SUM(sales) sum_sales,
      GROUPING_ID(grouping-columns) gid
   FROM sales, products, time
   WHERE join-condition
   GROUP BY
 month, division)
WHERE division = 25
  AND month = 200201
  AND gid = gid-for-Division-Month;
```

The bold items highlight the changed SQL. The inner query now has a simple GROUP BY clause of month, division. The columns year, quarter, brand and item have been converted to null to match the simplified GROUP BY clause. Because the query now requests just one group, fifteen out of sixteen groups are removed from the processing, greatly reducing the work. For a cube with more dimensions and more levels, the savings possible through group pruning can be far greater. Note that the group pruning transformation works with all the GROUP BY extensions: ROLLUP, CUBE, and GROUPING SETS.

While the Oracle optimizer has simplified the previous query to a simple GROUP BY, faster response times can be achieved if the group is precomputed and stored in a materialized view. Because OLAP queries can ask for any slice of the cube many groups may need to be precomputed and stored in a materialized view. This is discussed in the next section.

SQL for Creating Materialized Views to Store OLAP Cubes

OLAP requires fast response times for multiple users, and this in turn demands that significant parts of an OLAP cube be precomputed and held in materialized views. Oracle9*i* enables great flexibility in the use of materialized views for OLAP.

Data warehouse designers can choose exactly how much data to materialize. A data warehouse can have the full OLAP cube materialized. While this will take the most storage space, it ensures quick response for any query within the cube. On the other hand, a warehouse could have just partial materialization, saving storage space, but allowing only a subset of possible queries to be answered at highest speed. If an OLAP environment's queries cover the full range of aggregate groupings possible in its data set, it may be best to materialize the whole hierarchical cube.

This means that each dimension's aggregation hierarchy is precomputed in combination with each of the other dimensions. Naturally, precomputing a full hierarchical cube requires more disk space and higher creation and refresh times than a small set of aggregate groups. The trade-off in processing time and disk space versus query performance needs to be considered before deciding to create it. An additional possibility you could consider is to use data compression to lessen your disk space requirements.

Examples of Hierarchical Cube Materialized Views

This section shows complete and partial hierarchical cube materialized views.

Example 3.15 : Complete Hierarchical Cube Materialized View

```
CREATE MATERIALIZED VIEW sales_hierarchical_cube_mv
REFRESH FAST ON DEMAND
ENABLE QUERY REWRITE
AS
SELECT country_id, cust_state_province, cust_city, prod_category,
prod_subcategory, prod_name, calendar_month_number,
day_number_in_month, day_number_in_week,
GROUPING_ID(country_id, cust_state_province, cust_city,
prod_category, prod_subcategory, prod_name,
calendar_month_number, day_number_in_month,
day_number_in_week) gid,
SUM(amount_sold) s_sales,
COUNT(amount_sold) c_sales,
COUNT(*) c_star
FROM sales s, products p, customers c, times t
WHERE s.cust_id = c.cust_id AND s.prod_id = p.prod_id
    AND s.time_id = t.time_id
GROUP BY
  ROLLUP(country_id, (cust_state_province, cust_city)),
  ROLLUP(prod_category, (prod_subcategory, prod_name)),
  ROLLUP(calendar_month_number, (day_number_in_month,
    day_number_in_week))
PARTITION BY LIST (gid)
...;
```

This creates a complete hierarchical cube stored in a list-partitioned materialized view.

Example 3.16 : Partial Hierarchical Cube Materialized View

```
CREATE MATERIALIZED VIEW sales_mv
REFRESH FAST ON DEMAND
ENABLE QUERY REWRITE
AS
SELECT country_id, cust_state_province, cust_city,
prod_category, prod_subcategory, prod_name,
GROUPING_ID(country_id, cust_state_province, cust_city,
prod_category, prod_subcategory, prod_name) gid,
SUM(amount_sold) s_sales,
COUNT(amount_sold) c_sales,
```

```
COUNT(*) c_star
FROM sales s, products p, customers c
WHERE s.cust_id = c.cust_id and s.prod_id = p.prod_id
GROUP BY GROUPING SETS
((country_id, cust_state_province, cust_city),
(country_id, prod_category, prod_subcategory, prod_name),
(prod_category, prod_subcategory, prod_name),(country_id,
prod_category))
PARTITION BY LIST (gid)
...;
```

This creates a partial hierarchical cube stored in a list-partitioned materialized view. Note that it explicitly lists the groups needed using the GROUPING SETS extension to GROUP BY.

Partitioning Materialized Views for OLAP

Materialized views with multiple aggregate groups will give their best performance when partitioned appropriately. The most effective partitioning scheme for these materialized views is to use list partitioning, especially with the GROUPING_ID column. By partitioning the materialized views this way, you enable partition pruning for queries rewritten against this materialized view: only relevant aggregate groups will be accessed, greatly reducing the query processing cost.

Compressing Materialized Views for OLAP

You should consider data compression when using highly redundant data, such as tables with many foreign keys. In particular, materialized views created with the ROLLUP clause are likely candidates.

Materialized Views with Set Operators

Oracle provides some support for materialized views whose defining query involves set operators. Materialized views with set operators can now be created enabled for query rewrite. Query rewrite with such materialized views is supported using full exact text match. You can refresh the materialized view using either ON COMMIT or ON DEMAND refresh.

Fast refresh is supported if the defining query has the UNION ALL operator at the top level and each query block in the UNION ALL, meets the requirements of a materialized view with aggregates or materialized view with joins only. Further, the materialized view must include a constant column (known as a UNION ALL marker) that has a distinct value in each query block, which, in the following example, is columns 1 marker and 2 marker.

Examples of Materialized Views Using UNION ALL

The following examples illustrate creation of fast refreshable materialized views involving UNION ALL.

Example 3.17 : Materialized View Using UNION ALL

To create a UNION ALL materialized view with two join views, the materialized view logs must have the rowid column and, in the following example, the UNION ALL marker is the columns, 1 marker and 2 marker.

```
CREATE MATERIALIZED VIEW LOG ON sales
WITH ROWID;
CREATE MATERIALIZED VIEW LOG ON customers
WITH ROWID;
```

```
CREATE MATERIALIZED VIEW unionall_sales_cust_joins_mv
BUILD DEFERRED
REFRESH FAST ON COMMIT
ENABLE QUERY REWRITE
AS
(SELECT c.rowid crid, s.rowid srid, c.cust_id, s.amount_sold, 1 marker
FROM sales s, customers c
WHERE s.cust_id = c.cust_id AND c.cust_last_name = 'Smith')
UNION ALL
(SELECT c.rowid crid, s.rowid srid, c.cust_id, s.amount_sold, 2 marker
FROM sales s, customers c
WHERE s.cust_id = c.cust_id AND c.cust_last_name = 'Brown');
```

Example 3.18 : Materialized View Using UNION ALL

The following example shows a UNION ALL of a materialized view with joins and a materialized view with aggregates. A couple of things can be noted in this example. Nulls or constants can be used to ensure that the data types of the corresponding SELECT list columns match. Also the UNION ALL marker column can be a string literal, which is 'Year' umarker, 'Quarter' umarker, or 'Daily' umarker in the following example:

```
DROP MATERIALIZED VIEW LOG ON sales;
CREATE MATERIALIZED VIEW LOG ON sales WITH ROWID, SEQUENCE
(amount_sold, time_id)
INCLUDING NEW VALUES;

DROP MATERIALIZED VIEW LOG ON times;
CREATE MATERIALIZED VIEW LOG ON times WITH ROWID, SEQUENCE
   (time_id, fiscal_year, fiscal_quarter_number, day_number_in_week)
INCLUDING NEW VALUES;

DROP MATERIALIZED VIEW unionall_sales_mix_mv;
CREATE MATERIALIZED VIEW unionall_sales_mix_mv
BUILD DEFERRED
REFRESH FAST ON DEMAND
AS
(SELECT 'Year' umarker, NULL, NULL, t.fiscal_year,
        SUM(s.amount_sold) amt, COUNT(s.amount_sold), COUNT(*)
 FROM sales s, times t
 WHERE s.time_id = t.time_id
 GROUP BY t.fiscal_year)
UNION ALL
(SELECT 'Quarter' umarker, NULL, NULL, t.fiscal_quarter_number,
        SUM(s.amount_sold) amt, COUNT(s.amount_sold), COUNT(*)
FROM sales s, times t
WHERE s.time_id = t.time_id and t.fiscal_year = 2001
GROUP BY t.fiscal_quarter_number)
UNION ALL
(SELECT 'Daily' umarker, s.rowid rid, t.rowid rid2, t.day_number_in_week,
        s.amount_sold amt, 1, 1
FROM sales s, times t
WHERE s.time_id = t.time_id
  and t.time_id between '01-Jan-01' and '01-Dec-31');
```

CHOOSING INDEXES FOR MATERIALIZED VIEWS

The two most common operations on a materialized view are query execution and fast refresh, and each operation has different performance requirements. Query execution might need to access any subset of the materialized view key columns, and might need to join and aggregate over a subset of those columns. Consequently, query execution usually performs best if a single-column bitmap index is defined on each materialized view key column.

In the case of materialized views containing only joins using fast refresh, Oracle recommends that indexes be created on the columns that contain the rowids to improve the performance of the refresh operation.

If a materialized view using aggregates is fast refreshable, then an index is automatically created unless `USING NO INDEX` is specified in the `CREATE MATERIALIZED VIEW` statement.

INVALIDATING MATERIALIZED VIEWS

Dependencies related to materialized views are automatically maintained to ensure correct operation. When a materialized view is created, the materialized view depends on the detail tables referenced in its definition. Any DML operation, such as a `INSERT`, or `DELETE`, `UPDATE`, or DDL operation on any dependency in the materialized view will cause it to become invalid. To revalidate a materialized view, use the `ALTER MATERIALIZED VIEW COMPILE` statement.

A materialized view is automatically revalidated when it is referenced. In many cases, the materialized view will be successfully and transparently revalidated. However, if a column has been dropped in a table referenced by a materialized view or the owner of the materialized view did not have one of the query rewrite privileges and that privilege has now been granted to the owner, you should use the following statement to revalidate the materialized view:

```
ALTER MATERIALIZED VIEW mview_name ENABLE QUERY REWRITE;
```

The state of a materialized view can be checked by querying the data dictionary views `USER_MVIEWS` or `ALL_MVIEWS`. The column `STALENESS` will show one of the values `FRESH`, `STALE`, `UNUSABLE`, `UNKNOWN`, or `UNDEFINED` to indicate whether the materialized view can be used. The state is maintained automatically, but it can be manually updated by issuing an `ALTER MATERIALIZED VIEW` *name* `COMPILE` statement.

SECURITY ISSUES WITH MATERIALIZED VIEWS

To create a materialized view in your own schema, you must have the `CREATE MATERIALIZED VIEW` privilege and the `SELECT` privilege to any tables referenced that are in another schema. To create a materialized view in another schema, you must have the `CREATE ANY MATERIALIZED VIEW` privilege and the owner of the materialized view needs `SELECT` privileges to the tables referenced if they are from another schema.

Moreover, if you enable query rewrite on a materialized view that references tables outside your schema, you must have the `GLOBAL QUERY REWRITE` privilege or the `QUERY REWRITE` object privilege on each table outside your schema.

If the materialized view is on a prebuilt container, the creator, if different from the owner, must have `SELECT WITH GRANT` privilege on the container table.

If you continue to get a privilege error while trying to create a materialized view and you believe that all the required privileges have been granted, then the problem is most likely due to a privilege not being granted explicitly and trying to inherit the privilege from a role instead. The owner of the materialized view must have explicitly been granted `SELECT` access to the referenced tables if the tables are in a different schema.

If the materialized view is being created with `ON COMMIT REFRESH` specified, then the owner of the materialized view requires an additional privilege if any of the tables in the defining query are outside the owner's schema. In that case, the owner requires the `ON COMMIT REFRESH` system privilege or the `ON COMMIT REFRESH` object privilege on each table outside the owner's schema.

ALTERING MATERIALIZED VIEWS

Five modifications can be made to a materialized view. You can:

- Change its refresh option (`FAST/FORCE/COMPLETE/NEVER`)
- Change its refresh mode (`ON COMMIT/ON DEMAND`)
- Recompile it
- Enable or disable its use for query rewrite
- Consider it fresh.

All other changes are achieved by dropping and then re-creating the materialized view.

The `COMPILE` clause of the `ALTER MATERIALIZED VIEW` statement can be used when the materialized view has been invalidated. This compile process is quick, and allows the materialized view to be used by query rewrite again.

DROPPING MATERIALIZED VIEWS

Use the `DROP MATERIALIZED VIEW` statement to drop a materialized view. For example:

```
DROP MATERIALIZED VIEW sales_sum_mv;
```

This statement drops the materialized view `sales_sum_mv`. If the materialized view was prebuilt on a table, then the table is not dropped, but it can no longer be maintained with the refresh mechanism or used by query rewrite. Alternatively, you can drop a materialized view using Oracle Enterprise Manager.

ANALYZING MATERIALIZED VIEW CAPABILITIES

You can use the `DBMS_MVIEW.EXPLAIN_MVIEW` procedure to learn what is possible with a materialized view or potential materialized view. In particular, this procedure enables you to determine:

- If a materialized view is fast refreshable
- What types of query rewrite you can perform with this materialized view
- Whether PCT refresh is possible.

Using this procedure is straightforward. You simply call DBMS_MVIEW.EXPLAIN_MVIEW, passing in as a single parameter the schema and materialized view name for an existing materialized view. Alternatively, you can specify the SELECT string for a potential materialized view. The materialized view or potential materialized view is then analyzed and the results are written into either a table called MV_CAPABILITIES_TABLE, which is the default, or to an array called MSG_ARRAY.

Note that you must run the utlxmv.sql script prior to calling EXPLAIN_MVIEW except when you are placing the results in MSG_ARRAY. The script is found in the admin directory. In addition, you must create MV_CAPABILITIES_TABLE in the current schema. An explanation of the various capabilities is in table 3.7, and all the possible messages are listed in table 3.8.

Using the DBMS_MVIEW.EXPLAIN_MVIEW Procedure

The DBMS_MVIEW.EXPLAIN_MVIEW procedure has the following parameters:

- stmt_id
  An optional parameter. A client-supplied unique identifier to associate output rows with specific invocations of EXPLAIN_MVIEW.
- mv
  The name of an existing materialized view or the query definition of a potential materialized view you want to analyze.
- msg-array
  The PL/SQL varray that receives the output.

DBMS_MVIEW.EXPLAIN_MVIEW analyzes the specified materialized view in terms of its refresh and rewrite capabilities and inserts its results (in the form of multiple rows) into MV_CAPABILITIES_TABLE or MSG_ARRAY.

DBMS_MVIEW.EXPLAIN_MVIEW Declarations

The following PL/SQL declarations that are made for you in the DBMS_MVIEW package show the order and datatypes of these parameters for explaining an existing materialized view and a potential materialized view with output to a table and to a VARRAY.

Explain an existing or potential materialized view with output to MV_CAPABILITIES_TABLE:

```
DBMS_MVIEW.EXPLAIN_MVIEW
(mv             IN VARCHAR2,
 stmt_id IN VARCHAR2:= NULL);
```

Explain an existing or potential materialized view with output to a VARRAY:

```
DBMS_MVIEW.EXPLAIN_MVIEW
(mv          IN VARCHAR2,
 msg_array    OUT SYS.ExplainMVArrayType);
```

Using MV_CAPABILITIES_TABLE

One of the simplest ways to use DBMS_MVIEW.EXPLAIN_MVIEW is with the MV_CAPABILITIES_TABLE, which has the following structure:

```
CREATE  TABLE  MV_CAPABILITIES_TABLE
```

```
STMT_ID              VARCHAR(30),     - client-supplied unique statement
                                        identifier
MV                   VARCHAR(30),     - NULL for SELECT based EXPLAIN_MVIEW
CAPABILITY_NAME      VARCHAR(30),     - A descriptive name of particular
                                      - capabilities, such as REWRITE.
                                      - See Table 3.7
POSSIBLE             CHARACTER(1),    - Y = capability is possible
                                      - N = capability is not possible
RELATED_TEXT         VARCHAR(2000),   - owner.table.column, and so on re-
                                        lated to
                                      - this message
RELATED_NUM          NUMBER,          - When there is a numeric value
                                      - associated with a row, it goes here.
MSGNO                INTEGER,         - When available, message # explain-
                                        ing
                                      - why disabled or more details when
                                      - enabled.
MSGTXT               VARCHAR(2000),   - Text associated with MSGNO
SEQ                  NUMBER);         - Useful in ORDER BY clause when
                                      - selecting from this table.
```

You can use the utlxmv.sql script found in the admin directory to create MV_CAPABILITIES_TABLE.

Example of DBMS_MVIEW.EXPLAIN_MVIEW

First, create the materialized view. Alternatively, you can use EXPLAIN_MVIEW on a potential materialized view using its SELECT statement.

```
CREATE MATERIALIZED VIEW cal_month_sales_mv
BUILD IMMEDIATE
REFRESH FORCE
ENABLE QUERY REWRITE
AS
SELECT t.calendar_month_desc,  SUM(s.amount_sold) AS dollars
FROM sales s,  times t
WHERE s.time_id = t.time_id
GROUP BY t.calendar_month_desc;
```

Then, you invoke EXPLAIN_MVIEW with the materialized view to explain. You need to use the SEQ column in an ORDER BY clause so the rows will display in a logical order. If a capability is not possible, N will appear in the P column and an explanation in the MSGTXT column. If a capability is not possible for more than one reason, a row is displayed for each reason.

```
EXECUTE DBMS_MVIEW.EXPLAIN_MVIEW  ('SH.CAL_MONTH_SALES_MV');
SELECT capability_name,  possible, SUBSTR(related_text,1,8) AS rel_text,
SUBSTR(msgtxt,1,60) AS msgtxt
FROM MV_CAPABILITIES_TABLE
ORDER BY seq;
```

CAPABILITY_NAME	P	REL_TEXT	MSGTXT
PCT	N		
REFRESH_COMPLETE	Y		
REFRESH_FAST	N		
REWRITE	Y		
PCT_TABLE	N	SALES	no partition key or PMARKER in select list
PCT_TABLE	N	TIMES	relation is not a partitioned table
REFRESH_FAST_AFTER_INSERT	N	SH.TIMES	mv log must have new values
REFRESH_FAST_AFTER_INSERT	N	SH.TIMES	mv log must have ROWID
REFRESH_FAST_AFTER_INSERT	N	SH.TIMES	mv log does not have all necessary columns
REFRESH_FAST_AFTER_INSERT	N	SH.SALES	mv log must have new values
REFRESH_FAST_AFTER_INSERT	N	SH.SALES	mv log must have ROWID
REFRESH_FAST_AFTER_INSERT	N	SH.SALES	mv log does not have all necessary columns
REFRESH_FAST_AFTER_ONETAB_DML	N	DOLLARS	SUM(expr) without COUNT(expr)
REFRESH_FAST_AFTER_ONETAB_DML	N		see the reason why REFRESH_FAST_AFTER_INSERT is disabled
REFRESH_FAST_AFTER_ONETAB_DML	N		COUNT(*) is not present in the select list
REFRESH_FAST_AFTER_ONETAB_DML	N		SUM(expr) without COUNT(expr)
REFRESH_FAST_AFTER_ANY_DML	N		see the reason why REFRESH_FAST_AFTER_ONETAB_DML is disabled
REFRESH_FAST_AFTER_ANY_DML	N	SH.TIMES	mv log must have sequence
REFRESH_FAST_AFTER_ANY_DML	N	SH.SALES	mv log must have sequence
REFRESH_PCT	N		PCT is not possible on any of the detail tables in the materialized view
REWRITE_FULL_TEXT_MATCH	Y		
REWRITE_PARTIAL_TEXT_MATCH	Y		
REWRITE_GENERAL	Y		
REWRITE_PCT	N		PCT is not possible on any detail tables

MV_CAPABILITIES_TABLE.CAPABILITY_NAME Details

Table 3.7 lists explanations for values in the CAPABILITY_NAME column.

Table 3.7 CAPABILITY_NAME Column Details

CAPABILITY_NAME	Description
PCT	If this capability is possible, Partition Change Tracking is possible on at least one detail relation. If this capability is not possible, PCT is not possible with any detail relation referenced by the materialized view.
REFRESH_COMPLETE	If this capability is possible, complete refresh of the materialized view is possible.
REFRESH_FAST	If this capability is possible, fast refresh is possible at least under certain circumstances.

REWRITE	If this capability is possible, at least full text match query rewrite is possible. If this capability is not possible, no form of query rewrite is possible.
PCT_TABLE	If this capability is possible, it is possible with respect to a particular partitioned table in the top level FROM list. When possible, PCT applies to the partitioned table named in the RELATED_TEXT column. PCT is needed to support fast fresh after partition maintenance operations on the table named in the RELATED_TEXT column. PCT may also support fast refresh with regard to updates to the table named in the RELATED_TEXT column when fast refresh from a materialized view log is not possible. (PCT-based fast refresh generally does not perform as well as fast refresh from a materialized view log.) PCT is also needed to support query rewrite in the presence of partial staleness of the materialized view with regard to the table named in the RELATED_TEXT column. When disabled, PCT does not apply to the table named in the RELATED_TEXT column. In this case, fast refresh is not possible after partition maintenance operations on the table named in the RELATED_TEXT column. In addition, PCT-based refresh of updates to the table named in the RELATED_TEXT column is not possible. Finally, query rewrite cannot be supported in the presence of partial staleness of the materialized view with regard to the table named in the RELATED_TEXT column.
REFRESH_FAST_AFTER_INSERT	If this capability is possible, fast refresh from a materialized view log is possible at least in the case where the updates are restricted to INSERT operations; complete refresh is also possible. If this capability is not possible, no form of fast refresh from a materialized view log is possible.
REFRESH_FAST_AFTER_ONETAB_DML	If this capability is possible, fast refresh from a materialized view log is possible regardless of the type of update operation, provided all update operations are performed on a single table. If this capability is not possible, fast refresh from a materialized view log may not be possible when the update operations are performed on multiple tables.
REFRESH_FAST_AFTER_ANY_DML	If this capability is possible, fast refresh from a materialized view log is possible regardless of the type of update operation or the number of tables updated. If this capability is not possible, fast refresh from a materialized view log may not be possible when the update operations (other than INSERT) affect multiple tables.
REFRESH_FAST_PCT	If this capability is possible, fast refresh using PCT is possible. Generally, this means that refresh is possible after partition maintenance operations on those detail tables where PCT is indicated as possible.

REWRITE_FULL_TEXT_MATCH	If this capability is possible, full text match query rewrite is possible. If this capability is not possible, full text match query rewrite is not possible.
REWRITE_PARTIAL_TEXT_MATCH	If this capability is possible, at least full and partial text match query rewrite are possible. If this capability is not possible, at least partial text match query rewrite and general query rewrite are not possible.
REWRITE_GENERAL	If this capability is possible, all query rewrite capabilities are possible, including general query rewrite and full and partial text match query rewrite. If this capability is not possible, at least general query rewrite is not possible.
REWRITE_PCT	If this capability is possible, query rewrite can use a partially stale materialized view even in QUERY_REWRITE_INTEGRITY = enforced or trusted modes. When this capability is not possible, query rewrite can use a partially stale materialized view only in QUERY_REWRITE_INTEGRITY = stale_tolerated mode.

MV_CAPABILITIES_TABLE Column Details

The following table lists the semantics for RELATED_TEXT and RELATED_NUM columns.

Table 3.8 MV_CAPABILITIES_TABLE Column Details

MSGNO	MSGTXT	RELATED_NUM	RELATED_TEXT
NULL	NULL		For PCT capability only: [*owner*.]*name* of the table upon which PCT is enabled
2066	This statement resulted in an Oracle error	Oracle error number that occurred	
2067	No partition key or PMARKER in select list		[*owner*.]*name* of relation for which PCT is not supported
2068	Relation is not partitioned		[*owner*.]*name* of relation for which PCT is not supported
2069	PCT not supported with multicolumn partition key		[*owner*.]*name* of relation for which PCT is not supported
2070	PCT not supported with this type of partitioning		[*owner*.]*name* of relation for which PCT is not supported
2071	Internal error: undefined PCT failure code	The unrecognized numeric PCT failure code	[*owner*.]*name* of relation for which PCT is not supported
2077	Mv log is newer than last full refresh		[*owner*.]*table_name* of table upon which the mv log is needed
2078	Mv log must have new values		[*owner*.]*table_name* of table upon which the mv log is needed

2079	Mv log must have ROWID		[*owner.*] *table_name* of table upon which the mv log is needed
2080	Mv log must have primary key		[*owner.*] *table_name* of table upon which the mv log is needed
2081	Mv log does not have all necessary columns		[*owner.*] *table_name* of table upon which the mv log is needed
2082	Problem with mv log		[*owner.*] *table_name* of table upon which the mv log is needed
2099	Mv references a remote table or view in the FROM list	Offset from the SELECT keyword to the table or view in question	[*owner.*] *name* of the table or view in question
2126	Multiple master sites		Name of the first different node, or NULL if the first different node is local
2129	Join or filter condition(s) are complex		[*owner.*] *name* of the table involved with the join or filter condition (or NULL when not available)
2130	Expression not supported for fast refresh	Offset from the SELECT keyword to the expression in question	The alias name in the select list of the expression in question
2150	Select lists must be identical across the UNION operator	Offset from the SELECT keyword to the first different select item in the SELECT list	The alias name of the first different select item in the SELECT list

❑❑❑

4 DIMENSIONS

A **dimension** is a structure that categorizes data in order to enable users to answer business questions. Commonly used dimensions are `customers`, `products`, and `time`. For example, each sales channel of a clothing retailer might gather and store data regarding sales and reclamations of their cloth assortment. The retail chain management can build a data warehouse to analyze the sales of its products across all stores over time and help answer questions such as:

- What is the effect of promoting one product on the sale of a related product that is not promoted?
- What are the sales of a product before and after a promotion?
- How does a promotion affect the various distribution channels?

The data in the retailer's data warehouse system has two important components: dimensions and facts. The dimensions are products, customers, promotions, channels, and time. One approach for identifying your dimensions is to review your reference tables, such as a product table that contains everything about a product, or a promotion table containing all information about promotions. The facts are sales (units sold) and profits. A data warehouse contains facts about the sales of each product at on a daily basis.

A typical relational implementation for such a data warehouse is a Star Schema. The fact information is stored in the so-called fact table, whereas the dimensional information is stored in the so-called dimension tables. In our example, each sales transaction record is uniquely defined as for each customer, for each product, for each sales channel, for each promotion, and for each day (time).

In Oracle9*i*, the dimensional information itself is stored in a dimension table. In addition, the database object dimension helps to organize and group dimensional information into hierarchies. This represents natural `1:n` relationships between columns or column groups (the levels of a hierarchy) that cannot be represented with constraint conditions. Going up a level in the hierarchy is called rolling up the data and going down a level in the hierarchy is called drilling down the data. In the retailer example:

- Within the `time` dimension, months roll up to quarters, quarters roll up to years, and years roll up to all years.
- Within the `product` dimension, products roll up to subcategories, subcategories roll up to categories, and categories roll up to all products.
- Within the `customer` dimension, customers roll up to `city`. Then `city` rolls up to `state`. Then states roll up to `country`. Then countries roll up to `subregion`. Finally, subregions roll up to `region`, as shown in figure 4.1.

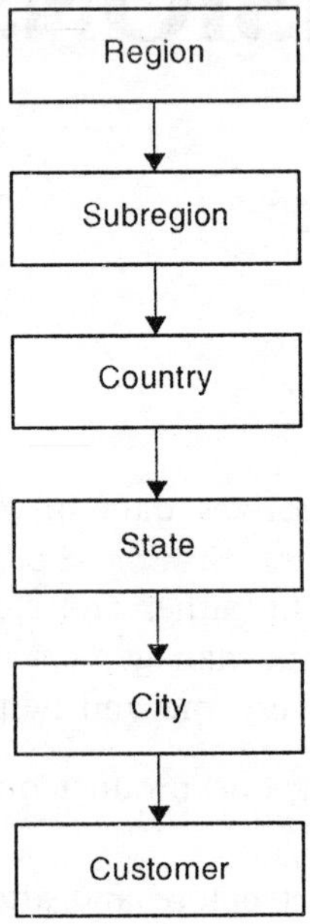

Figure 4.1 Sample Rollup for a Customer Dimension.

Data analysis typically starts at higher levels in the dimensional hierarchy and gradually drills down if the situation warrants such analysis.

Dimensions do not have to be defined, but spending time creating them can yield significant benefits, because they help query rewrite perform more complex types of rewrite. They are mandatory if you use the Summary Advisor (a GUI tool for materialized view management) to recommend which materialized views to create, drop, or retain.

You must not create dimensions in any schema that does not satisfy these relationships. Incorrect results can be returned from queries otherwise.

CREATING DIMENSIONS

Before you can create a dimension object, the dimension tables must exist in the database, containing the dimension data. For example, if you create a customer dimension, one or more tables must exist that contain the city, state, and country information. In a star schema data warehouse, these dimension tables already exist. It is therefore a simple task to identify which ones will be used.

Now you can draw the hierarchies of a dimension as shown in figure 4.1. For example, `city` is a child of `state` (because you can aggregate city-level data up to state), and `country`. This hierarchical information will be stored in the database object dimension.

In the case of normalized or partially normalized dimension representation (a dimension that is stored in more than one table), identify how these tables are joined. Note whether the joins between the dimension tables can guarantee that each child-side row joins with one and only one parent-side row. In the case of denormalized dimensions, determine whether the child-side columns uniquely determine the parent-side (or attribute) columns. These constraints can be enabled with the `NOVALIDATE` and `RELY` clauses if the relationships represented by the constraints are guaranteed by other means.

You create a dimension using either the `CREATE DIMENSION` statement or the Dimension Wizard in Oracle Enterprise Manager. Within the `CREATE DIMENSION` statement, use the `LEVEL` clause to identify the names of the dimension levels.

This customer dimension contains a single hierarchy with a geographical rollup, with arrows drawn from the child level to the parent level, as shown in figure 4.1.

Each arrow in this graph indicates that for any child there is one and only one parent. For example, each city must be contained in exactly one state and each state must be contained in exactly one country. States that belong to more than one country, or that belong to no country, violate hierarchical integrity. Hierarchical integrity is necessary for the correct operation of management functions for materialized views that include aggregates.

For example, you can declare a dimension `products_dim`, which contains levels `product`, `subcategory`, and `category`:

```
CREATE  DIMENSION  products_dim
        LEVEL  product              IS  (products.prod_id)
        LEVEL  subcategory          IS  (products.prod_subcategory)
        LEVEL  category             IS  (products.prod_category)  ...
```

Each level in the dimension must correspond to one or more columns in a table in the database. Thus, level `product` is identified by the column `prod_id` in the products table and level `subcategory` is identified by a column called `prod_subcategory` in the same table.

In this example, the database tables are denormalized and all the columns exist in the same table. However, this is not a prerequisite for creating dimensions. "Using Normalized Dimension Tables" shows how to create a dimension `customers_dim` that has a normalized schema design using the `JOIN KEY` clause.

The next step is to declare the relationship between the levels with the `HIERARCHY` statement and give that hierarchy a name. A hierarchical relationship is a functional dependency from one level of a hierarchy to the next level in the hierarchy. Using the level names defined previously, the `CHILD OF` relationship denotes that each child's level value is associated with one and only one parent level value. The following statements declare a hierarchy `prod_rollup` and define the relationship between `products`, `subcategory`, and `category`.

```
HIERARCHY  prod_rollup
  (product                          CHILD  OF
   subcategory                      CHILD  OF
   category)
```

In addition to the 1:n hierarchical relationships, dimensions also include 1:1 attribute relationships between the hierarchy levels and their dependent, determined dimension attributes. For example the dimension times_dim, as defined in *Oracle9i Sample Schemas*, has columns fiscal_month_desc, fiscal_month_name, and days_in_fiscal_month. Their relationship is defined as follows:

```
LEVEL  fis_month     IS  TIMES.FISCAL_MONTH_DESC
...
ATTRIBUTE  fis_month  DETERMINES
          (fiscal_month_name,  days_in_fiscal_month)
```

The ATTRIBUTE ... DETERMINES clause relates fis_month to fiscal_month_name and days_in_fiscal_month. Note that this is a unidirectional determination. It is only guaranteed, that for a specific fiscal_month, for example, 1999-11, you will find exactly one matching value for fiscal_month_name, for example, November and days_in_fiscal_month, for example, 28. You cannot determine a specific fiscal_month_desc based on the fiscal_month_name, which is November for every fiscal year.

In this example, suppose a query were issued that queried by fiscal_month_name instead of fiscal_month_desc. Because this 1:1 relationship exists between the attribute and the level, an already aggregated materialized view containing fiscal_month_desc can be joined back to the dimension information and used to identify the data.

A sample dimension definition follows:

```
CREATE DIMENSION products_dim
        LEVEL product                      IS (products.prod_id)
        LEVEL subcategory                  IS (products.prod_subcategory)
        LEVEL category                     IS (products.prod_category)
        HIERARCHY prod_rollup
        (
        product     CHILD OF
        subcategory CHILD OF
        category
        )
        ATTRIBUTE product DETERMINES
         (products.prod_name, products.prod_desc,
         prod_weight_class, prod_unit_of_measure,
         prod_pack_size,prod_status, prod_list_price, prod_min_price)
        ATTRIBUTE subcategory DETERMINES
         (prod_subcategory, prod_subcat_desc)
        ATTRIBUTE category DETERMINES
         (prod_category, prod_cat_desc);
```

The design, creation, and maintenance of dimensions is part of the design, creation, and maintenance of your data warehouse schema. Once the dimension has been created, check that it meets these requirements:

- There must be a 1:n relationship between a parent and children. A parent can have one or more children, but a child can have only one parent.
- There must be a 1:1 attribute relationship between hierarchy levels and their dependent dimension attributes. For example, if there is a column fiscal_month_desc, then a possible attribute relationship would be fiscal_month_desc to fiscal_month_name.

- If the columns of a parent level and child level are in different relations, then the connection between them also requires a 1:n join relationship. Each row of the child table must join with one and only one row of the parent table. This relationship is stronger than referential integrity alone, because it requires that the child join key must be non-null, that referential integrity must be maintained from the child join key to the parent join key, and that the parent join key must be unique.
- You must ensure (using database constraints if necessary) that the columns of each hierarchy level are non-null and that hierarchical integrity is maintained.
- The hierarchies of a dimension can overlap or be disconnected from each other. However, the columns of a hierarchy level cannot be associated with more than one dimension.
- Join relationships that form cycles in the dimension graph are not supported. For example, a hierarchy level cannot be joined to itself either directly or indirectly.

NOTE *The information stored with a dimension objects is only declarative. The previously discussed relationships are not enforced with the creation of a dimension object. You should validate any dimension definition with the* `DBMS_MVIEW.VALIDATE_DIMENSION` *procedure, as discussed on "Validating Dimensions".*

Multiple Hierarchies

A single dimension definition can contain multiple hierarchies. Suppose our retailer wants to track the sales of certain items over time. The first step is to define the time dimension over which sales will be tracked. Figure 4.2 illustrates a dimension `times_dim` with two time hierarchies.

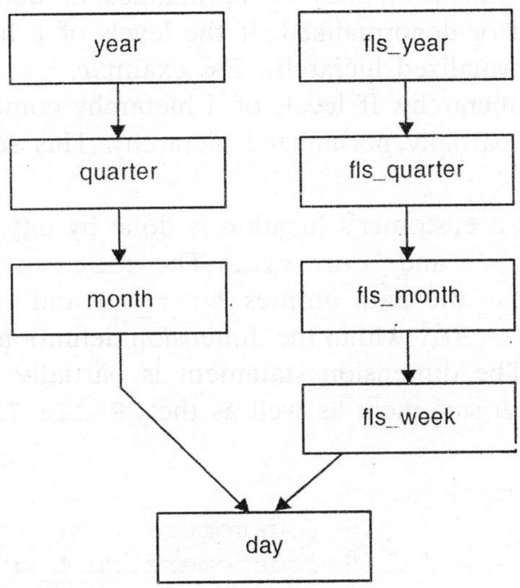

Figure 4.2 times_dim Dimension with Two Time Hierarchies.

From the illustration, you can construct the hierarchy of the denormalized `time_dim` dimension's `CREATE DIMENSION` statement as follows. The complete `CREATE DIMENSION` statement as well as the `CREATE TABLE` statement are shown in *Oracle9i Sample Schemas.*

```
CREATE DIMENSION times_dim
     LEVEL day                IS TIMES.TIME_ID
     LEVEL month              IS TIMES.CALENDAR_MONTH_DESC
     LEVEL quarter            IS TIMES.CALENDAR_QUARTER_DESC
     LEVEL year               IS TIMES.CALENDAR_YEAR
     LEVEL fis_week           IS TIMES.WEEK_ENDING_DAY
     LEVEL fis_month          IS TIMES.FISCAL_MONTH_DESC
     LEVEL fis_quarter        IS TIMES.FISCAL_QUARTER_DESC
     LEVEL fis_year           IS TIMES.FISCAL_YEAR
     HIERARCHY cal_rollup     (
              day             CHILD OF
              month           CHILD OF
              quarter         CHILD OF
              year
   )
   HIERARCHY fis_rollup     (
              day             CHILD OF
              fis_week        CHILD OF
              fis_month       CHILD OF
              fis_quarter     CHILD OF
              fis_year
   ) <attribute determination clauses>...
```

Using Normalized Dimension Tables

The tables used to define a dimension may be normalized or denormalized and the individual hierarchies can be normalized or denormalized. If the levels of a hierarchy come from the same table, it is called a fully denormalized hierarchy. For example, `cal_rollup` in the `times_dim` dimension is a denormalized hierarchy. If levels of a hierarchy come from different tables, such a hierarchy is either a fully or partially normalized hierarchy. This section shows how to define a normalized hierarchy.

Suppose the tracking of a customer's location is done by city, state, and country. This data is stored in the tables `customers` and `countries`. The `customer` dimension `customers_dim` is partially normalized because the data entities `cust_id` and `country_id` are taken from different tables. The clause `JOIN KEY` within the dimension definition specifies how to join together the levels in the hierarchy. The dimension statement is partially shown in the following. The complete `CREATE DIMENSION` statement as well as the `CREATE TABLE` statement are shown in *Oracle9i Sample Schemas.*

```
CREATE DIMENSION customers_dim
     LEVEL customer           IS (customers.cust_id)
     LEVEL city               IS (customers.cust_city)
     LEVEL state              IS (customers.cust_state_province)
     LEVEL country            IS (countries.country_id)
     LEVEL subregion          IS (countries.country_subregion)
     LEVEL region             IS (countries.country_region)
     HIERARCHY geog_rollup (
              customer        CHILD OF
              city            CHILD OF
              state           CHILD OF
```

```
        country         CHILD OF
        subregion       CHILD OF
        region
    JOIN KEY (customers.country_id) REFERENCES country
    ) ...attribute determination clause;
```

VIEWING DIMENSIONS

Dimensions can be viewed through one of two methods:

- Using the DEMO_DIM package
- Using Oracle enterprise manager.

Using The DEMO_DIM Package

Two procedures allow you to display the dimensions that have been defined. First, the file `smdim.sql`, located under `$ORACLE_HOME/rdbms/demo`, must be executed to provide the `DEMO_DIM` package, which includes:

- `DEMO_DIM.PRINT_DIM` to print a specific dimension
- `DEMO_DIM.PRINT_ALLDIMS` to print all dimensions accessible to a user.

The `DEMO_DIM.PRINT_DIM` procedure has only one parameter: the name of the dimension to display. The following example shows how to display the dimension `TIMES_DIM`.

```
SET SERVEROUTPUT ON;
EXECUTE DEMO_DIM.PRINT_DIM ('TIMES_DIM');
```

To display all of the dimensions that have been defined, call the procedure `DEMO_DIM.PRINT_ALLDIMS` without any parameters, which is illustrated as follows.

```
EXECUTE DBMS_OUTPUT.ENABLE(10000);
EXECUTE DEMO_DIM.PRINT_ALLDIMS;
```

Regardless of which procedure is called, the output format is identical. A sample display is shown here.

```
DIMENSION SH.PROMO_DIM
LEVEL CATEGORY IS SH.PROMOTIONS.PROMO_CATEGORY
LEVEL PROMO IS SH.PROMOTIONS.PROMO_ID
LEVEL SUBCATEGORY IS SH.PROMOTIONS.PROMO_SUBCATEGORY
HIERARCHY PROMO_ROLLUP ( PROMO
CHILD OF SUBCATEGORY
CHILD OF CATEGORY)
ATTRIBUTE CATEGORY DETERMINES SH.PROMOTIONS.PROMO_CATEGORY
ATTRIBUTE PROMO DETERMINES SH.PROMOTIONS.PROMO_BEGIN_DATE
ATTRIBUTE PROMO DETERMINES SH.PROMOTIONS.PROMO_COST
ATTRIBUTE PROMO DETERMINES SH.PROMOTIONS.PROMO_END_DATE
ATTRIBUTE PROMO DETERMINES SH.PROMOTIONS.PROMO_NAME
ATTRIBUTE SUBCATEGORY DETERMINES SH.PROMOTIONS.PROMO_SUBCATEGORY
```

Using Oracle Enterprise Manager

All of the dimensions that exist in the data warehouse can be viewed by using Oracle Enterprise Manager. Select the **Dimension** object from within the **Schema** icon to display all of the dimensions. Select a specific dimension to graphically display its hierarchy, levels, and any attributes that have been defined.

USING DIMENSIONS WITH CONSTRAINTS

Constraints play an important role with dimensions. Full referential integrity is sometimes enabled in data warehouses, but not always. This is because operational databases normally have full referential integrity and you can ensure that the data flowing into your warehouse never violates the already established integrity rules.

Oracle recommends that constraints be enabled and, if validation time is a concern, then the NOVALIDATE clause should be used as follows:

```
ENABLE NOVALIDATE CONSTRAINT pk_time;
```

Primary and foreign keys should be implemented also. Referential integrity constraints and NOT NULL constraints on the fact tables provide information that query rewrite can use to extend the usefulness of materialized views.

In addition, you should use the RELY clause to inform query rewrite that it can rely upon the constraints being correct as follows:

```
ALTER TABLE time MODIFY CONSTRAINT pk_time RELY;
```

This information is also used for query rewrite.

VALIDATING DIMENSIONS

The information of a dimension object is declarative only and not enforced by the database. If the relationships described by the dimensions are incorrect, incorrect results could occur. Therefore, you should verify the relationships specified by CREATE DIMENSION using the DBMS_OLAP.VALIDATE_DIMENSION procedure periodically.

This procedure is easy to use and has only five parameters:

- Dimension name
- Owner name
- Set to TRUE to check only the new rows for tables of this dimension
- Set to TRUE to verify that all columns are not null
- Unique run ID obtained by calling the DBMS_OLAP.CREATE_ID procedure. The ID is used to identify the result of each run.

The following example validates the dimension TIME_FN in the grocery schema

```
VARIABLE RID NUMBER;
EXECUTE DBMS_OLAP.CREATE_ID(:RID);
EXECUTE DBMS_OLAP.VALIDATE_DIMENSION ('TIME_FN', 'GROCERY',
FALSE, TRUE, :RID);
```

If the VALIDATE_DIMENSION procedure encounters any errors, they are placed in a system table. The table can be accessed from the view SYSTEM.MVIEW_EXCEPTIONS. Querying this view will identify the exceptions that were found. For example:

```
SELECT * FROM SYSTEM.MVIEW_EXCEPTIONS
WHERE RUNID = :RID;
RUNID  OWNER   TABLE_NAME DIMENSION_NAME  RELATIONSHIP  BAD_ROWID
-----  -----   ---------- --------------  ------------  ---------
678    GROCERY MONTH      TIME_FN         FOREIGN KEY
AAAAuwAAJAAAARwAAA
```

However, rather than query this view, it may be better to query the rowid of the invalid row to retrieve the actual row that has violated the constraint. In this example, the dimension TIME_FN is checking a table called month. It has found a row that violates the constraints. Using the rowid, you can see exactly which row in the month table is causing the problem, as in the following:

```
SELECT  *  FROM  month
WHERE  rowid  IN  (SELECT  bad_rowid
                          FROM  SYSTEM.MVIEW_EXCEPTIONS
                          WHERE  RUNID  =  :RID);

MONTH   QUARTER  FISCAL_QTR   YEAR   FULL_MONTH_NAME   MONTH_NUMB
-----   -------  ----------   ----   ---------------   ----------
199903  19981    19981        1998   March             3
```

Finally, to remove results from the system table for the current run:

```
EXECUTE  DBMS_OLAP.PURGE_RESULTS(:RID);
```

ALTERING DIMENSIONS

You can modify the dimension using the ALTER DIMENSION statement. You can add or drop a level, hierarchy, or attribute from the dimension using this command.

Referring to the time dimension in figure 4.2, you can remove the attribute fis_year, drop the hierarchy fis_rollup, or remove the level fiscal_year. In addition, you can add a new level called foyer as in the following:

```
ALTER DIMENSION times_dim DROP ATTRIBUTE fis_year;
ALTER DIMENSION times_dim DROP HIERARCHY fis_rollup;
ALTER DIMENSION times_dim DROP LEVEL fis_year;
ALTER DIMENSION times_dim ADD LEVEL f_year IS times.fiscal_year;
```

If you try to remove anything with further dependencies inside the dimension, Oracle rejects the altering of the dimension. A dimension becomes invalid if you change any schema object that the dimension is referencing. For example, if the table on which the dimension is defined is altered, the dimension becomes invalid.

To check the status of a dimension, view the contents of the column invalid in the ALL_DIMENSIONS data dictionary view.

To revalidate the dimension, use the COMPILE option as follows:

```
ALTER  DIMENSION  times_dim  COMPILE;
```

Dimensions can also be modified using Oracle Enterprise Manager.

DELETING DIMENSIONS

A dimension is removed by using the DROP DIMENSION statement. For example:

```
DROP DIMENSION times_dim;
```

Dimensions can also be deleted by using Oracle Enterprise Manager.

USING THE DIMENSION WIZARD

An alternative method for creating and viewing dimensions is to use Oracle Enterprise Manager, which graphically displays the dimension definition, thus making it easier to see the hierarchy and a dimension wizard is provided to facilitate easy definition of the dimension object.

The Dimension Wizard is automatically invoked whenever a request is made to create a dimension object in Oracle Enterprise Manager. You are then guided step by step through the information required for a dimension.

A dimension created using the Wizard can contain any of the attributes described in "Creating Dimensions", such as join keys, multiple hierarchies, and attributes. You might prefer to use the Wizard because it graphically displays the hierarchical relationships as they are being constructed. When it is time to describe the hierarchy, the Wizard automatically displays a default hierarchy based on the column values, which you can subsequently amend.

Managing the Dimension Object

The dimension object is located within the **Warehouse** section for a database. Selecting a specific dimension results in 5 sheets of information becoming available. The **General Property** sheet shown in figure 4.3 displays the dimension definition in a graphical form.

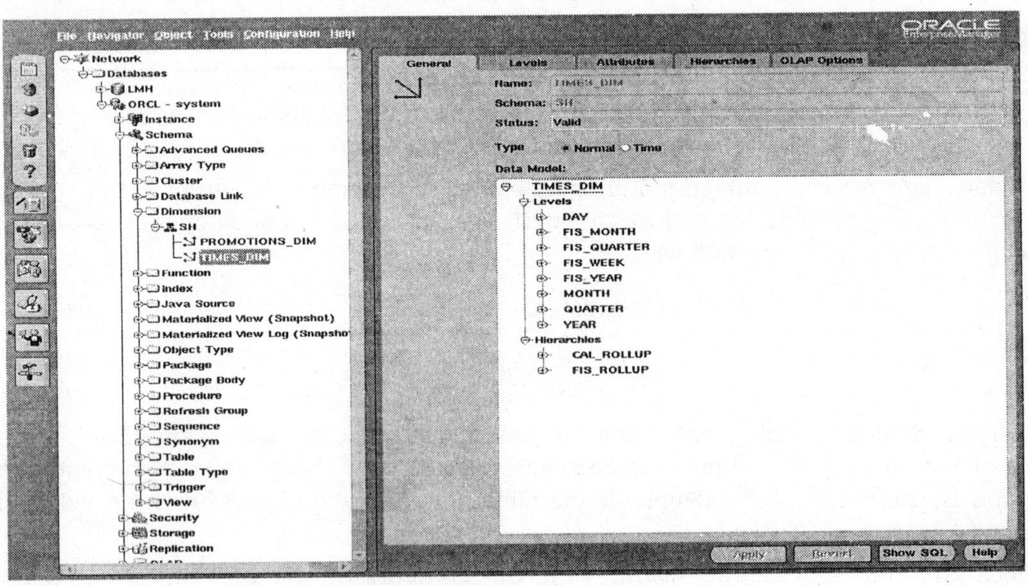

Figure 4.3 Dimension General Property Sheet.

The levels in the dimension can either be shown on the **General Property** sheet, or by selecting the **Levels** property sheet, levels can be deleted, displayed or new ones defined for this dimension as illustrated in figure 4.4.

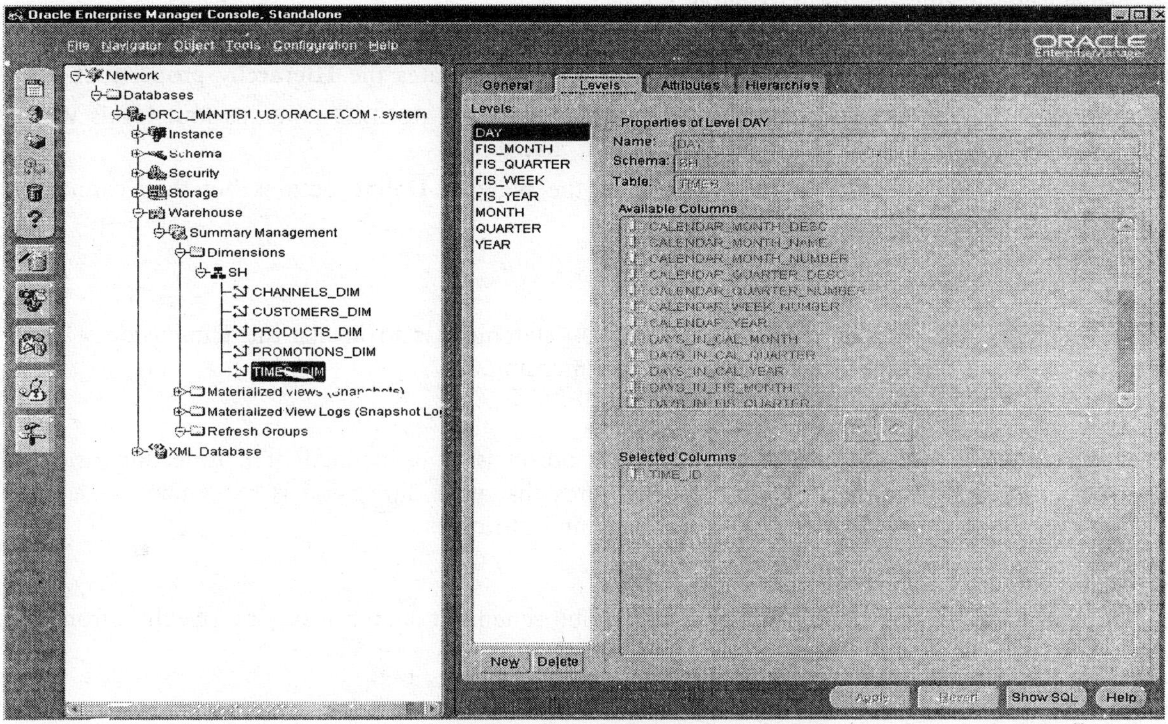

Figure 4.4 Dimension Levels Property Sheet.

By selecting the level name from the list on the left of the property sheet, the columns used for this level are displayed in the **Selected Columns** window in the lower half of the property sheet.

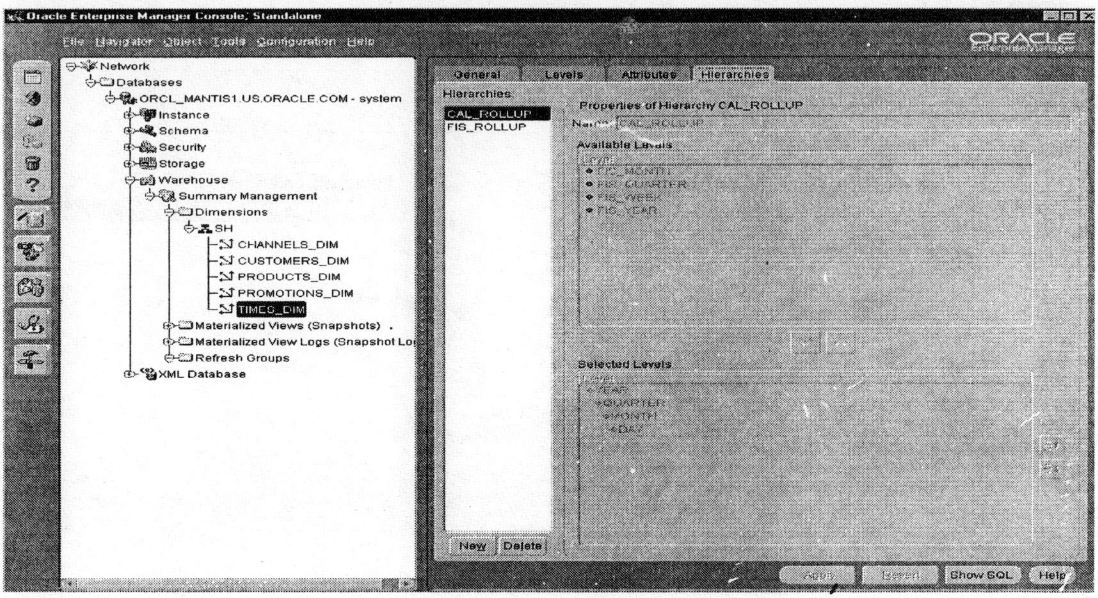

Figure 4.5 Dimension Hierarchy Property Sheet.

Levels can be added or removed by pressing the **New** or **Delete** buttons but they cannot be modified.

A similar property sheet to that for **Levels** is provided for the attributes in the dimension and is selected by clicking on the **Attributes** tab.

One of the main advantages of using Oracle Enterprise Manager to define the dimension is that the hierarchies can be easily displayed. Figure 4.5 illustrates the **Hierarchy** property sheet.

In figure 4.5, you can see that the hierarchy called CAL_ROLLUP contains four levels where the top level is year, followed by quarter, month, and day.

You can add or remove hierarchies by pressing the **New** or **Delete** buttons but they cannot be modified.

Creating a Dimension

An alternative to writing the CREATE DIMENSION statement is to invoke the Dimension wizard, which guides you through 6 steps to create a dimension.

Step 1

First, you must define which type of dimension object is to be defined. If a time dimension is required, selecting the time dimension type ensures that your dimension is recognized as a time dimension that has specific types of hierarchies and attributes.

Step 2

Specify the name of your dimension and into which schema it should reside by selecting from the drop down list of schemas.

Step 3

The levels in the dimension are defined in Step 3 as shown in figure 4.6.

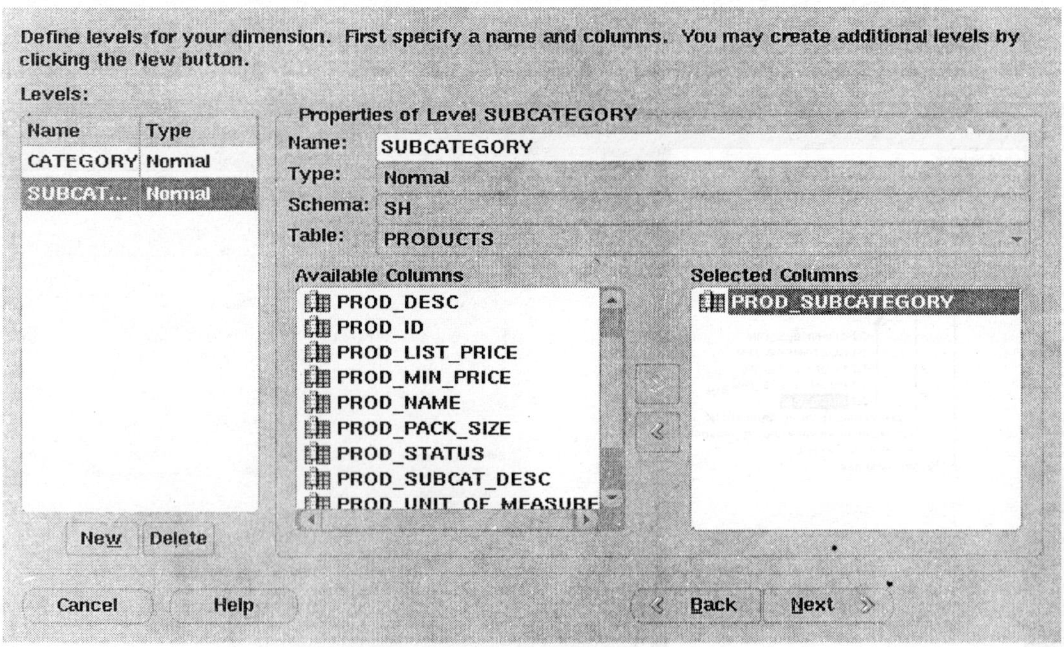

Figure 4.6 Dimension Wizard: Define Levels.

First, give the level a name and then select the table from where the columns which define this level are located. Now, select one or more columns from the available list and using the > key move them into the **Selected Columns** area. Your level will now appear in the list on the left side of the property sheet.

To define another level, click the **New** button, or, if all the levels have been defined, click the **Next** button to proceed to the next step. If a mistake is made when defining a level, simply click the **Delete** button to remove it and start again.

Step 4

The levels in the dimension can also have attributes. Give the attribute a name and then select the level on which this attribute is to be defined and using the > button move it into the **Selected Levels** column. Now choose the column from the drop down list for this attribute.

Levels can be added or removed by pressing the **New** or **Delete** buttons but they cannot be modified.

Step 5

A hierarchy is defined as illustrated in figure 4.7.

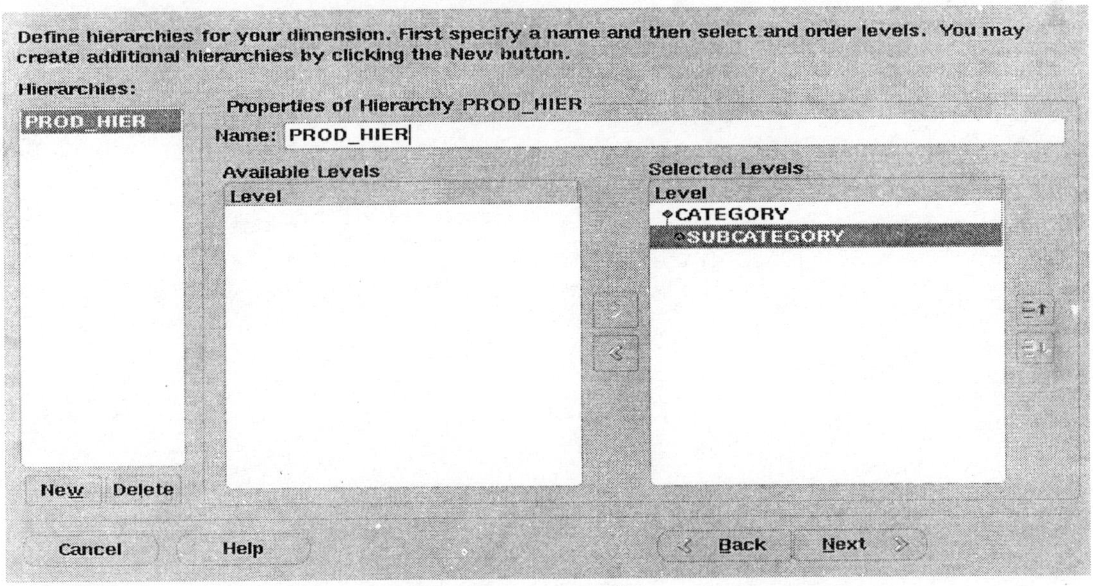

Figure 4.7 Dimension Wizard: Define Hierarchies.

First, give the hierarchy a name and then select the levels to be used in this hierarchy and move them to the **Selected Levels** column using the > button.

The level name at the top of the list defines the top of the hierarchy. Use the up and down buttons to move the levels into the required order. Note that each level will indent so you can see the relationships between the levels.

Step 6

Finally, the summary screen is displayed as shown in figure 4.8 where a graphical representation of the dimension is shown on the left side of the property sheet and on the right side the `CREATE DIMENSION` statement is shown. Clicking on the **Finish** button will create the dimension.

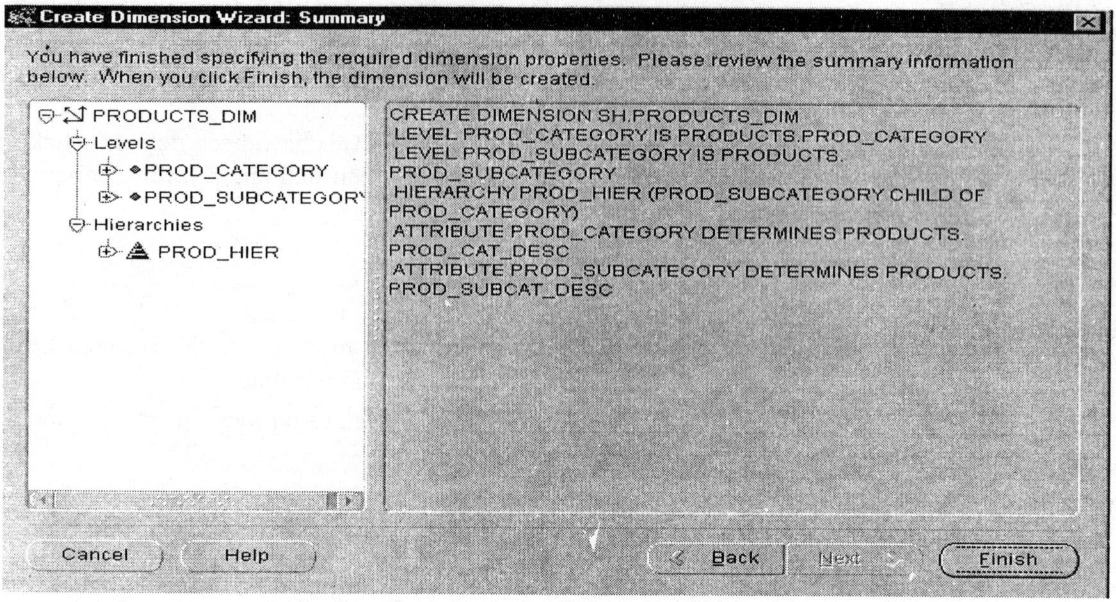

Figure 4.8 Dimension Wizard: Summary Screen.

❑❑❑

5 LOADING AND TRANSFORMATION

OVERVIEW OF LOADING AND TRANSFORMATION IN DATA WAREHOUSES

Data transformations are often the most complex and, in terms of processing time, the most costly part of the ETL process. They can range from simple data conversions to extremely complex data scrubbing techniques. Many, if not all, data transformations can occur within an Oracle9*i* database, although transformations are often implemented outside of the database (for example, on flat files) as well.

This chapter introduces techniques for implementing scalable and efficient data transformations within Oracle9*i*. The examples in this chapter are relatively simple. Real-world data transformations are often considerably more complex. However, the transformation techniques introduced in this chapter meet the majority of real-world data transformation requirements, often with more scalability and less programming than alternative approaches.

This chapter does not seek to illustrate all of the typical transformations that would be encountered in a data warehouse, but to demonstrate the types of fundamental technology that can be applied to implement these transformations and to provide guidance in how to choose the best techniques.

Transformation Flow

From an architectural perspective, you can transform your data in two ways:

- Multistage data transformation
- Pipelined data transformation.

Multistage Data Transformation

The data transformation logic for most data warehouses consists of multiple steps. For example, in transforming new records to be inserted into a sales table, there may be separate logical transformation steps to validate each dimension key.

Figure 5.1 offers a graphical way of looking at the transformation logic.

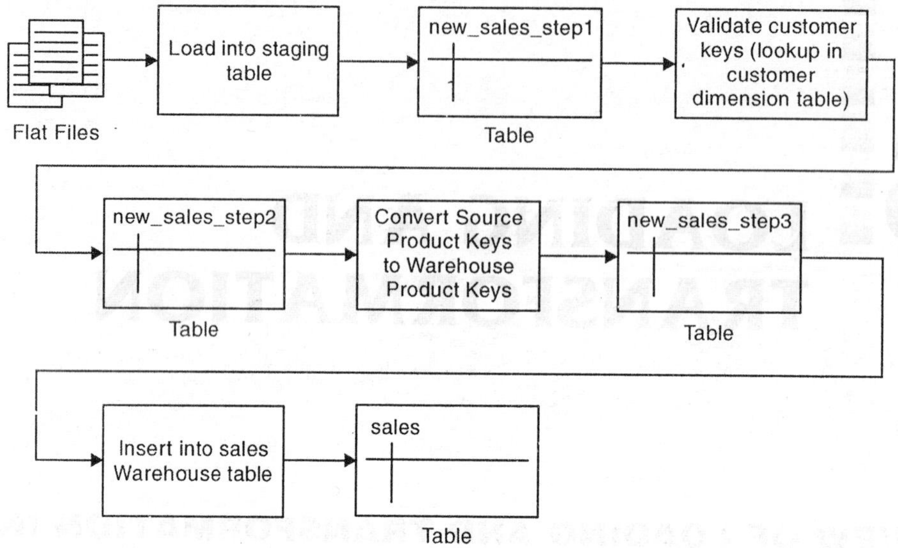

Figure 5.1 Multistage Data Transformation.

When using Oracle9*i* as a transformation engine, a common strategy is to implement each distinct transformation as a separate SQL operation and to create a separate, temporary staging table (such as the tables `new_sales_step1` and `new_sales_step2` in figure 5.1) to store the incremental results for each step. This load-then-transform strategy also provides a natural checkpointing scheme to the entire transformation process, which enables the process to be more easily monitored and restarted. However, a disadvantage multistaging is that the space and time requirements increase.

It may also be possible to combine many simple logical transformations into a single SQL statement or single PL/SQL procedure. Doing so may provide better performance than performing each step independently, but it may also introduce difficulties in modifying, adding, or dropping individual transformations, as well as recovering from failed transformations.

Pipelined Data Transformation

With the introduction of Oracle9*i*, Oracle's database capabilities have been significantly enhanced to address specifically some of the tasks in ETL environments. The ETL process flow can be changed dramatically and the database becomes an integral part of the ETL solution.

The new functionality renders some of the former necessary process steps obsolete whilst some others can be remodeled to enhance the data flow and the data transformation to become more scalable and non-interruptive. The task shifts from serial transform-then-load process (with most of the tasks done outside the database) or load-then-transform process, to an enhanced transform-while-loading.

Oracle9*i* offers a wide variety of new capabilities to address all the issues and tasks relevant in an ETL scenario. It is important to understand that the database offers toolkit functionality rather than trying to address a one-size-fits-all solution. The underlying database has to enable the most appropriate ETL process flow for a specific customer need, and not dictate or constrain it from a technical perspective. Figure 5.2 illustrates the new functionality, which is discussed throughout later sections.

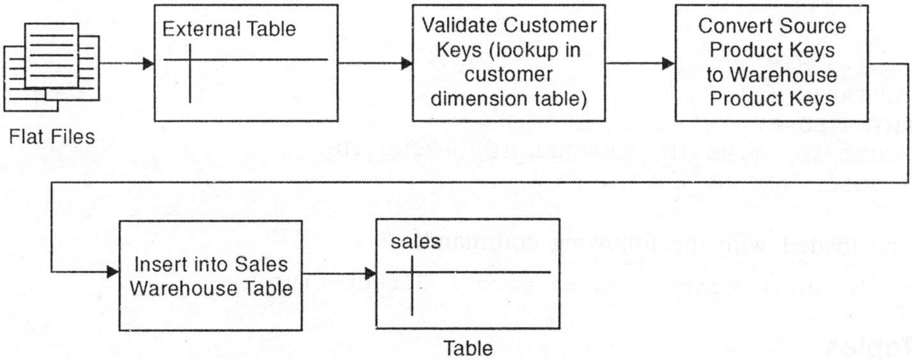

Figure 5.2 Pipelined Data Transformation.

LOADING MECHANISMS

You can use the following mechanisms for loading a warehouse:

- SQL*Loader
- External tables
- OCI and direct-path APIs
- Export/Import.

SQL*Loader

Before any data transformations can occur within the database, the raw data must become accessible for the database. One approach is to load it into the database. The chapter "Transportation in Data Warehouses", discusses several techniques for transporting data to an Oracle data warehouse. Perhaps the most common technique for transporting data is by way of flat files.

SQL*Loader is used to move data from flat files into an Oracle data warehouse. During this data load, SQL*Loader can also be used to implement basic data transformations. When using direct-path SQL*Loader, basic data manipulation, such as datatype conversion and simple `NULL` handling, can be automatically resolved during the data load. Most data warehouses use direct-path loading for performance reasons.

Oracle's conventional-path loader provides broader capabilities for data transformation than a direct-path loader: SQL functions can be applied to any column as those values are being loaded. This provides a rich capability for transformations during the data load. However, the conventional-path loader is slower than direct-path loader. For these reasons, the conventional-path loader should be considered primarily for loading and transforming smaller amounts of data.

The following is a simple example of an SQL*Loader controlfile to load data into the `sales` table of the `sh` sample schema from an external file `sh_sales.dat`. The external flat file `sh_sales.dat` consists of sales transaction data, aggregated on a daily level. Not all columns of this external file are loaded into `sales`. This external file will also be used as a source for loading the second fact table of the `sh` sample schema, which is done by using an external table:

The following shows the controlfile (`sh_sales.ctl`) to load the `sales` table:

```
LOAD DATA
INFILE sh_sales.dat
APPEND INTO TABLE sales
FIELDS TERMINATED BY "|"
(PROD_ID, CUST_ID, TIME_ID, CHANNEL_ID, PROMO_ID,
  QUANTITY_SOLD, AMOUNT_SOLD)
```

It can be loaded with the following command:

```
$  sqlldr sh/sh control=sh_sales.ctl direct=true.
```

External Tables

Another approach for handling external data sources is using external tables. Oracle9*i*'s external table feature enables you to use external data as a virtual table that can be queried and joined directly and in parallel without requiring the external data to be first loaded in the database. You can then use SQL, PL/SQL, and Java to access the external data.

External tables enable the pipelining of the loading phase with the transformation phase. The transformation process can be merged with the loading process without any interruption of the data streaming. It is no longer necessary to stage the data inside the database for further processing inside the database, such as comparison or transformation. For example, the conversion functionality of a conventional load can be used for a direct-path `INSERT AS SELECT` statement in conjunction with the `SELECT` from an external table.

The main difference between external tables and regular tables is that externally organized tables are read-only. No DML operations (`UPDATE/INSERT/DELETE`) are possible and no indexes can be created on them.

Oracle9*i*'s external tables are a complement to the existing SQL*Loader functionality, and are especially useful for environments where the complete external source has to be joined with existing database objects and transformed in a complex manner, or where the external data volume is large and used only once. SQL*Loader, on the other hand, might still be the better choice for loading of data where additional indexing of the staging table is necessary. This is true for operations where the data is used in independent complex transformations or the data is only partially used in further processing.

You can create an external table named `sales_transactions_ext`, representing the structure of the complete sales transaction data, represented in the external file `sh_sales.dat`. The product department is especially interested in a cost analysis on product and time. We thus create a fact table named `cost` in the `sales history` schema. The operational source data is the same as for the `sales` fact table. However, because we are not investigating every dimensional information that is provided, the data in the cost fact table has a coarser granularity than in the sales fact table, for example, all different distribution channels are aggregated.

We cannot load the data into the cost fact table without applying the previously mentioned aggregation of the detailed information, due to the suppression of some of the dimensions.

Oracle's external table framework offers a solution to solve this. Unlike SQL*Loader, where you would have to load the data before applying the aggregation, you can combine the loading and transformation within a single SQL DML statement, as shown in the following. You do not have to stage the data temporarily before inserting into the target table.

The Oracle object directories must already exist, and point to the directory containing the `sh_sales.dat` file as well as the directory containing the bad and log files.

```
CREATE TABLE sales_transactions_ext
(
  PROD_ID NUMBER(6),
  CUST_ID NUMBER,
  TIME_ID DATE,
  CHANNEL_ID CHAR(1),
  PROMO_ID NUMBER(6),
  QUANTITY_SOLD NUMBER(3),
  AMOUNT_SOLD NUMBER(10,2),
  UNIT_COST NUMBER(10,2),
  UNIT_PRICE NUMBER(10,2)
)
ORGANIZATION external
(
  TYPE oracle_loader
  DEFAULT DIRECTORY data_file_dir
  ACCESS PARAMETERS
  (
    RECORDS DELIMITED BY NEWLINE CHARACTERSET US7ASCII
    BADFILE log_file_dir:'sh_sales.bad_xt'
    LOGFILE log_file_dir:'sh_sales.log_xt'
    FIELDS TERMINATED BY "|" LDRTRIM
  )
  location
  (
    'sh_sales.dat'
  )
)REJECT LIMIT UNLIMITED;
```

The external table can now be used from within the database, accessing some columns of the external data only, grouping the data, and inserting it into the `costs` fact table:

```
INSERT /*+ APPEND */ INTO COSTS
(
  TIME_ID,
  PROD_ID,
  UNIT_COST,
  UNIT_PRICE
)
SELECT
  TIME_ID,
  PROD_ID,
  SUM(UNIT_COST),
  SUM(UNIT_PRICE)
FROM sales_transactions_ext
GROUP BY time_id, prod_id;
```

OCI and Direct-Path APIs

OCI and direct-path APIs are frequently used when the transformation and computation are done outside the database and there is no need for flat file staging.

Export/Import

Export and import are used when the data is inserted as is into the target system. No large volumes of data should be handled and no complex extractions are possible.

TRANSFORMATION MECHANISMS

You have the following choices for transforming data inside the database:

- Transformation using SQL.
- Transformation using PL/SQL.
- Transformation using Table Functions.

Transformation Using SQL

Once data is loaded into an Oracle9*i* database, data transformations can be executed using SQL operations. There are four basic techniques for implementing SQL data transformations within Oracle9*i*:

- CREATE TABLE ... AS SELECT And INSERT /*+APPEND*/ AS SELECT
- Transformation using UPDATE
- Transformation using MERGE
- Transformation using multitable INSERT.

CREATE TABLE ... AS SELECT and INSERT /*+APPEND*/ AS SELECT

The `CREATE TABLE ... AS SELECT` statement (CTAS) is a powerful tool for manipulating large sets of data. As shown in the following example, many data transformations can be expressed in standard SQL, and CTAS provides a mechanism for efficiently executing a SQL query and storing the results of that query in a new database table. The `INSERT /*+APPEND*/ ... AS SELECT` statement offers the same capabilities with existing database tables.

In a data warehouse environment, CTAS is typically run in parallel using `NOLOGGING` mode for best performance.

A simple and common type of data transformation is data substitution. In a data substitution transformation, some or all of the values of a single column are modified. For example, our `sales` table has a `channel_id` column. This column indicates whether a given sales transaction was made by a company's own sales force (a direct sale) or by a distributor (an indirect sale).

You may receive data from multiple source systems for your data warehouse. Suppose that one of those source systems processes only direct sales, and thus the source system does not know indirect sales channels. When the data warehouse initially receives sales data from this system, all sales records have a `NULL` value for the `sales.channel_id` field. These `NULL` values must be set to the proper key value. For example, you can do this efficiently by using an SQL function as part of the insertion into the target sales table statement:

The structure of source table `sales_activity_direct` is as follows:

```
SQL> DESC sales_activity_direct
Name            Null?    Type
------------    ------   ------------------
SALES_DATE               DATE
PRODUCT_ID               NUMBER
```

```
CUSTOMER_ID                NUMBER
PROMOTION_ID               NUMBER
AMOUNT                     NUMBER
QUANTITY                   NUMBER

INSERT /*+ APPEND NOLOGGING PARALLEL */
INTO sales
SELECT product_id, customer_id, TRUNC(sales_date), 'S',
  promotion_id, quantity, amount
FROM sales_activity_direct;
```

Transformation Using UPDATE

Another technique for implementing a data substitution is to use an `UPDATE` statement to modify the `sales.channel_id` column. An `UPDATE` will provide the correct result. However, if the data substitution transformations require that a very large percentage of the rows (or all of the rows) be modified, then, it may be more efficient to use a CTAS statement than an `UPDATE`.

Transformation Using MERGE

Oracle's merge functionality extends SQL, by introducing the SQL keyword `MERGE`, in order to provide the ability to update or insert a row conditionally into a table or out of line single table views. Conditions are specified in the `ON` clause. This is, besides pure bulk loading, one of the most common operations in data warehouse synchronization.

Prior to Oracle9*i*, merges were expressed either as a sequence of DML statements or as PL/SQL loops operating on each row. Both of these approaches suffer from deficiencies in performance and usability. The new merge functionality overcomes these deficiencies with a new SQL statement. This syntax has been proposed as part of the upcoming SQL standard.

When to Use Merge

There are several benefits of the new `MERGE` statement as compared with the two other existing approaches.

- The entire operation can be expressed much more simply as a single SQL statement
- You can parallelize statements transparently
- You can use bulk DML
- Performance will improve because your statements will require fewer scans of the source table.

Merge Examples

The following examples discuss various implementations of a merge. The examples assume that new data for the dimension table products is propagated to the data warehouse and has to be either inserted or updated. The table `products_delta` has the same structure as `products`.

Example 5.1 : Merge Operation Using SQL in Oracle9i

```
MERGE INTO products t
USING products_delta s
ON (t.prod_id=s.prod_id)
WHEN MATCHED THEN
UPDATE SET
```

```
t.prod_list_price=s.prod_list_price,
t.prod_min_price=s.prod_min_price
WHEN NOT MATCHED THEN
INSERT
(prod_id, prod_name, prod_desc,
prod_subcategory, prod_subcat_desc, prod_category,
prod_cat_desc, prod_status, prod_list_price, prod_min_price)
VALUES
(s.prod_id, s.prod_name, s.prod_desc,
s.prod_subcategory, s.prod_subcat_desc,
s.prod_category, s.prod_cat_desc,
s.prod_status, s.prod_list_price, s.prod_min_price);
```

Example 5.2 : Merge Operation Using SQL Prior to Oracle9i

A regular join between source `products_delta` and target `products`.

```
UPDATE products t
SET
(prod_name, prod_desc, prod_subcategory, prod_subcat_desc, prod_category,
prod_cat_desc, prod_status, prod_list_price,
prod_min_price) =
(SELECT prod_name, prod_desc, prod_subcategory, prod_subcat_desc,
prod_category, prod_cat_desc, prod_status, prod_list_price,
prod_min_price from products_delta s WHERE s.prod_id=t.prod_id);
```

An antijoin between source `products_delta` and target `products`.

```
INSERT INTO products t
SELECT * FROM products_delta s
WHERE s.prod_id NOT IN
(SELECT prod_id FROM products);
```

The advantage of this approach is its simplicity and lack of new language extensions. The disadvantage is its performance. It requires an extra scan and a join of both the `products_delta` and the `products` tables.

Example 5.3 : Pre-9i Merge Using PL/SQL

```
CREATE OR REPLACE PROCEDURE merge_proc
IS
CURSOR cur IS
SELECT prod_id, prod_name, prod_desc, prod_subcategory, prod_subcat_desc,
      prod_category, prod_cat_desc, prod_status, prod_list_price,
       prod_min_price
FROM products_delta;
crec cur%rowtype;
BEGIN
  OPEN cur;
  LOOP
    FETCH cur INTO crec;
    EXIT WHEN cur%notfound;
    UPDATE products SET
```

```
        prod_name = crec.prod_name, prod_desc = crec.prod_desc,
        prod_subcategory = crec.prod_subcategory,
        prod_subcat_desc = crec.prod_subcat_desc,
        prod_category = crec.prod_category,
        prod_cat_desc = crec.prod_cat_desc,
        prod_status = crec.prod_status,
        prod_list_price = crec.prod_list_price,
        prod_min_price = crec.prod_min_price
      WHERE crec.prod_id = prod_id;

    IF SQL%notfound THEN
    INSERT INTO products
    (prod_id, prod_name, prod_desc, prod_subcategory,
    prod_subcat_desc, prod_category,
      prod_cat_desc, prod_status, prod_list_price, prod_min_price)
    VALUES
    (crec.prod_id, crec.prod_name, crec.prod_desc, crec.prod_subcategory,
    crec.prod_subcat_desc, crec.prod_category,
    crec.prod_cat_desc, crec.prod_status, crec.prod_list_price, crec.prod_min_
price);
    END IF;
  END LOOP;
  CLOSE cur;
END merge_proc;
/
```

Transformation Using Multitable INSERT

Many times, external data sources have to be segregated based on logical attributes for insertion into different target objects. It's also frequent in data warehouse environments to fan out the same source data into several target objects. Multitable inserts provide a new SQL statement for these kinds of transformations, where data can either end up in several or exactly one target, depending on the business transformation rules. This insertion can be done conditionally based on business rules or unconditionally.

It offers the benefits of the `INSERT ... SELECT` statement when multiple tables are involved as targets. In doing so, it avoids the drawbacks of the alternatives available to you using functionality prior to Oracle9*i*. You either had to deal with *n* independent `INSERT ... SELECT` statements, thus processing the same source data *n* times and increasing the transformation workload *n* times. Alternatively, you had to choose a procedural approach with a per-row determination how to handle the insertion. This solution lacked direct access to high-speed access paths available in SQL.

As with the existing `INSERT ... SELECT` statement, the new statement can be parallelized and used with the direct-load mechanism for faster performance.

Example 5.4 : Unconditional Insert

The following statement aggregates the transactional sales information, stored in `sales_activity_direct`, on a per daily base and inserts into both the `sales` and the `costs` fact table for the current day.

```
INSERT ALL
  INTO sales VALUES (product_id, customer_id, today, 'S', promotion_id,
                     quantity_per_day, amount_per_day)
```

```
   INTO costs VALUES (product_id, today, product_cost, product_price)
SELECT TRUNC(s.sales_date) AS today,
   s.product_id, s.customer_id, s.promotion_id,
   SUM(s.amount_sold) AS amount_per_day, SUM(s.quantity) quantity_per_day,
   p.product_cost, p.product_price
   FROM sales_activity_direct s, product_information p
   WHERE s.product_id = p.product_id
   AND trunc(sales_date)=trunc(sysdate)
   GROUP BY trunc(sales_date), s.product_id,
        s.customer_id, s.promotion_id, p.product_cost,
p.product_price;
```

Example 5.5 : Conditional ALL Insert

The following statement inserts a row into the sales and cost tables for all sales transactions with a valid promotion and stores the information about multiple identical orders of a customer in a separate table cum_sales_activity. It is possible two rows will be inserted for some sales transactions, and none for others.

```
INSERT ALL
WHEN promotion_id IN (SELECT promo_id FROM promotions) THEN
   INTO sales VALUES (product_id, customer_id, today, 'S', promotion_id,
                      quantity_per_day, amount_per_day)
   INTO costs VALUES (product_id, today, product_cost, product_price)
WHEN num_of_orders > 1 THEN
   INTO cum_sales_activity VALUES (today, product_id, customer_id,
                                   promotion_id, quantity_per_day, amount_per_day,
                                   num_of_orders)
SELECT TRUNC(s.sales_date) AS today, s.product_id, s.customer_id,
   s.promotion_id, SUM(s.amount) AS amount_per_day, SUM(s.quantity)
   quantity_per_day, COUNT(*) num_of_orders,
   p.product_cost, p.product_price
FROM sales_activity_direct s, product_information p
WHERE s.product_id = p.product_id
AND TRUNC(sales_date) = TRUNC(sysdate)
GROUP BY TRUNC(sales_date), s.product_id, s.customer_id,
   s.promotion_id, p.product_cost, p.product_price;
```

Example 5.6 : Conditional FIRST Insert

The following statement inserts into an appropriate shipping manifest according to the total quantity and the weight of a product order. An exception is made for high value orders, which are also sent by express, unless their weight classification is not too high. It assumes the existence of appropriate tables large_freight_shipping, express_shipping, and default_shipping.

```
INSERT FIRST
  WHEN (sum_quantity_sold > 10 AND prod_weight_class < 5) OR
       (sum_quantity_sold > 5 AND prod_weight_class > 5) THEN
    INTO large_freight_shipping VALUES
       (time_id, cust_id, prod_id, prod_weight_class, sum_quantity_sold)
  WHEN sum_amount_sold > 1000 THEN
    INTO express_shipping VALUES
       (time_id, cust_id, prod_id, prod_weight_class,
        sum_amount_sold, sum_quantity_sold)
```

```
  ELSE
    INTO default_shipping VALUES
        (time_id, cust_id, prod_id, sum_quantity_sold)
  SELECT s.time_id, s.cust_id, s.prod_id, p.prod_weight_class,
    SUM(amount_sold) AS sum_amount_sold,
    SUM(quantity_sold) AS sum_quantity_sold
FROM sales s, products p
WHERE s.prod_id = p.prod_id
AND s.time_id = TRUNC(sysdate)
GROUP BY s.time_id, s.cust_id, s.prod_id, p.prod_weight_class;
```

Example 5.7 : Mixed Conditional and Unconditional Insert

The following example inserts new customers into the customers table and stores all new customers with `cust_credit_limit` higher then 4500 in an additional, separate table for further promotions.

```
INSERT FIRST
  WHEN cust_credit_limit >= 4500 THEN
    INTO customers
      INTO customers_special VALUES (cust_id, cust_credit_limit)
  ELSE
    INTO customers
SELECT * FROM customers_new;
```

Transformation Using PL/SQL

In a data warehouse environment, you can use procedural languages such as PL/SQL to implement complex transformations in the Oracle9*i* database. Whereas CTAS operates on entire tables and emphasizes parallelism, PL/SQL provides a row-based approach and can accommodate very sophisticated transformation rules. For example, a PL/SQL procedure could open multiple cursors and read data from multiple source tables, combine this data using complex business rules, and finally insert the transformed data into one or more target tables. It would be difficult or impossible to express the same sequence of operations using standard SQL statements.

Using a procedural language, a specific transformation (or number of transformation steps) within a complex ETL processing can be encapsulated, reading data from an intermediate staging area and generating a new table object as output. A previously generated transformation input table and a subsequent transformation will consume the table generated by this specific transformation. Alternatively, these encapsulated transformation steps within the complete ETL process can be integrated seamlessly, thus streaming sets of rows between each other without the necessity of intermediate staging. You can use Oracle9*i*'s table functions to implement such behavior.

Transformation Using Table Functions

Oracle9*i*'s table functions provide the support for pipelined and parallel execution of transformations implemented in PL/SQL, C, or Java. Scenarios as mentioned earlier can be done without requiring the use of intermediate staging tables, which interrupt the data flow through various transformations steps.

What is a Table Function?

A table function is defined as a function that can produce a set of rows as output. Additionally, table functions can take a set of rows as input. Prior to Oracle9*i*, PL/SQL functions:

- Could not take cursors as input
- Could not be parallelized or pipelined.

Starting with Oracle9*i*, functions are not limited in these ways. Table functions extend database functionality by allowing:

- Multiple rows to be returned from a function
- Results of SQL subqueries (that select multiple rows) to be passed directly to functions
- Functions take cursors as input
- Functions can be parallelized
- Returning result sets incrementally for further processing as soon as they are created. This is called incremental pipelining.

Table functions can be defined in PL/SQL using a native PL/SQL interface, or in Java or C using the Oracle Data Cartridge Interface (ODCI).

Figure 5.3 illustrates a typical aggregation where you input a set of rows and output a set of rows, in that case, after performing a SUM operation.

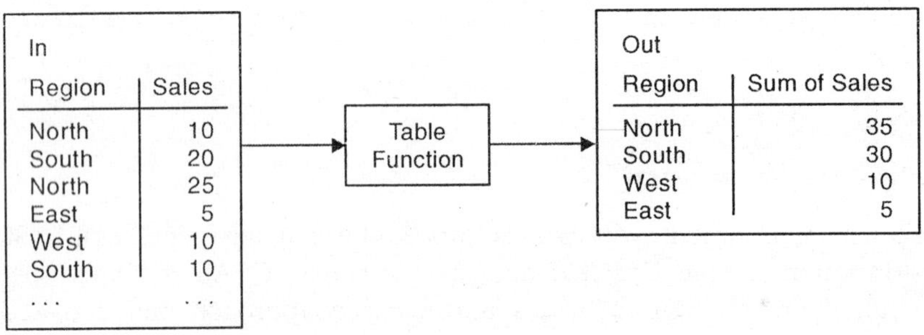

Figure 5.3 Table Function Example.

The pseudocode for this operation would be similar to:

```
INSERT INTO out
SELECT * FROM ("Table Function"(SELECT * FROM in));
```

The table function takes the result of the SELECT on In as input and delivers a set of records in a different format as output for a direct insertion into Out.

Additionally, a table function can fan out data within the scope of an atomic transaction. This can be used for many occasions like an efficient logging mechanism or a fan out for other independent transformations. In such a scenario, a single staging table will be needed.

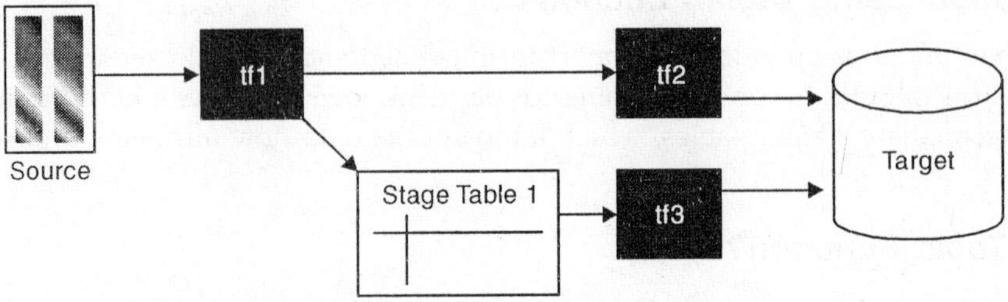

Figure 5.4 Pipelined Parallel Transformation with Fanout.

The pseudocode for this would be similar to:

```
INSERT INTO target SELECT * FROM (tf2(SELECT *
FROM (tf1(SELECT * FROM source))));
```

This will insert into `target` and, as part of `tf1`, into `Stage Table 1` within the scope of an atomic transaction.

```
INSERT INTO target SELECT * FROM tf3(SELECT * FROM stage_table1);
```

Example 5.8 : Table Functions Fundamentals

The following examples demonstrate the fundamentals of table functions, without the usage of complex business rules implemented inside those functions. They are chosen for demonstration purposes only, and are all implemented in PL/SQL.

Table functions return sets of records and can take cursors as input. Besides the `Sales History` schema, you have to set up the following database objects before using the examples:

```
REM object types
CREATE TYPE product_t AS OBJECT (
    prod_id                 NUMBER(6),
    prod_name               VARCHAR2(50),
    prod_desc               VARCHAR2(4000),
    prod_subcategory        VARCHAR2(50),
    prod_subcat_desc        VARCHAR2(2000).
    prod_category           VARCHAR2(50),
    prod_cat_desc           VARCHAR2(2000),
    prod_weight_class       NUMBER(2),
    prod_unit_of_measure    VARCHAR2(20),
    prod_pack_size          VARCHAR2(30),
    supplier_id             NUMBER(6),
    prod_status             VARCHAR2(20),
    prod_list_price         NUMBER(8,2),
    prod_min_price          NUMBER(8,2)
);
/
CREATE TYPE product_t_table AS TABLE OF product_t;
/
COMMIT;

REM package of all cursor types
REM we have to handle the input cursor type and the output cursor collection
REM type
CREATE OR REPLACE PACKAGE cursor_PKG as
  TYPE product_t_rec IS RECORD (
    prod_id                 NUMBER(6),
    prod_name               VARCHAR2(50),
    prod_desc               VARCHAR2(4000),
    prod_subcategory        VARCHAR2(50),
    prod_subcat_desc        VARCHAR2(2000),
    prod_category           VARCHAR2(50),
    prod_cat_desc           VARCHAR2(2000),
    prod_weight_class       NUMBER(2),
```

```
    prod_unit_of_measure  VARCHAR2(20),
    prod_pack_size        VARCHAR2(30),
    supplier_id           NUMBER(6),
    prod_status           VARCHAR2(20),
    prod_list_price       NUMBER(8,2),
    prod_min_price        NUMBER(8,2));
  TYPE product_t_rectab IS TABLE OF product_t_rec;
  TYPE strong_refcur_t IS REF CURSOR RETURN product_t_rec;
  TYPE refcur_t IS REF CURSOR;
END;
/

REM artificial help table, used to demonstrate figure 13-4
CREATE TABLE obsolete_products_errors (prod_id NUMBER, msg VARCHAR2(2000));
```

The following example demonstrates a simple filtering; it shows all obsolete products except the `prod_category` Boys. The table function returns the result set as a set of records and uses a weakly typed ref cursor as input.

```
CREATE OR REPLACE FUNCTION obsolete_products(cur cursor_pkg.refcur_t)
    RETURN product_t_table
  IS
    prod_id               NUMBER(6);
    prod_name             VARCHAR2(50);
    prod_desc             VARCHAR2(4000);
    prod_subcategory      VARCHAR2(50);
    prod_subcat_desc      VARCHAR2(2000);
    prod_category         VARCHAR2(50);
    prod_cat_desc         VARCHAR2(2000);
    prod_weight_class     NUMBER(2);
    prod_unit_of_measure  VARCHAR2(20);
    prod_pack_size        VARCHAR2(30);
    supplier_id           NUMBER(6);
    prod_status           VARCHAR2(20);
    prod_list_price       NUMBER(8,2);
    prod_min_price        NUMBER(8,2);
  sales NUMBER:=0;
  objset product_t_table := product_t_table();
  i NUMBER := 0;
BEGIN
  LOOP
    -- Fetch from cursor variable
    FETCH cur INTO prod_id, prod_name, prod_desc, prod_subcategory,
    prod_subcat_desc,  prod_category, prod_cat_desc, prod_weight_class,
    prod_unit_of_measure,  prod_pack_size, supplier_id, prod_status,
    prod_list_price, prod_min_price;
    EXIT WHEN cur%NOTFOUND; – exit when last row is fetched
    IF prod_status='obsolete' AND prod_category != 'Boys' THEN
    -- append to collection
    i:=i+1;
    objset.extend;
```

```
    objset(i):=product_t( prod_id, prod_name, prod_desc, prod_subcategory,
prod_subcat_desc,  prod_category, prod_cat_desc, prod_weight_class, prod_unit_
of_measure,  prod_pack_size, supplier_id, prod_status, prod_list_price, prod_
min_price);
    END IF;
  END LOOP;
  CLOSE cur;
  RETURN objset;
END;
/
```

You can use the table function in a SQL statement to show the results. Here we use additional SQL functionality for the output.

```
SELECT DISTINCT UPPER(prod_category), prod_status
FROM TABLE(obsolete_products(CURSOR(SELECT * FROM products)));

UPPER(PROD_CATEGORY)       PROD_STATUS
--------------------       -------------
GIRLS                      obsolete
MEN                        obsolete

2 rows selected.
```

The following example implements the same filtering than the first one. The main differences between these two are:

- This example uses a strong typed REF cursor as input and can be parallelized based on the objects of the strong typed cursor, as shown in one of the following examples.
- The table function returns the result set incrementally as soon as records are created.

```
REM Same example, pipelined implementation
REM strong ref cursor (input type is defined)
REM a table without a strong typed input ref cursor cannot be parallelized
REM
CREATE OR
REPLACE FUNCTION obsolete_products_pipe(cur cursor_pkg.strong_refcur_t)
RETURN product_t_table
PIPELINED
PARALLEL_ENABLE (PARTITION cur BY ANY) IS
    prod_id                NUMBER(6);
    prod_name              VARCHAR2(50);
    prod_desc              VARCHAR2(4000);
    prod_subcategory       VARCHAR2(50);
    prod_subcat_desc       VARCHAR2(2000);
    prod_category          VARCHAR2(50);
    prod_cat_desc          VARCHAR2(2000);
      prod_weight_class      NUMBER(2);
    prod_unit_of_measure VARCHAR2(20);
    prod_pack_size         VARCHAR2(30);
    supplier_id            NUMBER(6);
    prod_status            VARCHAR2(20);
```

```
    prod_list_price        NUMBER(8,2);
    prod_min_price         NUMBER(8,2);
  sales NUMBER:=0;
BEGIN
  LOOP
    — Fetch from cursor variable
  FETCH cur INTO prod_id, prod_name, prod_desc, prod_subcategory, prod_subcat_
desc, prod_category, prod_cat_desc, prod_weight_class, prod_unit_of_measure,
prod_pack_size, supplier_id, prod_status, prod_list_price, prod_min_price;
  EXIT WHEN cur%NOTFOUND; — exit when last row is fetched
    IF prod_status='obsolete' AND prod_category !='Boys' THEN
  PIPE ROW (product_t(prod_id, prod_name, prod_desc, prod_subcategory, prod_
subcat_desc, prod_category, prod_cat_desc, prod_weight_class, prod_unit_of_
measure, prod_pack_size, supplier_id, prod_status, prod_list_price, prod_min_
price));
    END IF;
  END LOOP;
  CLOSE cur;
  RETURN;
END;
/
```

You can use the table function as follows:

```
SELECT DISTINCT prod_category, DECODE(prod_status, 'obsolete', 'NO LONGER
REMOVE_AVAILABLE', 'N/A')
FROM TABLE(obsolete_products_pipe(CURSOR(SELECT * FROM products)));

PROD_CATEGORY        DECODE(PROD_STATUS,
----------------     ------------------------
Girls                NO LONGER AVAILABLE
Men                  NO LONGER AVAILABLE

2 rows selected.
```

We now change the degree of parallelism for the input table products and issue the same statement again:

```
ALTER TABLE products PARALLEL 4;
```

The session statistics show that the statement has been parallelized:

```
SELECT * FROM V$PQ_SESSTAT WHERE statistic='Queries Parallelized';

STATISTIC                   LAST_QUERY         SESSION_TOTAL
---------------------       --------------     -------------
Queries Parallelized                     1                 3

1 row selected.
```

Table functions are also capable to fanout results into persistent table structures. This is demonstrated in the next example. The function filters returns all obsolete products except a those of a specific `prod_category` (default `Men`), which was set to status obsolete by error. The detected wrong prod_id's are stored in a separate table structure. Its result set consists of all other obsolete product categories. It furthermore demonstrates how normal variables can be used in conjunction with table functions:

```
CREATE OR REPLACE FUNCTION obsolete_products_dml(cur cursor_pkg.strong_refcur_t,
prod_cat VARCHAR2 DEFAULT 'Men') RETURN product_t_table
PIPELINED
PARALLEL_ENABLE (PARTITION cur BY ANY) IS
    PRAGMA AUTONOMOUS_TRANSACTION;
    prod_id              NUMBER(6);
    prod_name            VARCHAR2(50);
    prod_desc            VARCHAR2(4000);
    prod_subcategory     VARCHAR2(50);
    prod_subcat_desc     VARCHAR2(2000);
    prod_category        VARCHAR2(50);
    prod_cat_desc        VARCHAR2(2000);
    prod_weight_class    NUMBER(2);
    prod_unit_of_measure VARCHAR2(20);
    prod_pack_size       VARCHAR2(30);
    supplier_id          NUMBER(6);
    prod_status          VARCHAR2(20);
    prod_list_price      NUMBER(8,2);
    prod_min_price       NUMBER(8,2);
  sales NUMBER:=0;
BEGIN
  LOOP
    – Fetch from cursor variable
    FETCH cur INTO prod_id, prod_name, prod_desc, prod_subcategory, prod_subcat_
desc, prod_category, prod_cat_desc, prod_weight_class, prod_unit_of_measure,
prod_pack_size, supplier_id, prod_status, prod_list_price, prod_min_price;
    EXIT WHEN cur%NOTFOUND; – exit when last row is fetched
    IF prod_status='obsolete' THEN
      IF prod_category=prod_cat THEN
        INSERT INTO obsolete_products_errors VALUES
        (prod_id, 'correction: category '||UPPER(prod_cat)||' still available');
      ELSE
    PIPE ROW (product_t( prod_id, prod_name, prod_desc, prod_subcategory, prod_
subcat_desc, prod_category, prod_cat_desc, prod_weight_class, prod_unit_of_
measure, prod_pack_size, supplier_id, prod_status, prod_list_price, prod_min_
price));
      END IF;
    END IF;
  END LOOP;
  COMMIT;
  CLOSE cur;
  RETURN;
END;
/
```

The following query shows all obsolete product groups except the prod_category Men, which was wrongly set to status obsolete.

```
SELECT DISTINCT prod_category, prod_status FROM TABLE(obsolete_products_
dml(CURSOR(SELECT * FROM products)));

PROD_CATEGORY           PROD_STATUS
---------------         --------------
Boys                    obsolete
Girls                   obsolete

2 rows selected.
```

As you can see, there are some products of the `prod_category Men` that were obsoleted by accident:

```
SELECT DISTINCT msg FROM obsolete_products_errors;

MSG
----------------------------------------
correction: category MEN still available

1 row selected.
```

Taking advantage of the second input variable changes the result set as follows:

```
SELECT DISTINCT prod_category, prod_status FROM TABLE(obsolete_products_
dml(CURSOR(SELECT * FROM products), 'Boys'));

PROD_CATEGORY     PROD_STATUS
-------------     -----------
Girls             obsolete
Men               obsolete

2 rows selected.

SELECT DISTINCT msg FROM obsolete_products_errors;

MSG
-----------------------------------------
correction: category BOYS still available

1 row selected.
```

Because table functions can be used like a normal table, they can be nested, as shown in the following:

```
SELECT DISTINCT prod_category, prod_status
FROM TABLE(obsolete_products_dml(CURSOR(SELECT *
      FROM TABLE(obsolete_products_pipe(CURSOR(SELECT *    FROM products))))));

PROD_CATEGORY      PROD_STATUS
-------------      ------------
Girls              obsolete

1 row selected.
```

Because the table function obsolete_products_pipe filters out all products of the prod_category Boys, our result does no longer include products of the prod_category Boys. The prod_category Men is still set to be obsolete by accident.

```
SELECT COUNT(*) FROM obsolete_products_errors;
MSG
----------------------------------------
correction: category MEN still available
```

The biggest advantage of Oracle9*i* ETL is its toolkit functionality, where you can combine any of the latter discussed functionality to improve and speed up your ETL processing. For example, you can take an external table as input, join it with an existing table and use it as input for a parallelized table function to process complex business logic. This table function can be used as input source for a MERGE operation, thus streaming the new information for the data warehouse, provided in a flat file within one single statement through the complete ETL process.

LOADING AND TRANSFORMATION SCENARIOS

The following sections offer examples of typical loading and transformation tasks:

- Parallel load scenario
- Key lookup scenario
- Exception handling scenario
- Pivoting scenarios.

Parallel Load Scenario

This section presents a case study illustrating how to create, load, index, and analyze a large data warehouse fact table with partitions in a typical star schema. This example uses SQL*Loader to explicitly stripe data over 30 disks.

- The example 120 GB table is named facts.
- The system is a 10-CPU shared memory computer with more than 100 disk drives.
- Thirty disks (4 GB each) are used for base table data, 10 disks for indexes, and 30 disks for temporary space. Additional disks are needed for rollback segments, control files, log files, possible staging area for loader flat files, and so on.
- The facts table is partitioned by month into 12 partitions. To facilitate backup and recovery, each partition is stored in its own tablespace.
- Each partition is spread evenly over 10 disks, so a scan accessing few partitions or a single partition can proceed with full parallelism. Thus there can be intra-partition parallelism when queries restrict data access by partition pruning.
- Each disk has been further subdivided using an operating system utility into 4 operating system files with names like /dev/D1.1, /dev/D1.2, ... , /dev/D30.4.
- Four tablespaces are allocated on each group of 10 disks. To better balance I/O and parallelize table space creation (because Oracle writes each block in a datafile when it is added to a tablespace), it is best if each of the four tablespaces on each group of 10 disks has its first datafile on a different disk. Thus the first tablespace has /dev/D1.1 as its first datafile, the second tablespace has /dev/D4.2 as its first datafile, and so on, as illustrated in figure 5.5.

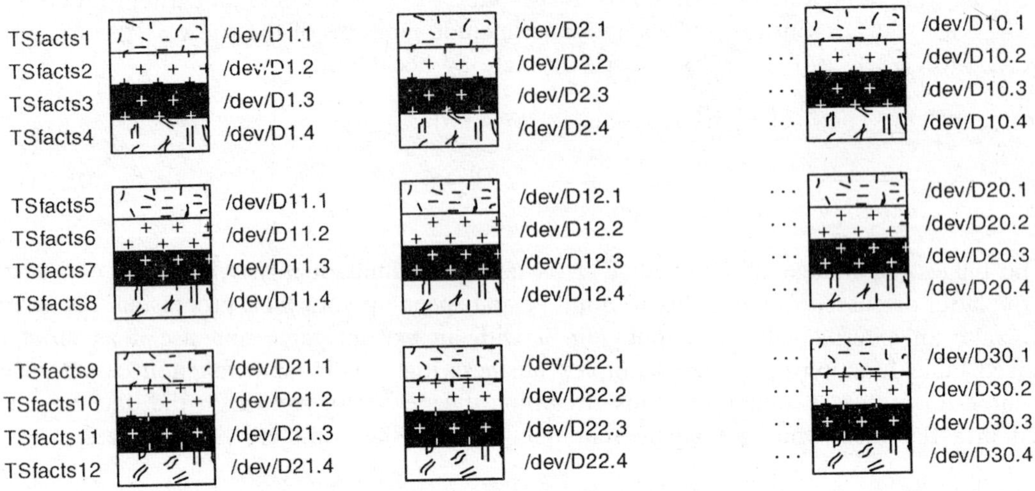

Figure 5.5 Datafile Layout for Parallel Load Example.

Step 1: Create the Tablespaces and Add Datafiles in Parallel

The following is the command to create a tablespace named `Tsfacts1`. Other tablespaces are created with analogous commands. On a 10-CPU machine, it should be possible to run all 12 `CREATE TABLESPACE` statements together. Alternatively, it might be better to run them in two batches of 6 (two from each of the three groups of disks).

```
CREATE TABLESPACE TSfacts1
DATAFILE /dev/D1.1'  SIZE 1024MB REUSE,
DATAFILE /dev/D2.1'  SIZE 1024MB REUSE,
DATAFILE /dev/D3.1'  SIZE 1024MB REUSE,
DATAFILE /dev/D4.1'  SIZE 1024MB REUSE,
DATAFILE /dev/D5.1'  SIZE 1024MB REUSE,
DATAFILE /dev/D6.1'  SIZE 1024MB REUSE,
DATAFILE /dev/D7.1'  SIZE 1024MB REUSE,
DATAFILE /dev/D8.1'  SIZE 1024MB REUSE,
DATAFILE /dev/D9.1'  SIZE 1024MB REUSE,
DATAFILE /dev/D10.1  SIZE 1024MB REUSE,
DEFAULT STORAGE (INITIAL 100MB NEXT 100MB PCTINCREASE 0);
...

CREATE TABLESPACE TSfacts2
DATAFILE /dev/D4.2'  SIZE 1024MB REUSE,
DATAFILE /dev/D5.2'  SIZE 1024MB REUSE,
DATAFILE /dev/D6.2'  SIZE 1024MB REUSE,
DATAFILE /dev/D7.2'  SIZE 1024MB REUSE,
DATAFILE /dev/D8.2'  SIZE 1024MB REUSE,
DATAFILE /dev/D9.2'  SIZE 1024MB REUSE,
DATAFILE /dev/D10.2  SIZE 1024MB REUSE,
DATAFILE /dev/D1.2'  SIZE 1024MB REUSE,
DATAFILE /dev/D2.2'  SIZE 1024MB REUSE,
DATAFILE /dev/D3.2'  SIZE 1024MB REUSE,
DEFAULT STORAGE (INITIAL 100MB NEXT 100MB PCTINCREASE 0);
...
```

```
CREATE TABLESPACE TSfacts4
DATAFILE /dev/D10.4' SIZE 1024MB REUSE,
DATAFILE /dev/D1.4'  SIZE 1024MB REUSE,
DATAFILE /dev/D2.4'  SIZE 1024MB REUSE,
DATAFILE /dev/D3.4   SIZE 1024MB REUSE,
DATAFILE /dev/D4.4'  SIZE 1024MB REUSE,
DATAFILE /dev/D5.4'  SIZE 1024MB REUSE,
DATAFILE /dev/D6.4'  SIZE 1024MB REUSE,
DATAFILE /dev/D7.4'  SIZE 1024MB REUSE,
DATAFILE /dev/D8.4'  SIZE 1024MB REUSE,
DATAFILE /dev/D9.4'  SIZE 1024MB REUSE,
DEFAULT STORAGE (INITIAL 100MB NEXT 100MB PCTINCREASE 0);
...

CREATE TABLESPACE TSfacts12
DATAFILE /dev/D30.4'  SIZE 1024MB REUSE,
DATAFILE /dev/D21.4'  SIZE 1024MB REUSE,
DATAFILE /dev/D22.4'  SIZE 1024MB REUSE,
DATAFILE /dev/D23.4   SIZE 1024MB REUSE,
DATAFILE /dev/D24.4'  SIZE 1024MB REUSE,
DATAFILE /dev/D25.4'  SIZE 1024MB REUSE,
DATAFILE /dev/D26.4'  SIZE 1024MB REUSE,
DATAFILE /dev/D27.4'  SIZE 1024MB REUSE,
DATAFILE /dev/D28.4'  SIZE 1024MB REUSE,
DATAFILE /dev/D29.4'  SIZE 1024MB REUSE,
DEFAULT STORAGE (INITIAL 100MB NEXT 100MB PCTINCREASE 0);
```

Extent sizes in the `STORAGE` clause should be multiples of the multiblock read size, where blocksize * `MULTIBLOCK_READ_COUNT` = multiblock read size.

`INITIAL` and `NEXT` should normally be set to the same value. In the case of parallel load, make the extent size large enough to keep the number of extents reasonable, and to avoid excessive overhead and serialization due to bottlenecks in the data dictionary. When `PARALLEL=TRUE` is used for parallel loader, the `INITIAL` extent is not used. In this case you can override the `INITIAL` extent size specified in the tablespace default storage clause with the value specified in the loader control file, for example, 64KB.

Tables or indexes can have an unlimited number of extents, provided you have set the `COMPATIBLE` initialization parameter to match the current release number, and use the `MAXEXTENTS` keyword on the `CREATE` or `ALTER` statement for the tablespace or object. In practice, however, a limit of 10,000 extents for each object is reasonable. A table or index has an unlimited number of extents, so set the `PERCENT_INCREASE` parameter to zero to have extents of equal size.

NOTE

If possible, do not allocate extents faster than about 2 or 3 for each minute. Thus, each process should get an extent that lasts for 3 to 5 minutes. Normally, such an extent is at least 50 MB for a large object. Too small an extent size incurs significant overhead, which affects performance and scalability of parallel operations. The largest possible extent size for a 4 GB disk evenly divided into 4 partitions is 1 GB. 100 MB extents should perform well. Each partition will have 100 extents. You can then customize the default storage parameters for each object created in the tablespace, if needed.

Step 2: Create the Partitioned Table

We create a partitioned table with 12 partitions, each in its own tablespace. The table contains multiple dimensions and multiple measures. The partitioning column is named `dim_2` and is a date. There are other columns as well.

```
CREATE TABLE facts (dim_1 NUMBER, dim_2 DATE, ...
  meas_1 NUMBER, meas_2 NUMBER, ... )
PARALLEL
PARTITION BY RANGE (dim_2)
(PARTITION jan95 VALUES LESS THAN ('02-01-1995') TABLESPACE
TSfacts1,
PARTITION feb95 VALUES LESS THAN ('03-01-1995') TABLESPACE
TSfacts2,
...
PARTITION dec95 VALUES LESS THAN ('01-01-1996') TABLESPACE
TSfacts12);
```

Step 3: Load the Partitions in Parallel

This section describes four alternative approaches for loading partitions in parallel. The different approaches to loading help you manage the ramifications of the `PARALLEL=TRUE` keyword of SQL*Loader that controls whether individual partitions are loaded in parallel. The `PARALLEL` keyword entails the following restrictions:

- Indexes cannot be defined
- You must set a small initial extent, because each loader session gets a new extent when it begins, and it does not use any existing space associated with the object
- Space fragmentation issues arise.

However, regardless of the setting of this keyword, if you have one loader process for each partition, you are still effectively loading into the table in parallel.

Example 5.9 : Loading Partitions in Parallel Case 1

In this approach, assume 12 input files are partitioned in the same way as your table. You have one input file for each partition of the table to be loaded. You start 12 SQL*Loader sessions concurrently in parallel, entering statements like these:

```
SQLLDR DATA=jan95.dat DIRECT=TRUE CONTROL=jan95.ctl
SQLLDR DATA=feb95.dat DIRECT=TRUE CONTROL=feb95.ctl
 . . .
SQLLDR DATA=dec95.dat DIRECT=TRUE CONTROL=dec95.ctl
```

In the example, the keyword `PARALLEL=TRUE` is *not* set. A separate control file for each partition is necessary because the control file must specify the partition into which the loading should be done. It contains a statement such as the following:

```
LOAD INTO facts partition(jan95)
```

The advantage of this approach is that local indexes are maintained by SQL*Loader. You still get parallel loading, but on a partition level—without the restrictions of the `PARALLEL` keyword. A disadvantage is that you must partition the input prior to loading manually.

Example 5.10 : Loading Partitions in Parallel Case 2

In another common approach, assume an arbitrary number of input files that are not partitioned in the same way as the table. You can adopt a strategy of performing parallel load for each input file individually. Thus if there are seven input files, you can start seven SQL*Loader sessions, using statements like the following:

```
SQLLDR DATA=file1.dat DIRECT=TRUE PARALLEL=TRUE
```

Oracle partitions the input data so that it goes into the correct partitions. In this case all the loader sessions can share the same control file, so there is no need to mention it in the statement.

The keyword `PARALLEL=TRUE` must be used, because each of the seven loader sessions can write into every partition. In Case 1, every loader session would write into only one partition, because the data was partitioned prior to loading. Hence all the `PARALLEL` keyword restrictions are in effect.

In this case, Oracle attempts to spread the data evenly across all the files in each of the 12 tablespaces—however an even spread of data is not guaranteed. Moreover, there could be I/O contention during the load when the loader processes are attempting to write to the same device simultaneously.

Example 5.11 : Loading Partitions in Parallel Case 3

In this example, you want precise control over the load. To achieve this, you must partition the input data in the same way as the datafiles are partitioned in Oracle.

This example uses 10 processes loading into 30 disks. To accomplish this, you must split the input into 120 files beforehand. The 10 processes will load the first partition in parallel on the first 10 disks, then the second partition in parallel on the second 10 disks, and so on through the 12th partition. You then run the following commands concurrently as background processes:

```
SQLLDR DATA=jan95.file1.dat DIRECT=TRUE PARALLEL=TRUE FILE=/dev/D1.1
...
SQLLDR DATA=jan95.file10.dat DIRECT=TRUE PARALLEL=TRUE FILE=/dev/D10.1
WAIT;
...
SQLLDR DATA=dec95.file1.dat DIRECT=TRUE PARALLEL=TRUE FILE=/dev/D30.4
...
SQLLDR DATA=dec95.file10.dat DIRECT=TRUE PARALLEL=TRUE FILE=/dev/D29.4
```

For Oracle Real Application Clusters, divide the loader session evenly among the nodes. The datafile being read should always reside on the same node as the loader session.

The keyword `PARALLEL=TRUE` must be used, because multiple loader sessions can write into the same partition. Hence all the restrictions entailed by the `PARALLEL` keyword are in effect. An advantage of this approach, however, is that it guarantees that all of the data is precisely balanced, exactly reflecting your partitioning.

NOTE

Although this example shows parallel load used with partitioned tables, the two features can be used independent of one another.

Example 5.12 : Loading Partitions in Parallel Case 4

For this approach, all partitions must be in the same tablespace. You need to have the same number of input files as datafiles in the tablespace, but you do not need to partition the input the same way in which the table is partitioned.

For example, if all 30 devices were in the same tablespace, then you would arbitrarily partition your input data into 30 files, then start 30 SQL*Loader sessions in parallel. The statement starting up the first session would be similar to the following:

```
SQLLDR DATA=file1.dat DIRECT=TRUE PARALLEL=TRUE FILE=/dev/D1
. . .
SQLLDR DATA=file30.dat DIRECT=TRUE PARALLEL=TRUE FILE=/dev/D30
```

The advantage of this approach is that as in Case 3, you have control over the exact placement of datafiles because you use the `FILE` keyword. However, you are not required to partition the input data by value because Oracle does that for you.

A disadvantage is that this approach requires all the partitions to be in the same tablespace. This minimizes availability.

Example 5.13 : Loading External Data

This is probably the most basic use of external tables where the data volume is large and no transformations are applied to the external data. The load process is performed as follows:

1. You create the external table. Most likely, the table will be declared as parallel to perform the load in parallel. Oracle will dynamically perform load balancing between the parallel execution servers involved in the query.
2. Once the external table is created (remember that this only creates the metadata in the dictionary), data can be converted, moved and loaded into the database using either a `PARALLEL CREATE TABLE AS SELECT` or a `PARALLEL INSERT` statement.

```
CREATE TABLE products_ext
(prod_id NUMBER, prod_name VARCHAR2(50), ...,
 price NUMBER(6.2), discount NUMBER(6.2))
ORGANIZATION EXTERNAL
(
DEFAULT DIRECTORY (stage_dir)
ACCESS PARAMETERS
( RECORDS FIXED 30
BADFILE 'bad/bad_products_ext'
LOGFILE 'log/log_products_ext'
( prod_id POSITION (1:8) CHAR,
  prod_name POSITION (*,+50) CHAR,
  prod_desc  POSITION (*,+200) CHAR,
  . . .)
REMOVE_LOCATION ('new/new_prod1.txt','new/new_prod2.txt'))
PARALLEL 5
```

```
REJECT LIMIT 200;
# load it in the database using a parallel insert
ALTER SESSION ENABLE PARALLEL DML;
INSERT INTO TABLE products SELECT * FROM products_ext;
```

In this example, stage_dir is a directory where the external flat files reside.

Note that loading data in parallel can be performed in Oracle9*i* by using SQL*Loader. But external tables are probably easier to use and the parallel load is automatically coordinated. Unlike SQL*Loader, dynamic load balancing between parallel execution servers will be performed as well because there will be intra-file parallelism. The latter implies that the user will not have to manually split input files before starting the parallel load. This will be accomplished dynamically.

Key Lookup Scenario

Another simple transformation is a key lookup. For example, suppose that sales transaction data has been loaded into a retail data warehouse. Although the data warehouse's sales table contains a product_id column, the sales transaction data extracted from the source system contains Uniform Price Codes (UPC) instead of product IDs. Therefore, it is necessary to transform the UPC codes into product IDs before the new sales transaction data can be inserted into the sales table.

In order to execute this transformation, a lookup table must relate the product_id values to the UPC codes. This table might be the product dimension table, or perhaps another table in the data warehouse that has been created specifically to support this transformation. For this example, we assume that there is a table named product, which has a product_id and an upc_code column.

This data substitution transformation can be implemented by using the following CTAS statement:

```
CREATE TABLE temp_sales_step2
   NOLOGGING PARALLEL AS
   SELECT
      sales_transaction_id,
      product.product_id sales_product_id,
      sales_customer_id,
      sales_time_id,
      sales_channel_id,
      sales_quantity_sold,
      sales_dollar_amount
   FROM  temp_sales_step1, product
   WHERE temp_sales_step1.upc_code = product.upc_code;
```

This CTAS statement will convert each valid UPC code to a valid product_id value. If the ETL process has guaranteed that each UPC code is valid, then this statement alone may be sufficient to implement the entire transformation.

Exception Handling Scenario

In the preceding example, if you must also handle new sales data that does not have valid UPC codes, you can use an additional CTAS statement to identify the invalid rows:

```
CREATE TABLE temp_sales_step1_invalid NOLOGGING PARALLEL AS
   SELECT * FROM temp_sales_step1
   WHERE temp_sales_step1.upc_code NOT IN (SELECT upc_code FROM product);
```

This invalid data is now stored in a separate table, `temp_sales_step1_invalid`, and can be handled separately by the ETL process.

Another way to handle invalid data is to modify the original CTAS to use an outer join:

```
CREATE TABLE temp_sales_step2
   NOLOGGING PARALLEL AS
   SELECT
          sales_transaction_id,
          product.product_id sales_product_id,
          sales_customer_id,
          sales_time_id,
          sales_channel_id,
          sales_quantity_sold,
          sales_dollar_amount
   FROM  temp_sales_step1, product
   WHERE temp_sales_step1.upc_code = product.upc_code (+);
```

Using this outer join, the sales transactions that originally contained invalidated UPC codes will be assigned a `product_id` of `NULL`. These transactions can be handled later.

Additional approaches to handling invalid UPC codes exist. Some data warehouses may choose to insert null-valued `product_id` values into their `sales` table, while other data warehouses may not allow any new data from the entire batch to be inserted into the `sales` table until all invalid UPC codes have been addressed. The correct approach is determined by the business requirements of the data warehouse. Regardless of the specific requirements, exception handling can be addressed by the same basic SQL techniques as transformations.

Pivoting Scenarios

A data warehouse can receive data from many different sources. Some of these source systems may not be relational databases and may store data in very different formats from the data warehouse. For example, suppose that you receive a set of sales records from a nonrelational database having the form:

```
product_id, customer_id, weekly_start_date, sales_sun, sales_mon, sales_tue,
  sales_wed, sales_thu, sales_fri, sales_sat
```

The input table looks like this:

```
SELECT * FROM sales_input_table;
```

PRODUCT_ID	CUSTOMER_ID	WEEKLY_ST	SALES_SUN	SALES_MON	SALES_TUE	SALES_WED	SALES_THU	SALES_FRI	SALES_SAT
111	222	01-OCT-00	100	200	300	400	500	600	700
222	333	08-OCT-00	200	300	400	500	600	700	800
333	444	15-OCT-00	300	400	500	600	700	800	900

In your data warehouse, you would want to store the records in a more typical relational form in a fact table `sales` of the `Sales History` sample schema:

```
prod_id, cust_id, time_id, amount_sold
```

NOTE

A number of constraints on the `sales` table have been disabled for purposes of this example, because the example ignores a number of table columns for the sake of brevity.

Thus, you need to build a transformation such that each record in the input stream must be converted into seven records for the data warehouse's `sales` table. This operation is commonly referred to as **pivoting**, and Oracle offers several ways to do this.

The result of the previous example will resemble the following:

```
SELECT prod_id, cust_id, time_id, amount_sold FROM sales;

   PROD_ID    CUST_ID   TIME_ID     AMOUNT_SOLD
---------- ---------- ----------- -----------
       111        222  01-OCT-00          100
       111        222  02-OCT-00          200
       111        222  03-OCT-00          300
       111        222  04-OCT-00          400
       111        222  05-OCT-00          500
       111        222  06-OCT-00          600
       111        222  07-OCT-00          700
       222        333  08-OCT-00          200
       222        333  09-OCT-00          300
       222        333  10-OCT-00          400
       222        333  11-OCT-00          500
       222        333  12-OCT-00          600
       222        333  13-OCT-00          700
       222        333  14-OCT-00          800
       333        444  15-OCT-00          300
       333        444  16-OCT-00          400
       333        444  17-OCT-00          500
       333        444  18-OCT-00          600
       333        444  19-OCT-00          700
       333        444  20-OCT-00          800
       333        444  21-OCT-00          900
```

Examples of Pre-Oracle9i Pivoting

The pre-Oracle9*i* way of pivoting involved using CTAS (or parallel `INSERT AS SELECT`) or PL/SQL is shown in this section.

Example 5.14 : Pre-Oracle9i Pivoting Using a CTAS Statement

```
CREATE table temp_sales_step2 NOLOGGING PARALLEL AS
  SELECT product_id, customer_id, time_id, amount_sold
  FROM
   (SELECT product_id, customer_id, weekly_start_date, time_id,
        sales_sun amount_sold FROM sales_input_table
   UNION ALL
    SELECT product_id, customer_id, weekly_start_date+1, time_id,
        sales_mon amount_sold FROM sales_input_table
```

```
UNION ALL
SELECT product_id, cust_id, weekly_start_date+2, time_id,
       sales_tue amount_sold FROM sales_input_table
UNION ALL
SELECT product_id, customer_id, weekly_start_date+3, time_id,
       sales_web amount_sold FROM sales_input_table
UNION ALL
SELECT product_id, customer_id, weekly_start_date+4, time_id,
       sales_thu amount_sold FROM sales_input_table
UNION ALL
SELECT product_id, customer_id, weekly_start_date+5, time_id,
       sales_fri amount_sold FROM sales_input_table
UNION ALL
SELECT product_id, customer_id, weekly_start_date+6, time_id,
       sales_sat amount_sold FROM sales_input_table);
```

Like all CTAS operations, this operation can be fully parallelized. However, the CTAS approach also requires seven separate scans of the data, one for each day of the week. Even with parallelism, the CTAS approach can be time-consuming.

Example 5.15 : Pre-Oracle9i Pivoting Using PL/SQL

PL/SQL offers an alternative implementation. A basic PL/SQL function to implement a pivoting operation is shown in the following statement:

```
DECLARE
   CURSOR c1 is
      SELECT product_id, customer_id, weekly_start_date, sales_sun,
      sales_mon, sales_tue, sales_wed, sales_thu, sales_fri, sales_sat
      FROM sales_input_table;
BEGIN
   FOR crec IN c1 LOOP
      INSERT INTO sales (prod_id, cust_id, time_id, amount_sold)
      VALUES (crec.product_id, crec.customer_id, crec.weekly_start_date,
             crec.sales_sun );
      INSERT INTO sales (prod_id, cust_id, time_id, amount_sold)
      VALUES (crec.product_id, crec.customer_id, crec.weekly_start_date+1,
             crec.sales_mon );
      INSERT INTO sales (prod_id, cust_id, time_id, amount_sold)
      VALUES (crec.product_id, crec.customer_id, crec.weekly_start_date+2,
              crec.sales_tue );
      INSERT INTO sales (prod_id, cust_id, time_id, amount_sold)
      VALUES (crec.product_id, crec.customer_id, crec.weekly_start_date+3,
              crec.sales_wed );
      INSERT INTO sales (prod_id, cust_id, time_id, amount_sold)
       VALUES (crec.product_id, crec.customer_id, crec.weekly_start_date+4,
              crec.sales_thu );
       INSERT INTO sales (prod_id, cust_id, time_id, amount_sold)
       VALUES (crec.product_id, crec.customer_id, crec.weekly_start_date+5,
              crec.sales_fri );
       INSERT INTO sales (prod_id, cust_id, time_id, amount_sold)
       VALUES (crec.product_id, crec.customer_id, crec.weekly_start_date+6,
              crec.sales_sat );
   END LOOP;
   COMMIT;
END;
```

This PL/SQL procedure can be modified to provide even better performance. Array inserts can accelerate the insertion phase of the procedure. Further performance can be gained by parallelizing this transformation operation, particularly if the `temp_sales_step1` table is partitioned, using techniques similar to the parallelization of data unloading described in Chapter 11, "Extraction in Data Warehouses". The primary advantage of this PL/SQL procedure over a CTAS approach is that it requires only a single scan of the data.

Example of Oracle9i Pivoting

Oracle9*i* offers a faster way of pivoting your data by using a multitable insert.

The following example uses the multitable insert syntax to insert into the demo table `sh.sales` some data from an input table with a different structure. The multitable insert statement looks like this:

```
INSERT ALL
      INTO sales (prod_id, cust_id, time_id, amount_sold)
      VALUES (product_id, customer_id, weekly_start_date, sales_sun)
      INTO sales (prod_id, cust_id, time_id, amount_sold)
      VALUES (product_id, customer_id, weekly_start_date+1, sales_mon)
      INTO sales (prod_id, cust_id, time_id, amount_sold)
      VALUES (product_id, customer_id, weekly_start_date+2, sales_tue)
      INTO sales (prod_id, cust_id, time_id, amount_sold)
      VALUES (product_id, customer_id, weekly_start_date+3, sales_wed)
      INTO sales (prod_id, cust_id, time_id, amount_sold)
      VALUES (product_id, customer_id, weekly_start_date+4, sales_thu)
      INTO sales (prod_id, cust_id, time_id, amount_sold)
      VALUES (product_id, customer_id, weekly_start_date+5, sales_fri)
      INTO sales (prod_id, cust_id, time_id, amount_sold)
      VALUES (product_id, customer_id, weekly_start_date+6, sales_sat)
SELECT product_id, customer_id, weekly_start_date, sales_sun,
      sales_mon, sales_tue, sales_wed, sales_thu, sales_fri, sales_sat
FROM sales_input_table;
```

This statement only scans the source table once and then inserts the appropriate.

❑❑❑

6 EXTRACTION, TRANSFORMATION AND LOADING

OVERVIEW OF ETL

You need to load your data warehouse regularly so that it can serve its purpose of facilitating business analysis. To do this, data from one or more operational systems needs to be extracted and copied into the warehouse. The process of extracting data from source systems and bringing it into the data warehouse is commonly called **ETL,** which stands for extraction, transformation, and loading. The acronym ETL is perhaps too simplistic, because it omits the transportation phase and implies that each of the other phases of the process is distinct. We refer to the entire process, including data loading, as ETL. You should understand that ETL refers to a broad process, and not three well-defined steps.

The methodology and tasks of ETL have been well known for many years, and are not necessarily unique to data warehouse environments: a wide variety of proprietary applications and database systems are the IT backbone of any enterprise. Data has to be shared between applications or systems, trying to integrate them, giving at least two applications the same picture of the world. This data sharing was mostly addressed by mechanisms similar to what we now call ETL.

Data warehouse environments face the same challenge with the additional burden that they not only have to exchange but to integrate, rearrange and consolidate data over many systems, thereby providing a new unified information base for business intelligence. Additionally, the data volume in data warehouse environments tends to be very large.

What happens during the ETL process? During extraction, the desired data is identified and extracted from many different sources, including database systems and applications. Very often, it is not possible to identify the specific subset of interest, therefore more data than necessary has to be extracted, so the identification of the relevant data will be done at a later point in time. Depending on the source system's capabilities (for example, operating system resources), some transformations may take place during this extraction process. The size of the extracted data varies from hundreds of kilobytes up to gigabytes, depending on the source system and the business situation. The same is true for the time delta between two (logically) identical extractions: the time span may vary between days/hours and minutes to near real-time. Web server log files for example can easily become hundreds of megabytes in a very short period of time.

After extracting data, it has to be physically transported to the target system or an intermediate system for further processing. Depending on the chosen way of transportation, some transformations can be done during this process, too. For example, an SQL statement which directly accesses a remote target through a gateway can concatenate two columns as part of the `SELECT` statement.

The emphasis in many of the examples in this section is scalability. Many long-time users of Oracle are experts in programming complex data transformation logic using PL/SQL. These chapters suggest alternatives for many such data manipulation operations, with a particular emphasis on implementations that take advantage of Oracle's new SQL functionality, especially for ETL and the parallel query infrastructure.

ETL TOOLS

Designing and maintaining the ETL process is often considered one of the most difficult and resource-intensive portions of a data warehouse project. Many data warehousing projects use ETL tools to manage this process. Oracle Warehouse Builder (OWB), for example, provides ETL capabilities and takes advantage of inherent database abilities. Other data warehouse builders create their own ETL tools and processes, either inside or outside the database.

Besides the support of extraction, transformation, and loading, there are some other tasks that are important for a successful ETL implementation as part of the daily operations of the data warehouse and its support for further enhancements. Besides the support for designing a data warehouse and the data flow, these tasks are typically addressed by ETL tools such as OWB.

Oracle9*i* is not an ETL tool and does not provide a complete solution for ETL. However, Oracle9*i* does provide a rich set of capabilities that can be used by both ETL tools and customized ETL solutions. Oracle9*i* offers techniques for transporting data between Oracle databases, for transforming large volumes of data, and for quickly loading new data into a data warehouse.

Daily Operations

The successive loads and transformations must be scheduled and processed in a specific order. Depending on the success or failure of the operation or parts of it, the result must be tracked and subsequent, alternative processes might be started. The control of the progress as well as the definition of a business workflow of the operations are typically addressed by ETL tools such as OWB.

Evolution of the Data Warehouse

As the data warehouse is a living IT system, sources and targets might change. Those changes must be maintained and tracked through the lifespan of the system without overwriting or deleting the old ETL process flow information. To build and keep a level of trust about the information in the warehouse, the process flow of each individual record in the warehouse can be reconstructed at any point in time in the future in an ideal case.

OVERVIEW OF EXTRACTION IN DATA WAREHOUSES

Extraction is the operation of extracting data from a source system for further use in a data warehouse environment. This is the first step of the ETL process. After the extraction, this data can be transformed and loaded into the data warehouse.

The source systems for a data warehouse are typically transaction processing applications. For example, one of the source systems for a sales analysis data warehouse might be an order entry system that records all of the current order activities.

Designing and creating the extraction process is often one of the most time-consuming tasks in the ETL process and, indeed, in the entire data warehousing process. The source systems might be very complex and poorly documented, and thus determining which data needs to be extracted can be difficult. The data has to be extracted normally not only once, but several times in a periodic manner to supply all changed data to the warehouse and keep it up-to-date. Moreover, the source system typically cannot be modified, nor can its performance or availability be adjusted, to accommodate the needs of the data warehouse extraction process.

These are important considerations for extraction and ETL in general. This chapter, however, focuses on the technical considerations of having different kinds of sources and extraction methods. It assumes that the data warehouse team has already identified the data that will be extracted, and discusses common techniques used for extracting data from source databases.

Designing this process means making decisions about the following two main aspects:

- Which extraction method do I choose?

  This influences the source system, the transportation process, and the time needed for refreshing the warehouse.

- How do I provide the extracted data for further processing?

  This influences the transportation method, and the need for cleaning and transforming the data.

INTRODUCTION TO EXTRACTION METHODS IN DATA WAREHOUSES

The extraction method you should choose is highly dependent on the source system and also from the business needs in the target data warehouse environment. Very often, there's no possibility to add additional logic to the source systems to enhance an incremental extraction of data due to the performance or the increased workload of these systems. Sometimes even the customer is not allowed to add anything to an out-of-the-box application system.

The estimated amount of the data to be extracted and the stage in the ETL process (initial load or maintenance of data) may also impact the decision of how to extract, from a logical and a physical perspective. Basically, you have to decide how to extract data logically and physically.

Logical Extraction Methods

There are two kinds of logical extraction:

- Full extraction
- Incremental extraction.

Full Extraction

The data is extracted completely from the source system. Since this extraction reflects all the data currently available on the source system, there's no need to keep track of changes to the data source since the last successful extraction. The source data will be provided as-is and no additional logical information (for example, timestamps) is necessary on the source site. An example for a full extraction may be an export file of a distinct table or a remote SQL statement scanning the complete source table.

Incremental Extraction

At a specific point in time, only the data that has changed since a well-defined event back in history will be extracted. This event may be the last time of extraction or a more complex business event like the last booking day of a fiscal period. To identify this delta change there must be a possibility to identify all the changed information since this specific time event. This information can be either provided by the source data itself like an application column, reflecting the last-changed timestamp or a change table where an appropriate additional mechanism keeps track of the changes besides the originating transactions. In most cases, using the latter method means adding extraction logic to the source system.

Many data warehouses do not use any change-capture techniques as part of the extraction process. Instead, entire tables from the source systems are extracted to the data warehouse or staging area, and these tables are compared with a previous extract from the source system to identify the changed data. This approach may not have significant impact on the source systems, but it clearly can place a considerable burden on the data warehouse processes, particularly if the data volumes are large.

Oracle's Change Data Capture mechanism can extract and maintain such delta information.

Physical Extraction Methods

Depending on the chosen logical extraction method and the capabilities and restrictions on the source side, the extracted data can be physically extracted by two mechanisms. The data can either be extracted online from the source system or from an offline structure. Such an offline structure might already exist or it might be generated by an extraction routine.

There are the following methods of physical extraction:

- Online extraction
- Offline extraction.

Online Extraction

The data is extracted directly from the source system itself. The extraction process can connect directly to the source system to access the source tables themselves or to an intermediate system that stores the data in a preconfigured manner (for example, snapshot logs or change tables). Note that the intermediate system is not necessarily physically different from the source system.

With online extractions, you need to consider whether the distributed transactions are using original source objects or prepared source objects.

Offline Extraction

The data is not extracted directly from the source system but is staged explicitly outside the original source system. The data already has an existing structure (for example, redo logs, archive logs or transportable tablespaces) or was created by an extraction routine.

You should consider the following structures:

- Flat files
  Data in a defined, generic format. Additional information about the source object is necessary for further processing.
- Dump files
  Oracle-specific format. Information about the containing objects is included.
- Redo and archive logs
  Information is in a special, additional dump file.
- Transportable tablespaces
  A powerful way to extract and move large volumes of data between Oracle databases. A more detailed example of using this feature to extract and transport data is provided later in this chapter . Oracle Corporation recommends that you use transportable tablespaces whenever possible, because they can provide considerable advantages in performance and manageability over other extraction techniques.

Change Data Capture

An important consideration for extraction is incremental extraction, also called Change Data Capture. If a data warehouse extracts data from an operational system on a nightly basis, then the data warehouse requires only the data that has changed since the last extraction (that is, the data that has been modified in the past 24 hours).

When it is possible to efficiently identify and extract only the most recently changed data, the extraction process (as well as all downstream operations in the ETL process) can be much more efficient, because it must extract a much smaller volume of data. Unfortunately, for many source systems, identifying the recently modified data may be difficult or intrusive to the operation of the system. Change Data Capture is typically the most challenging technical issue in data extraction.

Because change data capture is often desirable as part of the extraction process and it might not be possible to use Oracle's Change Data Capture mechanism, this section describes several techniques for implementing a self-developed change capture on Oracle source systems:

- Timestamps
- Partitioning
- Triggers.

These techniques are based upon the characteristics of the source systems, or may require modifications to the source systems. Thus, each of these techniques must be carefully evaluated by the owners of the source system prior to implementation.

Each of these techniques can work in conjunction with the data extraction technique discussed previously. For example, timestamps can be used whether the data is being unloaded to a file or accessed through a distributed query.

Timestamps

The tables in some operational systems have timestamp columns. The timestamp specifies the time and date that a given row was last modified. If the tables in an operational system have columns containing timestamps, then the latest data can easily be identified using the timestamp columns. For example, the following query might be useful for extracting today's data from an `orders` table:

```
SELECT * FROM orders WHERE TRUNC(CAST(order_date AS date),'dd') = TO_
DATE(SYSDATE,'dd-mon-yyyy');
```

If the timestamp information is not available in an operational source system, you will not always be able to modify the system to include timestamps. Such modification would require, first, modifying the operational system's tables to include a new timestamp column and then creating a trigger to update the timestamp column following every operation that modifies a given row.

Partitioning

Some source systems might use Oracle range partitioning, such that the source tables are partitioned along a date key, which allows for easy identification of new data. For example, if you are extracting from an `orders` table, and the `orders` table is partitioned by week, then it is easy to identify the current week's data.

Triggers

Triggers can be created in operational systems to keep track of recently updated records. They can then be used in conjunction with timestamp columns to identify the exact time and date when a given row was last modified. You do this by creating a trigger on each source table that requires change data capture. Following each DML statement that is executed on the source table, this trigger updates the timestamp column with the current time. Thus, the timestamp column provides the exact time and date when a given row was last modified.

A similar internalized trigger-based technique is used for Oracle materialized view logs. These logs are used by materialized views to identify changed data, and these logs are accessible to end users. A materialized view log can be created on each source table requiring change data capture. Then, whenever any modifications are made to the source table, a record is inserted into the materialized view log indicating which rows were modified. If you want to use a trigger-based mechanism, use change data capture.

Materialized view logs rely on triggers, but they provide an advantage in that the creation and maintenance of this change-data system is largely managed by Oracle.

However, Oracle recommends the usage of synchronous Change Data Capture for trigger based change capture, since CDC provides an externalized interface for accessing the change information and provides a framework for maintaining the distribution of this information to various clients

Trigger-based techniques affect performance on the source systems, and this impact should be carefully considered prior to implementation on a production source system.

DATA WAREHOUSING EXTRACTION EXAMPLES

You can extract data in two ways:

- Extraction using data files
- Extraction via distributed operations

Extraction Using Data Files

Most database systems provide mechanisms for exporting or unloading data from the internal database format into flat files. Extracts from mainframe systems often use COBOL programs, but many databases, as well as third-party software vendors, provide export or unload utilities.

Data extraction does not necessarily mean that entire database structures are unloaded in flat files. In many cases, it may be appropriate to unload entire database tables or objects. In other cases, it may be more appropriate to unload only a subset of a given table such as the changes on the source system since the last extraction or the results of joining multiple tables together. Different extraction techniques vary in their capabilities to support these two scenarios.

When the source system is an Oracle database, several alternatives are available for extracting data into files:

- Extracting into flat files using SQL*Plus
- Extracting into flat files using OCI or Pro*C Programs
- Exporting into Oracle export files using Oracle's export utility.

Extracting into Flat Files Using SQL*Plus

The most basic technique for extracting data is to execute an SQL query in SQL*Plus and direct the output of the query to a file. For example, to extract a flat file, `country_city.log`, with the pipe sign as delimiter between column values, containing a list of the cities in the US in the tables countries and customers, the following SQL script could be run:

```
SET echo off SET pagesize 0
SPOOL country_city.log
SELECT distinct t1.country_name ||'|'|| t2.cust_city
FROM countries t1, customers t2
WHERE t1.country_id = t2.country_id
AND t1.country_name= 'United States of America';
SPOOL off
```

The exact format of the output file can be specified by using SQL*Plus system variables.

This extraction technique offers the advantage of being able to extract the output of any SQL statement. The example previously extracts the results of a join.

This extraction technique can be parallelized by initiating multiple, concurrent SQL*Plus sessions, each session running a separate query representing a different portion of the data to be extracted. For example, suppose that you wish to extract data from an `orders` table, and that the `orders` table has been range partitioned by month, with partitions `orders_jan1998`, `orders_feb1998`, and so on. To extract a single year of data from the `orders` table, you could initiate 12 concurrent SQL*Plus sessions, each extracting a single partition. The SQL script for one such session could be:

```
SPOOL order_jan.dat
SELECT * FROM orders PARTITION (orders_jan1998);
SPOOL OFF
```

These 12 SQL*Plus processes would concurrently spool data to 12 separate files. You can then concatenate them if necessary (using operating system utilities) following the extraction. If you are planning to use SQL*Loader for loading into the target, these 12 files can be used as is for a parallel load with 12 SQL*Loader sessions

Even if the `orders` table is not partitioned, it is still possible to parallelize the extraction either based on logical or physical criteria. The logical method is based on logical ranges of column values, for example:

```
SELECT ... WHERE order_date
BETWEEN TO_DATE('01-JAN-99') AND TO_DATE('31-JAN-99');
```

The physical method is based on a range of values. By viewing the data dictionary, it is possible to identify the Oracle data blocks that make up the `orders` table. Using this information, you could then derive a set of rowid-range queries for extracting data from the `orders` table:

```
SELECT * FROM orders WHERE rowid BETWEEN value1 and value2;
```

Parallelizing the extraction of complex SQL queries is sometimes possible, although the process of breaking a single complex query into multiple components can be challenging. In particular, the coordination of independent processes to guarantee a globally consistent view can be difficult.

NOTE *All parallel techniques can use considerably more CPU and I/O resources on the source system, and the impact on the source system should be evaluated before parallelizing any extraction technique.*

Extracting into Flat Files Using OCI or Pro*C Programs

OCI programs (or other programs using Oracle call interfaces, such as Pro*C programs), can also be used to extract data. These techniques typically provide improved performance over the SQL*Plus approach, although they also require additional programming. Like the SQL*Plus approach, an OCI program can extract the results of any SQL query. Furthermore, the parallelization techniques described for the SQL*Plus approach can be readily applied to OCI programs as well.

When using OCI or SQL*Plus for extraction, you need additional information besides the data itself. At minimum, you need information about the extracted columns. It is also helpful to know the extraction format, which might be the separator between distinct columns.

Exporting into Oracle Export Files Using Oracle's Export Utility

Oracle's export utility allows tables (including data) to be exported into Oracle export files. Unlike the SQL*Plus and OCI approaches, which describe the extraction of the results of a SQL statement, Export provides a mechanism for extracting database objects. Thus, export differs from the previous approaches in several important ways:

- The export files contain metadata as well as data. An export file contains not only the raw data of a table, but also information on how to re-create the table, potentially including any indexes, constraints, grants, and other attributes associated with that table.
- A single export file may contain a subset of a single object, many database objects, or even an entire schema.
- Export cannot be directly used to export the results of a complex SQL query. Export can be used only to extract subsets of distinct database objects.
- The output of the Export utility must be processed using the Oracle import utility.

Oracle provides a direct-path export, which is quite efficient for extracting data. However, in Oracle8*i*, there is no direct-path import, which should be considered when evaluating the overall performance of an export-based extraction strategy.

Extraction Via Distributed Operations

Using distributed-query technology, one Oracle database can directly query tables located in various different source systems, such as another Oracle database or a legacy system connected with the Oracle gateway technology. Specifically, a data warehouse or staging database can directly access tables and data located in a connected source system. Gateways are another form of distributed-query technology. Gateways allow an Oracle database (such as a data warehouse) to access database tables stored in remote, non-Oracle databases. This is the simplest method for moving data between two Oracle databases because it combines the extraction and transformation into a single step, and requires minimal programming. However, this is not always feasible.

Continuing our example, suppose that you wanted to extract a list of employee names with department names from a source database and store this data into the data warehouse. Using an Oracle Net connection and distributed-query technology, this can be achieved by using a single SQL statement:

```
CREATE TABLE country_city
AS
SELECT distinct t1.country_name, t2.cust_city
FROM countries@source_db t1, customers@source_db t2
WHERE t1.country_id = t2.country_id
AND t1.country_name='United States of America';
```

This statement creates a local table in a data mart, `country_city`, and populates it with data from the `countries` and `customers` tables on the source system.

This technique is ideal for moving small volumes of data. However, the data is transported from the source system to the data warehouse through a single Oracle Net connection. Thus, the scalability of this technique is limited. For larger data volumes, file-based data extraction and transportation techniques are often more scalable and thus more appropriate.

OVERVIEW OF TRANSPORTATION IN DATA WAREHOUSES

Transportation is the operation of moving data from one system to another system. In a data warehouse environment, the most common requirements for transportation are in moving data from:

- A source system to a staging database or a data warehouse database
- A staging database to a data warehouse
- A data warehouse to a data mart.

Transportation is often one of the simpler portions of the ETL process, and can be integrated with other portions of the process.

INTRODUCTION TO TRANSPORTATION MECHANISMS IN DATA WAREHOUSES

You have three basic choices for transporting data in warehouses:

Transportation using flat files

- Transportation through distributed operations
- Transportation using transportable tablespaces.

Transportation Using Flat Files

The most common method for transporting data is by the transfer of flat files, using mechanisms such as FTP or other remote file system access protocols. Data is unloaded or exported from the source system into flat files then transported to the target platform using FTP or similar mechanisms.

Because source systems and data warehouses often use different operating systems and database systems, using flat files is often the simplest way to exchange data between heterogeneous systems with minimal transformations. However, even when transporting data between homogeneous systems, flat files are often the most efficient and most easy-to-manage mechanism for data transfer.

Transportation Through Distributed Operations

Distributed queries, either with or without gateways, can be an effective mechanism for extracting data. These mechanisms also transport the data directly to the target systems, thus providing both extraction and transformation in a single step. Depending on the tolerable impact on time and system resources, these mechanisms can be well suited for both extraction and transformation.

As opposed to flat file transportation, the success or failure of the transportation is recognized immediately with the result of the distributed query or transaction.

Transportation Using Transportable Tablespaces

Oracle8*i* introduced an important mechanism for transporting data: transportable tablespaces. This feature is the fastest way for moving large volumes of data between two Oracle databases.

Previous to Oracle8*i*, the most scalable data transportation mechanisms relied on moving flat files containing raw data. These mechanisms required that data be unloaded or exported into files from the source database, Then, after transportation, these files were loaded or imported into the target database. Transportable tablespaces entirely bypass the unload and reload steps.

Using transportable tablespaces, Oracle data files (containing table data, indexes, and almost every other Oracle database object) can be directly transported from one database to another. Furthermore, like import and export, transportable tablespaces provide a mechanism for transporting metadata in addition to transporting data.

Transportable tablespaces have some notable limitations: source and target systems must be running Oracle8*i* (or higher), must be running the same operating system, must use the same character set, and, prior to Oracle9*i*, must use the same block size. Despite these limitations, transportable tablespaces can be an invaluable data transportation technique in many warehouse environments.

The most common applications of transportable tablespaces in data warehouses are in moving data from a staging database to a data warehouse, or in moving data from a data warehouse to a data mart.

Transportable Tablespaces Example

Suppose that you have a data warehouse containing sales data, and several data marts that are refreshed monthly. Also suppose that you are going to move one month of sales data from the data warehouse to the data mart.

Step 1: Place the Data to be Transported into its own Tablespace

The current month's data must be placed into a separate tablespace in order to be transported. In this example, you have a tablespace `ts_temp_sales`, which will hold a copy of the current month's data. Using the `CREATE TABLE ... AS SELECT` statement, the current month's data can be efficiently copied to this tablespace:

```
CREATE TABLE temp_jan_sales
NOLOGGING
TABLESPACE ts_temp_sales
AS
SELECT * FROM sales
WHERE time_id BETWEEN '31-DEC-1999' AND '01-FEB-2000';
```

Following this operation, the tablespace `ts_temp_sales` is set to read-only:

```
ALTER TABLESPACE ts_temp_sales READ ONLY;
```

A tablespace cannot be transported unless there are no active transactions modifying the tablespace. Setting the tablespace to read-only enforces this.

The tablespace `ts_temp_sales` may be a tablespace that has been especially created to temporarily store data for use by the transportable tablespace features. Following "Step 3: Copy the Datafiles and Export File to the Target System", this tablespace can be set to read/write, and, if desired, the table `temp_jan_sales` can be dropped, or the tablespace can be re-used for other transportations or for other purposes.

In a given transportable tablespace operation, all of the objects in a given tablespace are transported. Although only one table is being transported in this example, the tablespace `ts_temp_sales` could contain multiple tables. For example, perhaps the data mart is refreshed not only with the new month's worth of sales transactions, but also with a new copy of the customer table. Both of these tables could be transported in the same tablespace. Moreover, this tablespace could also contain other database objects such as indexes, which would also be transported.

Additionally, in a given transportable-tablespace operation, multiple tablespaces can be transported at the same time. This makes it easier to move very large volumes of data between databases. Note, however, that the transportable tablespace feature can only transport a set of tablespaces which contain a complete set of database objects without dependencies on other tablespaces. For example, an index cannot be transported without its table, nor can a partition be transported without the rest of the table. You can use the `DBMS_TTS` package to check that a tablespace is transportable.

In this step, we have copied the January sales data into a separate tablespace; however, in some cases, it may be possible to leverage the transportable tablespace feature without even moving data to a separate tablespace. If the sales table has been partitioned by month in the data warehouse and if each partition is in its own tablespace, then it may be possible to directly transport the tablespace containing the January data. Suppose the January partition, `sales_jan2000`, is located in the tablespace `ts_sales_jan2000`. Then the tablespace `ts_sales_jan2000` could potentially be transported, rather than creating a temporary copy of the January sales data in the `ts_temp_sales`.

However, the same conditions must be satisfied in order to transport the tablespace `ts_sales_jan2000` as are required for the specially created tablespace. First, this tablespace must be set to `READ ONLY`. Second, because a single partition of a partitioned table cannot be transported without the remainder of the partitioned table also being transported, it is necessary to exchange the January partition into a separate table (using the `ALTER TABLE` statement) to transport the January data. The `EXCHANGE` operation is very quick, but the January data will no longer be a part of the underlying `sales` table, and thus may be unavailable to users until this data is exchanged back into the `sales` table after the export of the metadata. The January data can be exchanged back into the `sales` table after you complete step 3.

Step 2: Export the Metadata

The export utility is used to export the metadata describing the objects contained in the transported tablespace. For our example scenario, the export command could be:

```
EXP  TRANSPORT_TABLESPACE=y
       TABLESPACES=ts_temp_sales
       FILE=jan_sales.dmp
```

This operation will generate an export file, `jan_sales.dmp`. The export file will be small, because it contains only metadata. In this case, the export file will contain information describing the table `temp_jan_sales`, such as the column names, column datatype, and all other information that the target Oracle database will need in order to access the objects in `ts_temp_sales`.

Step 3: Copy the Datafiles and Export File to the Target System

Copy the data files that make up `ts_temp_sales`, as well as the export file `jan_sales.dmp` to the data mart platform, using any transportation mechanism for flat files.

Once the datafiles have been copied, the tablespace `ts_temp_sales` can be set to `READ WRITE` mode if desired.

Step 4: Import the Metadata

Once the files have been copied to the data mart, the metadata should be imported into the data mart:

```
IMP  TRANSPORT_TABLESPACE=y  DATAFILES='/db/tempjan.f'
      TABLESPACES=ts_temp_sales
      FILE=jan_sales.dmp
```

At this point, the tablespace `ts_temp_sales` and the table `temp_sales_jan` are accessible in the data mart. You can incorporate this new data into the data mart's tables.

You can insert the data from the `temp_sales_jan` table into the data mart's sales table in one of the two ways:

```
INSERT  /*+  APPEND  */  INTO  sales  SELECT  *  FROM  temp_sales_jan;
```

Following this operation, you can delete the `temp_sales_jan` table (and even the entire `ts_temp_sales` tablespace).

Alternatively, if the data mart's sales table is partitioned by month, then the new transported tablespace and the `temp_sales_jan` table can become a permanent part of the data mart. The `temp_sales_jan` table can become a partition of the data mart's sales table:

```
ALTER TABLE sales ADD PARTITION sales_00jan VALUES
   LESS THAN (TO_DATE('01-feb-2000','dd-mon-yyyy'));
```

```
ALTER TABLE sales EXCHANGE PARTITION sales_00jan
  WITH TABLE temp_sales_jan
INCLUDING INDEXES WITH VALIDATION;
```

Other Uses of Transportable Tablespaces

The previous example illustrates a typical scenario for transporting data in a data warehouse. However, transportable tablespaces can be used for many other purposes. In a data warehousing environment, transportable tablespaces should be viewed as a utility (much like Import/Export or SQL*Loader), whose purpose is to move large volumes of data between Oracle databases. When used in conjunction with parallel data movement operations such as the `CREATE TABLE ... AS SELECT` and `INSERT ... AS SELECT` statements, transportable tablespaces provide an important mechanism for quickly transporting data for many purposes.

❑❑❑

7 MAINTAINING THE DATA WAREHOUSE

ETL (Extraction, Transformation and Loading) is done on a scheduled basis to reflect changes made to the original source system. During this step, you physically insert the new, clean data into the production data warehouse schema, and take all of the other steps necessary (such as building indexes, validating constraints, taking backups) to make this new data available to the end users. Once all of this data has been loaded into the data warehouse, the materialized views have to be updated to reflect the latest data.

The partitioning scheme of the data warehouse is often crucial in determining the efficiency of refresh operations in the data warehouse load process. In fact, the load process is often the primary consideration in choosing the partitioning scheme of data warehouse tables and indexes.

The partitioning scheme of the largest data warehouse tables (for example, the fact table in a star schema) should be based upon the loading paradigm of the data warehouse.

Most data warehouses are loaded with new data on a regular schedule. For example, every night, week, or month, new data is brought into the data warehouse. The data being loaded at the end of the week or month typically corresponds to the transactions for the week or month. In this very common scenario, the data warehouse is being loaded by time. This suggests that the data warehouse tables should be partitioned on a date column. In our data warehouse example, suppose the new data is loaded into the `sales` table every month. Furthermore, the `sales` table has been partitioned by month. These steps show how the load process will proceed to add the data for a new month (January 2001) to the table `sales`.

1. Place the new data into a separate table, `sales_01_2001`. This data can be directly loaded into `sales_01_2001` from outside the data warehouse, or this data can be the result of previous data transformation operations that have already occurred in the data warehouse. `sales_01_2001` has the exact same columns, datatypes, and so forth, as the `sales` table. Gather statistics on the `sales_01_2001` table.
2. Create indexes and add constraints on `sales_01_2001`. Again, the indexes and constraints on `sales_01_2001` should be identical to the indexes and constraints on `sales`. Indexes can be built in parallel and should use the `NOLOGGING` and the `COMPUTE`

STATISTICS options. For example:

3. CREATE BITMAP INDEX sales_01_2001_customer_id_bix
4. ON sales_01_2001(customer_id)
5. TABLESPACE sales_idx NOLOGGING PARALLEL 8 COMPUTE STATISTICS;

   Apply all constraints to the sales_01_2001 table that are present on the sales table. This includes referential integrity constraints. A typical constraint would be:

```
ALTER TABLE sales_01_2001 ADD CONSTRAINT sales_customer_id
      REFERENCES customer(customer_id) ENABLE NOVALIDATE;
```

   If the partitioned table sales has a primary or unique key that is enforced with a global index structure, ensure that the constraint on sales_pk_jan01 is validated without the creation of an index structure, as in the following:

```
ALTER TABLE sales_01_2001 ADD CONSTRAINT sales_pk_jan01
PRIMARY KEY (sales_transaction_id) DISABLE VALIDATE;
```

   The creation of the constraint with ENABLE clause would cause the creation of a unique index, which does not match a local index structure of the partitioned table. You must not have any index structure built on the nonpartitioned table to be exchanged for existing global indexes of the partitioned table. The exchange command would fail.

6. Add the sales_01_2001 table to the sales table.

   In order to add this new data to the sales table, we need to do two things. First, we need to add a new partition to the sales table. We will use the ALTER TABLE ... ADD PARTITION statement. This will add an empty partition to the sales table:

```
ALTER TABLE sales ADD PARTITION sales_01_2001
VALUES LESS THAN (TO_DATE('01-FEB-2001', 'DD-MON-YYYY'));
```

   Then, we can add our newly created table to this partition using the EXCHANGE PARTITION operation. This will exchange the new, empty partition with the newly loaded table.

```
ALTER TABLE sales EXCHANGE PARTITION sales_01_2001 WITH TABLE
sales_01_2001
INCLUDING INDEXES WITHOUT VALIDATION UPDATE GLOBAL INDEXES;
```

   The EXCHANGE operation will preserve the indexes and constraints that were already present on the sales_01_2001 table. For unique constraints (such as the unique constraint on sales_transaction_id), you can use the UPDATE GLOBAL INDEXES clause, as shown previously. This will automatically maintain your global index structures as part of the partition maintenance operation and keep them accessible throughout the whole process. If there were only foreign-key constraints, the exchange operation would be instantaneous.

The benefits of this partitioning technique are significant. First, the new data is loaded with minimal resource utilization. The new data is loaded into an entirely separate table, and the index processing and constraint processing are applied only to the new partition. If the sales table was 50 GB and had 12 partitions, then a new month's worth of data contains approximately 4 GB. Only the new month's worth of data needs to be indexed. None of the indexes on the remaining 46 GB of data needs to be modified at all. This partitioning scheme additionally ensures that the load processing time is directly proportional to the amount of new data being loaded, not to the total size of the sales table.

Second, the new data is loaded with minimal impact on concurrent queries. All of the operations associated with data loading are occurring on a separate sales_01_2001 table. Therefore, none of the existing data or indexes of the sales table is affected during this data refresh process. The sales table and its indexes remain entirely untouched throughout this refresh process.

Third, in case of the existence of any global indexes, those are incrementally maintained as part of the exchange command. This maintenance does not affect the availability of the existing global index structures.

The exchange operation can be viewed as a publishing mechanism. Until the data warehouse administrator exchanges the sales_01_2001 table into the sales table, end users cannot see the new data. Once the exchange has occurred, then any end user query accessing the sales table will immediately be able to see the sales_01_2001 data.

Partitioning is useful not only for adding new data but also for removing and archiving data. Many data warehouses maintain a rolling window of data. For example, the data warehouse stores the most recent 36 months of sales data. Just as a new partition can be added to the sales table (as described earlier), an old partition can be quickly (and independently) removed from the sales table. These two benefits (reduced resources utilization and minimal end-user impact) are just as pertinent to removing a partition as they are to adding a partition.

Removing data from a partitioned table does not necessarily mean that the old data is physically deleted from the database. There are two alternatives for removing old data from a partitioned table:

You can physically delete all data from the database by dropping the partition containing the old data, thus freeing the allocated space:

```
ALTER TABLE sales DROP PARTITION sales_01_1998;
```

You can exchange the old partition with an empty table of the same structure; this empty table is created equivalent to step1 and 2 described in the load process. Assuming the new empty table stub is named sales_archive_01_1998, the following SQL statement will 'empty' partition sales_01_1998:

```
ALTER TABLE sales EXCHANGE PARTITION sales_01_1998 WITH TABLE
sales_archive_01_
1998 INCLUDING INDEXES WITHOUT VALIDATION UPDATE GLOBAL INDEXES;
```

Note that the old data is still existent, as the exchanged, nonpartitioned table sales_archive_01_1998.

If the partitioned table was setup in a way that every partition is stored in a separate tablespace, you can archive (or transport) this table using Oracle's transportable tablespace framework before dropping the actual data (the tablespace).

In some situations, you might not want to drop the old data immediately, but keep it as part of the partitioned table; although the data is no longer of main interest, there are still potential queries accessing this old, read-only data. You can use Oracle's data compression to minimize the space usage of the old data. We also assume that at least one compressed partition is already part of the partitioned table.

Refresh Scenarios

A typical scenario might not only need to compress old data, but also to merge several old partitions to reflect the granularity for a later backup of several merged partitions. Let's assume that a backup (partition) granularity is on a quarterly base for any quarter, where the oldest month is more than 36 months behind the most recent month. In this case, we are therefore compressing and merging sales_01_1998, sales_02_1998, and sales_03_1998 into a new, compressed partition sales_q1_1998.

1. Create the new merged partition in parallel another tablespace. The partition will be compressed as part of the MERGE operation:

```
ALTER TABLE sales MERGE PARTITION sales_01_1998, sales_02_1998, sales_03_
1998 INTO PARTITION sales_q1_1998 TABLESPACE archive_q1_1998 COMPRESS
UPDATE
GLOBAL INDEXES PARALLEL 4;
```

2. The partition MERGE operation invalidates the local indexes for the new merged partition. We therefore have to rebuild them:

```
ALTER TABLE sales MODIFY PARTITION sales_1_1998 REBUILD UNUSABLE
LOCAL
INDEXES;
```

Alternatively, you can choose to create the new compressed data segment outside the partitioned table and exchange it back. The performance and the temporary space consumption is identical for both methods:

1. Create an intermediate table to hold the new merged information. The following statement inherits all NOT NULL constraints from the origin table by default:

```
CREATE TABLE sales_q1_1998_out TABLESPACE archive_q1_1998 NOLOGGING
COMPRESS
PARALLEL 4 AS SELECT * FROM sales
WHERE time_id >=  TO_DATE('01-JAN-1998','dd-mon-yyyy')
AND time_id < TO_DATE('01-JUN-1998','dd-mon-yyyy');
```

2. Create the equivalent index structure for table sales_q1_1998_out than for the existing table sales.
3. Prepare the existing table sales for the exchange with the new compressed table sales_q1_1998_out. Because the table to be exchanged contains data actually covered in three partition, we have to 'create one matching partition, having the range boundaries we are looking for. You simply have to drop two of the existing partitions. Note that you have to drop the lower two partitions sales_01_1998 and sales_02_1998; the lower boundary of a range partition is always defined by the upper (exclusive) boundary of the previous partition:

```
ALTER TABLE sales DROP PARTITION sales_01_1998;
ALTER TABLE sales DROP PARTITION sales_02_1998;
```

4. You can now exchange table sales_q1_1998_out with partition sales_03_1998. Unlike what the name of the partition suggests, its boundaries cover Q1-1998.

```
ALTER TABLE sales EXCHANGE PARTITION sales_03_1998
WITH TABLE sales_q1_1998_out INCLUDING INDEXES WITHOUT VALIDATION
UPDATE GLOBAL INDEXES;
```

Both methods apply to slightly different business scenarios: Using the MERGE PARTITION approach invalidates the local index structures for the affected partition, but it keeps all data accessible all the time. Any attempt to access the affected partition through one of the unusable index structures raises an error. The limited availability time is approximately the time for re-creating the local bitmap index structures. In most cases this can be neglected, since this part of the partitioned table shouldn't be touched too often.

The CTAS approach, however, minimizes unavailability of any index structures close to zero, but there is a specific time window, where the partitioned table does not have all the data, because we dropped two partitions. The limited availability time is approximately the time for exchanging the table. Depending on the existence and number of global indexes, this time window varies. Without any existing global indexes, this time window a matter of a fraction to few seconds.

NOTE *Before you add a single or multiple compressed partitions to a partitioned table for the very first time, all local bitmap indexes must be either dropped or marked unusable. After the first compressed partition is added, no additional actions are necessary for all subsequent operations involving compressed partitions. It is irrelevant how the compressed partitions are added to the partitioned table.*

This example is a simplification of the data warehouse rolling window load scenario. Real-world data warehouse refresh characteristics are always more complex. However, the advantages of this rolling window approach are not diminished in more complex scenarios.

Scenarios for Using Partitioning for Refreshing Data Warehouses

This section contains two typical scenarios.

Refresh Scenario 1

Data is loaded daily. However, the data warehouse contains two years of data, so that partitioning by day might not be desired.

Solution: Partition by week or month (as appropriate). Use `INSERT` to add the new data to an existing partition. The `INSERT` operation only affects a single partition, so the benefits described previously remain intact. The `INSERT` operation could occur while the partition remains a part of the table. Inserts into a single partition can be parallelized:

```
INSERT /*+ APPEND*/ INTO sales PARTITION (sales_01_2001)
SELECT * FROM new_sales;
```

The indexes of this `sales` partition will be maintained in parallel as well. An alternative is to use the `EXCHANGE` operation. You can do this by exchanging the `sales_01_2001` partition of the `sales` table and then using an `INSERT` operation. You might prefer this technique when dropping and rebuilding indexes is more efficient than maintaining them.

Refresh Scenario 2

New data feeds, although consisting primarily of data for the most recent day, week, and month, also contain some data from previous time periods.

Solution 1: Use parallel SQL operations (such as `CREATE TABLE ... AS SELECT`) to separate the new data from the data in previous time periods. Process the old data separately using other techniques.

New data feeds are not solely time based. You can also feed new data into a data warehouse with data from multiple operational systems on a business need basis. For example, the sales data from direct channels may come into the data warehouse separately from the data from indirect channels. For business reasons, it may furthermore make sense to keep the direct and indirect data in separate partitions.

Solution 2: Oracle supports composite range list partitioning. The primary partitioning strategy of the sales table could be range partitioning based on `time_id` as shown in the example. However, the subpartitioning is a list based on the channel attribute. Each subpartition can now be loaded independently of each other (for each distinct channel) and added in a rolling window operation as discussed before. The partitioning strategy addresses the business needs in the most optimal manner.

OPTIMIZING DML OPERATIONS DURING REFRESH

You can optimize DML performance through the following techniques:

- Implementing an efficient MERGE operation
- Maintaining referential integrity
- Purging data.

Implementing an Efficient MERGE Operation

Commonly, the data that is extracted from a source system is not simply a list of new records that needs to be inserted into the data warehouse. Instead, this new data set is a combination of new records as well as modified records. For example, suppose that most of data extracted from the OLTP systems will be new sales transactions. These records will be inserted into the warehouse's `sales` table, but some records may reflect modifications of previous transactions, such as returned merchandise or transactions that were incomplete or incorrect when initially loaded into the data warehouse. These records require updates to the `sales` table.

As a typical scenario, suppose that there is a table called `new_sales` that contains both inserts and updates that will be applied to the `sales` table. When designing the entire data warehouse load process, it was determined that the `new_sales` table would contain records with the following semantics:

- If a given `sales_transaction_id` of a record in `new_sales` already exists in `sales`, then update the `sales` table by adding the `sales_dollar_amount` and `sales_quantity_sold` values from the `new_sales` table to the existing row in the `sales` table.
- Otherwise, insert the entire new record from the `new_sales` table into the `sales` table.

This `UPDATE-ELSE-INSERT` operation is often called a merge. A merge can be executed using one SQL statement in Oracle9*i*, though it required two earlier.

Example 7.1 : Merging Prior to Oracle9i

The first SQL statement updates the appropriate rows in the `sales` tables, while the second SQL statement inserts the rows:

```
UPDATE
  (SELECT
   s.sales_quantity_sold AS s_quantity,
   s.sales_dollar_amount AS s_dollar,
   n.sales_quantity_sold AS n_quantity,
   n.sales_dollar_amount AS n_dollar
   FROM sales s, new_sales n
```

```
   WHERE s.sales_transaction_id = n.sales_transaction_id) sales_view
 SET s_quantity = s_quantity + n_quantity, s_dollar = s_dollar + n_dollar;
INSERT INTO sales
SELECT * FROM new_sales s
WHERE NOT EXISTS
(SELECT 'x' FROM FROM sales t
 WHERE s.sales_transaction_id = t.sales_transaction_id);
```

The new, faster way of merging data is illustrated in example 7.2 as follows.

Example 7.2 : MERGE Operation in Oracle9i

```
MERGE INTO sales s
USING new_sales n
ON (s.sales_transaction_id = n.sales_transaction_id)
WHEN MATCHED THEN
UPDATE s_quantity = s_quantity + n_quantity, s_dollar = s_dollar + n_dollar
WHEN NOT MATCHED THEN
INSERT (sales_quantity_sold, sales_dollar_amount)
VALUES (n.sales_quantity_sold, n.sales_dollar_amount);
```

An alternative implementation of upserts is to utilize a PL/SQL package, which successively reads each row of the `new_sales` table and applies if-then logic to either update or insert the new row into the `sales` table. A PL/SQL-based implementation is effective when the `new_sales` table is small, although the SQL approach will often be more efficient for larger data volumes.

Maintaining Referential Integrity

In some data warehousing environments, you might want to insert new data into tables in order to guarantee referential integrity. For example, a data warehouse may derive `sales` from an operational system that retrieves data directly from cash registers. `sales` is refreshed nightly. However, the data for the `product` dimension table may be derived from a separate operational system. The `product` dimension table may only be refreshed once for each week, because the `product` table changes relatively slowly. If a new product was introduced on Monday, then it is possible for that product's `product_id` to appear in the `sales` data of the data warehouse before that `product_id` has been inserted into the data warehouses `product` table.

Although the sales transactions of the new product may be valid, this sales data will not satisfy the referential integrity constraint between the `product` dimension table and the `sales` fact table. Rather than disallow the new sales transactions, you might choose to insert the sales transactions into the `sales` table.

However, you might also wish to maintain the referential integrity relationship between the `sales` and `product` tables. This can be accomplished by inserting new rows into the `product` table as placeholders for the unknown products.

As in previous examples, we assume that the new data for the `sales` table will be staged in a separate table, `new_sales`. Using a single `INSERT` statement (which can be parallelized), the `product` table can be altered to reflect the new products:

```
INSERT INTO PRODUCT_ID
  (SELECT sales_product_id, 'Unknown Product Name', NULL, NULL ...
   FROM new_sales WHERE sales_product_id NOT IN
  (SELECT product_id FROM product));
```

Purging Data

Occasionally, it is necessary to remove large amounts of data from a data warehouse. A very common scenario is the rolling window discussed previously, in which older data is rolled out of the data warehouse to make room for new data.

However, sometimes other data might need to be removed from a data warehouse. Suppose that a retail company has previously sold products from `MS Software`, and that `MS Software` has subsequently gone out of business. The business users of the warehouse may decide that they are no longer interested in seeing any data related to `MS Software`, so this data should be deleted.

One approach to removing a large volume of data is to use parallel delete as shown in the following statement:

```
DELETE FROM sales WHERE sales_product_id IN
  (SELECT product_id
   FROM product WHERE product_category = 'MS Software');
```

This SQL statement will spawn one parallel process for each partition. This approach will be much more efficient than a serial `DELETE` statement, and none of the data in the `sales` table will need to be moved.

However, this approach also has some disadvantages. When removing a large percentage of rows, the `DELETE` statement will leave many empty row-slots in the existing partitions. If new data is being loaded using a rolling window technique (or is being loaded using direct-path `INSERT` or load), then this storage space will not be reclaimed. Moreover, even though the `DELETE` statement is parallelized, there might be more efficient methods. An alternative method is to re-create the entire `sales` table, keeping the data for all product categories except `MS Software`.

```
CREATE TABLE sales2 AS
SELECT * FROM sales, product
WHERE sales.sales_product_id = product.product_id
AND product_category <> 'MS Software'
NOLOGGING PARALLEL (DEGREE 8)
#PARTITION ... ; #create indexes, constraints, and so on
DROP TABLE SALES;
RENAME SALES2 TO SALES;
```

This approach may be more efficient than a parallel delete. However, it is also costly in terms of the amount of disk space, because the `sales` table must effectively be instantiated twice.

An alternative method to utilize less space is to re-create the `sales` table one partition at a time:

```
CREATE TABLE sales_temp AS SELECT * FROM sales WHERE 1=0;
INSERT INTO sales_temp PARTITION (sales_99jan)
SELECT * FROM sales, product
WHERE sales.sales_product_id = product.product_id
AND product_category <> 'MS Software';
<create appropriate indexes and constraints on sales_temp>
ALTER TABLE sales EXCHANGE PARTITION sales_99jan WITH TABLE sales_temp;
```

Continue this process for each partition in the `sales` table.

REFRESHING MATERIALIZED VIEWS

When creating a materialized view, you have the option of specifying whether the refresh occurs ON DEMAND or ON COMMIT. In the case of ON COMMIT, the materialized view is changed every time a transaction commits, which changes data used by the materialized view, thus ensuring that the materialized view always contains the latest data. Alternatively, you can control the time when refresh of the materialized views occurs by specifying ON DEMAND. In this case, the materialized view can only be refreshed by calling one of the procedures in the DBMS_MVIEW package.

DBMS_MVIEW provides three different types of refresh operations.

- DBMS_MVIEW.REFRESH

  Refresh one or more materialized views.
- DBMS_MVIEW.REFRESH_ALL_MVIEWS

  Refresh all materialized views.
- DBMS_MVIEW.REFRESH_DEPENDENT

  Refresh all table-based materialized views that depend on a specified detail table or list of detail tables.

Performing a refresh operation requires temporary space to rebuild the indexes and can require additional space for performing the refresh operation itself. Some sites might prefer not to refresh all of their materialized views at the same time: as soon as some underlying detail data has been updated, all materialized views using this data will become stale. Therefore, if you defer refreshing your materialized views, you can either rely on your chosen rewrite integrity level to determine whether or not a stale materialized view can be used for query rewrite, or you can temporarily disable query rewrite with an ALTER SYSTEM SET QUERY_REWRITE_ENABLED = false statement. After refreshing the materialized views, you can re-enable query rewrite as the default for all sessions in the current database instance by specifying ALTER SYSTEM SET QUERY_REWRITE_ENABLED as true. Refreshing a materialized view automatically updates all of its indexes. In the case of full refresh, this requires temporary sort space to rebuild all indexes during refresh. This is because the full refresh truncates or deletes the table before inserting the new full data volume. If insufficient temporary space is available to rebuild the indexes, then you must explicitly drop each index or mark it UNUSABLE prior to performing the refresh operation.

If you anticipate performing insert, update or delete operations on tables referenced by a materialized view concurrently with the refresh of that materialized view, and that materialized view includes joins and aggregation, Oracle recommends you use ON COMMIT fast refresh rather than ON DEMAND fast refresh.

Complete Refresh

A complete refresh occurs when the materialized view is initially defined as BUILD IMMEDIATE, unless the materialized view references a prebuilt table. For materialized views using BUILD DEFERRED, a complete refresh must be requested before it can be used for the first time. A complete refresh may be requested at any time during the life of any materialized view. The refresh involves reading the detail tables to compute the results for the materialized view. This can be a very time-consuming process, especially if there are huge amounts of data to be read and processed. Therefore, you should always consider the time required to process a complete refresh before requesting it.

However, there are cases when the only refresh method available for an already built materialized view is complete refresh because the materialized view does not satisfy the conditions specified in the following section for a fast refresh.

Fast Refresh

Most data warehouses have periodic incremental updates to their detail data. As described in "Materialized View Schema Design", you can use the SQL*Loader or any bulk load utility to perform incremental loads of detail data. Fast refresh of your materialized views is usually efficient, because instead of having to recompute the entire materialized view, the changes are applied to the existing data. Thus, processing only the changes can result in a very fast refresh time.

ON COMMIT Refresh

A materialized view can be refreshed automatically by using the `ON COMMIT` method. Therefore, whenever a transaction commits which has updated the tables on which a materialized view is defined, those changes will be automatically reflected in the materialized view. The advantage of using this approach is you never have to remember to refresh the materialized view. The only disadvantage is the time required to complete the commit will be slightly longer because of the extra processing involved. However, in a data warehouse, this should not be an issue because there is unlikely to be concurrent processes trying to update the same table.

Manual Refresh Using the DBMS_MVIEW Package

When a materialized view is refreshed `ON DEMAND`, one of three refresh methods can be specified as shown in the following table. You can define a default option during the creation of the materialized view. Table 7.1 details the refresh options.

Table 7.1 ON DEMAND Refresh Methods

Refresh Option	Parameter	Description
`COMPLETE`	C	Refreshes by recalculating the defining query of the materialized view
`FAST`	F	Refreshes by incrementally applying changes to the materialized view
`FORCE`	?	Attempts a fast refresh. If that is not possible, it does a complete refresh

Three refresh procedures are available in the `DBMS_MVIEW` package for performing `ON DEMAND` refresh. Each has its own unique set of parameters.

Refresh Specific Materialized Views with REFRESH

Use the `DBMS_MVIEW.REFRESH` procedure to refresh one or more materialized views. Some parameters are used only for replication, so they are not mentioned here. The required parameters to use this procedure are:

- The comma-delimited list of materialized views to refresh
- The refresh method: F-Fast, ?-Force, C-Complete
- The rollback segment to use
- Refresh after errors (`true` or `false`).

A Boolean parameter. If set to `true`, the `number_of_failures` output parameter will be set to the number of refreshes that failed, and a generic error message will indicate that failures occurred. The alert log for the instance will give details of refresh errors. If set to `false`, the default, then refresh will stop after it encounters the first error, and any remaining materialized views in the list will not be refreshed.

- The following four parameters are used by the replication process. For warehouse refresh, set them to `false, 0,0,0`.
- Atomic refresh (`true` or `false`).

  If set to `TRUE`, then all refreshes are done in one transaction. If set to `FALSE`, then the refresh of each specified materialized view is done in a separate transaction.

For example, to perform a fast refresh on the materialized view `cal_month_sales_mv`, the `DBMS_MVIEW` package would be called as follows:

```
DBMS_MVIEW.REFRESH('CAL_MONTH_SALES_MV', 'F', '', TRUE, FALSE, 0,0,0, FALSE);
```

Multiple materialized views can be refreshed at the same time, and they do not all have to use the same refresh method. To give them different refresh methods, specify multiple method codes in the same order as the list of materialized views (without commas). For example, the following specifies that `cal_month_sales_mv` be completely refreshed and `fweek_pscat_sales_mv` receive a fast refresh.

```
DBMS_MVIEW.REFRESH('CAL_MONTH_SALES_MV, FWEEK_PSCAT_SALES_MV', 'CF', '',
  TRUE, FALSE, 0,0,0, FALSE);
```

If the refresh method is not specified, the default refresh method as specified in the materialized view definition will be used.

Refresh All Materialized Views with REFRESH_ALL_MVIEWS

An alternative to specifying the materialized views to refresh is to use the procedure `DBMS_MVIEW.REFRESH_ALL_MVIEWS`. This procedure refreshes all materialized views. If any of the materialized views fails to refresh, then the number of failures is reported.

The parameters for this procedure are:

- The number of failures (this is an `OUT` variable)
- The refresh method: F-Fast, ?-Force, C-Complete
- Refresh after errors (`true` or `false`)

  A Boolean parameter. If set to `true`, the `number_of_failures` output parameter will be set to the number of refreshes that failed, and a generic error message will indicate that failures occurred. The alert log for the instance will give details of refresh errors. If set to `false`, the default, then refresh will stop after it encounters the first error, and any remaining materialized views in the list will not be refreshed.
- Atomic refresh (`true` or `false`)

  If set to `true`, then all refreshes are done in one transaction. If set to `false`, then the refresh of each specified materialized view is done in a separate transaction.

An example of refreshing all materialized views is:

```
DBMS_MVIEW.REFRESH_ALL_MVIEWS(failures,'C','', TRUE, FALSE);
```

Refresh Dependent Materialized Views with REFRESH_DEPENDENT

The third procedure, DBMS_MVIEW.REFRESH_DEPENDENT, refreshes only those materialized views that depend on a specific table or list of tables. For example, suppose the changes have been received for the orders table but not for customer payments. The refresh dependent procedure can be called to refresh only those materialized views that reference the orders table.

The parameters for this procedure are:

- The number of failures (this is an OUT variable)
- The dependent table
- The refresh method: F-Fast, ?-Force, C-Complete
- The rollback segment to use
- Refresh after errors (true or false)

  A Boolean parameter. If set to true, the number_of_failures output parameter will be set to the number of refreshes that failed, and a generic error message will indicate that failures occurred. The alert log for the instance will give details of refresh errors. If set to false, the default, then refresh will stop after it encounters the first error, and any remaining materialized views in the list will not be refreshed.
- Atomic refresh (true or false)

  If set to TRUE, then all refreshes are done in one transaction. If set to false, then the refresh of each specified materialized view is done in a separate transaction.

To perform a full refresh on all materialized views that reference the customers table, specify:

```
DBMS_MVIEW.REFRESH_DEPENDENT(failures, 'CUSTOMERS', 'C', '', FALSE, FALSE );
```

To obtain the list of materialized views that are directly dependent on a given object (table or materialized view), use the procedure DBMS_MVIEW.GET_MV_DEPENDENCIES to determine the dependent materialized views for a given table, or for deciding the order to refresh nested materialized views.

```
DBMS_MVIEW.GET_MV_DEPENDENCIES(mvlist IN  VARCHAR2, deplist OUT  VARCHAR2)
```

The input to this function is the name or names of the materialized view. The output is a comma separated list of the materialized views that are defined on it. For example, the following statement:

```
GET_MV_DEPENDENCIES("JOHN.SALES_REG, SCOTT.PROD_TIME", deplist)
```

This populates deplist with the list of materialized views defined on the input arguments. For example:

```
deplist <= "JOHN.SUM_SALES_WEST, JOHN.SUM_SALES_EAST, SCOTT.SUM_PROD_MONTH".
```

Using Job Queues for Refresh

Job queues can be used to refresh multiple materialized views in parallel. If queues are not available, fast refresh will sequentially refresh each view in the foreground process. The order in which the materialized views are refreshed cannot be guaranteed. To make queues available, you must set the JOB_QUEUE_PROCESSES parameter. This parameter defines the number of background job queue processes and determines how many materialized views can be refreshed concurrently. This parameter is only effective when atomic_refresh is set to false.

If the process that is executing DBMS_MVIEW.REFRESH is interrupted or the instance is shut down, any refresh jobs that were executing in job queue processes will be requeued and will continue running. To remove these jobs, use the DBMS_JOB.REMOVE procedure.

When Refresh is Possible

Not all materialized views may be fast refreshable. Therefore, use the package DBMS_MVIEW.EXPLAIN_MVIEW to determine what refresh methods are available for a materialized view.

Recommended Initialization Parameters for Parallelism

The following initialization parameters need to be set properly for parallelism to be effective:

- PARALLEL_MAX_SERVERS should be set high enough to take care of parallelism. You need to consider the number of slaves needed for the refresh statement. For example, with a DOP of eight, you need 16 slave processes.
- PGA_AGGREGATE_TARGET should be set for the instance to manage the memory usage for sorts and joins automatically. If the memory parameters are set manually, SORT_AREA_SIZE should be less than HASH_AREA_SIZE.
- OPTIMIZER_MODE should equal all_rows (cost-based optimization).

Remember to analyze all tables and indexes for better cost-based optimization.

Monitoring a Refresh

While a job is running, you can query the V$SESSION_LONGOPS view to tell you the progress of each materialized view being refreshed.

```
SELECT * FROM V$SESSION_LONGOPS;
```

To look at the progress of which jobs are on which queue, use:

```
SELECT * FROM DBA_JOBS_RUNNING;
```

Checking the Status of a Materialized View

Three views are provided for checking the status of a materialized view:

- USER_MVIEWS
- DBA_MVIEWS
- ALL_MVIEWS.

To check if a materialized view is fresh or stale, issue the following statement:

```
SELECT MVIEW_NAME, STALENESS, LAST_REFRESH_TYPE, COMPILE_STATE
FROM USER_MVIEWS ORDER BY MVIEW_NAME;
MVIEW_NAME              STALENESS    LAST_REF    COMPILE_STATE
----------              ---------    --------    -------------
CUST_MTH_SALES_MV       FRESH        FAST        NEEDS_COMPILE
PROD_YR_SALES_MV        FRESH        FAST        VALID
```

If the compile_state column shows NEEDS COMPILE, the other displayed column values cannot be trusted as reflecting the true status. To revalidate the materialized view, issue the following statement:

```
ALTER MATERIALIZED VIEW [materialized_view_name] COMPILE;
```

Then reissue the SELECT statement.

Tips for Refreshing Materialized Views with Aggregates

Following are some guidelines for using the refresh mechanism for materialized views with aggregates.

- For fast refresh, create materialized view logs on all detail tables involved in a materialized view with the ROWID, SEQUENCE and INCLUDING NEW VALUES clauses.

  Include all columns from the table likely to be used in materialized views in the materialized view logs.

  Fast refresh may be possible even if the SEQUENCE option is omitted from the materialized view log. If it can be determined that only inserts or deletes will occur on all the detail tables, then the materialized view log does not require the SEQUENCE clause. However, if updates to multiple tables are likely or required or if the specific update scenarios are unknown, make sure the SEQUENCE clause is included.

- Use Oracle's bulk loader utility or direct-path INSERT (INSERT with the APPEND hint for loads).

  This is a lot more efficient than conventional insert. During loading, disable all constraints and re-enable when finished loading. Note that materialized view logs are required regardless of whether you use direct load or conventional DML.

  Try to optimize the sequence of conventional mixed DML operations, direct-path INSERT and the fast refresh of materialized views. You can use fast refresh with a mixture of conventional DML and direct loads. Fast refresh can perform significant optimizations if it finds that only direct loads have occurred, as illustrated in the following:

  1. Direct-path INSERT (SQL*Loader or INSERT /*+ APPEND */) into the detail table
  2. Refresh materialized view
  3. Conventional mixed DML
  4. Refresh materialized view.

  You can use fast refresh with conventional mixed DML (INSERT, UPDATE, and DELETE) to the detail tables. However, fast refresh will be able to perform significant optimizations in its processing if it detects that only inserts or deletes have been done to the tables, such as:

  - DML INSERT or DELETE to the detail table
  - Refresh materialized views
  - DML update to the detail table
  - Refresh materialized view.

  Even more optimal is the separation of INSERT and DELETE.

  If possible, refresh should be performed after each type of data change (as shown earlier) rather than issuing only one refresh at the end. If that is not possible, restrict the conventional DML to the table to inserts only, to get much better refresh performance. Avoid mixing deletes and direct loads.

Furthermore, for refresh ON COMMIT, Oracle keeps track of the type of DML done in the committed transaction. Therefore, do not perform direct-path INSERT and DML to other tables in the same transaction, as Oracle may not be able to optimize the refresh phase.

For ON COMMIT materialized views, where refreshes automatically occur at the end of each transaction, it may not be possible to isolate the DML statements, in which case keeping the transactions short will help. However, if you plan to make numerous modifications to the detail table, it may be better to perform them in one transaction, so that refresh of the materialized view will be performed just once at commit time rather than after each update.

- Oracle recommends partitioning the tables because it enables you to use:
  - Parallel DML

    For large loads or refresh, enabling parallel DML will help shorten the length of time for the operation.
  - Partition Change Tracking (PCT) fast refresh

    You can refresh your materialized views fast after partition maintenance operations on the detail tables. "Partition Change Tracking" for details on enabling PCT for materialized views.
- Partitioning the materialized view will also help refresh performance as refresh can update the materialized view using parallel DML. For example, assume that the detail tables and materialized view are partitioned and have a parallel clause. The following sequence would enable Oracle to parallelize the refresh of the materialized view.

  1. Bulk load into the detail table
  2. Enable parallel DML with an ALTER SESSION ENABLE PARALLEL DML statement
  3. Refresh the materialized view.
- For a complete refresh using DBMS_MVIEW.REFRESH, set the parameter atomic to false. This will use TRUNCATE to delete existing rows in the materialized view, which is faster than a delete.
- When using DBMS_MVIEW.REFRESH with JOB_QUEUES, remember to set atomic to false. Otherwise, JOB_QUEUES will not get used. Set the number of job queue processes greater than the number of processors.

  If job queues are enabled and there are many materialized views to refresh, it is faster to refresh all of them in a single command than to call them individually.
- Use REFRESH FORCE to ensure getting a refreshed materialized view that can definitely be used for query rewrite. If a fast refresh cannot be done, a complete refresh will be performed.

Tips for Refreshing Materialized Views Without Aggregates

If a materialized view contains joins but no aggregates, then having an index on each of the join column rowids in the detail table will enhance refresh performance greatly, because this type of materialized view tends to be much larger than materialized views containing aggregates. For example, consider the following materialized view:

```
CREATE MATERIALIZED VIEW  detail_fact_mv
BUILD IMMEDIATE
```

```
AS
SELECT
   s.rowid "sales_rid", t.rowid "times_rid", c.rowid "cust_rid",
   c.cust_state_province, t.week_ending_day, s.amount_sold
FROM sales s, times t, customers c
WHERE s.time_id = t.time_id AND
      s.cust_id = c.cust_id;
```

Indexes should be created on columns sales_rid, times_rid and cust_rid. Partitioning is highly recommended, as is enabling parallel DML in the session before invoking refresh, because it will greatly enhance refresh performance.

This type of materialized view can also be fast refreshed if DML is performed on the detail table. It is recommended that the same procedure be applied to this type of materialized view as for a single table aggregate. That is, perform one type of change (direct-path INSERT or DML) and then refresh the materialized view. This is because Oracle can perform significant optimizations if it detects that only one type of change has been done.

Also, Oracle recommends that the refresh be invoked after each table is loaded, rather than load all the tables and then perform the refresh.

For refresh ON COMMIT, Oracle keeps track of the type of DML done in the committed transaction. Oracle therefore recommends that you do not perform direct-path and conventional DML to other tables in the same transaction because Oracle may not be able to optimize the refresh phase. For example, the following is not recommended:

1. Direct load new data into the fact table
2. DML into the store table
3. Commit.

Also, try not to mix different types of conventional DML statements if possible. This would again prevent using various optimizations during fast refresh. For example, try to avoid the following:

1. Insert into the fact table
2. Delete from the fact table
3. Commit.

If many updates are needed, try to group them all into one transaction because refresh will be performed just once at commit time, rather than after each update.

When you use the DBMS_MVIEW package to refresh a number of materialized views containing only joins with the ATOMIC parameter set to true, if you disable parallel DML, refresh performance may degrade.

In a data warehousing environment, assuming that the materialized view has a parallel clause, the following sequence of steps is recommended:

1. Bulk load into the fact table
2. Enable parallel DML
3. An ALTER SESSION ENABLE PARALLEL DML statement
4. Refresh the materialized view.

Tips for Refreshing Nested Materialized Views

All underlying objects are treated as ordinary tables when refreshing materialized views. If the ON COMMIT refresh option is specified, then all the materialized views are refreshed in the appropriate order at commit time.

Assume all the materialized views are defined for ON COMMIT refresh. If table sales changes, then, at commit time, join_sales_cust_time would refresh first, and then sum_sales_cust_time and join_sales_cust_time_prod. No specific order would apply for sum_sales_cust_time and join_sales_cust_time_prod as they do not have any dependencies between them.

In other words, Oracle builds a partially ordered set of materialized views and refreshes them such that, after the successful completion of the refresh, all the materialized views are fresh. The status of the materialized views can be checked by querying the appropriate USER_, DBA_, or ALL_MVIEWS view.

If any of the materialized views are defined as ON DEMAND refresh (irrespective of whether the refresh method is FAST, FORCE, or COMPLETE), you will need to refresh them in the correct order (taking into account the dependencies between the materialized views) because the nested materialized view will be refreshed with respect to the current contents of the other materialized views (whether fresh or not).

If a refresh fails during commit time, the list of materialized views that has not been refreshed is written to the alert log, and you must manually refresh them along with all their dependent materialized views.

Use the same DBMS_MVIEW procedures on nested materialized views that you use on regular materialized views.

These procedures have the following behavior when used with nested materialized views:

- If REFRESH is applied to a materialized view my_mv that is built on other materialized views, then my_mv will be refreshed with respect to the current contents of the other materialized views (that is, they will not be made fresh first).
- If REFRESH_DEPENDENT is applied to materialized view my_mv, then only materialized views that directly depend on my_mv will be refreshed (that is, a materialized view that depends on a materialized view that depends on my_mv will not be refreshed).
- If REFRESH_ALL_MVIEWS is used, the order in which the materialized views will be refreshed is not guaranteed.
- GET_MV_DEPENDENCIES provides a list of the immediate (or direct) materialized view dependencies for an object.

Tips for Fast Refresh with UNION ALL

You can use fast refresh for materialized views that use the UNION ALL operator by providing a maintenance column in the definition of the materialized view. For example, a materialized view with a UNION ALL operator such as the following:

```
CREATE MATERIALIZED VIEW union_all_mv
AS
SELECT x.rowid AS r1, y.rowid AS r2, a, b, c
FROM x, y
WHERE x.a = y.b
```

```
UNION ALL
SELECT p.rowid, r.rowid, a, c, d
WHERE p.a = r.y;
```

This can be made fast refreshable as follows:

```
CREATE MATERIALIZED VIEW fast_rf_union_all_mv
AS
SELECT x.rowid AS r1, y.rowid AS r2, a, b, c, 1 AS MARKER
FROM x, y
WHERE x.a = y.b
UNION ALL
SELECT p.rowid, r.rowid, a, c, d, 2 AS MARKER
FROM p, r
WHERE p.a = r.y;
```

The form of the maintenance marker column must be: `numeric_or_string_literal AS column_alias`, where each `UNION ALL` member has a distinct value for `numeric_or_string_literal`.

Tips After Refreshing Materialized Views

After you have performed a load or incremental load and rebuilt the detail table indexes, you need to re-enable integrity constraints (if any) and refresh the materialized views and materialized view indexes that are derived from that detail data. In a data warehouse environment, referential integrity constraints are normally enabled with the `NOVALIDATE` or `RELY` options. An important decision to make before performing a refresh operation is whether the refresh needs to be recoverable. Because materialized view data is redundant and can always be reconstructed from the detail tables, it might be preferable to disable logging on the materialized view. To disable logging and run incremental refresh non-recoverably, use the `ALTER MATERIALIZED VIEW ... NOLOGGING` statement prior to refreshing.

If the materialized view is being refreshed using the `ON COMMIT` method, then, following refresh operations, consult the alert log `alert_`*SID*`.log` and the trace file `ora_`*SID*`_number.trc` to check that no errors have occurred.

USING MATERIALIZED VIEWS WITH PARTITIONED TABLES

A major maintenance component of a data warehouse is synchronizing (refreshing) the materialized views when the detail data changes. Partitioning the underlying detail tables can reduce the amount of time taken to perform the refresh task. This is possible because partitioning enables refresh to use parallel DML to update the materialized view. Also, it enables the use of Partition Change Tracking.

Fast Refresh with Partition Change Tracking

In a data warehouse, changes to the detail tables can often entail partition maintenance operations, such as `DROP`, `EXCHANGE`, `MERGE`, and `ADD PARTITION`. To maintain the materialized view after such operations in Oracle8*i* required the use of manual maintenance (see also `CONSIDER FRESH`) or complete refresh. Oracle9*i* introduces an addition to fast refresh known as Partition Change Tracking (PCT) refresh.

For PCT to be available, the detail tables must be partitioned. The partitioning of the materialized view itself has no bearing on this feature. If PCT refresh is possible, it will occur automatically and no user intervention is required in order for it to occur.

The following examples will illustrate the use of this feature. In "PCT Fast Refresh Scenario 1", assume `sales` is a partitioned table using the `time_id` column and `products` is partitioned by the `prod_category` column. The table `times` is not a partitioned table.

PCT Fast Refresh Scenario 1

1. All detail tables must have materialized view logs. To avoid redundancy, only the materialized view log for the `sales` table is provided in the following:

```
CREATE materialized view LOG on SALES
WITH ROWID, SEQUENCE
   (prod_id, time_id, quantity_sold, amount_sold)
INCLUDING NEW VALUES;
```

2. The following materialized view satisfies requirements for PCT.

```
CREATE MATERIALIZED VIEW cust_mth_sales_mv
BUILD IMMEDIATE
REFRESH FAST ON DEMAND
  ENABLE QUERY REWRITE
  AS
  SELECT s.time_id, s.prod_id, SUM(s.quantity_sold), SUM(s.amount_sold),
         p.prod_name, t.calendar_month_name, COUNT(*),
         COUNT(s.quantity_sold), COUNT(s.amount_sold)
  FROM sales s, products p, times t
  WHERE  s.time_id = t.time_id AND
         s.prod_id = p.prod_id
  GROUP BY t.calendar_month_name, s.prod_id, p.prod_name, s.time_id;
```

3. You can use the `DBMS_MVIEW.EXPLAIN_MVIEW` procedure to determine which tables will allow PCT refresh.

MVNAME	CAPABILITY_NAME	POSSIBLE	RELATED_TEXT	MSGTXT
CUST_MTH_SALES_MV	PCT	Y	SALES	
CUST_MTH_SALES_MV	PCT_TABLE	Y	SALES	
CUST_MTH_SALES_MV	PCT_TABLE	N	PRODUCTS	no
partition key or PMARKER				in
SELECT list				
CUST_MTH_SALES_MV	PCT_TABLE	N	TIMES	
relation is not a				
partitioned table				

As can be seen from the partial sample output from `EXPLAIN_MVIEW`, any partition maintenance operation performed on the `sales` table will allow PCT fast refresh. However, PCT is not possible after partition maintenance operations or updates to the `products` table as there is insufficient information contained in `cust_mth_sales_mv` for PCT refresh to be possible. Note that the `times` table is not partitioned and hence can never allow for PCT refresh. Oracle will apply PCT refresh if it can determine that the materialized view has sufficient information to support PCT for all the updated tables.

4. Suppose at some later point, a SPLIT operation of one partition in the sales table becomes necessary.

```
ALTER TABLE SALES
SPLIT PARTITION month3 AT (TO_DATE('05-02-1998', 'DD-MM-YYYY'))
  INTO (
  PARTITION month3_1
  TABLESPACE summ,
  PARTITION month3
      TABLESPACE summ
  );
```

5. Insert some data into the sales table.

Fast refresh cust_mth_sales_mv using the DBMS_MVIEW.REFRESH procedure.

```
EXECUTE DBMS_MVIEW.REFRESH('CUST_MTH_SALES_MV', 'F',
     '',TRUE,FALSE,0,0,0,FALSE);
```

Fast refresh will automatically do a PCT refresh as it is the only fast refresh possible in this scenario. However, fast refresh will not occur if a partition maintenance operation occurs when any update has taken place to a table on which PCT is not enabled. This is shown in "PCT Fast Refresh Scenario 2".

"PCT Fast Refresh Scenario 1" would also be appropriate if the materialized view was created by using the PMARKER clause as illustrated in the following.

```
CREATE MATERIALIZED VIEW cust_sales_marker_mv
       BUILD IMMEDIATE
       REFRESH FAST ON DEMAND
       ENABLE QUERY REWRITE
       AS
        SELECT DBMS_MVIEW.PMARKER(s.rowid) s_marker,
               SUM(s.quantity_sold), SUM(s.amount_sold),
                   p.prod_name, t.calendar_month_name, COUNT(*),
               COUNT(s.quantity_sold), COUNT(s.amount_sold)
       FROM sales s, products p, times t
       WHERE  s.time_id = t.time_id AND
              s.prod_id = p.prod_id
       GROUP BY DBMS_MVIEW.PMARKER(s.rowid),
              p.prod_name, t.calendar_month_name;
```

PCT Fast Refresh Scenario 2

In "PCT Fast Refresh Scenario 2", the first four steps are the same as in "PCT Fast Refresh Scenario 1". Then, the SPLIT partition operation to the sales table is performed, but before the materialized view refresh occurs, records are inserted into the times table.

1. The same as in "PCT Fast Refresh Scenario 1".
2. The same as in "PCT Fast Refresh Scenario 1".
3. The same as in "PCT Fast Refresh Scenario 1".
4. The same as in "PCT Fast Refresh Scenario 1".
5. After issuing the same SPLIT operation, as shown in "PCT Fast Refresh Scenario 1", some data will be inserted into the times table.

```
ALTER TABLE SALES
  SPLIT PARTITION month3 AT (TO_DATE('05-02-1998', 'DD-MM-YYYY'))
  INTO (
     PARTIITION month3_1
     TABLESPACE summ,
     PARTITION month3
     TABLESPACE summ);
```

6. Refresh cust_mth_sales_mv.

```
EXECUTE DBMS_MVIEW.REFRESH('CUST_MTH_SALES_MV', 'F',
    '',TRUE,FALSE,0,0,0,FALSE);
ORA-12052: cannot fast refresh materialized view SH.CUST_MTH_SALES_MV
```

The materialized view is not fast refreshable because DML has occurred to a table on which PCT fast refresh is not possible. To avoid this occurring, Oracle recommends performing a fast refresh immediately after any partition maintenance operation on detail tables for which partition tracking fast refresh is available.

If the situation in "PCT Fast Refresh Scenario 2" occurs, there are two possibilities; perform a complete refresh or switch to the CONSIDER FRESH option outlined in the following, if suitable. However, it should be noted that CONSIDER FRESH and partition change tracking fast refresh are not compatible. Once the ALTER MATERIALIZED VIEW cust_mth_sales_mv CONSIDER FRESH statement has been issued, PCT refresh will no longer be applied to this materialized view, until a complete refresh is done.

A common situation in a warehouse is the use of rolling windows of data. In this case, the detail table and the materialized view may contain say the last 12 months of data. Every month, new data for a month is added to the table and the oldest month is deleted (or maybe archived). PCT refresh provides a very efficient mechanism to maintain the materialized view in this case.

PCT Fast Refresh Scenario 3

The new data is usually added to the detail table by adding a new partition and exchanging it with a table containing the new data.

```
ALTER TABLE sales ADD PARTITION month_new ...
ALTER TABLE sales EXCHANGE PARTITION month_new month_new_table
```

Next, the oldest partition is dropped or truncated.

```
ALTER TABLE sales DROP PARTITION month_oldest;
```

Now, if the materialized view satisfies all conditions for PCT refresh.

```
EXECUTE DBMS_MVIEW.REFRESH('CUST_MTH_SALES_MV', 'F', '',
   TRUE, FALSE,0,0,0,FALSE);
```

Fast refresh will automatically detect that PCT is available and perform a PCT refresh.

Fast Refresh with CONSIDER FRESH

If the materialized view and a detail table have the same partitioning criteria, then you could use CONSIDER FRESH to maintain the materialized view after partition maintenance operations.

The following example demonstrates how you can manually maintain an unsynchronized detail table and materialized view. Assume the sales table and the cust_mth_sales_mv are partitioned identically, and contain say 12 months of data, one month in each partition.

- Suppose the oldest month is to be removed from the table.

```
ALTER TABLE sales DROP PARTITION month_oldest;
```

- You could manually resynchronize the materialized view by doing a corresponding partition operation on the materialized view.

```
ALTER MATERIALIZED VIEW cust_mth_sales_mv DROP PARTITION month_oldest;
```

- Use CONSIDER FRESH to declare that the materialized view has been refreshed.

```
ALTER MATERIALIZED VIEW cust_mth_sales_mv CONSIDER FRESH;
```

In a data warehouse, you may often wish to accumulate historical information in the materialized view even though this information is no longer in the detailed tables. In this case, you could maintain the materialized view using the ALTER MATERIALIZED VIEW *materialized view name* CONSIDER FRESH statement.

Note that CONSIDER FRESH declares that the contents of the materialized view are FRESH (in sync with the detail tables). Care must be taken when using this option in this scenario in conjunction with query rewrite because you may see unexpected results.

After using CONSIDER FRESH in an historical scenario, you will be able to apply traditional fast refresh after DML and direct loads to the materialized view, but not PCT fast refresh. This is because if the detail table partition at one time contained data that is currently kept in aggregated form in the materialized view, PCT refresh in attempting to resynchronize the materialized view with that partition could delete historical data which cannot be recomputed.

Assume the sales table stores the prior year's data and the cust_mth_sales_mv keeps the prior 10 years of data in aggregated form.

1. Remove old data from a partition in the sales table:

   ```
   ALTER TABLE sales TRUNCATE PARTITION month1;
   ```

   The materialized view is now considered stale and requires a refresh because of the partition operation. However, as the detail table no longer contains all the data associated with the partition fast refresh cannot be attempted.

2. Therefore, alter the materialized view to tell Oracle to consider it fresh.

   ```
   ALTER MATERIALIZED VIEW cust_mth_sales_mv CONSIDER FRESH;
   ```

   This statement informs Oracle that cust_mth_sales_mv is fresh for your purposes. However, the materialized view now has a status that is neither known fresh nor known stale. Instead, it is UNKNOWN. If the materialized view has query rewrite enabled in QUERY_REWRITE_INTEGRITY=stale_tolerated mode, it will be used for rewrite.

3. Insert data into sales.

4. Refresh the materialized view.

   ```
   EXECUTE DBMS_MVIEW.REFRESH('CUST_MTH_SALES_MV', 'F',
     '', TRUE, FALSE,0,0,0,FALSE);
   ```

   Because the fast refresh detects that only INSERT statements occurred against the sales table it will update the materialized view with the new data. However, the status of the materialized view will remain UNKNOWN. The only way to return the materialized view to FRESH status is with a complete refresh which, also will remove the historical data from the materialized view.

❑❑❑

8 CHANGE DATA CAPTURE

ABOUT CHANGE DATA CAPTURE

Oftentimes, data warehousing involves the extraction and transportation of relational data from one or more source databases, into the data warehouse for analysis. Change Data Capture quickly identifies and processes only the data that has changed, not entire tables, and makes the change data available for further use.

Without Change Data Capture, database extraction is a cumbersome process in which you move the entire contents of tables into flat files, and then load the files into the data warehouse. This ad hoc approach is expensive in a number of ways.

Change Data Capture does not depend on intermediate flat files to stage the data outside of the relational database. It captures the change data resulting from `INSERT`, `UPDATE`, and `DELETE` operations made to user tables. The change data is then stored in a database object called a change table, and the change data is made available to applications in a controlled way.

Table 8.1 describes the advantages of performing database extraction with Change Data Capture.

Table 8.1 Database Extraction With and Without Change Data Capture

Database Extraction	With Change Data Capture	Without Change Data Capture
Extraction	Database extraction from `INSERT`, `UPDATE`, and `DELETE` operations occurs immediately, at the same time the changes occur to the source tables.	Database extraction is marginal at best for `INSERT` operations, and problematic for `UPDATE` and `DELETE` operations, because the data is no longer in the table.
Staging	Stages data directly to relational tables; there is no need to use flat files.	The entire contents of tables are moved into flat files.
Interface	Provides an easy-to-use publish and subscribe interface using `DBMS_LOGMNR_CDC_PUBLISH` and `DBMS_LOGMNR_CDC_SUBSCRIBE` packages.	Error prone and manpower intensive to administer.
Cost	Supplied with the Oracle9*i* (and later) database server. Reduces overhead cost by simplifying the extraction of change data.	Expensive because you must write and maintain the capture software yourself, or purchase it from a third-party vendors.

A Change Data Capture system is based on the interaction of a publisher and subscribers to capture and distribute change data, as described in the next section.

Publish and Subscribe Model

Most Change Data Capture systems have one publisher that captures and publishes change data for any number of Oracle source tables. There can be multiple subscribers accessing the change data. Change Data Capture provides PL/SQL packages to accomplish the publish and subscribe tasks.

Publisher

The **publisher** is usually a database administrator (DBA) who is in charge of creating and maintaining schema objects that make up the Change Data Capture system. The publisher performs these tasks:

- Determines the relational tables (called source tables) from which the data warehouse application is interested in capturing change data.
- Uses the Oracle supplied package, `DBMS_LOGMNR_CDC_PUBLISH`, to set up the system to capture data from one or more source tables.
- Publishes the change data in the form of change tables.
- Allows controlled access to subscribers by using the SQL `GRANT` and `REVOKE` statements to grant and revoke the `SELECT` privilege on change tables for users and roles.

Subscribers

The **subscribers**, usually applications, are consumers of the published change data. Subscribers subscribe to one or more sets of columns in source tables. Subscribers perform the following tasks:

- Use the Oracle supplied package, `DBMS_LOGMNR_CDC_SUBSCRIBE`, to subscribe to source tables for controlled access to the published change data for analysis.
- Extend the subscription window and create a new subscriber view when the subscriber is ready to receive a set of change data.
- Use `SELECT` statements to retrieve change data from the subscriber views.
- Drop the subscriber view and purge the subscription window when finished processing a block of changes.
- Drop the subscription when the subscriber no longer needs its change data.

Example of a Change Data Capture System

The Change Data Capture system captures the effects of DML statements, including `INSERT`, `DELETE`, and `UPDATE`, when they are performed on the source table. As these operations are performed, the change data is captured and published to corresponding change tables.

To capture change data, the publisher creates and administers change tables, which are special database tables that capture change data from a source table.

For example, for each source table for which you want to capture data, the publisher creates a corresponding change table. Change Data Capture ensures that none of the updates are missed or duplicated.

Each subscriber has its own view of the change data. This makes it possible for multiple subscribers to simultaneously subscribe to the same change table without interfering with one another.

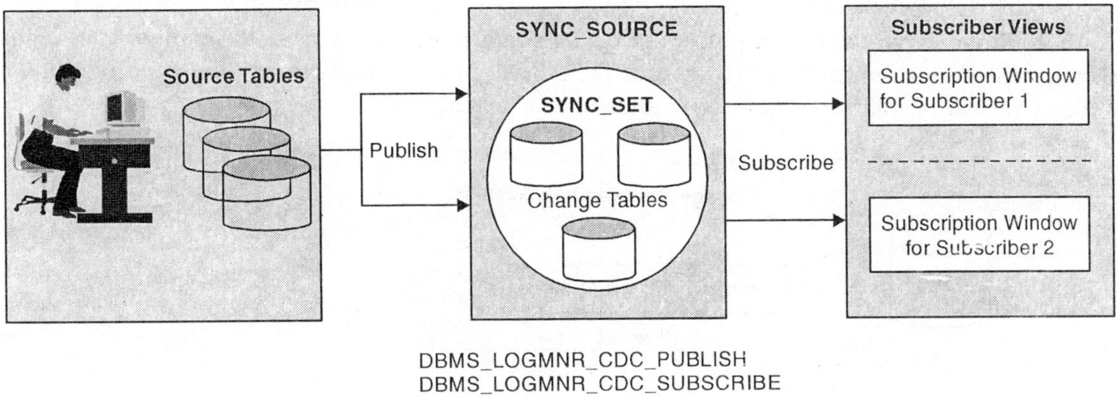

Figure 8.1 Publish and Subscribe Model in a Change Data Capture System.

For example, assume that the change tables in figure 8.1 contains all of the changes that occurred between Monday and Friday, and also assume that:

- Subscriber 1 is viewing and processing data from Tuesday.
- Subscriber 2 is viewing and processing data from Wednesday to Thursday.

Subscribers 1 and 2 each have a unique **subscription window** that contains a block of transactions. Change Data Capture manages the subscription window for each subscriber by creating a subscriber view that returns a range of transactions of interest to that subscriber. The subscriber accesses the change data by performing `SELECT` statements on the subscriber view that was generated by Change Data Capture.

When a subscriber needs to read additional change data, the subscriber makes procedure calls to *extend* the window and to create a new subscriber view. Each subscriber can *walk* through the data at its own pace, while Change Data Capture manages the data storage. As each subscriber finishes processing the data in its subscription window, it calls procedures to drop the subscriber view and *purge* the contents of the subscription window. Extending and purging windows is necessary to prevent the change table from growing indefinitely, and to prevent the subscriber from seeing the same data again.

Thus, Change Data Capture provides the following benefits for subscribers:

- Guarantees that each subscriber sees all of the changes, does not miss any changes, and does not see the same change data more than once.
- Keeps track of multiple subscribers and gives each subscriber shared access to change data.
- Handles all of the storage management, automatically removing data from change tables when it is no longer required by any of the subscribers.

Components and Terminology for Synchronous Change Data Capture

This section describes the Change Data Capture components shown in figure 8.2. The publisher is responsible for all of the components shown in figure 8.2, except for the subscriber views. The publisher creates and maintains all of the schema objects that make up the Change Data Capture system, and publishes change data so that subscribers can use it.

Subscribers are the consumers of change data and are granted controlled access to the change +data by the publisher. Subscribers subscribe to one or more columns in source tables.

With synchronous data capture, the change data is generated as data manipulation language (DML) operations are made to the source table. Every time a DML operation occurs on a source table, a record of that operation is written to the change table.

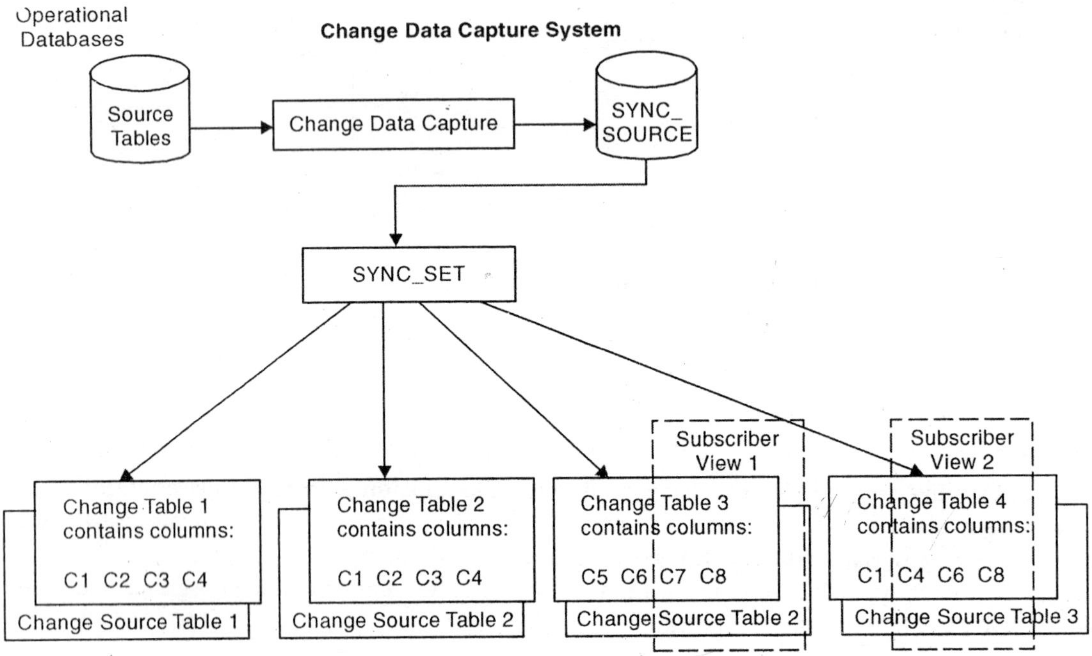

Figure 8.2 Components in a Synchronous Change Data Capture System.

The following subsections describe Change Data Capture components in more detail.

Source System

A source system is a production database that contains source tables for which Change Data Capture will capture changes.

Source Table

A source table is a database table that resides on the source system that contains the data you want to capture. Changes made to the source table are immediately reflected in the change table.

Change Source

A change source represents a source system. There is a system-generated change source named SYNC_SOURCE.

Change Set

A change set represents the collection of change tables. There is a system-generated change set named SYNC_SET.

Change Table

A change table contains the change data resulting from DML statements made to a single source table. A change table consists of two things: the change data itself, which is stored in a database table, and the system metadata necessary to maintain the change table. A given change table can capture changes from only one source table. In addition to published columns, the change table contains control columns that are managed by Change Data Capture.

Publication

A publication provides a way for publishers to publish multiple change tables on the same source table, and control subscriber access to the published change data. For example, Publication A consists of a change table that contains all the columns from the `EMPLOYEE` source table, while Publication B contains all the columns except the salary column from the `EMPLOYEE` source table. Because each change table is a separate publication, the publisher can implement security on the salary column by allowing only selected subscribers to access Publication A.

Subscriber View

A subscriber view is a view created by Change Data Capture that returns all of the rows in the subscription window. In figure 8.2, the subscribers have created two views: one on columns 7 and 8 of Source Table 3 and one on columns 4, 6, and 8 of Source Table 4. The columns included in the view are based on the actual columns that the subscribers subscribed to in the source table.

Subscription Window

A subscription window defines the time range of change rows that the subscriber can currently see. The oldest row in the window is the low watermark; the newest row in the window is the high watermark. Each subscriber has a subscription window.

INSTALLATION AND IMPLEMENTATION

Change Data Capture comes pre-packaged with the appropriate Oracle9*i* drivers already installed with which you can implement synchronous data capture.

In addition, note that Change Data Capture uses Java. Therefore, when you install the Oracle9*i* database server, ensure that Java is enabled.

Change Data Capture installs systemwide triggers on the `CREATE TABLE`, `ALTER TABLE`, and `DROP TABLE` statements. If system triggers are disabled on the database instance, Change Data Capture will not function correctly. Therefore, you should never disable system triggers.

To remove Change Data Capture from the database, the SQL script `rmcdc.sql` is provided in the `admin` directory. This will remove the system triggers that CDC installs on the `CREATE TABLE`, `ALTER TABLE` and `DROP` table statements. In addition, `rmcdc.sql` removes all Java classes used by Change Data Capture. Note that after `rmcdc.sql` is called, CDC will no longer operate on the system. If the system administrator decides to remove the Java Virtual Machine from a database instance, `rmcdc.sql` must be called before `rmjvm` is called.

To re-install Change Data Capture, the SQL script `initcdc.sql` is provided in the `admin` directory. It creates the CDC system triggers and Java classes that are required by Change Data Capture.

Change Data Capture Restriction on Direct-Path INSERT

Change Data Capture does not support the direct-path `INSERT` statement (and, by association, the `multi_table_insert` statement) feature in parallel DML mode.

When you create a change table, Change Data Capture creates triggers on the source table. Because a direct-path `INSERT` disables all database triggers, any rows inserted into the source table using the SQL statement for direct-path `INSERT` in parallel DML mode will not be captured in the change table.

Similarly, Change Data Capture cannot capture the inserted rows from multitable insert operations because the SQL `multi_table_insert` statement in parallel DML mode uses direct-path `INSERT`. Also, note that the multitable insert operation does not return an error message to indicate that the triggers used by Change Data Capture did not fire.

SECURITY

You grant privileges for a change table separately from the privileges you grant for a source table. For example, a subscriber that has privileges to perform a `SELECT` operation on a source table might not have privileges to perform a `SELECT` operation on a change table.

The publisher controls subscribers' access to change data by using the SQL `GRANT` and `REVOKE` statements to grant and revoke the `SELECT` privilege on change tables for users and roles. The publisher must grant the `SELECT` privilege before a user or application can subscribe to the change table.

The publisher must not grant any DML access (using either the `INSERT`, `UPDATE`, or `DELETE` statements) to the subscribers on the change tables because of the risk that a subscriber might inadvertently change the data in the change table, making it inconsistent with its source. Furthermore, the publisher should avoid creating change tables in schemas to which users have DML access.

COLUMNS IN A CHANGE TABLE

A change table contains the change data resulting from DML statements. A change table consists of two things: the change data itself, which is stored in a database table and the system metadata necessary to maintain the change table.

The change table contains control columns that are managed by Change Data Capture. Table 8.2 describes the contents of a change table.

Table 8.2 Control Columns for a Change Table

Column	Datatype	Nullable?	Description
RSID$	NUMBER	N	Unique row sequence ID.
OPERATION$	CHAR(2)	N	I: Insert UO or UU: Update old value UN: Update new value UL: Update LOB D: Delete
CSCN$	NUMBER	N	Commit SCN.

COMMIT_TIMESTAMP$	DATE	Y	Commit time of this transaction.
SOURCE_COLMAP$	NUMBER	N	Bit mask of updated columns; source table relative (optional column).
TARGET_COLMAP$	NUMBER	N	Bit mask of updated columns; change table relative (optional column).
USERNAME$	VARCHAR2(30)	N	Name of the user who caused the operation (optional column).
TIMESTAMP$	DATE	N	Time when the operation occurred in the source table (optional column).
ROW_ID$	ROW_ID	N	Row ID of affected row in source table (optional column).
SYS_NC_OID$	RAW(16)	Y	Object ID (optional column).

CHANGE DATA CAPTURE VIEWS

Information about the Change Data Capture environment is provided in the views described in table 8.3.

Table 8.3 View Names for Change Data Capture

View Name	Description
CHANGE_SOURCES	Allows a publisher to see existing change sources
CHANGE_SETS	Allows a publisher to see existing change sets
CHANGE_TABLES	Allows a publisher to see existing change tables
ALL_SOURCE_TABLES	Allows subscribers to see all of the published source tables for which the subscribers have privileges to subscribe
DBA_SOURCE_TABLES	Allows a publisher to see all of the existing (published) source tables
USER_SOURCE_TABLES	Allows the user to see all of the published source tables for which this user has privileges to subscribe
ALL_SOURCE_TAB_COLUMNS	Allows subscribers to see all of the source table columns that have been published, as well as the schema name and table name of the source table
DBA_SOURCE_TAB_COLUMNS	Allows subscribers to see all of the source table columns that have been published, as well as the schema name and table name of the source table
USER_SOURCE_TAB_COLUMNS	Allows users to see all of the source table columns that have been published, as well as the schema name and table name of the source table
ALL_PUBLISHED_COLUMNS	Allows a subscriber to see all of the published source table columns for which the subscriber has privileges

DBA_PUBLISHED_COLUMNS	Allows a subscriber to see all of the published source table columns for which the subscriber has privileges
USER_PUBLISHED_COLUMNS	Allows a user to see all of the published source table columns for which the user has privileges
ALL_SUBSCRIPTIONS	Allows a user to see all current subscriptions
DBA_SUBSCRIPTIONS	Allows a publisher to see all of the subscriptions
USER_SUBSCRIPTIONS	Allows a subscriber to see all of their current subscriptions
ALL_SUBSCRIBED_TABLES	Allows a user to see all of the published tables for which there are subscribers
DBA_SUBSCRIBED_TABLES	Allows a publisher to see all of the published tables to which subscribers have subscribed
USER_SUBSCRIBED_TABLES	Allows a subscriber to see all of the published tables to which the subscriber has subscribed
ALL_SUBSCRIBED_COLUMNS	Allows a user to see all of the published columns for which there are subscribers
DBA_SUBSCRIBED_COLUMNS	Allows a publisher to see all of the columns of published tables to which subscribers have subscribed
USER_SUBSCRIBED_COLUMNS	Allows a publisher to see all of the columns of published tables to which the subscriber has subscribed

SYNCHRONOUS MODE OF DATA CAPTURE

Synchronous data capture provides up-to-the-second accuracy because the changes are being captured continuously and in real time on the production system. The change tables are populated after DML operations occur on the source table.

While synchronous mode data capture adds overhead to the system at capture time, it can reduce cost by simplifying the extraction of change data.

PUBLISHING CHANGE DATA

This section provides step-by-step instructions for setting up a Change Data Capture system to capture and publish data from one or more Oracle relational source tables. Change Data Capture captures and publishes only committed data.

NOTE *To use the* DBMS_LOGMNR_CDC_PUBLISH *package, you must have the* EXECUTE_CATALOG_ROLE *privilege, and you must have the* SELECT_CATALOG_ROLE *privilege to look at all of the views. Also, you must be able to* GRANT SELECT *in the change tables to subscribers.*

Step 1: Decide which Oracle Instance will be the Source System

You need to decide which Oracle instance will be the source system that will provide the change data. The publisher needs to gather requirements from the subscribers and determine which source system contains the relevant source tables.

Step 2: Create the Change Tables that will Contain the Changes

You need to create the change tables that will contain the changes to individual source tables. Use the `DBMS_LOGMNR_CDC_PUBLISH.CREATE_CHANGE_TABLE` procedure to create change tables.

> NOTE: *For synchronous data capture, Change Data Capture automatically generates a change source, called `SYNC_SOURCE`, and a change set called `SYNC_SET`. Change tables are contained in the predefined `SYNC_SET` change set.*

Create a change table for each source table to be published, and decide which columns should be included. For update operations, decide whether to capture old values, new values, or both.

The publisher can set the `options_string` field of the `DBMS_LOGMNR_CDC_PUBLISH.CREATE_CHANGE_TABLE` procedure to have more control over the physical properties and tablespace properties of the change tables. The `options_string` field can contain any option available on the `CREATE TABLE DDL` statement.

Example 8.1 : Creating a Change Table

The following example creates a change table that captures changes that happen to a source table. The example uses the sample table `SCOTT.EMP`.

```
EXECUTE DBMS_LOGMNR_CDC_PUBLISH.CREATE_CHANGE_TABLE (OWNER => 'cdc',\
CHANGE_TABLE_NAME => 'emp_ct', \
CHANGE_SET_NAME => 'SYNC_SET', \
SOURCE_SCHEMA => 'scott', \
SOURCE_TABLE => 'emp' ,\
COLUMN_TYPE_LIST => 'empno number, ename varchar2(10), job varchar2(9), mgr
number, hiredate date, deptno number', \
CAPTURE_VALUES => 'both', \
RS_ID => 'y' \
ROW_ID => 'n', \
USER_ID => 'n', \
TIMESTAMP => 'n', \
OBJECT_ID => 'n', \
SOURCE_COLMAP => 'y', \
TARGET_COLMAP => 'y', \
OPTIONS_STRING => null);
```

This statement creates a change table named `emp_ct` within the change set `SYNC_SET`. The `column_type_list` parameter identifies the columns captured by the change table. The `source_schema` and `source_table` parameters identify the schema and source table that reside on the production system.

The `capture_values` setting in the example indicates that for `UPDATE` operations, the change data will contain two separate rows for each row that changed: one row will contain the row values before the update occurred, and the other row will contain the row values after the update occurred.

MANAGING CHANGE TABLES AND SUBSCRIPTIONS

This section describes storage management and how the publisher is able to manage change tables and subscriptions.

To ensure that the size of change tables does not grow without limit, Change Data Capture manages the data in change tables and automatically purges change data that is no longer needed. The DBMS_CDC_PUBLISH.PURGE procedure should be called periodically to remove data from change tables that is no longer required. PURGE looks at all active subscription windows to determine which change data is still in use. It will not purge any data as long as subscribers have active subscription windows that reference the change data.

Subscribers must call DBMS_CDC_SUBSCRIBE.PURGE_WINDOW when they are finished using change data. This indicates to CDC that the change data is no longer needed, and that PURGE may safely remove the unneeded rows. Conversely, until all subscribers have called PURGE_WINDOW on their subscription windows, the change data is considered still in use: PURGE will not remove those rows from the change table.

It is possible that a subscriber could fail to call PURGE_WINDOW, with the end result being that a change table would not be purged. The DBA_SUBSCRIPTIONS view helps the publisher determine if this is happening. In extreme circumstances a publisher may decide to drop an active subscription so that space can be reclaimed. An example might be that the subscriber is an application's program that is not calling PURGE_WINDOW as needed. The DBA_CDC_PUBLISH.DROP_SUBSCRIPTION procedure lets the publisher drop active subscriptions if circumstances require it: however, the publisher should first consider that subscribers may still be using the change data. You must use DBMS_CDC_PUBLISH.DROP_SUBSCRIBER_VIEW to drop any subscriber views prior to dropping a subscription using the DBMS_CDC_PUBLISH.DROP_SUBSCRIPTION procedure.

The PURGE procedure normally runs in a job queue, therefore it runs automatically. The publisher can execute PURGE manually at any time however.

Note that it is not possible to drop change tables by using the conventional DROP TABLE statement. If it is necessary to drop a change table, the procedure DBMS_CDC_PUBLISH.DROP_CHANGE_TABLE must be called. This procedure ensures that both the change table itself as well as the CDC metadata for it are both dropped. If you try to use DROP TABLE on a change table, it will raise the error:

```
ORA-31496 must use DBMS_CDC_PUBLISH.DROP_CHANGE_TABLE to drop change tables
```

DROP_CHANGE_TABLE procedure also safeguards the publisher from inadvertently dropping a change table while there are active subscribers that are using the change table. If DROP_CHANGE_TABLE is dropped while subscriptions are active, the procedure will fail with the Oracle error:

```
ORA-31424 change table has active subscriptions
```

If the publisher really wants to drop the change table in spite of active subscriptions, DROP_CHANGE_TABLE procedure must be called using the parameter FORCE => 'Y'. This tells CDC to override its normal safeguards and allow the change table to be dropped despite active subscriptions. The subscriptions will no longer be valid, and subscribers will lose access to the change data.

NOTE

The DROP USER CASCADE statement will drop all of a user's change tables by using the FORCE => 'Y' option. Therefore, if any other users have active subscriptions to the (dropped) change table, these will no longer be valid. In addition to dropping the user's change tables, DROP USER CASCADE also drops any subscriptions that were held by that user.

SUBSCRIBING TO CHANGE DATA

The subscribers, typically applications, register their interest in one or more source tables, and obtain subscriptions to these tables. Assuming sufficient access privileges, the subscribers may subscribe to any source tables that the publisher has published.

Steps Required to Subscribe to Change Data

The primary role of the subscriber is to access and use the change data. To do this, the subscriber must first determine which source tables are of interest, and then call the procedures in the `DBMS_LOGMNR_CDC_SUBSCRIBE` package to access them.

Step 1: Find the Source Tables for which the Subscriber has Access Privileges

Query the `ALL_SOURCE_TABLES` view to see all of the published source tables for which the subscriber has access privileges.

Step 2: Obtain a Subscription Handle

Call the `DBMS_LOGMNR_CDC_SUBSCRIBE.GET_SUBSCRIPTION_HANDLE` procedure to create a subscription.

The following example shows how the subscriber first names the change set of interest (`SYNC_SET`), and then returns a unique subscription handle that will be used throughout the session.

```
EXECUTE SYS.DBMS_LOGMNR_CDC_SUBSCRIBE.GET_SUBSCRIPTION_HANDLE ( \
CHANGE_SET => 'SYNC_SET',\
DESCRIPTION => 'Change data for emp',\
SUBSCRIPTION_HANDLE => :subhandle);
```

Step 3: Subscribe to a Source Table and Columns in the Source Table

Use the `DBMS_LOGMNR_CDC_SUBSCRIBE.SUBSCRIBE` procedure to specify which columns of the source tables are of interest to the subscriber and are to be captured.

The subscriber identifies the columns of the source table that are of interest. A subscription can contain one source table or multiple tables from the same change set. To see all of the published source table columns for which the subscriber has privileges, query the `ALL_PUBLISHED_COLUMNS` view.

In the following example, the subscriber wants to see only one source table.

```
EXECUTE SYS.DBMS_LOGMNR_CDC_SUBSCRIBE.SUBSCRIBE (\
SUBSCRIPTION_HANDLE => :subhandle, \
SOURCE_SCHEMA => 'scott', \
SOURCE_TABLE => 'emp', \
COLUMN_LIST => 'empno, ename, hiredate');
```

Step 4: Activate the Subscription

Use the `DBMS_LOGMNR_CDC_SUBSCRIBE.ACTIVATE_SUBSCRIPTION` procedure to activate the subscription.

Subscribers call this procedure when they are finished subscribing to source tables, and are ready to receive change data. Whether subscribing to one or multiple source tables, the subscriber needs to call the `ACTIVATE_SUBSCRIPTION` procedure only once.

In the following example, the ACTIVATE_SUBSCRIPTION procedure sets the subscription window to empty. At this point, no additional source tables can be added to the subscription.

```
EXECUTE  SYS.DBMS_LOGMNR_CDC_SUBSCRIBE.ACTIVATE_SUBSCRIPTION  ( \
SUBSCRIPTION_HANDLE  =>  :subhandle);
```

Step 5: Set the Boundaries to See New Data

Call the DBMS_LOGMNR_CDC_SUBSCRIBE.EXTEND_WINDOW procedure to set the upper boundary (called a high-water mark) for a subscription window.

For example:

```
EXECUTE  SYS.DBMS_LOGMNR_CDC_SUBSCRIBE.EXTEND_WINDOW  (\
SUBSCRIPTION_HANDLE  =>  :subhandle);
```

At this point, the subscriber has created a new window that begins where the previous window ends. The new window contains any data that was added to the change table. If no new data has been added, the EXTEND_WINDOW procedure has no effect. To access the new change data, the subscriber must call the CREATE_SUBSCRIBER_VIEW procedure, and select from the new subscriber view that is generated by Change Data Capture.

Step 6: Prepare a Subscriber View

Use the DBMS_LOGMNR_CDC_SUBSCRIBE.PREPARE_SUBSCRIBER_VIEW procedure to create and prepare a subscriber view. (You must do this for each change table in the subscription.)

Subscribers do not access data directly from a change table; subscribers see the change data through subscriber views and perform SELECT operations against them. The reason for this is because Change Data Capture generates a view that restricts the data to only the columns to which the application has subscribed, and returns only the rows that the application has not viewed previously. The contents of the subscriber view will not change.

The following example shows how to prepare a subscriber view:

```
EXECUTE  SYS.DBMS_LOGMNR_CDC_SUBSCRIBE.PREPARE_SUBSCRIBER_VIEW  ( \
SUBSCRIPTION_HANDLE  =>  :subhandle,  \
SOURCE_SCHEMA  =>  'scott',\
SOURCE_TABLE  =>  'emp',  \
VIEW_NAME  =>  :viewname);
```

Step 7: Read and Query the Contents of the Change Tables

Use the SQL SELECT statement on the subscriber view to read and query the contents of change tables (within the boundaries of the subscription window). You must do this for each change table in the subscription. For example:

```
SELECT  *  FROM  CDC#CV$119490;
```

The subscriber view name, CDC#CV$119490, is a generated name.

Step 8: Drop the Subscriber View

Use the DBMS_LOGMNR_CDC_SUBSCRIBE.DROP_SUBSCRIBER_VIEW procedure to drop the subscriber views.

Change Data Capture guarantees not to change the subscriber view, even if new data has been added. Subscribers continue to have access to a subscriber view until calling the DROP_SUBSCRIBER_VIEW procedure, which indicates the subscriber is finished using the view. For example:

```
EXECUTE SYS.DBMS_LOGMNR_CDC_SUBSCRIBE.DROP_SUBSCRIBER_VIEW (\
SUBSCRIPTION_HANDLE => :subhandle, \
SOURCE_SCHEMA => 'scott', \
SOURCE_TABLE => 'emp');
```

Step 9: Empty the Old Data from the Subscription Window

Use the DBMS_LOGMNR_CDC_SUBSCRIBE.PURGE_WINDOW procedure to let the Change Data Capture software know that the subscriber no longer needs the data in the current subscription window.

For example:

```
EXECUTE SYS.DBMS_LOGMNR_CDC_SUBSCRIBE.PURGE_WINDOW (\
SUBSCRIPTION_HANDLE => :subhandle);
```

Step 10: Repeat Steps 5 through 9

Repeat steps 5 though 9 as long as you are interested in additional change data.

Step 11: End the Subscription

Use the DBMS_LOGMNR_CDC_SUBSCRIBE.DROP_SUBSCRIPTION procedure to end the subscription. This is necessary to prevent the change tables from growing without bound. For example:

```
EXECUTE SYS.DBMS_LOGMNR_CDC_SUBSCRIBE.DROP_SUBSCRIPTION (\
SUBSCRIPTION_HANDLE => :subhandle);
```

What Happens to Subscriptions when the Publisher Makes Changes

The Change Data Capture environment is dynamic in nature. The publisher can add and drop change tables at any time. The publisher can also add to and drop columns from existing change tables at any time. The following list describes how changes to the Change Data Capture environment affect subscriptions:

- Subscribers do not get explicit notification if the publisher adds a new change table. The views can be checked to see if new change tables have been added, and whether or not you have access to them.
- If a publisher drops a change table that is currently being subscribed to, the publisher must use the force flag to get a successful drop. It is expected that the publisher will warn subscribers before the force flag is actually used. If the subscribers are unaware of the dropped table, then when the subscriber calls PREPARE_SUBSCRIBER_VIEW procedure, an appropriate exception is generated. This becomes the notification mechanism.
- If the publisher adds a user column to a change table and a new subscription includes this column, then the subscription window starts at the point the column was added.
- If the publisher adds a user column to a change table and a new subscription does not include this newly added column, then the subscription window starts at the low-water mark for the change table thus enabling the subscriber to see the entire table.

- If the publisher adds a user column to a change table, and old subscriptions exist, then the subscription windows remain unchanged.
- Subscribers subscribe to source columns and never to control columns. They can see the control columns that were present at the time of the subscription.
- If the publisher adds a control column to a change table and there is a new subscription, then the subscription window starts at the low-water mark for the change table. The subscription can see the control column immediately. All rows that existed in the change table prior to adding the control column will have the value `NULL` for the newly added control column field.
- If the publisher adds a control column to a change table, then any existing subscriptions can see the new control column when the window is extended (`DBMS_LOGMNR_CDC_PUBLISH.EXTEND_WINDOW` procedure) such that the low watermark for the window crosses over the point when the control column was added.

EXPORT AND IMPORT CONSIDERATIONS

When exporting or importing change tables for Change Data Capture, consider the following information:

- When change tables are imported, the job queue is checked for a Change Data Capture purge job. If no purge job is found, then one is submitted automatically (using the `DBMS_CDC_PUBLISH.PURGE` procedure). If a change table is imported, but no subscriptions are taken out before the purge job runs (24 hours later, by default), then all rows in the table will be purged.

  Choose one of the following methods to prevent the purging of data from a change table:
- Suspend the purge job using the `DBMS_JOB` package to either disable the job (using the `BROKEN` procedure) or execute the job sometime in the future when there are subscriptions (using the `NEXT_DATE` procedure).

NOTE

If you disable the purge job by marking it as broken, you need to remember to reset it once subscriptions have been activated. This prevents the change table from growing without bound.

- Take out a *dummy* subscription to preserve the change table data until real subscriptions appear. Then, you can drop the dummy subscription.
- When importing data into a source table for which a change table already exists, the imported data is also recorded in any associated change tables.

  Assume that you have a source table `Employees` that has an associated change table `CT_Employees`. When you import data into `Employees`, that data is also recorded in `CT_Employees`.
- When importing a source table and its change table to a database where the tables did not previously exist, Change Data Capture for that source table will not be established until the import process completes. This protects you from duplicating activity in the change table.
- When exporting a source table and its associated change table, and then importing them into a new instance, the imported source table data is not recorded in the change table because it is already in the change table.

- When importing a change table having the optional control ROW_ID column, the ROW_ID columns stored in the change table have meaning only if the associated source table has *not* been imported. If a source table is re-created or imported, each row will have a new ROW_ID that is unrelated to the ROW_ID that was previously recorded in a change table.
- Any time a table is exported from one database and imported to another, there is a risk that the import target already has tables or objects with the same name. Moving a change table to a different database where a table exists that has the same name as the source table may result in import errors.
- If you need to move a synchronous change table or its source table, then move both tables together and check the import log for error messages.

❑❑❑

9 SUMMARY ADVISOR

OVERVIEW OF THE SUMMARY ADVISOR IN THE DBMS_OLAP PACKAGE

Materialized views provide high performance for complex, data-intensive queries. The Summary Advisor helps you achieve this performance benefit by choosing the proper set of materialized views for a given workload. In general, as the number of materialized views and space allocated to materialized views is increased, query performance improves. But the additional materialized views have some cost: they consume additional storage space and must be refreshed, which increases maintenance time. The Summary Advisor considers these costs and makes the most cost-effective trade-offs when recommending the creation of new materialized views and evaluating the performance of existing materialized views.

To help you select from among the many possible materialized views in your schema, Oracle provides a collection of materialized view analysis and advisory functions and procedures in the DBMS_OLAP package. Collectively, these functions are called the Summary Advisor, and they are callable from any PL/SQL program. Figure 9.1 shows how the Summary Advisor recommends materialized views from a hypothetical or user-defined workload or one obtained from the SQL cache, or Oracle Trace. You can run the Summary Advisor from Oracle Enterprise Manager or by invoking the DBMS_OLAP package. You must have Java enabled to use the Summary Advisor.

All data and results generated by the Summary Advisor is stored in a set of tables referred to as the Summary Advisor repository. These tables are owned by SYSTEM and start with MVIEW$_ADV_*. Only DBAs can access these tables directly, but other users can access the data relevant to them using a set of read-only views. These views start with MVIEW_. Thus, the table MVIEW$_ADV_WORKLOAD stores the workload of all users, but a user accesses his workload through the MVIEW_WORKLOAD view.

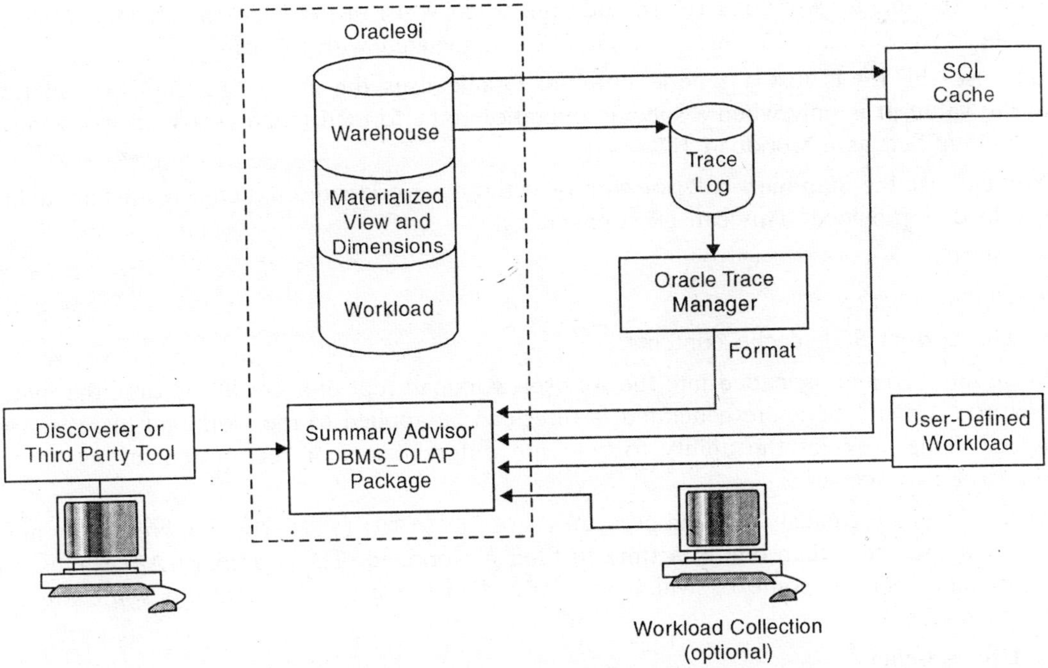

Figure 9.1 Materialized Views and the Summary Advisor.

Using the Summary Advisor or the DBMS_OLAP package, you can:

- Estimate the size of a materialized view
- Recommend a materialized view
- Recommend materialized views based on collected workload information
- Report actual utilization of materialized views based on collected workload
- Define a filter to use against a workload
- Load and validate a workload
- Purge filters, workloads, and results
- Generate a unique identifier (for example, run ID, filter ID, or workload ID).

All of these tasks can be performed independently of one another. However, sometimes you need to use several procedures from the DBMS_OLAP package to complete a task. For example, to recommend a set of materialized views based on a workload, you have to first load the workload and then generate the set of recommendations.

Before you can use any of these procedures, you must create a unique identifier for the data they are about to create. This number is obtained by calling the procedure CREATE_ID and the unique number is known subsequently as a run ID, workload ID or filter ID depending on the procedure it is given.

The identifier is used to store the Advisor artifacts in the repository. Each activity in the Advisor requires a unique identifier to distinguish it from other objects. For example, when you add a filter item, you associate the item with a filter ID. When you load a workload, the data gets stored using the unique workload ID. In addition, when you run RECOMMEND_MVIEW_STRATEGY or EVALUATE_MVIEW_STRATEGY, a unique ID is associated with the run.

Because the ID is just a unique number, Oracle uses the same CREATE_ID function to acquire the value. It is only when a specific operation is performed (such as a load workload) that the ID is identified as a workload ID.

You can use the Summary Advisor with or without a workload, but better results are achieved if a workload is provided. This can be supplied by:

- The user
- Oracle trace
- The current SQL cache contents.

Once the workload is loaded into the Advisor workload repository or at the time the materialized view recommendations are generated, a filter can be applied to the workload to restrict what is analyzed. This provides the ability to generate different sets of recommendations based on different workload scenarios.

These filters are created using the procedure ADD_FILTER_ITEM. You can create any number of filters, and use more than one at a time to filter a workload. The Summary Advisor uses four types of schema objects, some of which are defined in the user's schema and some are in the system schema:

- **User schema**

  For both V-table and workload tables, before the workload is available to the recommendation process. It must be loaded into the advisor workload repository.

  - V-tables

    V-tables are generated by Oracle Trace for storing results of formatting server-collected trace. Please note that these V-tables are different from the V$ tables.

  - Workload tables

    Workload tables are user tables that store workload information, and can reside in any schema.

- **System schema**

  - Result tables

    Result tables are internal tables that store both intermediate and final results from all Summary Advisor components.

  - Read-only views

    Read-only views allow you to access recommendations, filters and workloads.These views are MVIEW_RECOMMENDATIONS, MVIEW_EVALUATIONS, MVIEW_FILTER, and MVIEW_WORKLOAD.

    Whenever the Summary Advisor is run, the results, with the exception of estimated size, are placed in internal tables, which can be accessed from read-only views in the database. These results can be queried, so you do not have to keep running the Advisor process.

If you want to view the results of the last materialized view recommendation, you can issue the following statement:

```
SELECT MVIEW_OWNER, MVIEW_NAME, RECOMMENDED_ACTION,
PCT_PERFORMANCE_GAIN,
    BENEFIT_TO_COST_RATIO
FROM  SYSTEM.MVIEW_RECOMMENDATIONS
WHERE RUNID= (SELECT MAX(RUNID) FROM SYSTEM.MVIEW_RECOMMENDATIONS)
   ORDER BY RECOMMENDATION_NUMBER ASC
```

The advisory functions and procedures of the DBMS_OLAP package require you to gather structural statistics about fact and dimension table cardinalities, and the distinct cardinalities of every dimension level column, JOIN KEY column, and fact table key column. You do this by loading your data warehouse, then gathering either exact or estimated statistics with the DBMS_STATS package or the ANALYZE TABLE statement. Because gathering statistics is time-consuming and extreme statistical accuracy is not required, it is generally preferable to estimate statistics.

Using information from the system workload table, schema metadata and statistical information generated by the DBMS_STATS package, the Advisor engine generates summary recommendations and summary usage evaluations and stores the results in result tables.

To use the Summary Advisor with a workload, some or all of the following steps must be followed:

- Optionally obtain an identifier number as a filter ID and define one or more filter items.
- Obtain an identifier number as a workload ID and load a workload. If a filter was defined in step 1, then it can be used during the operation to refine the SQL statements as they are collected from the workload source. Load the workload.
- Call the procedure RECOMMEND_MVIEW_STRATEGY to generate the recommendations.

These steps can be repeated several times with different workloads to see the effect on the materialized views.

USING THE SUMMARY ADVISOR

The following sections will help you use the Advisor:

- Identifier numbers
- Workload management
- Loading a user-defined workload
- Loading a trace workload
- Loading a SQL cache workload
- Validating a workload
- Removing a workload
- Using filters with the summary advisor
- Removing a filter
- Recommending materialized views
- Summary data report
- When Recommendations are no longer required
- Stopping the recommendation process
- Summary advisor sample sessions

- Summary advisor and missing statistics
- Summary advisor privileges and ORA-30446.

Identifier Numbers

Most of the DBMS_OLAP procedures require a unique identifier as one of their parameters. You obtain this by calling the procedure CREATE_ID, which is illustrated in the following section.

DBMS_OLAP.CREATE_ID Procedure

Table 9.1 DBMS_OLAP.CREATE_ID Procedure Parameters

Parameter	Datatype	Description
id	NUMBER	The unique identifier that can be used to create a filter, load a workload, or create an analysis

With a SQL utility such as SQL*Plus, do the following:

1. Declare an output variable to receive the new identifier.
```
VARIABLE MY_ID NUMBER;
```
2. Call the CREATE_ID function to generate a new identifier.
```
EXECUTE DBMS_OLAP.CREATE_ID(:MY_ID);
```

Workload Management

The Advisor performs best when a workload based on usage is available. The Advisor Workload Repository is capable of storing multiple workloads, so that the different uses of a real-world data warehousing environment can be viewed over a long period of time and across the life cycle of database instance startup and shutdown.

To facilitate wider use of the Summary Advisor, three types of workload are supported:

- Current contents of the SQL cache
- Oracle Trace collection
- User-specified workload.

When the workload is loaded using the appropriate load_workload procedure, it is stored in a new workload repository in the SYSTEM schema called MVIEW_WORKLOAD whose format is shown in table 9.2. A specific workload can be removed by calling the PURGE_WORKLOAD routine and passing it a valid workload ID. To remove all workloads for the current user, call PURGE_WORKLOAD and pass the constant value DBMS_OLAP.WORKLOAD_ALL.

Table 9.2 MVIEW_WORKLOAD Table

Column	Datatype	Description
APPLICATION	VARCHAR2(30)	Optional application name for the query
CARDINALITY	NUMBER	Total cardinality of all of tables in query
WORKLOADID	NUMBER	Workload id identifying a unique sampling
FREQUENCY	NUMBER	Number of times query executed
IMPORT_TIME	DATE	Date at which item was collected
LASTUSE	DATE	Last date of execution
OWNER	VARCHAR2(30)	User who last executed query

PRIORITY	NUMBER	User-supplied ranking of query
QUERY	LONG	Query text
QUERYID	NUMBER	Id number identifying a unique query
RESPONSETIME	NUMBER	Execution time in seconds
RESULTSIZE	NUMBER	Total bytes selected by the query

Once the workload has been collected using the appropriate LOAD_WORKLOAD routine, there is also a filter mechanism that may be applied, this lets you specify the portion of workload that is to be loaded into the repository. You can also use the same filter mechanism to restrict workload-based summary recommendation and evaluation to a subset of the queries contained in the workload repository. Once the workload has been loaded, the Summary Advisor is run by calling the procedure RECOMMEND_MVIEW_STRATEGY. A major benefit of this approach is that it is easy to model different workloads by simply modifying the frequency column, removing some SQL queries, or adding new queries.

Summary Advisor can retrieve workload information from the SQL cache as well as Oracle Trace. If the collected data was retrieved from a server with the instance parameter cursor_sharing set to SIMILAR or FORCE, then user queries with embedded literal values will be converted to a statement that contains system-generated bind variables.

NOTE *Oracle Trace will be deprecated in a future release.*

In Oracle9*i*, it is not possible to retrieve the bind-variable data in order to reconstruct the statement in the form originally submitted by the user. This will, in turn, cause Summary Advisor to not consider the query for rewrite and potentially miss a critical statement in the user's workload. As a work-around, if the Advisor will be used to recommend materialized views, then the server should set the instance parameter CURSOR_SHARING to EXACT.

Loading a User-Defined Workload

A user-defined workload is loaded using the procedure LOAD_WORKLOAD_USER. The workload_id is obtained by calling the procedure CREATE_ID. The value of the flags parameter determines whether the workload is considered to be new, should be used to overwrite an existing workload, or should be appended to an existing workload. The optional filter_id can be supplied to specify the filter that is to be used against this workload. Where the filter would have been defined using the ADD_FILTER_ITEM procedure.

DBMS_OLAP.LOAD_WORKLOAD_USER Procedure

Table 9.3 DBMS_OLAP.LOAD_WORKLOAD_USER Procedure Parameters

Parameter	Datatype	Description
workload_id	NUMBER	The required workload id that was returned by the create_id call
flags	NUMBER	Can take one of the following values: DBMS_OLAP.WORKLOAD_OVERWRITE The load routine will explicitly remove any existing queries from the workload that are owned by the specified collection ID DBMS_OLAP.WORKLOAD_APPEND

		The load routine preserves any existing queries in the workload. Any queries collected by the load operation will be appended to the end of the specified workload DBMS_OLAP.WORKLOAD_NEW The load routine assumes there are no existing queries in the workload. If it finds an existing workload element, the call will fail with an error Note: the flags have the same behavior irrespective of the LOAD_WORKLOAD operation
filter_id	NUMBER	Specify filter for the workload to be loaded
owner_name	VARCHAR2	The schema that contains the user supplied table or view
table_name	VARCHAR2	The table or view name containing valid workload data

The actual workload is defined in a separate table and the two parameters owner_name and table_name describe where it is stored. There is no restriction on which schema the workload resides in, the name for the table, or how many of these user-defined tables exist. The only restriction is that the format of the user table must correspond to the USER_WORKLOAD table, as described in table 9.4 :

Table 9.4 USER_WORKLOAD

Column	Datatype	Optional/ Required	Description
QUERY	Can be any VARCHAR or LONG type. All character types are supported	Required	SQL statement
OWNER	VARCHAR2(30)	Required	User who last executed query
APPLICATION	VARCHAR2(30)	Optional	Application name for the query
FREQUENCY	NUMBER	Optional	Number of times query executed
LASTUSE	DATE	Optional	Last date of execution
PRIORITY	NUMBER	Optional	User-supplied ranking of query
RESPONSETIME	NUMBER	Optional	Execution time in seconds
RESULTSIZE	NUMBER	Optional	Total bytes selected by the query
SQL_ADDR	NUMBER	Optional	Cache address
SQL_HASH	NUMBER	Optional	Cache hash value

The following is an example of loading a user workload.

1. Declare an output variable to receive the new identifier.

   VARIABLE MY_ID NUMBER;

2. Call the CREATE_ID function to generate a new identifier.

   EXECUTE DBMS_OLAP.CREATE_ID(:MY_ID);

3. Insert into the MY_WORKLOAD tables the queries you want advice on.

   INSERT INTO advisor_user_workload VALUES
   (
   'SELECT SUM(s.quantity_sold)
   FROM sales s, products p

WHERE s.prod_id = p.prod_id AND p.prod_category = ''Boys''

GROUP BY p.prod_category', 'SH', 'app1', 10, NULL, 5, NULL, NULL)

4. Load the workload from a target table or view.

EXECUTE DBMS_OLAP.LOAD_WORKLOAD_USER(:MY_ID, DBMS_OLAP.WORKLOAD_NEW,

DBMS_OLAP.FILTER_NONE, 'SH', 'MY_WORKLOAD');

Loading a Trace Workload

Alternatively, you can collect a Trace workload from Oracle Enterprise Manager to gather dynamic information about your query workload, which can be used by an advisory function. If Oracle Trace is available, consider using it to collect materialized view usage. Doing so enables you to see which materialized views are in use. It also lets the Advisor detect any unusual query requests from users that would result in recommending some different materialized views.

A workload collected by Oracle Trace is loaded by using the procedure LOAD_WORKLOAD_TRACE. You obtain workload_id by calling the procedure CREATE_ID. The value of the flags parameter will determine whether the workload is considered new, should be used to overwrite an existing workload or should be appended to an existing workload. The optional filter ID can be supplied to specify the filter that is to be used against this workload. In addition, you can specify an application name to describe this workload and give every query a default priority. The application name is simply a tag that enables you to classify the workload query. The name can later be used to filter the workload during a RECOMMEND_MVIEW_STRATEGY or EVALUATE_MVIEW_STRATEGY operation.

The priority is an important piece of information. It tells the Advisor how important the query is to the business. When recommendations are formed, the priority will determine its value and will cause the Advisor to make decisions that favor higher ranking queries.

If the owner_name parameter is not defined, then the procedure will expect to find the formatted trace tables in the schema for the current user.

DBMS_OLAP.LOAD_WORKLOAD_TRACE Procedure

Table 9.5. DBMS_OLAP.LOAD_WORKLOAD_TRACE Procedure Parameters

Parameter	Datatype	Description
workload_id	NUMBER	The required id that was returned by the CREATE_ID call
flags	NUMBER	Can take one of the following values: DBMS_OLAP.WORKLOAD_OVERWRITE The load routine will explicitly remove any existing queries from the workload that are owned by the specified collection ID DBMS_OLAP.WORKLOAD_APPEND The load routine preserves any existing queries in the workload. Any queries collected by the load operation will be appended to the end of the specified workload DBMS_OLAP.WORKLOAD_NEW The load routine assumes there are no existing queries in the workload. If it finds an existing workload element, the call will fail with an error

		Note: the flags have the same behavior irrespective of the LOAD_WORKLOAD operation
filter_id	NUMBER	Specify filter for the workload to be loaded
application	VARCHAR2	The default business application name. This value will be used for a query if one is not found in the target workload
priority	NUMBER	The default business priority to be assigned to every query in the target workload
owner_name	VARCHAR2	The schema that contains the Oracle Trace data. If omitted, the current user will be used

Oracle Trace collects two types of data. One is a duration event which causes a data item to be collected twice: once at the start of the operation and once at the end of the operation. The duration of the data item is the difference between the start and end of the operation. For example, execution time is collected as a duration event. It first collects the clock time when the operation starts. Then it collects the clock time when the operation ends. Execution time is calculated by subtracting the start time from the end time.

A point event is a static data item that doesn't change over time. For example, an owner name is a static data item that would be the same at the start and the end of an operation.

To collect, analyze and load the summary event set, you must do the following:

1. Set six initialization parameters to collect data using Oracle Trace. Enabling these parameters incurs some additional overhead at database connection, but is otherwise transparent.
   - ORACLE_TRACE_COLLECTION_NAME = oraclesm or oraclee

     ORACLEE is the Oracle Expert collection which contains Summary Advisor data and additional data that is only used by Oracle Expert. ORACLESM is the Summary Advisor collection that contains only Summary Advisor data and is the preferred collection type.
   - ORACLE_TRACE_COLLECTION_PATH = location of collection files
   - ORACLE_TRACE_COLLECTION_SIZE = 0
   - ORACLE_TRACE_ENABLE = TRUE
   - ORACLE_TRACE_FACILITY_NAME = oraclesm or oralcee
   - ORACLE_TRACE_FACILITY_PATH = location of trace facility files.
2. Run the Oracle Trace Manager, specify a collection name, and select the SUMMARY_EVENT set. Oracle Trace Manager reads information from the associated configuration file and registers events to be logged with Oracle. While collection is enabled, the workload information defined in the event set gets written to a flat log file.
3. When collection is complete, Oracle Trace automatically formats the Oracle Trace log file into a set of relations, which have the predefined synonyms beginning with V_192216243_. Alternatively, the collection file, which usually has an extension of CDF, can be formatted manually using the otrcfmt utility, as shown in this example:

   otrcfmt collection_name.cdf user/password@database.

The trace data can be formatted in any schema. The LOAD_WORKLOAD_TRACE call lets you specify the location of the data.

4. Run the GATHER_TABLE_STATS procedure of the DBMS_STATS package or ANALYZE ... ESTIMATE STATISTICS to collect cardinality statistics on all fact tables, dimension tables, and key columns (any column that appears in a dimension LEVEL clause or JOIN clause of a CREATE DIMENSION statement).
5. Run the CREATE_ID procedure of the DBMS_OLAP package to get a unique workload_id for this workload.
6. Run the LOAD_WORKLOAD_TRACE procedure of the DBMS_OLAP package to load this workload into the repository.

   Once these six steps have been completed, you will be ready to make recommendations about your materialized views. An example of how to load a trace workload is illustrated as follows.

   (*a*) Declare an output variable to receive the new identifier.

   ```
   VARIABLE MY_ID NUMBER:
   ```

   (*b*) Call the CREATE_ID function to generate a new identifier.

   ```
   EXECUTE DBMS_OLAP.CREATE_ID(:MY_ID);
   ```

   (*c*) Load the workload from the formatted trace collection.

   ```
   EXECUTE DBMS_OLAP.LOAD_WORKLOAD_TRACE(:MY_ID, DBMS_OLAP.WORKLOAD_NEW,
   DBMS_
   OLAP.FILTER_NONE,    'myapp',  7,    'SH');
   ```

Loading a SQL Cache Workload

You obtain a SQL cache workload using the procedure LOAD_WORKLOAD_CACHE. At the time this procedure is called, the current contents of the SQL cache are analyzed and placed into the read-only view SYSTEM.MVIEW_WORKLOAD.

You obtain workload_id by calling the procedure CREATE_ID. The value of the flags parameter determines whether the workload is treated as new, should be used to overwrite an existing workload, or should be appended to an existing workload. The optional filter ID can be supplied to specify the filter that is to be used against this workload. Where the filter would have been defined using the ADD_FILTER_ITEM procedure. In addition, you can specify an application name to describe this workload and give every query a default priority.

DBMS_OLAP.LOAD_WORKLOAD_CACHE Procedure

Table 9.6 DBMS_OLAP.LOAD_WORKLOAD_CACHE Procedure Parameters

Parameter	Datatype	Description
workload_id	NUMBER	The required ID that was returned by the CREATE_ID call
flags	NUMBER	Can take one of the following values: DBMS_OLAP.WORKLOAD_OVERWRITE The load routine will explicitly remove any existing queries from the workload that are owned by the specified collection ID DBMS_OLAP.WORKLOAD_APPEND:

		The load routine preserves any existing queries in the workload. Any queries collected by the load operation will be appended to the end of the specified workload DBMS_OLAP.WORKLOAD_NEW: The load routine assumes there are no existing queries in the workload. If it finds an existing workload element, the call will fail with an error Note: the flags have the same behavior irrespective of the LOAD_WORKLOAD operation
filter_id	NUMBER	Specify filter for the workload to be loaded. The value DBMS_OLAP.FILTER_NONE indicates no filtering
application	VARCHAR2	String workload's application column. Not used by SQL Cache workload
priority	NUMBER	The default business priority to be assigned to every query in the target workload

An example of how to load a SQL Cache workload is as follows.

1. Declare an output variable to receive the new identifier.
   ```
   VARIABLE MY_ID NUMBER:
   ```
2. Call the CREATE_ID function to generate a new identifier.
   ```
   EXECUTE DBMS_OLAP.CREATE_ID(:MY_ID);
   ```
3. Load the workload from the SQL cache.
   ```
   EXECUTE DBMS_OLAP.LOAD_WORKLOAD_CACHE(:MY_ID, DBMS_OLAP.WORKLOAD_NEW, DBMS_
   OLAP.FILTER_NONE, 'Payroll', 7);
   ```

Validating a Workload

Prior to loading a workload, you can call one of the three VALIDATE_WORKLOAD procedures to check that the workload exists:

- VALIDATE_WORKLOAD_USER
- VALIDATE_WORKLOAD_CACHE
- VALIDATE_WORKLOAD_TRACE.

These procedures do not check that the contents of the workload are valid, they merely check that the workload exists.

Examples of Validating Workloads

The following are examples of validating the three types of workload:

```
DECLARE
   isitgood      NUMBER;
   err_text      VARCHAR2(200);
BEGIN
   DBMS_OLAP.VALIDATE_WORKLOAD_CACHE (isitgood, err_text);
END;
```

```
DECLARE
  isitgood         NUMBER;
  err_text         VARCHAR2(200);
BEGIN
   DBMS_OLAP.VALIDATE_WORKLOAD_TRACE  ('SH',  isitgood,  err_text);
END;

DECLARE
   isitgood        NUMBER;
   err_text        VARCHAR2(200);
BEGIN
    DBMS_OLAP.VALIDATE_WORKLOAD_USER  ('SH',  'USER_WORKLOAD',  isitgood,
err_text);
END;
```

Removing a Workload

When workloads are no longer needed, they can be removed using the procedure PURGE_WORKLOAD. You can delete all workloads or a specific collection.

DBMS_OLAP.PURGE_WORKLOAD Procedure

Table 9.7 DBMS_OLAP.PURGE_WORKLOAD Procedure Parameters

Parameter	Datatype	Description
workload_id	NUMBER	An ID number originally assigned by the create_id call. If the value of workload_id is set to DBMS_OLAP.WORKLOAD_ALL, then all workload collections for the current user will be deleted

The following is an example of removing a specific workload:

```
VARIABLE  workload_id  NUMBER;
DBMS_OLAP.PURGE_WORKLOAD(:workload_id);
```

The following example removes all workloads:

```
EXECUTE    DBMS_OLAP.PURGE_WORKLOAD(DBMS_OLAP.WORKLOAD_ALL);
```

Using Filters with the Summary Advisor

The entire contents of a workload do not have to be used during the recommendation process. Any workload can be filtered by creating a filter item using the procedure ADD_FILTER_ITEM, which is described is table 9.8.

DBMS_OLAP.ADD_FILTER_ITEM Procedure

Table 9.8 DBMS_OLAP.ADD_FILTER_ITEM Procedure Parameters

Parameter	Datatype	Description
filter_id	NUMBER	An ID that uniquely describes the filter. It is generated by the create_id call
filter_name	VARCHAR2	APPLICATION String-workload's application column BASETABLE String-based tables referenced by workload queries. Name must be fully qualified including owner and table name (for example, SH.SALES)

		CARDINALITY Numerical-sum of cardinality of the referenced base tables FREQUENCY Numerical-workload's frequency column LASTUSE Date-workload's lastuse column. Not used by SQL Cache workload OWNER String-workload's owner column. Expected in uppercase unless owner defined explicitly to be not all in uppercase PRIORITY Numerical-workload's priority column. Not used by SQL Cache workload RESPONSETIME Numerical-workload's responsetime column. Not used by SQL Cache workload SCHEMA String-based schema referenced be workload queries. TRACENAME String-list of oracle trace collection names. Only used by a Trace Workload
string_list	VARCHAR2	A comma-delimited list of strings
number_min	NUMBER	The lower bound of a numerical range. NULL represents the lowest possible value
number_max	NUMBER	The upper bound of a numerical range, NULL for no upper bound. NULL represents the highest possible value
date_min	VARCHAR2	The lower bound of a date range. NULL represents the lowest possible date value
date_max	VARCHAR2	The upper bound of a date range. NULL represents the highest possible date value

The Advisor supports ten different filter item types. For each filter item, Oracle stores an attribute that tells Advisor how to apply the selection rule. For example, an APPLICATION item requires a string attribute that can be either a single name as in GREG, or it can be a comma-delimited list of names like GREG, ROSE, KALLIE, HANNAH. For a single name, the Advisor takes the value and only accepts the workload query if the application name exactly matches the supplied name. For a list of names, the queries application name must appear in the list. Referring to my example, a query whose application name is GREG would match either a single application filter item containing GREG or the list GREG, ROSE, KALLIE, HANNAH. Conversely, a query whose application is KALLIE will only match the filter item list GREG, ROSE, KALLIE, HANNAH.

For numeric filter items such as CARDINALITY, the attribute represents a possible range of values. Advisor will determine if the filter item represents a bounded range such as 500 to 1000000, or it could be an exact match like 1000 to 1000. When the range value is specified as NULL, then the value is infinitely small or large, depending upon which attribute is set.

Data filters, such as LASTUSE behave similar to numeric filter except Advisor treats the range test as two dates. A value of NULL indicates infinity.

You can define a number of different types of filter as shown in table 9.9.

Table 9.9 Workload Filters and Attribute Types

Filter Item Name	string_list	number_min	number_max	date_min	date_max	Description
APPLICATION	Required	N/A	N/A	N/A	N/A	Query should be from the list applications defined in string_list. Multiple application names must be separated by commas
CARDINALITY	N/A	Required	Required	N/A	N/A	Sum of cardinalities of base tables found in a query
LASTUSE	N/A	N/A	N/A	Required	Required	Last execution date of the query
FREQUENCY	N/A	Required	Required	N/A	N/A	Number of executions for the query
OWNER	Required	N/A	N/A	N/A	N/A	List of database users who executed queries. Multiple owners must be separated by commas
PRIORITY	N/A	Required	Required	N/A	N/A	User-supplied priority value
BASETABLE	Required	N/A	N/A	N/A	N/A	List of fully qualified tables that appear in a candidate query. Multiple tables must be separated by commas
RESPONSETIME	N/A	Required	Required	N/A	N/A	Query response time in seconds
SCHEMA	Required	N/A	N/A	N/A	N/A	Query should be from the list schemas defined in string_list. Multiple schema names must separated by commas
TRACENAME	Required	N/A	N/A	N/A	N/A	List of Oracle Trace collection names. If this filter is not used, then the collection operation will choose the entire Oracle Trace collection, regardless of its collection name. Multiple names must be separated by commas

When dealing with a workload, the client can optionally attach a filter to reduce or refine the set of target SQL statements. If no filter is attached, then all target SQL statements will be collected or used.

A new filter can be created with the CREATE_ID call. Filter items can be added to the filter by using the ADD_FILTER_ITEM call. When a filter is created, an entry is stored in the read-only view SYSTEM.MVIEW_FILTER.

The following is an example illustrating how to add three different types of filter

1. Declare an output variable to receive the new identifier.

```
VARIABLE MY_ID NUMBER:
```

2. Call the CREATE_ID function to generate a new identifier.

```
EXECUTE DBMS_OLAP.CREATE_ID(:MY_ID);
```

3. Add filter items.

```
EXECUTE DBMS_OLAP.ADD_FILTER_ITEM(:MY_ID,'BASETABLE', 'SCOTT.EMP',NULL,
NULL, NULL, NULL);

EXECUTE DBMS_OLAP.ADD_FILTER_ITEM(:MY_ID, 'OWNER', 'SCOTT, PAYROLL,
PERSONNEL', NULL, NULL, NULL, NULL);

EXECUTE DBMS_OLAP.ADD_FILTER_ITEM(:MY_ID, 'FREQUENCY', NULL,

500, NULL, NULL, NULL);
```

This example defines a filter with three filter items. The first filter will only allow queries that reference the table SCOTT.EMP. The second item will accept queries that were executed by one of the users SCOTT, PAYROLL or PERSONNEL. Finally, the third filter item accepts queries that execute at least 500 times.

Note, all filter items must match for a single query to be accepted. If any of the items fails to match, then the query will not be accepted.

In the previous example, three filters will be applied against the data. However, each filter item could have created with its only unique filter id, thus creating three different filters as illustrated in the following:

```
VARIABLE MY_ID NUMBER:
EXECUTE DBMS_OLAP.CREATE_ID(:MY_ID);
EXECUTE DBMS_OLAP.ADD_FILTER_ITEM(:MY_ID,'BASETABLE',
        'SCOTT.EMP', NULL, NULL, NULL, NULL);
EXECUTE DBMS_OLAP.CREATE_ID(:MY_ID);
EXECUTE DBMS_OLAP.ADD_FILTER_ITEM(:MY_ID, 'OWNER',
       'SCOTT, PAYROLL,PERSONNEL', NULL, NULL, NULL, ULL);
EXECUTE DBMS_OLAP.CREATE_ID(:MY_ID);
EXECUTE DBMS_OLAP.ADD_FILTER_ITEM(:MY_ID, 'FREQUENCY', NULL, 500,NULL,
  NULL,NULL);
```

Removing a Filter

A filter can be removed at anytime by calling the procedure PURGE_FILTER, which is described in the following table. You can delete a specific filter or all filters. You can remove all filters using the purge_filter call by specifying DBMS_OLAP.FILTER_ALL as the filter ID.

DBMS_OLAP.PURGE_FILTER Procedure

Table 9.10 DBMS_OLAP.PURGE_FILTER Procedure Parameters

Parameter	Datatype	Description
filterid	NUMBER	A filter ID number used to identify the filter to be deleted

DBMS_OLAP.PURGE_FILTER Example

```
VARIABLE     MY_FILTER_ID NUMBER:
EXECUTE      DBMS_OLAP.PURGE_FILTER(:MY_FILTER_ID);
EXECUTE      DBMS_OLAP.PURGE_FILTER(DBMS_OLAP.FILTER_ALL);
```

Recommending Materialized Views

The analysis and advisory procedure for materialized views is RECOMMEND_MVIEW_STRATEGY in the DBMS_OLAP package. This procedure automatically recommends which materialized view to create, retain, or drop. RECOMMEND_MVIEW_STRATEGY uses structural statistics and optionally workload statistics.

You can call this procedure to obtain a list of materialized view recommendations that you can select, modify, or reject. Alternatively, you can use the DBMS_OLAP package directly in your PL/SQL programs for the same purpose.

To use the Summary Advisor, you must have the SELECT ANY TABLE privilege.

The parameters for RECOMMEND_MVIEW_STRATEGY and their descriptions are given in table 9.11.

RECOMMEND_MVIEW_STRATEGY Procedure Parameters

Table 9.11 RECOMMEND_MVIEW_STRATEGY Parameters

Parameter	I/O	Datatype	Description
run_id	IN	NUMBER	A return value that uniquely identifies the current operation
workoad_id	IN	NUMBER	An optional workload ID that maps to a workload in the current repository
filter_id	IN	NUMBER	An optional filter ID that maps to a set of user-supplied filter items
storage_in_bytes	IN	NUMBER	Maximum storage, in bytes, that can be used for storing materialized views. This number must be non-negative
retention_pct	IN	NUMBER	Number between 0 and 100 that specifies the percent of existing materialized view storage that must be retained, based on utilization on the actual or hypothetical workload A materialized view is retained if the cumulative space, ranked by utilization, is within the retention threshold specified (or if it is explicitly listed in retention_list). Materialized views that have a NULL utilization (for example, non-dimensional materialized views) are always retained

retention_list	IN	VARCHAR2	Comma-delimited list of materialized view table names A drop recommendation is not made for any materialized view that appears in this list
fact_table_filter	IN	VARCHAR2	Comma-delimited list of fact table names to analyze, or NULL to analyze all fact tables

The results from calling this package are put in the table SYSTEM.MVIEW_RECOMMENDATIONS shown in table 9.12. The output can be queried directly by using the MVIEW_RECOMMENDATION table or a structured report can be generated by using the DBMS_OLAP.GENERATE_MVIEW_REPORT procedure.

Table 9.12. MVIEW_RECOMMENDATIONS

Column	Datatype	Description
RUNID	NUMBER	Run ID identifying a unique advisor call
FACT_TABLES	VARCHAR2(1000)	A comma-delimited list of fully qualified table names for structured recommendations
GROUPING_LEVELS	VARCHAR2(2000)	A comma-delimited list of grouping levels, if any, for structured recommendations
QUERY_TEXT	LONG	Query text of materialized view if RECOMMENDED_ACTION is CREATE; NULL otherwise
RECOMMENDATION_NUMBER	NUMBER	Unique identifier for this recommendation
RECOMMENDED_ACTION	VARCHAR(6)	CREATE, RETAIN, or DROP
MVIEW_OWNER	VARCHAR2(30)	Owner of the materialized view summary if RECOMMENDED_ACTION is RETAIN or DROP; NULL otherwise
MVIEW_NAME	VARCHAR2(30)	Name of the materialized view if RECOMMENDED_ACTION is RETAIN or DROP; NULL otherwise
STORAGE_IN_BYTES	NUMBER	Actual or estimated storage in bytes storage
PCT_PERFORMANCE_GAIN	NUMBER	The expected incremental improvement in performance obtained by accepting this recommendation relative to the initial condition, assuming that all previous recommendations have been accepted, or NULL if unknown. Performance gain
BENEFIT_TO_COST_RATIO	NUMBER	Ratio of the incremental improvement in performance to the size of the materialized view in bytes, or NULL if unknown. Benefit/Cost

Summary Advisor Usage Examples

The following are several examples of how you can use the Summary Advisor recommendation process.

Example 9.1 : Summary Advisor (USER_WORKLOAD)

In this example, a workload is loaded from the table USER_WORKLOAD and no filtering is applied to the workload. The fact table is called sales.

```
DECLARE
  workload_id         NUMBER;
  run_id              NUMBER;

BEGIN
– load the workload
  DBMS_OLAP.CREATE_ID (workload_id);
  DBMS_OLAP.LOAD_WORKLOAD_USER(workload_id, DBMS_OLAP.WORKLOAD_NEW,
        DBMS_OLAP.FILTER_NONE,'SH','USER_WORKLOAD' );
– run recommend_mv
  DBMS_OLAP.CREATE_ID (run_id);
  DBMS_OLAP.RECOMMEND_MVIEW_STRATEGY(run_id, workload_id, NULL, 1000000, 100,
NULL, 'sales');
END;
```

Example 9.2 : Summary Advisor (SQL Cache)

In this example, the workload is derived from the current contents of the SQL cache and then filtered for only the application called sales_hist:

```
DECLARE
  workload_id         NUMBER;
  filter_id           NUMBER;
  run_id              NUMBER;
BEGIN
– add a filter for application sales_hist
  DBMS_OLAP.CREATE_ID(filter_id);
  DBMS_OLAP.ADD_FILTER_ITEM(filter_id, 'APPLICATION', 'sales_hist', NULL, NULL,
NULL, NULL);
– load the workload
  DBMS_OLAP.CREATE_ID(workload_id);
  DBMS_OLAP.LOAD_WORKLOAD_CACHE (workload_id, DBMS_OLAP.WORKLOAD_NEW, DBMS_
OLAP.FILTER_NONE, NULL
,NULL);
– run recommend_mv
  DBMS_OLAP.CREATE_ID (run_id );
  DBMS_OLAP.RECOMMEND_MVIEW_STRATEGY(run_id, workload_id, NULL, 1000000, 100,
NULL, 'sales');
END;
```

Example 9.3 : Summary Advisor (Oracle Trace)

In this example, the workload is from Oracle Trace without filtering.

```
DECLARE
  workload_id         NUMBER;
  run_id              NUMBER;
BEGIN
  DBMS_OLAP.CREATE_ID (workload_id);
```

```
   DBMS_OLAP.LOAD_WORKLOAD_TRACE (workload_id, DBMS_OLAP.WORKLOAD_NEW, DBMS_
OLAP.FILTER_NONE, NULL,NULL,NULL );
– run recommend_mv
   DBMS_OLAP.CREATE_ID(run_id);
   DBMS_OLAP.RECOMMEND_MVIEW_STRATEGY(run_id, workload_id, NULL,10000000, 100,
NULL, 'sales');
END;
```

SQL Script Generation

When the Summary Advisor is run using Oracle Enterprise Manager the facility is provided to implement the advisors recommendations. But when the procedure `RECOMMEND_MVIEW_STRATEGY` is called directly the procedure `GENERATE_MVIEW_SCRIPT` must be used to create a script which will implement the advisors recommendations. The parameters are as follows:

```
GENERATE_MVIEW_SCRIPT (filename VARCHAR2,
id NUMBER, tablespace_name VARCHAR2)
```

Table 9.13. GENERATE_MVIEW_SCRIPT Parameters

Parameter	Contents
filename	The fully-specified output file name
id	The Advisor run ID for which the script will be created
tablespace_name	An optional tablespace in which new materialized views will be placed

The resulting script is an executable SQL file that can contain `DROP` and `CREATE` statements for materialized views. For new materialized views, the name of the materialized views is auto-generated by combining the user-specified ID and the Rank value of the materialized views. It is recommended that the user must review the generated SQL script before attempting to execute it.

The filename specification requires the same security model as described in the `GENERATE_MVIEW_REPORT` routine.

Summary Advisor Sample Output

```
/*  Oracle Summary Advisor 9i - Production
 Summary Advisor Recommendation Script Recommendations
 for run ID #9999
  Rank 1
  Storage 0 bytes
  Gain 0.00%
  Benefit Ratio 0.00
  SELECT COUNT(*), AVG(dollar_cost)
  FROM sales
  GROUP BY store_key
*/

CREATE MATERIALIZED VIEW mv_id_9999_rank_1
  TABLESPACE user
  BUILD IMMEDIATE
  REFRESH COMPLETE
  ENABLE QUERY REWRITE AS
    SELECT COUNT(*),AVG(dollar_cost) FROM sales GROUP BY store_key;
```

```
/*Rank 2
Storage 6,000 bytes
Gain 13.00%
Benefit Ratio 874.00
*/

DROP MATERIALIZED VIEW sh.mview_fact_01;

/*
Rank 3
Storage 6,000 bytes
Gain 76.00%
Benefit Ratio 8,744.00
SELECT COUNT(*), MAX(dollar_cost), MIN(dollar_cost)
FROM sh.sales
WHERE store_key IN (10, 23)
AND unit_sales > 5000
ROUP BY store_key, promotion_key
*/

CREATE MATERIALIZED VIEW mv_id_9999_rank_3
  TABLESPACE user
  BUILD IMMEDIATE
  REFRESH COMPLETE
  ENABLE QUERY REWRITE AS
    SELECT COUNT(*), MAX(dollar_cost), MIN(dollar_cost) FROM sh.sales
    WHERE store_key IN (10,23) AND unit_sales > 5000 GROUP BY
       store_key, promotion_key;
```

Summary Data Report

A Summary Data Report offers you data about workloads and filters, and then generates recommendations. The report format is HTML and the contents are the following:

- Activity Journal Details

  This section describes the recorded data. A journal is simply a mechanism to permit the Advisor to record any interesting event that may occur during processing. During processing, many decisions can be made by the Advisor that are not necessarily visible to you. The journal enables you to see the internal processes and steps taken by the Summary Advisor. It contains work-in-progress messages, debugging messages and error messages for a particular Advisor element.

- Activity Log Details

  This section describes the various Advisor activities that have been executed by the current user. Activities include workload filter maintenance, workload collections and analysis operations.

- Materialized View Recommendations

  This section contains detail information regarding Advisor analysis sessions. It presents various recommendations on the creation of new materialized views as well as the removal of inappropriate or expensive materialized views.

- Materialized View Usage

  This section describes the Advisor's results from an evaluation of existing materialized views.
- Workload Collection Details

  The workload report lists the details of each SQL query for the current user's workload collections. The report is arranged by table references.
- Workload Filter Details

  The workload filter report lists details of workload filters for the current user.
- Workload Query Details

  This report contains the actual SQL queries for the current user's workload collections. Each query can be linked back to an entry in the Workload report.

PL/SQL Interface Syntax

```
PROCEDURE  GENERATE_MVIEW_REPORT
    (file_name IN VARCHAR2,
     id        IN NUMBER,
     flags     IN NUMBER)
```

Table 9.14 GENERATE_MVIEW_REPORT Parameters

Parameter	Description
`file_name`	A valid output file specification. Note, the Oracle9*i* restricts file access within Oracle Stored Procedures. This means that file locations and names must adhere to the known file permissions in the Policy Table.
`id`	The Advisor ID number used to collect or analyze data. `NULL` indicates all data for the requested section

`flags`	Report flags to indicate required detail sections. Multiple sections can be selected by referencing the following constants.
	`RPT_ALL`
	`RPT_ACTIVITY`
	`RPT_JOURNAL`
	`RPT_RECOMMENDATION`
	`RPT_USAGE`
	`RPT_WORKLOAD_DETAIL`
	`RPT_WORKLOAD_FILTER`
	`RPT_WORKLOAD_QUERY`

Because of the Oracle security model, report output file directories must be granted read and write permission prior to executing this call.

```
EXECUTE  DBMS_JAVA.GRANT_PERMISSION('Oracle-user-goes-here',
    'java.io.FilePermission', 'directory-spec-goes-here/*', 'read, write');
```

The following is an example of how to call this report:

```
EXECUTE  DBMS_OLAP.GENERATE_MVIEW_REPORT(
 '/usr/mydev/myname/report.html', 0, DBMS_OLAP.RPT_ALL);
```

This produces the HTML file `/usr/mydev/myname/report.html`. In this example, `report.html` is the Table of Contents for the report. It will contain links to each section of the report, which are found in external files with names derived from the original filename. Because no ID was specified for the second parameter, all data for the current user will be reported. If, for example, you want only a report on a particular recommendation run, then that run ID should be passed into the call. The report can generate the following HTML files:

HTML File	Description
xxxx.html	Table of Contents
xxxx_log.html	Activity Section
xxxx_jou.html	Journal Section
xxxx_fil.html	Workload Filter Section
xxxx_wrk.html	Workload Section
xxxx_rec.html	Materialized View Recommendation Section
xxxx_usa.html	Materialized View Usage Section

In this table, `xxxx` is the filename portion of the user-supplied file specification. All files appear in the same directory, which is the one you specify.

When Recommendations are No Longer Required

Every time the Summary Advisor is run, a new set of recommendations is created. When they are no longer required, they should be removed using the procedure `PURGE_RESULTS`. You can remove all results or those for a specific run.

DBMS_OLAP.PURGE_RESULTS Procedure

Table 9.15 DBMS_OLAP.PURGE_RESULTS Procedure Parameters

Parameter	Datatype	Description
run_id	NUMBER	An ID used to identify the results to delete
EXECUTE	DBMS_OLAP.PURGE_RESULTS	(DBMS_OLAP.RUNID_ALL);

Stopping the Recommendation Process

If the Summary Advisor takes too long to make its recommendations by using the procedure `RECOMMEND_MVIEW_STRATEGY`, you can stop it by calling the procedure `SET_CANCELLED` and passing in the `run_id` for this recommendation process.

DBMS_OLAP.SET_CANCELLED Procedure

Table 9.16. DBMS_OLAP.SET_CANCELLED Procedure Parameters

Parameter	Datatype	Description
run_id	NUMBER	Id that uniquely identifies an advisor analysis operation. This call can be used to cancel a long running workload collection as well as an Advisor analysis session

Summary Advisor Sample Sessions

Here are some complete examples of how to use the Summary Advisor.

Sample Session Setup

```
REM===============================================================
REM Setup for demos
REM===============================================================
CONNECT system/manager
GRANT SELECT ON mview_recommendations to sh;
GRANT SELECT ON mview_workload to sh;
GRANT SELECT ON mview_filter to sh;
DISCONNECT
```

Sample Session 1

```
    REM***************************************************************
    REM * Demo 1: Materialized View Recommendation With User Workload*
    REM***************************************************************
    REM===============================================================
    REM Step 1. Define user workload table and add artificial workload queries.
    REM===============================================================
CONNECT sh/sh
CREATE TABLE user_workload(
  query          VARCHAR2(40),
  owner          VARCHAR2(40),
  application    VARCHAR2(30),
  frequency      NUMBER,
  lastuse        DATE,
  priority       NUMBER,
  responsetime   NUMBER,
  resultsize     NUMBER
)
/
INSERT INTO user_workload values
(
   'SELECT SUM(s.quantity_sold)
    FROM sales s, products p
    WHERE s.prod_id = p.prod_id and p.prod_category = "Boys"
    GROUP BY p.prod_category',  'SH', 'app1', 10, NULL, 5, NULL, NULL
)
/
INSERT INTO user_workload values
(
   'SELECT SUM(s.amount)
    FROM sales s, products p
    WHERE s.prod_id = p.prod_id AND
      p.prod_category = "Girls"
    GROUP BY p.prod_category',
   'SH', 'app1', 10, NULL, 6, NULL, NULL
)
```

```
/
INSERT INTO user_workload values
(
  'SELECT SUM(quantity_sold)
   FROM sales s, products p
   WHERE s.prod_id = p.prod_id and
     p.prod_category = "Men"
   GROUP BY p.prod_category
  ',
  'SH', 'app1', 11, NULL, 3, NULL, NULL
)
/
INSERT INTO user_workload VALUES
(
  'SELECT SUM(quantity_sold)
   FROM sales s, products p
   WHERE s.prod_id = p.prod_id and
     p.prod_category in ("Women", "Men")
   GROUP BY p.prod_category  ', 'SH', 'app1', 1, NULL, 8, NULL, NULL
)
/

REM===========================================================================
REM Step 2. Create a new identifier to identify a new collection in the
REM         internal repository and load the user-defined workload into the
REM         workload collection without filtering the workload.
REM
===========================================================================
VARIABLE WORKLOAD_ID NUMBER;
EXECUTE  DBMS_OLAP.CREATE_ID(:workload_id);
EXECUTE  DBMS_OLAP.LOAD_WORKLOAD_USER(:workload_id,\
    DBMS_OLAP.WORKLOAD_NEW,\
    DBMS_OLAP.FILTER_NONE, 'SH', 'USER_WORKLOAD');
SELECT COUNT(*) FROM SYSTEM.MVIEW_WORKLOAD
   WHERE workloadid = :workload_id;

REM===========================================================================
REM Step 3. Create a new identifier to identify a new filter object. Add
REM         two filter items such that the filter can filter out workload
REM         queries with priority >= 5 and frequency <= 10.
REM===========================================================================
VARIABLE filter_id NUMBER;
EXECUTE  DBMS_OLAP.CREATE_ID(:filter_id);
EXECUTE  DBMS_OLAP.ADD_FILTER_ITEM(:filter_id,  'PRIORITY',
   NULL, 5, NULL, NULL, NULL);
EXECUTE DBMS_OLAP.ADD_FILTER_ITEM(:filter_id, 'FREQUENCY',    NULL,
   NULL, 10, NULL, NULL);
```

```
SELECT COUNT(*) FROM SYSTEM.MVIEW_FILTER
WHERE filterid = :filter_id;

REM===========================================================================
REM Step 4. Recommend materialized views with part of the previous workload
REM         collection that satisfy the filter conditions. Create a new
REM         identifier to identify the recommendation output.
REM===========================================================================
VARIABLE RUN_ID NUMBER;
EXECUTE DBMS_OLAP.CREATE_ID(:run_id);
EXECUTE DBMS_OLAP.RECOMMEND_MVIEW_STRATEGY(:run_id, :workload_id, :filter_id,
100000, 100, NULL, NULL);
SELECT COUNT(*) FROM SYSTEM.MVIEW_RECOMMENDATIONS;

REM===========================================================================
REM Step 5. Generate HTML reports on the output.
REM===========================================================================
EXECUTE DBMS_OLAP.GENERATE_MVIEW_REPORT('/tmp/output1.html', :run_id, DBMS_
OLAP.RPT_RECOMMENDATION);

REM===========================================================================
REM Step 6. Cleanup current output, filter and workload collection
REM         FROM the internal repository, truncate the user workload table
REM         for new user workloads.
REM===========================================================================
EXECUTE DBMS_OLAP.PURGE_RESULTS(:run_id);
EXECUTE DBMS_OLAP.PURGE_FILTER(:filter_id);
EXECUTE DBMS_OLAP.PURGE_WORKLOAD(:workload_id);
SELECT COUNT(*) FROM SYSTEM.MVIEW_WORKLOAD
   WHERE workloadid = :WORKLOAD_ID;
TRUNCATE TABLE user_workload;

DROP TABLE user_workload;
DISCONNECT
```

Sample Session 2

```
REM***************************************************************************
REM * Demo 2: Materialized View Recommendation With SQL Cache.   *
REM***************************************************************************
CONNECT sh/sh

REM===========================================================================
REM Step 1. Run some applications or some SQL queries, so that the
REM         Oracle SQL Cache is populated with target queries.
```

```
REM==================================================================
REM Clear Pool of SQL queries

ALTER SYSTEM FLUSH SHARED_POOL;

SELECT  SUM(s.quantity_sold)
FROM sales s, products p
WHERE s.prod_id = p.prod_id
 GROUP BY p.prod_category;

SELECT  SUM(s.amount_sold)
FROM sales s, products p
WHERE s.prod_id = p.prod_id
GROUP BY p.prod_category,

SELECT t.calendar_month_desc, SUM(s.amount_sold) AS dollars
FROM sales s, times t
WHERE s.time_id = t.time_id
GROUP BY t.calendar_month_desc;

SELECT t.calendar_month_desc, SUM(s.amount_sold) AS dollars
FROM sales s, times t
WHERE s.time_id = t.time_id
GROUP BY t.calendar_month_desc;
  .
REM==================================================================
REM Step 2. Create a new identifier to identify a new collection in the
REM         internal repository and grab a snapshot of the Oracle SQL cache
REM         into the new collection.
REM==================================================================
EXECUTE  DBMS_OLAP.CREATE_ID(:WORKLOAD_ID);
EXECUTE  DBMS_OLAP.LOAD_WORKLOAD_CACHE(:WORKLOAD_ID,
   DBMS_OLAP.WORKLOAD_NEW, DBMS_OLAP.FILTER_NONE, NULL, 1);
SELECT COUNT(*) FROM SYSTEM.MVIEW_WORKLOAD
   WHERE workloadid = :WORKLOAD_ID;

REM==================================================================
REM Step 3. Recommend materialized views with all of the workload workload
REM         and no filtering.
REM==================================================================
EXECUTE DBMS_OLAP.RECOMMEND_MVIEW_STRATEGY(:run_id, :workload_id, DBMS_
OLAP.FILTER_NONE, 10000000, 100, NULL, NULL);
SELECT COUNT(*) FROM SYSTEM.MVIEW_RECOMMENDATIONS;

REM==================================================================
REM Step 4. Generate HTML reports on the output.
```

```
REM=============================================================================
EXECUTE DBMS_OLAP.GENERATE_MVIEW_REPORT('/tmp/output2.html', :run_id,
    DBMS_OLAP.RPT_RECOMMENDATION);

REM=============================================================================
REM Step 5. Evaluate materialized views.
REM=============================================================================
EXECUTE DBMS_OLAP.CREATE_ID(:run_id);
EXECUTE DBMS_OLAP.EVALUATE_MVIEW_STRATEGY(:run_id, :workload_id, DBMS_
OLAP.FILTER_NONE);

REM=============================================================================
REM Step 5. Cleanup current output, and workload collection
REM         FROM the internal repository.
REM=============================================================================
EXECUTE DBMS_OLAP.PURGE_RESULTS(:run_id);
EXECUTE DBMS_OLAP.PURGE_WORKLOAD(:workload_id);
DISCONNECT
```

Sample Session Cleanup

```
REM=============================================================================
REM Cleanup for demos.
REM=============================================================================
CONNECT system/manager
REVOKE SELECT ON MVIEW_RECOMMENDATIONS FROM sh;
REVOKE SELECT ON MVIEW_WORKLOAD FROM sh;
REVOKE SELECT ON MVIEW_FILTER FROM sh;
DISCONNECT
```

Summary Advisor and Missing Statistics

The Summary Advisor will only perform materialized view analysis on table objects that contain a complete set of statistics as generated by the SQL `ANALYZE` statement or the `DBMS_STATS` package. While running Summary Advisor, the following Oracle error can occur:

```
QSM-00508: statistics missing on tables/columns
```

If this error occurs, then at least one table or column is missing the required statistics. To determine which object has missing statistics, issue the following statement:

```
SELECT runid#, text FROM system.mview$_adv_journal
```

The text column will contain information regarding missing statistics.

Database statistics are required for both the table and its set of defined columns. A common mistake occurs when the user only checks for valid table statistics, unaware that the column statistics have not been set.

Summary Advisor Privileges and ORA-30446

When processing a workload, the Summary Advisor attempts to validate each statement in order to identify table and column references. If the current database user does not have select privileges to a particular table, the Advisor bypasses the statement referencing the table. This may cause many statements to be excluded from analysis. If the Advisor excludes all statements in a workload, the workload is invalid and the Advisor returns the following message:

```
ORA-30446, valid workload queries not found
```

To avoid missing critical workload queries, the current database user must have select privileges on the tables that are targeted for materialized view analysis. Moreover, these select privileges cannot be obtained through a role.

ESTIMATING MATERIALIZED VIEW SIZE

A materialized view occupies storage space in the database, so it is helpful to know how much space will be required before it is created. Rather than guess or wait until it has been created and then discover that insufficient space is available in the tablespace, use the procedure `ESTIMATE_MVIEW_SIZE`. Calling this procedure instantly returns an estimate of the size in bytes for the materialized view. Table 9.17 lists the parameters to this procedure.

ESTIMATE_MVIEW_SIZE Parameters

Table 9.17 ESTIMATE_MVIEW_SIZE Procedure Parameters

Parameter	Description
stmt_id	Arbitrary string used to identify the statement in an EXPLAIN PLAN
select_clause	The SELECT statement to be analyzed
num_rows	Estimated cardinality
num_bytes	Estimated number of bytes

`ESTIMATE_SUMMARY_SIZE` returns the following:

- The number of rows it expects in the materialized view
- The size of the materialized view in bytes

In the following example, the query specified in the materialized view is passed into the `ESTIMATE_SUMMARY_SIZE` procedure. Note that the SQL statement is passed in without a semicolon at the end.

```
DBMS_OLAP.ESTIMATE_SUMMARY_SIZE  ('simple_store',
    'SELECT  product_key1, product_key2,
     SUM(dollar_sales) AS sum_dollar_sales,
     SUM(unit_sales) AS sum_unit_sales,
     SUM(dollar_cost) AS sum_dollar_cost,
     SUM(customer_count) AS no_of_customers
     FROM fact GROUP BY product_key1, product_key2', no_of_rows, mv_size );
```

The procedure returns two values: an estimate for the number of rows, and the size of the materialized view in bytes, as illustrated in the following.

```
No of Rows: 17284
Size of Materialized view (bytes): 2281488
```

IS A MATERIALIZED VIEW BEING USED ?

One of the major administrative problems with materialized views is knowing whether they are being used. Some materialized views might be in regular use. Others could have been created for a one-time problem that has now been resolved. However, the users who requested this level of analysis might never have told you that it was no longer required, so the materialized views remain in the database occupying storage space and possibly being regularly refreshed.

If a workload is available, then it can advise you which materialized views are in use. The workload will report only on materialized views that were used while it was collecting statistics. Therefore, if too small a window is chosen, not all the materialized views that are in use will be reported. To obtain the information, the procedure EVALUATE_MVIEW_STRATEGY is called. It analyzes the data and then the results can be viewed through the SYSTEM_MVIEW_EVALUATIONS view.

DBMS_OLAP.EVALUATE_MVIEW_STRATEGY Procedure

Table 9.18. EVALUATE_MVIEW_STRATEGY Procedure Parameters

Parameter	Datatype	Description
run_id	NUMBER	The Advisor-assigned ID for the current session
workload_id	NUMBER	An optional workload ID that maps to a user-supplied workload
filter_id	NUMBER	The optional filter ID is used to identify a filter against the target workload

In the following example, the utilization of materialized views is analyzed and the results are displayed:

```
DBMS_OLAP.EVALUATE_MVIEW_STRATEGY(:run_id, NULL, DBMS_OLAP.FILTER_NONE);
```

The following is a sample output obtained by querying the view SYSTEM.MVIEW_ EVALUATIONS, which provides the following information:

- Materialized view owner and name
- Rank of this materialized view in descending benefit-to-cost ratio
- Size of the materialized view in bytes
- The number of times the materialized view appears in the workload
- The cumulative benefit (calculated each time the materialized view is used)
- The benefit-to-cost ratio (calculated as the incremental improvement in performance to the size of the materialized view)

MVIEW_OWNER	MVIEW_NAME	RANK	SIZE	FREQ	CUMULATIVE	BENEFIT
GROCERY	STORE_MIN_SUM	1	340	1	9001	26.4735294
GROCERY	STORE_MAX_SUM	2	380	1	9001	23.6868421
GROCERY	STORE_STDCNT_SUM	3	3120	1	3000.38333	.961661325
GROCERY	QTR_STORE_PROMO_SUM	4	196020	2	0	0
GROCERY	STORE_SALES_SUM	5	340	1	0	0
GROCERY	STORE_SUM	6	21	10	0	0

SUMMARY ADVISOR WIZARD

The Summary Advisor Wizard in Oracle Enterprise Manager provides an interactive environment to recommend and build materialized views. Using the Wizard, you will be asked where the materialized views are to be placed, which fact tables to use, and which of the existing materialized views are to be retained. If a workload exists, it may be automatically selected. Otherwise, the Wizard will display the recommendations that are generated from the RECOMMEND_MVIEW_STRATEGY procedure.

All of the steps required to maintain your materialized views can be completed by answering the Wizard's questions. No subsequent DML operations are required.

You cannot use it to review or delete the recommendations, display the reports, or purge the workloads or filters.

Summary Advisor Steps

The Summary Advisor requires only the completion of a few steps to generate the recommendations. In figure 9.2, you see the first step where you have to define the type of workload being used.

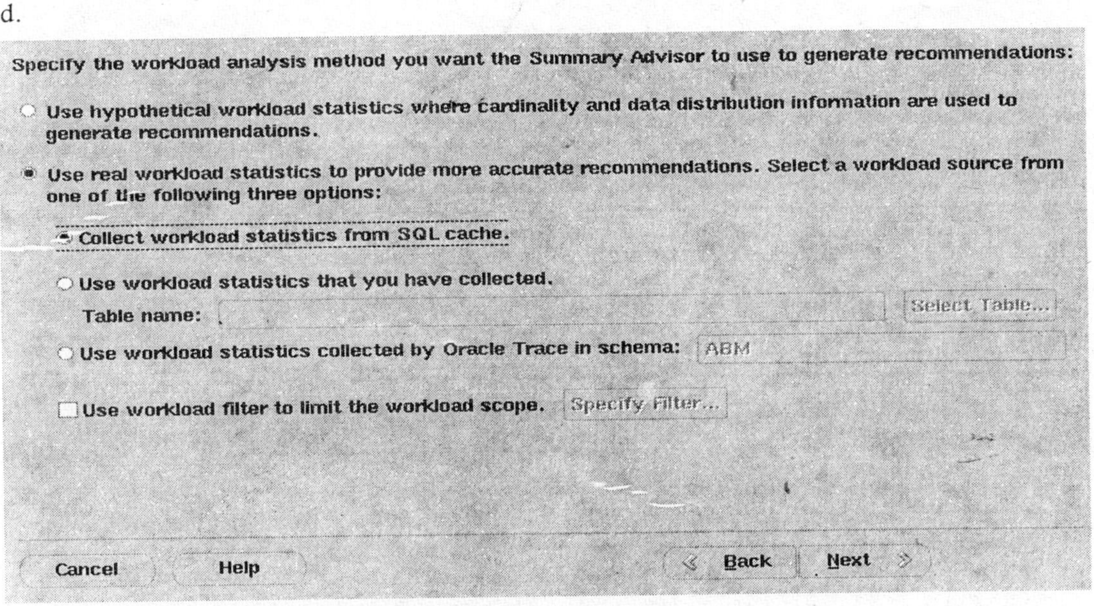

Figure 9.2 Summary Advisor Wizard: Workload Statistics.

If no workload is available, then select **Hypothetical**. Otherwise, specify where the workload comes from:

- The current contents of the SQL cache
- A user defined workload table which is selected from the drop down list
- An Oracle trace workload

Also, at this time, the workload can be filtered by selecting this option and clicking on the **Specify Filter** button. A new screen is displayed where the filters can be specified. There are four tabs: **General**, **SQL**, **Advanced**, and **Trace** where the filtering information is specified.

The Summary Advisor then attempts to determine which tables are the fact tables.

Step 2 displays these results and asks you to move the tables it has identified as fact tables and you want to be used as a fact table from the **Available Tables** column to the **Selected Tables** column using the **>** button as shown in figure 9.3. Alternatively, you can select which are your fact tables.

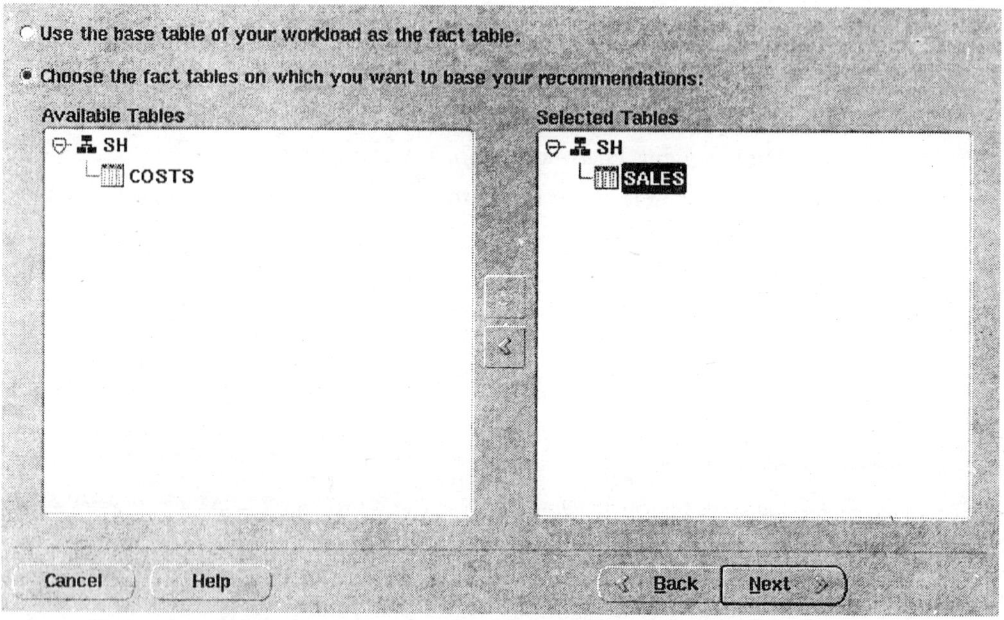

Figure 9.3 Summary Advisor: Select Fact Tables.

If there are any materialized views that already exist, the Summary Advisor wizard shows how much space they are using and asks if they should be retained. Then, it actually generates its recommendations and the screen shown in figure 9.4 is displayed.

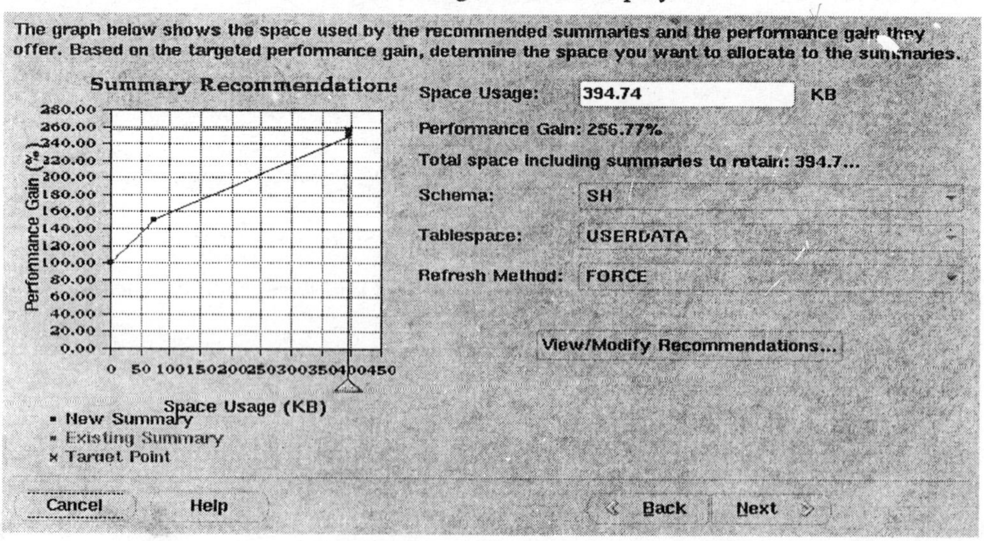

Figure 9.4 Summary Advisor: Recommendations.

The graph shown on the left of the screen shows the calculated gains for these recommendations. By sliding the marker along the line of the graph, depending on whether more performance is required or less storage space is used.

A set of materialized views will be recommended for that point on the graph. The actual recommendations are viewed by clicking on the **View/Modify Recommendations** button.

Default schema, tablespace and refresh method can be supplied for all recommendations. Then by pressing the **View/Modify Recommendations** button, each recommendation can be accepted or rejected and customized to your own requirements as to its name and other characteristics as shown in figure 9.5.

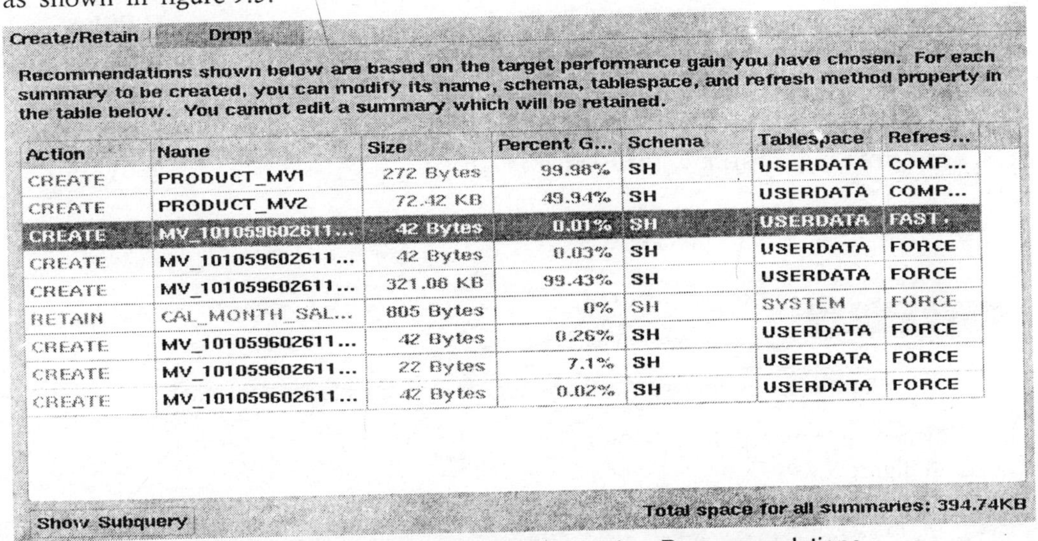

Figure 9.5 Summary Advisor: Customize Recommendations.

Finally, once you are satisfied with the recommendations, figure 9.6 is displayed where you can see the actual script which will be used to implement the recommendations. At this time, this script can be saved to a file and run later, or, if the **Finish** button is clicked, the recommendations are implemented.

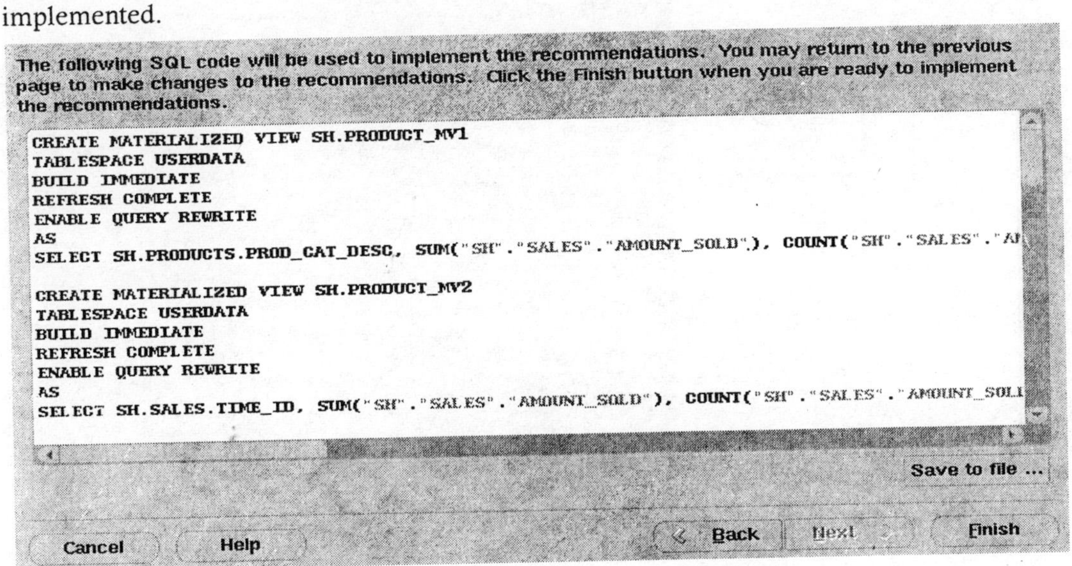

Figure 9.6 Summary Advisor: Final Screen.

Figure 9.7 shows the progress of the process implementing the recommendations.

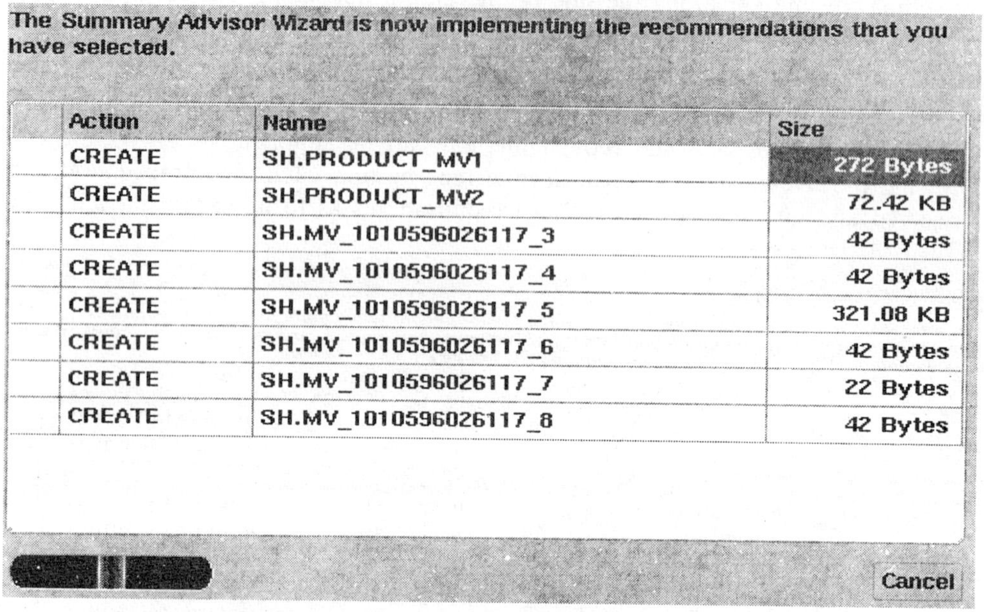

Figure 9.7 Summary Advisor: Monitor Implementation Process.

When finished, the materialized views can now be displayed in Oracle Enterprise Manager as illustrated in figure 9.8.

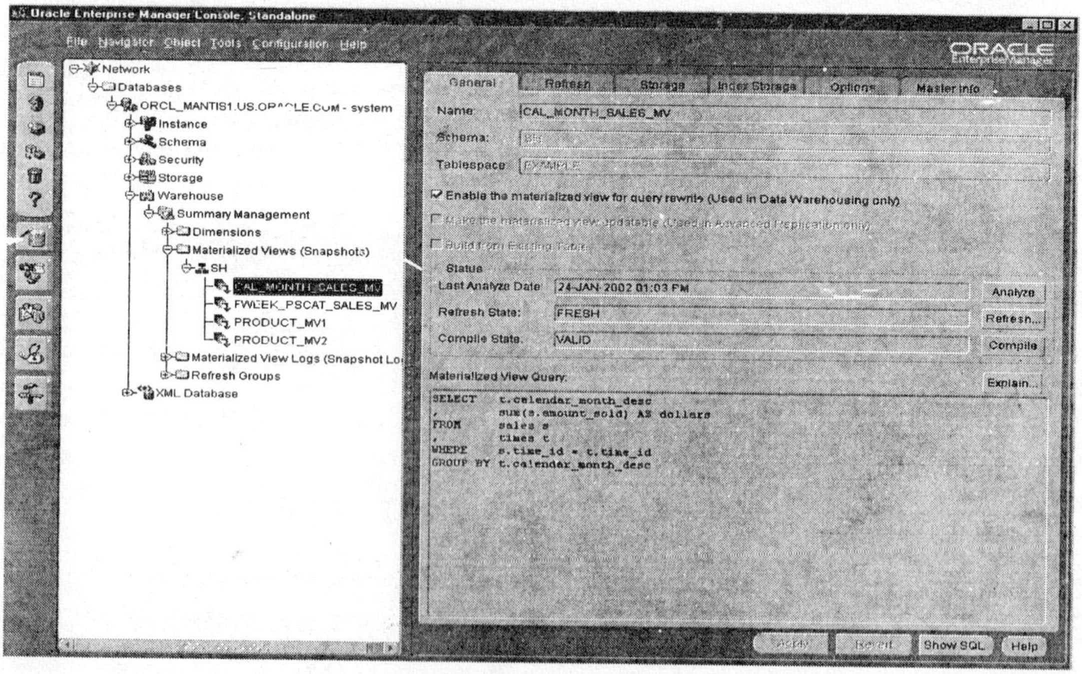

Figure 9.8 Materialized Views in Oracle Enterprise Manage.

❑❑❑

10 SQL FOR AGGREGATION IN DATA WAREHOUSES

OVERVIEW OF SQL FOR AGGREGATION IN DATA WAREHOUSES

Aggregation is a fundamental part of data warehousing. To improve aggregation performance in your warehouse, Oracle provides the following extensions to the GROUP BY clause:

- CUBE and ROLLUP extensions to the GROUP BY clause
- Three GROUPING functions
- GROUPING SETS expression.

The CUBE, ROLLUP, and GROUPING SETS extensions to SQL make querying and reporting easier and faster. ROLLUP calculates aggregations such as SUM, COUNT, MAX, MIN, and AVG at increasing levels of aggregation, from the most detailed up to a grand total. CUBE is an extension similar to ROLLUP, enabling a single statement to calculate all possible combinations of aggregations. CUBE can generate the information needed in cross-tabulation reports with a single query.

CUBE, ROLLUP, and the GROUPING SETS extension let you specify exactly the groupings of interest in the GROUP BY clause. This allows efficient analysis across multiple dimensions without performing a CUBE operation. Computing a full cube creates a heavy processing load, so replacing cubes with grouping sets can significantly increase performance. CUBE, ROLLUP, and grouping sets produce a single result set that is equivalent to a UNION ALL of differently grouped rows.

To enhance performance, CUBE, ROLLUP, and GROUPING SETS can be parallelized: multiple processes can simultaneously execute all of these statements. These capabilities make aggregate calculations more efficient, thereby enhancing database performance, and scalability.

The three GROUPING functions help you identify the group each row belongs to and enable sorting subtotal rows and filtering results.

Analyzing Across Multiple Dimensions

One of the key concepts in decision support systems is multidimensional analysis: examining the enterprise from all necessary combinations of dimensions. We use the term **dimension** to mean any category used in specifying questions. Among the most commonly specified dimensions are time, geography, product, department, and distribution channel, but the potential dimensions are as endless as the varieties of enterprise activity. The events or entities associated with a particular set of dimension values are usually referred to as **facts.** The facts might be sales in units or local currency, profits, customer counts, production volumes, or anything else worth tracking.

Here are some examples of multidimensional requests:

- Show total sales across all products at increasing aggregation levels for a geography dimension, from state to country to region, for 1999 and 2000.
- Create a cross-tabular analysis of our operations showing expenses by territory in South America for 1999 and 2000. Include all possible subtotals.
- List the top 10 sales representatives in Asia according to 2000 sales revenue for automotive products, and rank their commissions.

All these requests involve multiple dimensions. Many multidimensional questions require aggregated data and comparisons of data sets, often across time, geography or budgets.

To visualize data that has many dimensions, analysts commonly use the analogy of a data cube, that is, a space where facts are stored at the intersection of *n* dimensions. Figure 10.1 shows a data cube and how it can be used differently by various groups. The cube stores sales data organized by the dimensions of `product`, `market`, `sales`, and `time`. Note that this is only a metaphor: the actual data is physically stored in normal tables. The cube data consists of both detail and aggregated data.

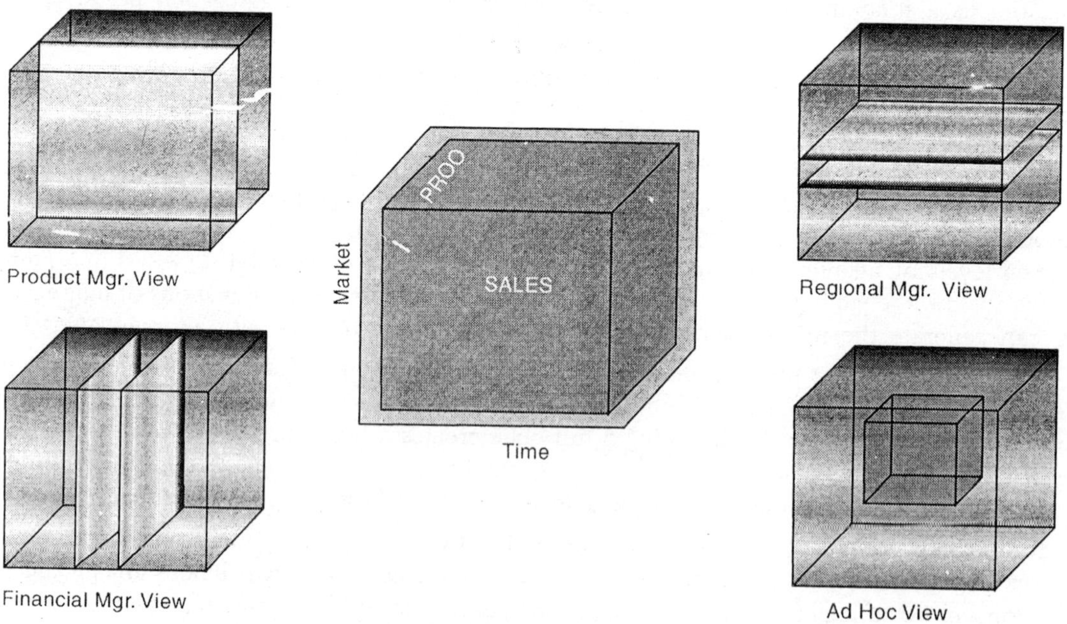

Figure 10.1 Logical Cubes and Views by Different Users.

You can retrieve slices of data from the cube. These correspond to cross-tabular reports such as the one shown in table 10.1. Regional managers might study the data by comparing slices of the cube applicable to different markets. In contrast, product managers might compare slices that apply to different products. An ad hoc user might work with a wide variety of constraints, working in a subset cube.

Answering multidimensional questions often involves accessing and querying huge quantities of data, sometimes in millions of rows. Because the flood of detailed data generated by large organizations cannot be interpreted at the lowest level, aggregated views of the information are essential. Aggregations, such as sums and counts, across many dimensions are vital to multidimensional analyses. Therefore, analytical tasks require convenient and efficient data aggregation.

Optimized Performance

Not only multidimensional issues, but all types of processing can benefit from enhanced aggregation facilities. Transaction processing, financial and manufacturing systems—all of these generate large numbers of production reports needing substantial system resources. Improved efficiency when creating these reports will reduce system load. In fact, any computer process that aggregates data from details to higher levels will benefit from optimized aggregation performance.

Oracle9i extensions provide aggregation features and bring many benefits, including:

- Simplified programming requiring less SQL code for many tasks
- Quicker and more efficient query processing
- Reduced client processing loads and network traffic because aggregation work is shifted to servers
- Opportunities for caching aggregations because similar queries can leverage existing work

An Aggregate Scenario

To illustrate the use of the `GROUP BY` extension, this chapter uses the `sh` data of the sample schema. All the examples refer to data from this scenario. The hypothetical company has sales across the world and tracks sales by both dollars and quantities information. Because there are many rows of data, the queries shown here typically have tight constraints on their `WHERE` clauses to limit the results to a small number of rows.

Example 10.1 : Simple Cross-Tabular Report With Subtotals

Table 10.1 is a sample cross-tabular report showing the total sales by `country_id` and `channel_desc` for the US and UK through the Internet and direct sales in September 2000.

Table 10.1 Simple Cross-Tabular Report With Subtotals

Channel	Country		
	UK	US	Total
Direct Sales	1,378,126	2,835,557	4,213,683
Internet	911,739	1,732,240	2,643,979
Total	2,289,865	4,567,797	6,857,662

Consider that even a simple report such as this, with just nine values in its grid, generates four subtotals and a grand total. The subtotals are the shaded numbers. Half of the values needed for this report would not be calculated with a query that requested SUM(amount_sold) and did a GROUP BY(channel_desc, country_id). To get the higher-level aggregates would require additional queries. Database commands that offer improved calculation of subtotals bring major benefits to querying, reporting, and analytical operations.

```
SELECT channel_desc,  country_id,
   TO_CHAR(SUM(amount_sold), '9,999,999,999') SALES$
FROM sales, customers, times, channels
WHERE sales.time_id=times.time_id AND
   sales.cust_id=customers.cust_id AND
   sales.channel_id= channels.channel_id AND
   channels.channel_desc IN ('Direct Sales', 'Internet') AND
   times.calendar_month_desc='2000-09'
   AND country_id IN ('UK', 'US')
GROUP BY CUBE(channel_desc, country_id);
```

CHANNEL_DESC	CO	SALES$
Direct Sales	UK	1,378,126
Direct Sales	US	2,835,557
Direct Sales		4,213,683
Internet	UK	911,739
Internet	US	1,732,240
Internet		2,643,979
	UK	2,289,865
	US	4,567,797
		6,857,662

Interpreting NULLs in Examples

NULLs returned by the GROUP BY extensions are not always the traditional null meaning value unknown. Instead, a NULL may indicate that its row is a subtotal. To avoid introducing another non-value in the database system, these subtotal values are not given a special tag.

ROLLUP EXTENSION TO GROUP BY

ROLLUP enables a SELECT statement to calculate multiple levels of subtotals across a specified group of dimensions. It also calculates a grand total. ROLLUP is a simple extension to the GROUP BY clause, so its syntax is extremely easy to use. The ROLLUP extension is highly efficient, adding minimal overhead to a query.

The action of ROLLUP is straightforward: it creates subtotals that roll up from the most detailed level to a grand total, following a grouping list specified in the ROLLUP clause. ROLLUP takes as its argument an ordered list of grouping columns. First, it calculates the standard aggregate values specified in the GROUP BY clause. Then, it creates progressively higher-level subtotals, moving from right to left through the list of grouping columns. Finally, it creates a grand total.

ROLLUP creates subtotals at n+1 levels, where n is the number of grouping columns. For instance, if a query specifies ROLLUP on grouping columns of time, region, and department (n = 3), the result set will include rows at four aggregation levels.

You might want to compress your data when using ROLLUP. This is particularly useful when there are few updates to older partitions.

When to Use ROLLUP

Use the ROLLUP extension in tasks involving subtotals.

- It is very helpful for subtotaling along a hierarchical dimension such as time or geography. For instance, a query could specify a ROLLUP(y, m, day) or ROLLUP(country, state, city).
- For data warehouse administrators using summary tables, ROLLUP can simplify and speed up the maintenance of summary tables.

ROLLUP Syntax

ROLLUP appears in the GROUP BY clause in a SELECT statement. Its form is:

```
SELECT ... GROUP BY ROLLUP(grouping_column_reference_list)
```

Example 10.2 : ROLLUP

This example uses the data in the sales history store data, the same data as was used in example 10.1. The ROLLUP is across three dimensions.

```
SELECT channel_desc, calendar_month_desc, country_id,
   TO_CHAR(SUM(amount_sold), '9,999,999,999') SALES$
FROM sales, customers, times, channels
WHERE sales.time_id=times.time_id AND
   sales.cust_id=customers.cust_id AND
   sales.channel_id= channels.channel_id AND
   channels.channel_desc IN ('Direct Sales', 'Internet') AND
   times.calendar_month_desc IN ('2000-09', '2000-10')
   AND country_id IN ('UK', 'US')
GROUP BY ROLLUP(channel_desc, calendar_month_desc, country_id);
```

```
CHANNEL_DESC         CALENDAR      CO          SALES$
-----------------------------------------------------
Direct Sales         2000-09       UK       1,378,126
Direct Sales         2000-09       US       2,835,557
Direct Sales         2000-09                4,213,683
Direct Sales         2000-10       UK       1,388,051
Direct Sales         2000-10       US       2,908,706
Direct Sales         2000-10                4,296,757
```

```
Direct  Sales                                            8,510,440
Internet            2000-09            UK                  911,739
Internet            2000-09            US                1,732,240
Internet            2000-09                              2,643,979
Internet            2000-10            UK                  876,571
Internet            2000-10            US                1,893,753
Internet            2000-10                              2,770,324
Internet                                                 5,414,303
                                                        13,924,743
```

Note that results do not always add due to rounding.

This query returns the following sets of rows:

- Regular aggregation rows that would be produced by GROUP BY without using ROLLUP
- First-level subtotals aggregating across country_id for each combination of channel_desc and calendar_month
- Second-level subtotals aggregating across calendar_month_desc and country_id for each channel_desc value
- A grand total row.

Partial Rollup

You can also roll up so that only some of the sub-totals will be included. This partial rollup uses the following syntax:

```
GROUP BY expr1, ROLLUP(expr2, expr3);
```

In this case, the GROUP BY clause creates subtotals at (2+1=3) aggregation levels. That is, at level (expr1, expr2, expr3), (expr1, expr2), and (expr1).

Example 10.3 : Partial ROLLUP

```
SELECT channel_desc, calendar_month_desc, country_id,
   TO_CHAR(SUM(amount_sold), '9,999,999,999') SALES$
FROM sales, customers, times, channels
WHERE sales.time_id=times.time_id AND
    sales.cust_id=customers.cust_id AND
    sales.channel_id= channels.channel_id AND
    channels.channel_desc IN ('Direct Sales', 'Internet') AND
    times.calendar_month_desc IN ('2000-09', '2000-10')
   AND country_id IN ('UK', 'US')
GROUP BY channel_desc, ROLLUP(calendar_month_desc, country_id);
   CHANNEL_DESC          CALENDAR          CO              SALES$
   ----------------------------------------------------------------
   Direct  Sales         2000-09           UK           1,378,126
   Direct  Sales         2000-09           US           2,835,557
   Direct  Sales         2000-09                        4,213,683
   Direct  Sales         2000-10           UK           1,388,051
   Direct  Sales         2000-10           US           2,908,706
```

```
Direct  Sales           2000-10                      4,296,757
Direct  Sales                                        8,510,440
Internet                2000-09        UK              911,739
Internet                2000-09        US            1,732,240
Internet                2000-09                      2,643,979
Internet                2000-10        UK              876,571
Internet                2000-10        US            1,893,753
Internet                2000-10                      2,770,324
Internet                                             5,414,303
```

This query returns the following sets of rows:

- Regular aggregation rows that would be produced by GROUP BY without using ROLLUP
- First-level subtotals aggregating across country_id for each combination of channel_desc and calendar_month_desc
- Second-level subtotals aggregating across calendar_month_desc and country_id for each channel_desc value
- It does *not* produce a grand total row.

CUBE EXTENSION TO GROUP BY

CUBE takes a specified set of grouping columns and creates subtotals for all of their possible combinations. In terms of multidimensional analysis, CUBE generates all the subtotals that could be calculated for a data cube with the specified dimensions. If you have specified CUBE(time, region, department), the result set will include all the values that would be included in an equivalent ROLLUP statement plus additional combinations. For instance, in example 10.1, the departmental totals across regions (279,000 and 319,000) would not be calculated by a ROLLUP(time, region, department) clause, but they would be calculated by a CUBE(time, region, department) clause. If *n* columns are specified for a CUBE, there will be 2 to the *n* combinations of subtotals returned. Example 10.3 gives an example of a three-dimension cube.

When to Use CUBE

Consider Using CUBE in any situation requiring cross-tabular reports. The data needed for cross-tabular reports can be generated with a single SELECT using CUBE. Like ROLLUP, CUBE can be helpful in generating summary tables. Note that population of summary tables is even faster if the CUBE query executes in parallel.

CUBE is typically most suitable in queries that use columns from multiple dimensions rather than columns representing different levels of a single dimension. For instance, a commonly requested cross-tabulation might need subtotals for all the combinations of month, state, and product. These are three independent dimensions, and analysis of all possible subtotal combinations is commonplace. In contrast, a cross-tabulation showing all possible combinations of year, month, and day would have several values of limited interest, because there is a natural hierarchy in the time dimension. Subtotals such as profit by day of month summed across year would be unnecessary in most analyses. Relatively few users need to ask "What were the total sales for the 16th of each month across the year?" See "Hierarchy Handling in ROLLUP and CUBE" for an example of handling rollup calculations efficiently.

CUBE Syntax

CUBE appears in the GROUP BY clause in a SELECT statement. Its form is:

```
SELECT ...   GROUP BY CUBE (grouping_column_reference_list)
```

Example 10.4 : CUBE

```
SELECT channel_desc, calendar_month_desc, country_id,
   TO_CHAR(SUM(amount_sold), '9,999,999,999') SALES$
FROM sales, customers, times, channels
WHERE sales.time_id=times.time_id AND
   sales.cust_id=customers.cust_id AND
   sales.channel_id= channels.channel_id AND
   channels.channel_desc IN ('Direct Sales', 'Internet') AND
   times.calendar_month_desc IN ('2000-09', '2000-10')
   AND country_id IN ('UK', 'US')
GROUP BY CUBE(channel_desc, calendar_month_desc, country_id);
```

CHANNEL_DESC	CALENDAR	CO	SALES$
Direct Sales	2000-09	UK	1,378,126
Direct Sales	2000-09	US	2,835,557
Direct Sales	2000-09		4,213,683
Direct Sales	2000-10	UK	1,388,051
Direct Sales	2000-10	US	2,908,706
Direct Sales	2000-10		4,296,757
Direct Sales		UK	2,766,177
Direct Sales		US	5,744,263
Direct Sales			8,510,440
Internet	2000-09	UK	911,739
Internet	2000-09	US	1,732,240
Internet	2000-09		2,643,979
Internet	2000-10	UK	876,571
Internet	2000-10	US	1,893,753
Internet	2000-10		2,770,324
Internet		UK	1,788,310
Internet		US	3,625,993
Internet			5,414,303
	2000-09	UK	2,289,865
	2000-09	US	4,567,797
	2000-09		6,857,662
	2000-10	UK	2,264,622
	2000-10	US	4,802,459
	2000-10		7,067,081
		UK	4,554,487
		US	9,370,256
			13,924,743

This query illustrates CUBE aggregation across three dimensions.

Partial CUBE

Partial CUBE resembles partial ROLLUP in that you can limit it to certain dimensions and precede it with columns outside the CUBE operator. In this case, subtotals of all possible combinations are limited to the dimensions within the cube list (in parentheses), and they are combined with the preceding items in the GROUP BY list.

Partial CUBE Syntax

```
GROUP BY expr1, CUBE(expr2, expr3)
```

This syntax example calculates 2*2, or 4, subtotals. That is:

- (expr1, expr2, expr3)
- (expr1, expr2)
- (expr1, expr3)
- (expr1)

Example 10.5 : Partial CUBE

Using the sales database, you can issue the following statement:

```
SELECT channel_desc, calendar_month_desc, country_id,
   TO_CHAR(SUM(amount_sold), '9,999,999,999') SALES$
FROM sales, customers, times, channels
WHERE sales.time_id=times.time_id AND
   sales.cust_id=customers.cust_id AND
   sales.channel_id= channels.channel_id AND
   channels.channel_desc IN ('Direct Sales', 'Internet') AND
   times.calendar_month_desc IN ('2000-09', '2000-10')
   AND country_id IN ('UK', 'US')
GROUP BY channel_desc, CUBE(calendar_month_desc, country_id);
```

CHANNEL_DESC	CALENDAR	CO	SALES$
Direct Sales	2000-09	UK	1,378,126
Direct Sales	2000-09	US	2,835,557
Direct Sales	2000-09		4,213,683
Direct Sales	2000-10	UK	1,388,051
Direct Sales	2000-10	US	2,908,706
Direct Sales	2000-10		4,296,757
Direct Sales		UK	2,766,177
Direct Sales		US	5,744,263
Direct Sales			8,510,440
Internet	2000-09	UK	911,739
Internet	2000-09	US	1,732,240
Internet	2000-09		2,643,979
Internet	2000-10	UK	876,571
Internet	2000-10	US	1,893,753
Internet	2000-10		2,770,324
Internet		UK	1,788,310
Internet		US	3,625,993
Internet			5,414,303

Calculating Subtotals Without CUBE

Just as for ROLLUP, multiple SELECT statements combined with UNION ALL statements could provide the same information gathered through CUBE. However, this might require many SELECT statements. For an n-dimensional cube, 2 to the *n* SELECT statements are needed. In the three-dimension example, this would mean issuing SELECT statements linked with UNION ALL. So many SELECT statements yield inefficient processing and very lengthy SQL.

Consider the impact of adding just one more dimension when calculating all possible combinations: the number of SELECT statements would double to 16. The more columns used in a CUBE clause, the greater the savings compared to the UNION ALL approach.

GROUPING FUNCTIONS

Two challenges arise with the use of ROLLUP and CUBE. First, how can you programmatically determine which result set rows are subtotals, and how do you find the exact level of aggregation for a given subtotal? You often need to use subtotals in calculations such as percent-of-totals, so you need an easy way to determine which rows are the subtotals. Second, what happens if query results contain both stored NULL values and "NULL" values created by a ROLLUP or CUBE? How can you differentiate between the two?

GROUPING Function

GROUPING handles these problems. Using a single column as its argument, GROUPING returns 1 when it encounters a NULL value created by a ROLLUP or CUBE operation. That is, if the NULL indicates the row is a subtotal, GROUPING returns a 1. Any other type of value, including a stored NULL, returns a 0.

GROUPING Syntax

GROUPING appears in the selection list portion of a SELECT statement. Its form is:

```
SELECT ...    [GROUPING(dimension_column)...]    ...
   GROUP BY ...     {CUBE | ROLLUP| GROUPING SETS}   (dimension_column)
```

Example 10.6 : GROUPING to Mask Columns

This example uses GROUPING to create a set of mask columns for the result set shown in example 10.3. The mask columns are easy to analyze programmatically.

```
SELECT channel_desc, calendar_month_desc, country_id,
    TO_CHAR(SUM(amount_sold), '9,999,999,999') SALES$,
    GROUPING(channel_desc) as Ch,
    GROUPING(calendar_month_desc) AS Mo,
    GROUPING(country_id) AS Co
FROM sales, customers, times, channels
WHERE sales.time_id=times.time_id AND
    sales.cust_id=customers.cust_id AND
    sales.channel_id= channels.channel_id AND
    channels.channel_desc IN ('Direct Sales', 'Internet') AND
    times.calendar_month_desc IN ('2000-09', '2000-10')
    AND country_id IN ('UK', 'US')
GROUP BY ROLLUP(channel_desc, calendar_month_desc, country_id);
```

CHANNEL_DESC	CALENDAR	CO	SALES$	CH	MO	CO
Direct Sales	2000-09	UK	1,378,126	0	0	0
Direct Sales	2000-09	US	2,835,557	0	0	0
Direct Sales	2000-09		4,213,683	0	0	1
Direct Sales	2000-10	UK	1,388,051	0	0	0
Direct Sales	2000-10	US	2,908,706	0	0	0
Direct Sales	2000-10		4,296,757	0	0	1
Direct Sales			8,510,440	0	1	1
Internet	2000-09	UK	911,739	0	0	0
Internet	2000-09	US	1,732,240	0	0	0
Internet	2000-09		2,643,979	0	0	1
Internet	2000-10	UK	876,571	0	0	0
Internet	2000-10	US	1,893,753	0	0	0
Internet	2000-10		2,770,324	0	0	1
Internet			5,414,303	0	1	1
			13,924,743	1	1	1

A program can easily identify the detail rows by a mask of "0 0 0" on the T, R, and D columns. The first level subtotal rows have a mask of "0 0 1", the second level subtotal rows have a mask of "0 1 1", and the overall total row has a mask of "1 1 1".

You can improve the readability of result sets by using the GROUPING and DECODE functions as shown in example 10.7.

Example 10.7 : GROUPING For Readability

```
SELECT DECODE(GROUPING(channel_desc), 1, 'All Channels', channel_desc)
   AS Channel,
   DECODE(GROUPING(country_id), 1, 'All Countries', country_id)
   AS Country, TO_CHAR(SUM(amount_sold), '9,999,999,999') SALES$
FROM sales, customers, times, channels
WHERE sales.time_id=times.time_id AND
   sales.cust_id=customers.cust_id AND
   sales.channel_id= channels.channel_id AND
   channels.channel_desc IN ('Direct Sales', 'Internet') AND
   times.calendar_month_desc= '2000-09'
   AND country_id IN ('UK', 'US')
GROUP BY CUBE(channel_desc, country_id);
```

CHANNEL	COUNTRY	SALES$
Direct Sales	UK	1,378,126
Direct Sales	US	2,835,557
Direct Sales	All Countries	4,213,683
Internet	UK	911,739
Internet	US	1,732,240
Internet	All Countries	2,643,979
All Channels	UK	2,289,865
All Channels	US	4,567,797
All Channels	All Countries	6,857,662

To understand the previous statement, note its first column specification, which handles the `channel_desc` column. Consider the first line of the previous statement:

```
SELECT DECODE(GROUPING(channel_desc), 1, 'All Channels', channel_desc)AS Channel
```

In this, the `channel_desc` value is determined with a `DECODE` function that contains a `GROUPING` function. The `GROUPING` function returns a 1 if a row value is an aggregate created by `ROLLUP` or `CUBE`, otherwise it returns a 0. The `DECODE` function then operates on the `GROUPING` function's results. It returns the text "All Channels" if it receives a 1 and the `channel_desc` value from the database if it receives a 0. Values from the database will be either a real value such as "Internet" or a stored `NULL`. The second column specification, displaying `country_id`, works the same way.

When to Use GROUPING

The `GROUPING` function is not only useful for identifying `NULLs`, it also enables sorting subtotal rows and filtering results. In example 10.8, you retrieve a subset of the subtotals created by a `CUBE` and none of the base-level aggregations. The `HAVING` clause constrains columns that use `GROUPING` functions.

Example 10.8 : GROUPING Combined with HAVING

```
SELECT channel_desc, calendar_month_desc, country_id,
   TO_CHAR(SUM(amount_sold), '9,999,999,999') SALES$,
   GROUPING(channel_desc) CH, GROUPING(calendar_month_desc)  MO,
GROUPING(country_id) CO
FROM sales, customers, times, channels
WHERE sales.time_id=times.time_id AND
   sales.cust_id=customers.cust_id AND
   sales.channel_id= channels.channel_id AND
   channels.channel_desc IN ('Direct Sales', 'Internet') AND
   times.calendar_month_desc IN ('2000-09', '2000-10')
   AND country_id IN ('UK', 'US')
GROUP BY CUBE(channel_desc, calendar_month_desc, country_id)
HAVING
     (GROUPING(channel_desc)=1 AND GROUPING(calendar_month_desc)= 1 AND
       GROUPING(country_id)=1) OR
     (GROUPING(channel_desc)=1 AND GROUPING(calendar_month_desc)= 1) OR
     (GROUPING(country_id)=1 AND GROUPING(calendar_month_desc)= 1);
```

CHANNEL_DESC	C	CO	SALES$	CH	MO	CO
		UK	4,554,487	1	1	0
		US	9,370,256	1	1	0
Direct Sales			8,510,440	0	1	1
Internet			5,414,303	0	1	1
			13,924,743	1	1	1

Compare the result set of example 10.8 with that in example 10.3 to see how example 10.8 is a precisely specified group: it contains only the yearly totals, regional totals aggregated over `time` and `department`, and the grand total.

GROUPING_ID Function

To find the GROUP BY level of a particular row, a query must return GROUPING function information for each of the GROUP BY columns. If we do this using the GROUPING function, every GROUP BY column requires another column using the GROUPING function. For instance, a four-column GROUP BY clause needs to be analyzed with four GROUPING functions. This is inconvenient to write in SQL and increases the number of columns required in the query. When you want to store the query result sets in tables, as with materialized views, the extra columns waste storage space.

To address these problems, Oracle9*i* introduces the GROUPING_ID function. GROUPING_ID returns a single number that enables you to determine the exact GROUP BY level. For each row, GROUPING_ID takes the set of 1's and 0's that would be generated if you use the appropriate GROUPING functions and concatenate them, forming a bit vector. The bit vector is treated as a binary number, and the number's base-10 value is returned by the GROUPING_ID function. For instance, if you group with the expression CUBE(a, b) the possible values are as shown in table 10.2.

Table 10.2 GROUPING_ID Example for CUBE(a, b)

Aggregation Level	Bit Vector	GROUPING_ID
a, b	0 0	0
a	0 1	1
b	1 0	2
Grand Total	1 1	3

GROUPING_ID clearly distinguishes groupings created by grouping set specification, and it is very useful during refresh and rewrite of materialized views.

GROUP_ID Function

While the extensions to GROUP BY offer power and flexibility, they also allow complex result sets that can include duplicate groupings. The GROUP_ID function lets you distinguish among duplicate groupings. If there are multiple sets of rows calculated for a given level, GROUP_ID assigns the value of 0 to all the rows in the first set. All other sets of duplicate rows for a particular grouping are assigned higher values, starting with 1. For example, consider the following query, which generates a duplicate grouping:

Example 10.9 : GROUP_ID

```
SELECT country_id, cust_state_province, SUM(amount_sold),
  GROUPING_ID(country_id, cust_state_province) GROUPING_ID, GROUP_ID()
FROM sales, customers, times
WHERE sales.time_id=times.time_id AND
   sales.cust_id=customers.cust_id AND
   times.time_id= '30-OCT-00'
   AND country_id IN ('FR', 'ES')
GROUP BY GROUPING SETS (country_id, ROLLUP(country_id, cust_state_province));
```

CO	CUST_STATE_PROVINCE	SUM(AMOUNT_SOLD)	GROUPING_ID	GROUP_ID()
ES	Alicante	8939	0	0
ES	Almeria	1053	0	0
ES	Barcelona	6312	0	0
ES	Girona	220	0	0
ES	Malaga	8137	0	0
ES	Salamanca	324	0	0
ES	Valencia	7588	0	0
FR	Alsace	5099	0	0
FR	Aquitaine	13183	0	0
FR	Brittany	3938	0	0
FR	Centre	2968	0	0
FR	Ile-de-France	16449	0	0
FR	Languedoc-Roussillon	20228	0	0
FR	Midi-Pyrenees	2322	0	0
FR	Pays de la Loire	1096	0	0
FR	Provence-Alpes-Cote d'Azur	1208	0	0
FR	Rhtne-Alpes	7637	0	0
		106701	3	0
ES		32573	1	0
FR		74128	1	0
ES		32573	1	1
FR		74128	1	1

This query generates the following groupings: (`country_id`, `cust_state_province`), (`country_id`), (`country_id`), and (). Note that the grouping (`country_id`) is repeated twice. The syntax for `GROUPING SETS` is explained in "GROUPING SETS Expression".

This function helps you filter out duplicate groupings from the result. For example, you can filter out duplicate (`region`) groupings from the previous example by adding a `HAVING` clause condition `GROUP_ID()=0` to the query.

GROUPING SETS EXPRESSION

You can selectively specify the set of groups that you want to create using a `GROUPING SETS` expression within a `GROUP BY` clause. This allows precise specification across multiple dimensions without computing the whole `CUBE`. For example, you can say:

```
SELECT channel_desc, calendar_month_desc, country_id,
   TO_CHAR(SUM(amount_sold), '9,999,999,999') SALES$
FROM sales, customers, times, channels
WHERE sales.time_id=times.time_id AND
   sales.cust_id=customers.cust_id AND
```

```
  sales.channel_id= channels.channel_id AND
  channels.channel_desc IN ('Direct Sales', 'Internet') AND
  times.calendar_month_desc IN ('2000-09', '2000-10')
  AND country_id IN ('UK', 'US')
GROUP BY GROUPING SETS((channel_desc, calendar_month_desc, country_id),
    (channel_desc, country_id), (calendar_month_desc, country_id));
```

Note that this statement uses composite columns, described in "Composite Columns". This statement calculates aggregates over three groupings:

- `(channel_desc, calendar_month_desc, country_id)`
- `(channel_desc, country_id)`
- `(calendar_month_desc, country_id).`

Compare the previous statement with the following alternative, which uses the `CUBE` operation and the `GROUPING_ID` function to return the desired rows:

```
SELECT channel_desc, calendar_month_desc, country_id,
   TO_CHAR(SUM(amount_sold), '9,999,999,999') SALES$,
   GROUPING_ID(channel_desc, calendar_month_desc, country_id)  gid
FROM sales, customers, times, channels
WHERE sales.time_id=times.time_id AND
   sales.cust_id=customers.cust_id AND
   sales.channel_id= channels.channel_id AND
   channels.channel_desc IN ('Direct Sales', 'Internet') AND
   times.calendar_month_desc IN ('2000-09', '2000-10')
   AND country_id IN ('UK', 'US')
GROUP BY CUBE(channel_desc, calendar_month_desc, country_id)
HAVING GROUPING_ID(channel_desc, calendar_month_desc, country_id)=0
  OR GROUPING_ID(channel_desc, calendar_month_desc, country_id)=2
  OR GROUPING_ID(channel_desc, calendar_month_desc, country_id)=4;
```

This statement computes all the 8 (2 *2 *2) groupings, though only the previous 3 groups are of interest to you.

Another alternative is the following statement, which is lengthy due to several unions. This statement requires three scans of the base table, making it inefficient. `CUBE` and `ROLLUP` can be thought of as grouping sets with very specific semantics. For example, consider the following statement:

```
CUBE(a, b, c)
```

This statement is equivalent to:

```
GROUPING SETS ((a, b, c), (a, b), (a, c), (b, c), (a), (b), (c), ())
ROLLUP(a, b, c)
```

And this statement is equivalent to:

```
GROUPING SETS ((a, b, c), (a, b), ())
```

GROUPING SETS Syntax

`GROUPING SETS` syntax lets you define multiple groupings in the same query. `GROUP BY` computes all the groupings specified and combines them with `UNION ALL`. For example, the following statement:

```
GROUP BY GROUPING sets (channel_desc, calendar_month_desc, country_id )
```

This statement is equivalent to:

```
GROUP BY channel_desc
UNION ALL
GROUP BY calendar_month_desc
UNION ALL country_id
```

Table 10.3 shows grouping sets specification and equivalent GROUP BY specification. Note that some examples use composite columns.

Table 10.3 GRCUPING SETS Statements and Equivalent GROUP BY

GROUPING SETS Statement	Equivalent GROUP BY Statement
GROUP BY GROUPING SETS(a, b, c)	GROUP BY a UNION ALL GROUP BY b UNION ALL GROUP BY c
GROUP BY GROUPING SETS(a, b, (b, c))	GROUP BY a UNION ALL GROUP BY b UNION ALL GROUP BY b, c
GROUP BY GROUPING SETS((a, b, c))	GROUP BY a, b, c
GROUP BY GROUPING SETS(a, (b), ())	GROUP BY a UNION ALL GROUP BY b UNION ALL GROUP BY ()
GROUP BY GROUPING SETS(a, ROLLUP(b, c))	GROUP BY a UNION ALL GROUP BY ROLLUP(b, c)

In the absence of an optimizer that looks across query blocks to generate the execution plan, a query based on UNION would need multiple scans of the base table, sales. This could be very inefficient as fact tables wiii normally be huge. Using GROUPING SETS statements, all the groupings of interest are available in the same query block.

COMPOSITE COLUMNS

A composite column is a collection of columns that are treated as a unit during the computation of groupings. You specify the columns in parentheses as in the following statement:

```
ROLLUP (year, (quarter, month), day)
```

In this statement, the data is not rolled up across year and quarter, but is instead equivalent to the following groupings of a UNION ALL:

- (year, quarter, month, day),
- (year, quarter, month),
- (year)
- ()

Here, (quarter, month) form a composite column and are treated as a unit. In general, composite columns are useful in ROLLUP, CUBE, GROUPING SETS, and concatenated groupings.

For example, in CUBE or ROLLUP, composite columns would mean skipping aggregation across certain levels. That is, the following statement:

```
GROUP BY ROLLUP(a, (b, c))
```

This is equivalent to:

```
GROUP BY a, b, c UNION ALL
GROUP BY a UNION ALL
GROUP BY ()
```

Here, (b, c) are treated as a unit and rollup will not be applied across (b, c). It is as if you have an alias, for example z, for (b, c) and the GROUP BY expression reduces to GROUP BY ROLLUP(a, z). Compare this with the normal rollup as in the following:

```
GROUP BY ROLLUP(a, b, c)
```

This would be the following:

```
GROUP BY a, b, c UNION ALL
GROUP BY a, b UNION ALL
GROUP BY a UNION ALL
GROUP BY ().
```

Similarly, the following statement:

```
GROUP BY CUBE((a, b), c)
```

This would be equivalent to:

```
GROUP BY a, b, c UNION ALL
GROUP BY a, b UNION ALL
GROUP BY c UNION ALL
GROUP By ()
```

In GROUPING SETS, a composite column is used to denote a particular level of GROUP BY. See table 10.3 for more examples of composite columns.

Example 10.10 : Composite Columns

You do not have full control over what aggregation levels you want with CUBE and ROLLUP. For example, the following statement:

```
SELECT channel_desc, calendar_month_desc, country_id,
   TO_CHAR(SUM(amount_sold), '9,999,999,999') SALES$
FROM sales, customers, times, channels
WHERE sales.time_id=times.time_id AND
   sales.cust_id=customers.cust_id AND
   sales.channel_id= channels.channel_id AND
      channels.channel_desc IN ('Direct Sales', 'Internet') AND
   times.calendar_month_desc IN ('2000-09', '2000-10')
   AND country_id IN ('UK', 'US')
GROUP BY ROLLUP(channel_desc, calendar_month_desc, country_id);
```

This statement results in Oracle computing the following groupings:

- (channel_desc, calendar_month_desc, country_id)
- (channel_desc, calendar_month_desc)

- (channel_desc)
- ()

If you are just interested in grouping of lines (1), (3) and (4) in this example, you cannot limit the calculation to those groupings without using composite columns. With composite columns, this is possible by treating month and country as a single unit while rolling up. Columns enclosed in parentheses are treated as a unit while computing CUBE and ROLLUP. Thus, you would say:

```
SELECT channel_desc, calendar_month_desc, country_id,
   TO_CHAR(SUM(amount_sold), '9,999,999,999') SALES$
FROM sales, customers, times, channels
WHERE sales.time_id=times.time_id AND
   sales.cust_id=customers.cust_id AND
   sales.channel_id= channels.channel_id  AND
      channels.channel_desc IN ('Direct Sales', 'Internet') AND
   times.calendar_month_desc IN ('2000-09', '2000-10')
   AND country_id IN ('UK', 'US')
GROUP BY ROLLUP(channel_desc, (calendar_month_desc, country_id));
```

CONCATENATED GROUPINGS

Concatenated groupings offer a concise way to generate useful combinations of groupings. Groupings specified with concatenated groupings yield the cross-product of groupings from each grouping set. The cross-product operation enables even a small number of concatenated groupings to generate a large number of final groups. The concatenated groupings are specified simply by listing multiple grouping sets, cubes, and rollups, and separating them with commas. Here is an example of concatenated grouping sets:

```
GROUP BY GROUPING SETS(a, b), GROUPING SETS(c, d)
```

This SQL defines the following groupings:

```
(a, c), (a, d), (b, c), (b, d)
```

Concatenation of grouping sets is very helpful for these reasons:

- Ease of query development

  You need not enumerate all groupings manually.
- Use by applications

  SQL generated by OLAP applications often involves concatenation of grouping sets, with each grouping set defining groupings needed for a dimension.

Example 10.11 : Concatenated Groupings

You can also specify more than one grouping in the GROUP BY clause. For example, if you want aggregated sales values for each product rolled up across all levels in the time dimension (year, month and day), and across all levels in the geography dimension (region), you can issue the following statement:

```
SELECT channel_desc, calendar_year, calendar_quarter_desc, country_id,
cust_state_province, TO_CHAR(SUM(amount_sold), '9,999,999,999') SALES$
FROM sales, customers, times, channels
WHERE sales.time_id=times.time_id AND
   sales.cust_id=customers.cust_id AND
   sales.channel_id= channels.channel_id AND
      channels.channel_desc IN ('Direct Sales', 'Internet') AND
times.calendar_month_desc IN ('2000-09', '2000-10')
AND country_id IN ('UK', 'US')
GROUP BY channel_desc,
GROUPING SETS (ROLLUP(calendar_year, calendar_quarter_desc),
               ROLLUP(country_id, cust_state_province));
```

This results in the following groupings:

- (channel_desc, calendar_year, calendar_quarter_desc)
- (channel_desc, calendar_year)
- (channel_desc)
- (channel_desc, country_id, cust_state_province)
- (channel_desc, country_id)
- (channel_desc)

This is the cross-product of the following:

- The expression, channel_desc
- ROLLUP(calendar_year, calendar_quarter_desc), which is equivalent to ((calendar_year, calendar_quarter_desc), (calendar_year), ())
- ROLLUP(country_id, cust_state_province), which is equivalent to ((country_id, cust_state_province), (country_id), ())

Note that the output contains two occurrences of (channel_desc) group. To filter out the extra (channel_desc) group, the query could use a GROUP_ID function.

Another concatenated join example is the following, showing the cross product of two grouping sets:

Example 10.12 : Concatenated Groupings (Cross-Product of Two Grouping Sets)

```
SELECT   country_id,  cust_state_province,
 calendar_year, calendar_quarter_desc,
 TO_CHAR(SUM(amount_sold), '9,999,999,999') SALES$
FROM sales, customers, times, channels
WHERE sales.time_id=times.time_id AND
 sales.cust_id=customers.cust_id AND
 sales.channel_id= channels.channel_id AND
 channels.channel_desc IN ('Direct Sales', 'Internet') AND
 times.calendar_month_desc IN ('2000-09', '2000-10')
 AND country_id IN ('UK', 'US')
GROUP BY
 GROUPING SETS (country_id, cust_state_province),
 GROUPING SETS (calendar_year, calendar_quarter_desc);
```

This statement results in the computation of groupings:

- (country_id, year), (country_id, calendar_quarter_desc), (cust_state_province, year) and (cust_state_province, calendar_quarter_desc)

Concatenated Groupings and Hierarchical Data Cubes

One of the most important uses for concatenated groupings is to generate the aggregates needed for a hierarchical cube of data. A hierarchical cube is a data set where the data is aggregated along the rollup hierarchy of each of its dimensions and these aggregations are combined across dimensions. It includes the typical set of aggregations needed for business intelligence queries. By using concatenated groupings, you can generate all the aggregations needed by a hierarchical cube with just *n* ROLLUPs (where *n* is the number of dimensions), and avoid generating unwanted aggregations.

Consider just three of the dimensions in the sh sample schema data set, each of which has a multilevel hierarchy:

- time: year, quarter, month, day (week is in a separate hierarchy)
- product: category, subcategory, prod_name
- geography: region, subregion, country, state, city

This data is represented using a column for each level of the hierarchies, creating a total of twelve columns for dimensions, plus the columns holding sales figures.

For our business intelligence needs, we would like to calculate and store certain aggregates of the various combinations of dimensions. In example 10.13, we create the aggregates for all levels, except for "day", which would create too many rows. In particular, we want to use ROLLUP within each dimension to generate useful aggregates. Once we have the ROLLUP-based aggregates within each dimension, we want to combine them with the other dimensions. This will generate our hierarchical cube. Note that this is not at all the same as a CUBE using all twelve of the dimension columns: that would create 2 to the 12th power (4,096) aggregation groups, of which we need only a small fraction. Concatenated grouping sets make it easy to generate exactly the aggregations we need. Example 10-13 shows where a GROUP BY clause is needed.

Example 10.13 : Concatenated Groupings and Hierarchical Cubes

```
SELECT
  calendar_year, calendar_quarter_desc,
  calendar_month_desc, country_region, country_subregion, countries.country_id,
  cust_state_province, cust_city,
   prod_cat_desc, prod_subcat_desc, prod_name,
   TO_CHAR(SUM(amount_sold), '9,999,999,999') SALES$
FROM sales, customers, times, channels, countries, products
WHERE
   sales.time_id=times.time_id AND
   sales.cust_id=customers.cust_id AND
   sales.channel_id= channels.channel_id AND
   sales.prod_id=products.prod_id  AND
   customers.country_id=countries.country_id AND
   channels.channel_desc IN ('Direct Sales', 'Internet') AND
   times.calendar_month_desc IN ('2000-09', '2000-10')  AND
   prod_name IN ('Ruckpart Eclipse', 'Ukko Plain Gortex Boot') AND
   countries.country_id IN ('UK', 'US')
GROUP BY
  ROLLUP(calendar_year, calendar_quarter_desc,
         calendar_month_desc),
```

```
ROLLUP(country_region, country_subregion, countries.country_id,
      cust_state_province, cust_city),
ROLLUP(prod_cat_desc, prod_subcat_desc, prod_name);
```

The ROLLUPs in the GROUP BY specification generate the following groups, four for each dimension.

Table 10.4 Hierarchical CUBE Example

ROLLUP By Time	ROLLUP By Product	ROLLUP By Geography
year, quarter, month	category, subcategory, name	region, subregion, country, state, city region, subregion, country, state region, subregion, country
year, quarter	category, subcategory	region, subregion
year	category	region
all times	all products	all geographies

The concatenated grouping sets specified in the previous SQL will take the ROLLUP aggregations listed in the table and perform a cross-product on them. The cross-product will create the 96 (4 × 4 × 6) aggregate groups needed for a hierarchical cube of the data. There are major advantages in using three ROLLUP expressions to replace what would otherwise require 96 grouping set expressions: the concise SQL is far less error-prone to develop and far easier to maintain, and it enables much better query optimization. You can picture how a cube with more dimensions and more levels would make the use of concatenated groupings even more advantageous.

CONSIDERATIONS WHEN USING AGGREGATION

This section discusses the following topics.

- Hierarchy handling in ROLLUP and CUBE
- Column capacity in ROLLUP and CUBE
- HAVING clause used with GROUP BY extensions
- ORDER BY clause used with GROUP BY extensions
- Using other aggregate functions with ROLLUP and CUBE.

Hierarchy Handling in ROLLUP and CUBE

The ROLLUP and CUBE extensions work independently of any hierarchy metadata in your system. Their calculations are based entirely on the columns specified in the SELECT statement in which they appear. This approach enables CUBE and ROLLUP to be used whether or not hierarchy metadata is available. The simplest way to handle levels in hierarchical dimensions is by using the ROLLUP extension and indicating levels explicitly through separate columns. The following code shows a simple example of this with months rolled up to quarters and quarters rolled up to years.

Example 10.14 : ROLLUP and CUBE Hierarchy Handling

```
SELECT calendar_year, calendar_quarter_number,
       calendar_month_number, SUM(amount_sold)
FROM sales, times, products, customers
WHERE sales.time_id=times.time_id AND
  sales.prod_id=products.prod_id AND
  sales.cust_id=customers.cust_id AND
 prod_name IN ('Ruckpart Eclipse', 'Ukko Plain Gortex Boot')
   AND country_id = 'US'
   AND calendar_year=1999
GROUP BY ROLLUP(calendar_year, calendar_quarter_number, calendar_month_number);
```

CALENDAR_YEAR	CALENDAR_QUARTER_NUMBER	CALENDAR_MONTH_NUMBER	SUM(AMOUNT_SOLD)
1999	1	2	79652
1999	1	3	156738
1999	1		236390
1999	2	4	97802
1999	2	5	116282
1999	2	6	85914
1999	2		299998
1999	3	7	113256
1999	3	8	79270
1999	3	9	103200
1999	3		295726
1999			832114
			832114

Column Capacity in ROLLUP and CUBE

CUBE, ROLLUP, and GROUPING SETS do not restrict the GROUP BY clause column capacity. The GROUP BY clause, with or without the extensions, can work with up to 255 columns. However, the combinatorial explosion of CUBE makes it unwise to specify a large number of columns with the CUBE extension. Consider that a 20-column list for CUBE would create 2 to the 20 combinations in the result set. A very large CUBE list could strain system resources, so any such query needs to be tested carefully for performance and the load it places on the system.

HAVING Clause Used with GROUP BY Extensions

The HAVING clause of SELECT statements is unaffected by the use of GROUP BY. Note that the conditions specified in the HAVING clause apply to both the subtotal and non-subtotal rows of the result set. In some cases a query may need to exclude the subtotal rows or the non-subtotal rows from the HAVING clause. This can be achieved by using a GROUPING or GROUPING_ID function together with the HAVING clause. See example 18.8 and its associated SQL statement for an example.

ORDER BY Clause Used with GROUP BY Extensions

In many cases, a query needs to order the rows in a certain way, and this is done with the ORDER BY clause. The ORDER BY clause of a SELECT statement is unaffected by the use of GROUP BY, since the ORDER BY clause is applied after the GROUP BY calculations are complete.

Note that the ORDER BY specification makes no distinction between aggregate and non-aggregate rows of the result set. For instance, you might wish to list sales figures in declining order, but still have the subtotals at the end of each group. Simply ordering sales figures in descending sequence will not be sufficient, since that will place the subtotals (the largest values) at the start of each group. Therefore, it is essential that the columns in the ORDER BY clause include columns that differentiate aggregate from non-aggregate columns. This requirement means that queries using ORDER BY along with aggregation extensions to GROUP BY will generally need to use one or more of the GROUPING functions.

Using Other Aggregate Functions with ROLLUP and CUBE

The examples in this chapter show ROLLUP and CUBE used with the SUM function. While this is the most common type of aggregation, these extensions can also be used with all other functions available to the GROUP BY clause, for example, COUNT, AVG, MIN, MAX, STDDEV, and VARIANCE. COUNT, which is often needed in cross-tabular analyses, is likely to be the second most commonly used function.

COMPUTATION USING THE WITH CLAUSE

The WITH clause (formally known as subquery_factoring_clause) enables you to reuse the same query block in a SELECT statement when it occurs more than once within a complex query. WITH is a part of the SQL-99 standard. This is particularly useful when a query has multiple references to the same query block and there are joins and aggregations. Using the WITH clause, Oracle retrieves the results of a query block and stores them in the user's temporary tablespace. Note that Oracle9*i* does not support recursive use of the WITH clause.

The following query is an example of where you can improve performance and write SQL more simply by using the WITH clause. The query calculates the sum of sales for each channel and holds it under the name channel_summary. Then it checks each channel's sales total to see if any channel's sales are greater than one third of the total sales. By using the WITH clause, the channel_summary data is calculated just once, avoiding an extra scan through the large sales table.

Example 10.15 : WITH Clause

```
WITH  channel_summary AS (
SELECT channels.channel_desc, SUM(amount_sold) AS channel_total
FROM sales, channels
WHERE sales.channel_id = channels.channel_id
GROUP BY channels.channel_desc
)
SELECT channel_desc, channel_total
FROM channel_summary
WHERE channel_total > (
SELECT SUM(channel_total) * 1/3
FROM channel_summary);
```

```
        CHANNEL_DESC                CHANNEL_TOTAL
        Direct  Sales               312829530
```

❑❑❑

11 SCHEMA MODELING TECHNIQUES

SCHEMAS IN DATA WAREHOUSES

A **schema** is a collection of database objects, including tables, views, indexes, and synonyms.

There is a variety of ways of arranging schema objects in the schema models designed for data warehousing. One data warehouse schema model is a star schema. The `Sales History` sample schema (the basis for most of the examples in this book) uses a star schema. However, there are other schema models that are commonly used for data warehouses. The most prevalent of these schema models is the **third normal form (3NF)** schema. Additionally, some data warehouse schemas are neither star schemas nor 3NF schemas, but instead share characteristics of both schemas; these are referred to as hybrid schema models.

The Oracle9*i* database is designed to support all data warehouse schemas. Some features may be specific to one schema model (such as the star transformation feature, described in "Using Star Transformation", which is specific to star schemas). However, the vast majority of Oracle's data warehousing features are equally applicable to star schemas, 3NF schemas, and hybrid schemas. Key data warehousing capabilities such as partitioning (including the rolling window load technique), parallelism, materialized views, and analytic SQL are implemented in all schema models.

The determination of which schema model should be used for a data warehouse should be based upon the requirements and preferences of the data warehouse project team. Comparing the merits of the alternative schema models is outside of the scope of this book; instead, this chapter will briefly introduce each schema model and suggest how Oracle can be optimized for those environments.

THIRD NORMAL FORM

Although this guide primarily uses star schemas in its examples, you can also use the third normal form for your data warehouse implementation.

Third normal form modeling is a classical relational-database modeling technique that minimizes data redundancy through normalization. When compared to a star schema, a 3NF schema typically has a larger number of tables due to this normalization process. For example, in figure 11.1, `orders` and `order items` tables contain similar information as `sales` table in the star schema in figure 11.2.

3NF schemas are typically chosen for large data warehouses, especially environments with significant data-loading requirements that are used to feed data marts and execute long-running queries.

The main advantages of 3NF schemas are that they:

- Provide a neutral schema design, independent of any application or data-usage considerations
- May require less data-transformation than more normalized schemas such as star schemas

figure 11.1 presents a graphical representation of a third normal form schema.

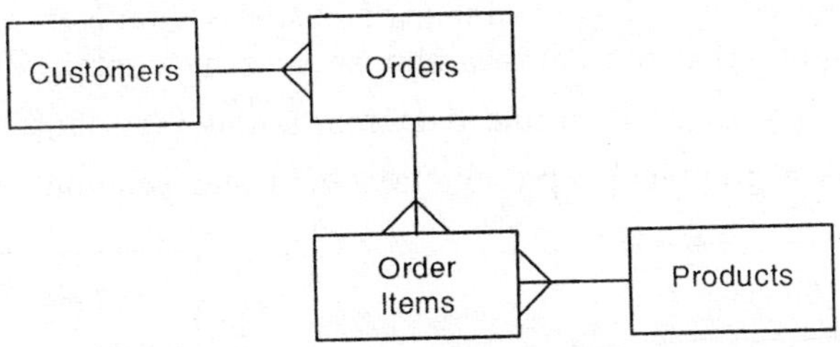

Figure 11.1 Third Normal Form Schema.

Optimizing Third Normal Form Queries

Queries on 3NF schemas are often very complex and involve a large number of tables. The performance of joins between large tables is thus a primary consideration when using 3NF schemas.

One particularly important feature for 3NF schemas is partition-wise joins. The largest tables in a 3NF schema should be partitioned to enable partition-wise joins. The most common partitioning technique in these environments is composite range-hash partitioning for the largest tables, with the most-common join key chosen as the hash-partitioning key.

Parallelism is often heavily utilized in 3NF environments, and parallelism should typically be enabled in these environments.

Star Schemas

The **star schema** is perhaps the simplest data warehouse schema. It is called a star schema because the entity-relationship diagram of this schema resembles a star, with points radiating from a central table. The center of the star consists of a large fact table and the points of the star are the dimension tables.

A star schema is characterized by one or more very large **fact** tables that contain the primary information in the data warehouse, and a number of much smaller **dimension** tables (or lookup tables), each of which contains information about the entries for a particular attribute in the fact table.

A **star query** is a join between a fact table and a number of dimension tables. Each dimension table is joined to the fact table by using a primary key to foreign key join, but the dimension tables are not joined to each other. The cost-based optimizer recognizes star queries and generates efficient execution plans for them.

A typical fact table contains keys and measures. For example, in the `sh` sample schema, the fact table, `sales`, contain the measures quantity_sold, amount, and cost, and the keys `cust_id`, `time_id`, `prod_id`, `channel_id`, and `promo_id`. The dimension tables are `customers`, `times`, `products`, `channels`, and `promotions`. The `product` dimension table, for example, contains information about each product number that appears in the fact table.

A star join is a primary key to foreign key join of the dimension tables to a fact table.

The main advantages of star schemas are that they:

- Provide a direct and intuitive mapping between the business entities being analyzed by end users and the schema design.
- Provide highly optimized performance for typical star queries.
- Are widely supported by a large number of business intelligence tools, which may anticipate or even require that the data-warehouse schema contain dimension tables.

Star schemas are used for both simple data marts and very large data warehouses.

Figure 11.2 presents a graphical representation of a star schema.

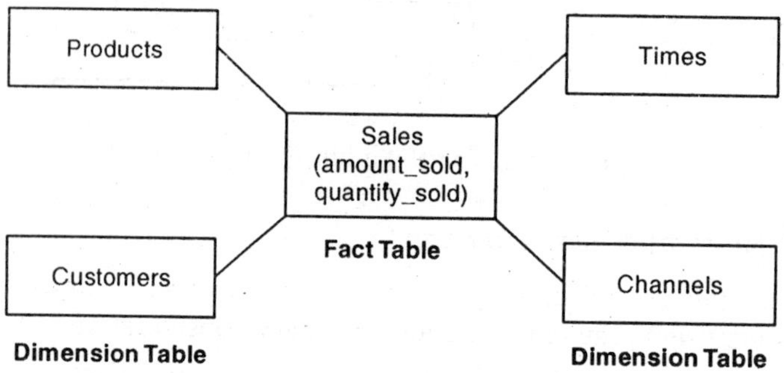

Figure 11.2 Star Schema.

Snowflake Schemas

The snowflake schema is a more complex data warehouse model than a star schema, and is a type of star schema. It is called a snowflake schema because the diagram of the schema resembles a snowflake.

Snowflake schemas normalize dimensions to eliminate redundancy. That is, the dimension data has been grouped into multiple tables instead of one large table. For example, a product dimension table in a star schema might be normalized into a `products` table, a `product_category` table, and a `product_manufacturer` table in a snowflake schema. While this saves space, it increases the number of dimension tables and requires more foreign key joins. The result is more complex queries and reduced query performance. Figure 11.3 presents a graphical representation of a snowflake schema.

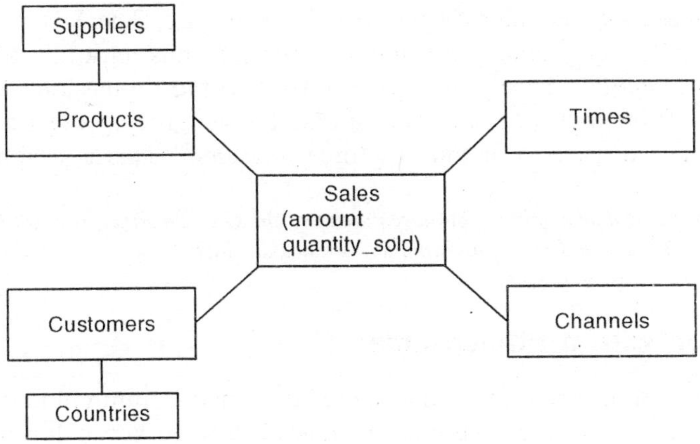

Figure 11.3 Snowflake Schema.

NOTE

Oracle Corporation recommends you choose a star schema over a snowflake schema unless you have a clear reason not to.

OPTIMIZING STAR QUERIES

You should consider the following when using star queries:

- Tuning star queries
- Using star transformation.

Tuning Star Queries

To get the best possible performance for star queries, it is important to follow some basic guidelines:

- A bitmap index should be built on each of the foreign key columns of the fact table or tables.
- The initialization parameter `STAR_TRANSFORMATION_ENABLED` should be set to `true`. This enables an important optimizer feature for star-queries. It is set to `false` by default for backward-compatibility.
- The cost-based optimizer should be used. This does not apply solely to star schemas: all data warehouses should always use the cost-based optimizer.

When a data warehouse satisfies these conditions, the majority of the star queries running in the data warehouse will use a query execution strategy known as the star transformation. The star transformation provides very efficient query performance for star queries.

Using Star Transformation

The star transformation is a powerful optimization technique that relies upon implicitly rewriting (or transforming) the SQL of the original star query. The end user never needs to know any of the details about the star transformation. Oracle's cost-based optimizer automatically chooses the star transformation where appropriate.

The star transformation is a cost-based query transformation aimed at executing star queries efficiently. Oracle processes a star query using two basic phases. The first phase retrieves exactly the necessary rows from the fact table (the result set). Because this retrieval utilizes bitmap indexes, it is very efficient. The second phase joins this result set to the dimension tables. An example of an end user query is: "What were the sales and profits for the grocery department of stores in the west and southwest sales districts over the last three quarters?" This is a simple star query.

NOTE *Bitmap indexes are available only if you have purchased the Oracle9i Enterprise Edition. In Oracle9i Standard Edition, bitmap indexes and star transformation are not available.*

Star Transformation with a Bitmap Index

A prerequisite of the star transformation is that there be a single-column bitmap index on every join column of the fact table. These join columns include all foreign key columns.

For example, the sales table of the `sh` sample schema has bitmap indexes on the `time_id`, `channel_id`, `cust_id`, `prod_id`, and `promo_id` columns.

Consider the following star query:

```
SELECT ch.channel_class, c.cust_city, t.calendar_quarter_desc,
   SUM(s.amount_sold) sales_amount
FROM sales s, times t, customers c, channels ch
WHERE  s.time_id = t.time_id
AND    s.cust_id = c.cust_id
AND    s.channel_id = ch.channel_id
AND    c.cust_state_province = 'CA'
AND    ch.channel_desc in ('Internet','Catalog')
AND    t.calendar_quarter_desc IN ('1999-Q1','1999-Q2')
GROUP BY ch.channel_class, c.cust_city, t.calendar_quarter_desc;
```

Oracle processes this query in two phases. In the first phase, Oracle uses the bitmap indexes on the foreign key columns of the fact table to identify and retrieve only the necessary rows from the fact table. That is, Oracle will retrieve the result set from the fact table using essentially the following query:

```
SELECT ... FROM sales
WHERE time_id IN
  (SELECT time_id FROM times
   WHERE calendar_quarter_desc IN('1999-Q1','1999-Q2'))
   AND cust_id IN
  (SELECT cust_id FROM customers WHERE cust_state_province='CA')
   AND channel_id IN
  (SELECT channel_id FROM channels WHERE channel_desc IN('Internet','Catalog'));
```

This is the transformation step of the algorithm, because the original star query has been transformed into this subquery representation. This method of accessing the fact table leverages the strengths of Oracle's bitmap indexes. Intuitively, bitmap indexes provide a set-based processing scheme within a relational database. Oracle has implemented very fast methods for doing set operations such as `AND` (an intersection in standard set-based terminology), `OR` (a set-based union), `MINUS`, and `COUNT`.

In this star query, a bitmap index on `time_id` is used to identify the set of all rows in the fact table corresponding to `sales` in `1999-Q1`. This set is represented as a bitmap (a string of 1's and 0's that indicates which rows of the fact table are members of the set).

A similar bitmap is retrieved for the fact table rows corresponding to the sale from `1999-Q2`. The bitmap `OR` operation is used to combine this set of `Q1` sales with the set of `Q2` sales.

Additional set operations will be done for the `customer` dimension and the `product` dimension. At this point in the star query processing, there are three bitmaps. Each bitmap corresponds to a separate dimension table, and each bitmap represents the set of rows of the fact table that satisfy that individual dimension's constraints.

These three bitmaps are combined into a single bitmap using the bitmap `AND` operation. This final bitmap represents the set of rows in the fact table that satisfy all of the constraints on the dimension table. This is the result set, the exact set of rows from the fact table needed to evaluate the query. Note that none of the actual data in the fact table has been accessed. All of these operations rely solely on the bitmap indexes and the dimension tables. Because of the bitmap indexes' compressed data representations, the bitmap set-based operations are extremely efficient.

Once the result set is identified, the bitmap is used to access the actual data from the sales table. Only those rows that are required for the end user's query are retrieved from the fact table. At this point, Oracle has effectively joined all of the dimension tables to the fact table using bitmap indexes. This technique provides excellent performance because Oracle is joining all of the dimension tables to the fact table with one logical join operation, rather than joining each dimension table to the fact table independently.

The second phase of this query is to join these rows from the fact table (the result set) to the dimension tables. Oracle will use the most efficient method for accessing and joining the dimension tables. Many dimension are very small, and table scans are typically the most efficient access method for these dimension tables. For large dimension tables, table scans may not be the most efficient access method. In the previous example, a bitmap index on `product.department` can be used to quickly identify all of those products in the grocery department. Oracle's cost-based optimizer automatically determines which access method is most appropriate for a given dimension table, based upon the cost-based optimizer's knowledge about the sizes and data distributions of each dimension table.

The specific join method (as well as indexing method) for each dimension table will likewise be intelligently determined by the cost-based optimizer. A hash join is often the most efficient algorithm for joining the dimension tables. The final answer is returned to the user once all of the dimension tables have been joined. The query technique of retrieving only the matching rows from one table and then joining to another table is commonly known as a semi-join.

Execution Plan for a Star Transformation with a Bitmap Index

The following typical execution plan might result from "Star Transformation with a Bitmap Index":

```
SELECT STATEMENT
 SORT GROUP BY
  HASH JOIN
   TABLE ACCESS FULL                               CHANNELS
   HASH JOIN
    TABLE ACCESS FULL                              CUSTOMERS
```

```
HASH JOIN
 TABLE ACCESS FULL                              TIMES
 PARTITION RANGE ITERATOR
  TABLE ACCESS BY LOCAL INDEX ROWID             SALES
   BITMAP CONVERSION TO ROWIDS
    BITMAP AND
     BITMAP MERGE
      BITMAP KEY ITERATION
       BUFFER SORT
        TABLE ACCESS FULL                       CUSTOMERS
       BITMAP INDEX RANGE SCAN                  SALES_CUST_BIX
     BITMAP MERGE
      BITMAP KEY ITERATION
       BUFFER SORT
        TABLE ACCESS FULL                       CHANNELS
       BITMAP INDEX RANGE SCAN                  SALES_CHANNEL_BIX
     BITMAP MERGE
      BITMAP KEY ITERATION
       BUFFER SORT
        TABLE ACCESS FULL                       TIMES
       BITMAP INDEX RANGE SCAN                  SALES_TIME_BIX
```

In this plan, the fact table is accessed through a bitmap access path based on a bitmap AND, of three merged bitmaps. The three bitmaps are generated by the BITMAP MERGE row source being fed bitmaps from row source trees underneath it. Each such row source tree consists of a BITMAP KEY ITERATION row source which fetches values from the subquery row source tree, which in this example is a full table access. For each such value, the BITMAP KEY ITERATION row source retrieves the bitmap from the bitmap index. After the relevant fact table rows have been retrieved using this access path, they are joined with the dimension tables and temporary tables to produce the answer to the query.

Star Transformation with a Bitmap Join Index

In addition to bitmap indexes, you can use a bitmap join index during star transformations. Assume you have the following additional index structure:

```
CREATE BITMAP INDEX sales_c_state_bjix
ON sales(customers.cust_state_province)
FROM sales, customers
WHERE sales.cust_id = customers.cust_id
LOCAL NOLOGGING COMPUTE STATISTICS;
```

The processing of the same star query using the bitmap join index is similar to the previous example. The only difference is that Oracle will utilize the join index, instead of a single-table bitmap index, to access the customer data in the first phase of the star query.

Execution Plan for a Star Transformation with a Bitmap Join Index

The following typical execution plan might result from "Execution Plan for a Star Transformation with a Bitmap Join Index":

```
SELECT STATEMENT
 SORT GROUP BY
  HASH JOIN
   TABLE ACCESS FULL                                    CHANNELS
   HASH JOIN
    TABLE ACCESS FULL                                   CUSTOMERS
    HASH JOIN
     TABLE ACCESS FULL                                  TIMES
     PARTITION RANGE ALL
      TABLE ACCESS BY LOCAL INDEX ROWID                 SALES
       BITMAP CONVERSION TO ROWIDS
        BITMAP AND
         BITMAP INDEX SINGLE VALUE                      SALES_C_STATE_BJIX
         BITMAP MERGE
          BITMAP KEY ITERATION
           BUFFER SORT
            TABLE ACCESS FULL                           CHANNELS
           BITMAP INDEX RANGE SCAN                      SALES_CHANNEL_BIX
         BITMAP MERGE
          BITMAP KEY ITERATION
           BUFFER SORT
            TABLE ACCESS FULL                           TIMES
           BITMAP INDEX RANGE SCAN                      SALES_TIME_BIX
```

The difference between this plan as compared to the previous one is that the inner part of the bitmap index scan for the `customer` dimension has no subselect. This is because the join predicate information on `customer.cust_state_province` can be satisfied with the bitmap join index `sales_c_state_bjix`.

How Oracle Chooses to Use Star Transformation

The star transformation is a cost-based transformation in the following sense. The optimizer generates and saves the best plan it can produce without the transformation. If the transformation is enabled, the optimizer then tries to apply it to the query and, if applicable, generates the best plan using the transformed query. Based on a comparison of the cost estimates between the best plans for the two versions of the query, the optimizer will then decide whether to use the best plan for the transformed or untransformed version.

If the query requires accessing a large percentage of the rows in the fact table, it might be better to use a full table scan and not use the transformations. However, if the constraining predicates on the dimension tables are sufficiently selective that only a small portion of the fact table needs to be retrieved, the plan based on the transformation will probably be superior.

Note that the optimizer generates a subquery for a dimension table only if it decides that it is reasonable to do so based on a number of criteria. There is no guarantee that subqueries will be generated for all dimension tables. The optimizer may also decide, based on the properties of the tables and the query, that the transformation does not merit being applied to a particular query. In this case the best regular plan will be used.

Star Transformation Restrictions

Star transformation is not supported for tables with any of the following characteristics:

- Queries with a table hint that is incompatible with a bitmap access path
- Queries that contain bind variables
- Tables with too few bitmap indexes. There must be a bitmap index on a fact table column for the optimizer to generate a subquery for it
- Remote fact tables. However, remote dimension tables are allowed in the subqueries that are generated
- Anti-joined tables
- Tables that are already used as a dimension table in a subquery
- Tables that are really unmerged views, which are not view partitions.

The star transformation may not be chosen by the optimizer for the following cases:

- Tables that have a good single-table access path
- Tables that are too small for the transformation to be worthwhile.

In addition, temporary tables will not be used by star transformation under the following conditions:

- The database is in read-only mode
- The star query is part of a transaction that is in serializable mode.

❑❑❑

12 SQL FOR ANALYSIS IN DATA WAREHOUSES

OVERVIEW OF SQL FOR ANALYSIS IN DATA WAREHOUSES

Oracle has enhanced SQL's analytical processing capabilities by introducing a new family of analytic SQL functions. These analytic functions enable you to calculate:

- Rankings and percentiles
- Moving window calculations
- Lag/lead analysis
- First/last analysis
- Linear regression statistics.

Ranking functions include cumulative distributions, percent rank, and N-tiles. Moving window calculations allow you to find moving and cumulative aggregations, such as sums and averages. Lag/lead analysis enables direct inter-row references so you can calculate period-to-period changes. First/last analysis enables you to find the first or last value in an ordered group.

Other enhancements to SQL include the CASE expression. CASE expressions provide if-then logic useful in many situations.

To enhance performance, analytic functions can be parallelized: multiple processes can simultaneously execute all of these statements. These capabilities make calculations easier and more efficient, thereby enhancing database performance, scalability, and simplicity.

Analytic functions are classified as described in table 12.1.

Table 12.1 Analytic Functions and Their Uses

Type	Used For
Ranking	Calculating ranks, percentiles, and n-tiles of the values in a result set.
Windowing	Calculating cumulative and moving aggregates. Works with these functions:

	SUM, AVG, MIN, MAX, COUNT, VARIANCE, STDDEV, FIRST_VALUE, LAST_VALUE, and new statistical functions
Reporting	Calculating shares, for example, market share. Works with these functions: SUM, AVG, MIN, MAX, COUNT (with/without DISTINCT), VARIANCE, STDDEV, RATIO_TO_REPORT, and new statistical functions
LAG/LEAD	Finding a value in a row a specified number of rows from a current row.
FIRST/LAST	First or last value in an ordered group.
Linear Regression	Calculating linear regression and other statistics (slope, intercept, and so on).
Inverse Percentile	The value in a data set that corresponds to a specified percentile.
Hypothetical Rank and Distribution	The rank or percentile that a row would have if inserted into a specified data set.

To perform these operations, the analytic functions add several new elements to SQL processing. These elements are build on existing SQL to allow flexible and powerful calculation expressions. With just a few exceptions, the analytic functions have these new elements. The processing flow is represented in figure 12.1.

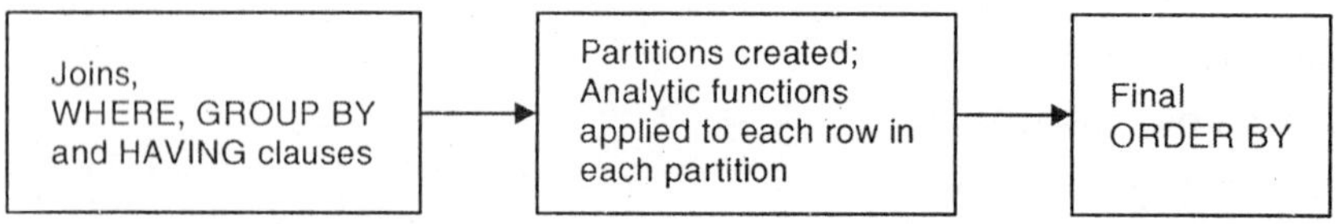

Figure 12.1 Processing Order.

The essential concepts used in analytic functions are:

- **Processing order**

  Query processing using analytic functions takes place in three stages. First, all joins, WHERE, GROUP BY and HAVING clauses are performed. Second, the result set is made available to the analytic functions, and all their calculations take place. Third, if the query has an ORDER BY clause at its end, the ORDER BY is processed to allow for precise output ordering. The processing order is shown in figure 12.1.

- **Result set partitions**

  The analytic functions allow users to divide query result sets into groups of rows called partitions. Note that the term **partitions** used with analytic functions is unrelated to Oracle's table partitions feature. Throughout this chapter, the term partitions refers to only the meaning related to analytic functions. Partitions are created after the groups defined with GROUP BY clauses, so they are available to any aggregate results such as sums and averages. Partition divisions may be based upon any desired columns or expressions. A query result set may be partitioned into just one partition holding all the rows, a few large partitions, or many small partitions holding just a few rows each.

- **Window**

  For each row in a partition, you can define a sliding window of data. This window determines the range of rows used to perform the calculations for the current row. Window sizes can be based on either a physical number of rows or a logical interval such as time. The window has a starting row and an ending row. Depending on its definition, the window may move at one or both ends. For instance, a window defined for a cumulative sum function would have its starting row fixed at the first row of its partition, and its ending row would slide from the starting point all the way to the last row of the partition. In contrast, a window defined for a moving average would have both its starting and end points slide so that they maintain a constant physical or logical range.

A window can be set as large as all the rows in a partition or just a sliding window of one row within a partition. When a window is near a border, the function returns results for only the available rows, rather than warning you that the results are not what you want.

When using window functions, the current row is included during calculations, so you should only specify (*n*–1) when you are dealing with *n* items.

- **Current row**

  Each calculation performed with an analytic function is based on a current row within a partition. The current row serves as the reference point determining the start and end of the window. For instance, a centered moving average calculation could be defined with a window that holds the current row, the six preceding rows, and the following six rows. This would create a sliding window of 13 rows, as shown in figure 12.2.

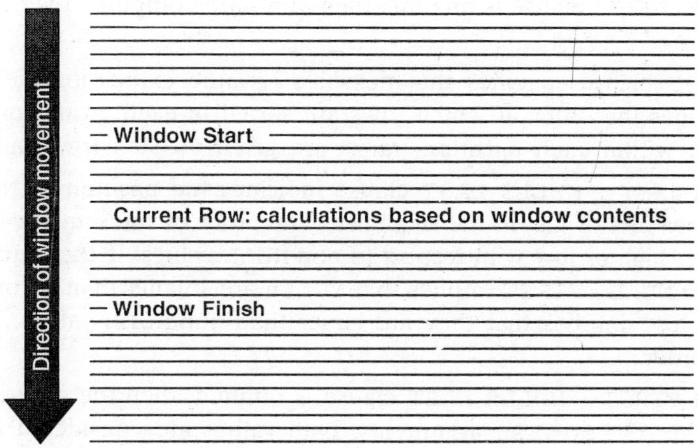

Figure 12.2 Sliding Window Example.

RANKING FUNCTIONS

A ranking function computes the rank of a record compared to other records in the dataset based on the values of a set of measures. The types of ranking function are:

- RANK and DENSE_RANK
- CUME_DIST and PERCENT_RANK
- NTILE
- ROW_NUMBER.

RANK and DENSE_RANK

The RANK and DENSE_RANK functions allow you to rank items in a group, for example, finding the top three products sold in California last year. There are two functions that perform ranking, as shown by the following syntax:

```
RANK ( ) OVER ( [query_partition_clause] order_by_clause )
DENSE_RANK ( ) OVER ( [query_partition_clause] order_by_clause )
```

The difference between RANK and DENSE_RANK is that DENSE_RANK leaves no gaps in ranking sequence when there are ties. That is, if you were ranking a competition using DENSE_RANK and had three people tie for second place, you would say that all three were in second place and that the next person came in third. The RANK function would also give three people in second place, but the next person would be in fifth place.

The following are some relevant points about RANK:

- Ascending is the default sort order, which you may want to change to descending.
- The expressions in the optional PARTITION BY clause divide the query result set into groups within which the RANK function operates. That is, RANK gets reset whenever the group changes. In effect, the value expressions of the PARTITION BY clause define the reset boundaries.
- If the PARTITION BY clause is missing, then ranks are computed over the entire query result set.
- The ORDER BY clause specifies the measures (<value expression>s) on which ranking is done and defines the order in which rows are sorted in each group (or partition). Once the data is sorted within each partition, ranks are given to each row starting from 1.
- The NULLS FIRST | NULLS LAST clause indicates the position of NULLs in the ordered sequence, either first or last in the sequence. The order of the sequence would make NULLs compare either high or low with respect to non-NULL values. If the sequence were in ascending order, then NULLS FIRST implies that NULLs are smaller than all other non-NULL values and NULLS LAST implies that they are larger than non-NULL values. It is the opposite for descending order.
- If the NULLS FIRST | NULLS LAST clause is omitted, then the ordering of the null values depends on the ASC or DESC arguments. Null values are considered larger than any other values. If the ordering sequence is ASC, then nulls will appear last; nulls will appear first otherwise. Nulls are considered equal to other nulls and, therefore, the order in which nulls are presented is non-deterministic.

Ranking Order

The following example shows how the [ASC | DESC] option changes the ranking order.

Example 12.1 : Ranking Order

```
SELECT channel_desc,
   TO_CHAR(SUM(amount_sold), '9,999,999,999') SALES$,
   RANK() OVER (ORDER BY SUM(amount_sold) ) AS default_rank,
   RANK() OVER (ORDER BY SUM(amount_sold) DESC NULLS LAST) AS custom_rank
FROM sales, products, customers, times, channels
WHERE sales.prod_id=products.prod_id AND
   sales.cust_id=customers.cust_id AND
   sales.time_id=times.time_id AND
```

```
    sales.channel_id=channels.channel_id AND
    times.calendar_month_desc IN ('2000-09', '2000-10')
     AND country_id='US'
GROUP BY channel_desc;
```

```
CHANNEL_DESC              SALES$          DEFAULT_RANK      CUSTOM_RANK
-----------------------------------------------------------------------
Direct Sales           5,744,263                     5                1
Internet               3,625,993                     4                2
Catalog                1,858,386                     3                3
Partners               1,500,213                     2                4
Tele Sales               604,656                     1                5
```

While the data in this result is ordered on the measure `SALES$`, in general, it is not guaranteed by the `RANK` function that the data will be sorted on the measures. If you want the data to be sorted on `SALES$` in your result, you must specify it explicitly with an `ORDER BY` clause, at the end of the `SELECT` statement.

Ranking on Multiple Expressions

Ranking functions need to resolve ties between values in the set. If the first expression cannot resolve ties, the second expression is used to resolve ties and so on. For example, here is a query ranking four of the sales channels over two months based on their dollar sales, breaking ties with the unit sales. (Note that the `TRUNC` function is used here only to create tie values for this query.)

Example 12.2 : Ranking On Multiple Expressions

```
SELECT channel_desc, calendar_month_desc,
    TO_CHAR(TRUNC(SUM(amount_sold),-6), '9,999,999,999') SALES$,
    TO_CHAR(SUM(quantity_sold), '9,999,999,999') SALES_Count,
    RANK() OVER (ORDER BY trunc(SUM(amount_sold), -6) DESC, SUM(quantity_sold)
DESC) AS col_rank
FROM sales, products, customers, times, channels
WHERE sales.prod_id=products.prod_id AND
    sales.cust_id=customers.cust_id AND
    sales.time_id=times.time_id AND
    sales.channel_id=channels.channel_id AND
    times.calendar_month_desc IN ('2000-09', '2000-10') AND
    channels.channel_desc<>'Tele Sales'
GROUP BY channel_desc, calendar_month_desc;
```

```
CHANNEL_DESC      CALENDAR          SALES$        SALES_COUNT     COL_RANK
---------------------------------------------------------------------------
Direct Sales      2000-10       10,000,000            192,551            1
Direct Sales      2000-09        9,000,000            176,950            2
Internet          2000-10        6,000,000            123,153            3
Internet          2000-09        6,000,000            113,006            4
Catalog           2000-10        3,000,000             59,782            5
Catalog           2000-09        3,000,000             54,857            6
Partners          2000-10        2,000,000             50,773            7
Partners          2000-09        2,000,000             46,220            8
```

The sales_count column breaks the ties for three pairs of values.

RANK and DENSE_RANK Difference

The difference between RANK and DENSE_RANK functions is illustrated as follows:

Example 12.3 : RANK and DENSE_RANK

```
SELECT channel_desc, calendar_month_desc,
   TO_CHAR(TRUNC(SUM(amount_sold),-6), '9,999,999,999') SALES$,
      RANK() OVER (ORDER BY trunc(SUM(amount_sold),-6) DESC)
               AS RANK,
DENSE_RANK() OVER (ORDER BY TRUNC(SUM(amount_sold),-6) DESC)
               AS DENSE_RANK
FROM sales, products, customers, times, channels
WHERE sales.prod_id=products.prod_id AND
   sales.cust_id=customers.cust_id AND
   sales.time_id=times.time_id AND
   sales.channel_id=channels.channel_id AND
   times.calendar_month_desc IN ('2000-09', '2000-10') AND
   channels.channel_desc<>'Tele Sales'
GROUP BY channel_desc, calendar_month_desc;
```

CHANNEL_DESC	CALENDAR	SALES$	RANK	DENSE_RANK
Direct Sales	2000-10	10,000,000	1	1
Direct Sales	2000-09	9,000,000	2	2
Internet	2000-09	6,000,000	3	3
Internet	2000-10	6,000,000	3	3
Catalog	2000-09	3,000,000	5	4
Catalog	2000-10	3,000,000	5	4
Partners	2000-09	2,000,000	7	5
Partners	2000-10	2,000,000	7	5

Note that, in the case of DENSE_RANK, the largest rank value gives the number of distinct values in the dataset.

Per Group Ranking

The RANK function can be made to operate within groups, that is, the rank gets reset whenever the group changes. This is accomplished with the PARTITION BY clause. The group expressions in the PARTITION BY subclause divide the dataset into groups within which RANK operates. For example, to rank products within each channel by their dollar sales, you say:

Example 12.4 : Per Group Ranking Example 1

```
SELECT channel_desc, calendar_month_desc,
   TO_CHAR(SUM(amount_sold), '9,999,999,999') SALES$,
      RANK() OVER (PARTITION BY channel_desc
      ORDER BY SUM(amount_sold) DESC) AS RANK_BY_CHANNEL
FROM sales, products, customers, times, channels
WHERE sales.prod_id=products.prod_id AND
```

```
   sales.cust_id=customers.cust_id AND
   sales.time_id=times.time_id AND
   sales.channel_id=channels.channel_id AND
   times.calendar_month_desc IN ('2000-08', '2000-09', '2000-10', '2000-11') AND
   channels.channel_desc IN ('Direct Sales', 'Internet')
GROUP BY channel_desc, calendar_month_desc;
```

A single query block can contain more than one ranking function, each partitioning the data into different groups (that is, reset on different boundaries). The groups can be mutually exclusive. The following query ranks products based on their dollar sales within each month (rank_of_product_per_region) and within each channel (rank_of_product_total).

Example 12.5 : Per Group Ranking Example 2

```
SELECT channel_desc, calendar_month_desc,
   TO_CHAR(SUM(amount_sold), '9,999,999,999') SALES$,
RANK() OVER (PARTITION BY calendar_month_desc
      ORDER BY SUM(amount_sold) DESC) AS RANK_WITHIN_MONTH,
 RANK() OVER (PARTITION BY channel_desc
      ORDER BY SUM(amount_sold) DESC) AS RANK_WITHIN_CHANNEL
FROM sales, products, customers, times, channels
WHERE sales.prod_id=products.prod_id AND
   sales.cust_id=customers.cust_id AND
   sales.time_id=times.time_id AND
   sales.channel_id=channels.channel_id AND
   times.calendar_month_desc IN ('2000-08', '2000-09', '2000-10', '2000-11')
   AND
   channels.channel_desc IN ('Direct Sales', 'Internet')
GROUP BY channel_desc, calendar_month_desc;
```

CHANNEL_DESC	CALENDAR	SALES$	RANK_WITHIN_MONTH	RANK_WITHIN_CHANNEL
Direct Sales	2000-08	9,588,122	1	4
Internet	2000-08	6,084,390	2	4
Direct Sales	2000-09	9,652,037	1	3
Internet	2000-09	6,147,023	2	3
Direct Sales	2000-10	10,035,478	1	2
Internet	2000-10	6,417,697	2	2
Direct Sales	2000-11	12,217,068	1	1
Internet	2000-11	7,821,208	2	1

Per Cube and Rollup Group Ranking

Analytic functions, RANK for example, can be reset based on the groupings provided by a CUBE, ROLLUP, or GROUPING SETS operator. It is useful to assign ranks to the groups created by CUBE, ROLLUP, and GROUPING SETS queries.

A sample CUBE and ROLLUP query is the following:

```
SELECT channel_desc,  country_id,
   TO_CHAR(SUM(amount_sold), '9,999,999,999') SALES$,
   RANK() OVER (PARTITION BY GROUPING_ID(channel_desc, country_id)
            ORDER BY SUM(amount_sold) DESC) AS RANK_PER_GROUP
FROM sales, customers, times, channels
WHERE sales.time_id=times.time_id AND
```

```
    sales.cust_id=customers.cust_id AND
    sales.channel_id= channels.channel_id AND
    channels.channel_desc IN ('Direct Sales', 'Internet') AND
    times.calendar_month_desc='2000-09'
   AND country_id IN ('UK', 'US', 'JP')
GROUP BY CUBE( channel_desc, country_id);
```

CHANNEL_DESC	CO	SALES$	RANK_PER_GROUP
Direct Sales	US	2,835,557	1
Internet	US	1,732,240	2
Direct Sales	UK	1,378,126	3
Internet	UK	911,739	4
Direct Sales	JP	91,124	5
Internet	JP	57,232	6
Direct Sales		4,304,807	1
Internet		2,701,211	2
	US	4,567,797	1
	UK	2,289,865	2
	JP	148,355	3
		7,006,017	1

Treatment of NULLs

NULLs are treated like normal values. Also, for rank computation, a NULL value is assumed to be equal to another NULL value. Depending on the ASC | DESC options provided for measures and the NULLS FIRST | NULLS LAST clause, NULLs will either sort low or high and hence, are given ranks appropriately. The following example shows how NULLs are ranked in different cases:

```
SELECT calendar_year AS YEAR, calendar_quarter_number AS QTR,
            calendar_month_number AS MO, SUM(amount_sold),
RANK()  OVER (ORDER BY SUM(amount_sold)  ASC NULLS FIRST) AS NFIRST,
RANK()  OVER (ORDER BY SUM(amount_sold)  ASC NULLS LAST) AS NLASST,
RANK()  OVER (ORDER BY SUM(amount_sold)  DESC NULLS FIRST) AS NFIRST_DESC,
RANK()  OVER (ORDER BY SUM(amount_sold)  DESC NULLS LAST) AS NLAST_DESC
FROM (
       SELECT sales.time_id, sales.amount_sold, products.*, customers.*
       FROM sales, products, customers
       WHERE
          sales.prod_id=products.prod_id AND
          sales.cust_id=customers.cust_id AND
          prod_name IN ('Ruckpart Eclipse', 'Ukko Plain Gortex Boot')
          AND country_id ='UK') v, times
 WHERE v.time_id (+) =times.time_id AND
      calendar_year=1999
 GROUP BY calendar_year, calendar_quarter_number, calendar_month_number;
```

YEAR	QTR	MO	SUM (AMOUNT_SOLD)	NFIRST	NLAST	NFIRST_DESC	NLAST_DESC
1999	1	3	51820	12	8	5	1
1999	2	6	45360	11	7	6	2
1999	3	9	43950	10	6	7	3

1999	3	8	41180	8	4	9	5
1999	2	5	27431	7	3	10	6
1999	2	4	20602	6	2	11	7
1999	3	7	15296	5	1	12	8
1999	1	1		1	9	1	9
1999	4	10		1	9	1	9
1999	4	11		1	9	1	9
1999	4	12		1	9	1	9

If the value for two rows is NULL, the next group expression is used to resolve the tie. If they cannot be resolved even then, the next expression is used and so on till the tie is resolved or else the two rows are given the same rank. For example:

Top N Ranking

You can easily obtain top N ranks by enclosing the RANK function in a subquery and then applying a filter condition outside the subquery. For example, to obtain the top five countries in sales for a specific month, you can issue the following statement:

```
SELECT * FROM
  (SELECT country_id,
     TO_CHAR(SUM(amount_sold), '9,999,999,999') SALES$,
     RANK() OVER (ORDER BY SUM(amount_sold)  DESC ) AS COUNTRY_RANK
   FROM sales, products, customers, times, channels
   WHERE sales.prod_id=products.prod_id AND
     sales.cust_id=customers.cust_id AND
     sales.time_id=times.time_id AND
     sales.channel_id=channels.channel_id AND
     times.calendar_month_desc='2000-09'
   GROUP BY country_id)
WHERE COUNTRY_RANK <= 5;
```

CO	SALES$	COUNTRY_RANK
US	6,517,786	1
NL	3,447,121	2
UK	3,207,243	3
DE	3,194,765	4
FR	2,125,572	5

Bottom N Ranking

Bottom N is similar to top N except for the ordering sequence within the rank expression. Using the previous example, you can order SUM(s_amount) ascending instead of descending.

CUME_DIST

The CUME_DIST function (defined as the inverse of percentile in some statistical books) computes the position of a specified value relative to a set of values. The order can be ascending or descending. Ascending is the default. The range of values for CUME_DIST is from greater than 0 to 1. To compute the CUME_DIST of a value x in a set S of size N, you use the formula:

```
CUME_DIST(x) = number of values in S coming before and including x
in the specified order/ N
```

Its syntax is:

```
CUME_DIST ( ) OVER ( [query_partition_clause] order_by_clause )
```

The semantics of various options in the CUME_DIST function are similar to those in the RANK function. The default order is ascending, implying that the lowest value gets the lowest CUME_DIST (as all other values come later than this value in the order). NULLs are treated the same as they are in the RANK function. They are counted toward both the numerator and the denominator as they are treated like non-NULL values. The following example finds cumulative distribution of sales by channel within each month:

```
SELECT calendar_month_desc AS MONTH, channel_desc,
    TO_CHAR(SUM(amount_sold) , '9,999,999,999') SALES$ ,
    CUME_DIST() OVER ( PARTITION BY calendar_month_desc ORDER BY
        SUM(amount_sold) ) AS
    CUME_DIST_BY_CHANNEL
  FROM sales, products, customers, times, channels
  WHERE sales.prod_id=products.prod_id AND
    sales.cust_id=customers.cust_id AND
    sales.time_id=times.time_id AND
    sales.channel_id=channels.channel_id AND
    times.calendar_month_desc IN ('2000-09', '2000-07','2000-08')
  GROUP BY calendar_month_desc, channel_desc;
```

MONTH	CHANNEL_DESC	SALES$	CUME_DIST_BY_CHANNEL
2000-07	Tele Sales	1,012,954	.2
2000-07	Partners	2,495,662	.4
2000-07	Catalog	2,946,709	.6
2000-07	Internet	6,045,609	.8
2000-07	Direct Sales	9,563,664	1
2000-08	Tele Sales	1,008,703	.2
2000-08	Partners	2,552,945	.4
2000-08	Catalog	3,061,381	.6
2000-08	Internet	6,084,390	.8
2000-08	Direct Sales	9,588,122	1
2000-09	Tele Sales	1,017,149	.2
2000-09	Partners	2,570,666	.4
2000-09	Catalog	3,025,309	.6
2000-09	Internet	6,147,023	.8
2000-09	Direct Sales	9,652,037	1

PERCENT_RANK

PERCENT_RANK is similar to CUME_DIST, but it uses rank values rather than row counts in its numerator. Therefore, it returns the percent rank of a value relative to a group of values. The function is available in many popular spreadsheets. PERCENT_RANK of a row is calculated as:

```
(rank of row in its partition - 1) / (number of rows in the partition - 1)
```

PERCENT_RANK returns values in the range zero to one. The row(s) with a rank of 1 will have a PERCENT_RANK of zero.

Its syntax is:

```
PERCENT_RANK ( ) OVER ( [query_partition_clause] order_by_clause )
```

NTILE

NTILE allows easy calculation of tertiles, quartiles, deciles and other common summary statistics. This function divides an ordered partition into a specified number of groups called **buckets** and assigns a bucket number to each row in the partition. NTILE is a very useful calculation because it lets users divide a data set into fourths, thirds, and other groupings.

The buckets are calculated so that each bucket has exactly the same number of rows assigned to it or at most 1 row more than the others. For instance, if you have 100 rows in a partition and ask for an NTILE function with four buckets, 25 rows will be assigned a value of 1, 25 rows will have value 2, and so on. These buckets are referred to as equiheight buckets.

If the number of rows in the partition does not divide evenly (without a remainder) into the number of buckets, then the number of rows assigned for each bucket will differ by one at most. The extra rows will be distributed one for each bucket starting from the lowest bucket number. For instance, if there are 103 rows in a partition which has an NTILE(5) function, the first 21 rows will be in the first bucket, the next 21 in the second bucket, the next 21 in the third bucket, the next 20 in the fourth bucket and the final 20 in the fifth bucket.

The NTILE function has the following syntax:

```
NTILE ( expr ) OVER ( [query_partition_clause] order_by_clause )
```

In this, the N in NTILE(N) can be a constant (for example, 5) or an expression.

This function, like RANK and CUME_DIST, has a PARTITION BY clause for per group computation, an ORDER BY clause for specifying the measures and their sort order, and NULLS FIRST | NULLS LAST clause for the specific treatment of NULLs. For example,

NTILE Example

The following is an example assigning each month's sales total into one of 4 buckets:

```
SELECT calendar_month_desc AS MONTH ,
     TO_CHAR(SUM(amount_sold), '9,999,999,999') SALES$,
     NTILE(4) OVER (ORDER BY SUM(amount_sold)) AS TILE4
   FROM sales, products, customers, times, channels
   WHERE sales.prod_id=products.prod_id AND
     sales.cust_id=customers.cust_id AND
     sales.time_id=times.time_id AND
     sales.channel_id=channels.channel_id AND
     times.calendar_year=1999 AND
     prod_category= 'Men'
   GROUP BY calendar_month_desc;
```

```
MONTH                SALES$              TILE4
----------------------------------------------
1999-10           4,373,102                  1
1999-01           4,754,622                  1
```

```
1999-11          5,367,943          1
1999-12          6,082,226          2
1999-07          6,161,638          2
1999-02          6,518,877          2
1999-06          6,634,401          3
1999-04          6,772,673          3
1999-08          6,954,221          3
1999-03          6,968,928          4
1999-09          7,030,524          4
1999-05          8,018,174          4
```

NTILE ORDER BY statements must be fully specified to yield reproducible results. Equal values can get distributed across adjacent buckets (75 is assigned to buckets 2 and 3 in the previous example) and buckets 1, 2, and 3 in the example have 3 elements - one more than the size of bucket 4. In this example. JEANS could as well be assigned to bucket 2 (instead of 3) and SWEATERS to bucket 3 (instead of 2), because there is no ordering on the p_product_key column. To ensure deterministic results, you must order on a unique key.

ROW_NUMBER

The ROW_NUMBER function assigns a unique number (sequentially, starting from 1, as defined by ORDER BY) to each row within the partition. It has the following syntax:

```
ROW_NUMBER ( ) OVER ( [query_partition_clause] order_by_clause )
```

ROW_NUMBER Example

```
SELECT channel_desc, calendar_month_desc,
    TO_CHAR(TRUNC(SUM(amount_sold), -6), '9,999,999,999') SALES$,
    ROW_NUMBER() OVER (ORDER BY TRUNC(SUM(amount_sold), -6) DESC)
      AS ROW_NUMBER
    FROM sales, products, customers, times, channels
    WHERE sales.prod_id=products.prod_id AND
    sales.cust_id=customers.cust_id AND
    sales.time_id=times.time_id AND
    sales.channel_id=channels.channel_id AND
    times.calendar_month_desc IN ('2000-09', '2000-10')
    GROUP BY channel_desc, calendar_month_desc;

    CHANNEL_DESC          CALENDAR        SALES$          ROW_NUMBER
    ----------------------------------------------------------------
    Direct Sales          2000-10       10,000,000                1
    Direct Sales          2000-09        9,000,000                2
    Internet              2000-09        6,000,000                3
    Internet              2000-10        6,000,000                4
    Catalog               2000-09        3,000,000                5
    Catalog               2000-10        3,000,000                6
    Partners              2000-09        2,000,000                7
    Partners              2000-10        2,000,000                8
    Tele Sales            2000-09        1,000,000                9
    Tele Sales            2000-10        1,000,000               10
```

Note that there are three pairs of tie values in these results. Like NTILE, ROW_NUMBER is a non-deterministic function, so each tied value could have its row number switched. To ensure deterministic results, you must order on a unique key. Inmost cases, that will require adding a new tie breaker column to the query and using it in the ORDER BY specification.

WINDOWING AGGREGATE FUNCTIONS

Windowing functions can be used to compute cumulative, moving, and centered aggregates. They return a value for each row in the table, which depends on other rows in the corresponding window. These functions include moving sum, moving average, moving min/max, cumulative sum, as well as statistical functions. They can be used only in the SELECT and ORDER BY clauses of the query. Two other functions are available: FIRST_VALUE, which returns the first value in the window; and LAST_VALUE, which returns the last value in the window. These functions provide access to more than one row of a table without a self-join. The syntax of the windowing functions is:

```
{SUM|AVG|MAX|MIN|COUNT|STDDEV|VARIANCE|FIRST_VALUE|LAST_VALUE}
  ({value expression1 | *}) OVER
    ([PARTITION BY value expression2[,...])
      ORDER BY value expression3 [collate clause>]
                 [ASC| DESC] [NULLS FIRST | NULLS LAST] [,...]
{ ROWS | RANGE }
{ BETWEEN
  { UNBOUNDED PRECEDING
  | CURRENT ROW
  | value_expr { PRECEDING | FOLLOWING }
  }
  AND
  { UNBOUNDED FOLLOWING
  | CURRENT ROW
  | value_expr { PRECEDING | FOLLOWING }
  }
| { UNBOUNDED PRECEDING
  | CURRENT ROW
  | value_expr PRECEDING
  }
}
```

Treatment of NULLs as Input to Window Functions

Window functions' NULL semantics match the NULL semantics for SQL aggregate functions. Other semantics can be obtained by user-defined functions, or by using the DECODE or a CASE expression within the window function.

Windowing Functions with Logical Offset

A logical offset can be specified with constants such as RANGE 10 PRECEDING, or an expression that evaluates to a constant, or by an interval specification like RANGE INTERVAL N DAY/MONTH/YEAR PRECEDING or an expression that evaluates to an interval. With logical offset, there can only be one expression in the ORDER BY expression list in the function, with type compatible to NUMERIC if offset is numeric, or DATE if an interval is specified.

Cumulative Aggregate Function Example

The following is an example of cumulative amount_sold by customer ID by quarter in 1999:

```
SELECT c.cust_id, t.calendar_quarter_desc,
TO_CHAR (SUM(amount_sold), '9,999,999,999') AS Q_SALES,
TO_CHAR(SUM(SUM(amount_sold)) OVER (PARTITION BY
c.cust_id ORDER BY c.cust_id, t.calendar_quarter_desc ROWS UNBOUNDED
PRECEDING), '9,999,999,999') AS CUM_SALES
FROM sales s, times t, customers c
WHERE
s.time_id=t.time_id AND
s.cust_id=c.cust_id AND
t.calendar_year=1999 AND
c.cust_id IN (6380, 6510)
GROUP BY c.cust_id, t.calendar_quarter_desc
ORDER BY c.cust_id, t.calendar_quarter_desc;
```

CUST_ID	CALENDA	Q_SALES	CUM_SALES
6380	1999-Q1	60,621	60,621
6380	1999-Q2	68,213	128,834
6380	1999-Q3	75,238	204,072
6380	1999-Q4	57,412	261,484
6510	1999-Q1	63,030	63,030
6510	1999-Q2	74,622	137,652
6510	1999-Q3	69,966	207,617
6510	1999-Q4	63,366	270,983

In this example, the analytic function SUM defines, for each row, a window that starts at the beginning of the partition (UNBOUNDED PRECEDING) and ends, by default, at the current row.

Nested SUMs are needed in this example since we are performing a SUM over a value that is itself a SUM. Nested aggregations are used very often in analytic aggregate functions.

Moving Aggregate Function Example

This example of a time-based window shows, for one customer, the moving average of sales for the current month and preceding two months:

```
SELECT c.cust_id, t.calendar_month_desc,
TO_CHAR (SUM(amount_sold), '9,999,999,999') AS SALES ,
TO_CHAR(AVG(SUM(amount_sold))
OVER (ORDER BY c.cust_id, t.calendar_month_desc  ROWS 2 PRECEDING),
'9,999,999,999') AS MOVING_3_MONTH_AVG
FROM sales s, times t, customers c
WHERE
s.time_id=t.time_id AND
s.cust_id=c.cust_id AND
t.calendar_year=1999 AND
c.cust_id IN (6380)
GROUP BY c.cust_id, t.calendar_month_desc
ORDER BY c.cust_id, t.calendar_month_desc;
```

```
CUST_ID        CALENDAR        SALES       MOVING_3_MONTH
----------------------------------------------------------
   6380        1999-01         19,642          19,642
   6380        1999-02         19,324          19,483
   6380        1999-03         21,655          20,207
   6380        1999-04         27,091          22,690
   6380        1999-05         16,367          21,704
   6380        1999-06         24,755          22,738
   6380        1999-07         31,332          24,152
   6380        1999-08         22,835          26,307
   6380        1999-09         21,071          25,079
   6380        1999-10         19,279          21,062
   6380        1999-11         18,206          19,519
   6380        1999-12         19,927          19,137
```

Note that the first two rows for the three month moving average calculation in the output data are based on a smaller interval size than specified because the window calculation cannot reach past the data retrieved by the query. You need to consider the different window sizes found at the borders of result sets. In other words, you may need to modify the query to include exactly what you want.

Centered Aggregate Function

Calculating windowing aggregate functions centered around the current row is straightforward. This example computes for a customer a centered moving average of the sales total for the one day preceding the current row and one day following the current row including the current row as well.

Example 12.6 : Centered Aggregate

```
SELECT cust_id, t.time_id,
TO_CHAR (SUM(amount_sold), '9,999,999,999') AS SALES,
TO_CHAR(AVG(SUM(amount_sold)) OVER
(PARTITION BY s.cust_id ORDER BY t.time_id
RANGE BETWEEN INTERVAL '1' DAY PRECEDING AND INTERVAL '1' DAY FOLLOWING),
'9,999,999,999') AS CENTERED_3_DAY_AVG
FROM sales s, times t
WHERE
s.time_id=t.time_id AND
t.calendar_week_number IN (51) AND
calendar_year=1999 AND cust_id IN (6380, 6510)
GROUP BY cust_id, t.time_id
ORDER BY cust_id, t.time_id;
```

```
CUST_ID        TIME_ID         SALES       CENTERED_3_DAY
----------------------------------------------------------
   6380        20-DEC-99       2,240           1,136
   6380        21-DEC-99          32             873
   6380        22-DEC-99         348             148
   6380        23-DEC-99          64             302
   6380        24-DEC-99         493             212
   6380        25-DEC-99          80             423
   6380        26-DEC-99         696             388
   6510        20-DEC-99         196             106
```

```
6510        21-DEC-99        16        155
6510        22-DEC-99       252        143
6510        23-DEC-99       160        305
6510        24-DEC-99       504        240
6510        25-DEC-99        56        415
6510        26-DEC-99       684        370
```

The starting and ending rows for each product's centered moving average calculation in the output data are based on just two days, since the window calculation cannot reach past the data retrieved by the query. Users need to consider the different window sizes found at the borders of result sets: the query may need to be adjusted.

Windowing Aggregate Functions in the Presence of Duplicates

The following example illustrates how window aggregate functions compute values when there are duplicates, that is, when multiple rows are returned for a single ordering value. The query retrieves the quantity sold in the US for two products during a specified time range. The query defines a moving window that runs from the date of the current row to 10 days earlier.

Note that the `RANGE` keyword is used to define the windowing clause of this example. This means that the window can potentially hold many rows for each value in the range. In this case, there are three rows with the duplicate ordering value of `'04-NOV-98'`.

Example 12.7 : Windowing Aggregate Functions with Logical Offsets

```
SELECT time_id, s.quantity_sold,
SUM(s.quantity_sold) OVER  (ORDER BY time_id
    RANGE  BETWEEN INTERVAL '10' DAY PRECEDING AND CURRENT ROW)
AS current_group_sum
FROM  customers c, products p, sales s
WHERE  p.prod_id=s.prod_id  AND  c.cust_id=s.cust_id
   AND c.country_id='US'  AND p.prod_id IN (250, 500)
   AND s.time_id BETWEEN  '24-OCT-98' AND  '14-NOV-98'
ORDER BY TIME_ID;

 TIME_ID     QUANTITY_SOLD  CURRENT_GROUP_SUM    /*      Source #s for row */
 ---------------------------------------------------------------------------
 24-OCT-98        19                 19          /*      19     */
 27-OCT-98        17                 36          /*      19+17  */
 04-NOV-98         2                 24          /*      17+(2+3+2)  */
 04-NOV-98         3                 24          /*      17+(2+3+2)  */
 04-NOV-98         2                 24          /*      17+(2+3+2)  */
 14-NOV-98        12                 19          /*      (2+3+2)+12  */
6 rows selected.
```

In the output, values within parentheses are from the rows with the tied ordering key value, `04-NOV-98`.

Consider the row with the output of `"04-NOV-98, 3, 24"`. In this case, all the other rows with `TIME_ID` of `04-NOV-98` (ties) are considered to belong to one group. Therefore, the `CURRENT_GROUP_SUM` should include this row (that is, 3) and its ties (that is, 2 and 2) in the window. It also includes any rows with dates up to 10 days earlier. In this data, that includes the row with date `27-OCT-98`. Hence the result is 17+(2+3+2) = 24. The calculation of

CURRENT_GROUP_SUM is identical for each of the tied rows, so the output shows three rows with the value 24.

Note that this example applies only when you use the RANGE keyword rather than the ROWS keyword. It is also important to remember that with RANGE, you can only use 1 ORDER BY expression in the analytic function's ORDER BY clause. With the ROWS keyword, you can use multiple order by expressions in the analytic function's order by clause.

Varying Window Size for Each Row

There are situations where it is useful to vary the size of a window for each row, based on a specified condition. For instance, you may want to make the window larger for certain dates and smaller for others. Assume that you want to calculate the moving average of stock price over three working days. If you have an equal number of rows for each day for all working days and no non-working days are stored, then you can use a physical window function. However, if the conditions noted are not met, you can still calculate a moving average by using an expression in the window size parameters.

Expressions in a window size specification can be made in several different sources. The expression could be a reference to a column in a table, such as a time table. It could also be a function that returns the appropriate boundary for the window based on values in the current row. The following statement for a hypothetical stock price database uses a user-defined function in its RANGE clause to set window size:

```
SELECT t_timekey,
    AVG(stock_price)
        OVER (ORDER BY t_timekey RANGE fn(t_timekey) PRECEDING) av_price
FROM stock, time
WHERE st_timekey = t_timekey
ORDER BY t_timekey;
```

In this statement, t_timekey is a date field. Here, *fn* could be a PL/SQL function with the following specification:

```
fn(t_timekey) returns
```

- 4 if t_timekey is Monday, Tuesday
- 2 otherwise
- If any of the previous days are holidays, it adjusts the count appropriately.

Note that, when window is specified using a number in a window function with ORDER BY on a date column, then it is converted to mean the number of days. You could have also used the interval literal conversion function, as NUMTODSINTERVAL(fn(t_timekey), 'DAY') instead of just fn(t_timekey) to mean the same thing. You can also write a PL/SQL function that returns an INTERVAL datatype value.

Windowing Aggregate Functions with Physical Offsets

For windows expressed in rows, the ordering expressions should be unique to produce deterministic results. For example, the following query is not deterministic because time_id is not unique in this result set.

Example 12.8 : Windowing Aggregate Functions With Physical Offsets

```
SELECT t.time_id,
TO_CHAR(amount_sold, '9,999,999,999') AS INDIV_SALE,
TO_CHAR(SUM(amount_sold) OVER
(PARTITION BY t.time_id ORDER BY t.time_id
ROWS UNBOUNDED PRECEDING), '9,999,999,999') AS CUM_SALES
FROM sales s, times t, customers c
WHERE
s.time_id=t.time_id AND
s.cust_id=c.cust_id AND
t.time_id IN (TO_DATE('11-DEC-1999'), TO_DATE('12-DEC-1999') )
 AND
c.cust_id BETWEEN 6500 AND 6600
ORDER BY t.time_id;
```

TIME_ID	INDIV_SALE	CUM_SALES
11-DEC-99	1,036	1,036
11-DEC-99	1,932	2,968
11-DEC-99	588	3,556
12-DEC-99	504	504
12-DEC-99	429	933
12-DEC-99	1,160	2,093

The statement could also yield the following:

TIME_ID	INDIV_SALE	CUM_SALES
11-DEC-99	1,932	2,968
11-DEC-99	588	3,556
11-DEC-99	1,036	1,036
12-DEC-99	504	504
12-DEC-99	1,160	2,093
12-DEC-99	429	933

One way to handle this problem would be to add the `prod_id` column to the result set and order on both `time_id` and `prod_id`.

FIRST_VALUE and LAST_VALUE

The `FIRST_VALUE` and `LAST_VALUE` functions allow you to select the first and last rows from a window. These rows are especially valuable because they are often used as the baselines in calculations. For instance, with a partition holding sales data ordered by day, you might ask "How much was each day's sales compared to the first sales day (`FIRST_VALUE`) of the period?" Or you might wish to know, for a set of rows in increasing sales order, "What was the percentage size of each sale in the region compared to the largest sale (`LAST_VALUE`) in the region?"

REPORTING AGGREGATE FUNCTIONS

After a query has been processed, aggregate values like the number of resulting rows or an average value in a column can be easily computed within a partition and made available to other reporting functions. Reporting aggregate functions return the same aggregate value for every row in a partition. Their behavior with respect to NULLs is the same as the SQL aggregate functions. The syntax is:

```
{SUM | AVG | MAX | MIN | COUNT | STDDEV | VARIANCE}
  ([ALL | DISTINCT] {value expression1 | *})
     OVER ([PARTITION BY value expression2[,...]])
```

In addition, the following conditions apply:

- An asterisk (*) is only allowed in `COUNT(*)`
- `DISTINCT` is supported only if corresponding aggregate functions allow it
- *value expression1* and *value expression2* can be any valid expression involving column references or aggregates.
- The `PARTITION BY` clause defines the groups on which the windowing functions would be computed. If the `PARTITION BY` clause is absent, then the function is computed over the whole query result set.

Reporting functions can appear only in the `SELECT` clause or the `ORDER BY` clause. The major benefit of reporting functions is their ability to do multiple passes of data in a single query block and speed up query performance. Queries such as "Count the number of salesmen with sales more than 10% of city sales" do not require joins between separate query blocks.

For example, consider the question "For each product category, find the region in which it had maximum sales". The equivalent SQL query using the `MAX` reporting aggregate function would be:

```
SELECT prod_category, country_region, sales FROM
(SELECT substr(p.prod_category,1,8), co.country_region, SUM(amount_sold)
  AS sales,
MAX(SUM(amount_sold)) OVER (partition BY prod_category) AS MAX_REG_SALES
FROM sales s, customers c, countries co, products p
WHERE s.cust_id=c.cust_id AND
c.country_id=co.country_id AND
s.prod_id=p.prod_id AND
s.time_id=to_DATE('11-OCT-2000')
GROUP BY prod_category, country_region)
WHERE sales=MAX_REG_SALES;
```

The inner query with the reporting aggregate function `MAX(SUM(amount_sold))` returns:

SUBSTR(P	COUNTRY_REGION	SALES	MAX_REG_SALES
Boys	Africa	594	41974
Boys	Americas	20353	41974
Boys	Asia	2258	41974
Boys	Europe	41974	41974
Boys	Oceania	1402	41974
Girls	Americas	13869	52963

Girls	Asia	1657	52963
Girls	Europe	52963	52963
Girls	Middle East	303	52963
Girls	Oceania	380	52963
Men	Africa	1705	123253
Men	Americas	69304	123253
Men	Asia	6153	123253
Men	Europe	123253	123253
Men	Oceania	2646	123253
Women	Africa	4037	255109
Women	Americas	145501	255109
Women	Asia	20394	255109
Women	Europe	255109	255109
Women	Middle East	350	255109
Women	Oceania	17408	255109

The full query results are:

PROD_CATEGORY	COUNTRY_REGION	SALES
Boys	Europe	41974
Girls	Europe	52963
Men	Europe	123253
Women	Europe	255109

Reporting Aggregate Example

Reporting aggregates combined with nested queries enable you to answer complex queries efficiently. For instance, what if we want to know the best selling products in our most significant product subcategories? We have 4 product categories which contain a total of 37 product subcategories, and there are 10,000 unique products. Here is a query which finds the 5 top-selling products for each product subcategory that contributes more than 20% of the sales within its product category.

```
SELECT SUBSTR(prod_category,1,8) AS CATEG, prod_subcategory, prod_id, SALES FROM
  (SELECT p.prod_category, p.prod_subcategory, p.prod_id,
     SUM(amount_sold) as SALES,
     SUM(SUM(amount_sold)) OVER (PARTITION BY p.prod_category) AS CAT_SALES,
     AUM(SUM(amount_sold)) OVER
        (PARTITION BY p.prod_subcategory) AS SUBCAT_SALES,
     RANK() OVER  (PARTITION BY p.prod_subcategory
        ORDER BY SUM(amount_sold) ) AS RANK_IN_LINE
    FROM sales s, customers c, countries co, products p
    WHERE s.cust_id=c.cust_id AND
       c.country_id=co.country_id AND  s.prod_id=p.prod_id AND
       s.time_id=to_DATE('11-OCT-2000')
    GROUP BY p.prod_category, p.prod_subcategory, p.prod_id
    ORDER BY prod_category, prod_subcategory)
  WHERE SUBCAT_SALES>0.2*CAT_SALES AND RANK_IN_LINE<=5;
```

RATIO_TO_REPORT

The RATIO_TO_REPORT function computes the ratio of a value to the sum of a set of values. If the expression value expression evaluates to NULL, RATIO_TO_REPORT also evaluates to NULL, but it is treated as zero for computing the sum of values for the denominator. Its syntax is:

```
RATIO_TO_REPORT ( expr ) OVER ( [query_partition_clause] )
```

In this, the following applies:

- expr can be any valid expression involving column references or aggregates.
- The PARTITION BY clause defines the groups on which the RATIO_TO_REPORT function is to be computed. If the PARTITION BY clause is absent, then the function is computed over the whole query result set.

Example 12.9 : RATIO_TO_REPORT

To calculate RATIO_TO_REPORT of sales per channel, you might use the following syntax:

```
SELECT ch.channel_desc,
    TO_CHAR(SUM(amount_sold),'9,999,999') as SALES,
    TO_CHAR(SUM(SUM(amount_sold)) OVER (), '9,999,999')
       AS TOTAL_SALES,
    TO_CHAR(RATIO_TO_REPORT(SUM(amount_sold)) OVER (), '9.999')
       AS RATIO_TO_REPORT
  FROM sales s, channels ch
  WHERE s.channel_id=ch.channel_id  AND
     s.time_id=to_DATE('11-OCT-2000')
  GROUP BY ch.channel_desc;
```

CHANNEL_DESC	SALES	TOTAL_SALE	RATIO_TO_REPORT
Catalog	111,103	781,613	.142
Direct Sales	335,409	781,613	.429
Internet	212,314	781,613	.272
Partners	91,352	781,613	.117
Tele Sales	31,435	781,613	.040

LAG/LEAD FUNCTIONS

The LAG and LEAD functions are useful for comparing values when the relative positions of rows can be known reliably. They work by specifying the count of rows which separate the target row from the current row. Since the functions provide access to more than one row of a table at the same time without a self-join, they can enhance processing speed. The LAG function provides access to a row at a given offset prior to the current position, and the LEAD function provides access to a row at a given offset after the current position.

LAG/LEAD Syntax

These functions have the following syntax:

```
{LAG | LEAD} ( value_expr [, offset] [, default] )
   OVER ( [query_partition_clause] order_by_clause )
```

offset is an optional parameter and defaults to 1. *default* is an optional parameter and is the value returned if *offset* falls outside the bounds of the table or partition.

Example 12.10 : LAG/LEAD

```
SELECT  time_id, TO_CHAR(SUM(amount_sold),'9,999,999') AS SALES,
TO_CHAR(LAG(SUM(amount_sold),1) OVER (ORDER BY time_id),'9,999,999') AS LAG1,
TO_CHAR(LEAD(SUM(amount_sold),1) OVER (ORDER BY time_id),'9,999,999') AS LEAD1
FROM sales
WHERE
time_id>=TO_DATE('10-OCT-2000') AND
time_id<=TO_DATE('14-OCT-2000')
GROUP BY time_id;
```

TIME_ID	SALES	LAG1	LEAD1
10-OCT-00	773,921		781,613
11-OCT-00	781,613	773,921	744,351
12-OCT-00	744,351	781,613	757,356
13-OCT-00	757,356	744,351	791,960
14-OCT-00	791,960	757,356	

FIRST/LAST FUNCTIONS

The FIRST/LAST aggregate functions allow you to return the result of an aggregate applied over a set of rows that rank as the first or last with respect to a given order specification. FIRST/LAST lets you order on column A but return an result of an aggregate applied on column B. This is valuable because it avoids the need for a self-join or subquery, thus improving performance. These functions begin with a tiebreaker function, which is a regular aggregate function (MIN, MAX, SUM, AVG, COUNT, VARIANCE, STDDEV) that produces the return value. The tiebreaker function is performed on the set rows (1 or more rows) that rank as first or last respect to the order specification to return a single value.

To specify the ordering used within each group, the FIRST/LAST functions add a new clause starting with the word KEEP.

FIRST/LAST Syntax

These functions have the following syntax:

```
aggregate_function KEEP
( DENSE_RANK LAST ORDER BY
  expr [ DESC | ASC ] [NULLS { FIRST | LAST }]
  [, expr [ DESC | ASC ] [NULLS { FIRST | LAST }]]...
)
[OVER query_partitioning_clause]
```

Note that the ORDER BY clause can take multiple expressions.

FIRST/LAST As Regular Aggregates

You can use the FIRST/LAST family of aggregates as regular aggregate functions.

Example 12.11 : FIRST/LAST Example 1

The following query lets us compare minimum price and list price of our products. For each product subcategory within the Men's clothing category, it returns the following:

- List price of the product with the lowest minimum price
- Lowest minimum price
- List price of the product with the highest minimum price
- Highest minimum price.

```
SELECT prod_subcategory, MIN(prod_list_price)
 KEEP (DENSE_RANK FIRST ORDER BY (prod_min_price))
AS LP_OF_LO_MINP,
MIN(prod_min_price) AS LO_MINP,
MAX(prod_list_price) KEEP (DENSE_RANK LAST ORDER BY (prod_min_price))
 AS LP_OF_HI_MINP,
MAX(prod_min_price) AS HI_MINP
FROM products
WHERE prod_category='Men'
GROUP BY prod_subcategory;
```

PROD_SUBCATEGORY	LP_OF_LO_MINP	LO_MINP	LP_OF_HI_MINP	HI_MINP
Casual Shirts - Men	39.9	16.92	88	59.4
Dress Shirts - Men	42.5	17.34	59.9	41.51
Jeans - Men	38	17.33	69.9	62.28
Outerwear - Men	44.9	19.76	495	334.12
Shorts - Men	34.9	15.36	195	103.54
Sportcoats - Men	195	96.53	595	390.92
Sweaters - Men	29.9	14.59	140	97.02
Trousers - Men	38	15.5	135	120.29
Underwear And Socks - Men	10.9	4.45	39.5	27.02

A query like this can be useful for understanding the sales patterns of your different channels. For instance, the result set here highlights that Telesales sell relatively small volumes.

FIRST/LAST As Reporting Aggregates

You can also use the `FIRST/LAST` family of aggregates as reporting aggregate functions. An example is calculating which months had the greatest and least increase in head count throughout the year. The syntax for these functions is similar to the syntax for any other reporting aggregate.

Consider the example in example 12.11 for `FIRST/LAST`. What if we wanted to find the list prices of individual products and compare them to the list prices of the products in their subcategory that had the highest and lowest minimum prices?

The following query lets us find that information for the Sportcoats - Men subcategory by using `FIRST/LAST` as reporting aggregates. Because there are over 100 products in this subcategory, we show only the first few rows of results.

Example 12.12 : FIRST/LAST Example 2

```
SELECT prod_id, prod_list_price,
MIN(prod_list_price) KEEP (DENSE_RANK FIRST ORDER BY (prod_min_price))
   OVER(PARTITION BY (prod_subcategory)) AS LP_OF_LO_MINP,
```

```
MAX(prod_list_price) KEEP (DENSE_RANK LAST ORDER BY (prod_min_price))
  OVER(PARTITION BY (prod_subcategory)) AS  LP_OF_HI_MINP
FROM products
WHERE prod_subcategory='Sportcoats - Men';
```

PROD_ID	PROD_LIST_PRICE	LP_OF_LO_MINP	LP_OF_HI_MINP
730	365	195	595
1165	365	195	595
1560	595	195	595
2655	195	195	595
2660	195	195	595
3840	275	195	595
3865	275	195	595
4035	319.9	195	595
4075	395	195	595
4245	195	195	595
4790	365	195	595
4800	365	195	595
5560	425	195	595
5575	425	195	595
5625	595	195	595
7915	275	195	595

....

Using the FIRST and LAST functions as reporting aggregates makes it easy to include the results in calculations such "Salary as a percent of the highest salary."

LINEAR REGRESSION FUNCTIONS

The regression functions support the fitting of an ordinary-least-squares regression line to a set of number pairs. You can use them as both aggregate functions or windowing or reporting functions. The functions are:

- REGR_COUNT
- REGR_AVGX
- REGR_AVGY
- REGR_SLOPE
- REGR_INTERCEPT
- REGR_R2
- REGR_SXX
- REGR_SYY
- REGR_SXY.

Oracle applies the function to the set of (e1, e2) pairs after eliminating all pairs for which either of e1 or e2 is null. e1 is interpreted as a value of the dependent variable (a "y value"), and e2 is interpreted as a value of the independent variable (an "x value"). Both expressions must be numbers.

The regression functions are all computed simultaneously during a single pass through the data. They are frequently combined with the COVAR_POP, COVAR_SAMP, and CORR functions.

REGR_COUNT

REGR_COUNT returns the number of non-null number pairs used to fit the regression line. If applied to an empty set (or if there are no (e1, e2) pairs where neither of e1 or e2 is null), the function returns 0.

REGR_AVGY and REGR_AVGX

REGR_AVGY and REGR_AVGX compute the averages of the dependent variable and the independent variable of the regression line, respectively. REGR_AVGY computes the average of its first argument (e1) after eliminating (e1, e2) pairs where either of e1 or e2 is null. Similarly, REGR_AVGX computes the average of its second argument (e2) after null elimination. Both functions return NULL if applied to an empty set.

REGR_SLOPE and REGR_INTERCEPT

The REGR_SLOPE function computes the slope of the regression line fitted to non-null (e1, e2) pairs.

The REGR_INTERCEPT function computes the y-intercept of the regression line. REGR_INTERCEPT returns NULL whenever slope or the regression averages are NULL.

REGR_R2

The REGR_R2 function computes the coefficient of determination (usually called "R-squared" or "goodness of fit") for the regression line.

REGR_R2 returns values between 0 and 1 when the regression line is defined (slope of the line is not null), and it returns NULL otherwise. The closer the value is to 1, the better the regression line fits the data.

REGR_SXX, REGR_SYY, and REGR_SXY

REGR_SXX, REGR_SYY and REGR_SXY functions are used in computing various diagnostic statistics for regression analysis. After eliminating (e1, e2) pairs where either of e1 or e2 is null, these functions make the following computations:

```
REGR_SXX:      REGR_COUNT(e1,e2)      *  VAR_POP(e2)
REGR_SYY:      REGR_COUNT(e1,e2)      *  VAR_POP(e1)
REGR_SXY:      REGR_COUNT(e1,e2)      *  COVAR_POP(e1, e2)
```

Linear Regression Statistics Examples

Some common diagnostic statistics that accompany linear regression analysis are given in table 12.2, "Common Diagnostic Statistics and Their Expressions". Note that Oracle's new functions allow you to calculate all of these.

Table 12.2 Common Diagnostic Statistics and Their Expressions

Type of Statistic	Expression
Adjusted R2	1-((1 - REGR_R2)*((REGR_COUNT-1)/(REGR_COUNT-2)))
Standard error	SQRT((REGR_SYY-(POWER(REGR_SXY,2)/REGR_SXX))/(REGR_COUNT-2))

Total sum of squares	REGR_SYY
Regression sum of squares	POWER(REGR_SXY,2) / REGR_SXX
Residual sum of squares	REGR_SYY - (POWER(REGR_SXY,2)/REGR_SXX)
t statistic for slope	REGR_SLOPE * SQRT(REGR_SXX) / (Standard error)
t statistic for y-intercept	REGR_INTERCEPT/((Standard error) * SQRT((1/REGR_COUNT)+(POWER(REGR_AVGX,2)/REGR_SXX))

Sample Linear Regression Calculation

In this example, we compute an ordinary-least-squares regression line that expresses the quantity sold of a product as a linear function of the product's list price. The calculations are grouped by sales channel. The values SLOPE, INTCPT, RSQR are slope, intercept, and coefficient of determination of the regression line, respectively. The (integer) value COUNT is the number of products in each channel for whom both quantity sold and list price data are available.

```
SELECT s.channel_id,
REGR_SLOPE(s.quantity_sold, p.prod_list_price) SLOPE,
REGR_INTERCEPT(s.quantity_sold, p.prod_list_price) INTCPT,
REGR_R2(s.quantity_sold, p.prod_list_price) RSQR,
REGR_COUNT(s.quantity_sold, p.prod_list_price) COUNT,
REGR_AVGX(s.quantity_sold, p.prod_list_price) AVGLISTP,
REGR_AVGY(s.quantity_sold, p.prod_list_price) AVGQSOLD
FROM sales s, products p
WHERE s.prod_id=p.prod_id
  AND p.prod_category='Men' AND s.time_id=to_DATE('10-OCT-2000')
GROUP BY s.channel_id;
```

```
C       SLOPE      INTCPT        RSQR    COUNT   AVGLISTP    AVGQSOLD
---------------------------------------------------------------------
C   -.0683687   16.627808   .05134258    20       65.495       12.15
I    .0197103   14.811392   .00163149    46    51.480435   15.826087
P   -.0124736   12.854546   .01703979    30        81.87   11.833333
S   .00615589   13.991924   .00089844    83    69.813253   14.421687
T   -.0041131   5.2271721   .00813224    27    82.244444   4.8888889
```

INVERSE PERCENTILE FUNCTIONS

Using the CUME_DIST function, you can find the cumulative distribution (percentile) of a set of values. However, the inverse operation (finding what value computes to a certain percentile) is neither easy to do nor efficiently computed. To overcome this difficulty, Oracle introduced the PERCENTILE_CONT and PERCENTILE_DISC functions. These can be used both as window reporting functions as well as normal aggregate functions.

These functions need a sort specification and a parameter that takes a percentile value between 0 and 1. The sort specification is handled by using an ORDER BY clause with one expression. When used as a normal aggregate function, it returns a single value for each ordered set.

PERCENTILE_CONT, which is a continuous function computed by interpolation, and PERCENTILE_DISC, which is a step function that assumes discrete values. Like other aggregates,

PERCENTILE_CONT and PERCENTILE_DISC operate on a group of rows in a grouped query, but with the following differences:

- They require a parameter between 0 and 1 (inclusive). A parameter specified out of this range will result in error. This parameter should be specified as an expression that evaluates to a constant.
- They require a sort specification. This sort specification is an ORDER BY clause with a single expression. Multiple expressions are not allowed.

Normal Aggregate Syntax

```
[PERCENTILE_CONT | PERCENTILE_DISC]( constant expression )
    WITHIN GROUP ( ORDER BY single order by expression
[ASC|DESC] [NULLS FIRST| NULLS LAST])
```

Inverse Percentile Example Basis

We use the following query to return the 17 rows of data used in the examples of this section:

```
SELECT cust_id, cust_credit_limit, CUME_DIST()
   OVER (ORDER BY cust_credit_limit) AS CUME_DIST
FROM customers
WHERE cust_city='Marshal';
```

CUST_ID	CUST_CREDIT_LIMIT	CUME_DIST
171630	1500	.23529412
346070	1500	.23529412
420830	1500	.23529412
383450	1500	.23529412
165400	3000	.35294118
227700	3000	.35294118
28340	5000	.52941176
215240	5000	.52941176
364760	5000	.52941176
184090	7000	.70588235
370990	7000	.70588235
408370	7000	.70588235
121790	9000	.76470588
22110	11000	.94117647
246390	11000	.94117647
40800	11000	.94117647
464440	15000	1

PERCENTILE_DISC(x) is computed by scanning up the CUME_DIST values in each group till you find the first one greater than or equal to x, where x is the specified percentile value. For the example query where PERCENTILE_DISC(0.5), the result is 5,000, as the following illustrates:

```
SELECT PERCENTILE_DISC(0.5) WITHIN GROUP
  (ORDER BY cust_credit_limit) AS perc_disc,
   PERCENTILE_CONT(0.5) WITHIN GROUP
  (ORDER BY cust_credit_limit) AS perc_cont
 FROM customers WHERE cust_city='Marshal';
```

```
PERC_DISC                 PERC_CONT
-----------------------------------
     5000                      5000
```

The result of PERCENTILE_CONT is computed by linear interpolation between rows after ordering them. To compute PERCENTILE_CONT(x), we first compute the row number = RN= (1+x*(n–1)), where n is the number of rows in the group and x is the specified percentile value. The final result of the aggregate function is computed by linear interpolation between the values from rows at row numbers CRN = CEIL(RN) and FRN = FLOOR(RN).

The final result will be: PERCENTILE_CONT(X) = if (CRN = FRN = RN), then (value of expression from row at RN) else (CRN – RN) * (value of expression for row at FRN) + (RN – FRN) * (value of expression for row at CRN).

Consider the previous example query, where we compute PERCENTILE_CONT(0.5). Here n is 17. The row number RN = (1 + 0.5*(n–1))= 9 for both groups. Putting this into the formula, (FRN=CRN=9), we return the value from row 9 as the result.

Another example is, if you want to compute PERCENTILE_CONT(0.66). The computed row number RN=(1 + 0.66*(n–1))= (1 + 0.66*16)= 11.67. PERCENTILE_CONT(0.66) = (12–11.67)*(value of row 11)+(11.67–11)*(value of row 12). These results are:

```
SELECT PERCENTILE_DISC(0.66) WITHIN GROUP
  (ORDER BY cust_credit_limit) AS perc_disc,
   PERCENTILE_CONT(0.66) WITHIN GROUP
  (ORDER BY cust_credit_limit) AS perc_cont
 FROM customers WHERE cust_city='Marshal';
```

```
PERC_DISC                 PERC_CONT
-----------------------------------
     7000                      7000
```

Inverse percentile aggregate functions can appear in the HAVING clause of a query like other existing aggregate functions.

As Reporting Aggregates

You can also use the aggregate functions PERCENTILE_CONT, PERCENTILE_DISC as reporting aggregate functions. When used as reporting aggregate functions, the syntax is similar to those of other reporting aggregates.

```
[PERCENTILE_CONT | PERCENTILE_DISC](constant expression)
WITHIN GROUP ( ORDER BY single order by expression
[ASC|DESC] [NULLS FIRST| NULLS LAST])
OVER ( [PARTITION BY value expression [,...]] )
```

This query computes the same thing (median credit limit for customers in this result set, but reports the result for every row in the result set, as shown in the following output:

```
SELECT cust_id, cust_credit_limit,
    PERCENTILE_DISC(0.5) WITHIN GROUP
      (ORDER BY cust_credit_limit) OVER () AS perc_disc,
    PERCENTILE_CONT(0.5) WITHIN GROUP
      (ORDER BY cust_credit_limit) OVER () AS perc_cont
 FROM customers WHERE cust_city='Marshal';
```

CUST_ID	CUST_CREDIT_LIMIT	PERC_DISC	PERC_CONT
171630	1500	5000	5000
346070	1500	5000	5000
420830	1500	5000	5000
383450	1500	5000	5000
165400	3000	5000	5000
227700	3000	5000	5000
28340	5000	5000	5000
215240	5000	5000	5000
364760	5000	5000	5000
184090	7000	5000	5000
370990	7000	5000	5000
408370	7000	5000	5000
121790	9000	5000	5000
22110	11000	5000	5000
246390	11000	5000	5000
40800	11000	5000	5000
464440	15000	5000	5000

Inverse Percentile Restrictions

For PERCENTILE_DISC, the expression in the ORDER BY clause can be of any data type that you can sort (numeric, string, date, and so on). However, the expression in the ORDER BY clause must be a numeric or datetime type (including intervals) because linear interpolation is used to evaluate PERCENTILE_CONT. If the expression is of type DATE, the interpolated result is rounded to the smallest unit for the type. For a DATE type, the interpolated value will be rounded to the nearest second, for interval types to the nearest second (INTERVAL DAY TO SECOND) or to the month(INTERVAL YEAR TO MONTH).

Like other aggregates, the inverse percentile functions ignore NULLs in evaluating the result. For example, when you want to find the median value in a set, Oracle ignores the NULLs and finds the median among the non-null values. You can use the NULLS FIRST/NULLS LAST option in the ORDER BY clause, but they will be ignored as NULLs are ignored.

HYPOTHETICAL RANK AND DISTRIBUTION FUNCTIONS

These functions provide functionality useful for what-if analysis. As an example, what would be the rank of a row, if the row was **hypothetically** inserted into a set of other rows?

This family of aggregates takes one or more arguments of a hypothetical row and an ordered group of rows, returning the RANK, DENSE_RANK, PERCENT_RANK or CUME_DIST of the row as if it was hypothetically inserted into the group.

Hypothetical Rank and Distribution Syntax

```
[RANK | DENSE_RANK | PERCENT_RANK | CUME_DIST]( constant expression [, ...] )
WITHIN GROUP ( ORDER BY order by expression [ASC|DESC] [NULLS FIRST|NULLS
LAST][, ...] )
```

Here, `constant expression` refers to an expression that evaluates to a constant, and there may be more than one such expressions that are passed as arguments to the function. The ORDER BY clause can contain one or more expressions that define the sorting order on which the ranking will be based. `ASC, DESC, NULLS FIRST, NULLS LAST` options will be available for each expression in the `ORDER BY`.

Example 12.13 : Hypothetical Rank and Distribution Example 1

Using the list price data from the `products` table used throughout this section, you can calculate the `RANK`, `PERCENT_RANK` and `CUME_DIST` for a hypothetical sweater with a price of $50 for how it fits within each of the sweater subcategories. The query and results are:

```
SELECT prod_subcategory,
 RANK(50) WITHIN GROUP  (ORDER BY prod_list_price DESC) AS HRANK,
  TO_CHAR(PERCENT_RANK(50) WITHIN GROUP
      (ORDER BY prod_list_price),'9.999') AS HPERC_RANK,
  TO_CHAR(CUME_DIST (50) WITHIN GROUP
      (ORDER BY prod_list_price),'9.999') AS HCUME_DIST
FROM products
WHERE prod_subcategory LIKE 'Sweater%'
GROUP BY prod_subcategory;
```

PROD_SUBCATEGORY	HRANK	HPERC_RANK	HCUME_DIST
Sweaters - Boys	16	.911	.912
Sweaters - Girls	1	1.000	1.000
Sweaters - Men	240	.351	.352
Sweaters - Women	21	783	.785

Unlike the inverse percentile aggregates, the `ORDER BY` clause in the sort specification for hypothetical rank and distribution functions may take multiple expressions. The number of arguments and the expressions in the `ORDER BY` clause should be the same and the arguments must be constant expressions of the same or compatible type to the corresponding `ORDER BY` expression. The following is an example using two arguments in several hypothetical ranking functions.

Example 12.14 : Hypothetical Rank and Distribution Example 2

```
SELECT prod_subcategory,
 RANK(45,30) WITHIN GROUP  (ORDER BY prod_list_price DESC,prod_min_price) AS
HRANK,
  TO_CHAR(PERCENT_RANK(45,30) WITHIN GROUP
      (ORDER BY prod_list_price, prod_min_price),'9.999') AS HPERC_RANK,
  TO_CHAR(CUME_DIST (45,30) WITHIN GROUP
      (ORDER BY prod_list_price, prod_min_price),'9.999') AS HCUME_DIST
FROM products
WHERE prod_subcategory
  LIKE 'Sweater%'
GROUP BY prod_subcategory;
```

PROD_SUBCATEGORY	HRANK	HPERC_RANK	HCUME_DIST
Sweaters - Boys	21	.858	.859
Sweaters - Girls	1	1.000	1.000
Sweaters - Men	340	.079	.081
Sweaters - Women	72	.228	.237

These functions can appear in the HAVING clause of a query just like other aggregate functions. They cannot be used as either reporting aggregate functions or windowing aggregate functions.

WIDTH_BUCKET FUNCTION

For a given expression, the WIDTH_BUCKET function returns the bucket number that the result of this expression will be assigned after it is evaluated. You can generate equiwidth histograms with this function. Equiwidth histograms divide data sets into buckets whose interval size (highest value to lowest value) is equal. The number of rows held by each bucket will vary. A related function, NTILE, creates equiheight buckets.

Equiwidth histograms can be generated only for numeric, date or datetime types. So the first three parameters should be all numeric expressions or all date expressions. Other types of expressions are not allowed. If the first parameter is NULL, the result is NULL. If the second or the third parameter is NULL, an error message is returned, as a NULL value cannot denote any end point (or any point) for a range in a date or numeric value dimension. The last parameter (number of buckets) should be a numeric expression that evaluates to a positive integer value; 0, NULL, or a negative value will result in an error.

Buckets are numbered from 0 to (n+1). Bucket 0 holds the count of values less than the minimum. Bucket(n+1) holds the count of values greater than or equal to the maximum specified value.

WIDTH_BUCKET Syntax

The WIDTH_BUCKET takes four expressions as parameters. The first parameter is the expression that the equiwidth histogram is for. The second and third parameters are expressions that denote the end points of the acceptable range for the first parameter. The fourth parameter denotes the number of buckets.

```
WIDTH_BUCKET(expression, minval expression, maxval expression, num buckets)
```

Consider the following data from table customers, that shows the credit limits of 17 customers. This data is gathered in the query shown in example 19.15.

CUST_ID	CUST_CREDIT_LIMIT
22110	11000
28340	5000
40800	11000
121790	9000
165400	3000
171630	1500
184090	7000
215240	5000
227700	3000
246390	11000
346070	1500

364760	5000
370990	7000
383450	1500
408370	7000
420830	1500
464440	15000

In the table customers, the column `cust_credit_limit` contains values between 1500 and 15000, and we can assign the values to four equiwidth buckets, numbered from 1 to 4, by using `WIDTH_BUCKET (cust_credit_limit, 0, 20000, 4)`. Ideally each bucket is a closed-open interval of the real number line, for example, bucket number 2 is assigned to scores between 5000.0000 and 9999.9999..., sometimes denoted [5000, 10000) to indicate that 5,000 is included in the interval and 10,000 is excluded. To accommodate values outside the range [0, 20,000), values less than 0 are assigned to a designated underflow bucket which is numbered 0, and values greater than or equal to 20,000 are assigned to a designated overflow bucket which is numbered 5 (num buckets + 1 in general). See figure 19.3 for a graphical illustration of how the buckets are assigned.

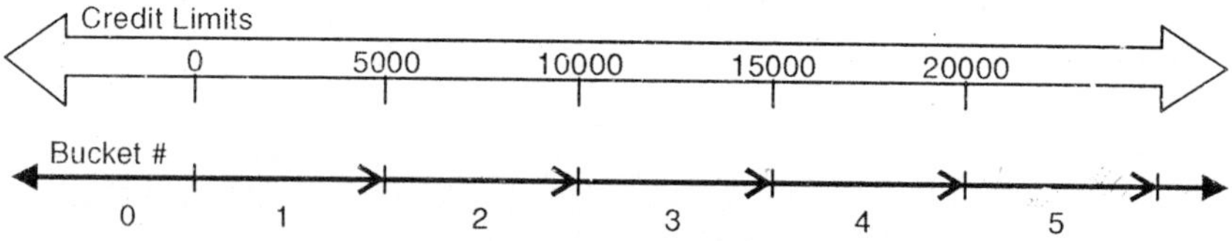

Figure 12.3 Bucket Assignments.

You can specify the bounds in the reverse order, for example, `WIDTH_BUCKET (cust_credit_limit, 20000, 0, 4)`. When the bounds are reversed, the buckets will be open-closed intervals. In this example, bucket number 1 is (`15000,20000`], bucket number 2 is (`10000,15000`], and bucket number 4, is (0,5000]. The overflow bucket will be numbered 0 (`20000, +infinity`), and the underflow bucket will be numbered 5 (`-infinity, 0`].

It is an error if the bucket count parameter is 0 or negative.

Example 12.15 : WIDTH_BUCKET

The following query shows the bucket numbers for the credit limits in the customers table for both cases where the boundaries are specified in regular or reverse order. We use a range of 0 to 20,000.

```
SELECT cust_id, cust_credit_limit,
  WIDTH_BUCKET(cust_credit_limit,0,20000,4) AS WIDTH_BUCKET_UP,
  WIDTH_BUCKET(cust_credit_limit,20000, 0, 4) AS WIDTH_BUCKET_DOWN
FROM customers WHERE cust_city = 'Marshal';
```

CUST_ID	CUST_CREDIT_LIMIT	WIDTH_BUCKET_UP	WIDTH_BUCKET_DOWN
22110	11000	3	2
28340	5000	2	4
40800	11000	3	2
121790	9000	2	3
165400	3000	1	4
171630	1500	1	4

```
184090        7000      2       3
215240        5000      2       4
227700        3000      1       4
246390       11000      3       2
346070        1500      1       4
364760        5000      2       4
370990        7000      2       3
383450        1500      1       4
408370        7000      2       3
420830        1500      1       4
464440       15000      4       2
```

USER-DEFINED AGGREGATE FUNCTIONS

Oracle offers a facility for creating your own functions, called user-defined aggregate functions. These functions are written in programming languages such as PL/SQL, Java, and C, and can be used as analytic functions or aggregates in materialized views.

The advantages of these functions are:

- Highly complex functions can be programmed using a fully procedural language.
- Higher scalability than other techniques when user-defined functions are programmed for parallel processing.
- Object datatypes can be processed.

As a simple example of a user-defined aggregate function, consider the skew statistic. This calculation measures if a data set has a lopsided distribution about its mean. It will tell you if one tail of the distribution is significantly larger than the other. If you created a user-defined aggregate called `udskew` and applied it to the credit limit data in the prior example, the SQL statement and results might look like this:

```
SELECT  USERDEF_SKEW(cust_credit_limit)
FROM customers  WHERE  cust_city='Marshal';

USERDEF_SKEW
============
0.583891
```

Before building user-defined aggregate functions, you should consider if your needs can be met in regular SQL. Many complex calculations are possible directly in SQL, particularly by using the `CASE` expression.

Staying with regular SQL will enable simpler development, and many query operations are already well-parallelized in SQL. Even the earlier example, the skew statistic, can be created by using standard, albeit lengthy, SQL.

CASE EXPRESSIONS

Oracle now supports simple and searched `CASE` statements. `CASE` statements are similar in purpose to the Oracle `DECODE` statement, but they offer more flexibility and logical power. They are also easier to read than traditional DECODE statements, and offer better performance as well. They are commonly used when breaking categories into buckets like age (for example, 20-29, 30-39, and so on). The syntax for simple statements is:

```
expr WHEN comparison_expr THEN return_expr
[, WHEN comparison_expr THEN return_expr]...
```

The syntax for searched statements is:

```
WHEN condition THEN return_expr [, WHEN condition THEN return_expr]...
```

You can specify only 255 arguments and each WHEN ... THEN pair counts as two arguments. For a workaround to this limit, see *Oracle9i SQL Reference*.

CASE Example

Suppose you wanted to find the average salary of all employees in the company. If an employee's salary is less than $2000, you want the query to use $2000 instead. With a CASE statement, you would have to write this query as follows,

```
SELECT AVG(foo(e.sal)) FROM emps e;
```

In this, foo is a function that returns its input if the input is greater than 2000, and returns 2000 otherwise. The query has performance implications because it needs to invoke a function for each row. Writing custom functions can also add to the development load.

Using CASE expressions in the database without PL/SQL, this query can be rewritten as:

```
SELECT AVG(CASE when e.sal > 2000 THEN e.sal ELSE 2000 end) FROM emps e;
```

Using a CASE expression lets you avoid developing custom functions and can also perform faster.

Creating Histograms With User-Defined Buckets

You can use the CASE statement when you want to obtain histograms with user-defined buckets (both in number of buckets and width of each bucket). The following are two examples of histograms created with CASE statements. In the first example, the histogram totals are shown in multiple columns and a single row is returned. In the second example, the histogram is shown with a label column and a single column for totals, and multiple rows are returned.

Histogram Example 1

```
SELECT
SUM(CASE WHEN cust_credit_limit BETWEEN  0 AND 3999 THEN 1 ELSE 0 END)
  AS "0-3999",
SUM(CASE WHEN cust_credit_limit BETWEEN  4000 AND 7999 THEN 1 ELSE 0 END)
  AS "4000-7999",
SUM(CASE WHEN cust_credit_limit BETWEEN  8000 AND 11999 THEN 1 ELSE 0 END)
  AS "8000-11999",
SUM(CASE WHEN cust_credit_limit BETWEEN  12000 AND 16000 THEN 1 ELSE 0 END)
  AS "12000-16000"
FROM customers WHERE cust_city='Marshal';

    0-3999        4000-7999        8000-11999      12000-16000
    ------------------------------------------------------------
      6               6                4                1
```

Histogram Example 2

```
SELECT
 (CASE WHEN cust_credit_limit BETWEEN  0 AND 3999
    THEN ' 0 - 3999'
   WHEN cust_credit_limit BETWEEN  4000 AND 7999 THEN ' 4000 - 7999'
   WHEN cust_credit_limit BETWEEN  8000 AND 11999 THEN  ' 8000 - 11999'
   WHEN cust_credit_limit BETWEEN  12000 AND 16000 THEN '12000 - 16000' END)
  AS BUCKET,
  COUNT(*) AS Count_in_Group
FROM customers.WHERE cust_city = 'Marshal'
GROUP BY
 (CASE WHEN cust_credit_limit BETWEEN  0 AND 3999
    THEN ' 0 - 3999'
 WHEN cust_credit_limit BETWEEN  4000 AND 7999 THEN ' 4000 - 7999'
 WHEN cust_credit_limit BETWEEN  8000 AND 11999 THEN  ' 8000 - 11999'
 WHEN cust_credit_limit BETWEEN  12000 AND 16000 THEN '12000 - 16000'
 END);
```

BUCKET	COUNT_IN_GROUP
0 - 3999	6
4000 - 7999	6
8000 - 11999	4
12000 - 16000	1

❑❑❑

13 ONLINE ANALYTICAL PROCESSING

In large data warehouse environments, many different types of analysis can occur. In addition to SQL queries, you may also apply more advanced analytical operations to your data. Two major types of such analysis are OLAP (On-Line Analytic Processing) and data mining. Rather than having a separate OLAP or data mining engine, Oracle has integrated OLAP and data mining capabilities directly into the database server. Oracle OLAP and Oracle Data Mining are options to the Oracle9*i* Database.

WHY OLAP?

Relational databases have dominated database technology by providing the online transactional processing (OLTP) that is essential for businesses to keep track of their affairs. Designed for efficient selection, storage, and retrieval of data, relational databases are ideal for housing gigabytes of detailed data.

The success of relational databases is apparent in their use to store information about an increasingly wide scope of activities. As a result, they contain a wealth of data that can yield critical information about a business. This information can provide a competitive edge in an increasingly competitive marketplace.

Analytical Processing Answers Business Questions

The challenge is in deriving answers to business questions from the available data, so that decision makers at all levels can respond quickly to changes in the business climate. While a standard transactional query might ask, "When did order 84305 ship?" A typical series of analytical queries might ask, "How do sales in the Southwestern region for this quarter compare with sales a year ago? What can we predict for sales next quarter? What factors can we alter to improve the sales forecast?"

The transactional query involves simple data selection and retrieval. However, the analytical queries involve inter-row calculations, time series analysis, and access to aggregated historical and current data. This is online analytical processing — OLAP.

The data processing required to answer analytical questions is fundamentally different from the data processing required to answer transactional questions. Table 13.1 highlights the major differences.

Table 13.1 Characteristics of Transactional And Analytical Queries

Characteristic	Transactional Query	Analytical Query
Typical operation	Update	Analyze
Age of data	Current	Historical
Level of data	Detail	Aggregate
Data required per query	Minimal	Extensive
Querying pattern	Individual queries	Iterative queries

Types of OLAP Applications

Applications that support business analyses fall into these major groups:

- Standard reporting
- Ad-hoc query and reporting
- Multidimensional analytical reporting
- Predictive analysis and planning.

Oracle provides the technology for all of these types of applications. Oracle OLAP and its development tools are particularly suited to analytical reporting and predictive analysis applications. This guide will introduce you to the tools for developing these types of applications.

Analytical Reporting

Analytic applications can support many facets of a business and offer high returns on the investment. Here are just a few examples of analytical applications:

- Accounting. Forecasting, budgeting, cost and profitability analyses, and consolidation
- Human Resources. Skills consolidation, labor scheduling and optimization
- Distribution. Scheduling and optimization
- Sales Force Automation. Cross-selling and territory analyses
- Marketing. Churn and market-based analyses
- Retailing. Site location and demographic analyses
- Manufacturing. Demand planning and forecasting
- Health Care. Outcomes analysis
- Financial Services. Risk assessment and management.

Predictive Analysis

Planning applications allow organizations to predict outcomes. They generate new data using predictive analytical tools such as models, forecasts, aggregation, allocation, and scenario management. Some examples of this type of application are corporate budgeting and financial analyses, and demand planning systems.

Budgeting and financial analyses systems allow organizations to analyze past performance, build revenue and spending plans, manage toward profit goals, and model the effects of change on the financial plan. Management can determine spending and investment levels that are appropriate for the anticipated revenue and profit levels. Financial analysts can prepare alternative budgets and investment plans contingent on factors such as fluctuations in currency values.

Demand planning systems allow organizations to predict market demand based on factors such as sales history, promotional plans, pricing models, and so forth. They can model different scenarios that forecast product demand and then determine appropriate manufacturing goals.

OLAP

Oracle9*i* OLAP adds the query performance and calculation capability previously found only in multidimensional databases to Oracle's relational platform. In addition, it provides a Java OLAP API that is appropriate for the development of internet-ready analytical applications. Unlike other combinations of OLAP and RDBMS technology, Oracle9*i* OLAP is not a multidimensional database using bridges to move data from the relational data store to a multidimensional data store. Instead, it is truly an OLAP-enabled relational database. As a result, Oracle9*i* provides the benefits of a multidimensional database along with the scalability, accessibility, security, manageability, and high availability of the Oracle9*i* database. The Java OLAP API, which is specifically designed for internet-based analytical applications, offers productive data access.

Benefits of OLAP and RDBMS Integration

Basing an OLAP system directly on the Oracle server offers the following benefits:

- Scalability
- Availability
- Manageability
- Backup and recovery
- Security.

Scalability

Oracle9*i* OLAP is highly scalable. In today's environment, there is tremendous growth along three dimensions of analytic applications: number of users, size of data, complexity of analyses. There are more users of analytical applications, and they need access to more data to perform more sophisticated analysis and target marketing. For example, a telephone company might want a customer dimension to include detail such as all telephone numbers as part of an application that is used to analyze customer turnover. This would require support for multi-million row dimension tables and very large volumes of fact data. Oracle9*i* can handle very large data sets using parallel execution and partitioning, as well as offering support for advanced hardware and clustering.

Availability

Oracle9*i* includes many features that support high availability. One of the most significant is partitioning, which allows management of precise subsets of tables and indexes, so that management operations affect only small pieces of these data structures. By partitioning tables and indexes, data management processing time is reduced, thus minimizing the time data is unavailable. Another feature supporting high availability is transportable tablespaces. With transportable tablespaces, large data sets, including tables and indexes, can be added with almost no processing to other databases. This enables extremely rapid data loading and updates.

Manageability

Oracle enables you to precisely control resource utilization. The Database Resource Manager, for example; provides a mechanism for allocating the resources of a data warehouse among different sets of end-users. Consider an environment where the marketing department and the sales department share an OLAP system. Using the Database Resource Manager, you could specify that the marketing department receive at least 60 percent of the CPU resources of the machines, while the sales department receive 40 percent of the CPU resources. You can also further specify limits on the total number of active sessions, and the degree of parallelism of individual queries for each department.

Another resource management facility is the progress monitor, which gives end users and administrators the status of long-running operations. Oracle9*i* maintains statistics describing the percent-complete of these operations. Oracle Enterprise Manager enables you to view a bar-graph display of these operations showing what percent complete they are. Moreover, any other tool or any database administrator can also retrieve progress information directly from the Oracle data server, using system views.

Backup and Recovery

Oracle provides a server-managed infrastructure for backup, restore, and recovery tasks that enables simpler, safer operations at terabyte scale. Some of the highlights are:

- Details related to backup, restore, and recovery operations are maintained by the server in a recovery catalog and automatically used as part of these operations. This reduces administrative burden and minimizes the possibility of human errors.
- Backup and recovery operations are fully integrated with partitioning. Individual partitions, when placed in their own tablespaces, can be backed up and restored independently of the other partitions of a table.
- Oracle includes support for incremental backup and recovery using Recovery Manager, enabling operations to be completed efficiently within times proportional to the amount of changes, rather than the overall size of the database.
- The backup and recovery technology is highly scalable, and provides tight interfaces to industry-leading media management subsystems. This provides for efficient operations that can scale up to handle very large volumes of data. Open platforms for more hardware options and enterprise-level platforms.

Security

Just as the demands of real-world transaction processing required Oracle to develop robust features for scalability, manageability and backup and recovery, they lead Oracle to create industry-leading security features. The security features in Oracle have reached the highest levels of U.S. government certification for database trustworthiness. Oracle's fine grained access control feature, enables cell-level security for OLAP users. Fine grained access control works with minimal burden on query processing, and it enables efficient centralized security management.

COMPONENTS OF ORACLE OLAP

Analytical queries and predictive analyses require a multidimensional OLAP solution. Oracle OLAP consists of the following components:

- Calculation engine
- Analytic workspaces
- OLAP DML
- PL/SQL table functions
- OLAP API
- OLAP catalog metadata.

This guide explains the relationships among these components from the perspectives of both database administrators and application developers.

Calculation Engine

The OLAP calculation engine supports the selection and rapid calculation of multidimensional data. The status of an individual session persists to support a series of queries, which is typical of analytical applications; the output from one query is easily used as input to the next query. The OLAP engine runs within the Oracle kernel.

Analytic Workspace

An analytic workspace stores multidimensional data objects and procedures written in the OLAP DML. Within a single database, many analytic workspaces can be created and shared among users. Like relational tables, an analytic workspace is owned by a particular user ID, and other users can be granted access to it. Because individual users can save a personal copy of their alterations to a workspace, the workspace environment is particularly conducive to planning applications.

An analytic workspace can be temporary (that is, for the life of the session) or it can be persistent, that is, saved from one session to the next. When an analytic workspace is persistent, the data is stored as LOBs in database tables. Analytic workspaces also provide an alternative to materialized views as a means of storing aggregate data.

OLAP DML

The OLAP DML is a data manipulation language that is understood by the Oracle OLAP calculation engine. The OLAP DML extends the analytical capabilities of querying languages such as SQL and the OLAP API to include forecasting, modeling, and what-if scenarios. Application developers can create stored procedures that use conditional logic and the extensive library of DML commands and functions to perform complex analyses of data. Moreover, the OLAP DML is a very accessible calculation language, similar to that of a spreadsheet, which is easy for power users and DBAs to learn and use.

OLAP DML commands and functions include the following categories:

- ☞ Aggregation
- ☞ Allocation
- ☞ Data Selection

- Date and Time Operations
- File Reading and Writing
- Financial Operations
- Forecasts and Regressions
- Numeric Manipulation
- Models
- Statistical Operations
- Text Manipulation
- Time Series Manipulation.

Both the OLAP API and PL/SQL can embed OLAP DML commands in their syntax. Using the OLAP DML, database administrators and application developers can create multidimensional data objects that are stored in an analytic workspace. The OLAP DML operates on data that is stored (permanently or temporarily) in these multidimensional objects.

SQL Table Functions

SQL table functions can take a set of rows as input and produce a set of rows as output that can be queried like a physical database table. Application developers who use SQL can access SQL packages that use table functions to create views of multidimensional data. SQL applications can then access these views. Thus, the calculation engine and multidimensional data sources are accessible to SQL, making analytic and predictive functions available to SQL-based applications. SQL applications can connect to the database using either the Oracle Call Interface (OCI) or Java Database Connectivity (JDBC).

OLAP API

The Oracle OLAP API is an application programming interface to Oracle OLAP. It is a querying language that selects and manipulates data for display in a Java client. Because the OLAP API is all Java, it supports deployment of analytical applications to large, geographically distributed user communities on the Internet. It is object oriented, so that application developers define the results they want, not the process by which the results are obtained. The OLAP API connects to the database using JDBC.

The OLAP API is the technology underlying the Oracle BI Beans for access to relational and multidimensional data. JavaBeans are the building blocks of application development. They are reusable pieces of Java code that can be assembled quickly into an application. The Oracle BI Beans provide pre-built OLAP-aware application building blocks: Connecting to a database; authenticating users' credentials; selecting and fetching data; and displaying the data in a variety of tabular and graphical formats. Using the BI Beans, developers can create applications with a common "look and feel," enabling users to gain expertise quickly in the new product.

The BI Beans can be used within Oracle JDeveloper or other Java development environments to build analytical applications, which can be deployed as either Java or HTML clients.

OLAP Catalog

Metadata is typically defined as "data about data." OLAP Catalog metadata is created and stored in relational tables in the database. OLAP applications can query this metadata repository to find out what data is available for analyses and display. The metadata contains information about the physical location of the data, that is, whether it is stored in a relational table or in an analytic workspace. The application does not need to be aware of the location of the data or alter its processing to accommodate the storage location. Since the data is queried using SQL, data from relational data and multidimensional data can be joined in a single SQL query.

Whether the data is stored in a relational schema or in an analytic workspace, the metadata identifies the data in terms of the multidimensional objects: measures, dimensions, levels, and attributes. The metadata provides information critical to the selection, manipulation, and display of that data.

WHAT IS THE OLAP DML?

The OLAP DML is a data manipulation language. You can use DML commands and functions to perform complex analysis of data. You can also write stored procedures that contain DML commands and functions.

Extensive Analytic Capabilities

The OLAP DML enables application developers to extend the analytical capabilities of querying languages such as SQL and the OLAP API. These are some situations in which you might use the OLAP DML:

- When you need to calculate data that cannot be calculated as part of your data warehouse extraction, transformation, and load (ETL) process or in SQL. Examples include forecasts, solving a model, some types of consolidations (aggregations), and allocations
- When your application needs to perform various calculations, but you do not want to immediately commit the results in SQL tables. For example, you might have a forecasting application where you want to allow users to save personal forecasts and reuse them during a later session, but you do not want users to commit the forecast to the SQL tables. Instead, you can just commit the data to the analytic workspace without committing it to SQL tables.
- When you want to manipulate data that is stored in an analytic workspace. An analytic workspace can be an alternative to materialized views for storing aggregate data. It may also be the preferred storage location for data that is frequently used in business analyses such as models and forecasts.

Features of the Multidimensional Model

There are inherent features of the multidimensional model that make it an appropriate environment for business intelligence. The multidimensional model:

- Enforces referential integrity. Each dimension member is unique and cannot be NA. If a measure has three dimensions, then each data value of that measure must be qualified by a member of each dimension.
- Promotes consistency. Dimensions are maintained as separate workspace objects and are shared by measures.
- Preserves the order of data. Each dimension has a default status list, which contains all of its members in the order they are stored. The default status list is always the same unless

it is purposefully altered by adding, deleting, or moving members. Within a session, the user can change the selection and order of the status list; this is called the current status list. The current status list remains the same until the user purposefully alters it by adding, removing, or changing the order of its members.

Because the order of dimension members is consistent and known, the selection of members can be relative. For example, the function call

```
lag(sales, 12, month)
```

compares the sales values of all months in the current status list against sales from a year ago (that is, 12 time periods earlier in the default status list for the month dimension).

- Presents data as fully solved. Applications do not need to define calculations. Because of the combination of power and ease-of-use of the OLAP DML, the analytic workspace can be prepared so that the data is presented as fully solved to the application.
- Manages calculated members and measures transparently. Users can define their own dimension members (often called **custom aggregates**), which function identically to the other dimension members and can be used transparently in any calculation. Similarly, users can define their own measures and assign values to them using any of the methods available in the OLAP DML. Throughout the session, these additions behave identically to the dimension members and objects originally provided in the workspace. Users can save their changes from one session to the next with a single DML command.

BASIC CATEGORIES OF OLAP DML COMMANDS

Following are descriptions of some of the basic categories of OLAP DML commands and functions.

Aggregation

The OLAP DML supports a variety of aggregation methods including first, last, average, weighted average, and sum. In a multidimensional data object, the aggregation method can vary by dimension. Some of the data can be aggregated and stored, while other data is aggregated at runtime. A technique called "skip level" aggregation pre-aggregates every other level in a dimension hierarchy. The DBA can choose whatever method seems appropriate: by level, individual member, member attribute, time range, data value, or other criteria.

Allocation

Allocations are a critical part of planning applications. Given a target for the organization — whether for sales quota, product growth, salary, or equipment — managers must allocate that target among its contributors. Some of the key features of the allocation system are:

- Support for hierarchies so the data is distributed based on parentage
- Support for arbitrary selections so that data is distributed among selected members, regardless of parentage or in the absence of a hierarchy
- A variety of allocation methods, including:
  - Copy methods (hierarchical copy, minimum, maximum, first, last)
  - Even distribution (even, hierarchical even)

  - Proportional distribution (including weighted distributions and user-defined multidimensional functions
- Cell-level locking prevents certain cells from being overwritten by the allocation. This feature is used when some values for the planning period are known
- Logging records how far an allocation has progressed and whether any errors have occurred.

Data Selection

Data selection within the analytic workspace is persistent throughout a session, which is a feature that supports the iterative nature of analytic queries. Users can select data in multiple steps, with each step refining the previous query. The OLAP DML provides data selection methods that are specifically designed for multidimensional data, such as hierarchical relations, levels of aggregation, attributes, time series functions, and data values.

Data Exchange

SQL statements can be embedded in the OLAP DML, which allows applications to select data from SQL tables and write data back to them. This can be done at runtime or as a data maintenance procedure. Access to SQL tables is controlled by the privileges and roles granted to the user's database ID.

The following embedded SQL statements define a cursor and fetch data from a relational table named `products` into a workspace dimension named `prod` and a measure named `prod_label`.

```
SQL DECLARE highprice CURSOR FOR SELECT prod_id, prod_name -
     FROM products WHERE suggested_price > :set_price
SQL OPEN highprice
SQL FETCH highprice LOOP INTO :prod, :prod_label
```

File Reading and Writing

Data can be read from flat files or spreadsheets into multidimensional objects. This is typically done as a data maintenance procedure. Access to external files is controlled by BFILE security. DBAs can set up aliases for directories and control which users and groups can use those aliases. The security system does not allow users to access directories without an alias.

The following program copies data from a file named `unit` and stores it in a dimensions named `month` and `productid` and variables named `productname` and `units.sold`. The DBA previously created a directory alias named `mydat`.

```
DEFINE read.product PROGRAM
PROGRAM
VARIABLE fi INT                  "Define a local integer variable
fi = FILEOPEN('mydat/unit' READ) "Store a file handle in the variable
FILEREAD fi COLUMN 1 WIDTH 5 month -
     COLUMN 6 WIDTH 6 productid -
     COLUMN 12 WIDTH 30 productname -
     COLUMN 44 WIDTH 22 units.sold
FILECLOSE fi
END
```

The next example creates a file named `custom.eif` as a private data store that contains the data and definitions for a custom measure named `mysales`. The user can import `mysales` during another session.

```
EXPORT mysales TO EIF FILE 'userdat/custom.eif' DATA DFNS
```

Financial Operations

The financial functions include interest rate calculations, depreciation, and payment schedules, similar to those provided in spreadsheets.

For example, the FPMTSCHED function calculates a payment schedule (principal plus interest) for paying off a series of fixed-rate installment loans over a specified number of time periods. The following call to FPMTSCHED calculates 36 payments based on the amounts listed in the loans variable, at the interest rates listed in the rates variable, for the month dimension of these variables.

```
FPMTSCHED(loans, rates, 36, month)
```

Forecasts and Regressions

The OLAP DML offers the most sophisticated and up-to-date forecasting and regression tools of Roadmap Geneva Forecasting, including simple linear regressions, non-linear regression methods, single exponential smoothing, double exponential smoothing, and the Holt-Winters method.

For example, the following FORECAST command uses the EXPONENTIAL method to forecast sales for the next 12 months based on historical data stored in the sales measure. It stores the results of the calculation in a second measure named fcst.sales.

```
FORECAST LENGTH 12 METHOD EXPONENTIAL FCNAME fcst.sales TIME month sales
```

Models

A model is a set of interrelated equations. These are some of the modeling features supported by the OLAP DML:

- You can perform calculations for individual dimension members following unique calculation rules.
- Oracle OLAP determines the order of the calculations, so you can list them in any order without concern for dependencies.
- Oracle OLAP solves simultaneous equations.

You can assign results either to a variable or to a dimension member. Dimension-based equations provide flexibility; since you do not need to specify the modeling variable until you solve a model, you can run the same model with any other measure with the same dimension. For example, you could run the same model on budget and actual, which both have a line dimension.

The following is an example of a modeling program.

```
'cost of goods' = 'raw materials'+labor+'fixed overhead'
'fixed overhead' = 'capital equipment'+'building costs'
'building costs' = 'building depreciation'+electric+heat+maintenance
'labor' = salary+benefits
'capital equipment' = 'equipment maintenance'+'equipment depreciation'
```

Numeric Computations

Functions are available to perform a wide variety of computations (such as sine, cosine, square root, minimum, and maximum) and data type conversions.

For example, the `CEIL` function returns the smallest whole number greater than or equal to a specified number. The function call

```
CEIL(-6.457).
```

returns a value of -6.

Statistical Operations

Statistical operations include standard deviation, rank, and correlation. For example, the `STDDEV` function calculates the standard deviation. The function call

```
STDDEV(units  month)
```

returns the standard deviation of values in the `units` measure for all months that are currently selected.

Text Manipulation

The OLAP DML provides support for manipulating both single- and multibyte character sets, with functions for concatenating strings, locating a string within a larger body of text, inserting a string, and so forth.

For example, the `EXTCHARS` function extracts a portion of text. The function call

```
EXTCHARS('lastname,firstname',  1,8)
```

extracts the first 8 characters, which contains the characters

```
lastname
```

Time Series Manipulation

The time series functions perform operations such as lead, lag, and moving average. For example, the `MOVINGTOTAL` function calculates a series of totals over time. The following example returns a 3-month total on the `sales` measure for all currently selected months.

```
MOVINGTOTAL(sales, -2, 0, 1, month)
```

METHODS OF EXECUTING OLAP DML COMMANDS

The OLAP DML can be used when you want to perform calculations that are not easily accomplished in the ETL process or using SQL (either directly or using the OLAP API). The results can be calculated as part of the data warehouse build and update process, and can optionally be written to SQL tables. Alternatively, applications developers can create OLAP DML programs using the OLAP Worksheet and execute them by embedding OLAP DML in their SQL- or Java-based applications.

OLAP Worksheet: The OLAP DML Development Tool

OLAP Worksheet is an interactive command line interface to Oracle that you can use to perform the following tasks:

- Connect to an analytic workspace
- Execute OLAP DML commands

- Execute SQL statements
- Create and populate data objects
- Create, modify, compile, and execute OLAP DML programs.

OLAP Worksheet has a command input window and a program edit window.

Procedure: Open OLAP Worksheet

To open OLAP Worksheet, use the following steps:

1. In Enterprise Manager, connect to a database that is enabled for OLAP.
2. Expand the database.
3. Choose **Warehouse.**
4. From the right mouse menu, choose **Oracle OLAP Worksheet.**

Once you have opened OLAP Worksheet, you can use its menus to establish a connection to Oracle, open a workspace, execute OLAP DML commands, execute SQL statements, or write OLAP DML programs, save any changes, and close the connection.

Embedding OLAP DML Commands in Programs

Applications developers can embed OLAP DML in their SQL- or Java-based applications:

- In SQL programs, you can embed OLAP DML commands using the procedures in the `DBMS_AW` package.
- In Java programs, you can embed OLAP DML commands using the `SPLExecutor` class in the OLAP API.

BUILDING SQL-BASED OLAP APPLICATIONS

SQL-based applications can access multidimensional data, which is stored in analytic workspaces. Two mechanisms in the database's object technology make this possible:

- Object types (also called abstract data types or ADT) are the basis for object-oriented programming in PL/SQL. An object type encapsulates a data structure along with the functions and procedures needed to manipulate the data. When you define an object type using the `CREATE TYPE` statement, you create an abstract template that corresponds to a real-world object.

  In OLAP, these "real-world objects" are measures, dimensions, hierarchies, attributes, and so forth. By defining object types for the objects in an analytic workspace, you can describe the format of multidimensional data to SQL as rows and columns.
- Table functions produce a collection of rows that can be queried like a physical database table. You use a table function instead of the name of a database table, in the `FROM` clause of a query. A table function can take a collection of rows as input.

  You can use table functions to fetch data from objects in an analytic workspace. The table functions require arguments that are passed to the OLAP engine, which selects, manipulates, and returns the data. By incorporating table functions into your application, you have the most power and flexibility in selecting and manipulating data in the analytic workspace.

If you overlay the table functions with relational views, then you can make the table functions (and thus the source of the data) transparent to SQL-based applications. Your applications can use standard SQL to run against these views of multidimensional data, the same way that they access other relational tables and views in the database.

Figure 13.1 shows how a SQL application can access multidimensional data (using table functions and views) as well as relational data.

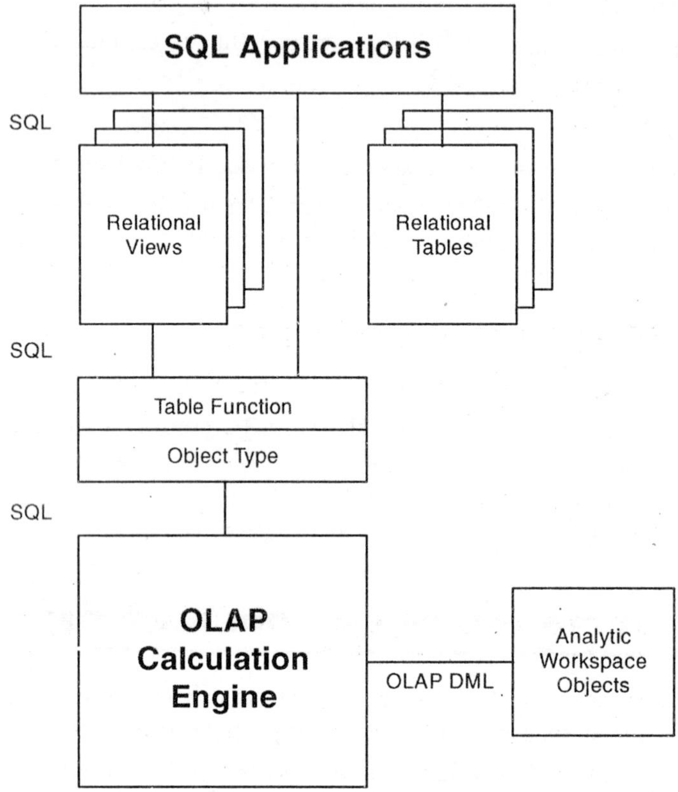

Figure 13.1 Components of a SQL-Based Analytical Application.

Methods of Accessing Multidimensional Data From SQL

There are several ways that SQL can access the multidimensional data of an analytic workspace. An abstract data type and the table functions underlie all of them. The method that you choose depends on how you want to use the data.

- Use the `CWM2_OLAP_AW_CREATE` package to create the analytic workspace from a star schema. Use other procedures in this package to define a star schema of dimension views and fact views, which represent the measures, dimensions, hierarchies, and attributes in the analytic workspace. You can then query these views using standard SQL `SELECT` statements. You can use other `CWM2` APIs to create OLAP Catalog metadata based on these views.

- If your analytic workspace did not originate from the AW_CREATE process, you can use the CWM2_OLAP_AW_ACCESS PL/SQL package to generate views of the workspace.
- Write object type definitions and then make relational queries and views of the analytic workspace data by using the OLAP_TABLE function in SQL SELECT statements. This method is more complex than using CWM2_OLAP_AW_CREATE or CWM2_OLAP_AW_ACCESS, but it provides more flexibility and power in an application than using predefined views.

Embedding OLAP DML Commands in SQL

Using the procedures and functions in the DBMS_AW package, SQL programmers can issue OLAP DML commands directly against analytic workspace data. They can move data from relational tables into an analytic workspace, perform advanced analysis of the data (for example, forecasting), and copy data from the analytic workspace back into relational tables.

While the data is in the analytic workspace, SQL programmers can also issue SELECT statements against the data in the analytic workspace using the OLAP_TABLE function.

Building Analytical Java Applications

Java is the language of the Internet. Using Java, an application developer can write a standalone application or an *applet*, which is a program that can be included in an HTML page and executed in a browser.

About Java

Java is the preferred programming language for an ever-increasing number of professional software developers. For those who have been programming in C or C++, the move to Java is easy because it provides a familiar environment while avoiding many of the shortcomings of the C language. Developed by Sun Microsystems, Java is fast superseding C++ and Visual Basic as the language of choice for application developers for the following reasons:

- Object oriented. Java allows application developers to focus on the data and methods of manipulating that data, rather than on abstract procedures; the programmer defines the desired object rather than the steps needed to create that object. Almost everything in Java is defined as an object.
- Platform independent. The Java compiler creates byte code that is interpreted at runtime by the Java Virtual Machine (JVM). As the result, the same software can run on all Windows, Unix, and Macintosh platforms where the JVM has been installed. All major browsers have the JVM built in.
- Network based. Java was designed to work over a network, which allows Java programs to handle remote resources as easily as local resources.
- Secure. Java code is either trusted or untrusted, and access to system resources is determined by this characteristic. Local code is trusted to have full access to system resources, but downloaded remote code (that is, an applet) is not trusted.

The Java "sandbox" security model provides a very restricted environment for untrusted code. For example, untrusted Java code cannot read to or write from files on the local file system, run programs, load libraries, define native method calls, or make network connections except to the originating host computer. A security manager determines the system resources that an applet can access. However, a signed applet, which identifies itself as being from a trusted source, has full access to system resources the same as local code.

Deploying Java Applications

With the rise in Internet technology, more and more businesses are recognizing the savings they can accrue just by changing the way they deploy their applications.

Traditional **thick client** applications implement many of their functions on the user's computer, thus requiring a large proportion of installed code. However, the days are gone when a team of technicians are required to install and maintain applications software on hundreds or thousands of individual desktop computers for a large user base. Instead, Java thick-client applications download the needed software to client computers automatically at run-time.

Alternatively, system administrators can deploy **thin client** applications that do not download any Java to client computers. These applications run on servers that users world wide can access using Java clients such as their Web browsers. By deploying thin client business intelligence applications on the Internet, businesses can distribute information both within their enterprise and externally to suppliers and customers.

Regardless of whether you choose a thick-client or a thin-client configuration, Java applications provide an immediate solution to the problems inherent in supporting large user communities, which typically are equipped with a variety of incompatible hardware and software platforms.

The Java Solution for OLAP

To develop an OLAP application, you can use the Java programming language. Java enables you to write applications that are platform-independent and easily deployed over the Internet.

The OLAP API is a Java-based application programming interface that provides access to multidimensional data for analytical business applications. The OLAP API fetches data stored in a data warehouse into the OLAP multidimensional data cache for manipulation by its analytical engine. Java classes in the OLAP API provide all of the functions required of an OLAP application: Connection to an OLAP instance; authentication of user credentials; access to data in the RDBMS controlled by the permissions granted to those credentials; and selection and manipulation of that data for business analysis.

The BI Beans simplify application development by providing these functions as JavaBeans. Moreover, the BI Beans include JavaBeans for presenting the data in graphs, crosstabs, and tables.

NOTE *Oracle JDeveloper and the BI Beans are applications and are not packaged with the Oracle RDBMS.*

Oracle Java Development Environment

Oracle JDeveloper provides an Integrated Development Environment (IDE) for developing Java applications. Although third-party Java IDEs can also be used effectively, only JDeveloper achieves full integration with the Oracle database and BI Beans wizards. The following are a few JDeveloper features:

- Remote graphical debugger with break points, watches, and an inspector
- Multiple Document Interface (MDI)
- *Codecoach* feature that helps you to optimize your code

- Generation of 100% Pure Java applications, applets, servlets, Java beans, and so forth with no proprietary code or markers
- Oracle database browser.

INTRODUCING THE BI BEANS

The BI Beans provide reusable components that are the basic building blocks for OLAP decision support applications. Using the BI Beans, developers can rapidly develop and deploy new applications, because these large functional units have already been developed and tested — not only for their robustness, but also for their ease of use. And because the BI Beans provide a common look and feel to OLAP applications, the learning curve for end users is greatly reduced.

Two groups of BI Beans are currently available:

- Presentation Beans display the data in a rich variety of formats so that trends and variations can easily be detected. Among the Presentation BI Beans currently available are Graph, Table, and Crosstabs.

  The Presentation Beans can be implemented as a thick client or a thin client. Thick clients best support users who do immersed analyses, that is, use the system for extensive periods of time with a lot of interaction. For example, users who create reports benefit from a thick client. Thin clients best support remote users who use a low bandwidth connection and have basic analytical needs. Thin clients can be embedded in a portal or other Web site for these users.
- OLAP BI Beans acquire and manipulate the data. The OLAP BI Beans use the OLAP API to connect to a data source, define a query, manipulate the resultant data set, and return the results to the Presentation BI Beans for display.

You can use the BI Beans in either thick-client or thin-client applications.

Thick-Client Configuration

The components of an OLAP thick-client application are grouped into three tiers, which can be on separate platforms or the same platform:

- Java client tier. A Java application can run either in a browser or directly in the Java Runtime Environment (JRE). The BI Beans that are dedicated to presenting the data and metadata also run on this tier.
- Application server tier. The "brains" of the application run on this tier, which includes the OLAP API and the OLAP BI Beans that are built using the OLAP API.
- Data server tier. The Oracle RDBMS and OLAP service form the data server tier, where the data is stored, selected, and manipulated. An OLAP API component also runs on the data server tier.

Figure 13.2 shows these relationships in a thick-client configuration.

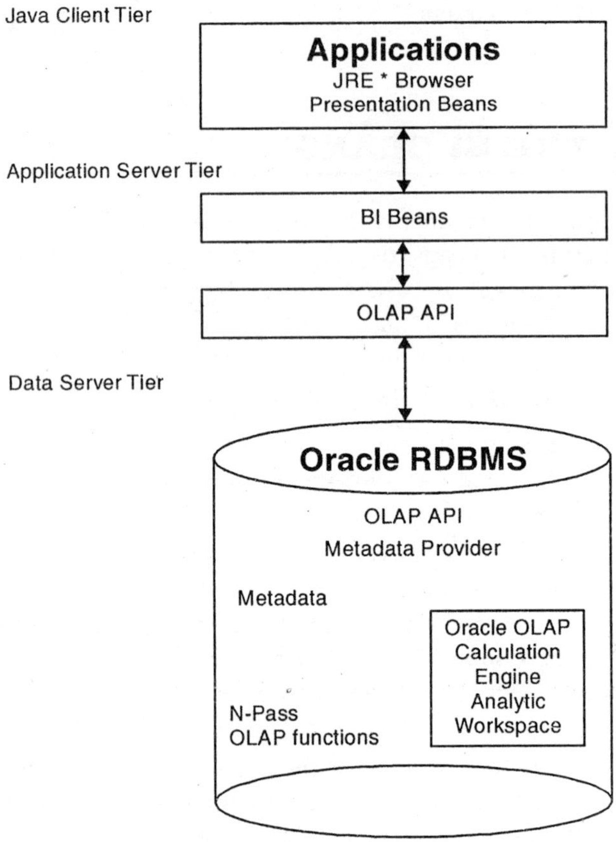

Figure 13.2 Thick Client Configuration.

Thin-Client Configuration

The components of an OLAP thin-client application are grouped into two tiers, which can be on separate platforms or the same platform:

- Application server tier. The "brains" of the application run on this tier, which includes a Web server, the OLAP API and the OLAP BI Beans (both presentation and analytical).
- Data server tier. The Oracle RDBMS is the data server tier, where the data is stored, selected, and manipulated either in relational tables or in the OLAP analytic workspace. An OLAP API component also runs on the data server tier.

Figure 13.3 shows these relationships in a thin-client configuration.

Metadata

The OLAP API and the BI Beans use the OLAP Catalog to provide the information they need about multidimensional objects defined in an Oracle data warehouse, such as measures and dimensions.

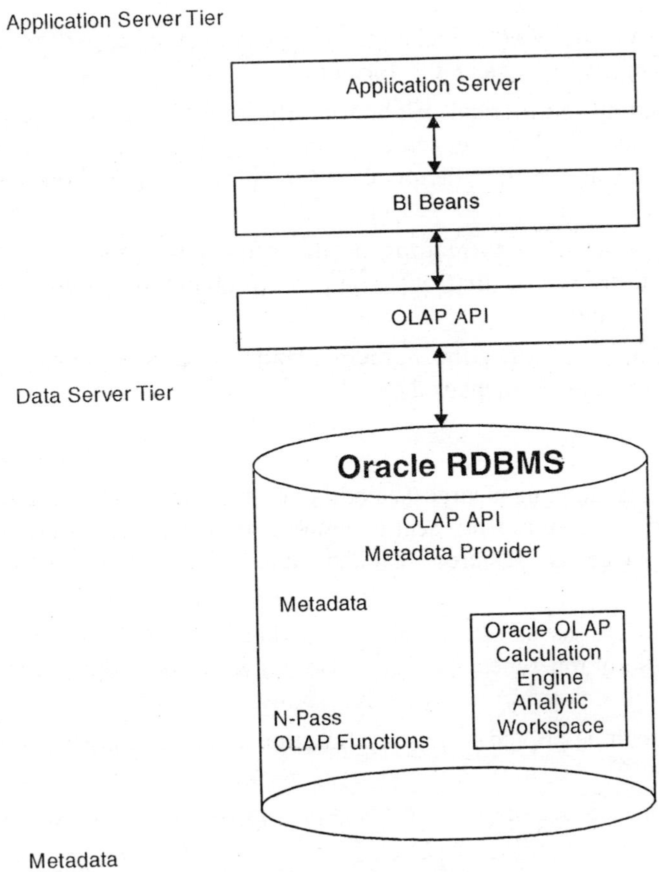

Figure 13.3 Thin-Client Configuration.

Runtime Repository

The BI Beans employ a runtime repository in the Oracle database that allows users to save their personal analyses and to share their discoveries with other users.

Navigation

The Presentation BI Beans support navigation techniques such as drilling, pivoting, and paging.

- *Drilling* displays lower-level values that contribute to a higher-level aggregate, such as the cities that contribute to a state total.
- *Pivoting* rotates the data cube so that the dimension members that appeared along the X-axis of a graph now appear along the Y-axis, or the dimension members that labeled columns in a crosstab now label rows instead. For example, if products label the rows and regions label the columns, then you can pivot the data cube so that products label the columns and regions label the rows.
- *Paging* handles additional dimensions by showing each member in a separate graph, crosstab, or table rather than nesting them in the columns or rows. For example, you might want to see each time period in a separate graph rather than all time periods on the same graph.

Formatting

The Presentation BI Beans allow you to change the appearance of a particular display. In addition, the values of the data itself can affect the format.

- Number formatting. Numerical displays can be modified by changing their scale, number of decimal digits and leading zeros, currency symbol, negative notation, and so forth. Currency symbols and scaling factors can be displayed in the column or row headers rather than in the cells.
- Stoplight formatting. The formatting of the cell background color, border, font, and so forth can be data driven so that outstanding or problematic results stand out visually from the other data values.
- Ranking. In ranking reports, the numerical rank of each dimension value, based on the value of the measure, is displayed.

Graphs

The Graph bean presents data in a large selection of two- and three-dimensional business chart types, such as bar, area, line, pie, ring, scatter, bubble, pyramid, and stock market. Many of the 2D graphs can be displayed as clustered, stacked, dual-Y, percentage, horizontal, vertical, or 3D effect.

Bar, line, and area graphs can be combined so that individual rows in the data cube can be specified as one of these graph types. You can also assign marker shape and type, data line type, color, and width, and fill colors on a row-by-row basis.

The graph image can be copied to the system clipboard and exported in GIF and other image formats.

Users can zoom in and out of selected areas of a graph. They can also scroll across the axes.

Crosstabs

The Crosstab bean presents data in a two-dimensional grid similar to a spreadsheet. Multiple dimensions can be nested along the rows or columns, and additional dimensions can appear as separate pages. Among the available customizations are: Font style, size, color and underlining; individual cell background colors; border formats; and text alignment.

Users can navigate through the data using either a mouse or the keyboard. They can insert rows and columns to display totals, and edit cells for what-if analysis.

Tables

The Table bean presents data in record format like a relational table or view. In contrast to the crosstab, the table display handles measures individually rather than as members of a measure dimension. Thus, each measure can be manipulated individually.

OLAP BI Beans

The OLAP BI Beans use the OLAP API to provide the basic services needed by an application. They enable clients to identify a database, present credentials for accessing that database, and make a connection. The application can then access the metadata and identify the available data. Users can select the measures they want to see and the specific slice of data that is of interest to them. That data can then be modified and manipulated.

Wizards

The BI Beans offer wizards that can be used both by application developers in creating an initial environment and by end users in customizing applications to suit their particular needs. The wizards lead you step-by-step so that you provide all of the information needed by an application. The following are some of the tasks that can be done by using wizards.

- Building a query. Fact tables and materialized views often contain much more data than users are interested in viewing. Fetching vast quantities of data can also degrade performance unnecessarily. In addition to selecting measures, you can limit the amount of data fetched in a query by selecting dimension members from a list or using a set of conditions. A selection can be saved and used again just by picking its name from a list.

  The BI Beans take advantage of all of the new OLAP functions in the database, including ranking, lag, lead, and windowing. End users can create powerful queries that ask sophisticated analytical questions without knowing SQL at all.

- Generating custom measures. You can define new "custom" measures whose values are calculated from data stored within the database. For example, a user might create a custom measure that shows the percent of change in sales from a year ago. The data in the custom measure would be calculated using the lag method on data in the Sales measure. Because a DBA cannot anticipate and create all of the calculations required by all users, the BI Beans enable users to create their own.

UNDERSTANDING THE OLAP API

OLAP applications typically have object-oriented user interfaces where users manipulate objects that represent organized groupings of their data. Thus, there is a natural relationship between an object-oriented user interface and an object-oriented API such as the Oracle OLAP API. The OLAP API exploits this natural relationship by providing objects that match the end-user behavior that an application needs.

Object-oriented languages such as Java manipulate data by applying methods on objects. This approach enables the objects to maintain a current state and support incremental modifications to that state. This approach provides excellent support for common OLAP actions such as drill and rotate.

For example, a central activity for users of OLAP applications is refining queries. A user has a question in mind and devises a query to answer that question. In most cases, the initial results of the query prompt the user to want to dig deeper for a solution, perhaps by drilling to see more detailed data or by rotating the report to highlight correlations in the data. The OLAP API is able to use the result of one query as the input to the next query.

How the OLAP API Accesses Multidimensional Data

The OLAP API accesses the data through the OLAP Catalog, that is, the relational tables that contain OLAP metadata. The application does not need to be aware of whether the data is located in relational tables or in an analytic workspace, nor does it need to know the mechanism for accessing that data.

Oracle OLAP translates all queries from the OLAP API into SQL; when a query is issued through the OLAP API, the SQL generator in Oracle OLAP issues a SELECT statement against a relational table or view. This has several advantages for application developers:

- The difficult task of writing the complex SQL needed to resolve multidimensional queries, and even more difficult task of optimizing that complex SQL, is left for Oracle OLAP to do. Application developers can be more productive writing in the OLAP API, which is designed for OLAP.
- Updates to SQL and the OLAP DML will be incorporated into new versions of the OLAP API. Applications can make use of new analytic and performance features without recoding.

Figure 13.4 shows how a query in the OLAP API that uses data from both a multidimensional workspace object and a relational table is resolved.

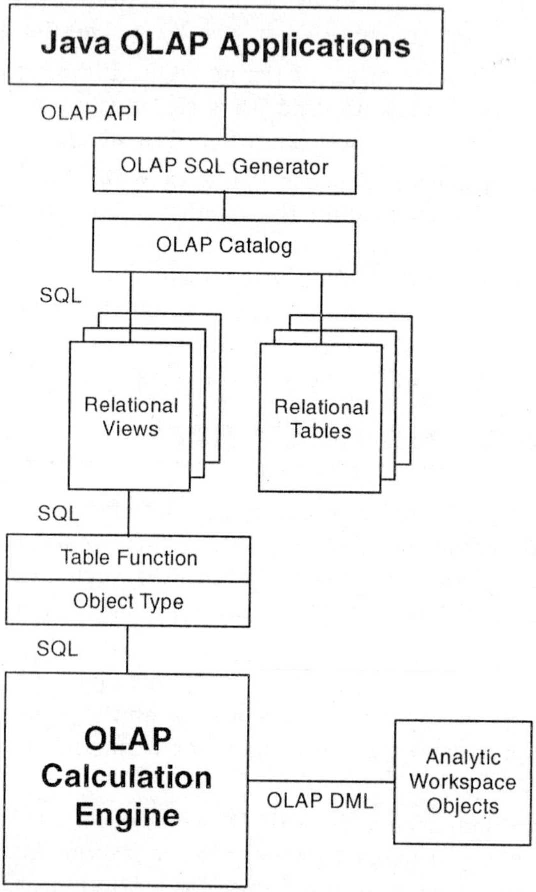

Figure 13.4 Accessing Relational and Multidimensional Data Using the OLAP API.

As an alternative access method, the OLAP API provides a way for a Java application to directly manipulate workspace data, without the need for any metadata and without the use of the OLAP API data manipulation classes. The Java application uses the `SPLExecutor` class in the OLAP API to send DML commands directly to Oracle OLAP for execution in the workspace.

Whichever access method is used, the application establishes a connection, opens the workspace, accesses the data (either through MDM metadata or through `SPLExecutor`), closes the workspace, and closes the connection.

Intelligent Caching

Analytical queries are by nature iterative. An analyst formulates a query, sees the results, and then formulates other queries based on those results. Since the likelihood is very high in business analysis of needing the same data to answer subsequent queries, the OLAP API caches the metadata so that it is available throughout the session without fetching it again. Moreover, the OLAP API defines the result set of a query geometrically. Using multidimensional cursors, the OLAP API can randomly access disparate regions of the result set. This allows an application to retrieve just the data currently of interest instead of all of the data in the result set. For example, you might scroll to the end of a page without having to fetch all of the data on the page.

To acquire data from a data warehouse, the OLAP API generates SQL statements. Data fetches use many of the newest innovations in Oracle9*i*, including concatenated rollup, scrollable cursors, and query rewrite.

Calculation Capabilities

The OLAP API generates SQL commands to select and manipulate data stored in the relational tables. These SQL commands can include the "N-pass" functions, such as `RANK`, `PERCENTILE`, `TOPN`, `BOTTOMN`, `LAG`, `LEAD`, `SUM`, `AVG`, `MIN`, `MAX`, `COUNT`, and `STDDEV`.

The OLAP API provides expanded calculation capabilities beyond those that can be handled efficiently in other OLAP solutions, such as:

- Totals broken out by multiple attributes
- Suppression of NA and zero rows, columns, and pages
- Row and column calculations
- Union dimensions
- Measures as dimensions
- Inter-row calculations such as the following book-to-bill ratio:

  ```
  Balance(Account "BOOKED", Period "PRIOR")/ Balance(Account "BILLED",
  Period "LAST")
  ```
- Asymmetric queries.

The OLAP engine performs additional calculations, such as:

- Modeling
- Forecasting
- What-if scenarios.

These types of analysis can be performed on data in the analytic workspace.

Example 13.1 : Selecting Values

This OLAP API code fragment demonstrates the selection of dimension values based on the data values of a measure. The Sales measure has four dimensions. The Geography, Channel, and Time dimensions are limited to one member each, then Product members are selected with Sales values greater than 20,000,000.

```
Source geographySel = geography.selectValue("BOSTON");
Source channelSel = channel.selectValue("TOTALCHANNEL");
Source timeSel = time.selectValue("1996");
Source prodSel = product.select(salesSel.gt(20000000));
Source result = sales.join(geographySel).
      join(channelSel).join(timeSel).join(prodSel);
```

❑❑❑

14 USING PARALLEL EXECUTION

INTRODUCTION TO PARALLEL EXECUTION TUNING

Parallel execution dramatically reduces response time for data-intensive operations on large databases typically associated with decision support systems (DSS) and data warehouses. You can also implement parallel execution on certain types of online transaction processing (OLTP) and hybrid systems. Parallel execution improves processing for:

- Queries requiring large table scans, joins, or partitioned index scans
- Creation of large indexes
- Creation of large tables (including materialized views)
- Bulk inserts, updates, merges, and deletes.

You can also use parallel execution to access object types within an Oracle database. For example, you can use parallel execution to access large objects (LOBs).

Parallel execution benefits systems with all of the following characteristics:

- Symmetric multiprocessors (SMPs), clusters, or massively parallel systems
- Sufficient I/O bandwidth
- Underutilized or intermittently used CPUs (for example, systems where CPU usage is typically less than 30%)
- Sufficient memory to support additional memory-intensive processes, such as sorts, hashing, and I/O buffers.

If your system lacks any of these characteristics, parallel execution might not significantly improve performance. In fact, parallel execution may reduce system performance on overutilized systems or systems with small I/O bandwidth.

When to Implement Parallel Execution

Parallel execution provides the greatest performance improvements in DSS and data warehousing environments. OLTP systems also benefit from parallel execution, but usually only during batch processing.

During the day, most OLTP systems should probably not use parallel execution. During off-hours, however, parallel execution can effectively process high-volume batch operations. For example, a bank might use parallelized batch programs to perform millions of updates to apply interest to accounts.

Operations That Can Be Parallelized

The Oracle server can use parallel execution for any of the following:

- Access methods

  For example, table scans, index full scans, and partitioned index range scans.

- Join methods

  For example, nested loop, sort merge, hash, and star transformation.

- DDL statements

  `CREATE TABLE AS SELECT`, `CREATE INDEX`, `REBUILD INDEX`, `REBUILD INDEX PARTITION`, and `MOVE SPLIT COALESCE PARTITION`

- DML statements

  For example, `INSERT AS SELECT`, updates, deletes, and `MERGE` operations.

- Miscellaneous SQL operations

  For example, `GROUP BY`, `NOT IN`, `SELECT DISTINCT`, `UNION`, `UNION ALL`, `CUBE`, and `ROLLUP`, as well as aggregate and table functions.

The Parallel Execution Server Pool

When an instance starts up, Oracle creates a pool of parallel execution servers which are available for any parallel operation. The initialization parameter `PARALLEL_MIN_SERVERS` specifies the number of parallel execution servers that Oracle creates at instance startup.

When executing a parallel operation, the parallel execution coordinator obtains parallel execution servers from the pool and assigns them to the operation. If necessary, Oracle can create additional parallel execution servers for the operation. These parallel execution servers remain with the operation throughout job execution, then become available for other operations. After the statement has been processed completely, the parallel execution servers return to the pool.

NOTE *The parallel execution coordinator and the parallel execution servers can only service one statement at a time. A parallel execution coordinator cannot coordinate, for example, a parallel query and a parallel DML statement at the same time.*

When a user issues a SQL statement, the optimizer decides whether to execute the operations in parallel and determines the degree of parallelism (DOP) for each operation. You can specify the number of parallel execution servers required for an operation in various ways.

If the optimizer targets the statement for parallel processing, the following sequence of events takes place:

1. The SQL statement's foreground process becomes a parallel execution coordinator.
2. The parallel execution coordinator obtains as many parallel execution servers as needed (determined by the DOP) from the server pool or creates new parallel execution servers as needed.
3. Oracle executes the statement as a sequence of operations. Each operation is performed in parallel, if possible.
4. When statement processing is completed, the coordinator returns any resulting data to the user process that issued the statement and returns the parallel execution servers to the server pool.

The parallel execution coordinator calls upon the parallel execution servers during the execution of the SQL statement, not during the parsing of the statement. Therefore, when parallel execution is used with the shared server, the server process that processes the EXECUTE call of a user's statement becomes the parallel execution coordinator for the statement.

Variations in the Number of Parallel Execution Servers

If the number of parallel operations processed concurrently by an instance changes significantly, Oracle automatically changes the number of parallel execution servers in the pool.

If the number of parallel operations increases, Oracle creates additional parallel execution servers to handle incoming requests. However, Oracle never creates more parallel execution servers for an instance than the value specified by the initialization parameter PARALLEL_MAX_SERVERS.

If the number of parallel operations decreases, Oracle terminates any parallel execution servers that have been idle for a threshold period of time. Oracle does not reduce the size of the pool less than the value of PARALLEL_MIN_SERVERS, no matter how long the parallel execution servers have been idle.

Processing Without Enough Parallel Execution Servers

Oracle can process a parallel operation with fewer than the requested number of processes.

If all parallel execution servers in the pool are occupied and the maximum number of parallel execution servers have been started, the parallel execution coordinator switches to serial processing.

How Parallel Execution Servers Communicate

To execute a query in parallel, Oracle generally creates a producer queue server and a consumer server. The producer queue server retrieves rows from tables and the consumer server performs operations such as join, sort, DML, and DDL on these rows. Each server in the producer execution process set has a connection to each server in the consumer set. This means that the number of virtual connections between parallel execution servers increases as the square of the DOP.

Each communication channel has at least one, and sometimes up to four memory buffers. Multiple memory buffers facilitate asynchronous communication among the parallel execution servers.

A single-instance environment uses at most three buffers for each communication channel. An Oracle Real Application Clusters environment uses at most four buffers for each channel. Figure 14.1 illustrates message buffers and how producer parallel execution servers connect to consumer parallel execution servers.

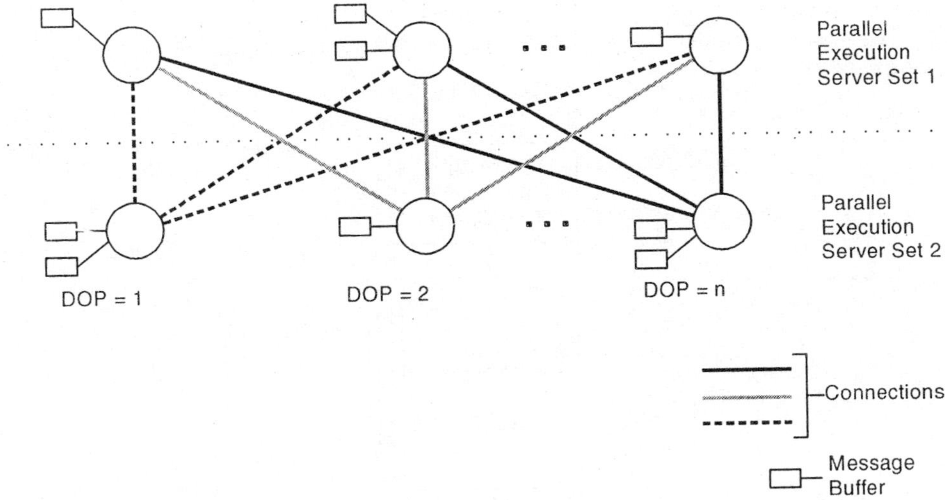

Figure 14.1 Parallel Execution Server Connections and Buffers.

When a connection is between two processes on the same instance, the servers communicate by passing the buffers back and forth. When the connection is between processes in different instances, the messages are sent by using external high-speed network protocols. In figure 14.1, the DOP is equal to the number of parallel execution servers, which in this case is *n*. figure 14.1 does not show the parallel execution coordinator. Each parallel execution server actually has an additional connection to the parallel execution coordinator.

Parallelizing SQL Statements

Each SQL statement undergoes an optimization and parallelization process when it is parsed. When the data changes, if a more optimal execution or parallelization plan becomes available, Oracle can automatically adapt to the new situation.

After the optimizer determines the execution plan of a statement, the parallel execution coordinator determines the parallelization method for each operation in the plan. For example, the parallelization method might be to parallelize a full table scan by block range or parallelize an index range scan by partition. The coordinator must decide whether an operation can be performed in parallel and, if so, how many parallel execution servers to enlist. The number of parallel execution servers is the DOP.

Dividing Work Among Parallel Execution Servers

The parallel execution coordinator examines the redistribution requirements of each operation. An operation's redistribution requirement is the way in which the rows operated on by the operation must be divided or redistributed among the parallel execution servers.

After determining the redistribution requirement for each operation in the execution plan, the optimizer determines the order in which the operations must be performed. With this information, the optimizer determines the data flow of the statement.

Figure 14.2 illustrates the data flow for a query to join the `employees` and `departments` tables:

```
SELECT department_name, MAX(salary), AVG(salary)
FROM employees, departments
WHERE employees.department_id = departments.department_id
GROUP BY department_name;
```

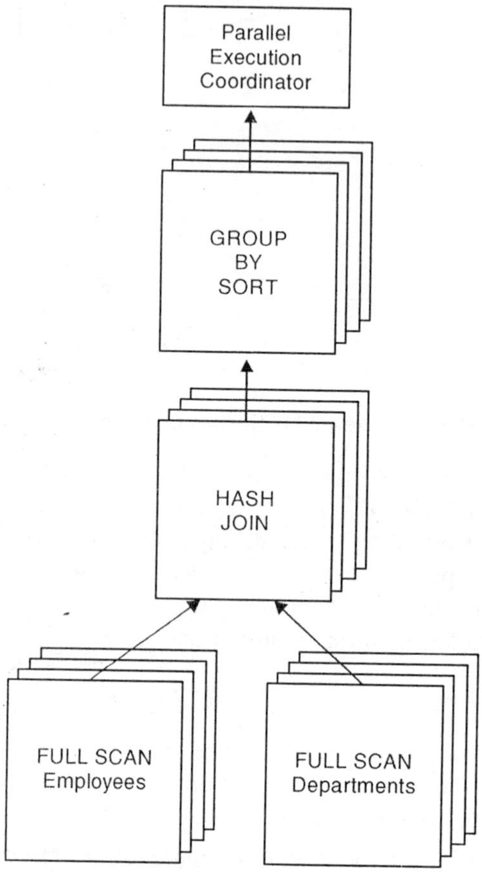

Figure 14.2 Data Flow Diagram for a Join of EMPLOYEES and DEPARTMENTS.

Parallelism Between Operations

Operations that require the output of other operations are known as parent operations. In figure 14.2 the GROUP BY SORT operation is the parent of the HASH JOIN operation because GROUP BY SORT requires the HASH JOIN output.

Parent operations can begin consuming rows as soon as the child operations have produced rows. In the previous example, while the parallel execution servers are producing rows in the FULL SCAN dept operation, another set of parallel execution servers can begin to perform the HASH JOIN operation to consume the rows.

Each of the two operations performed concurrently is given its own set of parallel execution servers. Therefore, both query operations and the data flow tree itself have parallelism. The parallelism of an individual operation is called intraoperation parallelism and the parallelism between operations in a data flow tree is called interoperation parallelism.

Due to the producer-consumer nature of the Oracle server's operations, only two operations in a given tree need to be performed simultaneously to minimize execution time.

To illustrate intraoperation and interoperation parallelism, consider the following statement:

```
SELECT * FROM employees ORDER BY last_name;
```

The execution plan implements a full scan of the `employees` table. This operation is followed by a sorting of the retrieved rows, based on the value of the `last_name` column. For the sake of this example, assume the `last_name` column is not indexed. Also assume that the DOP for the query is set to 4, which means that four parallel execution servers can be active for any given operation.

Figure 14.3 illustrates the parallel execution of the example query.

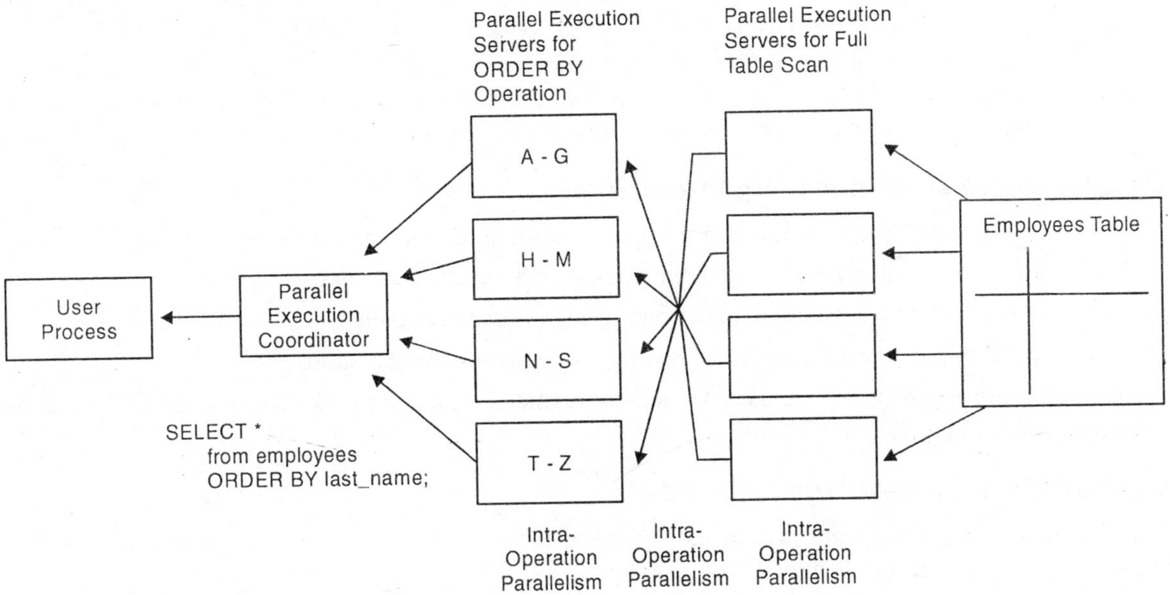

Figure 14.3 Interoperation Parallelism and Dynamic Partitioning.

As you can see from figure 14.3, there are actually eight parallel execution servers involved in the query even though the DOP is 4. This is because a parent and child operator can be performed at the same time (interoperation parallelism).

Also note that all of the parallel execution servers involved in the scan operation send rows to the appropriate parallel execution server performing the `SORT` operation. If a row scanned by a parallel execution server contains a value for the `ename` column between `A` and `G`, that row gets sent to the first `ORDER BY` parallel execution server. When the scan operation is complete, the sorting processes can return the sorted results to the coordinator, which, in turn, returns the complete query results to the user.

NOTE

When a set of parallel execution servers completes its operation, it moves on to operations higher in the data flow. For example, in figure 14.3, if there was another `ORDER BY` operation after the `ORDER BY`, the parallel execution servers performing the table scan would perform the second `ORDER BY` operation after completing the table scan.

TYPES OF PARALLELISM

The following types of parallelism are discussed in this section:

- Parallel query
- Parallel DDL
- Parallel DML
- Parallel execution of functions
- Other types of parallelism.

Parallel Query

You can parallelize queries and subqueries in SELECT statements. You can also parallelize the query portions of DDL statements and DML statements (INSERT, UPDATE, and DELETE).

However, you cannot parallelize the query portion of a DDL or DML statement if it references a remote object. When you issue a parallel DML or DDL statement in which the query portion references a remote object, the operation is automatically executed serially.

Parallel Queries on Index-Organized Tables

The following parallel scan methods are supported on index-organized tables:

- Parallel fast full scan of a nonpartitioned index-organized table
- Parallel fast full scan of a partitioned index-organized table
- Parallel index range scan of a partitioned index-organized table

These scan methods can be used for index-organized tables with overflow areas and for index-organized tables that contain LOBs.

Nonpartitioned Index-Organized Tables

Parallel query on a nonpartitioned index-organized table uses parallel fast full scan. The DOP is determined, in decreasing order of priority, by:

1. A PARALLEL hint (if present)
2. An ALTER SESSION FORCE PARALLEL QUERY statement
3. The parallel degree associated with the table, if the parallel degree is specified in the CREATE TABLE or ALTER TABLE statement

The allocation of work is done by dividing the index segment into a sufficiently large number of block ranges and then assigning the block ranges to parallel execution servers in a demand-driven manner. The overflow blocks corresponding to any row are accessed in a demand-driven manner only by the process which owns that row.

Partitioned Index-Organized Tables

Both index range scan and fast full scan can be performed in parallel. For parallel fast full scan, parallelization is exactly the same as for nonpartitioned index-organized tables. For parallel index range scan on partitioned index-organized tables, the DOP is the minimum of the degree picked up from the previous priority list (like in parallel fast full scan) and the number of partitions in the index-organized table. Depending on the DOP, each parallel execution server gets one or more partitions (assigned in a demand-driven manner), each of which contains the primary key index segment and the associated overflow segment, if any.

Parallel Queries on Object Types

Parallel queries can be performed on object type tables and tables containing object type columns. Parallel query for object types supports all of the features that are available for sequential queries on object types, including:

- Methods on object types
- Attribute access of object types
- Constructors to create object type instances
- Object views
- PL/SQL and OCI queries for object types.

There are no limitations on the size of the object types for parallel queries.

The following restrictions apply to using parallel query for object types.

- A `MAP` function is needed to parallelize queries involving joins and sorts (through `ORDER BY`, `GROUP BY`, or set operations). In the absence of a `MAP` function, the query will automatically be executed serially.
- Parallel queries on nested tables are not supported. Even if the table has a parallel attribute or parallel hints, the query will execute serially.
- Parallel DML and parallel DDL are not supported with object types. DML and DDL statements are always performed serially.

In all cases where the query cannot execute in parallel because of any of these restrictions, the whole query executes serially without giving an error message.

Parallel DDL

This section includes the following topics on parallelism for DDL statements:

- DDL Statements That Can Be Parallelized
- CREATE TABLE ... AS SELECT in Parallel
- Recoverability and Parallel DDL
- Space Management for Parallel DDL

DDL Statements That Can Be Parallelized

You can parallelize DDL statements for tables and indexes that are nonpartitioned or partitioned. Table 14.3 summarizes the operations that can be parallelized in DDL statements.

The parallel DDL statements for nonpartitioned tables and indexes are:

- `CREATE INDEX`
- `CREATE TABLE ... AS SELECT`
- `ALTER INDEX ... REBUILD.`

The parallel DDL statements for partitioned tables and indexes are:

- `CREATE INDEX`
- `CREATE TABLE ... AS SELECT`
- `ALTER TABLE ... MOVE PARTITION`
- `ALTER TABLE ... SPLIT PARTITION`
- `ALTER TABLE ... COALESCE PARTITION`
- `ALTER INDEX ... REBUILD PARTITION`
- `ALTER INDEX ... SPLIT PARTITION.`

This statement can be executed in parallel only if the (global) index partition being split is usable.

All of these DDL operations can be performed in no-logging mode for either parallel or serial execution.

`CREATE TABLE` for an index-organized table can be parallelized either with or without an `AS SELECT` clause.

Different parallelism is used for different operations (see table 14.3). Parallel `CREATE TABLE ... AS SELECT` statements on partitioned tables and parallel `CREATE INDEX` statements on partitioned indexes execute with a DOP equal to the number of partitions.

Partition parallel analyze table is made less necessary by the `ANALYZE {TABLE, INDEX} PARTITION` statements, since parallel analyze of an entire partitioned table can be constructed with multiple user sessions.

Parallel DDL cannot occur on tables with object columns. Parallel DDL cannot occur on non-partitioned tables with `LOB` columns.

CREATE TABLE ... AS SELECT in Parallel

For performance reasons, decision support applications often require large amounts of data to be summarized or rolled up into smaller tables for use with ad hoc, decision support queries. Rollup occurs regularly (such as nightly or weekly) during a short period of system inactivity.

Parallel execution lets you parallelize the query and create operations of creating a table as a subquery from another table or set of tables.

NOTE *Clustered tables cannot be created and populated in parallel.*

Figure 14.4 illustrates creating a table from a subquery in parallel.

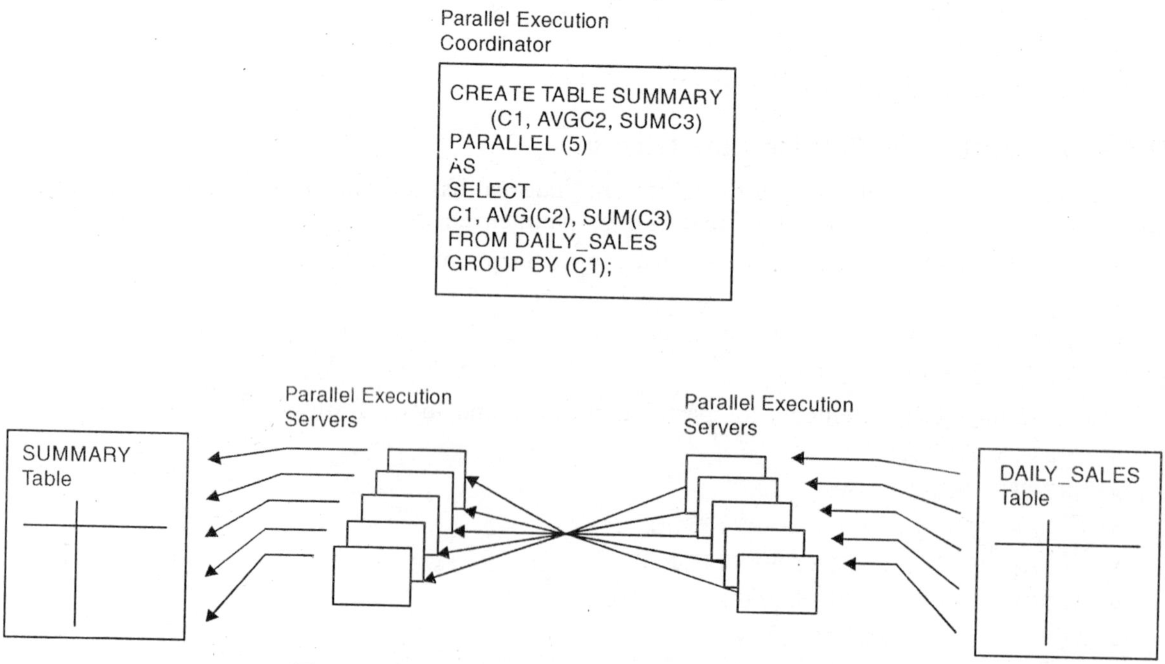

Figure 14.4 Creating a Summary Table in Parallel.

Recoverability and Parallel DDL

When summary table data is derived from other tables' data, recoverability from media failure for the smaller summary table may not be important and can be turned off during creation of the summary table.

If you disable logging during parallel table creation (or any other parallel DDL operation), you should back up the tablespace containing the table once the table is created to avoid loss of the table due to media failure.

Use the `NOLOGGING` clause of the `CREATE TABLE`, `CREATE INDEX`, `ALTER TABLE`, and `ALTER INDEX` statements to disable undo and redo log generation.

Space Management for Parallel DDL

Creating a table or index in parallel has space management implications that affect both the storage space required during a parallel operation and the free space available after a table or index has been created.

Storage Space When Using Dictionary-Managed Tablespaces

When creating a table or index in parallel, each parallel execution server uses the values in the `STORAGE` clause of the `CREATE` statement to create temporary segments to store the rows. Therefore, a table created with a `NEXT` setting of 5 MB and a `PARALLEL DEGREE` of 12 consumes at least 60 megabytes (MB) of storage during table creation because each process starts with an extent of 5 MB. When the parallel execution coordinator combines the segments, some of the segments may be trimmed, and the resulting table may be smaller than the requested 60 MB.

Free Space and Parallel DDL

When you create indexes and tables in parallel, each parallel execution server allocates a new extent and fills the extent with the table or index data. Thus, if you create an index with a DOP of 3, the index will have at least three extents initially. Allocation of extents is the same for rebuilding indexes in parallel and for moving, splitting, or rebuilding partitions in parallel.

Serial operations require the schema object to have at least one extent. Parallel creations require that tables or indexes have at least as many extents as there are parallel execution servers creating the schema object.

When you create a table or index in parallel, it is possible to create pockets of free space—either external or internal fragmentation. This occurs when the temporary segments used by the parallel execution servers are larger than what is needed to store the rows.

- If the unused space in each temporary segment is larger than the value of the `MINIMUM EXTENT` parameter set at the tablespace level, then Oracle trims the unused space when merging rows from all of the temporary segments into the table or index. The unused space is returned to the system free space and can be allocated for new extents, but it cannot be coalesced into a larger segment because it is not contiguous space (external fragmentation).
- If the unused space in each temporary segment is smaller than the value of the `MINIMUM EXTENT` parameter, then unused space cannot be trimmed when the rows in the temporary segments are merged. This unused space is not returned to the system free space; it becomes part of the table or index (internal fragmentation) and is available only for subsequent inserts or for updates that require additional space.

For example, if you specify a DOP of 3 for a `CREATE TABLE ... AS SELECT` statement, but there is only one datafile in the tablespace, then internal fragmentation may occur, as shown in figure 14.5. The pockets of free space within the internal table extents of a datafile cannot be coalesced with other free space and cannot be allocated as extents.

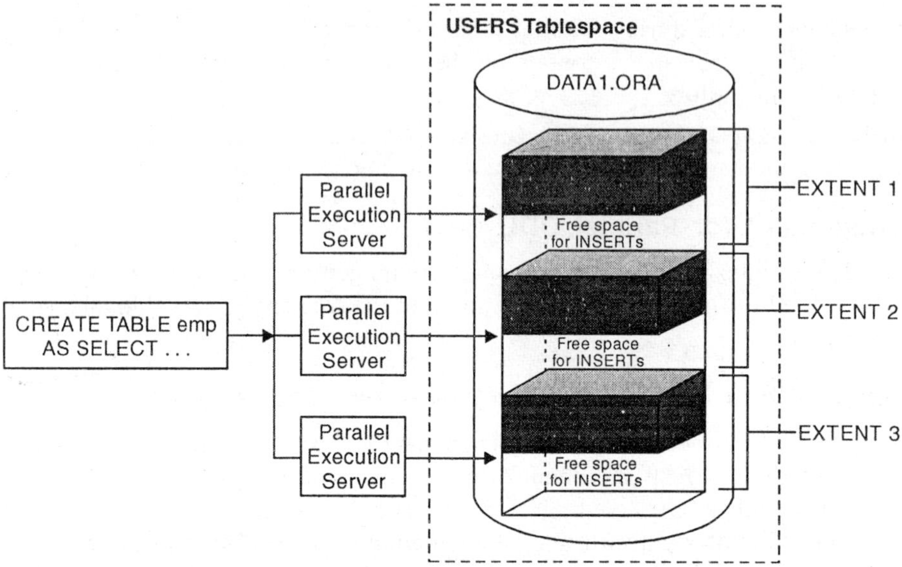

Figure 14.5 Unusable Free Space (Internal Fragmentation).

Parallel DML

Parallel DML (`PARALLEL`, `INSERT`, `UPDATE`, and `DELETE`) uses parallel execution mechanisms to speed up or scale up large DML operations against large database tables and indexes.

NOTE: *Although DML generally includes queries, in this chapter the term DML refers only to inserts, updates, merges, and deletes.*

This section discusses the following parallel DML topics:

- Advantages of parallel DML over manual parallelism
- When to use parallel DML
- Enabling parallel DML
- Transaction restrictions for parallel DML
- Rollback segments
- Recovery for parallel DML
- Space considerations for parallel DML
- Lock and enqueue resources for parallel DML
- Restrictions on parallel DML.

Advantages of Parallel DML over Manual Parallelism

You can parallelize DML operations manually by issuing multiple DML statements simultaneously against different sets of data. For example, you can parallelize manually by:

- Issuing multiple INSERT statements to multiple instances of an Oracle Real Application Clusters to make use of free space from multiple free list blocks.
- Issuing multiple UPDATE and DELETE statements with different key value ranges or rowid ranges.

However, manual parallelism has the following disadvantages:

- It is difficult to use. You have to open multiple sessions (possibly on different instances) and issue multiple statements.
- There is a lack of transactional properties. The DML statements are issued at different times; and, as a result, the changes are done with inconsistent snapshots of the database. To get atomicity, the commit or rollback of the various statements must be coordinated manually (may be across instances).
- The work division is complex. You may have to query the table in order to find out the rowid or key value ranges to correctly divide the work.
- The calculation is complex. The calculation of the degree of parallelism can be complex.
- There is a lack of affinity and resource information. You need to know affinity information to issue the right DML statement at the right instance when running an Oracle Real Application Clusters. You also have to find out about current resource usage to balance workload across instances.

Parallel DML removes these disadvantages by performing inserts, updates, and deletes in parallel automatically.

When to Use Parallel DML

Parallel DML operations are mainly used to speed up large DML operations against large database objects. Parallel DML is useful in a DSS environment where the performance and scalability of accessing large objects are important. Parallel DML complements parallel query in providing you with both querying and updating capabilities for your DSS databases.

The overhead of setting up parallelism makes parallel DML operations infeasible for short OLTP transactions. However, parallel DML operations can speed up batch jobs running in an OLTP database.

Some of the scenarios where parallel DML is used include:

- Refreshing tables in a data warehouse system
- Creating intermediate summary tables
- Using scoring tables
- Updating historical tables
- Running batch jobs.

Refreshing Tables in a Data Warehouse System

In a data warehouse system, large tables need to be refreshed (updated) periodically with new or modified data from the production system. You can do this efficiently by using parallel DML combined with updatable join views. You can also use the MERGE statement.

The data that needs to be refreshed is generally loaded into a temporary table before starting the refresh process. This table contains either new rows or rows that have been updated since the last refresh of the data warehouse. You can use an updatable join view with parallel UPDATE to refresh the updated rows, and you can use an anti-hash join with parallel INSERT to refresh the new rows.

Creating Intermediate Summary Tables

In a DSS environment, many applications require complex computations that involve constructing and manipulating many large intermediate summary tables. These summary tables are often temporary and frequently do not need to be logged. Parallel DML can speed up the operations against these large intermediate tables. One benefit is that you can put incremental results in the intermediate tables and perform parallel update.

In addition, the summary tables may contain cumulative or comparison information which has to persist beyond application sessions; thus, temporary tables are not feasible. Parallel DML operations can speed up the changes to these large summary tables.

Using Scoring Tables

Many DSS applications score customers periodically based on a set of criteria. The scores are usually stored in large DSS tables. The score information is then used in making a decision, for example, inclusion in a mailing list.

This scoring activity queries and updates a large number of rows in the large table. Parallel DML can speed up the operations against these large tables.

Updating Historical Tables

Historical tables describe the business transactions of an enterprise over a recent time interval. Periodically, the DBA deletes the set of oldest rows and inserts a set of new rows into the table. Parallel `INSERT ... SELECT` and parallel `DELETE` operations can speed up this rollover task.

Although you can also use parallel direct loader (SQL*Loader) to insert bulk data from an external source, parallel `INSERT ... SELECT` is faster for inserting data that already exists in another table in the database.

Dropping a partition can also be used to delete old rows. However, to do this, the table has to be partitioned by date and with the appropriate time interval.

Running Batch Jobs

Batch jobs executed in an OLTP database during off hours have a fixed time window in which the jobs must complete. A good way to ensure timely job completion is to parallelize their operations. As the work load increases, more machine resources can be added; the scaleup property of parallel operations ensures that the time constraint can be met.

Enabling Parallel DML

A DML statement can be parallelized only if you have explicitly enabled parallel DML in the session with the `ENABLE PARALLEL DML` clause of the `ALTER SESSION` statement. This mode is required because parallel DML and serial DML have different locking, transaction, and disk space requirements.

The default mode of a session is `DISABLE PARALLEL DML`. When parallel DML is disabled, no DML will be executed in parallel even if the `PARALLEL` hint is used.

When parallel DML is enabled in a session, all DML statements in this session will be considered for parallel execution. However, even if parallel DML is enabled, the DML operation may still execute serially if there are no parallel hints or no tables with a parallel attribute or if restrictions on parallel operations are violated.

The session's PARALLEL DML mode does not influence the parallelism of SELECT statements, DDL statements, and the query portions of DML statements. Thus, if this mode is not set, the DML operation is not parallelized, but scans or join operations within the DML statement may still be parallelized.

Transaction Restrictions for Parallel DML

To execute a DML operation in parallel, the parallel execution coordinator acquires or spawns parallel execution servers, and each parallel execution server executes a portion of the work under its own parallel process transaction.

- Each parallel execution server creates a different parallel process transaction.
- To reduce contention on the rollback segments, only a few parallel process transactions should reside in the same rollback segment. See "Rollback Segments".

The coordinator also has its own coordinator transaction, which can have its own rollback segment. In order to ensure user-level transactional atomicity, the coordinator uses a two-phase commit protocol to commit the changes performed by the parallel process transactions.

A session that is enabled for parallel DML may put transactions in the session in a special mode: If any DML statement in a transaction modifies a table in parallel, no subsequent serial or parallel query or DML statement can access the same table again in that transaction. This means that the results of parallel modifications cannot be seen during the transaction.

Serial or parallel statements that attempt to access a table that has already been modified in parallel within the same transaction are rejected with an error message.

If a PL/SQL procedure or block is executed in a parallel DML enabled session, then this rule applies to statements in the procedure or block.

Rollback Segments

Oracle assigns transactions to rollback segments that have the fewest active transactions. To speed up both forward and undo operations, you should create and bring online enough rollback segments so that at most two parallel process transactions are assigned to one rollback segment.

The SET TRANSACTION USE ROLLBACK SEGMENT statement is ignored when parallel DML is used because parallel DML requires more than one rollback segment for performance.

You should create the rollback segments in tablespaces that have enough space for them to extend when necessary. You can then set the MAXEXTENTS storage parameters for the rollback segments to UNLIMITED. Also, set the OPTIMAL value for the rollback segments so that after the parallel DML transactions commit, the rollback segments are shrunk to the OPTIMAL size.

Recovery for Parallel DML

The time required to roll back a parallel DML operation is roughly equal to the time it takes to perform the forward operation.

Oracle supports parallel rollback after transaction and process failures, and after instance and system failures. Oracle can parallelize both the rolling forward stage and the rolling back stage of transaction recovery.

Transaction Recovery for User-Issued Rollback

A user-issued rollback in a transaction failure due to statement error is performed in parallel by the parallel execution coordinator and the parallel execution servers. The rollback takes approximately the same amount of time as the forward transaction.

Process Recovery

Recovery from the failure of a parallel execution coordinator or parallel execution server is performed by the PMON process. If a parallel execution server or a parallel execution coordinator fails, PMON rolls back the work from that process and all other processes in the transaction roll back their changes.

System Recovery

Recovery from a system failure requires a new startup. Recovery is performed by the SMON process and any recovery server processes spawned by SMON. Parallel DML statements may be recovered by using parallel rollback. If the initialization parameter `COMPATIBLE` is set to 8.1.3 or greater, Fast-Start On-Demand Rollback enables terminated transactions to be recovered, on demand one block at a time.

Instance Recovery (Oracle Real Application Clusters)

Recovery from an instance failure in Oracle Real Application Clusters is performed by the recovery processes (that is, the SMON processes and any recovery server processes they spawn) of other live instances. Each recovery process of the live instances can recover the parallel execution coordinator or parallel execution server transactions of the failed instance independently.

Space Considerations for Parallel DML

Parallel `UPDATE` uses the space in the existing object, while direct-path `INSERT` gets new segments for the data.

Space usage characteristics may be different in parallel than sequential execution because multiple concurrent child transactions modify the object.

Lock and Enqueue Resources for Parallel DML

A parallel DML operation's lock and enqueue resource requirements are very different from the serial DML requirements. Parallel DML holds many more locks, so you should increase the starting value of the `ENQUEUE_RESOURCES` and `DML_LOCKS` parameters.

Restrictions on Parallel DML

The following restrictions apply to parallel DML (including direct-path `INSERT`):

- Intra-partition parallelism for `UPDATE`, `MERGE`, and `DELETE` operations require that the `COMPATIBLE` initialization parameter be set to 9.2 or greater.
- `INSERT`, `UPDATE`, `MERGE`, and `DELETE` operations on nonpartitioned tables are not parallelized if there is a bitmap index on the table. If the table is partitioned and there is a bitmap index on the table, the degree of parallelism will be restricted to at most the number of partitions accessed.
- A transaction can contain multiple parallel DML statements that modify different tables, but after a parallel DML statement modifies a table, no subsequent serial or parallel statement (DML or query) can access the same table again in that transaction.
    - This restriction also exists after a serial direct-path `INSERT` statement: no subsequent SQL statement (DML or query) can access the modified table during that transaction.
    - Queries that access the same table are allowed before a parallel DML or direct-path `INSERT` statement, but not after.

  - Any serial or parallel statements attempting to access a table that has already been modified by a parallel `UPDATE`, `DELETE`, or `MERGE`, or a direct-path `INSERT` during the same transaction are rejected with an error message.
- If the initialization parameter `ROW_LOCKING` is set to `intent`, then inserts, updates, merges, and deletes are not parallelized (regardless of the serializable mode).
- Parallel DML operations cannot be done on tables with triggers.
- Replication functionality is not supported for parallel DML.
- Parallel DML cannot occur in the presence of certain constraints: self-referential integrity, delete cascade, and deferred integrity. In addition, for direct-path `INSERT`, there is no support for any referential integrity.
- Parallel DML can be done on tables with object columns provided you are not touching the object columns.
- Parallel DML can be done on tables with `LOB` columns provided the table is partitioned. However, intra-partition parallelism is not supported.
- A transaction involved in a parallel DML operation cannot be or become a distributed transaction.
- Clustered tables are not supported.

Violations of these restrictions cause the statement to execute serially without warnings or error messages (except for the restriction on statements accessing the same table in a transaction, which can cause error messages). For example, an update is serialized if it is on a nonpartitioned table.

Partitioning Key Restriction

You can only update the partitioning key of a partitioned table to a new value if the update does not cause the row to move to a new partition. The update is possible if the table is defined with the row movement clause enabled.

Function Restrictions

The function restrictions for parallel DML are the same as those for parallel DDL and parallel query.

Data Integrity Restrictions

This section describes the interactions of integrity constraints and parallel DML statements.

NOT NULL and CHECK

These types of integrity constraints are allowed. They are not a problem for parallel DML because they are enforced on the column and row level, respectively.

UNIQUE and PRIMARY KEY

These types of integrity constraints are allowed.

FOREIGN KEY (Referential Integrity)

Restrictions for referential integrity occur whenever a DML operation on one table could cause a recursive DML operation on another table. These restrictions also apply when, in order to perform an integrity check, it is necessary to see simultaneously all changes made to the object being modified.

Table 14.1 lists all of the operations that are possible on tables that are involved in referential integrity constraints.

Table 14.1 Referential Integrity Restrictions

DML Statement	Issued on Parent	Issued on Child	Self-Referential
INSERT	(Not applicable)	Not parallelized	Not parallelized
MERGE	(Not applicable)	Not parallelized	Not parallelized
UPDATE No Action	Supported	Supported	Not parallelized
DELETE No Action	Supported	Supported	Not parallelized
DELETE Cascade	Not parallelized	(Not applicable)	Not parallelized

Delete Cascade

Delete on tables having a foreign key with delete cascade is not parallelized because parallel execution servers will try to delete rows from multiple partitions (parent and child tables).

Self-Referential Integrity

DML on tables with self-referential integrity constraints is not parallelized if the referenced keys (primary keys) are involved. For DML on all other columns, parallelism is possible.

Deferrable Integrity Constraints

If any deferrable constraints apply to the table being operated on, the DML operation will not be parallelized.

Trigger Restrictions

A DML operation will not be parallelized if the affected tables contain enabled triggers that may get fired as a result of the statement. This implies that DML statements on tables that are being replicated will not be parallelized.

Relevant triggers must be disabled in order to parallelize DML on the table. Note that, if you enable or disable triggers, the dependent shared cursors are invalidated.

Distributed Transaction Restrictions

A DML operation cannot be parallelized if it is in a distributed transaction or if the DML or the query operation is against a remote object.

Examples of Distributed Transaction Parallelization

This section contains several examples of distributed transaction processing.

Example 14.1 : Distributed Transaction Parallelization

In this example, the DML statement queries a remote object:

```
INSERT /* APPEND PARALLEL (t3,2) */ INTO t3 SELECT * FROM t4@dblink;
```

The query operation is executed serially without notification because it references a remote object.

Example 14.2 : Distributed Transaction Parallelization

In this example, the DML operation is applied to a remote object:

```
DELETE /*+ PARALLEL (t1, 2) */ FROM t1@dblink;
```

The DELETE operation is not parallelized because it references a remote object.

Example 14.3 : Distributed Transaction Parallelization

In this example, the DML operation is in a distributed transaction:

```
SELECT * FROM t1@dblink;
DELETE /*+ PARALLEL (t2,2) */ FROM t2;
COMMIT;
```

The DELETE operation is not parallelized because it occurs in a distributed transaction (which is started by the SELECT statement).

Parallel Execution of Functions

SQL statements can contain user-defined functions written in PL/SQL, in Java, or as external procedures in C that can appear as part of the SELECT list, SET clause, or WHERE clause. When the SQL statement is parallelized, these functions are executed on a per-row basis by the parallel execution server. Any PL/SQL package variables or Java static attributes used by the function are entirely private to each individual parallel execution process and are newly initialized when each row is processed, rather than being copied from the original session. Because of this, not all functions will generate correct results if executed in parallel.

User-written table functions can appear in the statement's FROM list. These functions act like source tables in that they output rows. Table functions are initialized once during the statement at the start of each parallel execution process. All variables are entirely private to the parallel execution process.

Functions in Parallel Queries

In a SELECT statement or a subquery in a DML or DDL statement, a user-written function may be executed in parallel if it has been declared with the PARALLEL_ENABLE keyword, if it is declared in a package or type and has a PRAGMA RESTRICT_REFERENCES that indicates all of WNDS, RNPS, and WNPS, or if it is declared with CREATE FUNCTION and the system can analyze the body of the PL/SQL code and determine that the code neither writes to the database nor reads or modifies package variables.

Other parts of a query or subquery can sometimes execute in parallel even if a given function execution must remain serial.

Functions in Parallel DML and DDL Statements

In a parallel DML or DDL statement, as in a parallel query, a user-written function may be executed in parallel if it has been declared with the PARALLEL_ENABLE keyword, if it is declared in a package or type and has a PRAGMA RESTRICT_REFERENCES that indicates all of RNDS, WNDS, RNPS, and WNPS, or if it is declared with CREATE FUNCTION and the system can analyze the body of the PL/SQL code and determine that the code neither reads nor writes to the database or reads nor modifies package variables.

For a parallel DML statement, any function call that cannot be executed in parallel causes the entire DML statement to be executed serially.

For an INSERT ... SELECT or CREATE TABLE ... AS SELECT statement, function calls in the query portion are parallelized according to the parallel query rules in the prior paragraph. The query may be parallelized even if the remainder of the statement must execute serially, or vice versa.

Other Types of Parallelism

In addition to parallel SQL execution, Oracle can use parallelism for the following types of operations:

- Parallel recovery
- Parallel propagation (replication)
- Parallel load (the SQL*Loader utility).

Like parallel SQL, parallel recovery and propagation are performed by a parallel execution coordinator and multiple parallel execution servers. Parallel load, however, uses a different mechanism.

The behavior of the parallel execution coordinator and parallel execution servers may differ, depending on what kind of operation they perform (SQL, recovery, or propagation). For example, if all parallel execution servers in the pool are occupied and the maximum number of parallel execution servers have been started:

- In parallel SQL, the parallel execution coordinator switches to serial processing.
- In parallel propagation, the parallel execution coordinator returns an error.

For a given session, the parallel execution coordinator coordinates only one kind of operation. A parallel execution coordinator can not coordinate, for example, parallel SQL and parallel recovery or propagation at the same time.

INITIALIZING AND TUNING PARAMETERS FOR PARALLEL EXECUTION

You can initialize and automatically tune parallel execution by setting the initialization parameter `PARALLEL_AUTOMATIC_TUNING` to `true`. Once enabled, automated parallel execution controls values for all parameters related to parallel execution. These parameters affect several aspects of server processing, namely, the DOP, the adaptive multiuser feature, and memory sizing.

With parallel automatic tuning enabled, Oracle determines parameter settings for each environment based on the number of CPUs on your system at database startup and the value set for `PARALLEL_THREADS_PER_CPU`. The default values Oracle sets for parallel execution processing when `PARALLEL_AUTOMATIC_TUNING` is `true` are usually optimal for most environments. In most cases, Oracle's automatically derived settings are at least as effective as manually derived settings.

You can also manually tune parallel execution parameters; however, Oracle recommends using automated parallel execution. Manual tuning of parallel execution is more complex than using automated tuning for two reasons: manual parallel execution tuning requires more attentive administration than automated tuning, and manual tuning is prone to user-load and system-resource miscalculations.

Initializing and tuning parallel execution involves the following steps:

- Selecting automated or manual tuning of parallel execution
- Using automatically derived parameter settings
- Setting the degree of parallelism
- How Oracle determines the degree of parallelism for operations
- Balancing the workload
- Parallelization rules for SQL statements

- Enabling parallelism for tables and queries
- Degree of parallelism and adaptive multiuser: how they interact
- Forcing parallel execution for a session
- Controlling performance with the degree of parallelism.

Selecting Automated or Manual Tuning of Parallel Execution

There are several ways to initialize and tune parallel execution. You can make your environment fully automated for parallel execution. As mentioned, by setting PARALLEL_AUTOMATIC_TUNING to true. You can further customize this type of environment by overriding some of the automatically derived values.

You can also leave PARALLEL_AUTOMATIC_TUNING at its default value of false and manually set the parameters that affect parallel execution. For most OLTP environments and other types of systems that would not benefit from parallel execution, do not enable parallel execution.

NOTE: *Well-established, manually tuned systems that achieve desired resource-use patterns might not benefit from automated parallel execution.*

Using Automatically Derived Parameter Settings

When PARALLEL_AUTOMATIC_TUNING is true, Oracle automatically sets other parameters, as shown in table 14.2. For most systems, you do not need to make further adjustments to have an adequately tuned, fully automated parallel execution environment.

Table 14.2 Parameters Affected by PARALLEL_AUTOMATIC_TUNING

Parameter	Default	ifPARALLEL_AUTOMATIC_TUNING = true	Comments
PARALLEL_ADAPTIVE_MULTI_USER	false	true	
PROCESSES	6	The greater of: 1.2 x PARALLEL_MAX_SERVERS or PARALLEL_MAX_SERVERS + 6 + 5 + (CPUs × 4)	Value is forced up to minimum if PARALLEL_ AUTOMATIC_TUNING is true.
SESSIONS	(PROCESSES × 1.1) + 5	(PROCESSES × 1.1) + 5	Automatic parallel tuning indirectly affects SESSIONS. If you do not set SESSIONS, Oracle sets it based on the value for PROCESSES.
PARALLEL_MAX_SERVERS	5	CPU × 10	Use this limit to maximize the number of processes that parallel execution uses. The value for this parameter is port-specific so processing can vary from system to system.

LARGE_POOL_SIZE	None	PARALLEL_EXECUTION_POOL + Shared Server heap requirements + Backup buffer requests + 300 KB	Oracle does not allocate parallel execution buffers from the SHARED_POOL when PARALLEL_AUTOMATIC_TUNING is set to false.
PARALLEL_EXECUTION_MESSAGE_SIZE	2 KB (port specific)	4 KB (port specific)	Default increases because Oracle allocates memory from the LARGE_POOL.

As mentioned, you can manually adjust the parameters shown in table 14.2, even if you set PARALLEL_AUTOMATIC_TUNING to true. You might need to do this if you have a highly customized environment or if your system does not perform optimally using the completely automated settings.

Setting the Degree of Parallelism

The parallel execution coordinator may enlist two or more of the instance's parallel execution servers to process an SQL statement. The number of parallel execution servers associated with a single operation is known as the degree of parallelism.

The DOP is specified in the following ways:

- At the statement level:
  - With hints
  - With the PARALLEL clause
- At the session level by issuing the ALTER SESSION FORCE PARALLEL statement
- At the table level in the table's definition
- At the index level in the index's definition.

The following example shows a statement that sets the DOP to 4 on a table:

```
ALTER TABLE employees PARALLEL 4;
```

This next example sets the DOP on an index to 4:

```
ALTER INDEX iemployees PARALLEL 4;
```

This last example sets a hint to 4 on a query:

```
SELECT /*+ PARALLEL(employees, 4) */ COUNT(*) FROM employees;
```

Note that the DOP applies directly only to intraoperation parallelism. If interoperation parallelism is possible, the total number of parallel execution servers for a statement can be twice the specified DOP. No more than two operations can be performed simultaneously.

Parallel execution is designed to effectively use multiple CPUs and disks to answer queries quickly. When multiple users employ parallel execution at the same time, available CPU, memory, and disk resources may be quickly exhausted. Oracle provides several ways to deal with resource utilization in conjunction with parallel execution, including:

- The adaptive multiuser algorithm, which reduces the DOP as the load on the system increases. You can turn this option on with the PARALLEL_ADAPTIVE_MULTI_USER parameter of the ALTER SYSTEM statement or in your initialization file.

- User resource limits and profiles, which allow you to set limits on the amount of various system resources available to each user as part of a user's security domain.
- The Database Resource Manager, which enables you to allocate resources to different groups of users.

How Oracle Determines the Degree of Parallelism for Operations

The parallel execution coordinator determines the DOP by considering several specifications. The coordinator:

1. Checks for hints or a `PARALLEL` clause specified in the SQL statement itself
2. Checks for a session value set by the `ALTER SESSION FORCE PARALLEL` statement
3. Looks at the table's or index's definition

After a DOP is found in one of these specifications, it becomes the DOP for the operation.

Hints, `PARALLEL` clauses, table or index definitions, and default values only determine the number of parallel execution servers that the coordinator requests for a given operation. The actual number of parallel execution servers used depends upon how many processes are available in the parallel execution server pool and whether interoperation parallelism is possible.

NOTE *You can specify hints in an SQL statement to set the DOP for a table or index and for the caching behavior of the operation.*

- The `PARALLEL` hint is used only for operations on tables. You can use it to parallelize queries and DML statements (`INSERT`, `UPDATE`, and `DELETE`).
- The `PARALLEL_INDEX` hint parallelizes an index range scan of a partitioned index. (In an index operation, the `PARALLEL` hint is not valid and is ignored.)

Table and Index Definitions

You can specify the DOP within a table or index definition by using one of the following statements: `CREATE TABLE`, `ALTER TABLE`, `CREATE INDEX`, or `ALTER INDEX`.

Default Degree of Parallelism

The default DOP is used when you ask to parallelize an operation but you do not specify a DOP in a hint or within the definition of a table or index. The default DOP is appropriate for most applications.

The default DOP for a SQL statement is determined by the following factors:

- The number of CPUs for all Oracle Real Application Clusters instances in the system, and the value of the parameter `PARALLEL_THREADS_PER_CPU`.
- For parallelizing by partition, the number of partitions that will be accessed, based on partition pruning.
- For parallel DML operations with global index maintenance, the minimum number of transaction free lists among all the global indexes to be updated. The minimum number of transaction free lists for a partitioned global index is the minimum number across all index partitions. This is a requirement to prevent self-deadlock.

NOTE *Oracle obtains the information about CPUs from the operating system.*

These factors determine the default number of parallel execution servers to use. However, the actual number of processes used is limited by their availability on the requested instances during run time. The initialization parameter PARALLEL_MAX_SERVERS sets an upper limit on the total number of parallel execution servers that an instance can have.

If a minimum fraction of the desired parallel execution servers is not available (specified by the initialization parameter PARALLEL_MIN_PERCENT), a user error is produced. The user can then retry the query with less parallelism.

Adaptive Multiuser Algorithm

When the adaptive multiuser algorithm is enabled, the parallel execution coordinator varies the DOP according to the system load. The Database Resource Manager determines the load by calculating the number of allocated threads. If the number of threads currently allocated is larger than the optimal number of threads, given the number of available CPUs, the algorithm reduces the DOP. This reduction improves throughput by avoiding overallocation of resources.

Minimum Number of Parallel Execution Servers

Oracle can perform an operation in parallel as long as at least two parallel execution servers are available. If too few parallel execution servers are available, your SQL statement may execute slower than expected. You can specify the minimum percentage of requested parallel execution servers that must be available in order for the operation to execute. This strategy ensures that your SQL statement executes with a minimum acceptable parallel performance. If the minimum percentage of requested parallel execution servers is not available, the SQL statement does not execute and returns an error.

The initialization parameter PARALLEL_MIN_PERCENT specifies the desired minimum percentage of requested parallel execution servers. This parameter affects DML and DDL operations as well as queries.

For example, if you specify 50 for this parameter, then at least 50 percent of the parallel execution servers requested for any parallel operation must be available in order for the operation to succeed. If 20 parallel execution servers are requested, then at least 10 must be available or an error is returned to the user. If PARALLEL_MIN_PERCENT is set to null, then all parallel operations will proceed as long as at least two parallel execution servers are available for processing.

Limiting the Number of Available Instances

In Oracle Real Application Clusters, instance groups can be used to limit the number of instances that participate in a parallel operation. You can create any number of instance groups, each consisting of one or more instances. You can then specify which instance group is to be used for any or all parallel operations. Parallel execution servers will only be used on instances which are members of the specified instance group.

Balancing the Workload

To optimize performance, all parallel execution servers should have equal work loads. For SQL statements parallelized by block range or by parallel execution servers, the workload is dynamically divided among the parallel execution servers. This minimizes workload skewing, which occurs when some parallel execution servers perform significantly more work than the other processes.

For SQL statements parallelized by partitions, if the workload is evenly distributed among the partitions, you can optimize performance by matching the number of parallel execution servers to the number of partitions or by choosing a DOP in which the number of partitions is a multiple of the number of processes.

For example, suppose a table has 10 partitions, and a parallel operation divides the work evenly among them. You can use 10 parallel execution servers (DOP equals 10) to do the work in approximately one-tenth the time that one process would take. You might also use five processes to do the work in one-fifth the time, or two processes to do the work in one-half the time.

If, however, you use nine processes to work on 10 partitions, the first process to finish its work on one partition then begins work on the 10th partition; and as the other processes finish their work, they become idle. This configuration does not provide good performance when the work is evenly divided among partitions. When the work is unevenly divided, the performance varies depending on whether the partition that is left for last has more or less work than the other partitions.

Similarly, suppose you use four processes to work on 10 partitions and the work is evenly divided. In this case, each process works on a second partition after finishing its first partition, but only two of the processes work on a third partition while the other two remain idle.

In general, you cannot assume that the time taken to perform a parallel operation on a given number of partitions (N) with a given number of parallel execution servers (P) will be N/P. This formula does not take into account the possibility that some processes might have to wait while others finish working on the last partitions. By choosing an appropriate DOP, however, you can minimize the workload skew and optimize performance.

Parallelization Rules for SQL Statements

A SQL statement can be parallelized if it includes a parallel hint or if the table or index being operated on has been declared `PARALLEL` with a `CREATE` or `ALTER` statement. In addition, a DDL statement can be parallelized by using the `PARALLEL` clause. However, not all of these methods apply to all types of SQL statements.

Parallelization has two components: the decision to parallelize and the DOP. These components are determined differently for queries, DDL operations, and DML operations.

To determine the DOP, Oracle looks at the reference objects:

- Parallel query looks at each table and index, in the portion of the query being parallelized, to determine which is the reference table. The basic rule is to pick the table or index with the largest DOP.
- For parallel DML (`INSERT`, `UPDATE`, `MERGE`, and `DELETE`), the reference object that determines the DOP is the table being modified by an insert, update, or delete operation. Parallel DML also adds some limits to the DOP to prevent deadlock. If the parallel DML statement includes a subquery, the subquery's DOP is the same as the DML operation.
- For parallel DDL, the reference object that determines the DOP is the table, index, or partition being created, rebuilt, split, or moved. If the parallel DDL statement includes a subquery, the subquery's DOP is the same as the DDL operation.

Rules for Parallelizing Queries

This section discusses some rules for parallelizing queries.

Decision to Parallelize

A `SELECT` statement can be parallelized only if the following conditions are satisfied:

- The query includes a parallel hint specification (PARALLEL or PARALLEL_INDEX) or the schema objects referred to in the query have a PARALLEL declaration associated with them.
  - At least one of the tables specified in the query requires one of the following:
  - A full table scan
  - An index range scan spanning multiple partitions.

Degree of Parallelism

The DOP for a query is determined by the following rules:

- The query uses the maximum DOP taken from all of the table declarations involved in the query and all of the potential indexes that are candidates to satisfy the query (the reference objects). That is, the table or index that has the greatest DOP determines the query's DOP (maximum query directive).
- If a table has both a parallel hint specification in the query and a parallel declaration in its table specification, the hint specification takes precedence over parallel declaration specification. See table 14.3 for precedence rules.

Rules for Parallelizing UPDATE, MERGE, and DELETE

UPDATE, MERGE, and DELETE operations are parallelized by partition or subpartition. Updates, merges, and deletes can only be parallelized on partitioned tables. Update, merge, and delete parallelism are not possible within a partition, nor on a nonpartitioned table.

You have two ways to specify parallel directives for UPDATE, MERGE, and DELETE operations (assuming that PARALLEL DML mode is enabled):

1. Use a parallel clause in the definition of the table being updated or deleted (the reference object).
2. Use an update, merge, or delete parallel hint in the statement.

Parallel hints are placed immediately after the UPDATE, MERGE, or DELETE keywords in UPDATE, MERGE, and DELETE statements. The hint also applies to the underlying scan of the table being changed.

You can use the ALTER SESSION FORCE PARALLEL DML statement to override parallel clauses for subsequent UPDATE, MERGE, and DELETE statements in a session. Parallel hints in UPDATE, MERGE, and DELETE statements override the ALTER SESSION FORCE PARALLEL DML statement.

Decision to Parallelize

The following rule determines whether the UPDATE, MERGE, or DELETE operation should be parallelized:

The UPDATE or DELETE operation will be parallelized if and only if at least one of the following is true:

- The table being updated or deleted has a PARALLEL specification.
- The PARALLEL hint is specified in the DML statement.
- An ALTER SESSION FORCE PARALLEL DML statement has been issued previously during the session.

If the statement contains subqueries or updatable views, then they may have their own separate parallel hints or clauses. However, these parallel directives do not affect the decision to parallelize the UPDATE, MERGE, or DELETE.

The parallel hint or clause on the tables is used by both the query and the UPDATE, MERGE, DELETE portions to determine parallelism, the decision to parallelize the UPDATE, MERGE, or DELETE portion is made independently of the query portion, and vice-versa.

Degree of Parallelism

The DOP is determined by the same rules as for the queries. Note that in the case of UPDATE and DELETE operations, only the target table to be modified (the only reference object) is involved. Thus, the UPDATE or DELETE parallel hint specification takes precedence over the parallel declaration specification of the target table. In other words, the precedence order is: MERGE, UPDATE, DELETE hint > Session > Parallel declaration specification of target table

See table 14.3 for precedence rules.

The maximum DOP you can achieve is equal to the number of partitions (or subpartitions in the case of composite subpartitions) in the table. A parallel execution server can update or merge into, or delete from multiple partitions, but each partition can only be updated or deleted by one parallel execution server.

If the DOP is less than the number of partitions, then the first process to finish work on one partition continues working on another partition, and so on until the work is finished on all partitions. If the DOP is greater than the number of partitions involved in the operation, then the excess parallel execution servers will have no work to do.

Example 14.4 : Parallelization

```
UPDATE tbl_1 SET c1=c1+1 WHERE c1>100;
```

If tbl_1 is a partitioned table and its table definition has a parallel clause, then the update operation is parallelized even if the scan on the table is serial (such as an index scan), assuming that the table has more than one partition with c1 greater than 100.

Example 14.5 : Parallelization

```
UPDATE /*+ PARALLEL(tbl_2,4) */ tbl_2 SET c1=c1+1;
```

Both the scan and update operations on tbl_2 will be parallelized with degree four.

Rules for Parallelizing INSERT ... SELECT

An INSERT ... SELECT statement parallelizes its INSERT and SELECT operations independently, except for the DOP.

You can specify a parallel hint after the INSERT keyword in an INSERT ... SELECT statement. Because the tables being queried are usually not the same as the table being inserted into, the hint enables you to specify parallel directives specifically for the insert operation.

You have the following ways to specify parallel directives for an INSERT ... SELECT statement (assuming that PARALLEL DML mode is enabled):

- SELECT parallel hints specified at the statement
- Parallel clauses specified in the definition of tables being selected
- INSERT parallel hint specified at the statement
- Parallel clause specified in the definition of tables being inserted into

You can use the ALTER SESSION FORCE PARALLEL DML statement to override parallel clauses for subsequent INSERT operations in a session. Parallel hints in insert operations override the ALTER SESSION FORCE PARALLEL DML statement.

Decision to Parallelize

The following rule determines whether the INSERT operation should be parallelized in an INSERT ... SELECT statement:

The INSERT operation will be parallelized if and only if at least one of the following is true:

- The PARALLEL hint is specified after the INSERT in the DML statement.
- The table being inserted into (the reference object) has a PARALLEL declaration specification.
- An ALTER SESSION FORCE PARALLEL DML statement has been issued previously during the session.

The decision to parallelize the INSERT operation is made independently of the SELECT operation, and vice versa.

Degree of Parallelism

Once the decision to parallelize the SELECT or INSERT operation is made, one parallel directive is picked for deciding the DOP of the whole statement, using the following precedence rule Insert hint directive > Session> Parallel declaration specification of the inserting table > Maximum query directive.

In this context, maximum query directive means that among multiple tables and indexes, the table or index that has the maximum DOP determines the parallelism for the query operation. The chosen parallel directive is applied to both the SELECT and INSERT operations.

Example 14.6 : Parallelization

The DOP used is 2, as specified in the INSERT hint:

```
INSERT /*+ PARALLEL(tbl_ins,2) */ INTO tbl_ins
SELECT /*+ PARALLEL(tbl_sel,4) */ * FROM tbl_sel;
```

Rules for Parallelizing DDL Statements

Decision to Parallelize

DDL operations can be parallelized if a PARALLEL clause (declaration) is specified in the syntax. In the case of CREATE INDEX and ALTER INDEX ... REBUILD or ALTER INDEX ... REBUILD PARTITION, the parallel declaration is stored in the data dictionary.

You can use the ALTER SESSION FORCE PARALLEL DDL statement to override the parallel clauses of subsequent DDL statements in a session.

Degree of Parallelism

The DOP is determined by the specification in the PARALLEL clause, unless it is overridden by an ALTER SESSION FORCE PARALLEL DDL statement. A rebuild of a partitioned index is never parallelized.

Parallel clauses in CREATE TABLE and ALTER TABLE statements specify table parallelism. If a parallel clause exists in a table definition, it determines the parallelism of DDL statements as well as queries. If the DDL statement contains explicit parallel hints for a table, however, those hints override the effect of parallel clauses for that table. You can use the `ALTER SESSION FORCE PARALLEL DDL` statement to override parallel clauses.

Rules for Parallelizing CREATE INDEX, REBUILD INDEX, MOVE or SPLIT PARTITION

The following rules apply:

Parallel CREATE INDEX or ALTER INDEX ... REBUILD

The `CREATE INDEX` and `ALTER INDEX ... REBUILD` statements can be parallelized only by a `PARALLEL` clause or an `ALTER SESSION FORCE PARALLEL DDL` statement.

`ALTER INDEX ... REBUILD` can be parallelized only for a nonpartitioned index, but `ALTER INDEX ... REBUILD PARTITION` can be parallelized by a `PARALLEL` clause or an `ALTER SESSION FORCE PARALLEL DDL` statement.

The scan operation for `ALTER INDEX ... REBUILD` (nonpartitioned), `ALTER INDEX ... REBUILD PARTITION`, and `CREATE INDEX` has the same parallelism as the `REBUILD` or `CREATE` operation and uses the same DOP. If the DOP is not specified for `REBUILD` or `CREATE`, the default is the number of CPUs.

Parallel MOVE PARTITION or SPLIT PARTITION

The `ALTER INDEX ... MOVE PARTITION` and `ALTER INDEX ... SPLIT PARTITION` statements can be parallelized only by a `PARALLEL` clause or an `ALTER SESSION FORCE PARALLEL DDL` statement. Their scan operations have the same parallelism as the corresponding `MOVE` or `SPLIT` operations. If the DOP is not specified, the default is the number of CPUs.

Rules for Parallelizing CREATE TABLE AS SELECT

The `CREATE TABLE ... AS SELECT` statement contains two parts: a `CREATE` part (DDL) and a `SELECT` part (query). Oracle can parallelize both parts of the statement. The `CREATE` part follows the same rules as other DDL operations.

Decision to Parallelize (Query Part)

The query part of a `CREATE TABLE ... AS SELECT` statement can be parallelized only if the following conditions are satisfied:

- The query includes a parallel hint specification (`PARALLEL` or `PARALLEL_INDEX`) or the `CREATE` part of the statement has a `PARALLEL` clause specification or the schema objects referred to in the query have a `PARALLEL` declaration associated with them.
- At least one of the tables specified in the query requires one of the following:
    - A full table scan
    - An index range scan spanning multiple partitions

Degree of Parallelism (Query Part)

The DOP for the query part of a `CREATE TABLE ... AS SELECT` statement is determined by one of the following rules:

- The query part uses the values specified in the `PARALLEL` clause of the `CREATE` part.
- If the `PARALLEL` clause is not specified, the default DOP is the number of CPUs.
- If the `CREATE` is serial, then the DOP is determined by the query.

Note that any values specified in a hint for parallelism are ignored.

Decision to Parallelize (CREATE Part)

The CREATE operation of CREATE TABLE ... AS SELECT can be parallelized only by a PARALLEL clause or an ALTER SESSION FORCE PARALLEL DDL statement.

When the CREATE operation of CREATE TABLE ... AS SELECT is parallelized, Oracle also parallelizes the scan operation if possible. The scan operation cannot be parallelized if, for example:

- The SELECT clause has a NOPARALLEL hint
- The operation scans an index of a nonpartitioned table

When the CREATE operation is not parallelized, the SELECT can be parallelized if it has a PARALLEL hint or if the selected table (or partitioned index) has a parallel declaration.

Degree of Parallelism (CREATE Part)

The DOP for the CREATE operation, and for the SELECT operation if it is parallelized, is specified by the PARALLEL clause of the CREATE statement, unless it is overridden by an ALTER SESSION FORCE PARALLEL DDL statement. If the PARALLEL clause does not specify the DOP, the default is the number of CPUs.

Summary of Parallelization Rules

Table 14.3 shows how various types of SQL statements can be parallelized and indicates which methods of specifying parallelism take precedence.

- The priority (1) specification overrides priority (2) and priority (3).
- The priority (2) specification overrides priority (3).

Table 14.3 Parallelization Rules

	Parallelized by Clause, Hint, or Underlying Table/Index Declaration (priority order: 1, 2, 3)			
Parallel Operation	**PARALLEL Hint**	**PARALLEL Clause**	**ALTER SESSION**	**PARALLEL Declaration**
Parallel query table scan (partitioned or nonpartitioned table)	(1) PARALLEL		(2) FORCE PARALLEL QUERY	(3) of table
Parallel query index range scan (partitioned index)	(1) PARALLEL_INDEX		(2) FORCE PARALLEL QUERY	(2) of index
Parallel UPDATE or DELETE (partitioned table only)	(1) PARALLEL		(2) FORCE PARALLEL DML	(3) of table being updated or deleted from
INSERT operation of parallel INSERT... SELECT (partitioned or nonpartitioned table)	(1) PARALLEL of insert		(2) FORCE PARALLEL DML	(3) of table being inserted into
SELECT operation of INSERT ... SELECT when INSERT is parallel	Takes degree from INSERT statement			

SELECT operation of INSERT ... SELECT when INSERT is serial	(1) PARALLEL			(2) of table being selected from
CREATE operation of parallel CREATE TABLE ...AS SELECT (partitioned or nonpartitioned table)	(Note: Hint in select clause does not affect the create operation.)	(2)	(1) FORCE PARALLEL DDL	
SELECT operation of CREATE TABLE ... AS SELECT when CREATE is parallel	Takes degree from CREATE statement			
SELECT operation of CREATE TABLE ... AS SELECT when CREATE is serial	(1) PARALLEL or PARALLEL_INDEX			(2) of querying tables or partitioned indexes
Parallel CREATE INDEX (partitioned or nonpartitioned index)		(2)	(1) FORCE PARALLEL DDL	
Parallel REBUILD INDEX (nonpartitioned index)		(2)	(1) FORCE PARALLEL DDL	
REBUILD INDEX (partitioned index)—never parallelized				
Parallel REBUILD INDEX partition		(2)	(1) FORCE PARALLEL DDL	
Parallel MOVE or SPLIT partition		(2)	(1) FORCE PARALLEL DDL	

Enabling Parallelism for Tables and Queries

The DOP of tables involved in parallel operations affect the DOP for operations on those tables. Therefore, after setting parallel tuning parameters, you must also enable parallel execution for each table you want parallelized, using the PARALLEL clause of the CREATE TABLE or ALTER TABLE statements. You can also use the PARALLEL hint with SQL statements to enable parallelism for that operation only, or use the FORCE option of the ALTER SESSION statement to enable parallelism for all subsequent operations in the session.

When you parallelize tables, you can also specify the DOP or allow Oracle to use a default DOP. The value of the default DOP is derived automatically, based on the value of PARALLEL_THREADS_PER_CPU and the number of CPUs available to Oracle.

```
ALTER TABLE employees PARALLEL;      – uses default DOP
ALTER TABLE employees PARALLEL 4;   – users DOP of 4
```

Degree of Parallelism and Adaptive Multiuser: How They Interact

The DOP specifies the number of available processes, or threads, used in parallel operations. Each parallel thread can use one or two query processes, depending on the query's complexity.

The adaptive multiuser feature adjusts the DOP based on user load. For example, you might have a table with a DOP of 5. This DOP might be acceptable with 10 users. However, if 10 more users enter the system and you enable the PARALLEL_ADAPTIVE_MULTI_USER feature, Oracle reduces the DOP to spread resources more evenly according to the perceived system load.

NOTE *Once Oracle determines the DOP for a query, the DOP does not change for the duration of the query.*

It is best to use the parallel adaptive multiuser feature when users process simultaneous parallel execution operations. If you enable PARALLEL_AUTOMATIC_TUNING, Oracle automatically sets PARALLEL_ADAPTIVE_MULTI_USER to true.

NOTE *Disable adaptive multiuser for single-user, batch processing systems or if your system already provides optimal performance.*

How the Adaptive Multiuser Algorithm Works

The adaptive multiuser algorithm has several inputs. The algorithm first considers the number of allocated threads as calculated by the Database Resource Manager. The algorithm then considers the default settings for parallelism as set in the initialization parameter file, as well as parallelism options used in CREATE TABLE and ALTER TABLE statements and SQL hints.

When a system is overloaded and the input DOP is larger than the default DOP, the algorithm uses the default degree as input. The system then calculates a reduction factor that it applies to the input DOP. For example, using a 16-CPU system, when the first user enters the system and it is idle, it will be granted a DOP of 32. The next user will be given a DOP of eight, the next four, and so on. If the system settles into a steady state of eight users issuing queries, all the users will eventually be given a DOP of 4, thus dividing the system evenly among all the parallel users.

Forcing Parallel Execution for a Session

If you are sure you want to execute in parallel and want to avoid setting the DOP for a table or modifying the queries involved, you can force parallelism with the following statement:

```
ALTER SESSION FORCE PARALLEL QUERY;
```

All subsequent queries will be executed in parallel provided no restrictions are violated. You can also force DML and DDL statements. This clause overrides any parallel clause specified in subsequent statements in the session, but is overridden by a parallel hint.

In typical OLTP environments, for example, the tables are not set parallel, but nightly batch scripts may want to collect data from these tables in parallel. By setting the DOP in the session, the user avoids altering each table in parallel and then altering it back to serial when finished.

Controlling Performance with the Degree of Parallelism

The initialization parameter PARALLEL_THREADS_PER_CPU affects algorithms controlling both the DOP and the adaptive multiuser feature. Oracle multiplies the value of PARALLEL_THREADS_PER_CPU by the number of CPUs for each instance to derive the number of threads to use in parallel operations.

The adaptive multiuser feature also uses the default DOP to compute the target number of query server processes that should exist in a system. When a system is running more processes than the target number, the adaptive algorithm reduces the DOP of new queries as required. Therefore, you can also use PARALLEL_THREADS_PER_CPU to control the adaptive algorithm.

PARALLEL_THREADS_PER_CPU enables you to adjust for hardware configurations with I/O subsystems that are slow relative to the CPU speed and for application workloads that perform few computations relative to the amount of data involved. If the system is neither CPU-bound nor I/O-bound, then the PARALLEL_THREADS_PER_CPU value should be increased. This increases the default DOP and allows better utilization of hardware resources. The default for PARALLEL_THREADS_PER_CPU on most platforms is 2. However, the default for machines with relatively slow I/O subsystems can be as high as eight.

TUNING GENERAL PARAMETERS FOR PARALLEL EXECUTION

This section discusses the following topics:

- Parameters establishing resource limits for parallel operations
- Parameters affecting resource consumption
- Parameters related to I/O.

Parameters Establishing Resource Limits for Parallel Operations

The parameters that establish resource limits are:

- PARALLEL_MAX_SERVERS
- PARALLEL_MIN_SERVERS
- LARGE_POOL_SIZE or SHARED_POOL_SIZE
- SHARED_POOL_SIZE
- PARALLEL_MIN_PERCENT
- CLUSTER_DATABASE_INSTANCES.

PARALLEL_MAX_SERVERS

The recommended value for the PARALLEL_MAX_SEVERS parameter is as follows:

```
2 x DOP x NUMBER_OF_CONCURRENT_USERS
```

The PARALLEL_MAX_SEVERS parameter sets a resource limit on the maximum number of processes available for parallel execution. If you set PARALLEL_AUTOMATIC_TUNING to false, you need to manually specify a value for PARALLEL_MAX_SERVERS.

Most parallel operations need at most twice the number of query server processes as the maximum DOP attributed to any table in the operation.

If PARALLEL_AUTOMATIC_TUNING is false, the default value for PARALLEL_MAX_SERVERS is 5. This is sufficient for some minimal operations, but not enough for effective use of parallel execution. If you manually set the PARALLEL_MAX_SERVERS parameter, set it to 16 times the number of CPUs. This is a reasonable starting value that will allow you to run four parallel queries simultaneously, assuming that each query is using a DOP of eight.

If the hardware system is neither CPU bound nor I/O bound, then you can increase the number of concurrent parallel execution users on the system by adding more query server processes. When the system becomes CPU or I/O-bound, however, adding more concurrent users becomes detrimental to the overall performance. Careful setting of PARALLEL_MAX_SERVERS is an effective method of restricting the number of concurrent parallel operations.

If users initiate too many concurrent operations, Oracle might not have enough query server processes. In this case, Oracle executes the operations sequentially or displays an error if PARALLEL_MIN_PERCENT is set to a value other than the default value of 0 (zero).

This condition can be verified through the GV$SYSSTAT view by comparing the statistics for parallel operations not downgraded and parallel operations downgraded to serial. For example:

```
SELECT * FROM GV$SYSSTAT WHERE name LIKE 'Parallel operation%';
```

When Users Have Too Many Processes

When concurrent users have too many query server processes, memory contention (paging), I/O contention, or excessive context switching can occur. This contention can reduce system throughput to a level lower than if parallel execution were not used. Increase the PARALLEL_MAX_SERVERS value only if the system has sufficient memory and I/O bandwidth for the resulting load.

You can use operating system performance monitoring tools to determine how much memory, swap space and I/O bandwidth are free. Look at the runq lengths for both your CPUs and disks, as well as the service time for I/Os on the system. Verify that the machine has sufficient swap space existing on the machine to add more processes. Limiting the total number of query server processes might restrict the number of concurrent users who can execute parallel operations, but system throughput tends to remain stable.

Increasing the Number of Concurrent Users

To increase the number of concurrent users, you can restrict the number of concurrent sessions that resource consumer groups can have. For example:

- You can enable PARALLEL_ADAPTIVE_MULTI_USER.
- You can set a large limit for users running batch jobs.
- You can set a medium limit for users performing analyses.
- You can prohibit a particular class of users from using parallelism.

Limiting the Number of Resources for a User

You can limit the amount of parallelism available to a given user by establishing a resource consumer group for the user. Do this to limit the number of sessions, concurrent logons, and the number of parallel processes that any one user or group of users can have.

Each query server process working on a parallel execution statement is logged on with a session ID. Each process counts against the user's limit of concurrent sessions. For example, to limit a user to 10 parallel execution processes, set the user's limit to 11. One process is for the parallel coordinator and the other 10 consist of two sets of query server servers. This would allow one session for the parallel coordinator and 10 sessions for the parallel execution processes.

PARALLEL_MIN_SERVERS

The recommended value for the PARALLEL_MIN_SERVERS parameter is 0 (zero), which is the default.

This parameter is used at startup and lets you specify in a single instance the number of processes to be started and reserved for parallel operations. The syntax is:

```
PARALLEL_MIN_SERVERS=n
```

The *n* variable is the number of processes you want to start and reserve for parallel operations.

Setting PARALLEL_MIN_SERVERS balances the startup cost against memory usage. Processes started using PARALLEL_MIN_SERVERS do not exit until the database is shut down. This way, when a query is issued the processes are likely to be available. It is desirable, however, to recycle query server processes periodically since the memory these processes use can become fragmented and cause the high water mark to slowly increase. When you do not set PARALLEL_MIN_SERVERS, processes exit after they are idle for five minutes.

LARGE_POOL_SIZE or SHARED_POOL_SIZE

The following discussion of how to tune the large pool also applies to tuning the shared pool, except as noted in "SHARED_POOL_SIZE". You must also increase the value for this memory setting by the amount you determine.

Parallel execution requires additional memory resources in addition to those required by serial SQL execution. Additional memory is used for communication and passing data between query server processes and the query coordinator.

There is no recommended value for LARGE_POOL_SIZE. Instead, Oracle recommends leaving this parameter unset and having Oracle set it for you by setting the PARALLEL_AUTOMATIC_TUNING parameter to true. The exception to this is when the system-assigned value is inadequate for your processing requirements.

NOTE: *When PARALLEL_AUTOMATIC_TUNING is set to true, Oracle allocates parallel execution buffers from the large pool. When this parameter is false, Oracle allocates parallel execution buffers from the shared pool.*

Oracle automatically computes LARGE_POOL_SIZE if PARALLEL_AUTOMATIC_TUNING is true. To manually set a value for LARGE_POOL_SIZE, query the V$SGASTAT view and increase or decrease the value for LARGE_POOL_SIZE depending on your needs. For example, suppose Oracle displays the following error on startup:

```
ORA-27102: out of memory
SVR4 Error: 12: Not enough space
```

You should reduce the value for LARGE_POOL_SIZE low enough so your database starts. After reducing the value of LARGE_POOL_SIZE, you might see the error:

```
ORA-04031: unable to allocate 16084 bytes of shared memory
    ("large pool","unknown object","large pool heap","PX msg pool")
```

If so, execute the following query to determine why Oracle could not allocate the 16,084 bytes:

```
SELECT NAME, SUM(BYTES)
FROM V$SGASTAT
WHERE POOL='LARGE POOL'
  GROUP BY ROLLUP (NAME);
```

Your output should resemble the following:

```
NAME                          SUM(BYTES)
----------------------------------------
PX msg pool                      1474572
free memory                       562132
                                 2036704

3 rows selected.
```

If you specify LARGE_POOL_SIZE and the amount of memory you need to reserve is bigger than the pool, Oracle does not allocate all the memory it can get. Instead, it leaves some space.

When the query runs, Oracle tries to get what it needs. Oracle uses the 560 KB and needs another 16KB when it fails. The error does not report the cumulative amount that is needed. The best way of determining how much more memory is needed is to use the formulas in "Adding Memory for Message Buffers".

To resolve the problem in the current example, increase the value for `LARGE_POOL_SIZE`. As shown in the sample output, the `LARGE_POOL_SIZE` is about 2 MB. Depending on the amount of memory available, you could increase the value of `LARGE_POOL_SIZE` to 4 MB and attempt to start your database. If Oracle continues to display an `ORA-4031` message, gradually increase the value for `LARGE_POOL_SIZE` until startup is successful.

Computing Additional Memory Requirements for Message Buffers

After you determine the initial setting for the large or shared pool, you must calculate additional memory requirements for message buffers and determine how much additional space you need for cursors.

Adding Memory for Message Buffers

You must increase the value for the `LARGE_POOL_SIZE` or the `SHARED_POOL_SIZE` parameters to accommodate message buffers. The message buffers allow query server processes to communicate with each other. If you enable automatic parallel tuning, Oracle allocates space for the message buffer from the large pool. Otherwise, Oracle allocates space from the shared pool.

Oracle uses a fixed number of buffers for each virtual connection between producer query servers and consumer query servers. Connections increase as the square of the DOP increases. For this reason, the maximum amount of memory used by parallel execution is bound by the highest DOP allowed on your system. You can control this value by using either the `PARALLEL_MAX_SERVERS` parameter or by using policies and profiles.

To calculate the amount of memory required, use one of the following formulas:

- For SMP systems:

  `mem in bytes = (3 × size × users × groups x connections)`

- For SMP Real Application Clusters and MPP systems:

  `mem in bytes = ((3 × local) + (2 × remote) × (size × users × groups))`

Each instance uses the memory computed by the formula.

The terms are:

- `SIZE` = `PARALLEL_EXECUTION_MESSAGE_SIZE`
- `USERS` = the number of concurrent parallel execution users that you expect to have running with the optimal DOP
- `GROUPS` = the number of query server process groups used for each query

  A simple SQL statement requires only one group. However, if your queries involve subqueries which will be processed in parallel, then Oracle uses an additional group of query server processes.

- `CONNECTIONS` = ($DOP^2 + 2 \times DOP$)

  If your system is a cluster or MPP, then you should account for the number of instances because this will increase the DOP. In other words, using a DOP of 4 on a two instance cluster results in a DOP of 8. A value of `PARALLEL_MAX_SERVERS` times the number of instances divided by four is a conservative estimate to use as a starting point.

- LOCAL = CONNECTIONS/INSTANCES
- REMOTE = CONNECTIONS - LOCAL

Add this amount to your original setting for the large or shared pool. However, before setting a value for either of these memory structures, you must also consider additional memory for cursors, as explained in the following section.

Calculating Additional Memory for Cursors

Parallel execution plans consume more space in the SQL area than serial execution plans. You should regularly monitor shared pool resource use to ensure that the memory used by both messages and cursors can accommodate your system's processing requirements.

Adjusting Memory After Processing Begins

The formulas in this section are just starting points. Whether you are using automated or manual tuning, you should monitor usage on an on-going basis to make sure the size of memory is not too large or too small. To do this, tune the large and shared pools after examining the size of structures in the large pool, using the following query:

```
SELECT POOL, NAME, SUM(BYTES)
FROM V$SGASTAT
WHERE POOL LIKE '%pool%'
  GROUP BY ROLLUP (POOL, NAME);
```

Your output should resemble the following:

```
POOL          NAME                              SUM(BYTES)
----------------------------------------------------------
large pool    PX msg pool                         38092812
large pool    free memory                           299988
large pool                                        38392800
shared pool   Checkpoint queue                       38496
shared pool   KGFF heap                               1964
shared pool   KGK heap                                4372
shared pool   KQLS heap                            1134432
shared pool   LRMPD SGA Table                        23856
shared pool   PLS non-lib hp                          2096
shared pool   PX subheap                            186828
shared pool   SYSTEM PARAMETERS                      55756
shared pool   State objects                        3907808
shared pool   character set memory                   30260
shared pool   db_block_buffers                      200000
shared pool   db_block_hash_buckets                  33132
shared pool   db_files                              122984
shared pool   db_handles                             52416
shared pool   dictionary cache                      198216
shared pool   dlm shared memory                    5387924
shared pool   enqueue_resources                      29016
shared pool   event statistics per sess             264768
shared pool   fixed allocation callback               1376
shared pool   free memory                         26329104
shared pool   gc_*                                   64000
shared pool   latch nowait fails or sle              34944
shared pool   library cache                        2176808
```

```
shared pool   log_buffer                         24576
shared pool   log_checkpoint_timeout             24700
shared pool   long op statistics array           30240
shared pool   message pool freequeue            116232
shared pool   miscellaneous                     267624
shared pool   processes                          76896
shared pool   session param values               41424
shared pool   sessions                          170016
shared pool   sql area                         9549116
shared pool   table columns                     148104
shared pool   trace_buffers_per_process        1476320
shared pool   transactions                       18480
shared pool   trigger inform                     24684
shared pool                                   52248968
                                              90641768
41 rows selected.
```

Evaluate the memory used as shown in your output, and alter the setting for LARGE_POOL_SIZE based on your processing needs.

To obtain more memory usage statistics, execute the following query:

```
SELECT * FROM V$PX_PROCESS_SYSSTAT WHERE STATISTIC LIKE 'Buffers%';
```

Your output should resemble the following:

```
STATISTIC                                        VALUE
-------------------------------------------------------
Buffers Allocated                                23225
Buffers Freed                                    23225
Buffers Current                                      0
Buffers HWM                                       3620
4 Rows selected.
```

The amount of memory used appears in the Buffers Current and Buffers HWM statistics. Calculate a value in bytes by multiplying the number of buffers by the value for PARALLEL_EXECUTION_MESSAGE_SIZE. Compare the high water mark to the parallel execution message pool size to determine if you allocate too much memory. For example, in the first output, the value for large pool as shown in px msg pool is 38,092,812 or 38 MB. The Buffers HWM from the second output is 3,620, which when multiplied by a parallel execution message size of 4,096 is 14,827,520, or approximately 15 MB. In this case, the high water mark has reached approximately 40 percent of its capacity.

SHARED_POOL_SIZE

As mentioned earlier, if PARALLEL_AUTOMATIC_TUNING is false, Oracle allocates query server processes from the shared pool. In this case, tune the shared pool as described under the previous heading for large pool, with the following exceptions:

- Allow for other clients of the shared pool, such as shared cursors and stored procedures
- Remember that larger values improve performance in multiuser systems, but smaller values use less memory

You must also take into account that using parallel execution generates more cursors. Look at statistics in the V$SQLAREA view to determine how often Oracle recompiles cursors. If the cursor hit ratio is poor, increase the size of the pool. This happens only when you have a large number of distinct queries.

You can then monitor the number of buffers used by parallel execution in the same way as explained previously, and compare the shared pool PX msg pool to the current high water mark reported in output from the view V$PX_PROCESS_SYSSTAT.

PARALLEL_MIN_PERCENT

The recommended value for the PARALLEL_MIN_PERCENT parameter is 0 (zero).

This parameter allows users to wait for an acceptable DOP, depending on the application in use. Setting this parameter to values other than 0 (zero) causes Oracle to return an error when the requested DOP cannot be satisfied by the system at a given time.

For example, if you set PARALLEL_MIN_PERCENT to 50, which translates to 50 percent, and the DOP is reduced by 50 percent or greater because of the adaptive algorithm or because of a resource limitation, then Oracle returns ORA-12827. For example:

```
SELECT /*+ PARALLEL(e, 8, 1) */ d.department_id, SUM(SAL)
FROM employees e, departments d WHERE e.department_id = d.department_id
GROUP BY d.department_id ORDER BY d.department_id;
```

Oracle responds with this message:

```
ORA-12827: insufficient parallel query slaves available
```

CLUSTER_DATABASE_INSTANCES

The CLUSTER_DATABASE_INSTANCES parameter should be set to a value that is equal to the number of instances in your Real Application Clusters environment.

The CLUSTER_DATABASE_INSTANCES parameter specifies the number of instances configured in an Oracle Real Application Clusters environment. Oracle uses the value of this parameter to compute values for LARGE_POOL_SIZE when PARALLEL_AUTOMATIC_TUNING is set to true.

Parameters Affecting Resource Consumption

The first group of parameters discussed in this section affects memory and resource consumption for all parallel operations, in particular, for parallel execution. These parameters are:

- PGA_AGGREGATE_TARGET
- PARALLEL_EXECUTION_MESSAGE_SIZE

A second subset of parameters discussed in this section explains parameters affecting parallel DML and DDL.

To control resource consumption, you should configure memory at two levels:

- At the Oracle level, so the system uses an appropriate amount of memory from the operating system.
- At the operating system level for consistency. On some platforms, you might need to set operating system parameters that control the total amount of virtual memory available, summed across all processes.

The SGA is typically part of real physical memory. The SGA is static and of fixed size; if you want to change its size, shut down the database, make the change, and restart the database. Oracle allocates the large and shared pools out of the SGA.

A large percentage of the memory used in data warehousing operations is more dynamic. This memory comes from process memory (PGA), and both the size of process memory and the number of processes can vary greatly. Use the PGA_AGGREGATE_TARGET parameter to control both the process memory and the number of processes.

PGA_AGGREGATE_TARGET

With Oracle9*i*, you can simplify and improve the way PGA memory is allocated, by enabling automatic PGA memory management. In this mode, Oracle dynamically adjusts the size of the portion of the PGA memory dedicated to work areas, based on an overall PGA memory target explicitly set by the DBA. To enable automatic PGA memory management, you have to set the initialization parameter `PGA_AGGREGATE_TARGET`.

HASH_AREA_SIZE

`HASH_AREA_SIZE` has been deprecated and you should use `PGA_AGGREGATE_TARGET` instead.

SORT_AREA_SIZE

`SORT_AREA_SIZE` has been deprecated and you should use `PGA_AGGREGATE_TARGET` instead.

PARALLEL_EXECUTION_MESSAGE_SIZE

The recommended value for `PARALLEL_EXECUTION_MESSAGE_SIZE` is 4 KB. If `PARALLEL_AUTOMATIC_TUNING` is `true`, the default is 4 KB. If `PARALLEL_AUTOMATIC_TUNING` is `false`, the default is slightly greater than 2 KB.

The `PARALLEL_EXECUTION_MESSAGE_SIZE` parameter specifies the upper limit for the size of parallel execution messages. The default value is operating system specific and this value should be adequate for most applications. Larger values for `PARALLEL_EXECUTION_MESSAGE_SIZE` require larger values for `LARGE_POOL_SIZE` or `SHARED_POOL_SIZE`, depending on whether you have enabled parallel automatic tuning.

While you might experience significantly improved response time by increasing the value for `PARALLEL_EXECUTION_MESSAGE_SIZE`, memory use also drastically increases. For example, if you double the value for `PARALLEL_EXECUTION_MESSAGE_SIZE`, parallel execution requires a message source pool that is twice as large.

Therefore, if you set `PARALLEL_AUTOMATIC_TUNING` to `false`, you must adjust the `SHARED_POOL_SIZE` to accommodate parallel execution messages. If you have set `PARALLEL_AUTOMATIC_TUNING` to `true`, but have set `LARGE_POOL_SIZE` manually, then you must adjust the `LARGE_POOL_SIZE` to accommodate parallel execution messages.

Parameters Affecting Resource Consumption for Parallel DML and Parallel DDL

The parameters that affect parallel DML and parallel DDL resource consumption are:

- TRANSACTIONS
- ROLLBACK_SEGMENTS
- FAST_START_PARALLEL_ROLLBACK
- LOG_BUFFER
- DML_LOCKS
- ENQUEUE_RESOURCES.

Parallel inserts, updates, and deletes require more resources than serial DML operations. Similarly, `PARALLEL CREATE TABLE ... AS SELECT` and `PARALLEL CREATE INDEX` can require more resources. For this reason, you may need to increase the value of several additional initialization parameters. These parameters do *not* affect resources for queries.

Transactions

For parallel DML and DDL, each query server process starts a transaction. The parallel coordinator uses the two-phase commit protocol to commit transactions; therefore, the number of transactions being processed increases by the DOP. As a result, you might need to increase the value of the `TRANSACTIONS` initialization parameter.

The `TRANSACTIONS` parameter specifies the maximum number of concurrent transactions. The default assumes no parallelism. For example, if you have a DOP of 20, you will have 20 more new server transactions (or 40, if you have two server sets) and 1 coordinator transaction. In this case, you should increase `TRANSACTIONS` by 21 (or 41) if the transactions are running in the same instance. If you do not set this parameter, Oracle sets it to a value equal to 1.1 x `SESSIONS`.

ROLLBACK_SEGMENTS

The increased number of transactions for parallel DML and DDL requires more rollback segments. For example, one command with a DOP of five uses 5 server transactions distributed among different rollback segments. The rollback segments should belong to tablespaces that have free space. The rollback segments should also be unlimited, or you should specify a high value for the `MAXEXTENTS` parameter of the `STORAGE` clause. In this way, the rollback segments can extend and not run out of space.

FAST_START_PARALLEL_ROLLBACK

If a system fails when there are uncommitted parallel DML or DDL transactions, you can speed up transaction recovery during startup by using the `FAST_START_PARALLEL_ROLLBACK` parameter.

This parameter controls the DOP used when recovering terminated transactions. Terminated transactions are transactions that are active before a system failure. By default, the DOP is chosen to be at most two times the value of the `CPU_COUNT` parameter.

If the default DOP is insufficient, set the parameter to the `HIGH`. This gives a maximum DOP of at most four times the value of the `CPU_COUNT` parameter. This feature is available by default.

LOG_BUFFER

Check the statistic `redo buffer allocation retries` in the `V$SYSSTAT` view. If this value is high relative to `redo blocks written`, try to increase the `LOG_BUFFER` size. A common `LOG_BUFFER` size for a system generating numerous logs is 3 MB to 5 MB. If the number of retries is still high after increasing `LOG_BUFFER` size, a problem might exist with the disk on which the log files reside. In that case, tune the I/O subsystem to increase the I/O rates for redo. One way of doing this is to use fine-grained striping across multiple disks. For example, use a stripe size of 16 KB. A simpler approach is to isolate redo logs on their own disk.

DML_LOCKS

This parameter specifies the maximum number of DML locks. Its value should equal the total number of locks on all tables referenced by all users. A parallel DML operation's lock and enqueue resource requirement is very different from serial DML. Parallel DML holds many more locks, so you should increase the value of the `ENQUEUE_RESOURCES` and `DML_LOCKS` parameters by equal amounts.

Table 14.4 shows the types of locks acquired by coordinator and parallel execution server processes for different types of parallel DML statements. Using this information, you can determine the value required for these parameters.

Table 14.4 Locks Acquired by Parallel DML Statements

Type of Statement	Coordinator Process Acquires	Each Parallel Execution Server Acquires
Parallel UPDATE or DELETE into partitioned table; WHERE clause pruned to a subset of partitions or subpartitions	1 table lock SX 1 partition lock X for each pruned (sub)partition	1 table lock SX 1 partition lock NULL for each pruned (sub)partition owned by the query server process 1 partition-wait lock S for each pruned (sub)parti-tion owned by the query server process
Parallel row-migrating UPDATE into partitioned table; WHERE clause pruned to a subset of (sub)partitions	1 table lock SX	1 table lock SX
	1 partition X lock for each pruned (sub)partition	1 partition lock NULL for each pruned (sub)partition owned by the query server process 1 partition-wait lock S for each pruned partition owned by the query server process
	1 partition lock SX for all other (sub)partitions	1 partition lock SX for all other (sub)partitions
Parallel UPDATE, MERGE, DELETE, or INSERT into partitioned table	1 table lock SX Partition locks X for all (sub)partitions	1 table lock SX 1 partition lock NULL for each (sub)partition 1 partition-wait lock S for each (sub)partition
Parallel INSERT into partitioned table; destination table with partition or subpartition clause	1 table lock SX 1 partition lock X for each specified (sub)partition	1 table lock SX 1 partition lock NULL for each specified (sub)partition 1 partition-wait lock S for each specified (sub)partition
Parallel INSERT into nonpartitioned table	1 table lock X	None

NOTE *Table, partition, and partition-wait DML locks all appear as TM locks in the* V$LOCK *view.*

Consider a table with 600 partitions running with a DOP of 100. Assume all partitions are involved in a parallel UPDATE or DELETE statement with no row-migrations.

The coordinator acquires:

- 1 table lock SX
- 600 partition locks X.

Total server processes acquires:

- 100 table locks SX
- 600 partition locks NULL
- 600 partition-wait locks S.

ENQUEUE_RESOURCES

This parameter sets the number of resources that can be locked by the lock manager. Parallel DML operations require many more resources than serial DML. Oracle allocates more enqueue resources as needed.

Parameters Related to I/O

The parameters that affect I/O are:

- DB_CACHE_SIZE
- DB_BLOCK_SIZE
- DB_FILE_MULTIBLOCK_READ_COUNT
- DISK_ASYNCH_IO and TAPE_ASYNCH_IO.

These parameters also affect the optimizer which ensures optimal performance for parallel execution I/O operations.

DB_CACHE_SIZE

When you perform parallel updates, merges, and deletes, the buffer cache behavior is very similar to any OLTP system running a high volume of updates.

DB_BLOCK_SIZE

The recommended value for this parameter is 8 KB or 16 KB.

Set the database block size when you create the database. If you are creating a new database, use a large block size such as 8 KB or 16 KB.

DB_FILE_MULTIBLOCK_READ_COUNT

The recommended value for this parameter is eight for 8 KB block size, or four for 16 KB block size. The default is 8.

This parameter determines how many database blocks are read with a single operating system `READ` call. The upper limit for this parameter is platform-dependent. If you set `DB_FILE_MULTIBLOCK_READ_COUNT` to an excessively high value, your operating system will lower the value to the highest allowable level when you start your database. In this case, each platform uses the highest value possible. Maximum values generally range from 64 KB to 1 MB.

DISK_ASYNCH_IO and TAPE_ASYNCH_IO

The recommended value for both of these parameters is `true`.

These parameters enable or disable the operating system's asynchronous I/O facility. They allow query server processes to overlap I/O requests with processing when performing table scans. If the operating system supports asynchronous I/O, leave these parameters at the default value of `true`. Figure 14.6 illustrates how asynchronous read works.

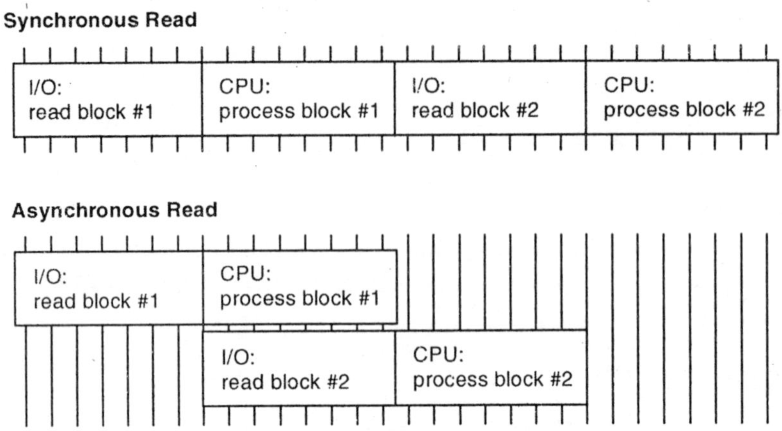

Figure 14.6 Asynchronous Read.

Asynchronous operations are currently supported for parallel table scans, hash joins, sorts, and serial table scans. However, this feature can require operating system specific configuration and may not be supported on all platforms. Check your Oracle operating system-specific documentation.

MONITORING AND DIAGNOSING PARALLEL EXECUTION PERFORMANCE

You should do the following tasks when diagnosing parallel execution performance problems:

- Quantify your performance expectations to determine whether there is a problem.
- Determine whether a problem pertains to optimization, such as inefficient plans that might require reanalyzing tables or adding hints, or whether the problem pertains to execution, such as simple operations like scanning, loading, grouping, or indexing running much slower than published guidelines.
- Determine whether the problem occurs when running in parallel, such as load imbalance or resource bottlenecks, or whether the problem is also present for serial operations.

Performance expectations are based on either prior performance metrics (for example, the length of time a given query took last week or on the previous version of Oracle) or scaling and extrapolating from serial execution times (for example, serial execution took 10 minutes while parallel execution took 5 minutes). If the performance does not meet your expectations, consider the following questions:

- Did the execution plan change?

  If so, you should gather statistics and decide whether to use index-only access and a `CREATE TABLE AS SELECT` statement. You should use index hints if your system is CPU-bound.

  You should also study the `EXPLAIN PLAN` output.
- Did the data set change?

  If so, you should gather statistics to evaluate any differences.

- Is the hardware overtaxed?

  If so, you should check CPU, I/O, and swap memory.

After setting your basic goals and answering these questions, you need to consider the following topics:

- Is there regression?
- Is there a plan change?
- Is there a parallel plan?
- Is there a serial plan?
- Is there parallel execution?
- Is the workload evenly distributed?

Is There Regression?

Does parallel execution's actual performance deviate from what you expected? If performance is as you expected, could there be an underlying performance problem? Perhaps you have a desired outcome in mind to which you are comparing the current outcome. Perhaps you have justifiable performance expectations that the system does not achieve. You might have achieved this level of performance or a particular execution plan in the past, but now, with a similar environment and operation, the system is not meeting this goal.

If performance is not as you expected, can you quantify the deviation? For data warehousing operations, the execution plan is key. For critical data warehousing operations, save the `EXPLAIN PLAN` results. Then, as you analyze and reanalyze the data, upgrade Oracle, and load new data, over time you can compare new execution plans with old plans. Take this approach either proactively or reactively.

Alternatively, you might find that plan performance improves if you use hints. You might want to understand why hints are necessary and determine how to get the optimizer to generate the desired plan without hints. Try increasing the statistical sample size: better statistics can give you a better plan.

Is There a Plan Change?

If there has been a change in the execution plan, determine whether the plan is or should be parallel or serial.

Is There a Parallel Plan?

If the execution plan is or should be parallel, study the `EXPLAIN PLAN` output. Did you analyze all the tables? Perhaps you need to use hints in a few cases. Verify that the hint provides better performance.

Is There a Serial Plan?

If the execution plan is or should be serial, consider the following strategies:

- Use an index. Sometimes adding an index can greatly improve performance. Consider adding an extra column to the index. Perhaps your operation could obtain all its data from the index, and not require a table scan. Perhaps you need to use hints in a few cases. Verify that the hint provides better results.

- Compute statistics. If you do not analyze often and you can spare the time, it is a good practice to compute statistics. This is particularly important if you are performing many joins, and it will result in better plans. Alternatively, you can estimate statistics.

NOTE *Using different sample sizes can cause the plan to change. Generally, the higher the sample size, the better the plan.*

- Use histograms for nonuniform distributions.
- Check initialization parameters to be sure the values are reasonable.
- Replace bind variables with literals unless `CURSOR_SHARING` is set to `force` or `similar`.
- Determine whether execution is I/O- or CPU-bound. Then check the optimizer cost model.
- Convert subqueries to joins.
- Use the `CREATE TABLE ... AS SELECT` statement to break a complex operation into smaller pieces. With a large query referencing five or six tables, it may be difficult to determine which part of the query is taking the most time. You can isolate bottlenecks in the query by breaking it into steps and analyzing each step.

Is There Parallel Execution?

If the cause of regression cannot be traced to problems in the plan, the problem must be an execution issue. For data warehousing operations, both serial and parallel, consider how the plan uses memory. Check the paging rate and make sure the system is using memory as effectively as possible. Check buffer, sort, and hash area sizing. After you run a query or DML operation, look at the `V$SESSTAT`, `V$PX_SESSTAT`, and `V$PQ_SYSSTAT` views to see the number of server processes used and other information for the session and system.

Is the Workload Evenly Distributed?

If you are using parallel execution, is there unevenness in workload distribution? For example, if there are 10 CPUs and a single user, you can see whether the workload is evenly distributed across CPUs. This can vary over time, with periods that are more or less I/O intensive, but in general each CPU should have roughly the same amount of activity.

The statistics in `V$PQ_TQSTAT` show rows produced and consumed for each parallel execution server. This is a good indication of skew and does not require single user operation.

Operating system statistics show you the per-processor CPU utilization and per-disk I/O activity. Concurrently running tasks make it harder to see what is going on, however. It may be useful to run in single-user mode and check operating system monitors that show system level CPU and I/O activity.

If I/O problems occur, you might need to reorganize your data by spreading it over more devices. If parallel execution problems occur, check to be sure you have followed the recommendation to spread data over at least as many devices as CPUs.

If there is no skew in workload distribution, check for the following conditions:

- Is there device contention?
- Is there controller contention?
- Is the system I/O-bound with too little parallelism? If so, consider increasing parallelism up to the number of devices.

- Is the system CPU-bound with too much parallelism? Check the operating system CPU monitor to see whether a lot of time is being spent in system calls. The resource might be overcommitted, and too much parallelism might cause processes to compete with themselves.
- Are there more concurrent users than the system can support?

Monitoring Parallel Execution Performance with Dynamic Performance Views

After your system has run for a few days, monitor parallel execution performance statistics to determine whether your parallel processing is optimal. Do this by using any of the views discussed in this section.

In Oracle Real Application Clusters, global versions of the views described in this section aggregate statistics from multiple instances. The global views have names beginning with `G`, such as `GV$FILESTAT` for `V$FILESTAT`, and so on.

V$PX_SESSION

The `V$PX_SESSION` view shows data about query server sessions, groups, sets, and server numbers. It also displays real-time data about the processes working on behalf of parallel execution. This table includes information about the requested DOP and the actual DOP granted to the operation.

V$PX_SESSTAT

The `V$PX_SESSTAT` view provides a join of the session information from `V$PX_SESSION` and the `V$SESSTAT` table. Thus, all session statistics available to a normal session are available for all sessions performed by using parallel execution.

V$PX_PROCESS

The `V$PX_PROCESS` view contains information about the parallel processes, including status, session ID, process ID, and other information.

V$PX_PROCESS_SYSSTAT

The `V$PX_PROCESS_SYSSTAT` view shows the status of query servers and provides buffer allocation statistics.

V$PQ_SESSTAT

The `V$PQ_SESSTAT` view shows the status of all current server groups in the system such as data about how queries allocate processes and how the multiuser and load balancing algorithms are affecting the default and hinted values. `V$PQ_SESSTAT` will be obsolete in a future release.

You might need to adjust some parameter settings to improve performance after reviewing data from these views. In this case, refer to the discussion of "Tuning General Parameters for Parallel Execution". Query these views periodically to monitor the progress of long-running parallel operations.

NOTE *For many dynamic performance views, you must set the parameter `TIMED_STATISTICS` to `true` in order for Oracle to collect statistics for each view. You can use the `ALTER SYSTEM` or `ALTER SESSION` statements to turn `TIMED_STATISTICS` on and off.*

V$FILESTAT

The V$FILESTAT view sums read and write requests, the number of blocks, and service times for every datafile in every tablespace. Use V$FILESTAT to diagnose I/O and workload distribution problems.

You can join statistics from V$FILESTAT with statistics in the DBA_DATA_FILES view to group I/O by tablespace or to find the filename for a given file number. Using a ratio analysis, you can determine the percentage of the total tablespace activity used by each file in the tablespace. If you make a practice of putting just one large, heavily accessed object in a tablespace, you can use this technique to identify objects that have a poor physical layout.

You can further diagnose disk space allocation problems using the DBA_EXTENTS view. Ensure that space is allocated evenly from all files in the tablespace. Monitoring V$FILESTAT during a long-running operation and then correlating I/O activity to the EXPLAIN PLAN output is a good way to follow progress.

V$PARAMETER

The V$PARAMETER view lists the name, current value, and default value of all system parameters. In addition, the view shows whether a parameter is a session parameter that you can modify online with an ALTER SYSTEM or ALTER SESSION statement.

V$PQ_TQSTAT

As a simple example, consider a hash join between two tables, with a join on a column with only 2 distinct values. At best, this hash function will have one hash value to parallel execution server A and the other to parallel execution server B. A DOP of two is fine, but, if it is 4, then at least 2 parallel execution servers have no work. To discover this type of skew, use a query similar to the following example:

```
SELECT dfo_number, tq_id, server_type, process, num_rows
FROM V$PQ_TQSTAT
ORDER BY dfo_number DESC, tq_id, server_type, process;
```

The best way to resolve this problem might be to choose a different join method; a nested loop join might be the best option. Alternatively, if one of the join tables is small relative to the other, a BROADCAST distribution method can be hinted using PQ_DISTRIBUTE hint. Note that the optimizer considers the BROADCAST distribution method, but requires OPTIMIZER_FEATURE_ENABLED set to 9.0.2 or higher.

Now, assume that you have a join key with high cardinality, but one of the values contains most of the data, for example, lava lamp sales by year. The only year that had big sales was 1968, and thus, the parallel execution server for the 1968 records will be overwhelmed. You should use the same corrective actions as described previously.

The V$PQ_TQSTAT view provides a detailed report of message traffic at the table queue level. V$PQ_TQSTAT data is valid only when queried from a session that is executing parallel SQL statements. A table queue is the pipeline between query server groups, between the parallel coordinator and a query server group, or between a query server group and the coordinator. Table queues are represented in EXPLAIN PLAN output by the row labels of PARALLEL_TO_PARALLEL, SERIAL_TO_PARALLEL, or PARALLEL_TO_SERIAL, respectively.

V$PQ_TQSTAT has a row for each query server process that reads from or writes to in each table queue. A table queue connecting 10 consumer processes to 10 producer processes has 20 rows in the view. Sum the bytes column and group by TQ_ID, the table queue identifier, to obtain the total number of bytes sent through each table queue. Compare this with the optimizer estimates; large variations might indicate a need to analyze the data using a larger sample.

Compute the variance of bytes grouped by `TQ_ID`. Large variances indicate workload imbalances. You should investigate large variances to determine whether the producers start out with unequal distributions of data, or whether the distribution itself is skewed. If the data itself is skewed, this might indicate a low cardinality, or low number of distinct values.

NOTE

The `V$PQ_TQSTAT` view will be renamed in a future release to `V$PX_TQSTSAT`.

V$SESSTAT and V$SYSSTAT

The `V$SESSTAT` view provides parallel execution statistics for each session. The statistics include total number of queries, DML and DDL statements executed in a session and the total number of intrainstance and interinstance messages exchanged during parallel execution during the session. `V$SYSSTAT` provides the same statistics as `V$SESSTAT`, but for the entire system.

Monitoring Session Statistics

These examples use the dynamic performance views described in "Monitoring Parallel Execution Performance with Dynamic Performance Views".

Use `GV$PX_SESSION` to determine the configuration of the server group executing in parallel. In this example, sessions 9 is the query coordinator, while sessions 7 and 21 are in the first group, first set. Sessions 18 and 20 are in the first group, second set. The requested and granted DOP for this query is 2, as shown by Oracle's response to the following query:

```
SELECT QCSID, SID, INST_ID "Inst",
  SERVER_GROUP "Group", SERVER_SET "Set",
  DEGREE "Degree", REQ_DEGREE "Req Degree"
FROM GV$PX_SESSION ORDER BY QCSID, QCINST_ID, SERVER_GROUP, SERVER_SET;
```

Your output should resemble the following:

QCSID	SID	Inst	Group	Set	Degree	Req Degree
9	9	1				
9	7	1	1	1	2	2
9	21	1	1	1	2	2
9	18	1	1	2	2	2
9	20	1	1	2	2	2

```
5 rows selected.
```

NOTE

For a single instance, use `SELECT FROM V$PX_SESSION` and do not include the column name `Instance ID`.

The processes shown in the output from the previous example using `GV$PX_SESSION` collaborate to complete the same task. The next example shows the execution of a join query to determine the progress of these processes in terms of physical reads. Use this query to track any specific statistic:

```
SELECT QCSID, SID, INST_ID "Inst",
  SERVER_GROUP "Group", SERVER_SET "Set",
  NAME "Stat Name", VALUE
```

```
FROM GV$PX_SESSTAT A, V$STATNAME B
WHERE A.STATISTIC# = B.STATISTIC#
  AND NAME LIKE 'PHYSICAL READS'
  AND VALUE > 0
ORDER BY QCSID, QCINST_ID, SERVER_GROUP, SERVER_SET;
```

Your output should resemble the following:

QCSIDSID	Inst	Group	Set	Stat	Name	VALUE
9	9	1			physical reads	3863
9	7	1	1	1	physical reads	2
9	21	1	1	1	physical reads	2
9	18	1	1	2	physical reads	2
9	20	1	1	2	physical reads	2

5 rows selected.

Use the previous type of query to track statistics in V$STATNAME. Repeat this query as often as required to observe the progress of the query server processes.

The next query uses V$PX_PROCESS to check the status of the query servers.

```
SELECT * FROM V$PX_PROCESS;
```

Your output should resemble the following:

SERV	STATUS	PID	SPID	SID	SERIAL
P002	IN USE	16	16955	21	7729
P003	IN USE	17	16957	20	2921
P004	AVAILABLE	18	16959		
P005	AVAILABLE	19	16962		
P000	IN USE	12	6999	18	4720
P001	IN USE	13	7004	7	234

6 rows selected.

Monitoring System Statistics

The V$SYSSTAT and V$SESSTAT views contain several statistics for monitoring parallel execution. Use these statistics to track the number of parallel queries, DMLs, DDLs, data flow operators (DFOs), and operations. Each query, DML, or DDL can have multiple parallel operations and multiple DFOs.

In addition, statistics also count the number of query operations for which the DOP was reduced, or downgraded, due to either the adaptive multiuser algorithm or the depletion of available parallel execution servers.

Finally, statistics in these views also count the number of messages sent on behalf of parallel execution. The following syntax is an example of how to display these statistics:

```
SELECT NAME, VALUE FROM GV$SYSSTAT
WHERE UPPER (NAME) LIKE '%PARALLEL OPERATIONS%'
OR UPPER (NAME) LIKE '%PARALLELIZED%'
OR UPPER (NAME) LIKE '%PX%';
```

Your output should resemble the following:

```
NAME                                                    VALUE
-------------------------------------------------------------
queries parallelized                                      347
DML statements parallelized                                 0
DDL statements parallelized                                 0
DFO trees parallelized                                    463
Parallel operations not downgraded                         28
Parallel operations downgraded to serial                   31
Parallel operations downgraded 75 to 99 pct               252
Parallel operations downgraded 50 to 75 pct               128
Parallel operations downgraded 25 to 50 pct                43
Parallel operations downgraded 1 to 25 pct                 12
PX local messages sent                                  74548
PX local messages recv'd                                74128
PX remote messages sent                                     0
PX remote messages recv'd                                   0

14 rows selected.
```

Monitoring Operating System Statistics

There is considerable overlap between information available in Oracle and information available though operating system utilities (such as `sar` and `vmstat` on UNIX-based systems). Operating systems provide performance statistics on I/O, communication, CPU, memory and paging, scheduling, and synchronization primitives. The `V$SESSTAT` view provides the major categories of operating system statistics as well.

Typically, operating system information about I/O devices and semaphore operations is harder to map back to database objects and operations than is Oracle information. However, some operating systems have good visualization tools and efficient means of collecting the data.

Operating system information about CPU and memory usage is very important for assessing performance. Probably the most important statistic is CPU usage. The goal of low-level performance tuning is to become CPU bound on all CPUs. Once this is achieved, you can work at the SQL level to find an alternate plan that might be more I/O intensive but use less CPU.

Operating system memory and paging information is valuable for fine tuning the many system parameters that control how memory is divided among memory-intensive warehouse subsystems like parallel communication, sort, and hash join.

AFFINITY AND PARALLEL OPERATIONS

NOTE: *The features described in this section are available only if you have purchased Oracle9i Enterprise Edition with the Real Application Clusters Option.*

In a shared-disk cluster or MPP configuration, an instance of the Oracle Real Application Clusters is said to have affinity for a device if the device is directly accessed from the processors on which the instance is running. Similarly, an instance has affinity for a file if it has affinity for the devices on which the file is stored.

Determination of affinity may involve arbitrary determinations for files that are striped across multiple devices. Somewhat arbitrarily, an instance is said to have affinity for a tablespace (or a partition of a table or index within a tablespace) if the instance has affinity for the first file in the tablespace.

Oracle considers affinity when allocating work to parallel execution servers. The use of affinity for parallel execution of SQL statements is transparent to users.

Affinity and Parallel Queries

Affinity in parallel queries increases the speed of scanning data from disk by doing the scans on a processor that is near the data. This can provide a substantial performance increase for machines that do not naturally support shared disks.

The most common use of affinity is for a table or index partition to be stored in one file on one device. This configuration provides the highest availability by limiting the damage done by a device failure and makes the best use of partition-parallel index scans.

DSS customers might prefer to stripe table partitions over multiple devices (probably a subset of the total number of devices). This configuration allows some queries to prune the total amount of data being accessed by using partitioning criteria and still obtain parallelism through rowid-range parallel table (partition) scans. If the devices are configured as a RAID, availability can still be very good. Even when used for DSS, indexes should probably be partitioned on individual devices.

Other configurations (for example, multiple partitions in one file striped over multiple devices) will yield correct query results, but you may need to use hints or explicitly set object attributes to select the correct DOP.

Affinity and Parallel DML

For parallel DML (inserts, updates, and deletes), affinity enhancements improve cache performance by routing the DML operation to the node that has affinity for the partition.

Affinity determines how to distribute the work among the set of instances or parallel execution servers to perform the DML operation in parallel. Affinity can improve performance of queries in several ways:

- For certain MPP architectures, Oracle uses device-to-node affinity information to determine on which nodes to spawn parallel execution servers (parallel process allocation) and which work granules (rowid ranges or partitions) to send to particular nodes (work assignment). Better performance is achieved by having nodes mainly access local devices, giving a better buffer cache hit ratio for every node and reducing the network overhead and I/O latency.
- For SMP, cluster, and MPP architectures, process-to-device affinity is used to achieve device isolation. This reduces the chances of having multiple parallel execution servers accessing the same device simultaneously. This process-to-device affinity information is also used in implementing stealing between processes.

For partitioned tables and indexes, partition-to-node affinity information determines process allocation and work assignment. For shared-nothing MPP systems, Oracle Real Application Clusters tries to assign partitions to instances, taking the disk affinity of the partitions into account. For shared-disk MPP and cluster systems, partitions are assigned to instances in a round-robin manner.

Affinity is only available for parallel DML when running in an Oracle Real Application Clusters configuration. Affinity information which persists across statements improves buffer cache hit ratios and reduces block pings between instances.

MISCELLANEOUS PARALLEL EXECUTION TUNING TIPS

This section contains some ideas for improving performance in a parallel execution environment and includes the following topics:

- Setting buffer cache size for parallel operations
- Overriding the default degree of parallelism
- Rewriting SQL statements
- Creating and populating tables in parallel
- Creating temporary tablespaces for parallel sort and hash join
- Executing parallel SQL statements
- Using EXPLAIN PLAN to show parallel operations plans
- Additional considerations for parallel DML
- Creating indexes in parallel
- Parallel DML tips
- Incremental data loading in parallel
- Using hints with cost-based optimization
- FIRST_ROWS(n) hint
- Enabling dynamic statistic sampling.

Setting Buffer Cache Size for Parallel Operations

With the exception of parallel update and delete, parallel operations do not generally benefit from larger buffer cache sizes. Other parallel operations can benefit only if you increase the size of the buffer pool and thereby accommodate the inner table or index for a nested loop join.

Overriding the Default Degree of Parallelism

The default DOP is appropriate for reducing response time while guaranteeing use of CPU and I/O resources for any parallel operations.

If it is memory-bound, or if several concurrent parallel operations are running, you might want to decrease the default DOP.

Oracle uses the default DOP for tables that have `PARALLEL` attributed to them in the data dictionary or that have the `PARALLEL` hint specified. If a table does not have parallelism attributed to it, or has `NOPARALLEL` (the default) attributed to it, and parallelism is not being forced through `ALTER SESSION FORCE PARALLEL`, then that table is never scanned in parallel. This override occurs regardless of the default DOP indicated by the number of CPUs, instances, and devices storing that table.

You can adjust the DOP by using the following guidelines:

- Modify the default DOP by changing the value for the `PARALLEL_THREADS_PER_CPU` parameter.
- Adjust the DOP either by using `ALTER TABLE`, `ALTER SESSION`, or by using hints.

- To increase the number of concurrent parallel operations, reduce the DOP, or set the parameter PARALLEL_ADAPTIVE_MULTI_USER to true.

Rewriting SQL Statements

The most important issue for parallel execution is ensuring that all parts of the query plan that process a substantial amount of data execute in parallel. Use EXPLAIN PLAN to verify that all plan steps have an OTHER_TAG of PARALLEL_TO_PARALLEL, PARALLEL_TO_SERIAL, PARALLEL_COMBINED_WITH_PARENT, or PARALLEL_COMBINED_WITH_CHILD. Any other keyword (or null) indicates serial execution and a possible bottleneck.

You can also use the utlxplp.sql script to present the EXPLAIN PLAN output with all relevant parallel information.

You can increase the optimizer's ability to generate parallel plans converting subqueries, especially correlated subqueries, into joins. Oracle can parallelize joins more efficiently than subqueries. This also applies to updates.

Creating and Populating Tables in Parallel

Oracle cannot return results to a user process in parallel. If a query returns a large number of rows, execution of the query might indeed be faster. However, the user process can only receive the rows serially. To optimize parallel execution performance for queries that retrieve large result sets, use PARALLEL CREATE TABLE ... AS SELECT or direct-path INSERT to store the result set in the database. At a later time, users can view the result set serially.

NOTE *Performing the SELECT in parallel does not influence the CREATE statement. If the CREATE is parallel, however, the optimizer tries to make the SELECT run in parallel also.*

When combined with the NOLOGGING option, the parallel version of CREATE TABLE ... AS SELECT provides a very efficient intermediate table facility, for example:

```
CREATE TABLE summary PARALLEL NOLOGGING
  AS SELECT dim_1, dim_2 ..., SUM (meas_1)
     FROM facts
  GROUP BY dim_1, dim_2;
```

These tables can also be incrementally loaded with parallel INSERT. You can take advantage of intermediate tables by using the following techniques:

- Common subqueries can be computed once and referenced many times. This can allow some queries against star schemas (in particular, queries without selective WHERE-clause predicates) to be better parallelized. Note that star queries with selective WHERE-clause predicates using the star-transformation technique can be effectively parallelized automatically without any modification to the SQL.
- Decompose complex queries into simpler steps in order to provide application-level checkpoint or restart. For example, a complex multitable join on a database 1 terabyte in size could run for dozens of hours. A failure during this query would mean starting over from the beginning. Using CREATE TABLE ... AS SELECT or PARALLEL INSERT AS SELECT, you can rewrite the query as a sequence of simpler queries that run for a few hours each. If a system failure occurs, the query can be restarted from the last completed step.
- Implement manual parallel deletes efficiently by creating a new table that omits the unwanted rows from the original table, and then dropping the original table. Alternatively, you can use the convenient parallel delete feature, which directly deletes rows from the original table.

- Create summary tables for efficient multidimensional drill-down analysis. For example, a summary table might store the sum of revenue grouped by month, brand, region, and salesman.
- Reorganize tables, eliminating chained rows, compressing free space, and so on, by copying the old table to a new table. This is much faster than export/import and easier than reloading.

NOTE *Be sure to use the* `DBMS_STATS` *package on newly created tables. Also consider creating indexes. To avoid I/O bottlenecks, specify a tablespace with at least as many devices as CPUs. To avoid fragmentation in allocating space, the number of files in a tablespace should be a multiple of the number of CPUs.*

Creating Temporary Tablespaces for Parallel Sort and Hash Join

For optimal space management performance, you should use locally managed temporary tablespaces. The following is an example:

```
CREATE TEMPORARY TABLESPACE TStemp TEMPFILE '/dev/D31'
SIZE 4096MB REUSE
EXTENT MANAGEMENT LOCAL
UNIFORM SIZE 10m;
```

You can associate temporary tablespaces to a database by issuing a statement such as:

```
ALTER DATABASE TEMPORARY TABLESPACE TStemp;
```

Once this is done, explicit assignment of users to tablespaces is not needed.

Size of Temporary Extents

When using a locally managed temporary tablespace, extents are all the same size because this helps avoid fragmentation. As a general rule, temporary extents should be smaller than permanent extents because there are more demands for temporary space, and parallel processes or other operations running concurrently must share the temporary tablespace. Normally, temporary extents should be in the range of 1MB to 10MB. Once you allocate an extent, it is available for the duration of an operation. If you allocate a large extent but only need to use a small amount of space, the unused space in the extent is unavailable.

At the same time, temporary extents should be large enough that processes do not have to wait for space. Temporary tablespaces use less overhead than permanent tablespaces when allocating and freeing a new extent. However, obtaining a new temporary extent still requires the overhead of acquiring a latch and searching through the SGA structures, as well as SGA space consumption for the sort extent pool.

Executing Parallel SQL Statements

After analyzing your tables and indexes, you should see performance improvements based on the DOP used.

As a general process, you should start with simple parallel operations and evaluate their total I/O throughput with a `SELECT COUNT(*) FROM facts` statement. Then, evaluate total CPU power by adding a complex `WHERE` clause to the statement. An I/O imbalance might suggest a better physical database layout. After you understand how simple scans work, add aggregation, joins, and other operations that reflect individual aspects of the overall workload. In particular, you should look for bottlenecks.

Besides query performance, you should also monitor parallel load, parallel index creation, and parallel DML, and look for good utilization of I/O and CPU resources.

Using EXPLAIN PLAN to Show Parallel Operations Plans

Use the `EXPLAIN PLAN` statement to see the execution plans for parallel queries. `EXPLAIN PLAN` output shows optimizer information in the `COST`, `BYTES`, and `CARDINALITY` columns. You can also use the `utlxplp.sql` script to present the `EXPLAIN PLAN` output with all relevant parallel information.

There are several ways to optimize the parallel execution of join statements. You can alter system configuration, adjust parameters as discussed earlier in this chapter, or use hints, such as the `DISTRIBUTION` hint.

The key points when using `EXPLAIN PLAN` are to:

- Verify optimizer selectivity estimates. If the optimizer thinks that only one row will be produced from a query, it tends to favor using a nested loop. This could be an indication that the tables are not analyzed or that the optimizer has made an incorrect estimate about the correlation of multiple predicates on the same table. A hint may be required to force the optimizer to use another join method. Consequently, if the plan says only one row is produced from any particular stage and this is incorrect, consider hints or gather statistics.
- Use hash join on low cardinality join keys. If a join key has few distinct values, then a hash join may not be optimal. If the number of distinct values is less than the DOP, then some parallel query servers may be unable to work on the particular query.
- Consider data skew. If a join key involves excessive data skew, a hash join may require some parallel query servers to work more than others. Consider using a hint to cause a `BROADCAST` distribution method if the optimizer did not choose it. Note that the optimizer will consider the `BROADCAST` distribution method only if the `OPTIMIZER_FEATURE_ENABLED` is set to 9.0.2 or higher.

Additional Considerations for Parallel DML

When you want to refresh your data warehouse database using parallel insert, update, or delete on a data warehouse, there are additional issues to consider when designing the physical database. These considerations do not affect parallel execution operations. These issues are:

- PDML and direct-path restrictions
- Limitation on the degree of parallelism
- Using local and global striping
- Increasing INITRANS and MAXTRANS
- Limitation on available number of transaction free lists for segments in dictionary-managed tablespaces
- Using multiple archivers
- Database writer process (DBWn) workload
- [NO]LOGGING clause.

PDML and Direct-Path Restrictions

If a parallel restriction is violated, the operation is simply performed serially. If a direct-path `INSERT` restriction is violated, then the `APPEND` hint is ignored and a conventional insert is performed. No error message is returned.

Limitation on the Degree of Parallelism

If you are performing parallel `UPDATE`, `MERGE`, or `DELETE` operations, the DOP is equal to or less than the number of partitions in the table.

Using Local and Global Striping

Parallel updates and deletes work only on partitioned tables. They can generate a high number of random I/O requests during index maintenance.

For local index maintenance, local striping is most efficient in reducing I/O contention because one server process only goes to its own set of disks and disk controllers. Local striping also increases availability in the event of one disk failing.

For global index maintenance (partitioned or nonpartitioned), globally striping the index across many disks and disk controllers is the best way to distribute the number of I/Os.

Increasing INITRANS and MAXTRANS

If you have global indexes, a global index segment and global index blocks are shared by server processes of the same parallel DML statement. Even if the operations are not performed against the same row, the server processes can share the same index blocks. Each server transaction needs one transaction entry in the index block header before it can make changes to a block. Therefore, in the `CREATE INDEX` or `ALTER INDEX` statements, you should set `INITRANS`, the initial number of transactions allocated within each data block, to a large value, such as the maximum DOP against this index. Leave `MAXTRANS`, the maximum number of concurrent transactions that can update a data block, at its default value, which is the maximum your system can support. This value should not exceed 255.

If you run a DOP of 10 against a table with a global index, all 10 server processes might attempt to change the same global index block. For this reason, you must set `MAXTRANS` to at least 10 so all server processes can make the change at the same time. If `MAXTRANS` is not large enough, the parallel DML operation fails.

Limitation on Available Number of Transaction Free Lists for Segments in Dictionary-Managed Tablespaces

Once a segment has been created, the number of process and transaction free lists is fixed and cannot be altered. If you specify a large number of process free lists in the segment header, you might find that this limits the number of transaction free lists that are available. You can abate this limitation the next time you re-create the segment header by decreasing the number of process free lists; this leaves more room for transaction free lists in the segment header.

For `UPDATE` and `DELETE` operations, each server process can require its own transaction free list. The parallel DML DOP is thus effectively limited by the smallest number of transaction free lists available on the table and on any of the global indexes the DML statement must maintain. For example, if the table has 25 transaction free lists and the table has two global indexes, one with 50 transaction free lists and one with 30 transaction free lists, the DOP is limited to 25. If the table had had 40 transaction free lists, the DOP would have been limited to 30.

The `FREELISTS` parameter of the `STORAGE` clause is used to set the number of process free lists. By default, no process free lists are created.

The default number of transaction free lists depends on the block size. For example, if the number of process free lists is not set explicitly, a 4 KB block has about 80 transaction free lists by default. The minimum number of transaction free lists is 25.

Using Multiple Archivers

Parallel DDL and parallel DML operations can generate a large amount of redo logs. A single ARCH process to archive these redo logs might not be able to keep up. To avoid this problem, you can spawn multiple archiver processes. This can be done manually or by using a job queue.

Database Writer Process (DBWn) Workload

Parallel DML operations dirty a large number of data, index, and undo blocks in the buffer cache during a short period of time. For example, suppose you see a high number of free_buffer_waits after querying the V$SYSTEM_EVENT view, as in the following syntax:

```
SELECT TOTAL_WAITS FROM V$SYSTEM_EVENT WHERE EVENT = 'FREE BUFFER WAITS';
```

In this case, you should consider increasing the DBW*n* processes. If there are no waits for free buffers, the query will not return any rows.

[NO]LOGGING Clause

The [NO]LOGGING clause applies to tables, partitions, tablespaces, and indexes. Virtually no log is generated for certain operations (such as direct-path INSERT) if the NOLOGGING clause is used. The NOLOGGING attribute is not specified at the INSERT statement level but is instead specified when using the ALTER or CREATE statement for a table, partition, index, or tablespace.

When a table or index has NOLOGGING set, neither parallel nor serial direct-path INSERT operations generate undo or redo logs. Processes running with the NOLOGGING option set run faster because no redo is generated. However, after a NOLOGGING operation against a table, partition, or index, if a media failure occurs before a backup is taken, then all tables, partitions, and indexes that have been modified might be corrupted.

NOTE *Direct-path INSERT operations (except for dictionary updates) never generate undo logs. The NOLOGGING attribute does not affect undo, only redo. To be precise, NOLOGGING allows the direct-path INSERT operation to generate a negligible amount of redo (range-invalidation redo, as opposed to full image redo).*

For backward compatibility, [UN]RECOVERABLE is still supported as an alternate keyword with the CREATE TABLE statement. This alternate keyword might not be supported, however, in future releases.

At the tablespace level, the logging clause specifies the default logging attribute for all tables, indexes, and partitions created in the tablespace. When an existing tablespace logging attribute is changed by the ALTER TABLESPACE statement, then all tables, indexes, and partitions created after the ALTER statement will have the new logging attribute; existing ones will not change their logging attributes. The tablespace-level logging attribute can be overridden by the specifications at the table, index, or partition level.

The default logging attribute is LOGGING. However, if you have put the database in NOARCHIVELOG mode, by issuing ALTER DATABASE NOARCHIVELOG, then all operations that can be done without logging will not generate logs, regardless of the specified logging attribute.

Creating Indexes in Parallel

Multiple processes can work together simultaneously to create an index. By dividing the work necessary to create an index among multiple server processes, Oracle can create the index more quickly than if a single server process created the index sequentially.

Parallel index creation works in much the same way as a table scan with an `ORDER BY` clause. The table is randomly sampled and a set of index keys is found that equally divides the index into the same number of pieces as the DOP. A first set of query processes scans the table, extracts key-rowid pairs, and sends each pair to a process in a second set of query processes based on key. Each process in the second set sorts the keys and builds an index in the usual fashion. After all index pieces are built, the parallel coordinator simply concatenates the pieces (which are ordered) to form the final index.

Parallel local index creation uses a single server set. Each server process in the set is assigned a table partition to scan and for which to build an index partition. Because half as many server processes are used for a given DOP, parallel local index creation can be run with a higher DOP.

You can optionally specify that no redo and undo logging should occur during index creation. This can significantly improve performance but temporarily renders the index unrecoverable. Recoverability is restored after the new index is backed up. If your application can tolerate a window where recovery of the index requires it to be re-created, then you should consider using the `NOLOGGING` clause.

The `PARALLEL` clause in the `CREATE INDEX` statement is the only way in which you can specify the DOP for creating the index. If the DOP is not specified in the parallel clause of `CREATE INDEX`, then the number of CPUs is used as the DOP. If there is no `PARALLEL` clause, index creation is done serially.

> NOTE
>
> *When creating an index in parallel, the* `STORAGE` *clause refers to the storage of each of the subindexes created by the query server processes. Therefore, an index created with an* `INITIAL` *of 5 MB and a DOP of 12 consumes at least 60 MB of storage during index creation because each process starts with an extent of 5 MB. When the query coordinator process combines the sorted subindexes, some of the extents might be trimmed, and the resulting index might be smaller than the requested 60 MB.*

When you add or enable a `UNIQUE` or `PRIMARY KEY` constraint on a table, you cannot automatically create the required index in parallel. Instead, manually create an index on the desired columns, using the `CREATE INDEX` statement and an appropriate `PARALLEL` clause, and then add or enable the constraint. Oracle then uses the existing index when enabling or adding the constraint.

Multiple constraints on the same table can be enabled concurrently and in parallel if all the constraints are already in the `ENABLE NOVALIDATE` state. In the following example, the `ALTER TABLE ... ENABLE CONSTRAINT` statement performs the table scan that checks the constraint in parallel:

```
CREATE TABLE a (a1 NUMBER CONSTRAINT ach CHECK (a1 > 0) ENABLE NOVALIDATE)
PARALLEL;
INSERT INTO a values (1);
COMMIT;
ALTER TABLE a ENABLE CONSTRAINT ach;
```

Parallel DML Tips

This section provides an overview of parallel DML functionality. The topics covered include:

- Parallel DML Tip 1: INSERT
- Parallel DML Tip 2: Direct-Path INSERT
- Parallel DML Tip 3: Parallelizing INSERT, MERGE, UPDATE, and DELETE

Parallel DML Tip 1: INSERT

Oracle INSERT functionality can be summarized as follows:

Table 14.5 Summary of INSERT Features

Insert Type	Parallel	Serial	NOLOGGING
Conventional	No	Yes	No
Direct-path INSERT (APPEND)	Yes, but requires: • ALTER SESSION ENABLE PARALLEL DML • Table PARALLEL attribute or PARALLEL hint • APPEND hint (optional)	Yes, but requires: • APPEND hint	Yes, but requires: • NOLOGGING attribute set for partition or table

If parallel DML is enabled and there is a PARALLEL hint or PARALLEL attribute set for the table in the data dictionary, then inserts are parallel and appended, unless a restriction applies. If either the PARALLEL hint or PARALLEL attribute is missing, the insert is performed serially.

Parallel DML Tip 2: Direct-Path INSERT

The append mode is the default during a parallel insert: data is always inserted into a new block which is allocated to the table. Therefore the APPEND hint is optional. You should use append mode to increase the speed of INSERT operations, but not when space utilization needs to be optimized. You can use NOAPPEND to override append mode.

The APPEND hint applies to both serial and parallel insert: even serial inserts are faster if you use this hint. APPEND, however, does require more space and locking overhead.

You can use NOLOGGING with APPEND to make the process even faster. NOLOGGING means that no redo log is generated for the operation. NOLOGGING is never the default; use it when you wish to optimize performance. It should not normally be used when recovery is needed for the table or partition. If recovery is needed, be sure to take a backup immediately after the operation. Use the ALTER TABLE [NO]LOGGING statement to set the appropriate value.

Parallel DML Tip 3: Parallelizing INSERT, MERGE, UPDATE, and DELETE

When the table or partition has the PARALLEL attribute in the data dictionary, that attribute setting is used to determine parallelism of INSERT, UPDATE, and DELETE statements as well as queries. An explicit PARALLEL hint for a table in a statement overrides the effect of the PARALLEL attribute in the data dictionary.

You can use the NOPARALLEL hint to override a PARALLEL attribute for the table in the data dictionary. In general, hints take precedence over attributes.

DML operations are considered for parallelization only if the session is in a PARALLEL DML enabled mode. (Use ALTER SESSION ENABLE PARALLEL DML to enter this mode.) The mode does not affect parallelization of queries or of the query portions of a DML statement.

Parallelizing INSERT ... SELECT

In the INSERT ... SELECT statement you can specify a PARALLEL hint after the INSERT keyword, in addition to the hint after the SELECT keyword. The PARALLEL hint after the INSERT keyword applies to the INSERT operation only, and the PARALLEL hint after the SELECT keyword applies to the SELECT operation only. Thus, parallelism of the INSERT and SELECT operations are independent of each other. If one operation cannot be performed in parallel, it has no effect on whether the other operation can be performed in parallel.

The ability to parallelize inserts causes a change in existing behavior if the user has explicitly enabled the session for parallel DML and if the table in question has a PARALLEL attribute set in the data dictionary entry. In that case, existing INSERT ... SELECT statements that have the select operation parallelized can also have their insert operation parallelized.

If you query multiple tables, you can specify multiple SELECT PARALLEL hints and multiple PARALLEL attributes.

Example 14.7 : Parallelizing INSERT ... SELECT

Add the new employees who were hired after the acquisition of ACME.

```
INSERT /*+ PARALLEL(EMP) */ INTO employees
SELECT /*+ PARALLEL(ACME_EMP) */ *
FROM ACME_EMP;
```

The APPEND keyword is not required in this example because it is implied by the PARALLEL hint.

Parallelizing UPDATE and DELETE

The PARALLEL hint (placed immediately after the UPDATE or DELETE keyword) applies not only to the underlying scan operation, but also to the UPDATE or DELETE operation. Alternatively, you can specify UPDATE or DELETE parallelism in the PARALLEL clause specified in the definition of the table to be modified.

If you have explicitly enabled parallel DML for the session or transaction, UPDATE or DELETE statements that have their query operation parallelized can also have their UPDATE or DELETE operation parallelized. Any subqueries or updatable views in the statement can have their own separate PARALLEL hints or clauses, but these parallel directives do not affect the decision to parallelize the update or delete. If these operations cannot be performed in parallel, it has no effect on whether the UPDATE or DELETE portion can be performed in parallel.

Tables must be partitioned in order to support parallel UPDATE and DELETE.

Example 14.8 : Parallelizing UPDATE and DELETE

Give a 10 percent salary raise to all clerks in Dallas.

```
UPDATE /*+ PARALLEL(EMP) */ employees
SET SAL=SAL * 1.1
  WHERE JOB='CLERK' AND DEPTNO IN
  (SELECT DEPTNO FROM DEPT WHERE LOCATION='DALLAS');
```

The PARALLEL hint is applied to the UPDATE operation as well as to the scan.

Example 14.9 : Parallelizing UPDATE and DELETE

Remove all products in the grocery category because the grocery business line was recently spun off into a separate company.

```
DELETE /*+ PARALLEL(PRODUCTS) */ FROM PRODUCTS
WHERE PRODUCT_CATEGORY ='GROCERY';
```

Again, the parallelism is applied to the scan as well as UPDATE operation on table employees.

Incremental Data Loading in Parallel

Parallel DML combined with the updatable join views facility provides an efficient solution for refreshing the tables of a data warehouse system. To refresh tables is to update them with the differential data generated from the OLTP production system.

In the following example, assume that you want to refresh a table named `customer` that has columns `c_key`, `c_name`, and `c_addr`. The differential data contains either new rows or rows that have been updated since the last refresh of the data warehouse. In this example, the updated data is shipped from the production system to the data warehouse system by means of ASCII files. These files must be loaded into a temporary table, named `diff_customer`, before starting the refresh process. You can use SQL*Loader with both the parallel and direct options to efficiently perform this task. You can use the `APPEND` hint when loading in parallel as well.

Once `diff_customer` is loaded, the refresh process can be started. It can be performed in two phases or by merging in parallel, as demonstrated in the following:

- Updating the table in parallel
- Inserting the new rows into the table in parallel
- Merging in parallel.

Updating the Table in Parallel

The following statement is a straightforward SQL implementation of the update using subqueries:

```
UPDATE customers
SET(c_name, c_addr) =
  (SELECT c_name, c_addr
   FROM diff_customer
   WHERE diff_customer.c_key = customer.c_key)
   WHERE c_key IN(SELECT c_key FROM diff_customer);
```

Unfortunately, the two subqueries in this statement affect performance.

An alternative is to rewrite this query using updatable join views. To do this, you must first add a primary key constraint to the `diff_customer` table to ensure that the modified columns map to a key-preserved table:

```
CREATE UNIQUE INDEX diff_pkey_ind ON diff_customer(c_key)
  PARALLEL NOLOGGING;
ALTER TABLE diff_customer ADD PRIMARY KEY (c_key);
```

You can then update the `customers` table with the following SQL statement:

```
UPDATE /*+ PARALLEL(cust_joinview) */
(SELECT /*+ PARALLEL(customers) PARALLEL(diff_customer) */
CUSTOMER.c_name AS c_name
CUSTOMER.c_addr AS c_addr,
diff_customer.c_name AS c_newname, diff_customer.c_addr AS c_newaddr
   WHERE customers.c_key = diff_customer.c_key) cust_joinview
   SET c_name = c_newname, c_addr = c_newaddr;
```

The base scans feeding the join view `cust_joinview` are done in parallel. You can then parallelize the update to further improve performance, but only if the `customer` table is partitioned.

Inserting the New Rows into the Table in Parallel

The last phase of the refresh process consists of inserting the new rows from the `diff_customer` temporary table to the `customer` table. Unlike the update case, you cannot avoid having a subquery in the `INSERT` statement:

```
INSERT /*+PARALLEL(customers)*/ INTO customers
SELECT * FROM diff_customer
s);
```

However, you can guarantee that the subquery is transformed into an anti-hash join by using the `HASH_AJ` hint. Doing so enables you to use parallel `INSERT` to execute the preceding statement efficiently. Parallel `INSERT` is applicable even if the table is not partitioned.

Merging in Parallel

In Oracle9*i*, you combine the previous updates and inserts into one statement, commonly known as a **merge**. The following statement achieves the same result as all of the statements in "Updating the Table in Parallel" and "Inserting the New Rows into the Table in Parallel":

```
MERGE INTO customers USING diff_customer
ON (diff_customer.c_key = customer.c_key)
WHEN MATCHED THEN
  UPDATE SET (c_name, c_addr) = (SELECT c_name, c_addr
  FROM diff_customer
  WHERE diff_customer.c_key = customers.c_key)
WHEN NOT MATCHED THEN
  INSERT VALUES (diff_customer.c_key,diff_customer.c_data);
```

Using Hints with Cost-Based Optimization

Cost-based optimization is a sophisticated approach to find the best execution plan for SQL statements. Oracle automatically uses cost-based optimization with parallel execution.

NOTE *You must use the* `DBMS_STATS` *package to gather current statistics for cost-based optimization. In particular, tables used in parallel should always be analyzed. Always keep your statistics current by using the* `DBMS_STATS` *package.*

Use discretion in employing hints. If used, hints should come as a final step in tuning and only when they demonstrate a necessary and significant performance advantage. In such cases, begin with the execution plan recommended by cost-based optimization, and go on to test the effect of hints only after you have quantified your performance expectations. Remember that hints are powerful. If you use them and the underlying data changes, you might need to change the hints. Otherwise, the effectiveness of your execution plans might deteriorate.

Always use cost-based optimization unless you have an existing application that has been hand-tuned for rule-based optimization. If you must use rule-based optimization, rewriting a SQL statement can greatly improve application performance.

NOTE *If any table in a query has a DOP greater than one (including the default DOP), Oracle uses the cost-based optimizer for that query, even if* `OPTIMIZER_MODE` *is set to* `RULE` *or if there is a* `RULE` *hint in the query itself.*

FIRST_ROWS(n) Hint

Starting with Oracle9*i*, a hint called `FIRST_ROWS(n)`, where *n* is a positive integer was added. This hint enables the optimizer to use a new optimization mode to optimize the query to return *n* rows in the shortest amount of time. Oracle Corporation recommends that you use this new hint in place of the old FIRST_ROWS hint for online queries because the new optimization mode may improve the response time compared to the old optimization mode.

Use the FIRST_ROWS(n) hint in cases where you want the first *n* number of rows in the shortest possible time. For example, to obtain the first 10 rows in the shortest possible time, use the hint as follows:

```
SELECT /*+ FIRST_ROWS(10) */ article_id
FROM articles_tab
WHERE CONTAINS(article, 'Oracle')>0
ORDER BY pub_date DESC;
```

Enabling Dynamic Statistic Sampling

Dynamic statistic sampling enables Oracle to test some data before running a query or transaction. This is particularly useful in data warehousing environments or when you expect long transactions or queries. In these situations, making sure that Oracle uses the best execution plan is important. Dynamic statistic sampling does, however, have a small cost, so you should use it when that cost is likely to be a small fraction of the total execution time.

If you enable dynamic statistic sampling, Oracle determines at compile time whether a query would benefit from dynamic sampling. If so, a recursive SQL statement is issued to scan a small, random sample of the table's blocks, and to apply the relevant single table predicates to estimate predicate selectivities. More accurate selectivity and statistics estimates allow the optimizer to produce better performing plans.

Dynamic sampling is controlled with the initialization parameter OPTIMIZER_DYNAMIC_SAMPLING, which can be set to a value between 0 and 10, inclusive. Increasing the value of the parameter will result in more aggressive application of dynamic sampling, in terms of both the type (unanalyzed/analyzed) of tables sampled and the amount of I/O spent on sampling.

The sample cardinality can also be used, in some cases, to estimate table cardinality. Depending on the value of the OPTIMIZER_DYNAMIC_SAMPLING initialization parameter, a certain number of blocks is read by the dynamic sampling query.

Oracle also provides the table-specific hint DYNAMIC_SAMPLING. If the table name is omitted, the hint is considered cursor-level. If a cursor-level hint is specified anywhere in the query (for example, in a subquery), it will apply to the entire query, so care should be taken when specifying a cursor-level hint in a view or subquery. The table-level hint forces dynamic sampling for the table.

❑❑❑

15 QUERY REWRITE

OVERVIEW OF QUERY REWRITE

One of the major benefits of creating and maintaining materialized views is the ability to take advantage of query rewrite, which transforms a SQL statement expressed in terms of tables or views into a statement accessing one or more materialized views that are defined on the detail tables. The transformation is transparent to the end user or application, requiring no intervention and no reference to the materialized view in the SQL statement. Because query rewrite is transparent, materialized views can be added or dropped just like indexes without invalidating the SQL in the application code.

Before the query is rewritten, it is subjected to several checks to determine whether it is a candidate for query rewrite. If the query fails any of the checks, then the query is applied to the detail tables rather than the materialized view. This can be costly in terms of response time and processing power.

The Oracle optimizer uses two different methods to recognize when to rewrite a query in terms of one or more materialized views. The first method is based on matching the SQL text of the query with the SQL text of the materialized view definition. If the first method fails, the optimizer uses the more general method in which it compares joins, selections, data columns, grouping columns, and aggregate functions between the query and a materialized view.

Query rewrite operates on queries and subqueries in the following types of SQL statements:

- `SELECT`
- `CREATE TABLE ... AS SELECT`
- `INSERT INTO ... SELECT.`

It also operates on subqueries in the set operators `UNION`, `UNION ALL`, `INTERSECT`, and `MINUS`, and subqueries in DML statements such as `INSERT`, `DELETE`, and `UPDATE`.

Several factors affect whether or not a given query is rewritten to use one or more materialized views:

- Enabling or disabling query rewrite:
    - by the CREATE or ALTER statement for individual materialized views
    - by the initialization parameter QUERY_REWRITE_ENABLED
    - by the REWRITE and NOREWRITE hints in SQL statements
- Rewrite integrity levels
- Dimensions and constraints.

There is also an explain rewrite procedure which will advise whether query rewrite is possible on a query and if so, which materialized views will be used.

Cost-Based Rewrite

Query rewrite is available with cost-based optimization. Oracle optimizes the input query with and without rewrite and selects the least costly alternative. The optimizer rewrites a query by rewriting one or more query blocks, one at a time.

If the rewrite logic has a choice between multiple materialized views to rewrite a query block, it will select the one which can result in reading in the least amount of data.

After a materialized view has been picked for a rewrite, the optimizer performs the rewrite, and then tests whether the rewritten query can be rewritten further with another materialized view. This process continues until no further rewrites are possible. Then the rewritten query is optimized and the original query is optimized. The optimizer compares these two optimizations and selects the least costly alternative.

Since optimization is based on cost, it is important to collect statistics both on tables involved in the query and on the tables representing materialized views. Statistics are fundamental measures, such as the number of rows in a table, that are used to calculate the cost of a rewritten query. They are created by using the DBMS_STATS package.

Queries that contain in-line or named views are also candidates for query rewrite. When a query contains a named view, the view name is used to do the matching between a materialized view and the query. When a query contains an inline view, the inline view can be merged into the query before matching between a materialized view and the query occurs.

In addition, if the inline view's text definition exactly matches with that of an inline view present in any eligible materialized view, general rewrite may be possible. This is because, whenever a materialized view contains exactly identical inline view text to the one present in a query, query rewrite treats such an inline view like a named view or a table.

Figure 15.1 presents a graphical view of the cost-based approach used during the rewrite process.

When Does Oracle Rewrite a Query?

A query is rewritten only when a certain number of conditions are met:

- Query rewrite must be enabled for the session.
- A materialized view must be enabled for query rewrite.
- The rewrite integrity level should allow the use of the materialized view. For example, if a materialized view is not fresh and query rewrite integrity is set to enforced, then the materialized view will not be used.

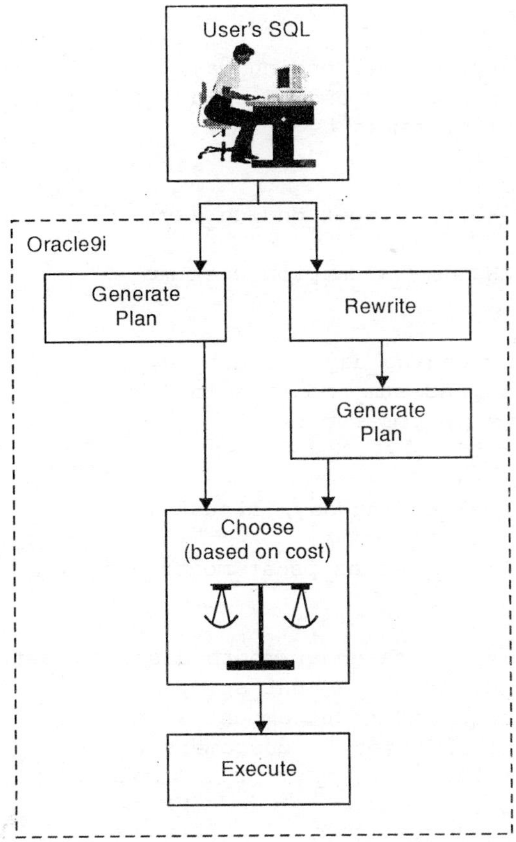

Figure 15.1 The Query Rewrite Process.

- Either all or part of the results requested by the query must be obtainable from the precomputed result stored in the materialized view.

To determine this, the optimizer may depend on some of the data relationships declared by the user using constraints and dimensions. Such data relationships include hierarchies, referential integrity, and uniqueness of key data, and so on.

Sample Schema and Materialized Views

The following sections use an example schema and a few materialized views to illustrate how the optimizer uses data relationships to rewrite queries. Oracle's sh sample schema consists of these tables:

```
COSTS, COUNTRIES, CUSTOMERS, PRODUCTS, PROMOTIONS, TIMES, CHANNELS, SALES
```

Examples of Materialized Views for Query Rewrite

The query rewrite examples in this chapter mainly refer to the following materialized views. Note that those materialized views do not necessarily represent the most efficient implementation for the `sh` sample schema. Instead, they are a base for demonstrating Oracle's rewrite capabilities. Further examples demonstrating specific functionality can be found in the specific context.

The following materialized views contain joins and aggregates:

```
CREATE MATERIALIZED VIEW sum_sales_pscat_week_mv
  ENABLE QUERY REWRITE
  AS
SELECT p.prod_subcategory, t.week_ending_day,
       SUM(s.amount_sold) AS sum_amount_sold
FROM   sales s, products p, times t
WHERE  s.time_id=t.time_id
AND    s.prod_id=p.prod_id
GROUP BY p.prod_subcategory, t.week_ending_day;

CREATE MATERIALIZED VIEW sum_sales_prod_week_mv
  ENABLE QUERY REWRITE
  AS
SELECT p.prod_id, t.week_ending_day, s.cust_id,
       SUM(s.amount_sold) AS sum_amount_sold
FROM   sales s, products p, times t
WHERE  s.time_id=t.time_id
AND    s.prod_id=p.prod_id
GROUP BY p.prod_id, t.week_ending_day, s.cust_id;

CREATE MATERIALIZED VIEW sum_sales_pscat_month_city_mv
  ENABLE QUERY REWRITE
  AS
SELECT p.prod_subcategory, t.calendar_month_desc, c.cust_city,
       SUM(s.amount_sold) AS sum_amount_sold,
       COUNT(s.amount_sold) AS count_amount_sold
FROM   sales s, products p, times t, customers c
WHERE  s.time_id=t.time_id
AND    s.prod_id=p.prod_id
AND    s.cust_id=c.cust_id
GROUP BY p.prod_subcategory, t.calendar_month_desc, c.cust_city;
```

- The following materialized views contain joins only:

```
CREATE MATERIALIZED VIEW join_sales_time_product_mv
  ENABLE QUERY REWRITE
  AS
SELECT p.prod_id, p.prod_name, t.time_id, t.week_ending_day,
       s.channel_id, s.promo_id, s.cust_id,
       s.amount_sold
FROM   sales s, products p, times t
WHERE  s.time_id=t.time_id
AND    s.prod_id = p.prod_id;

CREATE MATERIALIZED VIEW join_sales_time_product_oj_mv
  ENABLE QUERY REWRITE
  AS
SELECT p.prod_id, p.prod_name, t.time_id, t.week_ending_day,
       s.channel_id, s.promo_id, s.cust_id,
       s.amount_sold
FROM   sales s, products p, times t
WHERE  s.time_id=t.time_id
AND    s.prod_id=p.prod_id(+);
```

You must collect statistics on the materialized views so that the optimizer can determine whether to rewrite the queries. You can do this either on a per object base or for all newly created objects without statistics.

On a per object base, shown for `join_sales_time_product_mv`:

```
EXECUTE DBMS_STATS.GATHER_TABLE_STATS ('SH','JOIN_SALES_TIME_PRODUCT_MV',
      estimate_percent=>20,block_sample=>TRUE,cascade=>TRUE);
```

For all newly created objects without statistics, on schema level:

```
EXECUTE DBMS_STATS.GATHER_SCHEMA_STATS('SH', options => 'GATHER EMPTY',
      estimate_percent=>20, block_sample=>TRUE, cascade=>TRUE);
```

ENABLING QUERY REWRITE

Several steps must be followed to enable query rewrite:

1. Individual materialized views must have the `ENABLE QUERY REWRITE` clause.
2. The initialization parameter `QUERY_REWRITE_ENABLED` must be set to `true`.
3. Cost-based optimization must be used either by setting the initialization parameter `OPTIMIZER_MODE` to `all_rows` or `first_rows`, or by analyzing the tables and setting `OPTIMIZER_MODE` to `choose`.
4. The initialization parameter `OPTIMIZER_FEATURES_ENABLE` should be left unset for query rewrite to be possible. However, if it is given a value, then it must be set to at least 8.1.6 or query rewrite and explain rewrite will not be possible.

If step 1 has not been completed, a materialized view will never be eligible for query rewrite. `ENABLE QUERY REWRITE` can be specified either when the materialized view is created, as illustrated here, or with the `ALTER MATERIALIZED VIEW` statement.

```
CREATE MATERIALIZED VIEW join_sales_time_product_mv
ENABLE QUERY REWRITE
AS
SELECT p.prod_id, p.prod_name, t.time_id, t.week_ending_day,
       s.channel_id, s.promo_id, s.cust_id,
       s.amount_sold
FROM   sales s, products p, times t
WHERE  s.time_id=t.time_id
AND    s.prod_id = p.prod_id;
```

You can use the initialization parameter `QUERY_REWRITE_ENABLED` to disable query rewrite for all materialized views, or to enable it again for all materialized views that are individually enabled. However, the `QUERY_REWRITE_ENABLED` parameter cannot enable query rewrite for materialized views that have disabled it with the `CREATE` or `ALTER` statement.

The `NOREWRITE` hint disables query rewrite in a SQL statement, overriding the `QUERY_REWRITE_ENABLED` parameter, and the `REWRITE` hint (when used with `mv_name`) restricts the eligible materialized views to those named in the hint.

Initialization Parameters for Query Rewrite

Query rewrite requires the following initialization parameter settings:

- `OPTIMIZER_MODE = all_rows, first_rows, or choose`

- QUERY_REWRITE_ENABLED = true
- COMPATIBLE = 8.1.0 (or greater).

The QUERY_REWRITE_INTEGRITY parameter is optional, but must be set to stale_tolerated, trusted, or enforced if it is specified . It defaults to enforced if it is undefined.

Because the integrity level is set by default to enforced, all constraints must be validated. Therefore, if you use ENABLE NOVALIDATE, certain types of query rewrite might not work. To enable query rewrite in this environment, you should set your integrity level to a lower level of granularity such as trusted or stale_tolerated.

With OPTIMIZER_MODE set to choose, a query will not be rewritten unless at least one table referenced by it has been analyzed. This is because the rule-based optimizer is used when OPTIMIZER_MODE is set to choose and none of the tables referenced in a query have been analyzed.

Controlling Query Rewrite

A materialized view is only eligible for query rewrite if the ENABLE QUERY REWRITE clause has been specified, either initially when the materialized view was first created or subsequently with an ALTER MATERIALIZED VIEW statement.

The initialization parameters described previously can be set using the ALTER SYSTEM SET statement. For a given user's session, ALTER SESSION can be used to disable or enable query rewrite for that session only. For example:

```
ALTER SESSION SET QUERY_REWRITE_ENABLED = TRUE;
```

You can set the level of query rewrite for a session, thus allowing different users to work at different integrity levels. The possible statements are:

```
ALTER SESSION SET QUERY_REWRITE_INTEGRITY = stale_tolerated;
ALTER SESSION SET QUERY_REWRITE_INTEGRITY = trusted;
ALTER SESSION SET QUERY_REWRITE_INTEGRITY = enforced;
```

Rewrite Hints

Hints can be included in SQL statements to control whether query rewrite occurs. Using the NOREWRITE hint in a query prevents the optimizer from rewriting it.

The REWRITE hint with no argument in a query forces the optimizer to use a materialized view (if any) to rewrite it regardless of the cost.

The REWRITE(mv1,mv2,...) hint with arguments forces rewrite to select the most suitable materialized view from the list of names specified.

To prevent a rewrite, you can use the following statement:

```
SELECT /*+ NOREWRITE */ p.prod_subcategory, SUM(s.amount_sold)
FROM   sales s, products p
WHERE  s.prod_id=p.prod_id
GROUP BY p.prod_subcategory;
```

To force a rewrite using sum_sales_pscat_week_mv, you can use the following statement:

```
SELECT /*+ REWRITE (sum_sales_pscat_week_mv) */ p.prod_subcategory,
SUM(s.amount_sold)
```

```
FROM    sales s, products p
WHERE   s.prod_id=p.prod_id
GROUP BY p.prod_subcategory;
```

NOTE *That the scope of a rewrite hint is a query block. If an SQL statement consists of several query blocks (`SELECT` clauses), you might need to specify a rewrite hint on each query block to control the rewrite for the entire statement.*

Privileges for Enabling Query Rewrite

Use of a materialized view based not on privileges the user has on that materialized view, but on privileges the user has on detail tables or views in the query.

The system privilege `GRANT QUERY REWRITE` lets you enable materialized views in your own schema for query rewrite only if all tables directly referenced by the materialized view are in that schema. The `GRANT GLOBAL QUERY REWRITE` privilege allows you to enable materialized views for query rewrite even if the materialized view references objects in other schemas.

The privileges for using materialized views for query rewrite are similar to those for definer-rights procedures.

Accuracy of Query Rewrite

Query rewrite offers three levels of rewrite integrity that are controlled by the initialization parameter `QUERY_REWRITE_INTEGRITY`, which can either be set in your parameter file or controlled by using an `ALTER SYSTEM` or `ALTER SESSION` statement. The three values it can take are:

- `enforced`
  This is the default mode. The optimizer will only use materialized views that it knows contain fresh data and only use those relationships that are based on `ENABLED VALIDATED` primary/unique/foreign key constraints.
- `trusted`
  In `trusted` mode, the optimizer trusts that the data in the materialized views is fresh and the relationships declared in dimensions and `RELY` constraints are correct. In this mode, the optimizer will also use prebuilt materialized views or materialized views based on views, and it will use relationships that are not enforced as well as those that are enforced. In this mode, the optimizer also 'trusts' declared but not `ENABLED VALIDATED` primary/unique key constraints and data relationships specified using dimensions.
- `stale_tolerated`
  In `stale_tolerated` mode, the optimizer uses materialized views that are valid but contain stale data as well as those that contain fresh data. This mode offers the maximum rewrite capability but creates the risk of generating inaccurate results.

If rewrite integrity is set to the safest level, `enforced`, the optimizer uses only enforced primary key constraints and referential integrity constraints to ensure that the results of the query are the same as the results when accessing the detail tables directly. If the rewrite integrity is set to levels other than `enforced`, there are several situations where the output with rewrite can be different from that without it.

- A materialized view can be out of synchronization with the master copy of the data. This generally happens because the materialized view refresh procedure is pending following bulk load or DML operations to one or more detail tables of a materialized view. At some data warehouse sites, this situation is desirable because it is not uncommon for some materialized views to be refreshed at certain time intervals.

- The relationships implied by the dimension objects are invalid. For example, values at a certain level in a hierarchy do not roll up to exactly one parent value.
- The values stored in a prebuilt materialized view table might be incorrect.
- Partition operations such as DROP and MOVE PARTITION on the detail table could affect the results of the materialized view.
- A wrong answer can occur because of bad data relationships defined by unenforced table or view constraints.

HOW ORACLE REWRITES QUERIES

The optimizer uses a number of different methods to rewrite a query. The first, most important step is to determine if all or part of the results requested by the query can be obtained from the precomputed results stored in a materialized view.

The simplest case occurs when the result stored in a materialized view exactly matches what is requested by a query. The Oracle optimizer makes this type of determination by comparing the text of the query with the text of the materialized view definition. This method is most straightforward but the number of queries eligible for this type of query rewrite will be minimal.

When the text comparison test fails, the Oracle optimizer performs a series of generalized checks based on the joins, selections, grouping, aggregates, and column data fetched. This is accomplished by individually comparing various clauses (SELECT, FROM, WHERE, HAVING, or GROUP BY) of a query with those of a materialized view.

Text Match Rewrite Methods

The optimizer uses two methods:

- Full text match
- Partial text match.

In full text match, the entire text of a query is compared against the entire text of a materialized view definition (that is, the entire SELECT expression), ignoring the white space during text comparison. Given the following query:

```
SELECT  p.prod_subcategory, t.calendar_month_desc, c.cust_city,
SUM(s.amount_sold) AS sum_amount_sold,
COUNT(s.amount_sold) AS count_amount_sold
FROM    sales s, products p, times t, customers c
WHERE   s.time_id=t.time_id
AND     s.prod_id=p.prod_id
AND     s.cust_id=c.cust_id
GROUP BY p.prod_subcategory, t.calendar_month_desc, c.cust_city;
```

This query matches sum_sales_pscat_month_city_mv (white space excluded) and is rewritten as:

```
SELECT  prod_subcategory, calendar_month_desc, cust_city,
        sum_amount_sold, count_amount_sold
FROM    sum_sales_pscat_month_city_mv;
```

When full text match fails, the optimizer then attempts a partial text match. In this method, the text starting from the FROM clause of a query is compared against the text starting with the FROM clause of a materialized view definition. Therefore, the following query:

```
SELECT p.prod_subcategory, t.calendar_month_desc, c.cust_city,
       AVG(s.amount_sold)
FROM   sales s, products p, times t, customers c
WHERE  s.time_id=t.time_id
AND    s.prod_id=p.prod_id
AND    s.cust_id=c.cust_id
GROUP BY p.prod_subcategory, t.calendar_month_desc, c.cust_city;
```

This query is rewritten as:

```
SELECT prod_subcategory, calendar_month_desc, cust_city,
       sum_amount_sold/count_amount_sold
FROM   sum_sales_pscat_month_city_mv;
```

Note that, under the partial text match rewrite method, the average of sales aggregate required by the query is computed using the sum of sales and count of sales aggregates stored in the materialized view.

When neither text match succeeds, the optimizer uses a general query rewrite method.

Text Match Capabilities

Text match rewrite can distinguish uppercase from lowercase. For example, the following statement:

```
SELECT X, 'aBc' FROM Y
```

This statement matches this statement:

```
Select x, 'aBc' From y
```

Text match rewrite can support set operators (UNION ALL, UNION, MINUS, INTERSECT).

General Query Rewrite Methods

Oracle employs a number of checks to determine if a query can be rewritten to use a materialized view. These checks are as follows:

- Selection compatibility
- Join compatibility
- Data sufficiency
- Grouping compatibility
- Aggregate compatibility.

Table 15.1 illustrates how Oracle makes these five checks depending on the type of materialized view. Note that, depending on the composition of the materialized view, some or all of the checks may be made.

Table 15.1 Materialized View Types and General Query Rewrite Methods

Query Rewrite Checks	MV with Joins Only	MV with Joins and Aggregates	MV with Aggregates on a Single Table
Selection compatibility	X	X	X
Join compatibility	X	X	-
Data sufficiency	X	X	X
Grouping compatibility	-	X	X
Aggregate computability	-	X	X

To perform these checks, the optimizer uses data relationships on which it can depend. For example, primary key and foreign key relationships tell the optimizer that each row in the foreign key table joins with at most one row in the primary key table. Furthermore, if there is a NOT NULL constraint on the foreign key, it indicates that each row in the foreign key table must join to exactly one row in the primary key table.

Data relationships such as these are very important for query rewrite because they tell what type of result is produced by joins, grouping, or aggregation of data. Therefore, to maximize the rewritability of a large set of queries when such data relationships exist in a database, they should be declared by the user.

When are Constraints and Dimensions Needed?

To clarify when dimensions and constraints are required for the different types of query rewrite, refer to table 15.2.

Table 15.2 Dimension and Constraint Requirements for Query Rewrite

Rewrite Checks	Dimensions	Primary Key/Foreign Key/Not Null Constraints
Matching SQL text	Not Required	Not required
Join compatibility	Not Required	Required
Data sufficiency	Required OR	Required
Grouping compatibility	Required	Required
Aggregate computability	Not Required	Not required

View Constraints

Data warehouse applications recognize multi-dimensional cubes in the database by identifying integrity constraints in the relational schema. Integrity constraints represent primary and foreign key relationships between fact and dimension tables. By querying the data dictionary, applications can recognize integrity constraints and hence the cubes in the database. However, this does not work in an environment where DBAs, for schema complexity or security reasons, define views on fact and dimension tables. In such environments, applications cannot identify the cubes properly. By allowing constraint definitions between views, you can propagate base table constraints to the views, thereby allowing applications to recognize cubes even in a restricted environment.

View constraint definitions are declarative in nature, but operations on views are subject to the integrity constraints defined on the underlying base tables, and constraints on views can be enforced through constraints on base tables. Defining constraints on base tables is necessary, not only for data correctness and cleanliness, but also for materialized view query rewrite purposes using the original base objects.

Materialized view rewrite extensively uses constraints for query rewrite. They are used for determining lossless joins, which, in turn, determine if joins in the materialized view are compatible with joins in the query and thus if rewrite is possible.

`DISABLE NOVALIDATE` is the only valid state for a view constraint. However, you can choose `RELY` or `NORELY` as the view constraint state to enable more sophisticated query rewrites. For example, a view constraint in the `RELY` state allows query rewrite to occur when the query integrity level is set to `ENFORCED`. Table 15.3 illustrates when view constraints are used for determining lossless joins.

Note that view constraints cannot be used for query rewrite integrity level `TRUSTED`. This level enforces the highest degree of constraint enforcement `ENABLE VALIDATE`.

Table 15.3 View Constraints and Rewrite Integrity Modes

Constraint States	RELY	NORELY
ENFORCED	No	No
TRUSTED	Yes	No
STALE_TOLERATED	Yes	No

Example 15.1 : View Constraints

To demonstrate the rewrite capabilities on views, you have to extend the `sh` sample schema as follows:

```
CREATE VIEW time_view AS
SELECT time_id, TO_NUMBER(TO_CHAR(time_id, 'ddd')) AS day_in_year FROM times;
```

You can now establish a foreign-primary key relationship (in `RELY ON`) mode between the view and the fact table, and thus rewrite will take place as described in table 15.3, by adding the following constraints. Rewrite will then work for example in `TRUSTED` mode.

```
ALTER VIEW time_view ADD (CONSTRAINT time_view_pk
   PRIMARY KEY (time_id) DISABLE NOVALIDATE);
ALTER VIEW time_view MODIFY CONSTRAINT time_view_pk RELY;
ALTER TABLE sales ADD (CONSTRAINT time_view_fk FOREIGN key (time_id)
   REFERENCES time_view(time_id) DISABLE NOVALIDATE);
ALTER TABLE sales MODIFY CONSTRAINT time_view_fk RELY;
```

Consider the following materialized view definition:

```
CREATE MATERIALIZED VIEW sales_pcat_cal_day_mv
ENABLE QUERY REWRITE
AS
SELECT p.prod_category, t.day_in_year,
       SUM(s.amount_sold) as sum_amount_sold
FROM time_view t, sales s, products p
WHERE t.time_id = s.time_id
AND   p.prod_id = s.prod_id
GROUP BY p.prod_category, t.day_in_year;
```

The following query, omitting the dimension table `products`, will also be rewritten without the primary key/foreign key relationships, because the suppressed join between `sales` and `products` is known to be lossless.

```
SELECT t.day_in_year,
       SUM(s.amount_sold) AS sum_amount_sold
FROM time_view t, sales s
WHERE t.time_id = s.time_id
GROUP BY t.day_in_year;
```

However, if the materialized view `sales_pcat_cal_day_mv` were defined only in terms of the view `time_view`, then you could not rewrite the following query, suppressing then join between `sales` and `time_view`, because there is no basis for losslessness of the delta materialized view join. With the additional constraints as shown previously, this query will also rewrite.

```
SELECT p.prod_category,
       SUM(s.amount_sold) AS sum_amount_sold
FROM sales s, products p
WHEPE p.prod_id = s.prod_id
GROUP BY p.prod_category;
```

To revert the changes you have made to the sales history schema, apply the following SQL commands:

```
ALTER TABLE sales DROP CONSTRAINT time_view_fk;
DROP VIEW time_view;
```

View Constraints Restrictions

If the referential constraint definition involves a view, that is, either the foreign key or the referenced key resides in a view, the constraint can only be in `DISABLE NOVALIDATE` mode.

A `RELY` constraint on a view is allowed only if the referenced `UNIQUE` or `PRIMARY KEY` constraint in `DISABLE NOVALIDATE` mode is also a `RELY` constraint.

The specification of `ON DELETE` actions associated with a referential Integrity constraint, is not allowed (for example, `DELETE` cascade). However, `DELETE`, `UPDATE`, and `INSERT` operations are allowed on views and their base tables as view constraints are in `DISABLE NOVALIDATE` mode.

Expression Matching

An expression that appears in a query can be replaced with a simple column in a materialized view provided the materialized view column represents a precomputed expression that matches with the expression in the query. If a query can be rewritten to use a materialized view, it will be faster. This is because materialized views contain precomputed calculations and do not need to perform expression computation.

The expression matching is done by first converting the expressions into canonical forms and then comparing them for equality. Therefore, two different expressions will be matched as long as they are equivalent to each other. Further, if the entire expression in a query fails to match with an expression in a materialized view, then subexpressions of it are tried to find a match. The subexpressions are tried in a top-down order to get maximal expression matching.

Consider a query that asks for sum of sales by age brackets (1-10, 11-20, 21-30, and so on).

```
CREATE MATERIALIZED VIEW sales_by_age_bracket_mv
ENABLE QUERY REWRITE
AS
SELECT TO_CHAR((2000-c.cust_year_of_birth)/10-0.5,999) AS age_bracket,
       SUM(s.amount_sold) AS sum_amount_sold
FROM sales s, customers c
WHERE  s.cust_id=c.cust_id
```

```
GROUP BY TO_CHAR((2000-c.cust_year_of_birth)/10-0.5,999);
```

The following query rewrites, using expression matching:

```
SELECT TO_CHAR(((2000-c.cust_year_of_birth)/10)-0.5,999),
       SUM(s.amount_sold)
FROM sales s, customers c
WHERE  s.cust_id=c.cust_id
GROUP BY TO_CHAR((2000-c.cust_year_of_birth)/10-0.5,999);
```

This query is rewritten in terms of sum_sales_mv based on the matching of the canonical forms of the age bracket expressions (that is, 2000 - c.cust_year_of_birth)/10-0.5), as follows.

```
SELECT age_bracket, sum_amount_sold
FROM sales_by_age_bracket_mv;
```

Date Folding

Date folding rewrite is a specific form of expression matching rewrite. In this type of rewrite, a date range in a query is folded into an equivalent date range representing higher date granules. The resulting expressions representing higher date granules in the folded date range are matched with equivalent expressions in a materialized view. The folding of date range into higher date granules such as months, quarters, or years is done when the underlying datatype of the column is an Oracle DATE. The expression matching is done based on the use of canonical forms for the expressions.

DATE is a built-in datatype which represents ordered time units such as seconds, days, and months, and incorporates a time hierarchy (second -> minute -> hour -> day -> month -> quarter -> year). This hard-coded knowledge about DATE is used in folding date ranges from lower-date granules to higher-date granules. Specifically, folding a date value to the beginning of a month, quarter, year, or to the end of a month, quarter, year is supported. For example, the date value 1-jan-1999 can be folded into the beginning of either year 1999 or quarter 1999-1 or month 1999-01. And, the date value 30-sep-1999 can be folded into the end of either quarter 1999-03 or month 1999-09.

NOTE

Due to the way date folding works, you should be careful when using BETWEEN and date columns. The best way to use BETWEEN and date columns is to increment the later date by 1. In other words, instead of using date_col BETWEEN '1-jan-1999' AND '30-jun-1999', you should use date_col BETWEEN '1-jan-1999' AND '1-jul-1999'. You could also use the TRUNC function to get the equivalent result, as in TRUNC(date_col) BETWEEN '1-jan-1999' AND '30-jun-1999'. TRUNC will, however, strip time values.

Because date values are ordered, any range predicate specified on date columns can be folded from lower level granules into higher level granules provided the date range represents an integral number of higher level granules. For example, the range predicate date_col >= '1-jan-1999' AND date_col < '30-jun-1999' can be folded into either a month range or a quarter range using the TO_CHAR function, which extracts specific date components from a date value.

The advantage of aggregating data by folded date values is the compression of data achieved. Without date folding, the data is aggregated at the lowest granularity level, resulting in increased disk space for storage and increased I/O to scan the materialized view.

Consider a query that asks for the sum of sales by product types for the years 1998.

```
SELECT p.prod_category, SUM(s.amount_sold)
FROM sales s, products p
WHERE s.prod_id=p.prod_id
```

```
AND s.time_id >=  TO_DATE('01-jan-1998', 'dd-mon-yyyy')
AND s.time_id <   TO_DATE('01-jan-1999', 'dd-mon-yyyy')
GROUP BY p.prod_category;

CREATE MATERIALIZED VIEW sum_sales_pcat_monthly_mv
ENABLE QUERY REWRITE
AS
SELECT p.prod_category, TO_CHAR(s.time_id,'YYYY-MM') AS month,
       SUM(s.amount_sold) AS sum_amount
FROM sales s, products p
WHERE s.prod_id=p.prod_id
GROUP BY p.prod_category, TO_CHAR(s.time_id, 'YYYY-MM');

SELECT p.prod_category, SUM(s.amount_sold)
FROM sales s, products p
WHERE s.prod_id=p.prod_id
AND TO_CHAR(s.time_id, 'YYYY-MM') >= '01-jan-1998'
AND TO_CHAR(s.time_id, 'YYYY-MM') < '01-jan-1999'
GROUP BY p.prod_category;

SELECT mv.prod_category, mv.sum_amount
FROM sum_sales_pcat_monthly_mv mv
WHERE month >= '01-jan-1998' AND month < '01-jan-1999';
```

The range specified in the query represents an integral number of years, quarters, or months. Assume that there is a materialized view mv3 that contains pre-summarized sales by prod_type and is defined as follows:

```
CREATE MATERIALIZED VIEW mv3
  ENABLE QUERY REWRITE
AS
SELECT prod_type, TO_CHAR(sale_date,'yyyy-mm') AS month, SUM(sales) AS sum_sales
FROM fact, product
WHERE fact.prod_id = product.prod_id
GROUP BY prod_type, TO_CHAR(sale_date, 'yyyy-mm');
```

The query can be rewritten by first folding the date range into the month range and then matching the expressions representing the months with the month expression in mv3. This rewrite is shown in two steps (first folding the date range followed by the actual rewrite).

```
SELECT prod_type, SUM(sales) AS sum_sales
FROM fact, product
WHERE fact.prod_id = product.prod_id AND
      TO_CHAR(sale_date, 'yyyy-mm') >=
      TO_CHAR('01-jan-1998', 'yyyy-mm') AND < TO_CHAR('01-jan-1999', 'yyyy-mm')
GROUP BY prod_type;

SELECT prod_type, sum_sales
FROM mv3
WHERE month >=
     TO_CHAR('01-jan-1998', 'yyyy-mm') AND < TO_CHAR('01-jan-1999', 'yyyy-mm');
GROUP BY prod_type;
```

If mv3 had pre-summarized sales by prod_type and year instead of prod_type and month, the query could still be rewritten by folding the date range into year range and then matching the year expressions.

Selection Compatibility

Oracle supports rewriting of queries so that they will use materialized views in which the `HAVING` or `WHERE` clause of the materialized view contains a selection of a subset of the data in a table or tables. A materialized view's `WHERE` or `HAVING` clause can contain a join, a selection, or both, and still be used by a rewritten query. Predicate clauses containing expressions, or selecting rows based on the values of particular columns, are examples of non-join predicates.

To perform this type of query rewrite, Oracle must determine if the data requested in the query is contained in, or is a subset of, the data stored in the materialized view. This problem is sometimes referred to as the data containment problem or, in more general terms, the problem of a restricted subset of data in a materialized view. The following sections detail the conditions where Oracle can solve this problem and thus rewrite a query to use a materialized view that contains a restricted portion of the data in the detail table.

Selection compatibility is performed when both the query and the materialized view contain selections (non-joins). A selection compatibility check is done on the `WHERE` as well as the `HAVING` clause. If the materialized view contains selections and the query does not, then selection compatibility check fails because the materialized view is more restrictive than the query. If the query has selections and the materialized view does not then selection compatibility check is not needed. Regardless, selections and any columns mentioned in them must pass the data sufficiency check.

Definitions

The following definitions are introduced to help the discussion:

- *join relop*
  Is one of the following `(=, <, <=, >, >=)`
- *selection relop*
  Is `(=, <, <=, >, >=, !=, [NOT] BETWEEN | IN| LIKE |NULL)`
- *join predicate*
  Is of the form `(`*column1 join relop column2*`)`, where columns are from different tables within the same `FROM` clause in the current query block. So, for example, there cannot be an outer reference.
- *selection predicate*
  Is of the form *LHS-expression relop RHS-expression*, where LHS means left-hand side and RHS means right-hand side. All non-join predicates are selection predicates. The left-hand side usually contains a column and the right-hand side contains the values. For example, `color='red'` means the left-hand side is `color` and the right-hand side is `'red'` and the relational operator is `(=)`.
- *LHS-constrained*
  When comparing a selection from the query with a selection from the materialized view, the left-hand side of the selection is compared with the left-hand side of the query. If they match, they are said to be LHS-constrained or just constrained for short.
- *RHS-constrained*
  When comparing a selection from the query with a selection from the materialized view, the right-hand side of the selection is compared with the right-hand side of the query. If they match, they are said to be RHS-constrained or just constrained. Note that before comparing the selections, the LHS/RHS-expression is converted to a canonical form and then the comparison is done. This means that expressions such as *column1* + *5* and *5* + *column1* will match and be constrained.

Although selection compatibility does not restrict the general form of the WHERE, there is an optimal pattern and normally most queries fall into this pattern as follows:

```
(join predicate AND join predicate AND ....)  AND
 (selection predicate  AND|OR  selection predicate .... )
```

The join compatibility check operates on the joins and the selection compatibility operates on the selections. If the WHERE clause has an OR at the top, then the optimizer first checks for common predicates under the OR. If found, the common predicates are factored out from under the OR then joined with an AND back to the OR. This helps to put the WHERE into the optimal pattern. This is done only if OR occurs at the top of the WHERE clause. For example, if the WHERE clause is:

```
(sales.prod_id = prod.prod_id AND prod.prod_name = 'Kids Polo Shirt')
  OR (sales.prod_id = prod.prod_id  AND prod.prod_name = 'Kids Shorts')
```

The join is factored out and the WHERE becomes:

```
(sales.prod_id = prod.prod_id) AND (prod.prod_name = 'Kids Polo Shirt'
  OR prod.prod_name = 'Kids Shorts')
```

Thus putting the WHERE into the most optimal pattern.

If the WHERE is so complex that factoring cannot be done, all predicates under the OR are treated as selections and join compatibility is not performed but selection compatibility is still performed. In the HAVING clause, all predicates are considered selections.

Selection compatibility categorizes selections into the following cases:

- Simple

  Simple selections are of the form *expression relop constant.*
- Complex

  Complex selections are of the form *expression relop expression.*
- Range

  Range selections are of a form such as WHERE (cust_last_name BETWEEN 'abacrombe' AND 'anakin').

  Note that simple selections with relational operators (<, <=, >, >=) are also considered range selections.
- IN lists

  Single and multi-column IN lists such as WHERE(prod_id) IN (102, 233, ...).

  Note that selections of the form (column1='v1' OR column1='v2' OR column1='v3' OR ....) are treated as a group and classified as an IN list.
- IS [NOT] NULL
- [NOT] LIKE
- Other

  Other selections are when selection compatibility cannot determine containment of data. For example, EXISTS.

When comparing a selection from the query with a selection from the materialized view, the left-hand side of the selection is compared with the left-hand side of the query. If they match, they are said to be LHS-constrained or constrained for short.

If the selections are constrained, then the right-hand side values are checked for containment. That is, the RHS values of the query selection must be contained by right-hand side values of the materialized view selection.

Example 15.2 : Selection Compatibility

If the query contains the following:

```
WHERE prod_id = 102
```

And if a materialized view contains the following:

```
WHERE prod_id BETWEEN 0 AND 200
```

In this example, the selections are constrained on `prod_id` and the right-hand side value of the query `102` is within the range of the materialized view.

Example 15.3 : Selection Compatibility

A selection can be a bounded range (a range with an upper and lower value), for example:

If the query contains the following:

```
WHERE prod_id > 10 AND prod_id < 50
```

And if a materialized view contains the following:

```
WHERE prod_id BETWEEN 0 AND 200
```

In this example, the selections are constrained on `prod_id` and the query range is within the materialized view range. In this example, we notice that both query selections are constrained by the same materialized view selection. The left-hand side can be an expression.

Example 15.4 : Selection Compatibility

If the query contains the following:

```
WHERE (sales.amount_sold * .07) BETWEEN 1.00 AND 100.00
```

And if a materialized view contains the following:

```
WHERE (sales.amount_sold * .07) BETWEEN 0.0 AND 200.00
```

In this example, the selections are constrained on `(sales.amount_sold *.07)` and the right-hand side value of the query is within the range of the materialized view. Complex selections require that both the left-hand side and right-hand side be matched (for example, when the left-hand side and the right-hand side are constrained).

Example 15.5 : Selection Compatibility

If the query contains the following:

```
WHERE (cost.unit_price * 0.95) > (cost_unit_cost * 1.25)
```

And if a materialized view contains the following:

```
WHERE (cost.unit_price * 0.95) > (cost_unit_cost * 1.25)
```

If the left-hand side and the right-hand side are constrained and the `<selection relop>` is the same, then generally the selection can be dropped from the rewritten query. Otherwise, the selection must be keep to filter out extra data from the materialized view.

If query rewrite can drop the selection from the rewritten query, then any columns from the selection may not have to be in the materialized view so more rewrites can be done with less data.

Selection compatibility requires that all selections in the materialized view be LHS-constrained with some selection in the query. This ensures that the materialized view data is not more restrictive that the query.

Example 15.6 : Selection Compatibility

Selections in the query do not have to be constrained by any selections in the materialized view but if they are then the right-hand side values must be contained by the materialized view. For example,

If the query contains the following:

```
WHERE prod_name = 'Shorts' AND prod_category = 'Men'
```

And if a materialized view contains the following:

```
WHERE prod_category = 'Men'
```

In this example, selection with `prod_category` is constrained. The query has an extra selection that is not constrained but this is acceptable because the materialized view does have the data.

Example 15.7 : Selection Compatibility

If the query contains the following:

```
WHERE prod_category = 'Men'
```

And if a materialized view contains the following:

```
WHERE prod_name = 'Shorts' AND prod_category = 'Men'
```

In this example, the materialized view selection with `prod_name` is not constrained. The materialized view is more restrictive that the query because it only contains the product `Shorts`, therefore, query rewrite will not occur.

Example 15.8 : Selection Compatibility

Selection compatibility also checks for cases where the query has a multi-column in list where the columns are fully constrained by individual columns from the materialized view single column in lists. For example:

If the query contains the following:

```
WHERE (prod_id, cust_id) IN ((1022, 1000), (1033, 2000))
```

And if a materialized view contains the following:

```
WHERE prod_id IN (1022,1033) AND cust_id IN (1000, 2000)
```

In this example, the materialized view `IN` lists are constrained by the columns in the query multi-column in list. Furthermore, the right-hand side values of the query selection are contained by the materialized view so that rewrite will occur.

Example 15.9 : Selection Compatibility

Selection compatibility also checks for cases where the materialized view has a multi-column `IN`-list where the columns are fully constrained by individual columns or columns from `IN`-lists in the query. For example:

If the query contains the following:

```
WHERE prod_id = 1022 AND cust_id IN (1000, 2000)
```

And if a materialized view contains the following:

```
WHERE (prod_id, cust_id) IN ((1022, 1000), (1022, 2000))
```

In this example, the materialized view IN-list columns are fully constrained by the columns in the query selections. Furthermore, the right-hand side values of the query selection are contained by the materialized view. However, the following example fails selection compatibility check.

Example 15.10 : Selection Compatibility

If the query contains the following:

```
WHERE (prod_id = 1022 AND cust_id IN (1000, 2000)
```

And if a materialized view contains the following:

```
WHERE (prod_id, cust_id, cust_city)
  IN ((1022, 1000, 'Boston'), (1022, 2000, 'Nashua'))
```

In this example, the materialized view in list column cust_city is not constrained so the materialized view is more restrictive than the query. Selection compatibility also works with complex ORs. If we assume that the shape of the WHERE is as follows:

```
(selection AND selection AND ...) OR (selection AND selection AND ...)
```

Each group of selections separated by AND is related and the group is called a disjunct. The disjuncts are separated by ORs. Selection compatibility requires that every disjunct in the query be contained by some disjunct in the materialized view. Otherwise, the materialized view is more restrictive than the query. The materialized view disjuncts do not have to match any query disjunct. This just means that the materialized view has more data than the query requires. When comparing a disjunct from the query with a disjunct of the materialized view, the normal selection compatibility rules apply as specified in the previous discussion. For example;

Example 15.11 : Selection Compatibility

If the query contains the following:

```
WHERE (city_population > 15000 AND city_population < 25000
   AND state_name = 'New Hampshire')
```

And if a materialized view contains the following:

```
WHERE (city_population < 5000 AND state_name = 'New York') OR
   (city_population BETWEEN 10000 AND 50000 AND state_name = 'New Hampshire')
```

In this example, the query has a single disjunct (group of selections separated by AND). The materialized view has two disjuncts separated by OR. The query disjunct is contained by the second materialized view disjunct so selection compatibility succeeds. It is clear that the materialized view contains more data than needed by the query so the query can be rewritten. For example, here is a simple materialized view definition:

```
CREATE MATERIALIZED VIEW cal_month_sales_id_mv
BUILD IMMEDIATE
REFRESH FORCE
ENABLE QUERY REWRITE
AS
SELECT     t.calendar_month_desc,
           SUM(s.amount_sold) AS dollars
FROM       sales s,
           times t
WHERE     s.time_id = t.time_id AND s.cust_id = 10
GROUP BY t.calendar_month_desc;
```

The following query could be rewritten to use this materialized view because the query asks for the amount where the customer ID is 10 and this is contained in the materialized view.

```
SELECT    t.calendar_month_desc, SUM(s.amount_sold) AS dollars
FROM      times t, sales s
WHERE     s.time_id = t.time_id AND s.cust_id = 10
GROUP BY t.calendar_month_desc;
```

Because the predicate `s.cust_id = 10` selects the same data in the query and in the materialized view, it is dropped from the rewritten query. This means the rewritten query looks like:

```
SELECT mv.calendar_month_desc, mv.dollars FROM cal_month_sales_id_mv mv;
```

Query rewrite can also occur when the query specifies a range of values, such as `s.prod_id > 10000` and `s.prod_id < 20000`, as long as the range specified in the query is within the range specified in the materialized view. For example, if there is a materialized view defined as:

```
CREATE MATERIALIZED VIEW product_sales_mv
   BUILD IMMEDIATE
   REFRESH FORCE
   ENABLE QUERY REWRITE
   AS
   SELECT p.prod_name, SUM(s.amount_sold) AS dollar_sales
   FROM products p, sales s
   WHERE p.prod_id = s.prod_id
   GROUP BY prod_name
   HAVING SUM(s.amount_sold) BETWEEN 5000 AND 50000;
```

Then a query such as:

```
SELECT p.prod_name, SUM(s.amount_sold) AS dollar_sales
   FROM products p, sales s
   WHERE p.prod_id = s.prod_id
   GROUP BY prod_name
   HAVING SUM(s.amount_sold) BETWEEN 10000 AND 20000;
```

This query would be rewritten as follows:

```
SELECT prod_name, dollar_sales FROM product_sales_mv
WHERE dollar_sales > 10000 AND dollar_sales < 20000;
```

Rewrite with select expressions is also supported when the expression evaluates to a constant, such as `TO_DATE('12-SEP-1999','DD-Mon-YYYY')`. For example, if an existing materialized view is defined as:

```
CREATE MATERIALIZED VIEW sales_on_valentines_day_99_mv
BUILD IMMEDIATE
REFRESH FORCE
ENABLE QUERY REWRITE
AS
  SELECT prod_id, cust_id, amount_sold
  FROM sales s, times t
  WHERE s.time_id = t.time_id
  AND t.time_id = TO_DATE('04-FEB-1999', 'DD-MON-YYYY');
```

Then the following query:

```
SELECT prod_id, cust_id, amount_sold
  FROM sales s, times t
```

```
WHERE s.time_id = t.time_id
AND t.time_id = TO_DATE('14-FEB-1999', 'DD-MON-YYYY');
```

This query would be rewritten as follows:

```
SELECT * FROM sales_on_valentines_day_99_mv;
```

Rewrite can also occur against a materialized view when the selection is contained in an `IN` expression. For example, given the following materialized view definition:

```
CREATE MATERIALIZED VIEW popular_promo_sales_mv
BUILD IMMEDIATE
REFRESH FORCE
ENABLE QUERY REWRITE
AS
  SELECT p.promo_name, SUM(s.amount_sold) AS sum_amount_sold
  FROM  promotions p, sales s
  WHERE s.promo_id = p.promo_id
  AND promo_name IN ('coupon', 'premium', 'giveaway')
  GROUP BY promo_name;
```

The following query:

```
SELECT p.promo_name, SUM(s.amount_sold)
FROM  promotions p, sales s
WHERE s.promo_id = p.promo_id
AND promo_name IN ('coupon', 'premium')
GROUP BY promo_name;
```

This query is rewritten as follows:

```
SELECT * FROM popular_promo_sales_mv WHERE promo_name IN ('coupon', 'premium');
```

You can also use expressions in selection predicates. This process looks like the following example:

```
expression relational operator constant
```

where *expression* can be any arbitrary arithmetic expression allowed by Oracle. The expression in the materialized view and the query must match. Oracle attempts to discern expressions that are logically equivalent, such as `A+B` and `B+A`, and will always recognize identical expressions as being equivalent.

You can also use queries with an expression on both sides of the operator or user-defined functions as operators. Query rewrite occurs when the complex predicate in the materialized view and the query are logically equivalent. This means that, unlike exact text match, terms could be in a different order and rewrite can still occur, as long as the expressions are equivalent.

In addition, selection predicates can be joined with an `AND` operator in a query and the query can still be rewritten to use a materialized view as long as every restriction on the data selected by the query is matched by a restriction in the definition of the materialized view. Again, this does not mean an exact text match, but that the restrictions on the data selected must be a logical match. Also, the query may be more restrictive in its selection of data and still be eligible, but it can never be less restrictive than the definition of the materialized view and still be eligible for rewrite.

For example, given the preceding materialized view definition, a query such as:

```
SELECT p.promo_name, SUM(s.amount_sold)
FROM  promotions p, sales s
WHERE s.promo_id = p.promo_id
AND promo_name  = 'coupon'
  GROUP BY promo_name
  HAVING SUM(s.amount_sold) > 1000;
```

This query would be rewritten as follows:

```
SELECT * FROM popular_promo_sales_mv
WHERE promo_name = 'coupon' AND sum_amount_sold > 1000;
```

This is an example where the query is more restrictive than the definition of the materialized view, so rewrite can occur. However, if the query had selected `promo_category`, then it could not have been rewritten against the materialized view, because the materialized view definition does not contain that column.

For another example, if the definition of a materialized view restricts a city name column to `Boston`, then a query that selects `Seattle` as a value for this column can never be rewritten with that materialized view, but a query that restricts city name to `Boston` and restricts a column value that is not restricted in the materialized view could be rewritten to use the materialized view.

All the rules noted previously also apply when predicates are combined with an `OR` operator. The simple predicates, or simple predicates connect by `AND`s, are considered separately. Each predicate in the query must appear in the materialized view if rewrite is to occur.

For example, the query could have a restriction like `city='Boston' OR city ='Seattle'` and to be eligible for rewrite, the materialized view that the query might be rewritten against must have the same restriction. In fact, the materialized view could have additional restrictions, such as `city='Boston' OR city='Seattle' OR city='Cleveland'` and rewrite might still be possible.

Note, however, that the reverse is not true. If the query had the restriction `city = 'Boston' OR city='Seattle' OR city='Cleveland'` and the materialized view only had the restriction `city='Boston' OR city='Seattle'`, then rewrite would not be possible since the query seeks more data than is contained in the restricted subset of data stored in the materialized view.

Join Compatibility Check

In this check, the joins in a query are compared against the joins in a materialized view. In general, this comparison results in the classification of joins into three categories:

- Common joins that occur in both the query and the materialized view. These joins form the common subgraph.
- Delta joins that occur in the query but not in the materialized view. These joins form the query delta subgraph.
- Delta joins that occur in the materialized view but not in the query. These joins form the materialized view delta subgraph.

These can be visualized as shown in figure 15.2.

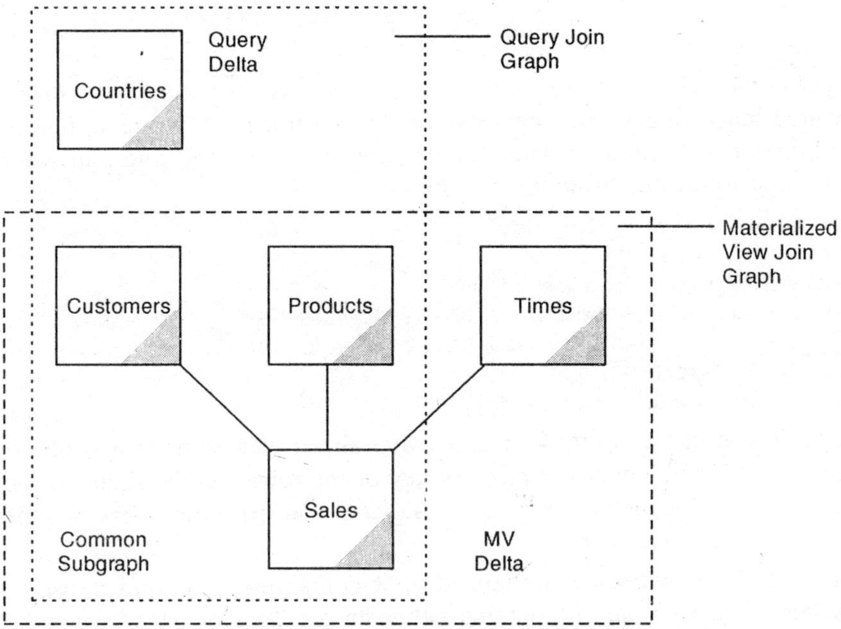

Figure 15.2 Query Rewrite Subgraphs.

Common Joins

The common join pairs between the two must be of the same type, or the join in the query must be derivable from the join in the materialized view. For example, if a materialized view contains an outer join of table `A` with table `B`, and a query contains an inner join of table `A` with table `B`, the result of the inner join can be derived by filtering the anti-join rows from the result of the outer join.

For example, consider the following query:

```
SELECT  p.prod_name, t.week_ending_day,
        SUM(amount_sold)
FROM    sales s, products p, times t
WHERE   s.time_id=t.time_id
AND     s.prod_id = p.prod_id
AND     t. week_ending_day BETWEEN TO_DATE('01-AUG-1999', 'DD-MON-YYYY')
                          AND     TO_DATE('10-AUG-1999', 'DD-MON-YYYY')
GROUP BY prod_name, week_ending_day;
```

The common joins between this query and the materialized view `join_sales_time_product_mv` are:

```
s.time_id = t.time_id AND s.prod_id = p.prod_id
```

They match exactly and the query can be rewritten as follows:

```
SELECT  prod_name, week_ending_day,
        SUM(amount_sold)
FROM    join_sales_time_product_mv
WHERE   week_ending_day BETWEEN TO_DATE('01-AUG-1999','DD-MON-YYYY')
```

```
                              AND      TO_DATE('10-AUG-1999','DD-MON-YYYY')
GROUP BY prod_name, week_ending_day;
```

The query could also be answered using the `join_sales_time_product_oj_mv` materialized view where inner joins in the query can be derived from outer joins in the materialized view. The rewritten version will (transparently to the user) filter out the anti-join rows. The rewritten query will have the following structure:

```
SELECT  prod_name,  week_ending_day,
        SUM(amount_sold)
FROM    join_sales_time_product_oj_mv
WHERE   week_ending_day BETWEEN TO_DATE('01-AUG-1999','DD-MON-YYYY')
                        AND     TO_DATE('10-AUG-1999','DD-MON-YYYY')
AND     prod_id IS NOT NULL
GROUP BY prod_name, week_ending_day;
```

In general, if you use an outer join in a materialized view containing only joins, you should put in the materialized view either the primary key or the rowid on the right side of the outer join. For example, in the previous example, `join_sales_time_product_oj_mv`, there is a primary key on both `sales` and `products`.

Another example of when a materialized view containing only joins is used is the case of a semi-join rewrites. That is, a query contains either an `EXISTS` or an `IN` subquery with a single table.

Consider this query, which reports the products that had sales greater than $1,000.

```
SELECT DISTINCT prod_name
FROM products p
WHERE EXISTS
  (SELECT *
   FROM sales s
   WHERE p.prod_id=s.prod_id
     AND s.amount_sold > 1000);
```

This query could also be seen as:

```
SELECT DISTINCT prod_name
FROM products p
WHERE p.prod_id IN (SELECT s.prod_id
                    FROM sales s
                    WHERE s.amount_sold > 1000
                       );
```

This query contains a semi-join between the `products` and the `sales` table:

```
s.prod_id = p.prod_id
```

This query can be rewritten to use either the `join_sales_time_product_mv` materialized view, if foreign key constraints are active or `join_sales_time_product_oj_mv` materialized view, if primary keys are active. Observe that both materialized views contain `s.prod_id=p.prod_id`, which can be used to derive the semi-join in the query.

The query is rewritten with `join_sales_time_product_mv` as follows:

```
SELECT prod_name
FROM (SELECT DISTINCT prod_name
      FROM  join_sales_time_product_mv
      WHERE amount_sold > 1000
      );
```

If the materialized view join_sales_time_product_mv is partitioned by time_id, then this query is likely to be more efficient than the original query because the original join between sales and products has been avoided.

The query could be rewritten using join_sales_time_product_oj_mv as follows.

```
SELECT prod_name
FROM (SELECT DISTINCT prod_name
      FROM  join_sales_time_product_oj_mv
      WHERE amount_sold > 1000
      AND prod_id IS NOT NULL
      );
```

Rewrites with semi-joins are currently restricted to materialized views with joins only and are not available for materialized views with joins and aggregates.

Query Delta Joins

A **query delta join** is a join that appears in the query but not in the materialized view. Any number and type of delta joins in a query are allowed and they are simply retained when the query is rewritten with a materialized view. Upon rewrite, the materialized view is joined to the appropriate tables in the query delta. For example, consider the following query:

```
SELECT p.prod_name, t.week_ending_day, c.cust_city,
       SUM(s.amount_sold)
FROM   sales s, products p, times t, customers c
WHERE  s.time_id=t.time_id
AND    s.prod_id = p.prod_id
AND    s.cust_id = c.cust_id
GROUP BY prod_name, week_ending_day, cust_city;
```

Using the materialized view join_sales_time_product_mv, common joins are: s.time_id=t.time_id and s.prod_id=p.prod_id. The delta join in the query is s.cust_id=c.cust_id.

The rewritten form will then join the join_sales_time_product_mv materialized view with the customers table as follows:

```
SELECT mv.prod_name, mv.week_ending_day, c.cust_city,
       SUM(mv.amount_sold)
FROM   join_sales_time_product_mv mv, customers c
WHERE  mv.cust_id = c.cust_id
GROUP BY prod_name, week_ending_day, cust_city;
```

Materialized View Delta Joins

A **materialized view delta join** is a join that appears in the materialized view but not the query. All delta joins in a materialized view are required to be lossless with respect to the result of common joins. A lossless join guarantees that the result of common joins is not restricted. A **lossless** join is one where, if two tables called A and B are joined together, rows in table A will always match with rows in table B and no data will be lost, hence the term lossless join. For example, every row with the foreign key matches a row with a primary key provided no nulls are allowed in the foreign key. Therefore, to guarantee a lossless join, it is necessary to have FOREIGN KEY, PRIMARY KEY, and NOT NULL constraints on appropriate join keys. Alternatively, if the join between tables A and B is an outer join (A being the outer table), it is lossless as it preserves all rows of table A.

All delta joins in a materialized view are required to be non-duplicating with respect to the result of common joins. A non-duplicating join guarantees that the result of common joins is not duplicated. For example, a non-duplicating join is one where, if table A and table B are joined together, rows in table A will match with at most one row in table B and no duplication occurs. To guarantee a non-duplicating join, the key in table B must be constrained to unique values by using a primary key or unique constraint.

Consider the following query that joins sales and times:

```
SELECT  t.week_ending_day,
        SUM(s.amount_sold)
FROM    sales s, times t
WHERE   s.time_id = t.time_id
AND     t.week_ending_day BETWEEN TO_DATE('01-AUG-1999', 'DD-MON-YYYY')
                          AND     TO_DATE('10-AUG-1999', 'DD-MON-YYYY')
GROUP BY week_ending_day;
```

The materialized view join_sales_time_product_mv has an additional join (s.prod_id=p.prod_id) between sales and products. This is the delta join in join_sales_time_product_mv. You can rewrite the query if this join is lossless and non-duplicating. This is the case if s.prod_id is a foreign key to p.prod_id and is not null. The query is therefore rewritten as:

```
SELECT  week_ending_day,
        SUM(amount_sold)
FROM    join_sales_time_product_mv
WHERE   week_ending_day BETWEEN TO_DATE('01-AUG-1999', 'DD-MON-YYYY')
                        AND     TO_DATE('10-AUG-1999', 'DD-MON-YYYY')
GROUP BY week_ending_day;
```

The query can also be rewritten with the materialized view join_sales_time_product_mv_oj where foreign key constraints are not needed. This view contains an outer join (s.prod_id=p.prod_id(+)) between sales and products. This makes the join lossless. If p.prod_id is a primary key, then the non-duplicating condition is satisfied as well and optimizer will rewrite the query as follows:

```
SELECT  week_ending_day,
        SUM(amount_sold)
FROM    join_sales_time_product_oj_mv
WHERE   week_ending_day BETWEEN TO_DATE('01-AUG-1999', 'DD-MON-YYYY')
  AND   TO_DATE('10-AUG-1999', 'DD-MON-YYYY')
GROUP BY week_ending_day;
```

Note that the outer join in the definition of join_sales_time_product_mv_oj is not necessary, because the parent key - foreign key relationship between sales and products in the Sales History schema is already lossless. It is used for demonstration purposes only, and would be necessary if sales.prod_id is nullable, thus violating the losslessness of the join condition sales.prod_id = products.prod_id.

Current limitations restrict most rewrites with outer joins to materialized views with joins only. There is limited support for rewrites with materialized aggregate views with outer joins, so those views should rely on foreign key constraints to assure losslessness of materialized view delta joins.

Join Equivalence Recognition

Query rewrite is able to make many transformations based upon the recognition of equivalent joins. Query rewrite recognizes the following construct as being equivalent to a join:

```
WHERE table1.column1 = F(args)    /* sub-expression A */
AND table2.column2 = F(args)      /* sub-expression B */
```

If `F(args)` is a PL/SQL function that is declared to be deterministic and the arguments to both invocations of `F` are the same, then the combination of sub-expression `A` with sub-expression `B` be can be recognized as a join between `table1.column1` and `table2.column2`. That is, the following expression is equivalent to the previous expression:

```
WHERE table1.column1 = F(args)           /* sub-expression A */
AND table2.column2 = F(args)             /* sub-expression B */
AND table1.column1 = table2.column2      /* join-expression J */
```

Because join-expression `J` can be inferred from sub-expression `A` and sub-expression `B`, the inferred join can be used to match a corresponding join of `table1.column1 = table2.column2` in a materialized view.

Data Sufficiency Check

In this check, the optimizer determines if the necessary column data requested by a query can be obtained from a materialized view. For this, the equivalence of one column with another is used. For example, if an inner join between table `A` and table `B` is based on a join predicate `A.X = B.X`, then the data in column `A.X` will equal the data in column `B.X` in the result of the join. This data property is used to match column `A.X` in a query with column `B.X` in a materialized view or vice versa. For example, consider this query:

```
SELECT p.prod_name, s.time_id, t.week_ending_day,
       SUM(s.amount_sold)
FROM   sales s, products p, times t
WHERE  s.time_id=t.time_id
AND    s.prod_id = p.prod_id
GROUP BY p.prod_name, s.time_id, t.week_ending_day;
```

This query can be answered with `join_sales_time_product_mv` even though the materialized view does not have `s.time_id`. Instead, it has `t.time_id`, which, through a join condition `s.time_id=t.time_id`, is equivalent to `s.time_id`. Thus, the optimizer might select this rewrite:

```
SELECT prod_name, time_id, week_ending_day,
       SUM(amount_sold)
FROM   join_sales_time_product_mv
GROUP BY prod_name, time_id, week_ending_day;
```

If some column data requested by a query cannot be obtained from a materialized view, the optimizer further determines if it can be obtained based on a data relationship called functional dependency. When the data in a column can determine data in another column, such a relationship is called functional dependency or functional determinance. For example, if a table contains a primary key column called `prod_id` and another column called `prod_name`, then, given a `prod_id` value, it is possible to look up the corresponding `prod_name`. The opposite is not true, which means a `prod_name` value need not relate to a unique `prod_id`.

When the column data required by a query is not available from a materialized view, such column data can still be obtained by joining the materialized view back to the table that contains required column data provided the materialized view contains a key that functionally determines the required column data. For example, consider the following query:

```
SELECT p.prod_category, t.week_ending_day,
       SUM(s.amount_sold)
FROM   sales s, products p, times t
WHERE  s.time_id=t.time_id
AND    s.prod_id=p.prod_id AND    p.prod_category='CD'
GROUP BY p.prod_category, t.week_ending_day;
```

The materialized view sum_sales_prod_week_mv contains p.prod_id, but not p.prod_category. However, we can join sum_sales_prod_week_mv back to products to retrieve prod_category because prod_id functionally determines prod_category. The optimizer rewrites this query using sum_sales_prod_week_mv as follows:

```
SELECT p.prod_category, mv.week_ending_day,
       SUM(mv.sum_amount_sold)
FROM   sum_sales_prod_week_mv mv, products p
WHERE  mv.prod_id=p.prod_id
AND    p.prod_category='CD'
GROUP BY p.prod_category, mv.week_ending_day;
```

Here the products table is called a joinback table because it was originally joined in the materialized view but joined again in the rewritten query. There are two ways to declare functional dependency:

- Using the primary key constraint (as shown in the previous example)
- Using the DETERMINES clause of a dimension.

The DETERMINES clause of a dimension definition might be the only way you could declare functional dependency when the column that determines another column cannot be a primary key. For example, the products table is a denormalized dimension table that has columns prod_id, prod_name, and prod_subcategory, and prod_subcategory functionally determines prod_subcat_desc and prod_category determines prod_cat_desc.

The first functional dependency can be established by declaring prod_id as the primary key, but not the second functional dependency because the prod_subcategory column contains duplicate values. In this situation, you can use the DETERMINES clause of a dimension to declare the second functional dependency. The following dimension definition illustrates how the functional dependencies are declared:

```
CREATE DIMENSION products_dim
       LEVEL product              IS (products.prod_id)
       LEVEL subcategory          IS (products.prod_subcategory)
       LEVEL category             IS (products.prod_category)
       HIERARCHY prod_rollup (
               product            CHILD OF
               subcategory        CHILD OF
               category
       )
       ATTRIBUTE product DETERMINES products.prod_name
       ATTRIBUTE product DETERMINES products.prod_desc
```

```
ATTRIBUTE subcategory DETERMINES products.prod_subcat_desc
ATTRIBUTE category    DETERMINES products.prod_cat_desc;
```

The hierarchy prod_rollup declares hierarchical relationships that are also 1:n functional dependencies. The 1:1 functional dependencies are declared using the DETERMINES clause, as seen when prod_subcategory functionally determines prod_subcat_desc.

Consider the following query:

```
SELECT p.prod_subcat_desc, t.week_ending_day,
       SUM(s.amount_sold)
FROM   sales s, products p, times t
WHERE  s.time_id=t.time_id
AND    s.prod_id=p.prod_id
AND    p.prod_subcat_desc LIKE '%Men'
GROUP BY p.prod_subcat_desc, t.week_ending_day;
```

This can be rewritten by joining sum_sales_pscat_week_mv to the products table so that prod_subcat_desc is available to evaluate the predicate. But the join will be based on the prod_subcategory column, which is not a primary key in the products table; therefore, it allows duplicates. This is accomplished by using an inline view that selects distinct values and this view is joined to the materialized view as shown in the rewritten query.

```
SELECT iv.prod_subcat_desc, mv.week_ending_day,
       SUM(mv.sum_amount_sold)
FROM   sum_sales_pscat_week_mv mv,
        (SELECT DISTINCT prod_subcategory, prod_subcat_desc
         FROM products) iv
WHERE   mv.prod_subcategory=iv.prod_subcategory
AND    iv.prod_subcat_desc LIKE '%Men'
GROUP BY iv.prod_subcat_desc, mv.week_ending_day;
```

This type of rewrite is possible because of the fact that prod_subcategory functionally determines prod_subcat_desc as declared in the dimension.

Grouping Compatibility Check

This check is required only if both the materialized view and the query contain a GROUP BY clause. The optimizer first determines if the grouping of data requested by a query is exactly the same as the grouping of data stored in a materialized view. In other words, the level of grouping is the same in both the query and the materialized view.

If the grouping of data requested by a query is at a coarser level compared to the grouping of data stored in a materialized view, the optimizer can still use the materialized view to rewrite the query. For example, the materialized view sum_sales_pscat_week_mv groups by week_ending_day, and prod_subcategory. This query groups by prod_subcategory, a coarser grouping granularity:

```
SELECT p.prod_subcategory, SUM(s.amount_sold) AS sum_amount
FROM   sales s, products p
WHERE  s.prod_id=p.prod_id
GROUP BY p.prod_subcategory;
```

Therefore, the optimizer will rewrite this query as:

```
SELECT p.prod_subcategory, SUM(sum_amount_sold)
FROM   sum_sales_pscat_week_mv mv,
GROUP BY p.prod_subcategory;
```

In another example, a query requests data grouped by prod_category whereas a materialized view stores data grouped by prod_subcategory. If prod_subcategory is a CHILD OF prod_category (see the dimension example earlier), the grouped data stored in the materialized view can be further grouped by prod_category when the query is rewritten. In other words, aggregates at prod_subcategory level (finer granularity) stored in a materialized view can be rolled up into aggregates at prod_category level (coarser granularity).

For example, consider the following query:

```
SELECT  p.prod_category, t.week_ending_day,
        SUM(s.amount_sold) AS sum_amount
FROM    sales s, products p, times t
WHERE   s.time_id=t.time_id
AND     s.prod_id=p.prod_id
GROUP BY p.prod_category, t.week_ending_day;
```

Because prod_subcategory functionally determines prod_category, sum_sales_pscat_week_mv can be used with a joinback to products to retrieve prod_category column data, and then aggregates can be rolled up to prod_category level, as shown here:

```
SELECT  pv.prod_subcategory, mv.week_ending_day, SUM(mv.sum_amount_sold)
FROM    sum_sales_pscat_week_mv mv,
        (SELECT DISTINCT prod_subcategory, prod_category
         FROM products) pv
WHERE  mv.prod_subcategory=mv.prod_subcategory
GROUP BY pv.prod_subcategory, mv.week_ending_day;
```

Note that, for this rewrite, the data sufficiency check determines that a joinback to the products table is necessary, and the grouping compatibility check determines that aggregate rollup is necessary.

Aggregate Computability Check

This check is required only if both the query and the materialized view contain aggregates. Here the optimizer determines if the aggregates requested by a query can be derived or computed from one or more aggregates stored in a materialized view. For example, if a query requests AVG(X) and a materialized view contains SUM(X) and COUNT(X), then AVG(X) can be computed as SUM(X)/COUNT(X).

If the grouping compatibility check has determined that the rollup of aggregates stored in a materialized view is required, then the aggregate computability check determines if it is possible to roll up each aggregate requested by the query using aggregates in the materialized view.

For example, SUM(sales) at the city level can be rolled up to SUM(sales) at the state level by summing all SUM(sales) aggregates in a group with the same state value. However, AVG(sales) cannot be rolled up to a coarser level unless COUNT(sales) is also available in the materialized view. Similarly, VARIANCE(sales) or STDDEV(sales) cannot be rolled up unless COUNT(sales) and SUM(sales) are also available in the materialized view. For example, given the query:

```
SELECT   p.prod_subcategory, AVG(s.amount_sold) AS avg_sales
FROM     sales s, products p
WHERE    s.prod_id = p.prod_id
GROUP BY p.prod_subcategory;
```

This statement can be rewritten with materialized view sum_sales_pscat_month_city_mv provided the join between sales and times and sales and customers are lossless and non-duplicating. Further, the query groups by prod_subcategory whereas the materialized view groups by prod_subcategory, calendar_month_desc and cust_city, which means the aggregates stored in the materialized view will have to be rolled up. The optimizer will rewrite the query as:

```
SELECT mv.prod_subcategory,
    SUM(mv.sum_amount_sold)/COUNT(mv.count_amount_sold)
  AS avg_sales
FROM sum_sales_pscat_month_city_mv mv
GROUP BY mv.prod_subcategory;
```

The argument of an aggregate such as SUM can be an arithmetic expression like A+B. The optimizer will try to match an aggregate SUM(A+B) in a query with an aggregate SUM(A+B) or SUM(B+A) stored in a materialized view. In other words, expression equivalence is used when matching the argument of an aggregate in a query with the argument of a similar aggregate in a materialized view. To accomplish this, Oracle converts the aggregate argument expression into a canonical form such that two different but equivalent expressions convert into the same canonical form. For example, A*(B-C), A*B-C*A, (B-C)*A, and -A*C+A*B all convert into the same canonical form and, therefore, they are successfully matched.

Query Rewrite with Inline Views

Oracle supports general query rewrite when the user query contains an inline view, or a subquery in the FROM list. Query rewrite matches inline views in the materialized view with inline views in the request query when the text of the two inline views exactly match. In this case, rewrite treats the matching inline view as it would a named view, and general rewrite processing is possible.

Here is an example where the materialized view contains an inline view, and the query has the same inline view, but the aliases for these views are different. Previously, this query could not be rewritten because neither exact text match nor partial text match is possible.

Here is the materialized view definition:

```
CREATE MATERIALIZED VIEW inline_example
ENABLE QUERY REWRITE AS
SELECT t.calendar_month_name, t.calendar_year  p.prod_category,
  SUM(V1.revenue) AS sum_revenue
FROM times t, products p,
     (SELECT time_id, prod_id, amount_sold*0.2 as revenue FROM sales) V1
WHERE t.time_id = V1.time_id
AND   p.prod_id = V1.prod_id
GROUP BY calendar_month_name, calendar_year, prod_category ;
```

And here is the query that will be rewritten to use the materialized view:

```
SELECT t.calendar_month_name, t.calendar_year, p.prod_category,
   SUM(X1.revenue) AS sum_revenue
FROM times t, products p,
     (SELECT time_id, prod_id, amount_sold*0.2 AS revenue FROM sales) X1
WHERE t.time_id = X1.time_id
AND   p.prod_id = X1.prod_id
GROUP BY calendar_month_name, calendar_year, prod_category
```

Query Rewrite with Selfjoins

Query rewrite of queries which contain multiple references to the same tables, or self joins are possible, to the extent that general rewrite can occur when the query and the materialized view definition have the same aliases for the multiple references to a table. This allows Oracle to provide a distinct identity for each table reference and this in turn allows query rewrite.

The following is an example of a materialized view and a query. In this example, the query is missing a reference to a column in a table so an exact text match will not work. But general query rewrite can occur because the aliases for the table references match.

To demonstrate the self-join rewriting possibility with the `Sales History` schema, we are assuming the following addition to include the actual shipping and payment date in the fact table, referencing the same dimension table times. This is for demonstration purposes only and will not return any results:

```
ALTER TABLE sales ADD (time_id_ship DATE);
ALTER TABLE sales ADD (CONSTRAINT time_id_book_fk FOREIGN key (time_id_ship)
REFERENCES times(time_id) ENABLE NOVALIDATE);
ALTER TABLE sales MODIFY CONSTRAINT time_id_book_fk RELY;
ALTER TABLE sales ADD (time_id_paid DATE);
ALTER TABLE sales ADD (CONSTRAINT time_id_paid_fk FOREIGN key (time_id_paid)
REFERENCES times(time_id) ENABLE NOVALIDATE);
ALTER TABLE sales MODIFY CONSTRAINT time_id_paid_fk RELY;
```

To reverse the changes, you can simply drop the columns:

```
ALTER TABLE sales DROP COLUMN time_id_ship;
ALTER TABLE sales DROP COLUMN time_id_paid;
```

Now, we can define a materialized view as follows:

```
CREATE MATERIALIZED VIEW sales_shipping_lag_mv
ENABLE QUERY REWRITE
AS
  SELECT t1.fiscal_week_number, s.prod_id,
        t2.fiscal_week_number - t1.fiscal_week_number as lag
  FROM times t1, sales s, times t2
  WHERE t1.time_id = s.time_id
  AND   t2.time_id = s.time_id_ship;
```

The following query fails the exact text match test but is rewritten because the aliases for the table references match:

```
SELECT s.prod_id,
       t2.fiscal_week_number - t1.fiscal_week_number AS lag
FROM times t1, sales s, times t2
WHERE t1.time_id = s.time_id
AND   t2.time_id = s.time_id_ship;
```

Note that Oracle performs other checks to insure the correct match of an instance of a multiply instanced table in the request query with the corresponding table instance in the materialized view. For instance, in the following example, Oracle correctly determines that the matching alias names used for the multiple instances of table `time` does not establish a match between the multiple instances of table `time` in the materialized view:

The following query cannot be rewritten using `sales_shipping_lag_mv` even though the alias names of the multiply instanced table `time` match because the joins are not compatible between the instances of `time` aliased by `t2`:

```
SELECT s.prod_id,
       t2.fiscal_week_number - t1.fiscal_week_number AS lag
```

```
FROM times t1, sales s, times t2
WHERE t1.time_id = s.time_id AND   t2.time_id = s.time_id_paid;
```

This request query joins the instance of the `time` table aliased by `t2` on the `s.time_id_paid` column, while the materialized views joins the instance of the `time` table aliased by `t2` on the `s.time_id_ship` column. Because the join conditions differ, Oracle correctly determines that rewrite cannot occur.

SPECIAL CASES FOR QUERY REWRITE

There are a few special cases when using query rewrite:

- Query rewrite using partially stale materialized views
- Query rewrite using complex materialized views
- Query rewrite using nested materialized views
- Query rewrite when using GROUP BY extensions.

Query Rewrite Using Partially Stale Materialized Views

In Oracle9*i*, when a certain partition of the detail table is updated, only specific sections of the materialized view are marked stale. The materialized view must have information that can identify the partition of the table corresponding to a particular row or group of the materialized view. The simplest scenario is when the partitioning key of the table is available in the `SELECT` list of the materialized view because this is the easiest way to map a row to a stale partition. The key points when using partially stale materialized views are:

- Query rewrite can use a materialized view in `ENFORCED` or `TRUSTED` mode if the rows from the materialized view used to answer the query are known to be `FRESH`.
- The fresh rows in the materialized view are identified by adding selection predicates to the materialized view's `WHERE` clause. We will rewrite a query with this materialized view if its answer is contained within this (restricted) materialized view. Note that support for materialized views with selection predicates is a prerequisite for this type of rewrite.

The fact table `sales` is partitioned based on ranges of `time_id` as follows:

```
PARTITION BY RANGE (time_id)
(PARTITION SALES_Q1_1998
          VALUES LESS THAN (TO_DATE('01-APR-1998', 'DD-MON-YYYY')),
 PARTITION SALES_Q2_1998
          VALUES LESS THAN (TO_DATE('01-JUL-1998', 'DD-MON-YYYY')),
 PARTITION SALES_Q3_1998
          VALUES LESS THAN (TO_DATE('01-OCT-1998', 'DD-MON-YYYY')),
...
```

Suppose you have a materialized view grouping by `time_id` as follows:

```
CREATE MATERIALIZED VIEW sum_sales_per_city_mv
ENABLE QUERY REWRITE
AS
SELECT s.time_id, p.prod_subcategory, c.cust_city,
      SUM(s.amount_sold) AS sum_amount_sold
FROM sales s, products p, customers c
WHERE s.cust_id = c.cust_id
```

```
AND    s.prod_id = p.prod_id
GROUP BY time_id, prod_subcategory, cust_city;
```

Suppose new data will be inserted for December 2000, which will end up in the partition `sales_q4_2000`. For testing purposes, you can apply an arbitrary DML operation on `sales`, changing a different partition than `sales_q1_2000` when this materialized view is fresh. For example:

```
INSERT INTO SALES VALUES(10,10,'01-dec-2000','S',10,123.45,54321);
```

Until a refresh is done, the materialized view is generically stale and cannot be used for unlimited rewrite in enforced mode. However, because the table `sales` is partitioned and not all partitions have been modified, Oracle can identify all partitions that have not been touched. The fresh rows in the materialized view, that means the data of all partitions where Oracle knows that no changes have occurred, can be represented by modifying the materialized view's defining query as follows:

```
SELECT s.time_id, p.prod_subcategory, c.cust_city,
       SUM(s.amount_sold) AS sum_amount_sold
FROM sales s, products p, customers c
WHERE s.cust_id = c.cust_id
AND    s.prod_id = p.prod_id
AND    s.time_id < TO_DATE('01-OCT-2000','DD-MON-YYYY')
GROUP BY time_id, prod_subcategory, cust_city;
```

Note that the freshness of partially stale materialized views is tracked on a per partition base, and not on a logical base. Since the partitioning strategy of the sales fact table is on a quarterly base, changes in December 2000 causes the complete partition `sales_q4_2000` to become stale.

Consider the following query which asks for sales in quarter 1 and 2 of 2000:

```
SELECT s.time_id, p.prod_subcategory, c.cust_city,
       SUM(s.amount_sold) AS sum_amount_sold
FROM sales s, products p, customers c
WHERE s.cust_id = c.cust_id
AND    s.prod_id = p.prod_id
AND    s.time_id BETWEEN TO_DATE('01-JAN-2000', 'DD-MON-YYYY')
AND TO_DATE('01-JUL-2000', 'DD-MON-YYYY')
GROUP BY time_id, prod_subcategory, cust_city;
```

Oracle knows that those ranges of rows in the materialized view are fresh and can therefore rewrite the query with the materialized view. The rewritten query looks as follows:

```
SELECT time_id, prod_subcategory, cust_city, sum_amount_sold
FROM sum_sales_per_city_mv
WHERE time_id BETWEEN TO_DATE('01-JAN-2000', 'DD-MON-YYYY')
AND TO_DATE('01-JUL-2000', 'DD-MON-YYYY');
```

Instead of the partitioning key, a partition marker (a function that identifies the partition given a rowid) can be present in the select (and `GROUP BY` list) of the materialized view. You can use the materialized view to rewrite queries that require data from only certain partitions (identifiable by the partition-marker), for instance, queries that reference a partition-extended table-name or queries that have a predicate specifying ranges of the partitioning keys containing entire partitions.

The following example illustrates the use of a partition marker in the materialized view instead of the direct usage of the partition key column.

```
CREATE MATERIALIZED VIEW sum_sales_per_city_2_mv
ENABLE QUERY REWRITE
AS
SELECT DBMS_MVIEW.PMARKER(s.rowid) AS pmarker,
       t.fiscal_quarter_desc, p.prod_subcategory, c.cust_city,
       SUM(s.amount_sold) AS sum_amount_sold
FROM sales s, products p, customers c, times t
WHERE s.cust_id = c.cust_id
AND   s.prod_id = p.prod_id
AND   s.time_id = t.time_id
GROUP BY DBMS_MVIEW.PMARKER(s.rowid),
         prod_subcategory, cust_city, fiscal_quarter_desc;
```

Suppose you know that the partition `sales_q1_2000` is fresh and DML changes have taken place for other partitions of the `sales` table. For testing purposes, you can apply an arbitrary DML operation on `sales`, changing a different partition than `sales_q1_2000` when the materialized view is fresh. For example:

```
INSERT INTO SALES VALUES(10,10,'01-dec-2000','S',10,123.45,54321);
```

Although the materialized view `sum_sales_per_city_2_mv` is now considered generically stale, Oracle can rewrite the following query using this materialized view. This query restricts the data to the partition `sales_q1_2000`, and selects only certain values of `cust_city`, as shown in the following:

```
SELECT p.prod_subcategory, c.cust_city,
SUM(s.amount_sold) AS sum_amount_sold
FROM sales s, products p, customers c
WHERE s.cust_id = c.cust_id
AND s.prod_id = p.prod_id
AND c.cust_city= 'Nuernberg'
AND s.time_id >= TO_DATE('01-JAN-2000','dd-mon-yyyy')
AND s.time_id <  TO_DATE('01-APR-2000','dd-mon-yyyy')
GROUP BY prod_subcategory, cust_city;
```

The same query could have been expressed with a partition-extended name as in the following statement:

```
SELECT p.prod_subcategory, c.cust_city,
SUM(s.amount_sold) AS sum_amount_sold
FROM sales partition (sales_q1_2000) s, products p, customers c
WHERE s.cust_id = c.cust_id
AND s.prod_id = p.prod_id
AND c.cust_city= 'Nuernberg'
GROUP BY prod_subcategory, cust_city;
```

Note that rewrite with a partially stale materialized view that contains a `PMARKER` function can only take place when the complete data content of one or more partitions is accessed and the predicate condition is on the partitioned fact table itself, as shown in the earlier example.

The `DBMS_MVIEW.PMARKER` function gives you exactly one distinct value for each partition. This dramatically reduces the number of rows in a potential materialized view compared to the partitioning key itself, but you are also giving up any detailed information about this key. The only thing you know is the partition number and, therefore, the lower and upper boundary values. This is the trade-off for reducing the cardinality of the range partitioning column and thus the number of rows.

Assuming the value of `p_marker` for partition `sales_q1_2000` is 31070, the previously shown queries can be rewritten against the materialized view as:

```
SELECT mv.prod_subcategory, mv.cust_city,
SUM(mv.sum_amount_sold)
FROM sum_sales_per_city_2_mv mv
WHERE mv.pmarker = 31070
AND mv.cust_city= 'Nuernberg'
GROUP BY prod_subcategory, cust_city;
```

So the query can be rewritten against the materialized view without accessing stale data.

Query Rewrite Using Complex Materialized Views

Complex materialized views are views that are not uniquely resolvable for query rewrite. Rewrite capability with complex materialized views is restricted to text match-based rewrite (partial or full). You can define a materialized view using arbitrarily complex SQL query expressions, but such a materialized view is treated as complex by query rewrite.

For example some of the constructs that make a materialized view complex are: set operators (`UNION`, `UNION ALL`, `INTERSECT`, `MINUS`), `START WITH` clause, `CONNECT BY` clause, and so on. Oracle currently supports general rewrite with inline views and self-joins on certain cases. These are the cases when the texts of inline view in the query and materialized view exactly match and the aliases of the duplicate tables in both the query and materialized view exactly match. All other cases involving inline views and self-joins will make a materialized view complex.

Query Rewrite Using Nested Materialized Views

Query rewrite is attempted iteratively to take advantage of nested materialized views. Oracle first tries to rewrite a query with a materialized view having aggregates and joins, then with a materialized join view. If any of the rewrites succeeds, Oracle repeats that process again until no rewrites have occurred. For example, assume that you had created a materialized views `join_sales_time_product_mv` and `sum_sales_time_product_mv`:

```
CREATE MATERIALIZED VIEW join_sales_time_product_mv
ENABLE QUERY REWRITE
AS
SELECT p.prod_id, p.prod_name, t.time_id, t.week_ending_day,
       s.channel_id, s.promo_id, s.cust_id,
       s.amount_sold
FROM   sales s, products p, times t
WHERE  s.time_id=t.time_id
AND    s.prod_id = p.prod_id;

CREATE MATERIALIZED VIEW sum_sales_time_product_mv
ENABLE QUERY REWRITE
AS
SELECT mv.prod_name, mv.week_ending_day,
       COUNT(*) cnt_all,
       SUM(mv.amount_sold) sum_amount_sold,
       COUNT(mv.amount_sold) cnt_amount_sold
FROM join_sales_time_product_mv mv
GROUP BY mv.prod_name, mv.week_ending_day;
```

Consider the following query:

```
SELECT p.prod_name, t.week_ending_day, SUM(s.amount_sold)
FROM sales s, products p, times t
WHERE s.time_id=t.time_id
AND s.prod_id=p.prod_id
GROUP BY p.prod_name, t.week_ending_day;
```

Oracle first tries to rewrite it with a materialized aggregate view and finds there is none eligible (note that single-table aggregate materialized view `sum_sales_store_time_mv` cannot yet be used), and then tries a rewrite with a materialized join view and finds that `join_sales_time_product_mv` is eligible for rewrite. The rewritten query has this form:

```
SELECT mv.prod_name, mv.week_ending_day, SUM(mv.amount_sold)
FROM join_sales_time_product_mv mv
GROUP BY mv.prod_name, mv.week_ending_day;
```

Because a rewrite occurred, Oracle tries the process again. This time the query can be rewritten with single-table aggregate materialized view `sum_sales_store_time` into this form:

```
SELECT mv.prod_name, mv.week_ending_day, mv.sum_amount_sold
FROM sum_sales_time_product_mv mv;
```

Query Rewrite When Using GROUP BY Extensions

Oracle9*i* introduced extensions to the `GROUP BY` clause in the form of `GROUPING SETS`, `ROLLUP`, and their concatenation. These extensions enable you to selectively specify the groupings of interest in the `GROUP BY` clause of the query. For example, the following is a typical query with Grouping Sets:

```
SELECT p.prod_subcategory, t.calendar_month_desc, c.cust_city,

  SUM(s.amount_sold) AS sum_amount_sold
FROM sales s, customers c, products p, times t
WHERE s.time_id=t.time_id
  AND s.prod_id = p.prod_id AND s.cust_id = c.cust_id
GROUP BY GROUPING SETS
(
    (p.prod_subcategory, t.calendar_month_desc),
    (c.cust_city, p.prod_subcategory)
);
```

The term **base grouping** for queries with `GROUP BY` extensions denotes all unique expressions present in the `GROUP BY` clause. In the previous query, the following grouping (p.prod_subcategory, t.calendar_month_desc, c.cust_city,) is a base grouping.

The extensions can be present in user queries and in the queries defining materialized views. In both cases, materialized view rewrite applies and you can distinguish rewrite capabilities into the following scenarios:

Materialized View Has Simple GROUP BY and Query Has Extended GROUP BY

When a query contains an extended `GROUP BY` clause, it can be rewritten with a materialized view if its base grouping can be rewritten using the materialized view as listed in the rewrite rules explained in "When Does Oracle Rewrite a Query?". For example, in the following query:

```
SELECT p.prod_subcategory, t.calendar_month_desc, c.cust_city,
  SUM(s.amount_sold) AS sum_amount_sold
FROM sales s, customers c, products p, times t
```

```
WHERE s.time_id=t.time_id
  AND s.prod_id = p.prod_id AND s.cust_id = c.cust_id
GROUP BY GROUPING SETS
(
    (p.prod_subcategory, t.calendar_month_desc),
    (c.cust_city, p.prod_subcategory)
);
```

The base grouping is: `(p.prod_subcategory, t.calendar_month_desc, c.cust_city, p.prod_subcategory))` and, consequently, Oracle can rewrite the query using `sum_sales_pscat_month_city_mv` as follows:

```
SELECT mv.prod_subcategory, mv.calendar_month_desc, mv.cust_city,
  SUM(mv.sum_amount_sold) AS sum_amount_sold
FROM sum_sales_pscat_month_city_mv mv
GROUP BY GROUPING SETS
(
   (mv.prod_subcategory, mv.calendar_month_desc),
   (mv.cust_city, mv.prod_subcategory)
);
```

A special situation arises if the query uses the `EXPAND_GSET_TO_UNION` hint.

Materialized View Has Extended GROUP BY and Query Has Simple GROUP BY

In order for a materialized view with an extended `GROUP BY` to be used for rewrite, it must satisfy two additional conditions:

- It must contain a grouping distinguisher, which is the `GROUPING_ID` function on all `GROUP BY` expressions. For example, if the `GROUP BY` clause of the materialized view is `GROUP BY CUBE(a, b)`, then the `SELECT` list should contain `GROUPING_ID(a, b)`.
- The `GROUP BY` clause of the materialized view should not result in any duplicate groupings. For example, `GROUP BY GROUPING SETS ((a, b), (a, b))` would disqualify an materialized view from general rewrite.

A materialized view with an extended `GROUP BY` contains multiple groupings. Oracle finds the grouping with the lowest cost from which the query can be computed and uses that for rewrite. For example, consider the materialized view:

```
CREATE MATERIALIZED VIEW sum_grouping_set_mv
ENABLE QUERY REWRITE
AS
SELECT
   p.prod_category, p.prod_subcategory, c.cust_state_province, c.cust_city,
   GROUPING_ID(p.prod_category,p.prod_subcategory,
               c.cust_state_province,c.cust_city) AS gid,
   SUM(s.amount_sold) AS sum_amount_sold
FROM sales s, products p, customers c
WHERE s.prod_id = p.prod_id AND s.cust_id = c.cust_id
GROUP BY GROUPING SETS
(
   (p.prod_category, p.prod_subcategory, c.cust_city),
   (p.prod_category, p.prod_subcategory, c.cust_state_province, c.cust_city),
   (p.prod_category, p.prod_subcategory)
);
```

In this case, the following query:

```
SELECT
  p.prod_subcategory, c.cust_city,
  SUM(s.amount_sold) AS sum_amount_sold
FROM sales s, products p, customers c
WHERE s.prod_id = p.prod_id AND s.cust_id = c.cust_id
GROUP BY p.prod_subcategory, c.cust_city;
```

This query will be rewritten with the closest matching grouping from the materialized view. That is, the `(prodcategory, prod_subcategory, cust_city)` grouping:

```
SELECT
  prod_subcategory, cust_city,
  SUM(sum_amount_sold) AS sum_amount_sold
FROM sum_grouping_set_mv
WHERE gid = grouping identifier of (prod_category,prod_subcategory, cust_city)
GROUP BY prod_subcategory, cust_city;
```

Both Materialized View and Query Have Extended GROUP BY

When both materialized view and the query contain `GROUP BY` extensions, Oracle uses two strategies for rewrite: grouping match and `UNION ALL` rewrite. First, Oracle tries grouping match. The groupings in the query are matched against groupings in the materialized view and if all are matched with no rollup, Oracle selects them from the materialized view. For example, the following query:

```
SELECT
  p.prod_category, p.prod_subcategory, c.cust_state_province, c.cust_city,
  SUM(s.amount_sold) AS sum_amount_sold
FROM sales s, products p, customers c
WHERE s.prod_id = p.prod_id AND s.cust_id = c.cust_id
GROUP BY GROUPING SETS
(
  (p.prod_category, p.prod_subcategory, c.cust_city),
  (p.prod_category, p.prod_subcategory)
);
```

This query matches two groupings from `sum_grouping_set_mv` and Oracle rewrites the query as:

```
SELECT
  prod_subcategory, cust_city, sum_amount_sold
FROM sum_grouping_set_mv
WHERE gid = grouping identifier of (prod_category,prod_subcategory, cust_city)
   OR gid = grouping identifier of (prod_category,prod_subcategory)
```

In Oracle9*i*, release 2, if grouping match fails, Oracle tries a general rewrite mechanism called `UNION ALL` rewrite. Oracle first represents the query with the extended `GROUP BY` clause as an equivalent `UNION ALL` query. Every grouping of the original query is placed in a separate `UNION ALL` branch. The branch will have a simple `GROUP BY` clause. For example, consider this query:

```
SELECT
  p.prod_category, p.prod_subcategory, c.cust_state_province,
  t.calendar_month_desc, SUM(s.amount_sold) AS sum_amount_sold
FROM sales s, products p, customers c
WHERE s.prod_id = p.prod_id AND s.cust_id = c.cust_id
```

```
GROUP BY GROUPING SETS
(
   (p.prod_subcategory, t.calendar_month_desc),
   (t.calendar_month_desc),
   (p.prod_category, p.prod_subcategory, c.cust_state_province),
   (p.prod_category, p.prod_subcategory)
);
```

This is first represented as UNION ALL with four branches:

```
SELECT
   null, p.prod_subcategory, null,
    t.calendar_month_desc, SUM(s.amount_sold) AS sum_amount_sold
FROM sales s, products p, customers c
WHERE s.prod_id = p.prod_id AND s.cust_id = c.cust_id
GROUP BY p.prod_subcategory, t.calendar_month_desc
UNION ALL
  SELECT
    null, null, null,
    t.calendar_month_desc, SUM(s.amount_sold) AS sum_amount_sold
FROM sales s, products p, customers c
WHERE s.prod_id = p.prod_id AND s.cust_id = c.cust_id
GROUP BY t.calendar_month_desc
SELECT
    p.prod_category, p.prod_subcategory, c.cust_state_province,
    null, SUM(s.amount_sold) AS sum_amount_sold
FROM sales s, products p, customers c
WHERE s.prod_id = p.prod_id AND s.cust_id = c.cust_id
GROUP BY p.prod_category, p.prod_subcategory, c.cust_state_province
UNION ALL
  SELECT
    p.prod_category, p.prod_subcategory, null,
    null, SUM(s.amount_sold) AS sum_amount_sold
  FROM sales s, products p, customers c
  WHERE s.prod_id = p.prod_id AND s.cust_id = c.cust_id
  GROUP BY p.prod_category, p.prod_subcategory
```

Each branch is then rewritten separately using the rules from "When Does Oracle Rewrite a Query?". Using the materialized view sum_grouping_set_mv, Oracle can rewrite only branches 3 (which requires materialized view rollup) and 4 (which matches the materialized view exactly). The unrewritten branches will be converted back to the extended GROUP BY form. Thus, eventually, the query is rewritten as:

```
SELECT
    null, p.prod_subcategory, null,
    t.calendar_month_desc, SUM(s.amount_sold) AS sum_amount_sold
FROM sales s, products p, customers c
WHERE s.prod_id = p.prod_id AND s.cust_id = c.cust_id
GROUP BY GROUPING SETS
  (
    (p.prod_subcategory, t.calendar_month_desc),
    (t.calendar_month_desc),
  )
UNION ALL
  SELECT
```

```
    prod_category, prod_subcategory, cust_state_province,
    null, SUM(sum_amount_sold) AS sum_amount_sold
  FROM sum_grouping_set_mv
  WHERE gid = <grouping id of (prod_category,prod_subcategory, cust_city)>
  GROUP BY p.prod_category, p.prod_subcategory, c.cust_state_province
UNION ALL
  SELECT
    prod_category, prod_subcategory, null,
    null, sum_amount_sold
  FROM sum_grouping_set_mv
  WHERE gid = <grouping id of (prod_category,prod_subcategory)>
```

Observe the following features of UNION ALL rewrite. First, a query with extended GROUP BY is represented as an equivalent UNION ALL and recursively submitted for rewrite optimization. The groupings that cannot be rewritten stay in the last branch of UNION ALL and access the base data instead.

Hint for Queries with Extended GROUP BY

Oracle9*i* introduced a new hint, the EXPAND_GSET_TO_UNION hint, to force expansion of the query with GROUP BY extensions into the equivalent UNION ALL query. This hint can be in an environment where materialized views have simple GROUP BY clauses only. In this case, we extend rewrite flexibility as each branch can be independently rewritten by a separate materialized view.

DID QUERY REWRITE OCCUR?

Because query rewrite occurs transparently, special steps have to be taken to verify that a query has been rewritten. Of course, if the query runs faster, this should indicate that rewrite has occurred, but that is not proof. Therefore, to confirm that query rewrite does occur, use the EXPLAIN PLAN statement or the DBMS_MVIEW.EXPLAIN_REWRITE procedure.

Explain Plan

For query rewrite, all you need to check is that the object_name column in PLAN_TABLE contains the materialized view name. If it does, then query rewrite will occur when this query is executed.

In this example, the materialized view cal_month_sales_mv has been created.

```
CREATE MATERIALIZED VIEW cal_month_sales_mv
ENABLE QUERY REWRITE
AS
SELECT  t.calendar_month_desc, SUM(s.amount_sold) AS dollars
FROM  sales s, times t
WHERE  s.time_id = t.time_id
GROUP BY t.calendar_month_desc;
```

If EXPLAIN PLAN is used on the following SQL statement, the results are placed in the default table PLAN_TABLE. However, PLAN_TABLE must first be created by using the utlxplan.sql script.

```
EXPLAIN PLAN
FOR
SELECT  t.calendar_month_desc, SUM(s.amount_sold)
```

```
FROM   sales s, times t
WHERE   s.time_id = t.time_id
GROUP BY t.calendar_month_desc;
```

For the purposes of query rewrite, the only information of interest from PLAN_TABLE is the OBJECT_NAME, which identifies the objects that will be used to execute this query. Therefore, you would expect to see the object name calendar_month_sales_mv in the output as illustrated here.

```
SELECT   object_name FROM plan_table;

        OBJECT_NAME

        CALENDAR_MONTH_SALES_MV
2 rows selected.
```

DBMS_MVIEW.EXPLAIN_REWRITE Procedure

It can be difficult to understand why a query did not rewrite. The rules governing query rewrite eligibility are quite complex, involving various factors such as constraints, dimensions, query rewrite integrity modes, freshness of the materialized views, and the types of queries themselves. In addition, you may want to know why query rewrite chose a particular materialized view instead of another. To help with this matter, Oracle provides a PL/SQL procedure (DBMS_MVIEW.EXPLAIN_REWRITE) to advise you when a query can be rewritten and, if not, why not. Using the results from DBMS_MVIEW.EXPLAIN_REWRITE, you can take the appropriate action needed to make a query rewrite if at all possible.

NOTE: *The query specified in the EXPLAIN_REWRITE statement is never actually executed.*

DBMS_MVIEW.EXPLAIN_REWRITE Syntax

You can obtain the output from DBMS_MVIEW.EXPLAIN_REWRITE in two ways. The first is to use a table, while the second is to create a varray. The following shows the basic syntax for using an output table:

```
DBMS_MVIEW.EXPLAIN_REWRITE  (
    query              VARCHAR2(2000),
    mv                 VARCHAR2(30),
    statement_id       VARCHAR2(30)
  );
```

You can create an output table named REWRITE_TABLE by executing the Oracle-supplied script utlxrw.sql.

The QUERY parameter is a text string representing the SQL query. The parameter, MV, is a fully qualified materialized view name in the form of SCHEMA.MV. This is an optional parameter. When it is not specified, EXPLAIN_REWRITE returns any relevant error messages regarding all the materialized views considered for rewriting the given query. When SCHEMA is omitted and only MV is specified, EXPLAIN_REWRITE looks for the materialized view in the current schema.

Therefore, to call the EXPLAIN_REWRITE procedure using an output table is as follows:

```
DBMS_MVIEW.EXPLAIN_REWRITE  (
    query              VARCHAR2(2000),
    mv                 VARCHAR2(30),
    statement_id       VARCHAR2(30)
  );
```

If you want to direct the output of EXPLAIN_REWRITE to a varray instead of a table, you should call the procedure as follows:

```
DBMS_MVIEW.EXPLAIN_REWRITE  (
    query              VARCHAR2(2000),
    mv                 VARCHAR2(30),
    output_array       SYS.RewriteArrayType
  );
```

NOTE *If the query is less than 256 characters long, EXPLAIN_REWRITE can be easily invoked by using the EXECUTE command from SQL*PLUS. Otherwise, the recommended method is to use a PL/SQL BEGIN... END block, as shown in the examples in /rdbms/demo/smxrw.sql.*

Further, the EXPLAIN_REWRITE cannot accept queries longer than 32627 characters. These restrictions also apply when passing a materialized view's defining query to the EXPLAIN_MVIEW procedure

Using REWRITE_TABLE

Output of EXPLAIN_REWRITE can be directed to a table named REWRITE_TABLE. You can create this output table by running the Oracle-supplied script utlxrw.sql. This script can be found in the admin directory. The format of REWRITE_TABLE is as follows.

```
CREATE TABLE REWRITE_TABLE(
  statement_id          VARCHAR2(30),   – ID for the query
  mv_owner              VARCHAR2(30),   – MV's schema
  mv_name               VARCHAR2(30),   – Name of the MV
  sequence              INTEGER,        – Seq # of error msg
  query                 VARCHAR2(2000),– user query
  message               VARCHAR2(512),  – EXPLAIN_REWRITE error msg
  pass                  VARCHAR2(3),    – Query Rewrite pass no
  flags                 INTEGER,        – For future use
  reserved1             INTEGER,        – For future use
  reserved2             VARCHAR2(256);  – For future use
);
```

Example 15.12 : EXPLAIN_REWRITE Using REWRITE_TABLE

An example PL/SQL invocation is:

```
EXECUTE DBMS_MVIEW.EXPLAIN_REWRITE \
('SELECT p.prod_name, SUM(amount_sold)  ' ||\
'FROM sales s, products p ' ||\
'WHERE s.prod_id = p.prod_id ' ||\
' AND prod_name > ''B%'' ' ||\
' AND prod_name < ''C%'' ' ||\
'GROUP BY prod_name', \
'TestXRW.PRODUCT_SALES_MV', \
'SH');

SELECT message FROM rewrite_table ORDER BY sequence;
MESSAGE
------------------------------------------------------------------------------------
------------
QSM-01033: query rewritten with materialized view, PRODUCT_SALES_MV
1 row selected.
```

Here is another example where you can see a more detailed explanation of why some materialized views were not considered and eventually the materialized view sales_mv was chosen as the best one.

```
DECLARE
    qrytext VARCHAR2(500)  :='SELECT cust_first_name, cust_last_name,
SUM(amount_sold) AS dollar_sales FROM sales s, customers c WHERE s.cust_id=
c.cust_id GROUP BY cust_first_name, cust_last_name';
    idno    VARCHAR2(30) :='ID1';
BEGIN
DBMS_MVIEW.EXPLAIN_REWRITE(querytxt, '', idno);
END;
/
SELECT message FROM rewrite_table ORDER BY sequence;

SQL>                              MESSAGE
--------------------------------------------------------------------------------
QSM-01082:      Joining materialized view, CAL_MONTH_SALES_MV, with table, SALES,
                not possible
QSM-01022:      a more optimal materialized view than PRODUCT_SALES_MV was used
                to rewrite
QSM-01022:      a more optimal materialized view than FWEEK_PSCAT_SALES_MV was
                used to rewrite
QSM-01033:      query rewritten with materialized view, SALES_MV
```

Using a VARRAY

You can save the output of EXPLAIN_REWRITE in a PL/SQL varray. The elements of this array are of the type RewriteMessage, which is defined in the SYS schema as shown in the following:

```
TYPE RewriteMessage IS record(
  mv_owner                VARCHAR2(30),     – MV's schema
  mv_name                 VARCHAR2(30),     – Name of the MV
  sequence                INTEGER,          – Seq # of error msg
  query                   VARCHAR2(2000),   – user query
  message                 VARCHAR2(512),    – EXPLAIN_REWRITE error msg
  pass                    VARCHAR2(3),      – Query Rewrite pass no
  flags                   INTEGER,          – For future use
  reserved1               INTEGER,          – For future use
  reserved2               VARCHAR2(256)     – For future use
);
```

The array type, RewriteArrayType, which is a varray of RewriteMessage objects, is defined in SYS schema as follows:

- TYPE RewriteArrayType AS VARRAY(256) OF RewriteMessage;
  Using this array type, now you can declare an array variable and specify it in the EXPLAIN_REWRITE statement.
- Each RewriteMessage record provides a message concerning rewrite processing.
  The parameters are the same as for REWRITE_TABLE, except for statement_id, which is not used when using a varray as output.
- The mv_owner field defines the owner of materialized view that is relevant to the message.
- The mv_name field defines the name of a materialized view that is relevant to the message.

- The `sequence` field defines the sequence in which messages should be ordered.
- The `query` field contains the first 2000 characters of the query text under analysis.
- The `message` field contains the text of message relevant to rewrite processing of `query`.
- The `flags`, `reserved1`, and `reserved2` fields are reserved for future use.

Example 15.13 : EXPLAIN_REWRITE Using VARRAY

Consider the following query:

```
SELECT  c.cust_state_province,
     AVG(s.amount_sold)
FROM sales s, customers c
WHERE s.cust_id = c.cust_id
GROUP BY c.cust_state_province;
```

If that is used with the following materialized view:

```
CREATE MATERIALIZED VIEW avg_sales_city_state_mv
  ENABLE QUERY REWRITE
  AS
   SELECT c.cust_city, c.cust_state_province,
            AVG(s.amount_sold)
   FROM sales s, customers c
   WHERE s.cust_id = c.cust_id
   GROUP BY c.cust_city, c.cust_state_province;
```

The query will not rewrite with this materialized view. This can be quite confusing to a novice user as it seems like all information required for rewrite is present in the materialized view. The user can find out from `DBMS_MVIEW.EXPLAIN_REWRITE` that `AVG` cannot be computed from the given materialized view. The problem is that a `ROLLUP` is required here and `AVG` requires a `COUNT` or a `SUM` to do `ROLLUP`.

An example PL/SQL block for the previous query, using a varray as its output medium, is as follows:

```
SET SERVEROUTPUT ON
DECLARE
  Rewrite_Array SYS.RewriteArrayType   := SYS.RewriteArrayType();
  querytxt VARCHAR2(1500) := 'SELECT S.CITY, AVG(F.DOLLAR_SALES)
          FROM STORE S, FACT F WHERE S.STORE_KEY = F.STORE_KEY
          GROUP BY S.CITY';
  i NUMBER;
BEGIN
   DBMS_MVIEW.Explain_Rewrite(querytxt, 'MV_CITY_STATE', Rewrite_Array);
  FOR i IN 1..Rewrite_Array.count
  LOOP
DBMS_OUTPUT.PUT_LINE(Rewrite_Array(i).message);
  END LOOP;
END;
/
```

Following is the output of this `EXPLAIN_REWRITE` statement:

```
>> MV_NAME   : MV_CITY_STATE
>> QUERY     : SELECT S.CITY, AVG(F.DOLLAR_SALES) FROM STORE S, FACT F
               WHERE S.ST ORE_KEY = F.STORE_KEY GROUP BY S.CITY
```

```
>> MESSAGE   : QSM-01065: materialized view, MV_CITY_STATE, cannot compute
               measure, AVG, in the query
DBMS_MVIEW.Explain_Rewrite(querytxt, 'ID1', 'MV_CITY_STATE',
     user_name, Rewrite_Array);
```

DESIGN CONSIDERATIONS FOR IMPROVING QUERY REWRITE CAPABILITIES

The following design considerations will help in getting the maximum benefit from query rewrite. They are not mandatory for using query rewrite and rewrite is not guaranteed if you follow them. They are general rules of thumb.

Query Rewrite Considerations: Constraints

Make sure all inner joins referred to in a materialized view have referential integrity (foreign key - primary key constraints) with additional `NOT NULL` constraints on the foreign key columns. Since constraints tend to impose a large overhead, you could make them `NO VALIDATE` and `RELY` and set the parameter `QUERY_REWRITE_INTEGRITY` to `stale_tolerated` or `trusted`. However, if you set `QUERY_REWRITE_INTEGRITY` to `enforced`, all constraints must be enforced to get maximum rewritability.

Query Rewrite Considerations: Dimensions

You can express the hierarchical relationships and functional dependencies in normalized or denormalized dimension tables using the `HIERARCHY` and `DETERMINES` clauses of a dimension. Dimensions can express intra-table relationships which cannot be expressed by any constraints. Set the parameter `QUERY_REWRITE_INTEGRITY` to `trusted` or `stale_tolerated` for query rewrite to take advantage of the relationships declared in dimensions.

Query Rewrite Considerations: Outer Joins

Another way of avoiding constraints is to use outer joins in the materialized view. Query rewrite will be able to derive an inner join in the query, such as `(A.a=B.b)`, from an outer join in the materialized view `(A.a = B.b(+))`, as long as the rowid of `B` or column `B.b` is available in the materialized view. Most of the support for rewrites with outer joins is provided for materialized views with joins only. To exploit it, a materialized view with outer joins should store the rowid or primary key of the inner table of an outer join. For example, the materialized view `join_sales_time_product_mv_oj` stores the primary keys `prod_id` and `time_id` of the inner tables of outer joins.

Query Rewrite Considerations: Text Match

If you need to speed up an extremely complex, long-running query, you could create a materialized view with the exact text of the query. Then the materialized view would contain the query results, thus eliminating the time required to perform any complex joins and search through all the data for that which is required.

Query Rewrite Considerations: Aggregates

To get the maximum benefit from query rewrite, make sure that all aggregates which are needed to compute ones in the targeted set of queries are present in the materialized view. The conditions on aggregates are quite similar to those for incremental refresh. For instance, if `AVG(x)` is in the query, then you should store `COUNT(x)` and `AVG(x)` or store `SUM(x)` and `COUNT(x)` in the materialized view.

Query Rewrite Considerations: Grouping Conditions

Aggregating data at lower levels in the hierarchy is better than aggregating at higher levels because lower levels can be used to rewrite more queries. Note, however, that doing so will also take up more space. For example, instead of grouping on state, group on city (unless space constraints prohibit it).

Instead of creating multiple materialized views with overlapping or hierarchically related `GROUP BY` columns, create a single materialized view with all those `GROUP BY` columns. For example, instead of using a materialized view that groups by city and another materialized view that groups by month, use a materialized view that groups by city and month.

Use `GROUP BY` on columns which correspond to levels in a dimension but not on columns that are functionally dependent, because query rewrite will be able to use the functional dependencies automatically based on the `DETERMINES` clause in a dimension. For example, instead of grouping on `prod_name`, group on `prod_id` (as long as there is a dimension which indicates that the attribute `prod_id` determines `prod_name`, you will enable the rewrite of a query involving `prod_name`).

Query Rewrite Considerations: Expression Matching

If several queries share the same common subexpression, it is advantageous to create a materialized view with the common subexpression as one of its `SELECT` columns. This way, the performance benefit due to precomputation of the common subexpression can be obtained across several queries.

Query Rewrite Considerations: Date Folding

When creating a materialized view which aggregates data by folded date granules such as months or quarters or years, always use the year component as the prefix but not as the suffix. For example, `TO_CHAR(date_col, 'yyyy-q')` folds the date into quarters, which collate in year order, whereas `TO_CHAR(date_col, 'q-yyyy')` folds the date into quarters, which collate in quarter order. The former preserves the ordering while the latter does not. For this reason, any materialized view created without a year prefix will not be eligible for date folding rewrite.

Query Rewrite Considerations: Statistics

Optimization with materialized views is based on cost and the optimizer needs statistics of both the materialized view and the tables in the query to make a cost-based choice. Materialized views should thus have statistics collected using the `DBMS_STATS` package.

❑❑❑

16 ORACLE9I DATA MINING

DATA MINING

There is an explosion of data in modern society and most organizations have large database that contains wealth of potentially accessible information. However it is usually very difficult to access this information. The unbridled growth of data will inevitably lead to a situation in which it is increasingly difficult to access the desired information. It is similar to looking for a needle in a haystack, only the amount of hay will be growing all the time.

Data mining is defined as the automated extraction of hidden predictive information from large database.

Oracle enables data mining inside the database for performance and scalability. Some of the capabilities are:

- An API that provides programmatic control and application integration
- Analytical capabilities with OLAP and statistical functions in the database
- Multiple algorithms: Naïve Bayes, decision trees, clustering, and association rules
- Real-time and batch scoring modes
- Multiple prediction types
- Association insights.

Enabling Data Mining Applications

Oracle9*i* Data Mining provides a Java API to exploit the data mining functionality that is embedded within the Oracle9*i* database.

By delivering complete programmatic control of the database in data mining, Oracle Data Mining (ODM) delivers powerful, scalable modeling and real-time scoring. This enables e-businesses to incorporate predictions and classifications in all processes and decision points throughout the business cycle.

ODM is designed to meet the challenges of vast amounts of data, delivering accurate insights completely integrated into e-business applications. This integrated intelligence enables the automation and decision speed that e-businesses require in order to compete today.

Predictions and Insights

Oracle Data Mining uses data mining algorithms to sift through the large volumes of data generated by e-businesses to produce, evaluate, and deploy predictive models. It also enriches mission critical applications in CRM, manufacturing control, inventory management, customer service and support, Web portals, wireless devices and other fields with context-specific recommendations and predictive monitoring of critical processes. ODM delivers real-time answers to questions such as:

- Which N items is person A most likely to buy or like?
- What is the likelihood tnat this product will be returned for repair?

Mining Within the Database Architecture

Oracle Data Mining performs all the phases of data mining within the database. In each data mining phase, this architecture results in significant improvements including performance, automation, and integration.

Data Preparation

Data preparation can create new tables or views of existing data. Both options perform faster than moving data to an external data mining utility and offer the programmer the option of snapshots or real-time updates.

Oracle Data Mining provides utilities for complex, data mining-specific tasks. Binning improves model build time and model performance, so ODM provides a utility for user-defined binning. ODM accepts data in either single record format or in transactional format and performs mining on transactional formats. Single record format is most common in applications, so ODM provides a utility for transforming single record format.

Associated analysis for preparatory data exploration and model evaluation is extended by Oracle's statistical functions and OLAP capabilities. Because these also operate within the database, they can all be incorporated into a seamless application that shares database objects. This allows for more functional and faster applications.

Model Building

Oracle Data Mining provides four algorithms: Naïve Bayes, Decision Tree, Clustering, and Association Rules. These algorithms address a broad spectrum of business problems, ranging from predicting the future likelihood of a customer purchasing a given product, to understand which products are likely be purchased together in a single trip to the grocery store. All model building takes place inside the database. Once again, the data does not need to move outside the database in order to build the model, and therefore the entire data-mining process is accelerated.

Model Evaluation

Models are stored in the database and directly accessible for evaluation, reporting, and further analysis by a wide variety of tools and application functions. ODM provides APIs for calculating traditional confusion matrixes and lift charts. It stores the models, the underlying data, and these analysis results together in the database to allow further analysis, reporting and application specific model management.

Scoring

Oracle Data Mining provides both batch and real-time scoring. In batch mode, ODM takes a table as input. It scores every record, and returns a scored table as a result. In real-time mode, parameters for a single record are passed in and the scores are returned in a Java object.

In both modes, ODM can deliver a variety of scores. It can return a rating or probability of a specific outcome. Alternatively it can return a predicted outcome and the probability of that outcome occurring. Some examples follow.

- How likely is this event to end in outcome A?
- Which outcome is most likely to result from this event?
- What is the probability of each possible outcome for this event?

Java API

The Oracle Data Mining API lets you build analytical models and deliver real-time predictions in any application that supports Java. The API is based on the emerging JSR-073 standard.

Data Mining Components

Oracle9*i* Data Mining has two main components:

- Oracle9*i* Data Mining API
- Data Mining Server (DMS).

Oracle9*i* Data Mining API

The Oracle9*i* Data Mining API is the component of Oracle9*i* Data Mining that allows users to write Java programs that mine data.

The ODM API provides an early look at concepts and approaches being proposed for the emerging standard Java Data Mining (JDM). JDM follows Sun Microsystem's Java Community Process as a Java Specification Request (JSR-73). JDM used design elements from several evolving data mining standards, including the Object Management Group's Common Warehouse Metadata (CWM), the Data Mining Group's Predictive Model Markup Language (PMML), and the International Standards Organization's SQL/MM for Data Mining. JDM has also influenced these standards. Oracle9*i* Data Mining will comply with the JDM standard when that standard is published.

Data Mining Server

The Data Mining Server (DMS) is the server-side, in-database component that performs the data mining operations within the 9*i* database, and thus benefits from RDBMS availability and scalability.

The DMS also provides a metadata repository consisting of mining input objects and result objects, along with the namespaces within which these objects are stored and retrieved.

DATA MINING FUNCTIONS

Data mining models are based on one of two kinds of learning: *supervised* and *unsupervised* (sometimes referred to as directed and undirected learning). Supervised learning functions are typically used to predict a value.Unsupervised learning functions are typically used to find the intrinsic structure, relations, or affinities in a body of data but no classes or labels are assigned a priori. Examples of unsupervised learning algorithms include *k*-means clustering and Apriori association rules. An example of supervised learning algorithms includes Naive Bayes for classification.

ODM supports the following data mining functions:

- Classification (supervised)
- Clustering (unsupervised)
- Association rules (unsupervised)
- Attribute importance (supervised).

Classification

In a classification problem, you have a number of cases (examples) and wish to predict which of several classes each case belongs to. Each case consists of multiple attributes, each of which takes on one of several possible values. The attributes consist of multiple predictor attributes (independent variables) and one target attribute (dependent variable). Each of the target attribute's possible values is a class to be predicted on the basis of that case's predictor attribute values.

Costs

Classification is used in customer segmentation, business modeling, credit analysis, and many other applications. For example, a credit card company may wish to predict which customers will default on their payments. Each customer corresponds to a case; data for each case might consist of a number of attributes that describe the customer's spending habits, income, demographic attributes, etc. These are the predictor attributes. The target attribute indicates whether or not the customer has defaulted; that is, there are two possible classes, corresponding to having defaulted or not. The build data are used to build a model that you then use to predict, for new cases, whether those customers are likely to default.

A classification task begins with build data for which the target values (or class assignments) are known. Different classification algorithms use different techniques for finding relations between the predictor attribute's values and the target attribute's values in the build data. These relations are summarized in a model, which can then be applied to new cases with unknown target values to predict target values. A classification model can also be used on build data with known target values, to compare the predictions to the known answers. This technique is used when testing a model to measure the model's predictive accuracy. The application of a classification model to new data is often called *scoring the data.*

In a classification problem, it may be important to specify the costs involved in making an incorrect decision. Doing so can be useful when the costs of different misclassifications varies significantly.

For example, suppose the problem is to predict whether a user will respond to a promotional mailing. The target has two categories: YES (the customer responds) and NO (the customer does not respond). Suppose a positive response to the promotion generates $500 and that it costs $5 to do the mailing. If the model predicts YES and the actual value is YES, the cost of misclassification is $0. If the model predicts YES and the actual value is NO, the cost of misclassification is $5. If the model predicts NO and the actual value is YES, the cost of misclassification is $500. If the model predicts NO and the actual value is NO, the cost is $0.

The row indexes of a cost matrix correspond to *actual values*; the column indexes correspond to *predicted values*. For any pair of actual/predicted indexes, the value indicates the number of records classified in that pairing.

Some algorithms, like Adaptive Bayes Network, optimize for the cost matrix directly, modifying the model structure so as to produce minimal cost solutions. Other algorithms, like Naive Bayes, that predict probabilities, use the cost matrix during scoring to propose the least expensive solution.

Priors

In building a classification model, you may need to balance the number of positive and negative cases for the target of a supervised model. This can happen either because a given target value is rare in the population, for example, fraud cases, or because the data you have does not accurately reflect the real population, that is, the data sample is skewed.

A classification model works best when it has a reasonable number of examples of each target value in its build data table. When only a few possible values exist, it works best with more or less equal numbers of each value.

For example, a data table may accurately reflect reality, yet have 99% negatives in its target classification and only 1% positives. A model could be 99% accurate if it predicted on the negative case, yet the model would be useless.

To work around this problem, you can create a build data table in which positive and negative target values are more or less evenly balanced, and then supply priors information to tell the model what the true balance of target values is.

Clustering

Clustering is a technique useful for exploring data. It is particularly useful where there are many cases and no obvious natural groupings. Here, clustering data mining algorithms can be used to find whatever natural groupings may exist.

Clustering analysis identifies clusters embedded in the data. A cluster is a collection of data objects that are similar in some sense to one another. A good clustering method produces high-quality clusters to ensure that the inter-cluster similarity is low and the intra-cluster similarity is high; in other words, members of a cluster are more like each other than they are like members of a different cluster.

Clustering can also serve as a useful data-preprocessing step to identify homogeneous groups on which to build predictive models. Clustering models are different from predictive models in that the outcome of the process is not guided by a known result, that is, there is no target attribute. Predictive models predict values for a target attribute, and an error rate between the target and predicted values can be calculated to guide model building. Clustering models, on the other hand, uncover natural groupings (clusters) in the data. The model can then be used to assign groupings labels (cluster IDs) to data points.

In ODM a cluster is characterized by its *centroid*, attribute histograms, and place in the clustering model hierarchical tree. ODM performs hierarchical clustering using an enhanced version of the *k*-means algorithm and O-Cluster, an Oracle proprietary algorithm. The clusters discovered by these algorithms are then used to create rules that capture the main characteristics of the data assigned to each cluster. The rules represent the hyperboxes (bounding boxes) that envelop the clusters discovered by the clustering algorithm. The antecedent of each rule describes the clustering bounding box. The consequent encodes the cluster ID for the cluster described by the rule. For example, for a dataset with two attributes: AGE and HEIGHT, the following rule represents most of the data assigned to cluster 10:

If AGE >= 25 and AGE <= 40

and HEIGHT >= 5.0 ft

and HEIGHT <= 5.5 ft

then CLUSTER = 10

The clusters are also used to generate a Bayesian probability model which is used during scoring for assigning data points to clusters.

Association Rules

The Association Rules model is often associated with "market basket analysis", which is used to discover relationships or correlations among a set of items. It is widely used in data analysis for direct marketing, catalog design, and other business decision-making processes. A typical association rule of this kind asserts the likelihood that, for example, "70% of the people who buy spaghetti, wine, and sauce also buy garlic bread."

Association rules capture the co-occurrence of items or events in large volumes of customer transaction data. Because of progress in bar-code technology, it is now possible for retail organizations to collect and store massive amounts of sales data, referred to as "basket data." Association rules were initially defined on basket data, even though they are applicable in several other applications. Finding all such rules is valuable for cross-marketing and mail-order promotions, but there are other applications as well: catalog design, add-on sales, store layout, customer segmentation, web page personalization, and target marketing.

Traditionally, association rules are used to discover business trends by analyzing customer transactions. However, they can also be used effectively to predict Web page accesses for personalization. For example, assume that after mining the Web access log we discovered an association rule "A and B implies C," with 80% confidence, where A, B, and C are Web page accesses. If a user has visited pages A and B, there is an 80% chance that he/she will visit page C in the same session. Page C may or may not have a direct link from A or B. This information can be used to create a link dynamically to page C from pages A or B so that the user can "click-through" to page C directly. This kind of information is particularly valuable for a Web server supporting an e-commerce site to link the different product pages dynamically, based on the customer interaction.

Association rule mining can be formally defined as follows: Let I = $\{i_1, i_2, ..., i_n\}$ be a set of literals (constants: either a number or a character) called *items* and D be a set of *transactions* where each transaction T is a set of items such that T is a subset of I. Associated with each transaction is an identifier, called its TID. An association rule is an implication of the form X implies Y, where X and Y are both subsets of I, and X intersect Y is empty. The rule has support *s* in the database D if *s*% of the transactions in D contain both X and Y, and confidence *c* if *c*% of transactions that contain X also contain Y. The problem of mining association rules is to generate all rules that have support and confidence greater than the user-specified minimum support and minimum confidence, respectively.

Algorithms that calculate association rules work in two phases. In the first phase, all combinations of items that have the required minimum support (called the "frequent item sets") are discovered. In the second phase, rules of the form X implies Y with the specified minimum confidence are generated from the frequent item sets. Typically the first phase is computationally expensive and has in recent years attracted attention from researchers all over the world. This has resulted in several innovative techniques for discovering frequent item sets.

There are several properties of association rules that can be calculated. ODM supports two:

- **Support:** Support of a rule is a measure of how frequently the items involved in it occur together. Using probability notation, support (A implies B) = P(A, B).
- **Confidence:** Confidence of a rule is the conditional probability of B given A; confidence (A implies B) = P (B given A), which is equal to P(A, B) or P(A).

These statistical measures can be used to rank the rules and hence the predictions.

Attribute Importance

Attribute Importance, also known as *feature selection*, provides an automated solution for improving the speed and possibly the accuracy of classification models built on data tables with a large number of attributes.

Attribute Importance ranks the predictive attributes by eliminating redundant, irrelevant, or uninformative attributes and identifying those predictor attributes that may have the most influence in making predictions. ODM examines data and constructs classification models that can be used to make predictions about subsequent data. The time required to build these models increases with the number of predictors. Attribute Importance helps a user identify a proper subset of these attributes that are most relevant to predicting the target. Model building can proceed using the selected attributes (predictor attributes) only.

Using fewer attributes decreases model building time, although sometimes at a cost in predictive accuracy. Using too many attributes (especially those that are "noise") can affect the model and degrade its performance and accuracy. By extracting as much information as possible from a given data table using the smallest number of attributes, a user can save significant computing time and often build better models.

Attribute Importance permits the user to specify a number or percentage of attributes to use; alternatively the user can specify a cutoff point. After an Attribute Importance model is built, the user can select the subset of attributes based on the ranking or the predictive value.

Attribute Importance can be applied to data tables with a very large set of attributes. However, the DBA may have to tune the database in various ways to ensure that a large Attribute Importance build executes efficiently. For example, it is important to ensure that there is adequate swap space and table space.

ODM ALGORITHMS

Oracle9*i* Data Mining supports the following data mining algorithms:

- Adaptive bayes network (classification)
- Naive bayes (classification)
- Model seeker (classification)
- *k*-Means (clustering)
- O-cluster (clustering)
- Predictor variance (attribute importance)
- Apriori (association rules).

The choice of data mining algorithm depends on the data and the conclusions to be reached.

For classification:

- Choose ABN if you
  - o have a large number of attributes
  - o need model *transparency*, that is, rules that explain the model
  - o want more options to control the amount of time required to build the model
- Choose NB for the fastest build time
- Choose Model Seeker if you
  - o are unsure which settings should be provided
  - o wish to compare Naive Bayes to Adaptive Bayes Network automatically
  - o the *figure of merit* for computing the "best" model is appropriate for your situation

For clustering:

- Choose O-Cluster if you
  - o want the number of clusters to be automatically determined
  - o have both categorical and numerical attributes
  - o have a large number of attributes >20)
  - o have a large number of cases (>1000)
- Choose *k*-means if you
  - o want to specify the number of clusters
  - o need to mine only numerical attributes
  - o have small tables (<100 rows)
  - o a small number of attributes (<100)

Adaptive Bayes Network

Adaptive Bayes Network (ABN) is an Oracle proprietary algorithm supporting decision-tree-like features in that it produces "rules". ABN provides a fast, scalable, non-parametric means of extracting predictive information from data with respect to a target attribute. (Non-parametric statistical techniques avoid assuming that the population is characterized by a family of simple distributional models, such as standard linear regression, where different members of the family are differentiated by a small set of parameters.)

ABN can provide such information in the form of human-understandable rules. For example, a rule may be "If income is \$70K-\$80K and household size is 3–5, the likelihood of owning a late-model minivan is YES." The rules produced by ABN are one of its main advantages over Naive Bayes. The business user, marketing professional, or business analyst can understand the basis of the model's predictions and can therefore be comfortable acting on them and explaining them to others.

In addition to explanatory rules, ABN provides performance and scalability, which are derived via a collection of user parameters controlling the trade-off of accuracy and build time.

ABN predicts binary as well as multiclass targets. Binary targets are those that take on only two values, for example, *buy* and *not buy*. Multiclass targets have more than two values, for example, products purchased (product A or product B or product C). Multiclass target values are not assumed to exist in an ordered relation to each other, for example, hair brush is not assumed to be greater or less than comb.

ABN can use costs and priors for both building and scoring . A key concept for ABN is *network feature*. Network features are like individual decision trees. Features are tree-like multi-attribute structures. From the standpoint of the network, features are conditionally independent components. Features contain at least one attribute (the root attribute). Conditional probabilities are computed for each value of the root predictor. A two-attribute feature will have, in addition to the root predictor conditional probabilities, computed conditional probabilities for each combination of values of the root and the depth 2 predictor. That is, if a root predictor, x, has i values and the depth 2 predictor, y, has j values, a conditional probability is computed for each combination of values {$x=a$, $y=b$ such that a is in the set [1,..,i] and b is in the set [1,..,j]}. Similarly, a depth 3 predictor, z, would have an additional associated conditional probability computed for each combination of values {$x=a$, $y=b$, $z=c$ such that a is in the set [1,..,i] and b is in the set [1,..,j] and c is in the set [1,..,k]}.

Build Parameters

To control the execution time of a build, ABN provides four user-settable parameters:

- **Maximum Network Feature Depth:** This parameter restricts the depth of any individual network feature in the model. At each depth for an individual network feature, there is only one predictor. Each depth level requires a scan of the data to accumulate the counts required for predictor selection and probability estimates and an apply operation on a sample to test for significance. Thus, the computational cost of deep feature builds may be high. The range for this parameter consists of the positive integers. The NULL or 0 value setting has special meaning: unrestricted depth. Builds beyond depth 7 are rare. Setting this parameter to 1 makes the algorithm act like a Naive Bayes model with stepwise attribute selection. ABN may stop model building well before reaching the maximum. The default is 10.
- **Maximum Number Of Network Features:** This controls the maximum number of features included in the model. It also controls the number of predictors in the Naive Bayes model it tests as a first step in its model selection procedure. Subsequent steps in the model build procedure construct multidimensional features by extending single-predictor "seed" features. Note that the seed features are extended in rank order. During stepwise selection, subsequent features must improve the model as measured by MDL (Minimum Description Length) relative to the current state of the model. Thus the likelihood of substantial benefit from extending later features declines rapidly. The default is 10.
- **Maximum Consecutive Pruned Network Features:** This is the maximum number of consecutive pruned features before halting the stepwise selection process. A negative value of -1 is used to indicate that only the Naive Bayes model and a single-feature model are constructed. If the Naive Bayes model is best, then it is selected. Otherwise, all as-yet untested features are pruned from the final feature tree array. The default is -1.
- **Maximum Build Time:** The maximum build time (in minutes) allows the user to build quick, possibly less accurate models for immediate use or simply to get a sense of how long it will take to build a model with a given set of data. To accomplish this, the algorithm divides the build into milestones (model states) representing complete functional models. The algorithm completes at least a single milestone and then projects whether it can reach the next one within the user-specified maximum build time. This decision is revisited at

each milestone achieved until either the model build is complete or the algorithm determines it cannot reach the next milestone within the user-specified time limit. The user has access to the statistics produced by the time estimation procedure. The default is NULL (no time limit):

Model States:

- **Complete Multi Feature:** Multiple features have been tested for inclusion in the model. MDL pruning has determined whether the model actually has one or more features. The model may have completed either because there is insufficient time to test an additional feature or because the number of consecutive features failing the stepwise selection criteria exceeded the maximum allowed or seed features have been extended and tested.
- **Complete Single Feature:** A single feature has been built to completion.
- **Incomplete Single Feature:** The model consists of a single feature of at least depth two (two predictors) but the attempts to extend this feature have not completed.
- **Naive Bayes:** The model consists of a subset of (single-predictor) features that individually pass MDL correlation criteria. No MDL pruning has occurred with respect to the joint model.

The algorithm outputs its current model state and statistics that provide an estimate of how long it would take for the model to build (and prune) a feature.

See table 16.1, below, for a comparison of the main characteristics of the two classification algorithms, Adaptive Bayes Network and Naive Bayes.

Naive Bayes Algorithm

The Naive Bayes algorithm (NB) makes predictions using Bayes' Theorem, which derives the probability of a prediction from the underlying evidence, as described below. NB affords fast model building and scoring.

NB can be used for both binary and multiclass classification problems to answer questions such as "Which customers will switch to a competitor? Which transaction patterns suggest fraud? Which prospects will respond to an advertising campaign?" For example, suppose a bank wants to promote its mortgage offering to its current customers and that, to reduce promotion costs, it wants to target the most likely prospects. The bank has historical data for its customers, including income, number of household members, money-market holdings, and information on whether a customer has recently obtained a mortgage through the bank. Using NB, the bank can predict how likely a customer is to respond positively to a mortgage offering. With this information, the bank can reduce its promotion costs by restricting the promotion to the most likely candidates.

Bayes' Theorem proves the following equation:

$$P(\textit{this-prediction} \mid \textit{this-evidence}) = \frac{\text{P(this-prediction) P(this-evidence} \mid \text{this-prediction)}}{\text{sumP(some-prediction) P(this-evidence} \mid \text{some-prediction)}}$$

where P means "probability of", " | " means "given", and "sum" means "sum of all these terms". Translated into English, the equation says that the probability of a particular predicted event, given the evidence in this instance, is computed from three other numbers: the probability of that prediction in similar situations in general, ignoring the specific evidence (this is called the prior probability); times the probability of seeing the evidence we have here, given that the particular prediction is correct; divided by the sum, for each possible prediction (including the present one), of a similar product for that prediction (i.e., the probability of that prediction in general, times the probability of seeing the current evidence given that possible prediction).

NB assumes that each attribute, or piece of evidence, is independent from the others. In practice, this assumption usually does not degrade the model's predictive accuracy significantly, and makes the difference between a computationally feasible algorithm and an intractable one.

It is useful to have a good estimate of the accuracy of any predictive model. An especially accurate estimate of accuracy is a type of cross-validation called "leave-one-out cross-validation", discussed below.

Naive Bayes cross-validation permits the user to test model accuracy on the same data that was used to build the model, rather than building the model on one portion of the data and testing it on a different portion. Not having to hold aside a portion of the data for testing is especially useful if the amount of build data is relatively small.

"Leave-one-out cross-validation" is a special case of cross-validation in which one record is left out of the build data when building each of several models. The number of models built equals the number of records (omitting a different build record for each model), which makes this procedure computationally expensive. With Naive Bayes models, however, the approach can be modified such that all build records are used for building a single model. Then, the model is repeatedly modified to quickly remove the effects of one build record, incrementally "unbuilding" the model for that record, as though that record had been omitted when building the model in the first place. The accuracy of the prediction for each build record can then be assessed against the model that would have been built from all the build records except that one, without having had to actually build a separate model for each build record.

To use Naive Bayes cross-validation, the user executes a MiningTaskCrossValidate task, specifying that a Naive Bayes model is to be built and tested. The execution of the cross-validate task creates a MiningTestResult object populated with the test results.

See table 16.1, below, for a comparison of the main characteristics of ABN and NB.

Table 16.1 Comparison of Adaptive Bayes Network and Naive Bayes

Feature	Adaptive Bayes Network	Naive Bayes
Number of cases	Any size	Any size
Number of attributes	Any number (built-in feature selection)	Best if less than 200
Speed	Not as fast	Faster
Accuracy	As accurate or more accurate than Naive Bayes	As accurate or less accurate than Adaptive Bayes Network
Attribute types	Numerical (binned) and categorical	Numerical (binned) and categorical
Automatic binning	Yes	Yes
Target attribute	Binary and multiclass	Binary and multiclass

Model Seeker

Model Seeker is a new feature of the ODM API that allows a user to build multiple classifications, evaluate the models, and select a "best" model, asynchronously.

The models to be built and evaluated can be a combination of Naive Bayes (NB) and Adaptive Bayes Network (ABN) models. Model Seeker does not build unsupervised models.

After building the specified models, Model Seeker evaluates each model by testing and calculating lift. Model Seeker generates a summary of information about each model built so that a user can manually select the "best" model using different criteria, if desired.

Model Seeker's criterion for the "best" model is the one with the largest value for the weighted target positive and total negative relative error rate. The weight is set as the relative importance of the positive category to the other categories treated as a single negative category. If the weight is set to 1.0, the positive category error rate has the same weight as all the other categories combined.

The following formula is used to calculate the figure of merit (FOM) for the "best" model, where FOM is the weighted sum of target positive relative accuracy and total negative relative accuracy:

$$FOM = \frac{W * (\text{number of correct positives})}{(W + 1) * (\text{number of actual positives})} + \frac{(\text{number of correct negatives})}{(W + 1) * (\text{number of actual negatives})}$$

where W is the user-specified *weight*, a value that must be > 0. The weight is the ratio of the false negative cost to the false positive cost. A weight of 1 means that the false positives and false negatives have equal weight.

Enhanced *k*-Means Algorithm

The *k*-means algorithm is a distance-based clustering algorithm that partitions the data into a predetermined number of clusters (provided there are enough distinct cases). The *k*-means algorithm works only with numerical attributes. Distance-based algorithms rely on a distance metric (function) to measure the similarity between data points. Data points are assigned to the nearest cluster according to the distance metric used.

ODM implements a hierarchical version of the *k*-means algorithm. The tree can either be grown one level at a time (balanced approach) or one node at the time (unbalanced approach). The node with the largest distortion (sum of distance to the node's centroid) is split to increase the size of the tree until the desired number of clusters is reached.

This incremental approach to *k*-means avoids the need for building multiple *k*-means models and provides clustering results that are consistently superior to the traditional *k*-means.

The choice between balanced and unbalanced approaches is controlled by the system parameter CL_ALG_SETTING_TREE_GROWTH in the ODM_CONFIGURATION table. The balanced approach is faster than the unbalanced approach, while the unbalanced approach generates models with smaller overall distortion.

Binning for *k*-Means

ODM-enhanced *k*-means bins the data internally, thus providing automatic data discretization. However, if manual binning is used, the bin values should be represented by contiguous integer numbers starting at 1. In addition, the same number of bins should be used for all attributes.

k-means works with numerical data only. As a result, if a user would like to cluster data with categorical attributes, he/she should "explode" the categorical attribute into multiple binary columns (one per unique value of the categorical attribute) before using ODM clustering *k*-means.

Scalability through Summarization

Because traditional *k*-means requires multiple passes through the data, it can be impractical for large data tables that don't fit in memory. In this case multiple expensive database scans would be required. ODM's enhanced *k*-means requires at most one database scan. For data tables that don't fit in memory, the enhanced *k*-means algorithm employs a smart summarization approach that creates a summary of the data table that can be stored in memory. This approach allows the enhanced *k*-means algorithm to handle data tables of any size. The summarization scheme can be seen as a smart sampling approach that first identifies the main partitions in the data and then generates summary points for each partition in proportion to their share of the total data. Each summary point has a weight that accounts for the proportion of the data it represents.

Scoring

The clusters discovered by enhanced *k*-means are used to generate a Bayesian probability model that is then used during scoring (model apply) for assigning data points to clusters. The traditional *k*-means algorithm can be interpreted as a mixture model where the mixture components are spherical multivariate normal distributions with the same variance for all components. (A mixture model is a type of density model that includes several component functions (usually Gaussian) that are combined to provide a multimodel density.)

In the mixture model created from the clusters discovered by enhanced *k*-means, on the other hand, the mixture components are a product of independent normal distribution with potentially different variances. Because of this greater flexibility, the probability model created by enhanced *k*-means provides a better description of the underlying data than the underlying model of traditional *k*-means.

See table 16.2, below, for a comparison of the main characteristics of the two clustering algorithms.

O-Cluster Algorithm

The O-Cluster algorithm creates a hierarchical grid-based clustering model, that is, it creates axis-parallel partitions in the input attribute space. The algorithm operates recursively. The resulting hierarchical structure represents an irregular grid that tessellates the attribute space into clusters. The resulting clusters define dense areas in the attribute space. The clusters are described by intervals along the attribute axes and the corresponding centroids and histograms. A parameter called *sensitivity* defines a baseline density level. Only areas with peak density above this baseline level can be identified as clusters.

Binning for O-Cluster

O-Cluster bins the data internally, thus providing automatic data discretization. However, if manual binning is used, the bin values should be represented by contiguous integer numbers starting at 1.

Attribute Type

Binary attributes should be declared as categorical. O-Cluster distinguishes between continuous and discrete numerical attributes. The two types of attributes undergo different binning procedures in order to capture the characteristics of the underlying distributions. For example, a discrete numerical attribute such as *age* should be declared of data type INTEGER. On the other hand, continuous numerical attributes such as height measured in feet should be declared of data type NUMBER.

Scoring

The clusters discovered by O-Cluster are used to generate a Bayesian probability model that is then used during scoring (model apply) for assigning data points to clusters. The generated probability model is a mixture model where the mixture components are represented by a product of independent normal distributions for numerical attributes and multinomial distributions for categorical attributes.

The main characteristics of the enhanced *k*-means and O-Cluster algorithms are summarized in table 16.2, below.

Table 16.2 Comparison of Enhanced k-Means and O-Cluster

Feature	Enhanced *k*-means	O-Cluster
Clustering methodology	Distance-based	Grid-based
Number of cases	Handles tables of any size. Uses summarization for tables that don't fit in the memory buffer.	Good for data tables that have more than 1,000 cases
Number of attributes	Good for datasets that have 10 or fewer attributes	Good for data tables that have more than 10 attributes
Number of clusters	User-specified	Automatically determined
Attribute type	Numerical attributes only	Numerical and categorical attributes
Hierarchical clustering	Yes	Yes
Probabilistic cluster assignment	Yes	Yes
Automatic data normalization	Yes	Yes

Predictor Variance Algorithm

ODM Attribute Importance is implemented by using the Predictor Variance algorithm. Predictor Variance estimates the variances of the predictor target combinations and the variance with respect to the other predictors.

The basic concept is that the higher the sum of the variances, the more informative the predictor attribute is in the build data table. These statistics give an idea of how correlated each predictor is with the target attribute. Predictor variance assesses the relative usefulness of each attribute for making predictions for rows in general, instead of making a prediction for any particular case.

For algorithms like ABN that perform automatic attribute selection, the attributes selected may differ significantly from Predictor Variance. This is because of the different techniques used to derive the important attributes.

Apriori Algorithm

The association rule mining problem can be decomposed into two subproblems:

- Find all combinations of items, called frequent itemsets, whose support is greater than minimum support.
- Use the frequent itemsets to generate the desired rules. The idea is that if, for example, ABCD and AB are frequent, then the rule AB implies CD holds if the ratio of support(ABCD)

to support(AB) is at least as large as the minimum confidence. Note that the rule will have minimum support because ABCD is frequent.

The Apriori algorithm for finding frequent itemsets makes multiple passes over the data. In the *k*th pass, it finds all itemsets having *k* items, called the *k*-itemsets. Each pass consists of two phases. Let F_k represent the set of frequent *k*-itemsets, and C_k the set of candidate *k*-itemsets (potentially frequent itemsets). First, is the candidate generation phase where the set of all frequent (*k*-1) itemsets, F_{k-1}, found in the (*k*-1)th pass, is used to generate the candidate itemsets C_k. The candidate generation procedure ensures that C_k is a superset of the set of all frequent *k*-itemsets. A specialized in-memory hash-tree data structure is used to store C_k. Then, data is scanned in the support counting phase. For each transaction, the candidates in C_k contained in the transaction are determined by using the hash-tree data structure and their support count is incremented. At the end of the pass, C_k is examined to determine which of the candidates are frequent, yielding F_k. The algorithm terminates when F_k or C_{k+1} becomes empty.

In ODM, we use an SQL-based implementation of the Apriori algorithm. The candidate generation and support counting steps are implemented using SQL queries. We do not use any specialized in-memory data structures. The SQL queries are fine-tuned to run efficiently in the database server by using various hints.

DATA MINING TASKS

Data mining tasks in ODM include model building, testing, computing lift, and applying (scoring), as well as importing and exporting a PMML representation of certain models.

All models go through a build process. Classification models also have a testing phase in which a different data table also containing known target values is presented to the model and the predicted value is compared with the known (or actual) target values. Association Rules, Attribute Importance, and clustering models do not have a testing phase, nor do they compute lift. Classification models and clustering models can both be used to score a data table, whereas an association rules model does not support scoring. ODM imports and exports PMML models for Naive Bayes classification and Association Rules. Attribute Importance supports only build since it produces an importance ordering of the attributes.

Table 16.3 compares data mining tasks performed for the different ODM functions.

Table 16.3 Data Mining Tasks per Function

Function	Build	Test	Compute Lift	Apply (Score)	Import PMML	Export PMML
Classification	X	X	X	X	Naive Bayes	Naive Bayes
Clustering	X			X		
Association rules	X				X	X
Attribute importance	X					

Model Build

ODM supports two levels of settings: *function* and *algorithm*. When the function level settings do not specify particular algorithm settings, ODM chooses an appropriate algorithm and provides defaults for the relevant parameters. In general, model building at the function level eliminates many of the technical details of data mining.

Models are built in the data mining server (DMS). After a model is built, it is persisted in the DMS and can be accessed by its user-specified unique name.

The typical steps for model building are as follows:

1. Specify input data by creating a physical data specification that references an existing data table or view. This data may or may not have been prepared (for example, binned) manually.
2. Create a mining function settings object, which specifies function-level parameters to the algorithm.
3. Create a logical data specification and associate it with the mining function settings.
4. Create mining algorithm settings (optional), which specifies algorithm-specific parameters to the algorithm.
5. Create a build task and invoke the execute method.

Figure 16.1 illustrates the build process. Raw data undergoes the transformations specified by the user and may also be manually binned (i.e., sorted into bins) according to user-specified bin boundaries. The resulting data table, that is, the *build data table*, is fed to the appropriate ODM algorithm, along with mining function settings. The algorithm performs further data preprocessing that may include automatic internal binning, and then performs the build. The resulting model includes bin boundary tables internal to the algorithm, i.e., the ones that resulted from automatic binning. They are not part of the model if you did not choose automatic binning.

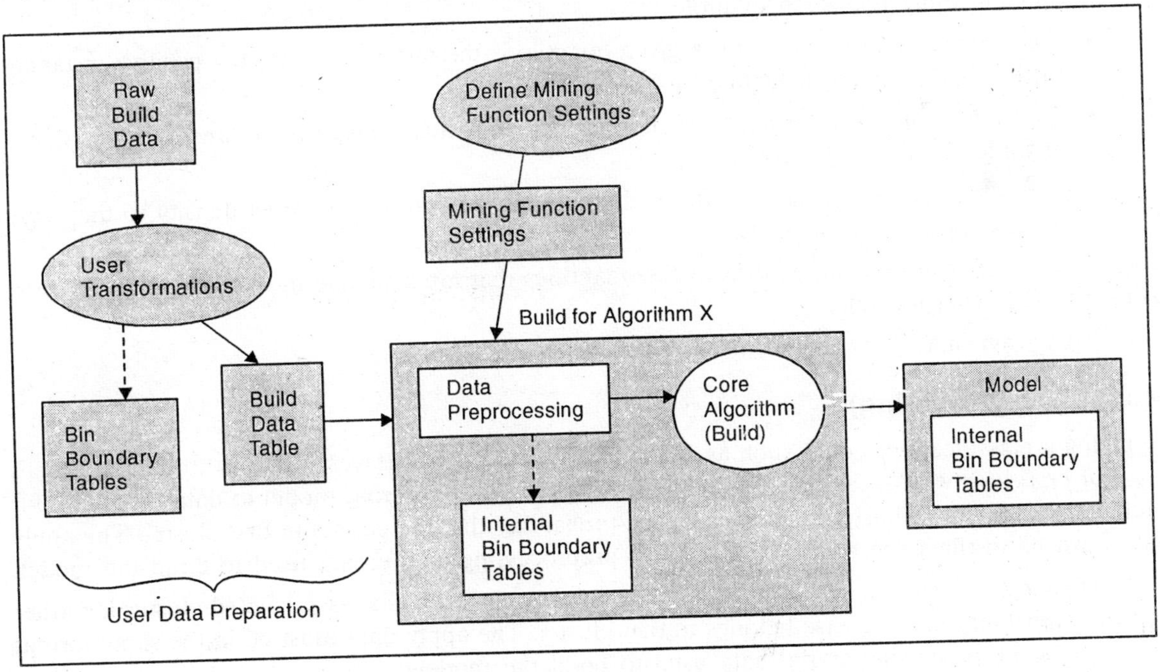

Figure 16.1 The Build Process.

Model Test

Classification models can be tested to get an estimate of their accuracy.

After a model is built, model testing estimates the accuracy of a model's predictions by applying it to a new data table that has the same format as the build data table . The test results are stored in a mining test result object. A classification test result includes a *confusion matrix* that allows a user to understand the type and number of classification errors made by the model.

Computing Lift

ODM supports computing lift for a classification model. Lift can be computed for binary (2 values) target fields and multiclass (more than 2 values) target fields. Given a designated positive target value, that is, the value of most interest for prediction, such as "buyer," or "has disease," test cases are sorted according to how confidently they are predicted to be pcsitive cases. Positive cases with highest confidence come first, followed by positive cases with lowest confidence. Negative cases with lowest confidence come next, followed by negative cases with highest confidence. Based on that ordering, they are partitioned into quantiles, and the following statistics are calculated:

- *Target density* of a quantile is the number of actually positive instances in that quantile divided by the total number of instances in the quantile.
- *Cumulative target density* is the target density computed over the first *n* quantiles.
- *Quantile lift* is the ratio of target density for the quantile to the target density over all the test data.
- *Cumulative percentage of records* for a given quantile is the percentage of all test cases represented by the first *n* quantiles, starting at the end that is most confidently positive, up to and including the given quantile.
- *Cumulative number of targets* for a given quantile is the number of actually positive instances in the first *n* quantiles (defined as above).
- *Cumulative number of nontargets* is the number of actually negative instances in the first *n* quantiles (defined as above).
- *Cumulative lift* for a given quantile is the ratio of the cumulative target density to the target density over all the test data.

Targets_cumulative can be computed from the quantities that are available in the *odm_lift_result_entry* using the following formula:

targets_cumulative = *lift_cumulative* * *percentage_records_cumulative*

Model Apply (Scoring)

Applying a classification model such as Naive Bayes or Adaptive Bayes Network to data produces *scores* or *predictions* with an associated probability. Applying a clustering model to data produces, for each case, a predicted cluster identifier and the probability that the case is in that cluster. The apply data must be in the same format and state of preprocessing as the data used to build the model.

Applying a clustering model to new data produces, for each case, a predicted cluster identifier and the probability that the case belongs to that cluster. The apply data must be in the same format and state of preprocessing as the data used to build the model.

Figure 16.2 shows the apply process. Note that the input data for the apply process must undergo the same preprocessing undergone by the build data table. The data to be scored must have attributes compatible with those of the build data, that is, it must have the same attributes with the same names and respective data types or there must be a suitable mapping of one to the other. The apply data table can have attributes not found in the build data table. The result of the apply operation is placed in the schema specified by the user.

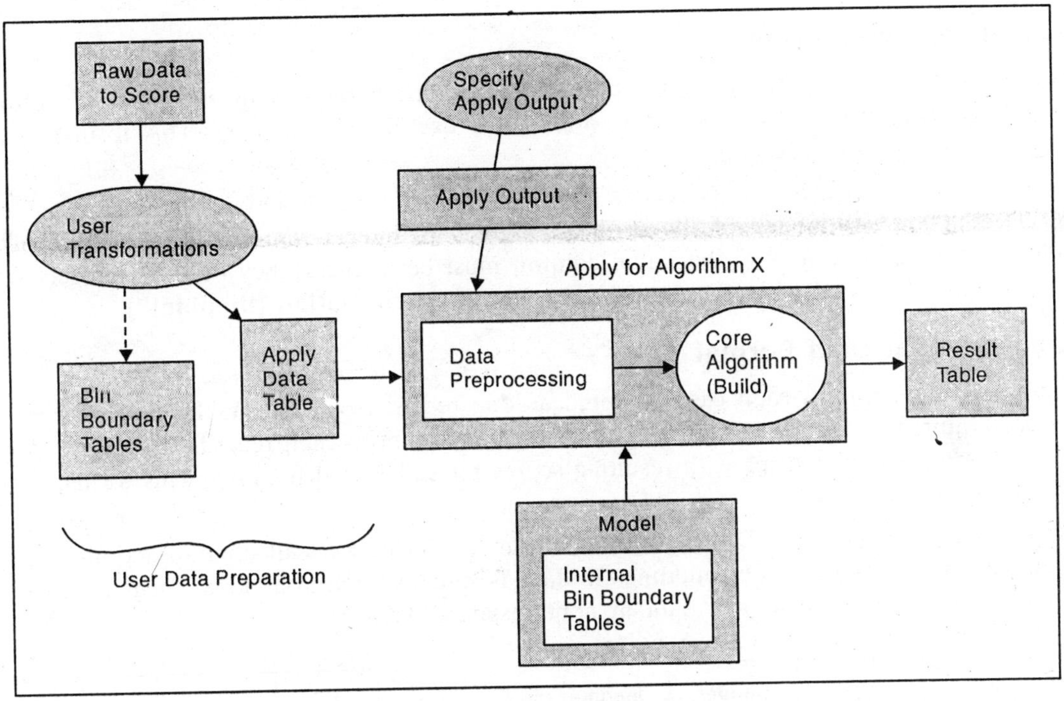

Figure 16.2 The Apply Process.

The ODM user specifies the result content. For example, a user may want the *customer identifier* attribute, along with the *score* and *probability*, to be output into a table for each record in the provided mining data. This is specified using the **MiningApplyOutput** class.

ODM supports the apply operation for a table (a set of cases) or a single case (represented by a Java object). ODM supports multicategory apply, obtaining multiple class values with their associated probabilities for each case.

ODM OBJECTS AND FUNCTIONALITY

The principal objects that constitute Oracle9*i* Data Mining are described below.

Physical Data Specification

A *physical data specification* object specifies the characteristics of the physical data to be used for mining, for example, whether the data is in *transactional* or *nontransactional* format and the roles the various data columns play. The data referenced by a physical data specification object can be used in several ways: model building, testing, computing lift, scoring, transformations, etc.

ODM physical data must be in one of two formats:

- Transactional
- Nontransactional

These formats describe how to interpret each case as stored in a given database table. See figure 16.3.

Transactional Data Format

In transactional data format, each case is stored as multiple records in a table with columns *sequenceID*, *attribute_name*, and *value* (these are names user-defined names). This format is also referred to as *multi-record case.*

sequenceID is an integer that associates multiple records in a transactional table. *attribute_name* is a string containing the name of the attribute. *value* is an integer representing the value of the attribute. Note that the values in the Value column must be integers; they become integers when they are binned, that is, the bin ID is an integer (see **"Discretization (Binning)"**).

Nontransactional Data Format

In nontransactional format, each case is stored as one record (row) in a table. Nontransactional data is not required to provide a key column to uniquely identify each record. However, a key is recommended to associate cases with resulting scores for supervised learning. This format is also referred to as *single-record case.*

Note that in Oracle 9*i*, ODM algorithms automatically convert all nontransactional data to transactional data prior to model building. If data is already in transactional format, algorithm performance can be enhanced over data in nontransactional format.

ID	Age	Gender	Income
1	25	M	30K
2	50	F	75K
3	40	M	50K
4	32	F	100K
5	75	M	25K

Nontransactional Data Format

→

ID	Attribute	Value
1	Age	25
1	Gender	M
1	Income	30K
2	Age	50
2	Gender	F

Transactional Data Format

Figure 16.3 Nontransactional and Transactional Data Format.

Mining Function Settings

A *mining function settings* (MFS) object contains the high-level parameters for building a mining model. Oracle9*i* Data Mining supports several mining algorithms for building a model.

The mining function settings allow a user to specify the type of problem to solve (for example, classification) without having to specify a particular algorithm. The ODM API allows a user to specify an algorithm; however, if none is specified, the data mining system selects an algorithm based on the function settings the user has specified. For example, if the user specifies clustering, the DMS may select *k*-means as the algorithm to build the model.

Each MFS object consists of the following:

- parameters specific to the mining function
- a logical data specification
- a data usage specification

ODM supports the persistence of mining function settings as independent, named entities in the Data Mining Server (DMS).

Table 16.4 displays function-level parameter settings and their default values.

Table 16.4 Parameter Settings by Function

Function	Parameter	Default
Classification	CostMatrix	NULL
	Priors	NULL
Clustering	MaxNumberOfClusters	20
Association rules	MinimumSupport	0.1
	MinimumConfidence	0.1
	MaximumRuleLength	2
Attribute importance	*None*	

Mining Algorithm Settings

A *mining algorithm settings* object contains the parameters associated with a particular algorithm for building a model. It allows expert data miners to fine-tune the behavior of the algorithm. Generally, not all parameters must be specified. Missing parameters are replaced with system default values. Algorithm parameters are algorithm-specific, along with their corresponding default values.

ODM's design, which separates mining algorithm settings from mining function settings, enables non-expert data miners to use ODM effectively, while expert data miners can have the control they need.

Table 16.5 displays the algorithm-level parameters and their default values. The default algorithm for a function appears in boldface type.

Table 16.5 Parameter Settings by Algorithm

Function	Algorithm	Parameter	Default
Classification	ABN	MaximumNetworkFeatureDepth	10
		MaximumNumberOfNetwork-Features	10
		MaximumConsecutivePruned-NetworkFeatures	–1
		MaximumBuildTime	NULL
	NB	SingletonThreshold	0.1

		PairwiseThreshold	0.1
Clustering	*k*-means	DistanceFunction	Euclidean
		Iterations	7
		Error	0.05
		StoppingCriterion	ErrorAnd-
			Iterations
	O-Cluster	Sensitivity	0.5
Association Rules	*N/A*		
Attribute	Predictor	*None*	
Importance	Variance		

Logical Data Specification

A *logical data specification* (LDS) object is a set of mining attribute instances that describes the logical nature of the data used as input for model building. This set of mining attributes is the basis for producing the *signature* of the model. Each mining attribute specified in a logical data specification must have a unique name.

As stored in the DMS, each MFS has its own copy of the LDS, even if references are shared in the API client process.

Mining Attributes

A *mining attribute* is a logical concept that describes a domain of data used as input to an ODM data mining operation. Mining attributes are either categorical or numerical. For example, domains of data include "age" ranging from 0 to 100, "buyer" with values true and false. A mining attribute specifies the name, data type, and attribute type (categorical or numeric).

Data Usage Specification

A *data usage specification* (DUS) object specifies how the attributes in a logical data specification (LDS) instance are used for building a model. A specification contains at most one data usage entry instance for each mining attribute in the LDS. If no data use is specified for an attribute, the default usage is active, implying that the attribute is used in building a model.

Usage includes specifying:

- whether an attribute is *active* (to be used in the model build process), *inactive* (ignored), or *supplementary* (an attribute for use with results output during scoring but not during model build)
- whether an attribute is a *target* for a supervised learning model.

ODM Attribute Names and Case

ODM's treatment of attribute names differs from that of Oracle SQL. Oracle SQL can treat attribute names in a case-insensitive manner; ODM attribute names, however, are *case-sensitive*. The implications of this for ODM users are:

- The specification of attribute names must be consistent across build, test, compute lift, and apply tasks. For example, if a given target attribute name is specified for build in mixed-case format, then the same format must be maintained while specifying the attribute for test, apply, and lift.
- For a MiningApply output specification, the API allows the specification of aliases for active and supplementary attributes; the results are based on these aliases. These aliases must be unique and case-insensitive.

Mining Model

A *mining model* object is the result of building a model based on a mining function settings object. The representation of the model depends on the algorithm specified by the user or selected by the DMS. Some models can be used for direct inspection, for example, to examine the rules produced from association rules or clusters, others to generate predictions, for example, using a classification model.

ODM supports the persistence of mining models as independent, named entities in the DMS. A mining model contains a copy of the mining function settings (MFS) used to build it. Models cannot be stored by the user.

Mining Results

A *mining result* object contains the end products of one of the following mining tasks: build, test, compute lift, or apply. ODM supports the persistence of mining results as independent, named entities in the DMS.

A mining result object contains the operation start time and end time, the name of the model used, input data location, and output data location (if any) for the data mining operation.

A *build result* contains the model details. It provides the function and algorithm name of the model.

An *apply result* names the destination table (schema and table name) for the result.

A*test result,* for classification models, contains the model accuracy and references the confusion matrix.

A lift result of the lift elements is calculated on a per-quantile basis.

Confusion Matrix

The row indexes of a confusion matrix correspond to *actual values* observed and used for model testing; the column indexes correspond to *predicted values* produced by applying the model to the test data. For any pair of actual/predicted indexes, the value indicates the number of records classified in that pairing. For example, a value of 25 for an actual value index of "buyer" and a predicted value index of "nonbuyer" indicates that the model incorrectly classified a "buyer" as a "nonbuyer" 25 times. A value of 516 for an actual/predicted value index of "buyer" indicates that the model correctly classified a "buyer" 516 times.

The predictions were correct 516 + 725 = 1241 times, and incorrect 25 + 10 = 35 times. The sum of the values in the matrix is equal to the number of scored records in the input data table. The number of scored records is the sum of correct and incorrect predictions, which is 1241 + 35 = 1276. The error rate is 35/1276 = 0.0274; the accuracy rate is 1241/1276 = 0.9725.

A *confusion matrix* provides a quick understanding of model accuracy and the types of errors the model makes when scoring records. It is the result of a test task for classification models.

		Predicted	
		Buyer	Non-Buyer
Actual	Buyer	516	25
	Non-Buyer	19	725

Figure 16.4 Confusion Matrix.

Mining Apply Output

A *mining apply output* instance contains several *items* that allow users to tailor the results of a model apply operation. Output can be in one or more of the following forms:

- scalar data to be passed through to the output from the input data table, for example, key attributes
- computed values from the apply itself such as score and probability
- for transactional input data, the sequence ID associated with a given case

The resulting data representation is in nontransactional form (one record per result).

Through the mining apply object, ODM supports specifying names for the resulting data columns.

There are two types of input to the apply mining operation: a *database table* for batch scoring and an *individual record* for record scoring. Apply input data must contain the same attributes that were used to build the model. However, the input data may contain additional attributes, which may appear in the output to describe the output (see source attribute, below).

Batch scoring using an input database table results in a table called the *apply output* table. An input record is represented as an instance of *RecordInstance* that contains a set of *AttributeInstance* objects, each of which describes the name of the attribute, the data type, and the value. The result of record scoring is also an instance of *RecordInstance.* The output of the apply mining operation is specified by *MiningApplyOutput.*

An instance of *MiningApplyOutput* is a specification of the data to be included in the apply output (either a table or a record) created as the result of the *apply* mining operation. The columns (or attributes) in the apply output are described by a combination of multiple *ApplyContentItem* objects. Each item can be one of the following:

- **Source attribute:** The apply output table (or record) may contain columns copied directly from the input table (or record). These are called *source attributes*, and each is represented by an instance of *ApplySourceAttributeItem.* Source attributes can be used to identify the individual source cases in the apply output, i.e., associate a key with each output record. There can be no more than 997 source attributes the output table.
- **Multiple predictions based on probability:** An instance of *ApplyMultipleScoringItem* results in top or bottom *n* predictions ordered by probability of the predictions, where *n* can range

from 1 to the total number of target values. One such item produces two columns in the output: prediction and probability, each of which is named by the user. There can be at most one instance of *ApplyMultipleScoringItem* in a *MiningApplyOutput* object.

Typically, users select "top" with $n = 1$ for obtaining the top likely prediction for each case from, for example, a classification model. However, other users may require seeing the top three predictions, for example, for recommending products to a customer.

- **Multiple predictions based on target values:** An instance of *ApplyTargetProbabilityItem* results in predictions for target values. Each such target value must be one of the original target values used to build the model. A given target value can be specified at most once. One such item produces up to three columns in the output: prediction, (optional) probability, and (optional) rank, each of which is named by the user. Probability and rank are optional. There can be at most one instance of *ApplyTargetProbabilityItem* or *ApplyMultipleScoringItem* in a *MiningApplyOutput* object. This option is useful when interested in the probability of a particular prediction, for example, if a retailer has many red sweaters, what is the probability the customer would buy something red?

The number of columns in the apply output table varies depending on the combination of items. When multiple target values are specified by *MiningApplyOutput* (if $n > 1$), n rows of output table correspond to the prediction for an input row.

Consider an input table of 15 rows. If the top 2 predictions ($n = 2$) with probabilities are specified in *MiningApplyOutput* with one source attribute from the input table, there will be 3 columns in the output table: the source attribute, the prediction, and its probability.The number of rows in the output table is 30 because the result of apply for each input row will be 2 rows (top 2) in the output table.

If the input data is transactional, the sequence ID is automatically included in the output table. However, explicit inclusion of source attributes is required for nontransactional data.

MISSING VALUES

In this section, we discuss ODM's handing of missing values.

Missing Values Handling

Data tables often contain missing values, that is, one or more of the attributes in a case have a null value. ODM handles missing values as follows, depending on the data format:

- For nontransactional data, an attribute name and value pair is used only if the value is not null; otherwise, it is ignored.
- For transactional data, the row is ignored if either the sequence ID, attribute name, or value is null.

Note that this means it is the empty "cell" that is ignored, not the entire record. By "cell", we mean the intersection of one row and one column (attribute name). For transactional data, it can be said that the "row" is ignored because in transactional format, each row contains the value for one attribute.

DISCRETIZATION (BINNING)

ODM algorithms require that input data be *discretized* (*binned*) before model building, testing, computing lift, and applying (scoring). Binning means grouping related values together to reduce the number of distinct values for an attribute. Having fewer bins typically leads to a more compact model and one that builds faster, but it can also lead to some loss in accuracy. The target attribute is typically not binned.

The decisions about the number of bins, the values that are to be assigned to each bin, where the bin boundaries are to be set, etc., can be made according to program defaults or can be specified by the user.

The best binning is done by an expert familiar with the data being binned and the problem to be solved. However, if there is no additional information that can inform decisions about binning or if what is wanted is an initial exploration of the data and problem, ODM can bin the data using default settings.

Numerical and Categorical Attributes

The distinction between categorical and numerical attributes depends on the application, that is, the application determines how to treat a particular attribute. The main difference is whether the values of an attribute have a certain order. Values of a categorical attribute do not have any meaningful order; values of a numerical attribute do have a meaningful order. This does not mean that the values of a categorical attribute cannot be ordered, but rather that the order does not matter. For example, since U.S. postal codes are numbers, they can be ordered; however, their order is not necessarily meaningful to an application, and they can therefore be considered categorical.

Automated Binning

Because binning can have an effect on a model's accuracy, it is better when an expert specifies the binning based on some information about the data or the problem. However, in cases where there is no additional information to inform binning decisions or when the purpose is to get an initial understanding of the problem, it makes sense to use some form of automatic binning that uses global defaults. For example, group all attributes into five bins, where five is a globally specified default. Then for categorical attributes, the five most frequent values are assigned to five different bins, and all remaining values are assigned to a sixth bin.

For numerical attributes, the values are divided into five groups of equal size according to their order.

An important advantage of automated binning is that it allows ODM to handle raw (unprepared) data, and thus simplifies what can be a daunting task for the user new to data mining. Automated binning also allows initial exploration of problems about which there is little or no information to guide binning decisions.

Data Preparation

ODM provides four ways to bin data:

- Explicit specification: The user provides the bin boundaries for one or more attributes. The user provides one of the following:
  - o for categorical data, a list of categorical values to be contained in each bin.
  - o for numerical data, a set of upper and lower boundaries for the bins

- Top N most frequent items: For categorical attributes only, the user selects the value N and the name of the "other" category. ODM determines the N most frequent values and puts all other values in the "other" category.
- Quantile binning: For numerical attributes only, the values are sorted, and the values are divided into the number of user-specified quantiles. ODM determines which values are in which bins.
- Automated binning: In cases where the user has no insight into how to define optimal bins or needs to get an initial understanding of the problem, ODM can perform the binning.

An example of binning is shown below. Table 16.6 displays original data, before binning. table 16.7 shows the bin boundaries for numeric data; table 16.8 shows bin boundaries for categorical data. Table 16.9 shows the results of binning.

Table 16.6 Binning Illustration: Data before Binning

PERSON_ID	Age	Work Class	Weight	Education	MARTIAL_ STATUS	Occupation
2	27	Private	160972	HS-grad	Married	Crafts
8	46	Private	116635	Bach.	Separ.	Prof.
10	34	Private	62124	HS-grad	Separ.	Agricultural
11	23	Sta-gov	103588	< Bach.	NeverM	Cleric.
41	30	Private	178835	< Bach.	Married	Sales

Table 16.7 Binning Illustration: Bin Boundaries for Numeric Data

COLUMN_NAME	LOWER_ BOUNDARY	UPPER_ BOUNDARY	BIN_ID	IS_ ATTRIBUTE	DISPLAY_NAME
AGE	17	24.3	1	T	17-24.3
AGE	24.3	31.6	2	T	24.3-31.6
AGE	31.6	38.9	3	T	31.6-38.9
AGE	38.9	46.2	4	T	38.9-46.2
AGE	46.2	53.5	5	T	46.2-53.5
WEIGHT	13769	122137.4	1	T	13769-122137.4
WEIGHT	122137.4	230505.8	2	T	122137.4-230505.8
WEIGHT	230505.8	338874.2	3	T	230505.8-338874.2
WEIGHT	338874.2	447242.6	4	T	338874.2-447242.6

Table 16.8 Binning Illustration: Bin Boundaries for Categorical Data

COLUMN_NAME	Category	BIN_ID	DISPLAY_NAME	IS_ATTRIBUTE
WORKCLASS	Loc-gov	100	Government	T
WORKCLASS	Fed-gov	100	Government	T
WORKCLASS	Sta-gov	100	Government	T
WORKCLASS	Private	300	Others	T
EDUCATION	HS-grad	1	HS-grad	T
EDUCATION	< Bach.	2	< Bach.	T

EDUCATION	Bach.	3	Bach.	T
EDUCATION	Masters	4	Masters	T
MARITAL_STATUS	Married	1	Married	T
MARITAL_ STATUS	NeverM	2	NeverM	T
MARITAL_ STATUS	Divorc.	3	Divorc.	T
MARITAL_ STATUS	Widowed	4	Widowed	T
MARITAL_ STATUS	Separ.	5	Separ.	T
OCCUPATION	Prof	1	Prof	T
OCCUPATION	Crafts	2	Crafts	T
OCCUPATION	Exec.	3	Exec.	T
OCCUPATION	Sales	4	Sales	T
OCCUPATION	Cleric	5	Cleric	T
OCCUPATION		6	Other_occ	T

Table 16.9 Binning Illustration: Assignment of Original Data to Bins

PERSON_ID	Age	Work Class	Weight	Education	MARITAL_STATUS	Occupation
2	2	300	2	1	1	2
8	4	300	1	3	5	1
10	3	300	1	1	5	6
11	1	100	1	2	2	5
41	2	300	2	2	1	4

NOTE

Currently automatic binning requires closed intervals for numerical bins. This can result in certain values being ignored. For example, if the salary range in the build data table is 0 to 1,000,000, any salary greater than 1,000,000 is ignored when the model is applied. If you are trying to identify likely purchasers of a high-end consumer product, attributes indicating the wealthiest individuals are likely to be deleted, and you probably won't find the best targets. Manual binning has the option of making extreme bins open-ended, that is, with infinite boundaries.

PMML SUPPORT

The Predictive Model Markup Language (PMML) specifies data mining models using an XML DTD (document type definition). PMML provides a standard representation for data mining models to facilitate model interchange among vendors. PMML is specified by the Data Mining Group (http://www.dmg.org).

ODM is both a producer and consumer of PMML models. That is, ODM can produce (generate) a PMML model that can be used by other software that can consume PMML. ODM can also consume PMML models, that is, ODM can convert certain PMML model representations to valid ODM models. ODM is a producer and consumer of two model types: Association Rules models and Naive Bayes classification models.

ODM consumes only models that use features supported by ODM.

❑❑❑

17 DATA MINING PROGRAMMING USING ORACLE

This chapter discusses two major topics:

- The requirements for compiling and executing ODM programs
- How to perform common data mining tasks using Oracle9*i* Data Mining (ODM)?

This chapter provides an overview of the steps required to perform basic ODM tasks. For detailed examples of how to perform these tasks, see the ODM sample programs. The ODM sample programs are distributed with the ODM documentation. This chapter does not include a detailed description of any of the ODM API classes and methods. For detailed information about the ODM API, see the ODM Javadoc in the directory $ORACLE_HOME/dm/doc on any system where ODM is installed.

Compiling and Executing ODM Programs

ODM depends on the following Oracle9*i* Java Archive (.jar) files:

$ORACLE_HOME/jdbc/lib/classes12.jar

$ORACLE_HOME/lib/xmlparserv2.jar

$ORACLE_HOME/rdbms/jlib/jmscommon.jar

$ORACLE_HOME/rdbms/jlib/aqapi.jar

$ORACLE_HOME/rdbms/jlib/xsu12.jar

$ORACLE_HOME/dm/lib/odmapi.jar

These files must be in your CLASSPATH to compile and execute ODM programs.

If you use a database character set that is *not* US7ASCII, WE8DEC, WE8ISO8859P1, or UTF8, you must also include the following in your CLASSPATH:

$ORACLE_HOME/jdbc/lib/nls_charset12.zip

If you do not include nls_charset12.zip in your CLASSPATH, an ODM program will fail with the following error:

oracle.jms.AQjmsException: Non supported character set:oracle-character-set-178

Using ODM to Perform Mining Tasks

This section describes the steps required to perform several common data mining tasks using ODM.

All work in ODM is done using MiningTask objects.

Build a Model

This section summarizes the steps required to build a model.

1. Prepocess the input data, as required.
2. Discretize (bin) the input data. (This step is optional, ODM algorithms can automatically bin input data.)
3. Construct and store a MiningFunctionSettings object.
4. Construct and store a MiningBuildTask object.
5. After successful construction of the build task object, call a store method to store the object in the data mining server.
6. Call the execute method; the execute method queues the work for asynchronous execution and returns a task identifier to the caller.
7. Periodically call the getCurrentStatus method to get the status of the task. Alternatively, use the waitForCompletion method to wait until all asynchronous activity for task completes.

After successful completion of the task, a build results object exists.

The following sample programs illustrate building ODM models:

- Sample_AdaptiveBayesNetworkBuild.java
- Sample_NaiveBayesBuild.java
- Sample_AssociationRulesBuild.java
- Sample_ClusteringBuild.java.

Perform Tasks in Sequence

Data mining tasks are usually performed in sequence. The following sequence of tasks is typical:

1. Collect and preprocess data
2. Build a model
3. Test the model
4. Calculate lift
5. Apply the model

To implement a sequence of dependent task executions, you may periodically check the asynchronous task execution status using the getCurrentStatus method or block for completion using the waitForCompletion method. You can then perform the dependent task after completion of the previous task.

For example, follow these steps to perform the build, test, and compute lift sequence:

1. Perform the build task as described above
2. After successful completion of the build task, start the test task by calling the execute method on a MiningTestTask object. Either periodically check the status of the test operation or block until the task completes.
3. After successful completion of the test task, execute the compute lift task by calling the execute method on a MiningComputeLiftTask object.

Find the Best Model

Model Seeker builds multiple models; it then evaluates and compares the models to find a "best" model.

Follow these steps to use Model Seeker:

1. Create a single ModelSeekerTask (MST) instance to hold the information needed to specify the models to build. The required information is defined in subclasses of the MiningFunctionSettings (MFS) and MiningAlgorithmSettings (MAS) classes.

You can specify a combination of as many instances of the following as desired:

- NaiveBayesAlgorithmSettings
- CombinationNaiveBayesSettings
- AdaptiveBayesNetworkAlgorithmSettings
- CombinationAdaptiveBayesNetSettings.

(You cannot specify clustering models or Association Rules models.)

2. Call the Model Seeker Task execute method. The method returns once the task is queued for asynchronous execution.

3. Periodically call the getCurrentStatus method to get the status of the task, using the task name. Alternatively, use the waitForCompletion method to wait until all asynchronous activity for the required work completes.

4. When the model seeker task completes, use the getResults method to view the summary information and the best model. Model Seeker discards all models that it builds except the best one.

The sample program Sample_ModelSeeker.java illustrates how to use Model Seeker.

Find and Use the Most Important Attributes

Models based on data sets with a large number of attributes can have very long build times. To minimize build time, you can use ODM Attribute Importance to identify the critical attributes and then build a model using these attributes only.

Identify the most important attributes by building an Attributes Importance model as follows:

1. Create a physical data specification for input data set.
2. Discretize the data if required.
3. Create and store mining settings for the attribute importance.
4. Build the attribute importance model.
5. Access the model and retrieve the attributes by threshold.

The sample program `Sample_AttributeImportanceBuild.java` illustrates how to build an attribute importance model.

After identifying the important attributes, build a model using the selected attributes as follows:

1. Access the model and retrieve the attributes by threshold or by rank.
2. Modify the Data Usage Specification by calling the function `adjustAttributeUsage` defined on `MiningFunctionSetting`. Only the attributes returned by Attribute Importance will be active for model building.
3. Build a model using the new Logical Data Specification and Data Usage Specification.

The sample program `Sample_AttributeImportanceUsage.java` illustrates how to build a model using the important attributes.

Apply a Model to New Data

You make predictions by applying a model to new data, that is, by *scoring* the data.

Any table that you score (apply a model to) must have the same format as the table used to build the model. If you build a model using a table that is in transactional format, any table that you apply that model to must be in transactional format. Similarly, if the table used to build the model was in nontransactional format, any table to which you apply the model must be in nontransactional format.

Note that you can score a single record, which must also be in the same format as the table used to build the model.

ODM Basic Usage

This chapter contains complete examples of using ODM to build a model and then score new data using that model. These examples illustrate the steps that are required in all code that uses ODM. The following two sample programs are discussed in this chapter:

- `Sample_NaiveBayesBuild_short.java`
- `Sample_NaiveBayesApply_short.java`.

The complete code for these examples is included in the ODM sample programs that are installed when ODM is installed.

The data that the sample programs use are included with sample programs: `Sample_NaiveBayesBuild_short.java` uses `census_2d_build_unbinned` and `Sample_NaiveBayesApply_short.java` uses `census_2d_apply_unbinned`.

This chapter does not include a detailed description of any of the ODM API classes and methods. For detailed information about the ODM API, see the ODM Javadoc in the directory `$ORACLE_HOME/dm/doc` on any system where ODM is installed.

The sample programs have a number of steps in common. Common steps are repeated for simplicity of reference.

These short sample programs use data tables that are used by the other ODM sample programs. The short sample program that builds a model uses the table `CENSUS_2D_BUILD_UNBINNED`; the short sample program that applies the model uses `CENSUS_2D_APPLY_UNBINNED`. For more information about these tables.

Note that these short sample programs do not use the property files that the other ODM use.

NOTE

If you execute `SampleNaiveBayesBuild.java` and then execute `SampleNaiveBayesBuild_short.java` or `Sample_NaiveBayesApply_short.java`, you must change the `buildtablename` to a new name. Otherwise, you get a unique constraint error because the model name, MFS name, and Mining Task name are identical in both programs.

USING THE SHORT SAMPLE PROGRAMS

The short sample programs must be compiled and then executed in the proper order; you must execute `SampleNaiveBayesBuild_short.java` (which builds the model) before you execute `SampleNaiveBayesApply_short.java` (which applies the model to data).

You can compile and execute these models in several ways:

- Using scripts provided with the sample programs
- Using Oracle9*i* JDeveloper.

Note that the short sample programs do not use property files.

BUILDING A MODEL

This section describes the steps that must be performed by any program that builds an ODM model.

The sample program `Sample_NaiveBayesBuild_short.java` is a complete executable program that illustrates these required steps. The data for the sample program is `CENSUS_2D_BUILD_UNBINNED`.

Before Building an ODM Model

Before you build an ODM model, ODM must be installed on your system. You need to know the URL of the database where the ODM Data Mining Server resides, the user name, and the password. (Ask the person who installed the program what the user name and password are.)

Before you execute an ODM program, the ODM Monitor must be running.

Before you build a model, you must identify the data to be used during model building. The data must reside in a table in an Oracle9*i* database. You should clean the data as necessary; for example, you may want to treat missing values and deal with outliers, that is, extreme values that are either errors or values that may skew the binning. The table that contains the data can be in either transactional or nontransactional form. The ODM sample programs include data tables to use for model building.

Before you start building a model, you must also know what data mining function you wish to perform; for example, you may wish to create a classification model. You may specify which algorithm to use or let ODM decide which algorithm to use. The sample programs described in this chapter build and apply a Naive Bayes model.

Main Steps in ODM Model Building

For ODM to build a model, ODM must know the answers to the following questions:

- Which server should be used to do the mining?
- Where is the data for mining and how is it organized?
- What type of model should be built? What is its function? Which algorithm should be used?

The following steps provide answers to the questions asked above:

1. Connect to the DMS (data mining server).
2. Create a `PhysicalDataSpecification` object for the build data.

3. Create a `MiningFunctionSettings` object (in this case, a `ClassificationFunctionSettings` object with no supplemental attributes).
4. Build the model.

The steps are illustrated below with code for building a Naive Bayes model.

Connect to the Data Mining Server

Before building a model, it is necessary to create an instance of `DataMiningServer`. This instance is used as a proxy to create connections to a Data Mining Server (DMS). The instance also maintains the connection. The DMS is the server-side, in-database component that performs the actual data mining operations within ODM. The DMS also provides a metadata repository consisting of mining input objects and result objects, along with the namespaces within which these objects are stored and retrieved.

```
//Create an instance of the DMS server.
//The mining server DB_URL, user_name, and password for your installation
//need to be specified
dms=new DataMiningServer("DB_URL", "user_name", "password");
//get the actual connection dmsConnection = dms.login();
```

Describe the Build Data

Before ODM can use data to build a model, it must know where the data is and how the data is organized. This is done through a `PhysicalDataSpecification` instance where you indicate whether the data is in nontransactional or transactional format and describe the roles the various data columns play.

Location Access Data for Build Data

Before you create a `PhysicalDataSpecification` instance, you must provide information about the location of the build data. This is accomplished using a `LocationAccessData` object.

```
//Create a LocationAccessData using the table_name
//(CENSUS_2D_BUILD_UNBINNED) and schema_name for your installation
LocationAccessData lad =
      new LocationAccessData("CENSUS_2D_BUILD_UNBINNED", "schema_name");
```

Next, create the actual `PhysicalDataSpecification` instance.

Physical Data Specification for Nontransactional Build Data

If the data is in nontransactional format, all the information needed to build a `PhysicalDataSpecification` is contained in the `LocationAccessData` object.

```
//Create the actual PhysicalDataSpecification for a
//NonTransactionalDataSpecification object since the
//data set is nontransactional
PhysicalDataSpecification m_PhysicalDataSpecification =
                     new NonTransactionalDataSpecification(lad);
```

Physical Data Specification for Transactional Build Data

If the data is in transactional format, you must specify the role that the various data columns play.

```
//Create the actual PhysicalDataSpecification for a transactional
//data case
```

```
PhysicalDataSpecification m_PhysicalDataSpecification =
        new TransactionalDataSpecification(
                "CASE_ID",          //column name for sequence id
                "ATTRIBUTES",       //column name for attribute name
                "VALUES",           //column name for value
                lad);
```

Create the MiningFunctionSettings Object

The `MiningFunctionSettings` (MFS) object tells the DMS the type of model to build, the function of the model, and the algorithm to use.

ODM supports the following mining functions:

- Association rules (unsupervised learning)
- Clustering (unsupervised learning)
- Classification (supervised learning)
- Attribute importance (supervised learning).

The MFS allows a user to specify the type of result desired without having to specify a particular algorithm. If an algorithm is not specified, the underlying DMS selects the algorithm based on user-provided parameters.

Specify the Default Algorithm for Classification

To build a model for classification using ODM's default classification algorithm, use a `ClassificationFunctionSettings` object with a null `MiningAlgorithmSettings` for the MFS. An easy way to create a `ClassificationFunctionSettings` object is to use the `create` method, as illustrated below. In this case, it is necessary to indicate the name of the target attribute, the type of the target attribute, and whether the data has been prepared (binned) by the user. Unprepared data will automatically be binned by ODM.

```
//Specify "class" as the target attribute name, categorical for the target
//attribute type, and set the DataPreparationStatus to unprepared.
//Automatic binning will be applied in this case.
ClassificationFunctionSettings m_ClassificationFunctionSettings =
        ClassificationFunctionSettings.create(
                dmsConnection,
                null,
                m_PhysicalDataSpecification,
                "class",
                AttributeType.categorical,
                DataPreparationStatus.getInstance("unprepared"));
```

Specify the Naive Bayes Algorithm

If a particular algorithm is to be used, the information about the algorithm is captured in a `MiningAlgorithmSettings` instance. For example, if you want to build a model for classification using the Naive Bayes algorithm, first create a `NaiveBayesSettings` instance to specify settings for the Naive Bayes algorithm. Two settings are available: `singleton threshold` and `pairwise threshold`. Then create a `ClassificationFunctionSettings` instance for the build operation.

```
//Create the Naive Bayes algorithm settings by setting the thresholds
//to 0.01.
```

```
NaiveBayesSettings algorithmSetting = new NaiveBayesSettings(0.01f 0.01f);

//Create the actual ClassificationFunctionSettings using
//algorithmSetting for MiningAlgorithmSettings. Specify "class" as
//the target attribute name, "categorical" for the target attribute
//type, and set the DataPreparationStatus to "unprepared".
//Automatic binning will be applied in this case.
ClassificationFunctionSettings m_ClassificationFunctionSettings =
        ClassificationFunctionSettings.create(
            dmsConnection,
            algorithmSetting,
            m_PhysicalDataSpecification,
            class,
            Attribute Type.categorical,
            DataPreparationStatus.getInstance(unprepared));
```

Validate the Mining Function Settings for Build

Because `MiningFunctionSettings` objects are complex objects, it is good practice to validate whether they were correctly created before starting the actual build task. If the `MiningFunctionSettings` object is a valid one, it should be persisted in the DMS for later use. This is illustrated below for the `ClassificationFunctionSettings` in our example.

```
//Validate and store the ClassificationFunctionSettings object
//with the name "Sample_NB_MFS".
m_ClassificationFunctionSettings.validate();
m_ClassificationFunctionSettings.store(dmsConnection, "Sample_NB_MFS");
```

Build the Model

Now that all the required information for building the model has been captured in an instance of `PhysicalDataSpecification` and `MiningFunctionSettings`, the last step needed is to decide whether the model should be built synchronously or asynchronously.

If you are calling ODM from an application, the design of the calling application may determine whether to build the model synchronously or asynchronously. Also, if the data used to build the model is large, it may take a significant amount of time to build the model; in such a case, you will probably want to build the model asynchronously.

Build the Model Synchronously

For a synchronous build, use the static `MiningModel.build` method. Note that this method is deprecated for ODM release 2.

```
//Build the model using the MFS named "Sample_NB_MFS" and store the
//model under the name "Sample_NB_Model".
MiningModel.build(
    dmsConn,
    lad,
    m_PhysicalDataSpecification,
    "Sample_NB_MFS",
    "Sample_NB_Model");
```

Build the Model Asynchronously

For an asynchronous build, create an instance of `MiningTask`. A mining task can be persisted in the DMS using the `store` method and executed at any time; however, it can be executed only once. Once the task is executing, query the current status information of a task by calling the `getCurrentStatus` method. This call returns a `MiningTaskStatus` object, which provides more details about the state. You can get the complete status history of a task by calling the `getStatusHistory` method.

```
//Create a Naive Bayes build task and execute it.
//MiningFunctionsSettings name (for example, "Sample_NB_MFS"), and
//the ModelName (for example, "Sample_NB_Model") need to be specified.
MiningBuildTask task =
     new MiningBuildTask(
          m_PhysicalDataSpecification,
          "Sample__NB_MFS",
          "Sample_NB_Model");

//Store the task under the name "Sample_NB_Build_Task"
task.store(dmsConnection, "Sample_NB_Build_Task");

//Execute the task
task.execute(dmsConnection);
```

After the `MiningModel.build` or the `task.execute` call successfully completes, the model will be stored by using the name that you specified (in this case, Sample_NB_Model) in the DMS.

SCORING DATA USING A MODEL

After you've created a model, you can apply it to new data to make predictions; the process is referred to as "scoring data."

ODM can be used to score multiple records specified in a single database table or to score a single record. This section describes scoring multiple records.

The sample program `Sample_NaiveBayesApply_short.java` is a complete executable program that illustrates these required steps. The data for this sample program is `CENSUS_2D_APPLY_UNBINNED`. Note that this sample program does not use a property file.

Before Scoring Data

Before scoring an ODM model, you must have built an ODM model. This implies that ODM is installed on your system, and that you know the location of the database, the user name, and the password.

Before executing an ODM program, the ODM Monitor must be running.

Before you score data, the data must reside in a table in an Oracle9*i* database. The data to score must be compatible with the build data that you used when you built the model. You should clean the data to be scored in the same way that you cleaned the build data. If the build data for the model was not binned, the data to score must also be not binned.

The table that contains the data to score can be in either transactional or nontransactional form.

Main Steps in ODM Scoring

For ODM to score data using a model, ODM must know the answers to the following questions:

- Which server should be used to do the scoring?

- Where is the data for scoring and how.is it organized?
- Where should the output be stored?
- What information do you want returned as the result of scoring?

The following steps provide answers to the questions above:

1. Connect to the DMS (data mining server).
2. Create a `PhysicalDataSpecification` object for the input data (the data that you want to score).
3. Create a `LocationAccessData` object for the input and output data.
4. Create a `MiningApplyOutput` object for the output data.
5. Score the data.

The steps above are illustrated in this section with code for scoring a Naive Bayes model.

Connect to the Data Mining Server

Before scoring data, it is necessary to create an instance of `DataMiningServer`. This instance is used as a proxy to create connections to a Data Mining Server (DMS). The instance also maintains the connection. The DMS is the server-side, in-database component that performs the actual data mining operations within ODM. The DMS also provides a metadata repository consisting of mining input objects and result objects, along with the namespaces within which these objects are stored and retrieved.

```
//Create an instance of the DMS server.
//The mining server DB_URL, user_name, and password for your installation
//need to be specified.
dms=new DataMiningServer("DB_URL", "user_name", "password");
```

//get the actual connection dmsConnection = dms.login(();

Describe the Input Data

Before ODM can apply a model to data, it must know the physical layout of the data. This is done through a `PhysicalDataSpecification` instance where you indicate whether the data is in nontransactional or transactional format and describe the roles the various data columns play.

Location Access Data for Apply Input

Before you create a `PhysicalDataSpecification` instance, you must provide information about the location of the input data. This is accomplished by using a `LocationAccessData` object.

```
//Create a LocationAccessData using the table_name
//(CENSUS_2D_APPLY_UNBINNED) and the schema_name for your installation
LocationAccessData lad =
    new LocationAccessData("CENSUS_2D_APPLY_UNBINNED", "schema_name)";
```

Next, create the `PhysicalDataSpecification` instance.

Physical Data Specification for Nontransactional Input Data

If the data is in nontransactional format, all the information needed to build a `PhysicalDataSpecification` is contained in the `LocationAccessData` object.

```
//Create the actual PhysicalDataSpecification for a
//NonTransactionalDataSpecification object since the
```

```
//data set is nontransactional
PhysicalDataSpecification m_PhysicalDataSpecification =
                    new NonTransactionalDataSpecification(lad);
```

Physical Data Specification for Transactional Input Data

If the data is in transactional format, you must specify the role that the various data columns play.

```
//Create the actual PhysicalDataSpecification for transactional
//data case
PhysicalDataSpecification m_PhysicalDataSpecification =
          new TransactionalDataSpecification(
                    "CASE_ID",         //column name for sequence id
                    "ATTRIBUTES",      //column name for attribute name
                    "VALUES",          //column name for value
                    lad);
```

Describe the Output Data

Before scoring the input data the DMS needs to know where to store the output of the scoring.

Location Access Data for Apply Output

Create a `LocationAccessData` object specifying where to store the apply output. The following code specifies writing to the output table CENSUS_NB_APPLY_RESULT.

```
// LocationAccessData for output table to store the apply results.
LocationAccessData ladOutput = new LocationAccessData ("CENSUS_NB_APPLY_RESULT",

                                             "output_schema_name");
```

Specify the Format of the Apply Output

The DMS also needs to know the content of the scoring output. This information is captured in a `MiningApplyOutput` (MAO) object. An instance of `MiningApplyOutput` specifies the data (columns) to be included in the apply output table that is created as the result of an apply operation. The columns in the apply output table are described by a combination of `ApplyContentItem` objects. These columns can be either from the input table or generated by the scoring task (for example, prediction and probability). The following steps are involved in creating a `MiningApplyOutput` object:

1. Create an empty `MiningApplyOutput` object.
2. Create an `ApplyContentItem` object describing which generated columns to be included in the output and add it to the `MiningApplyOutput` object.
3. Create `ApplyContentItem` objects describing columns from the input table to be included in the output and add them to the `MiningApplyOutput` object.
4. Validate the `MiningApplyOuput` that you created.

Create an Empty Mining Apply Output Object

Create an empty `MiningApplyOutput` object as follows:

```
// Create MiningApplyOutput object
MiningApplyOutput m_MiningApplyOutput = new MiningApplyOutput();
```

Specify the Generated Columns in the Apply Output

There are two options for generated columns, described by the following `ApplyContentItem` subclasses:

- `ApplyMultipleScoringItem`: used for generating a list of top or bottom *n* predictions ordered by their associated target value probability
- `ApplyTargetProbabilityItem`: used for generating a list of probabilities for particular target values.

For the current example, let's use an `ApplyTargetProbabilityItem` instance. Before creating an instance of `ApplyTargetProbabilityItem`, it is necessary to specify the names and the data types of the prediction, probability, and rank **columns** for the output. This is done through `Attribute` objects.

```
// Create Attribute objects that specify the names and data
// types of the prediction, probability, and rank columns for the
// output.
Attribute predictionAttribute =
new Attribute("myprediction", DataType.stringType);
Attribute probabilityAttribute =
new Attribute("myprobability", DataType.stringType);
Attribute rankAttr =
new Attribute("myrank", DataType.stringType);

// Create the ApplyTargetProbabilityItem instance
ApplyTargetProbabilityItem aTargetAttrItem =
new ApplyTargetProbabilityItem(predictionAttribute, probabilityAttribute,rankAttr);
```

An `ApplyTargetProbabilityItem` class contains a set of target values whose prediction and probability appear in the apply output table, regardless of their ranks. A target value is represented as a Category, and it must be one of the target values in the target attribute used when building the model to be applied. This step is not necessary for the `ApplyMultipleScoringItem` case.

```
// Create Category objects to represent the target values
// to be included in the apply output table. In this example
// two target values are specified.
Category target_category = new Category("positive_class", "0",

                    DataType.getInstance("int"));
Category target_category1 = new Category("positive_class", "1",

                    DataType.getInstance("int"));

// Add the target values to the ApplyTargetProbabilityItem
// instance
aTargetAttrItem.addTarget(target_category);
aTargetAttrItem.addTarget(target_category1);

// Add the ApplyTargetProbabilityItem to the MiningApplyOutput
// object
m_MiningApplyOutput.addItem(aTargetAttrItem);
```

Specify the Input Columns to be Included in Output

The input table columns to be included in the apply output are described by `ApplySourceAttributeItem` instances. Each instance maps a column in the input table to a column in the output table. These columns are described by a source Attribute and a destination Attribute.

```
// In this example, attribute "PERSON_ID" from the source table
// will be returned in the column "ID" in the output table.
// This specification is captured by the
// m_ApplySourceAttributeItem object.
MiningAttribute sourceAttribute = new MiningAttribute(
                "PERSON_ID",
                 DataType.intType,
                 AttributeType.notApplicable,
                 false,
                 false);

Attribute destinationAttribute = new Attribute(
                "ID",
                DataType.intType);

ApplySourceAttributeItem m_ ApplySourceAttributeItem =
            new ApplySourceAttributeItem(
            sourceAttribute,
            destinationAttribute)

// Add the ApplySourceAttributeItem object
// to the MiningApplyOutput object
m_MiningApplyOutput.addItem(m_ApplySourceAttributeItem);
```

Note that the source mining attribute could have been taken from the logical data of the model's function settings.

Validate the Mining Apply Output Object

Because `MiningApplyOutput` objects are complex objects, it is a good practice to validate that they were correctly created before you do the actual scoring. This is illustrated below for the `MiningApplyOutput` in our example.

```
// Validate the MiningApplyOutput
m_ MiningApplyOutput.validate();
```

Apply the Model

Now that all the required information for scoring the model has been captured in instances of `PhysicalDataSpecification`, `LocationAccessData`, and `MiningApplyOutput`, the last step is

- Specify how to score the data (synchronously or asynchronously)
- Tell the DMS which model to use for scoring

If you are calling ODM from an application, the design of the calling application may determine whether to apply the model synchronously or asynchronously. Also, if the input data has many cases, the apply operation may require a significant amount of time; in such a case ',' you will probably want to apply the model asynchronously.

Apply the Model Synchronously

For synchronous apply, use the static `SupervisedModel.Apply` method. Note that this method is deprecated for ODM release 2.

```
// Synchronous Apply
// Score the model using the model named "Sample_NB_Model" and
// store the results in the "Sample_NB_APPLY_RESULT"
public static void apply(
            dmsConn,
            lad,
            m_PhysicalDataSpecification,
            "Sample_NB_Model",
            m_MiningApplyOutput,
            ladOutput,
            "Sample_NB_APPLY_RESULT")
```

Apply the Model Asynchronously

For asynchronous apply, it is necessary to create an instance of `MiningTask`. A mining task can be persisted in the DMS using the `store(dmsConn, taskName)` method and executed at any time; such a task can be executed only once. The current status information of a task can be queried by calling the `getCurrentStatus(dmsConn, taskName)` method. This returns a `MiningTaskStatus` object, which provides more details about the state. You can get the complete status history of a task by calling the `getStatusHistory(dmsConn, taskName)` method.

```
// Asynchronous Apply
/ Create a Naive Bayes apply task and execute it.
// Result name (e.g., "Sample_NB_APPLY_RESULT"), and the
// model name (e.g., "Sample_NB_Model") need to be specified
MiningApplyTask task =  new MiningBuildTask(
                        m_PhysicalDataSpecification,
                        "Sample_NB_Model",
                        m_MiningApplyOutput,
                        ladOutput,
                        "Sample_NB_APPLY_RESULT");

// Store the task under the name "Sample_NB_APPLY_Task"
task.store(dmsConnection, "Sample_NB_APPLY_Task");

// Execute the task
task.execute(dmsConnection);
```

❑❑❑

GLOSSARY

additive Describes a fact (or **measure**) that can be summarized through addition. An additive fact is the most common type of fact. Examples include sales, cost, and profit. Contrast with **nonadditive** and **semi-additive.**

advisor See: **Summary Advisor.**

aggregate Summarized data. For example, unit sales of a particular product could be aggregated by day, month, quarter and yearly sales.

aggregation The process of consolidating data values into a single value. For example, sales data could be collected on a daily basis and then be aggregated to the week level, the week data could be aggregated to the month level, and so on. The data can then be referred to as aggregate data. **Aggregation** is synonymous with **summarization,** and aggregate data is synonymous with summary data.

ancestor A value at any level higher than a given value in a hierarchy. For example, in a Time dimension, the value `1999` might be the ancestor of the values `Q1-99` and `Jan-99`.

attribute A descriptive characteristic of one or more levels. For example, the product dimension for a clothing manufacturer might contain a level called item, one of whose attributes is color. Attributes represent logical groupings that enable end users to select data based on like characteristics.

Note that in relational modeling, an attribute is defined as a characteristic of an entity. In Oracle9i, an attribute is a column in a dimension that characterizes elements of a single level.

cardinality

From an OLTP perspective, this refers to the number of rows in a table. From a data warehousing perspective, this typically refers to the number of distinct values in a column. For most data warehouse DBAs, a more important issue is the **degree of cardinality.**

child

A value at the level under a given value in a hierarchy. For example, in a Time dimension, the value `Jan-99` might be the child of the value `Q1-99`. A value can be a child for more than one parent if the child value belongs to multiple hierarchies.

cleansing

The process of resolving inconsistencies and fixing the anomalies in source data, typically as part of the ETL process.

Common Warehouse Metadata (CWM)

A repository standard used by Oracle data warehousing, and decision support. The CWM repository schema is a standalone product that other products can share—each product owns only the objects within the CWM repository that it creates.

cross product

A procedure for combining the elements in multiple sets. For example, given two columns, each element of the first column is matched with every element of the second column. A simple example is illustrated as follows:

Col1	Col2	Cross Product
a	c	ac
b	d	ad
		bc
		bd

Cross products are performed when grouping sets are concatenated.

data mart

A data warehouse that is designed for a particular line of business, such as sales, marketing, or finance. In a dependent data mart, the data can be derived from an enterprise-wide data warehouse. In an independent data mart, data can be collected directly from sources.

data source

A database, application, repository, or file that contributes data to a warehouse.

data warehouse

A relational database that is designed for query and analysis rather than transaction processing. A data warehouse usually contains historical data that is derived from transaction data, but it can include data from other sources. It separates analysis workload from transaction workload and enables a business to consolidate data from several sources.

In addition to a relational database, a data warehouse environment often consists of an ETL solution, an OLAP engine, client analysis tools, and other applications that manage the process of gathering data and delivering it to business users.

degree of cardinality

The number of unique values of a column divided by the total number of rows in the table. This is particularly important when deciding which indexes to build. You typically want to use bitmap indexes on low degree of cardinality columns and B-tree indexes on high degree of cardinality columns. As a general rule, a cardinality of under 1% makes a good candidate for a bitmap index.

denormalize

The process of allowing redundancy in a table. Contrast with **normalize.**

derived fact (or measure)

A fact (or measure) that is generated from existing data using a mathematical operation or a data transformation. Examples include averages, totals, percentages, and differences.

detail

See: **fact table.**

detail table

See: **fact table.**

dimension

The term dimension is commonly used in two ways:

- A general term for any characteristic that is used to specify the members of a data set. The 3 most common dimensions in sales-oriented data warehouses are time, geography, and product. Most dimensions have hierarchies.
- An object defined in a database to enable queries to navigate dimensions. In Oracle9i, a dimension is a database object that defines hierarchical (parent/child) relationships between pairs of column sets. In Oracle Express, a dimension is a database object that consists of a list of values.

dimension table

Dimension tables describe the business entities of an enterprise, represented as hierarchical, categorical information such as time, departments, locations, and products. Dimension tables are sometimes called lookup or reference tables.

dimension value

One element in the list that makes up a dimension. For example, a computer company might have dimension values in the product dimension called `LAPPC` and `DESKPC`. Values in the geography dimension might include `Boston` and `Paris`. Values in the time dimension might include `MAY96` and `JAN97`.

drill

To navigate from one item to a set of related items. Drilling typically involves navigating up and down through the levels in a hierarchy. When selecting data, you can expand or collapse a hierarchy by drilling down or up in it, respectively.

drill down

To expand the view to include child values that are associated with parent values in the hierarchy.

drill up

To collapse the list of descendant values that are associated with a parent value in the hierarchy.

element An object or process. For example, a dimension is an object, a mapping is a process, and both are elements.

entity Entity is used in database modeling. In relational databases, it typically maps to a table.

ETL Extraction, transformation, and loading. ETL refers to the methods involved in accessing and manipulating source data and loading it into a data warehouse. The order in which these processes are performed varies.

Note that ETT (extraction, transformation, transportation) and ETM (extraction, transformation, move) are sometimes used instead of ETL.

extraction The process of taking data out of a source as part of an initial phase of ETL.

fact Data, usually numeric and additive, that can be examined and analyzed. Examples include sales, cost, and profit. **Fact** and **measure** are synonymous; fact is more commonly used with relational environments, measure is more commonly used with multidimensional environments.

fact table A table in a star schema that contains facts. A fact table typically has two types of columns: those that contain facts and those that are foreign keys to dimension tables. The primary key of a fact table is usually a composite key that is made up of all of its foreign keys.

A fact table might contain either detail level facts or facts that have been aggregated (fact tables that contain aggregated facts are often instead called **summary tables**). A fact table usually contains facts with the same level of aggregation.

fast refresh An operation that applies only the data changes to a materialized view, thus eliminating the need to rebuild the materialized view from scratch.

file-to-table mapping Maps data from flat files to tables in the warehouse.

hierarchy A logical structure that uses ordered levels as a means of organizing data. A hierarchy can be used to define data aggregation; for example, in a time dimension, a hierarchy might be used to aggregate data from the `Month` level to the `Quarter` level to the `Year` level. Hierarchies can be defined in Oracle9*i* as part of the dimension object. A hierarchy can also be used to define a navigational drill path, regardless of whether the levels in the hierarchy represent aggregated totals.

level A position in a hierarchy. For example, a time dimension might have a hierarchy that represents data at the `Month`, `Quarter`, and `Year` levels.

level value table A database table that stores the values or data for the levels you created as part of your dimensions and hierarchies.

mapping
The definition of the relationship and data flow between source and target objects.

materialized view
A pre-computed table comprising aggregated or joined data from fact and possibly dimension tables.. Also known as a summary or aggregate table.

measure
See: **fact.**

metadata
Data that describes data and other structures, such as objects, business rules, and processes. For example, the schema design of a data warehouse is typically stored in a repository as metadata, which is used to generate scripts used to build and populate the data warehouse. A repository contains metadata.

Examples include: for data, the definition of a source to target transformation that is used to generate and populate the data warehouse; for information, definitions of tables, columns and associations that are stored inside a relational modeling tool; for business rules, discount by 10 percent after selling 1,000 items.

model
An object that represents something to be made. A representative style, plan, or design. Metadata that defines the structure of the data warehouse.

nonadditive
Describes a fact (or measure) that cannot be summarized through addition. An example includes Average. Contrast with **additive** and **semi-additive.**

normalize
In a relational database, the process of removing redundancy in data by separating the data into multiple tables. Contrast with **denormalize.**

The process of removing redundancy in data by separating the data into multiple tables.

OLAP
See: **online analytical processing (OLAP).**

online analytical processing (OLAP)
OLAP functionality is characterized by dynamic, multidimensional analysis of historical data, which supports activities such as the following:

- Calculating across dimensions and through hierarchies
- Analyzing trends
- Drilling up and down through hierarchies
- Rotating to change the dimensional orientation

OLAP tools can run against a multidimensional database or interact directly with a relational database.

OLTP
See: **online transaction processing (OLTP).**

online transaction processing (OLTP)
Online transaction processing. OLTP systems are optimized for fast and reliable transaction handling. Compared to data warehouse systems, most OLTP interactions will involve a relatively small number of rows, but a larger group of tables.

parallelism Breaking down a task so that several processes do part of the work. When multiple CPUs each do their portion simultaneously, very large performance gains are possible.

parallel execution Breaking down a task so that several processes do part of the work. When multiple CPUs each do their portion simultaneously, very large performance gains are possible.

parent A value at the level above a given value in a hierarchy. For example, in a Time dimension, the value `Q1-99` might be the parent of the value `Jan-99`.

partition Very large tables and indexes can be difficult and time-consuming to work with. To improve manageability, you can break your tables and indexes into smaller pieces called partitions.

pivoting A transformation where each record in an input stream is converted to many records in the appropriate table in the data warehouse. This is particularly important when taking data from nonrelational databases.

publisher Usually a database administrator who is in charge of creating and maintaining schema objects that make up the Change Data Capture system.

refresh The mechanism whereby materialized views are changed to reflect new data.

schema A collection of related database objects. Relational schemas are grouped by database user ID and include tables, views, and other objects. Whenever possible, a sample schema called `sh` is used throughout this Guide.

semi-additive Describes a fact (or measure) that can be summarized through addition along some, but not all, dimensions. Examples include headcount and on hand stock. Contrast with **additive** and **nonadditive.**

slice and dice This is an informal term referring to data retrieval and manipulation. We can picture a data warehouse as a cube of data, where each axis of the cube represents a dimension. To "slice" the data is to retrieve a piece (a slice) of the cube by specifying measures and values for some or all of the dimensions. When we retrieve a data slice, we may also move and reorder its columns and rows as if we had diced the slice into many small pieces. A system with good slicing and dicing makes it easy to navigate through large amounts of data.

snowflake schema A type of star schema in which the dimension tables are partly or fully normalized.

source A database, application, file, or other storage facility from which the data in a data warehouse is derived.

source system A database, application, file, or other storage facility from which the data in a data warehouse is derived.

staging area A place where data is processed before entering the warehouse.

staging file A file used when data is processed before entering the warehouse.

star query A join between a fact table and a number of dimension tables. Each dimension table is joined to the fact table using a primary key to foreign key join, but the dimension tables are not joined to each other.

star schema A relational schema whose design represents a multidimensional data model. The star schema consists of one or more fact tables and one or more dimension tables that are related through foreign keys.

subject area A classification system that represents or distinguishes parts of an organization or areas of knowledge. A data mart is often developed to support a subject area such as sales, marketing, or geography.

subscribers Consumers of the published change data. These are normally applications.

summary See: **materialized view.**

summary advisor The summary advisor recommends which materialized views to retain, create, and drop. It helps database administrators manage materialized views. It is a GUI in Oracle Enterprise Manager, and has similar capabilities to the `DBMS_OLAP` package.

target Holds the intermediate or final results of any part of the ETL process. The target of the entire ETL process is the data warehouse.

third normal form (3NF) A classical relational database modeling technique that minimizes data redundancy through normalization.

third normal form schema A schema that uses the same kind of normalization as typically found in an OLTP system. Third normal form schemas are sometimes chosen for large data warehouses, especially environments with significant data loading requirements that are used to feed data marts and execute long-running queries.

transformation The process of manipulating data. Any manipulation beyond copying is a transformation. Examples include cleansing, aggregating, and integrating data from multiple sources.

transportation The process of moving copied or transformed data from a source to a data warehouse.

unique identifier An identifier whose purpose is to differentiate between the same item when it appears in more than one place.

update window The length of time available for updating a warehouse. For example, you might have 8 hours at night to update your warehouse.

update frequency How often a data warehouse is updated with new information. For example, a warehouse might be updated nightly from an OLTP system.

validation — The process of verifying metadata definitions and configuration parameters.

versioning — The ability to create new versions of a data warehouse project for new requirements and changes.

algorithm — A specific technique or procedure for producing a data mining model. An algorithm uses a specific model representation and may support one or more functional areas. Examples of algorithms used by ODM include Naive Bayes and Adaptive Bayes Networks for classification, *k*-means and O-Cluster for clustering, predictive variance for attribute importance, and Apriori for association rules.

algorithm settings — The settings that specify algorithm-specific behavior for model building.

apply output — A user specification describing the kind of output desired from applying a model to data. This output may include predicted values, associated probabilities, key values, and other supplementary data.

association rules — A data mining function that captures co-occurrence of items among transactions. A typical rule is an implication of the form A -> B, which means that the presence of itemset A implies the presence of itemset B with certain support and confidence. The support of the rule is the ratio of the number of transactions where the itemsets A and B are present to the total number of transactions. The confidence of the rule is the ratio of the number of transactions where the itemsets A and B are present to the number of transactions where itemset A is present. ODM uses the Apriori algorithm for association rules.

attribute — An instance of `Attribute` maps to a column with a name and data type. The attribute corresponds to a column in a database table. When assigned to a column, the column must have a compatible data type; if the data type is not compatible, a runtime exception is likely. Attributes are also called *variables*, *features*, *data fields*, or *table columns*.

attribute importance — A measure of the importance of an attribute in predicting a specified target. The measure of different attributes of a build data table enables users to select the attributes that are found to be most relevant to a mining model. A smaller set of attributes results in a faster model build; the resulting model could be more accurate. ODM uses the predictive variance algorithm for attribute importance. Also known as *feature selection* and *key fields*.

attribute usage — Specifies how a logical attribute is to be used when building a model, for example, active or supplementary, suppressing automatic data preprocessing, and assigning a weight to a particular attribute. See also **attributes usage set.**

attributes usage set A collection of attribute usage objects that together determine how the logical attributes specified in a logical data object are to be used.

binning See **discretization.**

case All the data collected about a specific transaction or related set of values.

categorical attribute An attribute where the values correspond to discrete categories. For example, *state* is a categorical attribute with discrete values (CA, NY, MA, etc.). Categorical attributes are either non-ordered (nominal) like state, gender, etc., or ordered (ordinal) such as high, medium, or low temperatures.

category Corresponds to a distinct value of a categorical attribute. Categories may have string or numeric values. String values must not exceed 64 characters in length.

centroid See **cluster centroid.**

classification A data mining function for predicting target values for new records using a model built from records with known target values. ODM supports two algorithms for classification, Naive Bayes and Adaptive Bayes Networks.

cluster centroid The cluster centroid is the vector that encodes, for each attribute, either the mean (if the attribute is numerical) or the mode (if the attribute is categorical) of the cases in the build data assigned to a cluster.

clustering A data mining function for finding naturally occurring groupings in data. More precisely, given a set of data points, each having a set of attributes, and a similarity measure among them, clustering is the process of grouping the data points into different clusters such that data points in the same cluster are more similar to one another and data points in different clusters are less similar to one another. ODM supports two algorithms for clustering, *k*-means and O-Cluster.

confusion matrix Measures the correctness of predictions made by a model from a text task. The row indexes of a confusion matrix correspond to *actual values* observed and provided in the test data. These were used for model building. The column indexes correspond to *predicted values* produced by applying the model. For any pair of actual/predicted indexes, the value indicates the number of records classified in that pairing.

When predicted value equals actual value, the model produces correct predictions. All other entries indicate errors.

cost matrix A two-dimensional, *n* by *n* table that defines the cost associated with a prediction versus the actual value. A cost matrix is typically used in classification models, where *n* is the number of distinct values in the target, and the columns and rows are labeled with target values. The rows are the actual values; the columns are the predicted values.

cross-validation
A technique of evaluating the accuracy of a classification or regression model. This technique is used when there are insufficient cases for model building and testing. The data table is divided into several parts, with each part in turn being used to evaluate a model built using the remaining parts. Cross-validation occurs automatically for Naive Bayes and Adaptive Bayes networks.

data mining
The process of discovering hidden, previously unknown, and usable information from a large amount of data. This information is represented in a compact form, often referred to as a *model.*

data mining server (DMS)
The component of the Oracle database that implements the data mining engine and persistent metadata repository.

discretization
Discretization groups related values together under a single value (or bin). This reduces the number of distinct values in a column. Fewer bins result in models that build faster. ODM algorithms require that input data be *discretized* prior to model building, testing, computing lift, and applying (scoring).

distance-based (clustering algorithm)
Distance-based algorithms rely on a distance metric (function) to measure the similarity between data points. Data points are assigned to the nearest cluster according to the distance metric used.

DMS
See **data mining server (DMS).**

feature
See **network feature.**

lift
A measure of how much better prediction results are using a model than could be obtained by chance. For example, suppose that 2% of the customers mailed a catalog without using the model would make a purchase. However, using the model to select catalog recipients, 10% would make a purchase. Then the lift is 10/2 or 5. Lift may also be used as a measure to compare different data mining models. Since lift is computed using a data table with actual outcomes, lift compares how well a model performs with respect to this data on predicted outcomes. Lift indicates how well the model improved the predictions over a random selection given actual results. Lift allows a user to infer how a model will perform on new data.

location access data
Specifies the location of data for a mining operation.

logical attribute
A description of a domain of data used as input to mining operations. Logical attributes may be categorical, ordinal, or numerical.

logical data
A set of mining attributes used as input to building a mining model.

MDL principle
See **minimum description length principle.**

minimum description length principle Given a sample of data and an effective enumeration of the appropriate alternative theories to explain the data, the best theory is the one that minimizes the sum of

- The length, in bits, of the description of the theory
- The length, in bits, of the data when encoded with the help of the theory.

mining apply output See **apply output.**

mining function ODM supports the following mining functions: classification, association rules, attribute importance, and clustering.

mining function settings An object that specifies the type of model to build, the function of the model, and the algorithm to use. ODM supports the following mining functions: classification, association rules, attribute importance, and clustering.

mining model The result of building a model from mining function settings. The representation of the model is specific to the algorithm specified by the user or selected by the DMS. A model can be used for direct inspection, e.g., to examine the rules produced from a decision tree or association rules, or to score data.

mining result The end product(s) of a mining operation. For example, a build task produces a mining model; a test task produces a test result.

missing value A data value that is missing because it was not measured (that is, has a null value), not answered, was unknown, or was lost. Data mining systems vary in the way they treat missing values. Typically, they ignore missing values, omit any records containing missing values, replace missing values with the mode or mean, or infer missing values from existing values. ODM ignores missing values during mining operations.

mixture model A mixture model is a type of density model that includes several component functions (usually Gaussian) that are combined to provide a multimodal density.

model An important function of data mining is the production of a model. A model can be descriptive or predictive. A descriptive model helps in understanding underlying processes or behavior. For example, an association model describes consumer behavior. A predictive model is an equation or set of rules that makes it possible to predict an unseen or unmeasured value (the dependent variable or output) from other, known values (independent variables or input). The form of the equation or rules is suggested by mining data collected from the process under study. Some training or estimation technique is used to estimate the parameters of the equation or rules. See also **mining model.**

multi-record case See **transactional format.**

network feature A network feature is a tree-like multi-attribute structure. From the standpoint of the network, features are conditionally independent components. Features contain at least one attribute (the root attribute). Conditional probabilities are computed for each value of the root predictor. A two-attribute feature will have, in addition to the root predictor conditional probabilities, computed conditional probabilities for each combination of values of the root and the depth 2 predictor. That is, if a root predictor, x, has i values and the depth 2 predictor, y, has j values, a conditional probability is computed for each combination of values $\{x=a, y=b$ such that a is in the set $\{1,..,i\}$ and b is in the set $\{1,..,j\}\}$. Similarly, a depth 3 predictor, z, would have additional associated conditional probability computed for each combination of values $\{x=a, y=b, z=c$ such that a is in the set $\{1,..,i\}$ and b is in the set $\{1,..,j\}$ and c is in the set $\{1,..,k\}\}$. Network features are used in the Adaptive Bayes Network algorithm.

nontransactional format Each case in the data is stored as one record (row) in a table. Also known as *single-record case*. See also **transactional format.**

numerical attribute An attribute whose values are numbers. The numeric value can be either an integer or a real number. Numerical attribute values can be manipulated as continuous values. See also **categorical attribute.**

outlier A data value that does not (or is not thought to have) come from the typical population of data; in other words, a data value that falls outside the boundaries that enclose most other data values in the data.

physical data Identifies data to be used as input to data mining. Through the use of attribute assignment, attributes of the physical data are mapped to logical attributes of a model's logical data. The data referenced by a *physical data* object can be used in model building, model application (scoring), lift computation, statistical analysis, etc.

physical data specification An object that specifies the characteristics of the physical data used in a mining operation. The physical data specification includes information about the format of the data (transactional or nontransactional) and the roles that the data columns play.

positive target value In binary classification problems, you may designate one of the two classes (target values) as positive, the other as negative. When ODM computes a model's lift, it calculates the density of positive target values among a set of test instances for which the model predicts positive values with a given degree of confidence.

predictor A logical attribute used as input to a supervised model or algorithm to build a model.

prior probabilities The set of prior probabilities specifies the distribution of examples of the various classes in data. Also referred to as *priors*, these could be different from the distribution observed in the data.

priors See **prior probabilities.**

rule An expression of the general form *if X, then Y*. An output of certain models, such as association rules models or decision tree models. The predicate *X* may be a compound predicate.

score Scoring data means applying a data mining model to new data to generate predictions. See **apply output.**

settings See **algorithm settings** and **mining function settings.**

single-record case See **nontransactional format.**

supervised mining (learning) The process of building data mining models using a known dependent variable, also referred to as the target. Classification techniques are supervised. See **unsupervised mining (learning).**

target In supervised learning, the identified logical attribute that is to be predicted. Sometimes called *target value* or *target attribute.*

task A container within which to specify arguments to data mining operations to be performed by the data mining system.

transactional format Each case in the data is stored as multiple records in a table with columns `sequenceID`, `attribute_name`, and `value`. Also known as *multi-record case.* See also **nontransactional format.**

transformation A function applied to data resulting in a new form or representation of the data. For example, discretization and normalization are transformations on data.

unsupervised mining (learning) The process of building data mining models without the guidance (supervision) of a known, correct result. Clustering and association rules are unsupervised mining functions. See **supervised mining (learning).**

INDEX

D

G

H

I

J

L

M

N

O

P

Q

R

S